# The
# Language of
# Real Estate
# Appraisal

The
# Language of
# Real Estate
# Appraisal

Jeffrey D. Fisher, Ph.D.
Robert S. Martin, MAI, SREA, CRE, SRPA
Paige Mosbaugh, M.B.A.

**Dearborn**™
Real Estate Education

This publication is designed to provide accurate and authoritative information in regard to the subject matter covered. It is sold with the understanding that a publisher is not engaged in rendering legal, accounting, or other professional service. If legal advice or other expert assistance is required, the services of a competent professional person should be sought.

**Senior Vice President and General Manager:** Roy Lipner
**Publisher and Director of Distance Learning:** Evan Butterfield
**Development Editor:** Amanda Rahn
**Production Manager:** Bryan Samolinski
**Creative Director:** Lucy Jenkins
**Typesetting:** Janet Schroeder

© 1991 by Dearborn Financial Publishing, Inc.®
2002 Printing
Published by Dearborn™ Real Estate Education
a division of Dearborn Financial Publishing, Inc.®
155 North Wacker Drive
Chicago, Illinois 60606-1719
http://www.dearbornRE.com

Printed in the United States of America.
       04   10   9   8

**Library of Congress Cataloging-in-Publication Data**

Fisher, Jeffrey D.
  The language of real estate appraisal / Jeffrey D. Fisher, Robert
S. Martin, Paige Mosbaugh.
     p. cm.
  ISBN 0-88462-983-X
  1. Real property—Valuation—Terminology.   I. Martin, Robert S.
II. Mosbaugh, Paige.   III. Title
HD1387.F53  1990
333.33'2'014—dc20                     90-46293
                                            CIP

# Table of Contents

# Preface

Every field of study uses words to explain concepts that are somewhat unique to that field. People use these words to communicate with each other in conversation, letters, reports, and legal documents. These words become part of the "language" of that field. Real estate in general, and the field of real estate appraisal in particular, uses many terms that are not commonly used outside the field. Examples include "highest and best use" and "capitalization rate." Also, many different words are used that mean essentially the same thing. For example, "equity dividend rate," "equity capitalization rate" and "cash on cash return" are three terms that are interchangeable.

With the passage of the Financial Institutions Reform, Recovery and Enforcement Act in 1989 and the creation of the Resolution Trust Corporation, many new real estate definitions and terms were created. Words such as *certified appraiser* and *licensed appraiser* are specifically defined in this law. Other words such as *fair value* may also have taken on a new meaning as defined by this legislature. Terms such as these were not included in previous publications, but since then have become an important part of appraisal terminology and are included in this book.

This book contains the terms and definitions commonly used in the appraisal industry that comprise the "language of appraisal." Considerable care has been taken to ensure that the definitions and explanations of the terms and concepts in this book reflect the currently accepted usage in the profession. Extensive cross-references to related terms are used to clarify both similarities and differences between related concepts.

This book is a valuable reference for anyone who is either currently practicing appraisal or considering entering the appraisal profession. Exams offered for state licensing and certification of appraisers as well as exams offered by professional organizations for designation purposes draw heavily upon the terms and concepts contained in this book. Because most of the exams are in a multiple choice format, understanding the similarities and differences between key terms and concepts is important in preparing for the exams.

Because this book is arranged in alphabetical order by the term or concept rather than by subject matter, it is a valuable reference tool to be used in conjunction with other study materials. This book differs from other references by including expanded discussion and illustration of the terms and concepts where necessary to clarify their usage and meaning. Examples and completed problems are also provided for many of the terms to further clarify their meaning. Thus, this book is an outstanding text for review of the field of appraisal.

Many symbols are used in the field of appraisal to represent certain terms, especially in mathematical calculations. For example, the symbol for the overall capitalization rate is $R_O$. Where appropriate, common symbols are provided along with the discussion of the term. A summary of these symbols also appears in Appendix A in the back of this book.

Appraisal problems often require the use of either financial tables or calculations. Appendix B includes tables for monthly compounding and Appendix C contains tables for annual compounding.

We would like to thank the following reviewers for their valuable suggestions as to what terms should be included in this book: Michael L. Austin, ASA, CAE, CMA; Robert Chaapel, National College of Appraisal and Property Management; William N. Kinnard, Jr., Ph.D., MAI, SREA; Dennis Tosh, Ph.D., University of Mississippi.

We would also like to thank Sherrie Henry, Jeri Rogers and Terri Blanton for their assistance in preparing the manuscript. Also thanks to Scott Rigney for checking the calculations in the book.

**a**  The symbol for *annualizer* in the general formula for a capitalization rate: $R = Y - \triangle_a$.

**abandonment**  The act of relinquishing or giving up all interests in real property and/or fixtures thereon, with no intention to reclaim or use the property again; not to be confused with simple discontinuance of use or vacating the property.

**abnormal sale**  A sale that is not typical of what is happening in the marketplace, at the time pertinent to the appraisal assignment.

**absorption analysis**  An analysis of the amount of space or the number of units that can be sold, leased, put into use or traded on the market during a predetermined period of time and at prevailing prices or rentals. *See also* feasibility analysis.

**absorption period**  An estimate of the total time period over which a property can be successfully sold, leased, put into use or traded in its market area at prevailing prices or rentals.

**absorption rate**  An estimate of the number of units or square feet per time period of a particular property type that can be successfully sold, leased, put into use or traded in its market area at prevailing prices or rentals. The rate is typically derived through an absorption analysis in a feasibility analysis.

**abstract of title**  A historical summary of all recorded instruments and proceedings, including conveyances, transfers and other evidence of title that affect or impair the title to property. *See also* title.

**abstraction**  *See* allocation.

**abutting property**  Property that is touching or contiguous to another property, as distinguished from lying near or adjacent to another property.

**accelerated depreciation**  A method of cost write-off or recovery in accounting practice or federal income tax laws in which allowances for

1

depreciation or cost recovery are greater in early years than a straight-line basis and decline according to a formula or prescribed format. The term is also used to describe specific depreciation methods, e.g., declining balance and sum-of-the-years'-digits, among others.

**acceleration clause**   A provision in a loan or mortgage that allows the lender to declare the loan balance immediately due and payable contingent on certain conditions happening, such as default of a covenant or sale of the property.

**access**   A path of entry to a property or the physical and legal means of entrance. Most property owners have a right to access to their property from a public street that includes the right to unimpeded flow of light and air. Landlords also have rights to access a rented property under reasonable conditions.

**accessibility**   The relative ease with which a person can enter or exit a site or building. Accessibility is important when determining the suitability of a site or a building for a particular use.

**accession**   The transfer of ownership of fixtures or land as a result of the attachment of those fixtures or land to another's property.

**accessory building**   A building on the same site or lot as a main building or an outbuilding used in connection with the main building, e.g., a garage, a pump house, or a well house.

**accrual system**   In accounting, a method of recording and apportioning items of expense and income to the period in which each is involved, regardless of the date of actual payment or collection. The accrual system is distinguishable from cash accounting, in which cash receipts and expenditures are reported and accounted for in the period in which receipt or expenditure occurs.

**accrued depreciation**   In real estate appraisal, the total deduction from cost new due to physical deterioration, functional obsolescence and/ or external obsolescence. Accrued depreciation represents the total difference between an improvement's reproduction cost or replacement cost and its contributing value in the cost approach. Typical methods of estimating accrued depreciation include the economic age-life method, the modified economic age-life method, and the breakdown method. *See also* economic age-life method, modified economic age-life method, breakdown method, curable physical deterioration, incurable physical deterioration, curable functional obsolescence, incurable functional obsolescence, external obsolescence.

**accrued interest payable**   Interest accumulated and payable on debt (borrowed money) but not yet paid. Depending on the contract terms, this amount may be added to the original principal amount.

**accumulated depreciation**　In accounting, the total amount of depreciation or cost recovery expense that has been claimed for a specific asset since purchase of the property to date. Upon sale of a property, the accumulated depreciation is subtracted from the original cost plus capital additions to a property to find the adjusted basis. The adjusted basis is then subtracted from the sale proceeds to find the capital gain for income tax purposes.

**accumulation of $1 per period ($S_{\overline{n}}$)**　*See* future value annuity of $1 per period ($S_{\overline{n}}$).

**acquisition**　The process of obtaining a property.

**acquisition appraisal**　An appraisal that estimates the market value of a property to be acquired for a public use by a government so that just compensation can be offered to the property owner. *See also* appraisal, condemnation.

**acquisition cost**　The outlay of funds needed to obtain rights in a property. In addition to the purchase price, acquisition cost includes expenses such as closing costs, mortgage loan origination fees, legal and appraisal fees, and title insurance.

**acre (ac)**　A land measure equal to 43,560 square feet. An acre is also equivalent to 4,840 square yards, 4,047 square meters, 0.4047 hectare, 160 square rods, or 10 square chains. A square mile or section contains 640 acres.

**acreage property**　A large and, for the most part, an unimproved tract of land; such land may be used for agricultural purposes, as well as for industrial, residential or commercial uses.

**actual age**　The amount of time that has passed since construction of a structure was completed. It is also called chronological, physical or historical age. *See also* effective age, economic life, physical life, remaining economic life, remaining physical life.

**ad valorem**　A Latin term that means "According to value."

**ad valorem tax**　A real property tax that is based on the assessed value of the property. The property tax burden is therefore proportionate to the value of the property, as opposed to taxes that are based on units or quantity sold. *See also* assessed value.

**adjustable rate mortgage (ARM)**　A mortgage loan in which the interest rate is adjusted periodically based on a specified index or formula. ARMs may include a limit on the amount that the interest rate can rise or fall in a given year as well as a limit on the total amount the rate can rise or fall over the life of the loan. Adjustable rate mortgages often have an initial interest rate that is lower than fixed rate mortgages because the risk of interest rate change is partially borne by the borrower with an adjustable rate loan. *See also* fixed rate mortgage.

**adjusted basis**   In income tax accounting, the amount used as the starting point for identifying capital gain on resale of a property. Adjusted basis can be calculated as the original cost plus any additional capital investment in the property minus accumulated depreciation or cost recovery. Also called basis. *See also* book value, capital gain.

For example, a property is purchased for $800,000. An additional $50,000 is invested in the property, and accumulated depreciation equals $110,000. The adjusted basis can be calculated as:

| | |
|---|---|
| Original cost | $800,000 |
| Capital investment (added) | + 50,000 |
| Accumulated depreciation | − 110,000 (Total cost recovery) |
| Adjusted basis | $740,000 |

**adjusted internal rate of return (AIRR)**   An internal rate of return analysis in which different reinvestment and discount rates for both positive and negative cash flows have been specified. The adjusted internal rate applies a "safe rate" to all negative cash flows, discounts them to time period zero, and adds them to the initial investment. The safe rate is the rate that could be earned on the funds until needed to cover negative cash flows. A market rate is applied to all positive cash flows, which are carried forward to the end of the investment holding period. The market rate is the rate that can be earned by investing the positive cash flows in other investments. The AIRR equals the internal rate of return (IRR) that equates the present value figure to the future value figure. The AIRR is usually less than the IRR for the same property because funds are assumed to be reinvested at a lower rate. Also called the modified internal rate of return. *See also* financial management rate of return, internal rate of return.

For example, assume a property produces a net operating income (NOI) of $10,000 in year 1, and this NOI increases by 4% a year over a 5-year holding period. The property is purchased for $100,000 and sold at $120,000 after 5 years. Cash flows from the property can be reinvested at 6%. The adjusted internal rate of return can be calculated as follows:

| Year | Cash Flow | Present Value | Future Value (6%) |
|---|---|---|---|
| 0 | (100,000) | (100,000) | |
| 1 | 10,000 | | 12,625 |
| 2 | 10,400 | | 12,387 |
| 3 | 10,816 | | 12,153 |
| 4 | 11,249 | | 11,924 |
| 5 | 131,699 | | 131,699 |
| Total | | (100,000) | 180,788 |

$$100,000 \times S^n_{(x\%, \ 5 \ years)} = 180,788$$

$$S^n_{(x\%, \ 5 \ years)} = 1.80788$$

1.80788 is between 12% and 13% by using an annual compound interest table.
Adjusted IRR = 12.57% by using a financial calculator.

**adjusted sales price**   The estimated sales price of a comparable property after additions and/or subtractions have been made to the actual sales price to allow for differences between the comparable and the subject property transaction. This is what the comparable property would have sold for if it had possessed all the characteristics of the subject property as of the effective date of the appraisal. *See also* adjustments, sales adjustment grid, direct sales comparison approach.

**adjustments**   The value changes added to or subtracted from the sales price of a comparable property to arrive at an indicated value for the property being appraised (subject property). Adjustments may be made by percentage changes or by specific dollar amounts. Real estate elements of comparison that are used to adjust the sales price of the comparable property include property rights, financing terms, conditions of sale, market conditions, location and physical characteristics. *See also* direct sales comparison approach, percentage adjustments, sales adjustment grid.

**administrative expenses**   The expenses incurred in directing or conducting a business (including the construction process), as distinguished from the expenses of manufacturing, selling, and financing. The items included depend upon the nature of the business, but usually encompass items such as salaries of officers, rent of offices, and office and general expenses. Also called general and administrative expenses or overhead expenses.

**adverse possession**   The acquiring of title to real property owned by another by means of open, actual, continuous, and hostile possession for a statutory period of time that is stipulated by state law.

**aesthetic value**   Aesthetic value is an intangible value created when a property possesses characteristics that are exceptionally attractive or pleasing. The aesthetic value may be protected through zoning ordinances or building codes, e.g., the regulation of signs in a commercial district.

**affinity groups**   Retail establishments that are perceived to be linked together by the consumer on the basis of the nature of the product or the consumer's shopping habits. Examples are women's clothing stores, accessory and shoe stores, family clothing stores, etc.

**after-tax cash flow (ATCF)**   The cash flow (either from operations or at resale) that remains from net operating income and net resale proceeds after deduction for debt service, loan repayment, and all ordinary income taxes applicable to each period. *See also* before-tax cash flow (BTCF), debt service, net operating income (NOI), tax liability, taxable income.

For example, if a property has a net operating income of $20,000, debt service of $5,000 and federal income taxes estimated to be $5,000, then the after-tax cash flow from operations is as follows:

| | |
|---|---:|
| NOI | $20,000 |
| Debt service | − 5,000 |
| Tax liability | − 5,000 |
| After-tax cash flow | $10,000 |

If the same property could be sold for $100,000 with a mortgage balance at the time of sale of $70,000 and a federal income tax liability from sale of $20,000 then the after-tax cash flow from sale would be as follows:

| | |
|---|---:|
| Sales price | $100,000 |
| Mortgage balance | − 70,000 |
| Tax liability | − 20,000 |
| After-tax cash flow | $ 10,000 |

**after-tax equity yield rate (Y$_t$)**    The annualized rate of return that discounts all expected after-tax cash flows (from operations and resale) to a present value equal to the original equity investment in the property. It represents the internal rate of return on equity after taxes. *See also* before-tax equity yield rate, equity yield rate (Y$_E$).

For example, a property is purchased for $200,000, with a mortgage of $160,000. The property produces an after-tax cash flow to the investor of $4,000 per year. At the end of 10 years, the property is sold. After closing costs, taxes, and repayment of the mortgage, the investor realizes an after-tax cash flow from sale of $45,000. The after-tax equity yield rate is calculated as follows:

$$\text{Equity invested} = \$200,000 - \$160,000 = \$40,000$$
$$40,000 = 4,000 \times a_{\overline{n}|(x\%, \ 10 \ \text{years})} + 45,000 \times 1/S^n_{(x\%, \ 10 \ \text{years})}$$

Using an annual compound interest table or financial calculator, the annual interest rate equals 10.76%.

**after-tax income**    *See* after-tax cash flow (ATCF).

**after-tax internal rate of return (ATIRR)**    The annualized rate of return, calculated after income taxes are deducted, on capital that is generated or capable of being generated within an investment or portfolio. *See also* internal rate of return (IRR), yield rate.

**after-tax proceeds from resale**    *See* after-tax cash flow (ATCF).

**after-tax yield rate**    *See* after-tax internal rate of return (ATIRR).

**age-life method**  *See* economic age-life method.

**agglomeration economies**  Spatial associations that generate cost reductions for a business activity. There are four categories of agglomeration economies. Transfer economies are those cost-reducing factors associated with a firm locating in an area where there are other firms that demand transport services and systems. Internal economies to scale are those cost-reducing factors that arise when a firm locates near the buyer of its output. Localization economies are those cost-reducing factors that arise from a firm locating in an area where there are other firms in the same industrial group. Urbanization economies are those cost-reducing factors that arise when a firm locates in an area where there are firms in all other industrial categories, i.e., an urban or metropolitan area.

**air rights**  The legal rights to use, occupy, control and regulate the airspace above a parcel of real estate. Air rights can be sold, leased and created through easements. *See also* avigation easement.

**AIRR**  *See* adjusted internal rate of return (AIRR).

**Akerson format**  An alternative way of writing the Ellwood formula; a series of calculations used to find an overall rate that is based on the mortgage equity analysis concept that allows for cash flow forecasts including the impact of financing. The process allows for a direct solution for value even though the loan amount is entered as a percentage of value, and any change in value (either appreciation or depreciation) may be entered as a percentage of value.

For example, an investor requires a 15% equity yield rate. The net operating income (NOI) of a property is $10,000 per year for a 5-year holding period. The value of the property will increase by 20% over 5 years, and the loan on the property equals 75% of value, with a 12% rate, 15-year term and monthly payments. The overall rate can be calculated as follows:

1. $M \times R_M =$      $.75 \times .14402 =$      $.10802$
2. $+(1-M) \times Y_E =$    $.25 \times .15 =$      $.03750$
3. $-M \times p \times 1/S_{\overline{n}|} =$   $-.75 \times .16348 \times .14832 =$   $-.01819$
4. $-\triangle_O \ 1/S_{\overline{n}|} =$      $-.20 \times .14832 =$      $-.02966$
5. $=$ Overall Rate $(R_O)$      $.09767$

where M equals the loan to value ratio, $R_M$ equals the mortgage capitalization rate, $Y_E$ equals the equity yield rate, p equals the percent of loan paid off, $1/S_{\overline{n}|}$ equals the sinking fund factor at the equity yield rate over the holding period, and $\triangle_O$ equals the total change in property value. The value of the property can now be found as follows:

$$V = NOI/R_O = \$10,000/.09767 = \$102,386$$

*See also* Ellwood formula.

**allocation**   The division of the value of a property between land and improvements; an appraisal method in which the land value is found by deducting the value of improvements from the overall sales price of the property. The value of the improvements may be established by developing a typical ratio of site value to total property value and applying this ratio to the property to be appraised. Allocation is most frequently used in appraisals of vacant lots in which comparable sales of vacant lots cannot be found and improved sites must be used as comparables, e.g., in urban areas where few vacant lots exist or in rural areas where few sales exist. Allocation is also called abstraction or extraction method. *See also* land.

**allowance for replacements**   A non-cash expense item included in many forecasted income and expense statements to compensate for the future replacement of building components that may wear out in the future, such as a new roof or replacement of heating, ventilating and air-conditioning (HVAC) equipment. The annual allowance for reserves should reflect the amount that must be set aside each year to have the funds required to replace the item at the time it must be replaced. Also called an allowance for reserves or a reserve for replacement.

**allowance for reserves**   *See* allowance for replacements.

**alternative mortgage instrument**   A type of mortgage that has different interest, repayment terms, principal or other features from the standard fixed rate mortgage, e.g., an adjustable rate mortgage or a graduated payment mortgage.

**amenities**   Features, both tangible and intangible, that enhance and therefore add value to a real estate property; e.g., tangible amenities such as recreation facilities and club facilities; or intangible amenities such as view and convenience.

**amenity value**   The value added to a real estate property by the presence of an amenity.

**amortization**   (1) The process of retiring a debt through repayment of principal. It occurs when the payment on the debt exceeds the required interest payment for a particular time period. For example, suppose a loan has a balance at the beginning of a year of $100,000, annual payments of $12,000, and a 10% interest rate. Interest for the year would be 10% of $100,000, or $10,000. Amortization would be equal to $12,000 less $10,000, or $2,000 per year. *See also* amortization schedule. (2) Annual deductions allowed in the calculation of federal income taxes. For example, points paid on a loan on income property are amortized over the loan term. If points amount to $25,000 and the loan has a 25-year term, then $1,000 can be deducted each year for tax purposes.

**amortization rate**  The ratio of the periodic amortization principal payment to the total principal amount to be amortized; corresponds to a sinking fund factor or rate. It is the difference between the mortgage (annual) constant ($R_M$) and the nominal rate of interest (I). *See also* amortization, amortization schedule.

**amortization schedule**  A table that shows the allocation of payments for principal and interest on a debt. Also referred to as a loan schedule. For example, the amortization schedule for a $100,000 loan at 10% interest for 25 years with monthly payments would look as follows:

| Month | Beginning Balance | Payment | Interest Paid | Principal Paid | Ending Balance |
|---|---|---|---|---|---|
| 0 | | | | | 100,000.00 |
| 1 | 100,000.00 | 908.70 | 833.33 | 75.37 | 99,924.63 |
| 2 | 99,924.63 | 908.70 | 832.71 | 75.99 | 99,848.64 |
| 3 | 99,848.64 | 908.70 | 832.07 | 76.63 | 99,772.01 |
| 4 | 99,772.01 | 908.70 | 831.43 | 77.27 | 99,694.74 |
| 5 | 99,694.74 | 908.70 | 830.79 | 77.91 | 99,616.83 |
| . | | | | | |
| . | | | | | |
| . | | | | | |
| 300 | 901.19 | 908.70 | 7.51 | 901.19 | 0.00 |

In this case, payments are equal over the life of the loan and are large enough to cover both interest and principal each period. The loan payment can be calculated by multiplying the loan amount by the installment to amortize $1 factor from column 6 of the compound interest monthly tables in Appendix B. Other types of loans may specify different methods of calculating the loan payment, however. The interest paid each period equals the monthly interest rate (0.83%) multiplied by the beginning balance. The principal paid equals the payment minus the interest paid. And the ending balance equals the beginning balance minus the principal paid.

**amortization term**  The length of time over which the periodic principal repayments are made to pay off a loan in its entirety. *See also* amortization, amortization schedule.

**amortizing mortgage**  A mortgage in which periodic payments cover both a partial repayment of principal and interest on the outstanding balance.

**amount of $1**  *See* future value of $1 ($S^n$).

**amount of $1 at compound interest ($S^n$)**  *See* future value of $1 ($S^n$).

**amount of $1 per period**  *See* future value annuity of $1 per period ($S_{\overline{n}}$).

$a_{\overline{n}|}$    *See* present value ordinary annuity $1 per period ($a_{\overline{n}|}$).

$1/a_{\overline{n}|}$    *See* installment to amortize $1 ($1/a_{\overline{n}|}$).

**analogue approach**    The process of finding existing, successful properties that are similar to the subject property. The comparison is made on the basis of physical, financial and locational features of the site and on customer profiles. *See* near twin approach.

**anchor tenant**    The major store that attracts or generates traffic within a shopping center. Anchors are strategically placed to maximize sales for all tenants. The type of anchor depends on the type of shopping center, e.g., a supermarket is a typical anchor for a neighborhood shopping center, whereas a major chain or department store is a typical anchor for a regional shopping mall. *See also* shopping center.

**annual constant**    *See* mortgage capitalization rate.

**annual debt service**    The total mortgage payments, including interest and principal, required in 1 year by a particular loan or for a particular property. *See also* amortization, amortization schedule.

**annual loan constant**    *See* mortgage capitalization rate ($R_M$).

**annual percentage rate (APR)**    A result of the federal Truth-in-Lending Act that requires lenders to reveal to borrowers the actual annual percentage rate being charged on a loan. The APR equals the effective rate of a loan after financing costs, such as origination fees and discount points, have been considered. Charges such as a prepayment penalty are not included in the calculation of the APR. For example, a mortgage for $100,000 with 2 discount points, 10% interest rate, 30-year term and payments of $877.57 has an APR of 10.24% ($98,000 = 877.57 \times a_{\overline{n}|(360 \text{ months}, x\%)}$, $x = 10.24\%$ using a monthly financial table or financial calculator). As in this example, the effect of financing fees is to raise the effective rate of the loan. *See also* effective rate.

**annualizer (a)**    A factor used in yield capitalization formulas to convert the total change in property value over a time period to an annual rate of change; the value of (a) varies depending on the pattern of income flow. *See* yield capitalization formulas, sinking fund factor ($1/S_{\overline{n}|}$).

**annuity**    A series of cash flows in which payments occur at regular intervals. The payments could be equal or could represent mathematically related or non-mathematically related patterns. A level annuity has equal payments. A straight-line annuity changes by fixed dollar amounts. A constant ratio annuity changes based on a constant percentage each period, and a variable annuity does not represent a mathematically related pattern of change. In an appraisal, the periodic payments are typically viewed as being received at the end of the period. *See also* annuity in advance, decreasing annuity, deferred annuity, increasing annuity, income stream, level annuity, life annuity, ordinary annuity, variable annuity.

**annuity due**   *See* annuity in advance.

**annuity in advance**   A series of payments that occur at the beginning of each period. Also called an annuity due. *See also* ordinary annuity.

**anticipated use method**   *See* subdivision analysis.

**anticipation**   The appraisal principle that states that value is created by the expectation of benefits to be received in the future. *See also* appraisal principles.

**apartment**   One or more rooms with complete living facilities used as a dwelling unit by 1 or more occupants.

**apartment building**   A building comprised of 4 or more dwelling units that share facilities such as a lobby, stairs, elevators, and utilities.

**apartment house**   A building comprised of 3 or more dwelling units that share facilities such as a lobby, stairs, elevators, and utilities.

**appointments**   Fixtures or personal property found in a building that may increase or decrease the intrinsic value of the property, e.g., equipment, lighting fixtures, furniture.

**appraisal**   According to the Uniform Standards of Professional Appraisal Practice, (1) The act or process of estimating value; an estimate of value. (2) Pertains to appraising and related functions, e.g., appraisal practice, appraisal services. *See also* acquisition appraisal, The Appraisal Foundation, appraisal principles, appraisal theories, approaches to value, consulting, review, report, reuse appraisal.

**appraisal date**   *See* date of appraisal.

**Appraisal Foundation, The**   An entity created by the appraisal profession for the purpose of regulating the appraisal industry. Given power by the Financial Institutions Reform, Recovery and Enforcement Act of 1989 to set minimum standards and qualifications for the appraisal profession. *See also* Financial Institutions Reform, Recovery and Enforcement Act (FIRREA), federally related transaction.

**appraisal practice**   According to the Uniform Standards of Professional Appraisal Practice, the work or services performed by appraisers, defined by 3 terms in these standards: appraisal, review, and consulting.

Comment: These 3 terms are intentionally generic and not mutually exclusive. For example, an estimate of value may be required as part of a review or consulting service. The use of other nomenclature by an appraiser (e.g., analysis, counseling, evaluation, study, submission, valuation) does not exempt an appraiser from adherence to these standards.

**appraisal principles**   The theories that attempt to explain the rationale of market behavior that affects value. Appraisal principles include the theories of anticipation, change, conformity supply and demand, substitution, and balance. *See also* appraisal, report.

**appraisal report**   *See* report.

**appraisal theories**   Different approaches occurring over time that tried to explain the creation and source of wealth and value. Well-known theories include the classical, mercantilism, physiocrat, and neoclassical theories.

**appraiser**   A person who possesses the education, training and experience necessary to render accurately an opinion as to the value of real estate. After the passage of the Financial Institutions Reform, Recovery and Enforcement Act of 1989, appraisers must be state-certified or licensed effective July 1, 1991, to appraise property involving a federally insured or regulated agency. *See also* Financial Institutions Reform, Recovery and Enforcement Act (FIRREA), certified appraiser, designated appraiser, fee appraiser, licensed appraiser, review appraiser.

**appreciation**   (1) An increase in the value of an asset over a specific time period due to changes in economic or market conditions. (2) An increase in the resale price of a property due to increase in demand or inflation. *See also* resale.

**approaches to value**   Various methods typically used by an appraiser in preparing an appraisal report. Of the three traditional approaches to value, the cost approach bases value on the reproduction or replacement cost of improvements, less depreciation, plus the value of the land. The income approach bases value on the capitalization of future cash flows from a property at an acceptable market rate. The direct sales comparison approach bases value on a comparative analysis of recent sales prices of similar properties, after making adjustments for seller concessions, property rights, time, and any differences in the properties.

**appurtenances**   Items that have been affixed to a property and thus become an inherent part of the property. Such items usually pass with the property when title is transferred although they are not part of the property, e.g., easements, water rights, condominium parking spaces. *See also* appointments.

**ARM**   *See* adjustable rate mortgage (ARM).

**APR**   *See* annual percentage rate (APR).

**arbitrator**   One who mediates a dispute to avoid a court determination.

**architectural style**   The design, structure, form and ornamentation of a building, e.g., cape cod, tudor, French provincial, bungalow. Some methods have been designed to provide a uniform classification system, e.g., the Class, Type, Style (CTS) System. *See also* formal architecture, vernacular architecture.

**architecture**   The art or trade of designing buildings, including the style, structure and character of construction.

**area**   The surface space defined by two-dimensional boundaries of a building, lot, market, city or other such space, measured in square units. For example, a rectangular building that measures 30 feet by 100 feet has an area of 3,000 square feet.

**area regulations**   The portion of the zoning ordinance that regulates the positioning of the improvement on the land. Area regulations are typically stated through the use of setback, sideline and backline requirements for residential property, with the addition of the parking ratio for commercial property. *See also* zoning.

**arithmetic mean**   *See* mean.

**ARM**   *See* adjustable rate mortgage (ARM).

**arm's-length transaction**   A transaction occurring in a competitive market with reasonable exposure under conditions requisite to a fair sale, with a willing buyer and seller each acting prudently, knowledgeably, and for self-interest, and assuming that neither is under undue duress. *See also* market value.

**arrears**   (1) Refers to a payment that is made at the end of a time period. (2) Delinquency in paying a debt.

**asbestos**   A material made of nonflammable, natural mineral fibers frequently used as a type of insulation and commonly used from 1930–1970 in residential, commercial, and industrial properties. The material is now perceived to be a serious health risk, and its usage has been limited by the Environmental Protection Agency since 1978. The presence of asbestos in a building may seriously affect its value depending on the need for removal or encapsulation of the asbestos.

**asking price**   *See* listing price.

**assemblage**   The act of combining 2 or more parcels of land into 1 large tract; usually done to allow the construction of a larger building in the hope that it will produce more income than several smaller buildings. An additional value (plottage value) may be created above and beyond the sum of the values of the separate parcels when the land is joined together. *See also* plottage.

**assess**   (1) The process of valuing real property for tax purposes. (2) The process of determining by a court or commission the compensation due to a property owner for the taking of real property.

**assessed valuation**   The process of valuing a property for tax purposes. The assessed value may or may not equal the market value.

**assessed value**   The value or worth of a property according to tax rolls on which ad valorem taxes are based. *See also* property tax.

**assessment**   (1) The valuation of real property for tax purposes based on appraisals by local government officials. (2) The distribution of proportionate individual shares of a common expense that is not regularly incurred, e.g., the division of expenses among condominium owners. (3) A specific charge levied against certain parcels of real estate for a definite purpose intended to benefit only those parcels, e.g., the addition of sidewalks or water lines in a neighborhood. *See* special assessment. *See also* central assessment, impact fees. (4) The valuation of real property to determine the just compensation to be paid a property owner for the taking of the property for a public purpose. *See also* condemnation.

**assessment base**   The total worth of all assessed properties in an assessment or tax district.

**assessment cycle**   *See* assessment period.

**assessment district**   The area under the authority of an assessor, which may consist of a single tax district or several districts.

**assessment frequency**   *See* assessment period.

**assessment period**   The time frame in which all property in the assessment district must be valued for tax purposes. Also called assessment cycle or assessment frequency.

**assessment ratio**   The ratio of assessed value divided by full market value. *See also* assessment/sales ratio.

**assessment roll**   An official listing of the property taxes paid by property owners in a jurisdiction. It usually lists the name of the owner, address, assessed value of land and improvements, total assessed value, application exemption codes and an identifier for each taxable parcel.

**assessment/sales ratio**   The ratio of the assessed value divided by the selling price. *See also* assessment ratio.

**assessor**   A person who determines real property values for ad valorem taxation.

**assessor's manual**   A handbook that provides guidelines and requirements for real property assessment procedures and is used to ensure uniform tax assessments for similar properties.

**assumable mortgage**   A mortgage that does not require approval from the lender to be transferred to a third party. The sales price of a property purchased with an assumable mortgage will probably have to be adjusted for the effects of financing. A property purchased with a below-market assumable mortgage will most likely sell at a higher price because of the lower mortgage payments assumed. *See also* mortgage.

**ATCF**   *See* after-tax cash flow (ATCF).

**ATIRR**   *See* after-tax internal rate of return (ATIRR).

**attic**   The accessible space between the roof rafters and the top floor ceiling joists.

**average**   A measure of central tendency for a group of data. Common measures include the mean, median and mode. The term *average* is sometimes used as if it was synonymous with *mean*.

**average deviation**   A number arrived at by finding the mean of a set of numbers, summing the absolute difference of this mean with each value, and dividing this sum by the total number of values in the set; gives an indication of the variation in the set of numbers. *See also* mean, standard deviation.

For example, consider the following set of numbers: 1, 5, 7, 3. The mean is:

$$\frac{1+5+7+3}{4}=4$$

The average deviation is:

$$\frac{|1-4|+|5-4|+|7-4|+|3-4|}{4}=2$$

**avigation easement**   A right purchased from owners of land near airports or gained through condemnation that allows aircraft to fly at low elevations over private property. It prevents property owners from building improvements or growing trees over a certain height. The amount of restriction is based on the glide angle required for the safe use of the airfield's runway. *See also* easement.

**award**   The total amount of compensation paid for a property through a condemnation proceeding. *See also* condemnation.

# B

**B** *See* building ratio, outstanding balance, loan balance.

**backfill** The subsurface material, usually soil or crushed stone, placed against structures, foundations or footings where excess soil was excavated during construction.

**balance** The appraisal principle that states that property value is created and maintained when contrasting, opposing or interacting elements are in a state of equilibrium. *See also* appraisal principles.

**balance sheet** A statement of the financial position of a business as of a specific date, prepared from books of account. It presents the current book values of the assets, liabilities, capital and surplus in a business as of a certain date.

**balcony** An open balustrade or platform that projects from the outside of an upper floor of a building. It is accessible through the building interior and is typically cantilevered or supported by columns.

**balloon framing** In construction, a type of framing common in older, multistory, brick buildings in which long studs extend from the top of the foundation wall to the roof. The second floor is supported by a horizontal ribbon or ledger board and joists that are nailed to the studs. This type of framing is rarely used today because of the poor fire resistance and high costs of long studs. *See also* framing, platform framing, post and beam framing.

**balloon payment** The remaining balance that is due at the end of a balloon mortgage. The final or balloon payment is substantially larger than the previous payments. A balloon payment is necessary in mortgages in which the periodic payment does not fully amortize the principal balance over the life of the loan. Also called a lump sum payment.

**baluster** In construction, a vertical post that extends from the handrail to the bottom rail or the stair on a stairway. *See also* balustrade.

17

**balustrade**   In construction, a railing on a stairway that consists of a handrail and balusters.

**band of investment technique**   A method of estimating either overall capitalization rates or overall discount rates by calculating the weighted average of capitalization or discount rates for various components that make up a total property investment. *See also* debt coverage ratio formula, direct capitalization, income capitalization approach, overall capitalization rate ($R_O$), discount rate.

*Mortgage-equity formula:* The weighted average of the mortgage capitalization rate (mortgage constant) and equity capitalization rate (equity dividend rate) results in an estimate of the overall capitalization rate for the property ($R_O = M \times R\hat{M} + (1 - M) \times R_E$).

For example, a property being appraised can be financed with a 75% loan. The loan has a 15-year term with monthly payments at 9% interest (indicated mortgage capitalization rate of 0.1217). Comparable sales indicate an equity capitalization rate of 10%. The overall capitalization rate can be estimated as follows:

$$R_O = (0.75 \times 0.1217) + (0.25 \times 0.10) = 0.116$$

*Land-building formula:* The weighted average of the land capitalization rate and the building capitalization rate results in an estimate of the overall capitalization rate for the property ($R_O = L \times R_L + B \times R_B$).

For example, comparable sales indicate that the land capitalization rate is 0.09, the building capitalization rate is 0.14, and land to value ratio of 30%. The indicated overall capitalization rate can be calculated as follows:

$$R_O = (0.30 \times 0.09) + (0.70 \times 0.14) = 0.125$$

**base rent**   The minimum rent stipulated in a lease. It is typically associated with leases that also allow for overage rent. *See also* rent, overage rent.

**baseboard**   In construction, a finishing board attached to the bottom of interior walls at the point where the base of the wall meets the floor.

**basement**   The lowest floor in a building. It may be partially or wholly underground. *See also* cellar.

**basic activities**   In economic base analysis, those productive activities with outputs primarily intended for export to other areas. Basic activities can be manufacturing, service or government. *See* basic industry.

**basic capitalization rate (r)**   *See* basic rate (r).

**basic employment**   Employment in basic industry. *See* basic industry.

**basic industry**    In economic base analysis, an industry that attracts income from outside the community. A basic industry is opposite of a nonbasic industry that is a support industry for a basic industry.

**basic rate (r)**    In the Ellwood equation, the basic rate is a preliminary estimate of the overall capitalization rate prior to adjusting the rate for expected appreciation or depreciation in property value. The formula is:

$$r = Y_E - M[Y_E + P(1/S_{\overline{n}}) - R_M]$$

where $Y_E$ = equity yield rate, M = loan to value ratio, P = percentage of loan paid off, $1/S_{\overline{n}}$ = sinking fund factor at the equity yield rate and $R_M$ equals the mortgage capitalization rate. The basic capitalization rate does not consider income and value changes and is not an estimate for the property discount rate $(Y_O)$. *See also* Ellwood techniques, J factor, K factor, overall capitalization rate $(R_O)$.

**basis**    *See* adjusted basis.

**basis point**    $1/100$ of 1%. Used to indicate a change in interest rates. For example, a rise in interest rates from 10% to 11% would equal an increase of 100 basis points.

**bathroom**    A room, if full-sized, that measures at least 35 square feet and usually includes a bathtub, sink and toilet. A three-quarter bathroom includes a shower stall, sink and toilet. A half-bath or two-thirds bath, which is also called a lavatory, lavette or powder room, includes a sink and toilet. The number of bathrooms per house is usually indicated by neighborhood standards. However, there should be at least one full-sized bathroom in the house and at least one bathroom per floor in a multi-story house. Bathrooms require the most heat and best ventilation of any other room in the house. *See also* building description, house zone.

**bay**    The area between four columns or piers.

**bay depth**    A floor area measurement that is the distance from the tenant side of the corridor wall to the exterior wall.

**bay window**    A window that extends outwardly from the wall creating a horizontal shelf area at the bottom and is supported by its own foundation. It is distinguished from an oriel or box bay window that lacks foundation support.

**beam**    A horizontal load-bearing structural member transmitting superimposed vertical loads to walls, columns, or heavier horizontal members. A beam may be made of wood, steel or concrete.

**bearing**    In surveying, a horizontal angle from 0° to 90° that specifies the direction of a course or angle in relation to true north or south.

**bearing beam**   A principal load-supporting member of a building that runs between foundation walls and is supported by poles, columns or pillars. It may be made of wood, steel or concrete.

**bearing wall**   A wall that supports part of a building, usually a floor or roof above it.

**bedrock**   The solid rock, usually lying a few feet beneath the topsoil, that serves as a good foundation support.

**bedroom**   A room, usually measuring at least 80 square feet that is used as a sleeping area in residential properties. The number of bedrooms in a house is usually indicated by neighborhood standards, with two- and three-bedroom homes being the most widely accepted. Each bedroom should have at least one closet with interior lighting. *See also* building description, house zone.

**before-and-after method**   A technique used to determine just compensation for land that has been partially taken through condemnation. In this method, the value of the property before condemnation and after condemnation is determined. The value of the remaining property not taken through the condemnation is the difference between the value before and after condemnation. Federal courts follow this method.

For example, assume a 50-acre parcel is worth $4 per square foot. The front 25 acres are then condemned. After the condemnation, the rear 25 acres are valued at $1 per square foot. Under the before-and-after method, the amount of compensation due to the owner would equal:

$$50 \text{ acres} \times \$4.00/\text{sf} \times 43{,}560 \text{ sf}/\text{acre} = \$8{,}712{,}000$$
$$- 25 \text{ acres} \times \$1.00/\text{sf} \times 43{,}560 \text{ sf}/\text{acre} = \underline{\$1{,}089{,}000}$$
$$\$7{,}623{,}000$$

The before-and-after method is also used to determine the feasibility of renovating a building. In this case, the value of the building before and after renovation is measured to determine if the value of the building increased more than the renovation costs. *See also* condemnation, federal rule, partial taking, state rule.

**before-tax cash flow (BTCF)**   Income that remains from net operating income (NOI) after debt service is paid but before ordinary income tax on operations is deducted. Also called equity dividend or pre-tax cash flow. *See also* after-tax cash flow (ATCF), net operating income (NOI).

For example, if a property has a net operating income (NOI) of $20,000 and debt service of $5,000, then the before-tax cash flow from operations can be calculated as follows:

|                      |            |
|----------------------|------------|
| NOI                  | $20,000    |
| Debt service         | − 5,000    |
| Before-tax cash flow | $15,000    |

If the same property could be sold for $100,000 with a mortgage balance of $70,000 at the time of sale and selling costs of $7,000, then the before-tax cash flow from sale can be calculated as follows:

|                      |            |
|----------------------|------------|
| Sales price          | $100,000   |
| Mortgage balance     | − 70,000   |
| Selling costs        | −  7,000   |
| Before-tax cash flow | $ 23,000   |

**before-tax equity yield rate**    The annualized rate of return that discounts all expected before-tax cash flows (either from operations or at re-sale) to a present value equal to the original equity investment in the property. It represents the internal rate of return on equity before taxes. *See also* after-tax equity yield rate ($Y_t$), equity yield rate ($Y_E$).

For example, a property is purchased for $200,000 with a mortgage of $160,000. The property produces a before-tax cash flow of $6,000 per year to the investor. At the end of 10 years, the property is sold. After closing costs and repayment of the mortgage, the investor realizes a before-tax cash flow from sale of $50,000. The before-tax equity yield rate is calculated as follows:

$$\text{Equity invested} = \$200,000 - \$160,000 = \$40,000$$
$$40,000 = 6,000 \times a_{\overline{n}|(x\%,\ 10\ \text{years})} + 50,000 \times 1/S^n_{(x\%,\ 10\ \text{years})}$$

Using an annual interest table or financial calculator, the annual interest rate equals 16.16%.

**before-tax income**    *See* before-tax cash flow (BTCF).

**before-tax internal rate of return (BTIRR)**    The annualized rate of return on capital that is generated or capable of being generated within an investment or portfolio. *See* internal rate of return (IRR).

**before-tax yield rate**    *See* before-tax internal rate of return (BTIRR).

**benefit-cost ratio**    *See* cost-benefit ratio.

**benefits**    In an eminent domain proceeding, benefits are the betterment gained from a public improvement for which private property was taken in the condemnation. *See also* condemnation, eminent domain, general benefits, special benefits.

**bent**    A rigid framing unit of a building, consisting of two columns and a horizontal truss, beam or girder.

**betterment**    An increase in the capital cost of a structure that increases the utility or market desirability of the property, and therefore its value. The measure of value increase is frequently the cost, but the cause is the enhanced utility. A capital improvement as distinguished from repairs or maintenance.

**bias**    The deviation of a statistical estimate from the true parameter the statistical procedure is designed to estimate. Bias is the systematic error introduced into an analysis by the failure to follow proper procedure or by other errors in the data program.

**blanket mortgage**    A loan that is secured by more than one property or lot. It is commonly used in construction financing for subdivision or condominium development. *See also* mortgage.

**blended rate**    An interest rate of newly refinanced debt that is lower than the current market rate but higher than the existing rate on the debt; used in instruments such as a wraparound mortgage.

**block group**    A census term that represents a combination of adjacent census blocks in urbanized areas that house approximately 1,000 individuals. A block group is equivalent to the enumeration district in geographic areas that do not have census blocks.

**blueprint**    An architectural draft or drawing of a building that provides the details of construction. Actual construction may vary slightly from the blueprint.

**board foot**    A lumber measurement that equals 12 inches by 12 inches by 1 inch, or 144 cubic inches.

**bona fide sale**    A sale in a competitive market at the current market price that represents good faith between the buyer and seller. *See also* arm's-length transaction.

**bond rating**    A classification assigned by financial reporting organizations reflecting their assessment of the relative financial risk of a bond issue.

**book depreciation**    On an owner's books, the amount of capital recapture written off for an asset for a specific period of time.

**book value**    The capital amount at which property is carried on the books of a company. It usually equals the original cost less reserves for depreciation plus any additions to capital. *See also* adjusted basis.

**borrower**    One who has temporarily used funds from another through the use of debt financing. Also called a mortgagor when the funds are borrowed through a mortgage.

**boundaries**    (1) The outer edges of a parcel of land. (2) The outer edges of an area, such as a neighborhood or district, which delineates the physical area that has influence on a property's value. Boundaries may refer to changes in prevailing land use, occupant characteristics or physical characteristics. *See also* neighborhood boundaries.

**BPI** *See* buying power index (BPI).

**breakdown method** A method of estimating accrued depreciation by which each cause of depreciation is analyzed and measured separately. (The five causes measured include curable physical deterioration, incurable physical deterioration, curable functional obsolescence, incurable functional obsolescence, and external obsolescence.) The different types of depreciation are then summed to find the total depreciation. *See also* accrued depreciation, curable physical deterioration, incurable physical deterioration, curable functional obsolescence, incurable functional obsolescence, external obsolescence.

**break-even point** *See* break-even ratio.

**break-even ratio** The ratio of the operating expenses plus annual debt service of a property divided by its gross income. The income figure used varies in practice and can be seen as either the effective gross income or the potential gross income. Use of the potential gross income in the ratio can give a rough estimate of how high the vacancy loss on the property could be to still break even. For example, the potential gross income of a property equals $150,000, operating expenses equal $90,000, and debt service equals $55,000. The break-even ratio equals: ($90,000 + $55,000)/$150,000 = 0.97. Vacancy on the property could then equal approximately 1 − 0.97 = 0.03, or 3% for the property to break even.

**bridge loan** A short-term loan used in the period of time between the termination of one loan and the beginning of another loan, such as the period between the termination of a construction loan and the origination of a permanent loan. Also used as temporary financing after the purchase of a property until it can be renovated or developed to qualify for a permanent loan. *See also* temporary financing.

**British Thermal Unit (BTU)** A measure of heat that represents the amount of heat required to raise the temperature of 1 pound of water 1 degree Fahrenheit at approximately 39.2°F. BTUs are used to measure the capacity of heating and air-conditioning equipment.

**BTCF** *See* before-tax cash flow (BTCF).

**BTIRR** *See* before-tax internal rate of return (BTIRR).

**BTU** *See* British Thermal Unit (BTU).

**buffer zone** A strip of land separating one type of zoning from another; it will sometimes be left vacant as a buffer from land that is incompatibly zoned. *See also* zoning.

**builder's breakdown method** *See* quantity survey method.

**building** A structure, usually roofed and walled, that is constructed for permanent use. It includes any permanent additions and structural components necessary for operation and maintenance of the structure.

**building cap rate**    *See* building capitalization rate ($R_B$).

**building capitalization rate ($R_B$)**    The capitalization rate that reflects the ratio of annual building income divided by the building value. Historically, the building capitalization rate was used to estimate building value in the building and land residual techniques. *See* band of investment technique, building residual technique, land residual technique.

**building codes**    Rules and ordinances created by local, state or municipal governments to set minimum building and construction standards to public safety. Building codes are a valid exercise of the state's police power and may be enforced by inspections, building permits and certificates of occupancy. Building codes address issues such as construction, quality, design, use, location, occupancy and maintenance of buildings.

**building cost**    The estimated funds required to construct a building. Common methods of estimating building cost include the comparative-unit method, unit-in-place method and quantity survey method. *See* replacement cost, reproduction cost.

**building description**    An explanation of property features and measurements and quality and condition of construction that is completed as a basis for an appraisal. It includes a description of features such as: the general placement of the improvements on the subject site and the effects of their location, the quality and condition of exterior building features and materials, exterior dimensions, a scale diagram of the improvement, exterior and interior photos, identification of the architectural style of the main improvement, compatibility of the subject with its environment, interior description of the number and type of rooms, functional utility of the layout, quality of workmanship and materials used, mechanical systems, air-conditioning, insulation, energy efficiency, garage, and outbuildings. *See also* architectural style, house zone.

**building height**    The total height measured from the bottom of the ground floor to the top of the outer surface of the roof.

**building ratio (B)**    The ratio of the building value divided by the total property value used in the income approach to appraisal in band of investment techniques. For example, a building costs $120,000 and the land costs $200,000. The building ratio equals: $120,000/ ($120,000 + $200,000) = 0.375. *See also* band of investment technique, building residual technique, land residual technique.

**building residual technique**    A method used to find total property value where the income attributable to the land is deducted from the net operating income and the remainder is divided by the building capitalization rate to arrive at an estimate of the building value. The building value is then added to the land value to arrive at an estimate of the total property value. This appraisal method reflects buyer concerns and actions prior to the 1970s. *See also* residual techniques.

For example, a property's land is valued at $100,000. Net operating income for the property equals $40,000. The land cap rate equals 0.09 and the building cap rate equals 0.13. The building value and property value can be calculated as follows:

| | | |
|---|---|---|
| Land value | | $100,000 |
| NOI | 40,000 | |
| Land value $\times R_L$ (100,000 $\times$ 0.09) | $-9,000$ | |
| Building income | 31,000 | |
| Building value (31,000/0.13) | | 238,462 |
| Total property value | | $338,462 |

**building restrictions** Regulations or controls used to limit the type and size of structures that can be constructed, e.g., deed restrictions and zoning ordinances. *See also* zoning.

**building service systems** The systems and components that provide plumbing, sewage, heating, ventilating, air-conditioning, lighting, power, vertical transport, fire protection and special services (public address, oxygen) to a building.

**building site** A parcel of land on which a building may be erected, including all surrounding land allocated to ancillary uses supportive of the building's use.

**built-up method** A method of developing a discount rate whereby a riskless rate is used and then increased to adjust for types of risk such as management, financial, and non-liquidity risks that are inherent in the property being analyzed. *See also* discount rate.

**built-up roofing** A roofing membrane composed of bitumens and felt, in which the membrane construction is "built-up" by the felt papers and interspersing bitumen layers. A viscoelastic membrane.

**bulk regulation** *See* area regulations.

**bullet loan** A short-term loan for leased-up properties used in the period between the expiration of a construction loan and the time that a permanent loan can be found. It is typically an interest-only loan lasting 2 to 10 years that cannot be prepaid. *See also* temporary financing.

**bundle of rights** An ownership concept that describes real property by the legal rights associated with owning the property. It specifies rights such as the rights to sell, lease, use, occupy, mortgage, and trade the property, among others. These rights are typically purchased by the buyer in a sales transaction unless specifically noted or limited in the sale.

**business park development**    A cluster of properties in which the tenant is offered office space with supporting warehouse space, research and development facilities, or production space.

**business risk**    The risk associated with the uncertainty of future income flows caused by the nature of a business. In real estate, business risk includes future variability in rents, vacancies, and operating expenses. *See also* risk.

**business valuation**    An estimate of the worth of complete or partial ownership rights in a business.

**business value**    The value resulting from business organization including such things as management skills, assembled work force, working capital, trade names, franchises, patents, trademarks, contracts, leases, and operating agreements. Business value is an intangible asset that is distinct from the real property and tangible personal property. It is also referred to as enterprise value or business enterprise value. *See also* going concern value.

**buydown**    A financing technique in which an annual lump-sum payment is made to the lender, typically by a third party such as a developer, in order to reduce the monthly payment of the borrower. The amount paid may remain level or change over several years. The buydown method is sometimes used by residential developers to lower the effective interest rate paid by the homebuyer. However, the cost of the buydown is typically reflected in the purchase price.

**buyer characteristics**    Demographic, economic and psychographic (attitudes, habits, lifestyle, tastes and preferences) characteristics of the buyer that underlie the demand for the property or the space on the property.

**buyer's market**    A marketplace characterized by a greater supply of a product than demand for that product. *See also* supply, demand.

**buying power index (BPI)**    A measure of demand in a local area relative to a benchmark value. One such index, the Survey of Buying Power BPI uses the United States as a benchmark in the following formulation:

$$BPI = 0.5 \text{ (local area's percentage of income)}$$
$$+ 0.3 \text{ (local area's percentage of U.S. retail sales)}$$
$$+ 0.2 \text{ (local area's percentage of U.S. population)}$$

Another form of the BPI could use a region or a state instead of the United States as the benchmark value.

# C

**C**  *See* mortgage coefficient (C).

**CAM**  *See* common area maintenance (CAM).

**cantilever**  In construction, a beam or other structural member that is supported only at one end and extends beyond the wall or building part that supports it.

**cap**  *See* interest rate cap.

**cap rate**  *See* capitalization rate.

**capital**  The accumulated wealth including money and/or property owned or used by a person or business.

**capital assets**  (1) Permanent property used to produce income, e.g., land, buildings, machinery, equipment. (2) In accounting, cash or property that can be easily converted to cash, e.g., accounts receivable, merchandise inventories.

**capital expenditure**  The cash outflow or creation of a liability used to invest in an asset, e.g., purchases of land, buildings, machinery, and equipment; as opposed to expenses that are considered a part of daily operations (capital expenses).

**capital gain**  The taxable profit derived from the sale of a capital asset. Equals the sales price minus the total of sales costs and the adjusted basis, where the adjusted basis equals the original cost plus capital additions minus accumulated depreciation. *See also* adjusted basis, tax liability.  For example:

| | |
|---|---|
| Sales price | $100,000 |
| Closing costs | 7,000 |
| Original cost | 85,000 |
| Capital additions | 5,000 |
| Accumulated depreciation | 30,000 |

Adjusted basis = $85,000 − 30,000 + 5,000 = $60,000
Capital gain = $100,000 − 7,000 − 60,000 = $33,000

Short-term capital gains (assets owned for 12 months or less) were treated as ordinary income for tax purposes prior to 1987, whereas long-term capital gains were not taxed. However, the exclusion was repealed in 1987. Effective January 1, 1987, the entire capital gain (short term or long term) is taxed at the ordinary income tax rate.

**capital loss**    The loss derived from the sale of a capital asset; it equals the sales price minus sales costs and the adjusted basis, where the adjusted basis equals the original cost plus capital additions minus accumulated depreciation. (See example in capital gain.) Current tax laws specify that short-term and long-term capital loss deductions from ordinary income are limited to $3,000 per year for tax purposes. The excess may be carried forward to future years at a rate of $3,000 per year until the loss has been fully deducted. A capital loss may not be used to adjust ordinary income if the loss arises from the sale of the taxpayer's personal residence. *See also* capital gain.

**capital market**    The market in which long-term or intermediate-term money instruments are traded by buyers and sellers.

**capital recovery**    *See* return of capital.

**capital recovery period**    The time span over which the capital invested in a project is returned.

**capitalization**    Any process of converting income into an estimate of value. *See also* capitalization rate, direct capitalization, yield capitalization, yield capitalization formulas.

**capitalization in perpetuity**    A capitalization procedure used to determine the value of a project in which an endless time period is considered. Provides for a return on investment but not a return of investment.

The formula to discount a perpetuity is: $PV = CF/Y$, where PV equals the present value, CF equals the cash flow and Y equals the discount rate. For instance, an annuity of $10,000 per year that lasts forever discounted at 10% has a present value of $100,000 ($10,000/.10). In the case of a perpetuity, the discount rate ($Y_O$) equals the overall capitalization rate ($R_O$).

**capitalization of ground rental**    *See* ground rent capitalization.

**capitalization rate**    A ratio that represents the relationship between a particular year's cash flow and the present value or the interest applicable to the cash flow. Usually assumed to be an overall capitalization rate unless stated otherwise. In appraisal, the term is typically preceded by a description that identifies the applicable interest. For example, the capitalization rate found by dividing first year net operating income by the overall property value is called the overall capitalization rate. One approach to estimating the value of a property is to divide the current annual income of the property by an appropriate capitalization rate. Also called cap rate.

For example, a property produces a net operating income (NOI) of $12,000 during the first year of operation. The value of the property is estimated to be $120,000. Therefore, the overall capitalization rate would equal 10% ($12,000/$120,000). A second comparable property may produce a first year NOI of $10,000. If other comparable properties also indicate capitalization rates of 10%, the value of the second property could be estimated at $100,000 ($10,000/.10). *See also* building capitalization rate ($R_B$), equity capitalization rate ($R_E$), going-in capitalization rate, land capitalization rate ($R_L$), terminal capitalization rate, mortgage capitalization rate ($R_M$), direct capitalization, yield capitalization, band of investment technique, debt coverage ratio formula.

**capitalized value**   A property value indication resulting from a direct or yield capitalization process; the present worth of anticipated future benefits, usually in the form of income, from ownership of the property. *See also* income capitalization approach.

**capture rate**   The estimated percentage of a total market that is currently absorbed by existing facilities or is projected to be absorbed by expected construction.

**capture rate analysis**   An analysis that assumes retail centers attract expenditure levels relative to their size and location. Thus, a center is more likely to attract a shopper if the center is larger, if it is located nearer the shopper's residence than other centers or both.

**carryback financing**   A financing technique in which the seller finances part of the purchase through a note secured by a junior mortgage or contract for deed.

**carrying charges**   Expenses incurred on a regular basis when holding idle property or property under construction, e.g., taxes, interest, insurance, utilities, and security.

**cash equivalency adjustment**   An adjustment made to a comparable sale that was financed in a manner atypical of the market. The adjustment eliminates the amount of the premium paid for beneficial financing. Once the adjustment is made, the adjusted sales price should reflect the price that would have been paid assuming financing typical of the market was used. The adjustment can be made through either the income approach or the direct sales comparison approach. In the income approach, the adjusted sales price is calculated by finding the value of the loan at current market interest rates and adding this figure to the down payment. In the direct sales comparison approach, comparable sales with typical financing are compared to sales with atypical financing. The difference in price after all other adjustments are made equals the adjustment to be made for atypical financing. *See also* direct sales comparison approach.

For example, using the income approach, a comparable single-family home sale is found, but it has below market financing. The home was sold at \$107,500 with a \$37,500 down payment and a \$70,000 assumable loan at a 9% interest rate with a remaining term of 15 years and payments of \$709.99 per month. Market interest rates on similar loans are currently 11%. Assume the buyer will hold the loan for the full term. To find the adjusted sales price, we first find the present value of the payments on the assumable loan at the market rate using the monthly present value interest factors (MPVIFA) in Appendix A.

$$PV = 709.99 \times (a_{\overline{n}|,\ 11\%,\ 15\ \text{years}})$$
$$a_{\overline{n}|,\ 11\%,\ 15\ \text{years}} = 87.981937$$
$$PV = 709.99 \times 87.981937$$
$$PV = \$62,466.30 = \text{cash equivalent of assumable loan}$$

Thus, the adjusted price of the home equals the present value of the loan at current interest rates (\$62,466) plus the down payment (\$37,500) that equals \$99,966. The cash equivalency adjustment would equal the original value of the loan (\$70,000) minus the value at current interest rates (\$62,466.30) or \$7,533.70. The adjusted price of the sale can also be found by subtracting the adjustment (\$7,534) from the sales price (\$107,500) that also equals \$99,966.

There are alternative methods of estimating the impact of below market financing. The method shown above is not the only method used today.

**cash equivalent**    A price expressed in terms of cash as distinguished from a price that is expressed all or partly in terms of the face or nominal amount of notes or other debt securities that cannot be sold on the market at their face amount. *See also* cash equivalency adjustment.

**cash flow**    The periodic income or loss arising from the operation and ultimate resale of an income-producing property. The cash flow could further be classified as either before-tax or after-tax cash flow and could also reflect the impact of financing. *See also* before-tax cash flow (BTCF), after-tax cash flow (ATCF), net operating income (NOI).

**cash flow analysis**    According to the Uniform Standards of Professional Appraisal Practice, a study of the anticipated movement of cash into or out of an investment.

**cash flow rate**    *See* equity capitalization rate ($R_E$).

**cash flow statement**  An annual financial report that shows income, expenses and profits and is often used to evaluate the return on the investment in the property.

**cash on cash return**  *See* equity capitalization rate ($R_E$).

**cash throw-off**  *See* cash flow.

**CBD**  *See* central business district (CBD).

**CCD**  *See* census county division (CCD).

**ceiling height**  The total height from the finished surface of the floor to the lower surface of the bottom chord of the roof truss (or to the bottom of the main beam supporting the roof in the absence of roof trusses). In multistory buildings, ceiling height is measured to the lower surface of the ceiling or ceiling joist.

**cellar**  (1) An underground room. (2) A storage space that is usually, but not always, underground. *See also* basement.

**census block**  Corresponds to the common usage of the term that refers to the physical or geographic area most often rectangular in shape and bounded by streets. A census block is the smallest statistical unit for which census data are available. The data are primarily housing variables. Block data are available for the urbanized area in a Metropolitan Statistical Area (MSA) but not for the MSA as a whole. *See also* census county division (CCD), census tract.

**census county division (CCD)**  A permanent subdivision of a county used for census purposes; established for areas that do not have local political subdivisions such as townships or MCDs (minor civil divisions). *See also* census block, census tract.

**census tract**  The smallest geographic area into which the Metropolitan Statistical Area (MSA) is divided for statistical purposes. Tract boundaries are established in cooperation with a local committee or organization and the Bureau of the Census. The boundaries are established with the intention of being stable over long periods of time but allowance is made for subdividing a single tract into subtracts bearing the same numerical identification. Tracts are designed to be relatively uniform with respect to demographic and economic conditions. Tracts include approximately 4,000 people. *See also* census county division, census block.

**central business district (CBD)**  The downtown area of a city or core that contains the primary business, retail, recreational and governmental activities of the community.

**central tendency**  In statistics, a measure of the tendency of values in a sample of numbers to cluster around a central point in a frequency distribution. Commonly used measures of central tendency are the mean, median and mode.

**certificate of convenience and necessity**    A grant of authority from a state or federal regulatory commission authorizing a company to render a public utility service, usually specifying the area and other conditions of service.

**certificate of reasonable value (CRV)**    A certificate issued by the Veterans Administration that states the estimated market value of a property based on a VA-approved appraisal. A CRV must be issued on any property in which VA financing is being used.

**certification**    (1) In an appraisal report, a certification of value which is signed, sealed and dated by the appraiser stating that the appraiser has personally conducted the appraisal in an unbiased and professional manner and that all assumptions and limiting conditions are set forth in the report. (2) *See* certified appraiser.

**certified appraiser**    As specified in the Financial Institutions Reform, Recovery and Enforcement Act (FIRREA), an appraiser who has been certified by the appropriate state to value property. Typically, the appraiser will have to pass a state-regulated exam and complete advanced education requirements to become certified. The FIRREA states that only certified appraisers may appraise property valued at $1 million or more that involves a federal agency. *See also* Financial Institutions Reform, Recovery and Enforcement Act (FIRREA); federally related transaction; licensed appraiser.

**chain store**    A retail store that is under the same ownership and management as several other stores that sell similar merchandise and are uniformly designed and managed.

**change**    An appraisal principle that recognizes the fact that a property and its environment are always in transition and are impacted by economic and social forces that are constantly at work. *See also* appraisal principles.

**change in property value ($\triangle_o$)**    The total change in property value over a holding period. For example, if a property increases from $100,000 to $110,000 in value over a 5-year holding period, then $\triangle_o = 10\%$ [(110,000 − 100,000)/100,000]. *See also* yield capitalization formulas.

**chattel**    A legal term for personal property. Tangible personal property (e.g., equipment or appliances) is called chattel personal whereas intangible personal property (e.g., leasehold estate) is called chattel real.

**chattel mortgage**    A mortgage that is secured by personal property.

**chimney** In construction, brick or other masonry that extends above the roof and carries the smoke outside. Smoke is carried inside the chimney through the flue. *See also* flue.

**chronological age** *See* actual age.

**city** A politically determined geographic area; the area contained within the political boundaries of a large incorporated municipality; a locale in which the inhabitants possess self-government.

**city growth** The nature in which a city grows outward from its point of origin (siting factor). City growth can be affected by availability of developable land, technology, transportation modes and the willingness and ability of the local government to provide needed services. For example, cities such as New York, which have relatively scarce land, grow with an increasing density of land use. *See also* siting factor.

**classical theory** An historical valuation theory that based value on the cost of production. Popular in the 1700s, it included capital, land, labor and productivity as the primary components of production. Utility and scarcity were also assumed to affect value. *See also* appraisal theories.

**clearing** The removal of unwanted vegetation by a bulldozer so that construction can begin on a site.

**client** According to the Uniform Standards of Professional Appraisal Practice, any party for whom an appraiser performs a service.

**closed mortgage** A mortgage that cannot be prepaid until a specified time or until maturity.

**closed-end mortgage** A mortgage that contains a "no further encumbrance" provision that prevents the mortgagor from using the property as security for further loans.

**closing costs** The expenses incurred when transferring property ownership, e.g., title fees, taxes, insurance premiums, legal fees and broker's commission. Closing costs may be incurred by the buyer or the seller. Also called selling costs.

**cloud on a title** An encumbrance on the title to a property that may affect the ownership or salability of the property.

**cluster development** An area in which housing units are built in groups on sites that are smaller than the typical site, and larger common areas are incorporated into the development.

**cluster sampling** (1) Analogous to stratified random sampling because both processes establish subgroups of the population. In cluster sampling, the subgroups, or clusters, are set up in such a way that there is a great deal of similarity between the clusters, and each cluster reflects the population as a whole. Dissimilarity occurs within each of the clusters. (2) A two-stage sampling procedure by which a population is divided into several groups, or clusters, a number of which are then drawn into the sample. A subsample of elements is then selected from each of the specified clusters. *See also* random sample, convenience sample.

**cluster zoning**    A type of zoning in which an allowable density of units for an entire area is stated, allowing development within the area to be clustered in different configurations, as opposed to more typical zoning in which zoning is based on a lot-by-lot basis, which specifies an allowable density per lot.

**CMO**    *See* collateralized mortgage obligation (CMO).

**CMSA**    *See* Consolidated Metropolitan Statistical Area (CMSA).

**coefficient of correlation (r)**    A statistical factor that measures the manner and degree in which variables change together. The correlation coefficient can range in value from $-1$ (perfect negative correlation) to 0 (independence) to $+1$ (perfect positive correlation). *See also* correlation, correlation analysis.

**coefficient of multiple determination ($R^2$)**    A statistical factor used in regression analysis that shows how much of the change in a dependent variable is determined by the independent variables used in the equation; the ratio of explained variance to total variance. For instance, $R^2$ of 0.80 would indicate that 80% of the variance in the dependent variable is explained by the independent variables. *See also* regression analysis.

**collateral**    Something of value offered as a guarantee or security for the fulfillment of a financial obligation.

**collateralized mortgage**    A mortgage secured by something of value in addition to real estate; an existing mortgage that is used as security or collateral for a loan.

**collateralized mortgage obligation (CMO)**    Debt instruments that are issued using a pool of mortgages for collateral. The issuer retains the ownership of the mortgage pool and issues bonds as debt against the mortgage pool. However, all amortization and prepayments flow through to investors. CMOs can be issued in multiple maturity classes against the same pool of mortgages to meet the needs of the different classes of investors. Therefore, securities are created with maturity and prepayment streams that may be vastly different from the underlying mortgage pool.

**collection loss**    Income that is lost when payment is not collected from tenants.

**column**    A vertical structural member that supports horizontal members (e.g., beams or girders) and is designed to transmit a load to bearing material at its base.

**commercial property**    Real estate used in the operation of a business, e.g., office buildings, retail stores, restaurants.

**commitment**    A pledge or promise by a lender regarding the terms and conditions under which a loan will be made. The sum of money to be loaned, date of payment and interest rate are specified. After a borrower applies for a loan, the lender writes a commitment letter that is a detailed offer to loan money according to specific terms. If accepted and fulfilled by the borrower, mortgage documentation is prepared by the lender.

**commitment fee**    A sum of money paid by a borrower to a lender who agrees to loan funds to the borrower at a future date; often calculated as a percentage of the expected loan and refunded from the closing costs when the loan is actually made.

**common area charges**    Fees charged to tenants or owners to reimburse the owner for expenses incurred in the maintenance and operation of areas that are used by all tenants; commonly used as part of shopping center rents.

**common area maintenance (CAM)**    Maintenance charges for items such as landscaping, snow removal, common area utilities, etc., that may be charged directly to tenants as reimbursement for these types of expenses on an income property.

**common areas**    Land or building areas that are mutually used by and benefit all tenants or owners; include areas such as halls, elevators and playgrounds. Frequently found in condominiums and shopping centers.

**common elements**    *See* common areas.

**common interest**    In condominium developments, the percentage of ownership held by one owner as compared to the whole property; may be measured on a square foot or price basis, e.g., the ratio of the square footage of one condominium as compared to the total square footage of all condominiums. The common interest measures the extent to which an owner will be charged for items such as real estate taxes, maintenance and operation of the common areas, and affects the number of votes an owner has in the condominium owners' association.

**common wall**    In construction, a wall that is shared by two or more buildings or by two sections of a single building.

**community shopping center**    A shopping center that measures approximately 100,000 to 300,000 square feet with 20 to 70 retail spaces and is typically anchored by a junior department store, discount store or supermarket. A community shopping center provides a broader range of facilities and merchandise than a neighborhood shopping center, but less than a regional shopping center. *See also* shopping center, neighborhood shopping center, regional shopping center, super-regional shopping center.

**comparable properties**    *See* comparables.

**comparable sales**    *See* comparables.

**comparable sales approach**    *See* direct sales comparison approach.

**comparables**    Properties that have been recently sold or leased and are similar to a subject property. Sales prices of these properties are used to estimate a value for the subject property. Comparable properties need not be identical to the subject but should be similar and relatively easy to adjust for differences in order to arrive at an indicated value for the subject after adjustment. Also called comparable sales, comparable properties, comps. *See also* direct sales comparison approach.

**comparative-unit method**    A method used to estimate the cost of a building based on the value of comparable properties that were recently constructed and adjusted for time and physical differences. The total value is based on the sum of the value per square foot or cubic foot. Values may also be determined through a recognized cost service. *See also* building cost.

**compatibility**    An appraisal concept that states that a building's form, construction, scale and size should be in harmony with its use and environment to maintain value.

**compensable damages**    In a condemnation proceeding, damages that are legally required to be paid to the owner or tenant of a property that is being wholly or partially condemned. Damages are usually limited to the loss of value in the property. Sentimental value, inconvenience, and loss of business not related to the real estate are not typically compensable. Physical invasion of the property by a condemning authority or the taking of some property right must usually occur before damages are considered compensable. *See also* damages.

**competition**    An appraisal concept that states that value is affected by the interaction of supply and demand in a market.

**competitive analysis**    *See* survey of competition.

**competitive area**  The physical space or geographic area in which the competition for a subject property operates and where economic and demographic changes can affect its revenues, expenses and value.

**competitive differential**  The process of identifying the special features that give one property a competitive edge over another. The data come from a survey of the competition.

**competitive market segment**  The group of properties that are in the same classification and compete directly with the subject property in the immediate market area.

**complex (industrial)**  A grouping of buildings, site improvements and support facilities organized to carry out a related set of industrial activities in one location.

**compound discount**  Successive deductions from a future sum or sums receivable at specified future dates, at specified rates of discount, to the present. Mathematically, compound discount is the obverse of compound interest. *See* discounted cash flow analysis (DCF).

**compound growth**  The process of increasing in amount by a certain percentage each period. Future growth is based on the original amount plus all accrued growth. For example, $10,000 that grows at a compound growth rate of 5% would equal $11,576 in three years $[(1.05)^3 \times 10,000]$. Also called exponential growth or constant ratio growth. *See also* compound interest.

**compound interest**  Continuous and systematic additions to a principal sum over a series of time periods. The additions are based on a specific periodic interest rate with additions based on the total prior accumulation of interest and principal. *See also* amortization schedule, simple interest.

**comps**  *See* comparables.

**concentric zone theory (model)**  A land development model that theorizes that a city grows by establishing additional rings around a pattern of existing rings of activity. At the center of the pattern is the central business district (CBD). The next ring is a "transition" ring containing manufacturing and warehousing activity, as well as some less-prestigious commercial activity. The third ring contains low-income housing, while the fourth ring contains middle-income housing. The new ring, the growth ring, will contain new housing units that are upper-income housing options.

**concessions**  A discount or service given to prospective tenants to induce them to sign a lease.

**condemnation**   The exercise of the power of eminent domain by the government, i.e., the right of the government to take private property for public use. *See also* acquisition appraisal, award, before-and-after method, benefits, compensable damages, consequential damages, damages, eminent domain, general benefits, partial taking, proximity damage, special benefits, value after the taking, value before the taking.

**condition (of construction)**   The amount of structural defects or physical deterioration present in a building. *See also* quality (of construction).

**condition of sale**   An element of comparison in the direct sales comparison approach that refers to the motivations of the buyer and seller in a sales transaction. Examples include the relationship between buyer and seller, financial needs of buyer and seller (a quick sale), and lack of exposure on the market. *See also* direct sales comparison approach.

**condominium**   A multi-unit structure or property in which persons hold fee simple title to individual units and an individual interest in common areas.

**condominium conversion**   The transformation of a rental property into condominium ownership, e.g., changing an apartment complex into condominiums.

**conduit**   In construction, a hollow metal or fiber pipe used to carry and protect electrical wires.

**conformity**   An appraisal principle that states that the more a property is in harmony with its surroundings, the greater the contributory value. *See also* appraisal principles.

**consequential damages**   Financial compensation made to a person who has suffered loss or injury as a result of a breach of contract, which could not reasonably have been prevented.

**consistent use**   An appraisal concept that states that land and improvements to that land must be valued on the same basis. Improvements to the land must contribute to the land value to have any value themselves.

**Consolidated Metropolitan Statistical Area (CMSA)**   A large geographic area that consists of two or more Primary Metropolitan Statistical Areas (PMSAs); designated under standards set in 1980 by the Federal Committee on MSAs. *See also* Metropolitan Statistical Area (MSA), Primary Metropolitan Statistical Area (PMSA).

**constant**   *See* mortgage capitalization rate ($R_M$).

**constant amortization mortgage**   A mortgage that requires equal periodic principal payments. Because the interest decreases as the loan is amortized, total payments decrease over the loan term. *See also* mortgage.

**constant dollar projections**   Dollar projections that account for only real growth and not for inflation.

**constant dollars**   A dollar figure that represents only real growth and does not include inflation.

**constant ratio growth**   *See* compound growth.

**construction cost**   The cost to build a structure including direct costs of labor and materials, contractor's overhead and profit plus indirect costs such as taxes and construction loan interest. Distinguished from original cost, which is the cost to the present owner who may have paid more or less than the cost of construction. Also called fixed capital costs, total cost of construction. *See also* building cost, replacement cost, reproduction cost.

**construction loan**   A short-term loan used to cover the construction costs of a project that is generally repaid with the proceeds from permanent financing. *See also* temporary financing.

**constructive notice**   The legal presumption that a person is responsible for knowing certain facts that may be discovered by diligence or inquiry into the public records.

**consulting**   According to the Uniform Standards of Professional Appraisal Practice, the act or process of providing information, analysis of real estate data and recommendations or conclusions on diversified problems in real estate, other than estimating value.

**consumer price index (CPI)**   A series of numbers released by the Bureau of Labor Statistics of the federal Department of Labor that represents the change in price levels of a predetermined mix of consumer goods and services. The CPI is often used to adjust rental payments in leases.

**consumer research**   The process of investigating the subgroups of the population who express a demand for real estate by analyzing their economic, demographic and psychographic characteristics (such as attitudes, habits, and lifestyles).

**contingency**   In a contract, a provision that states that the contract is binding only if a certain act or event occurs, for example, an offer to purchase a house may be binding only if financing can be obtained.

**contingency allowance**   A specific provision in a construction budget for unforeseeable elements of cost that may be encountered within a construction project. Contingencies are different from escalation costs which account for price-level changes over time.

**contingent fees**    Compensation that is paid only if certain acts or events occur.

**contour map**    A topographic map that depicts the features of the land by contour lines that represent land elevations.

**contract**    A legal agreement between two or more competent parties to do or not to do a particular act; an enforceable promise. In real estate, a contract is usually a written, signed and dated statement to do or not to do a legal act within a specific time.

**contract rent**    The actual rental payment specified in a lease. Contract rent may be greater than, less than or equal to economic rent and/or market rent.

**contractor's overhead**    Expenses incurred by a contractor to manage or administrate the construction of a project; a component of direct costs in comparison to the developer's overhead that is not part of direct costs. Contractor's overhead includes costs such as job supervision costs, liability insurance and unemployment insurance.

**contractor's profit**    The profit, above and beyond all construction costs, generally expressed as a percentage of direct construction costs, that is adequate to compensate a contractor for the time and effort required to construct an improvement; a component of direct costs in comparison to the developer's profit that is not part of direct costs.

**contribution**    An appraisal concept that states that the value of a particular component is equal to the amount it contributes to the property as a whole. The value of the component is not measured as its cost but by the amount that its absence would detract from the entire property value.

**convenience (or low-order) products**    Generally non-durable commodities that are needed immediately, relatively inexpensive and purchased frequently (daily, weekly, monthly) at the most convenient or accessible location without extensive comparison of style, price and quality. Because the consumer shops frequently at these stores, the quality of products and their prices is well-known.

**convenience sample**    A process by which the researcher identifies the elements in the population that are most accessible, most willing to respond or simply more convenient to interview. *See also* cluster sampling, random sample.

**conventional mortgage**    A mortgage that is not insured or guaranteed by a government agency but may be privately insured. *See also* mortgage.

**Converse's modification**    An enhanced version of Reilly's Model of Retail Gravitation used to determine the geographic trade area boundaries of a retail establishment, provides the ability to obtain an estimate of the distance from the site where its influence is equal to that of its competitors. *See also* Reilly's Model of Retail Gravitation.

**conversion**   The process of changing an income-producing property into another use.

**convertible mortgage**   A mortgage in which the lender may convert his debt position into equity by decreasing or forgoing cash amortization payments at some time during the life of the loan.

**conveyance**   A transfer of title or an interest in real property through a written document such as a deed or lease.

**cooperative apartment**   A unit in a building in which the resident purchases stock in the corporation or trust that owns the building in an amount representative of the value of a single apartment. The resident receives a lease for that apartment.

**cooperative conversion**   The transformation of rental property into cooperative ownership, e.g., changing an apartment complex into cooperative ownership.

**cooperative interest**   An ownership interest in a cooperative apartment. Cooperative interest does not include the owner's pro rata share of the blanket mortgage.

**cooperative ownership**   A form of ownership in which each resident of a cooperative apartment building has purchased shares in a corporation that holds title to the building. The individual pays a proportionate share of operating expenses and debt service on the building owned by the corporation, based on the amount of stock held in the corporation. In return for stock in the corporation, the individual receives a lease granting occupancy of a specific unit in the building.

**corner influence**   The effect on value when a property line abuts the intersection of two streets. The value may be greater or less than inside lots, depending on the utility associated with being located on a corner.

**corporation**   In law, an organization that acts as a single legal entity in performing certain activities and is held separate from the individuals involved.

**correlation**   In statistics, a measure of the closeness of fit or strength of a linear relationship between two or more variables. For example, if the values of two variables form a straight line when graphed, then the correlation between the two variables is high because the value of one variable can be determined by knowing the value of the other variable. *See also* coefficient of correlation (r).

**correlation analysis**  A statistical method used to determine the strength of relationship or closeness of fit between variables. Simple correlation analyzes the relationship between one dependent variable and one independent variable. Multiple correlation analyzes one dependent variable and two or more independent variables. *See also* coefficient of correlation, correlation, regression analysis.

**corrosion**  Direct chemical or electrochemical reaction of a metal with its environment and general destruction of any material resulting from reaction with environment.

**cost**  *See* construction cost, development cost, direct costs, indirect costs, reproduction cost, replacement cost, original cost.

**cost approach**  One of the three traditional appraisal approaches to estimating value. In this approach, value is based on adding the contributing value of any improvements (after deduction for accrued depreciation) to the value of the land as if it were vacant, based on its highest and best use. If the interest appraisal is other than fee simple, additional adjustments may be necessary for non-realty interest and/or the impact of existing leases or contracts. *See also* appraisal, building cost, replacement cost, reproduction cost.

**cost estimating**  In appraisal, an approximation of the reproduction or replacement cost of an improvement. Common methods of cost estimating include: comparative-unit method, quantity survey method and unit-in-place method (segregated cost method).

**cost index**  A multiplier used to estimate current costs, based on known historical costs.

**cost of development method**  *See* subdivision analysis.

**cost of friction**  (1) Travel costs that users of a site must incur to maintain the linkages they desire with land uses on other sites. (2) *See* transfer costs.

**cost recovery**  *See* depreciation.

**cost service index**  A table of multipliers that differs by region, used to estimate current costs based on known historical costs.

**cost to cure**  The dollar amount needed to restore an item of deferred maintenance to a new or reasonably new condition. *See also* curable physical deterioration.

**cost-benefit ratio**  The ratio of benefits generated by an improvement divided by the cost of that improvement. The ratio must exceed 1.00 for the improvement to be considered desirable. The alternative term, benefit-cost ratio, is actually more descriptive.

**cost-benefit study**   An analysis of the cost of creating an improvement versus the benefits that will be created by the improvement including nonmonetary issues. A cost-benefit study is typically used by public agencies to make decisions concerning capital improvements. *See also* cost-benefit ratio.

**cost-of-living index**   An index number that indicates the relative change in the cost of living throughout different periods of time.

**covenant**   A written agreement that specifies certain uses or acts allowable on a property; found in real estate documents such as leases, mortgages and deeds. Damages may be claimed for breach of a covenant.

**coverage ratio**   *See* debt coverage ratio (DCR).

**CPI**   *See* consumer price index (CPI).

**CPI adjustment**   An adjustment used in leases in which the rent payment is periodically adjusted by a percentage of the increase in the consumer price index (CPI). A CPI adjustment is used to help protect the lessor from unexpected increases in inflation.

**crawl space**   In construction, the unfinished space between the first floor and the ground, usually less than a full story in height, and present in buildings without a basement.

**creative financing**   A general term used to describe financing techniques atypical of the majority of transactions. Financing may differ by amount of principal, interest rate, or payment terms.

**credit rating**   (1) An estimate of the credit worthiness and responsibility assigned to borrower-applicants by credit investigating, rating and servicing organizations. (2) The amount, type, and terms of credit, if any, that a bank or rating agency estimates can safely and prudently be extended to a borrower or an applicant for credit.

**cross elasticity**   *See* elasticity.

**CRV**   *See* certificate of reasonable value (CRV).

**cul-de-sac**   A street that dead-ends into a large turnaround area, used primarily in residential areas to decrease traffic flow through the street.

**culvert**   A small drainage structure that provides access for water to drain under drives, parking lots or other areas.

**cumulative attraction**   Retail establishments located next to each other so that each establishment can benefit from the increased volume of potential customers drawn to the cluster of retail establishments.

**curable**    Reasonable and economically feasible to cure; refers to physical deterioration and functional obsolescence in which the cost to cure the item is less than or the same as the anticipated increase in value after the item is cured. *See also* curable functional obsolescence, curable physical deterioration.

**curable depreciation**    Items of physical deterioration and functional obsolescence in which the cost to cure the item is less than or the same as the anticipated increase in value after the item is cured. Curable depreciation is reasonable and economically feasible to cure. *See also* curable functional obsolescence, curable physical deterioration.

**curable functional obsolescence**    A loss in value due to a defect in design, in which the cost to cure the item is less than or the same as the anticipated increase in value after the item is cured, for example, flaws in materials or design or materials and design that have become obsolete over time; an element of accrued depreciation. Includes superadequacies and deficiencies requiring additions, substitutions or modernization.

Deficiencies requiring additions are measured by how much the cost of the addition exceeds the cost if it were installed new during construction. For example, an office building is hard to rent because it has no windows on the top floor. The cost to install new windows in the existing structure is $10,000. If the windows were installed in a new building, the cost would be $7,000. The loss in value, therefore, is $3,000.

Deficiencies requiring substitutions or modernization are measured as the cost of installing the modern component minus the remaining value of the existing component. For example, an office building has outdated tile on the floor in the lobby. New tile, including the cost of installation, will be $4,000. The remaining value of the outdated tile is $300. Therefore, the loss in value is $3,700.

Superadequacies are measured as the current *reproduction cost* of the item minus any physical deterioration already charged plus the cost to install a normally adequate or standard item. For example, a small office building lobby has 12-foot ceilings that cause the electrical bill to be too high. The cost of lowering the ceiling will be $1,000. The salvage value of the old ceiling is zero. The estimated savings from decreased electrical bills is $240 per year, which would equal a capitalized value of $1,846 at a 13% building capitalization rate. Since the capitalized gain in net operating income ($1,846) is greater than the cost to cure ($1,000), the superadequacy is deemed curable. The depreciation due to the superadequacy is estimated as follows: The current reproduction cost of the ceiling is $700 and the physical deterioration already charged is $200. Therefore, the loss in value is $1,500 ($700 − $200 + $1,000).

However, if a *replacement cost* is used as the basis of the current cost, the expenditure to reproduce the superadequacy and the charge for physical deterioration are not deducted. Therefore, the total amount of depreciation charged would be $1,000 (the cost to cure only).

**curable physical deterioration**    Items of deferred maintenance or in need of repair in which the cost to repair is reasonable and economically feasible, measured as the cost to restore the item to new or reasonably new condition. An element of accrued depreciation. For example, a building has wood siding and needs to be painted. The cost to restore the building to a reasonably new state is $1,500, which is the cost of curable physical deterioration.

**curb**    The edge of a sidewalk, paved street, floor or well opening, typically made of concrete or stone and often raised.

**curb appeal**    The initial impression one gains of a property, usually as seen from the street while driving by. Curb appeal may be good or bad.

**current dollar projections**    Dollar projections that account for both real growth and inflation.

**current use**    The present purpose for which a property is used. Current use may or may not be the highest and best use.

**current value**    In accounting, refers to market value at the present time.

**current yield**    *See* internal rate of return (IRR).

**curtain wall**    An exterior wall that encloses, but does not support, the structural frame of a building.

**customer**    An individual who purchases a product or a service from a retail establishment. In practice, the definition is difficult to measure. The analyst must establish how much a "customer" spends. For example, an individual may spend $1 per year in the establishment, while another individual may spend $100 per week. Obtaining information on the latter individual is more important than gathering data on the $1 per year spender.

# D

**dairy farm**   A business enterprise that depends primarily on the production of dairy cattle as a source of milk and dairy products. Primary considerations in appraising a dairy farm include the soil and its production capability, improvements, the feed balance, and the market for the farm's product.

**damages**   The compensation recoverable in a lawsuit by a person who has received personal or property injury through an act or default of another. *See also* condemnation, consequential damages, eminent domain, proximity damages.

**data**   The information pertinent to a specific assignment. Such data may be divided into four different classes: general (relating to the economic and demographic background, the region, the city and the neighborhood), specific (relating to the subject property and comparable properties in the market), primary (information gathered by the appraiser that is not available in a published source, such as property dimensions and characteristics), and secondary (published information such as census data). *See also* general data, primary data, secondary data.

**date of appraisal**   The date on which, or as of which, the value estimate applies. This date establishes the market conditions in terms of which value is estimated. The date of appraisal is not necessarily the same as the date when the appraisal report is written. Also called date of value, valuation date.

**date of value**   *See* date of appraisal.

**days on the market**   The time period between the point when a property is listed and advertised for sale on a multiple listing service and that point when it is sold or otherwise removed from market availability.

**DCR**   *See* debt coverage ratio (DCR).

**dead-load**    The weight of a structure plus any fixed weight. *See also* live-load floor capacity.

**debt**    A dollar amount that is borrowed from another party, usually under specific terms. Debt may be secured or unsecured.

**debt coverage ratio (DCR)**    The ratio of annual net operating income (NOI) divided by the annual debt service. Lenders usually specify a minimum DCR (e.g., 1.2) that they require the property to meet during the first year of a loan term. For example, if a property is estimated to have an NOI of $12,000 for a given year and debt service (principal and interest) during that year is $10,000, then the DCR is $12,000/$10,000, or 1.2.

**debt coverage ratio formula**    A method of developing the overall capitalization rate by multiplying the debt coverage ratio by the mortgage capitalization rate and the loan-to-value ratio for the property: $(R_O = DCR \times R_M \times M)$. *See also* band of investment technique.

For example, a property can be purchased with a 75 percent loan. The loan has a 15-year term with monthly payments at 9% interest (indicated mortgage capitalization rate of 0.1217). The lender requires a debt coverage ratio of 1.2. The overall capitalization rate can be estimated as follows:

$$R_O = 1.2 \times 0.1217 \times 0.75 = .1095$$

This method views the valuation problem from the point of view of the lender only. There is an implied equity dividend in the analysis. If the implied equity dividend reflects the requirement of a typical investor, this method may be used to estimate the overall rate for a market value appraisal.

**debt equity ratio**    The ratio of the total amount of the loan divided by the invested capital (equity) of the owner(s).

**debt financing**    The use of borrowed funds to acquire a capital investment, as opposed to investing one's own funds. In real estate, the property itself usually serves as the security for the debt.

**debt service**    The periodic payment specified in a loan contract that covers the repayment needed to amortize the outstanding debt. *See also* amortization.

**debtor**    A person who borrows money; a mortgagor.

**decentralization**    Dispersion from a central point. (1) The movement of people, industry and business from the city to the suburbs, rural-urban fringe, and/or smaller cities. (2) The breakdown of an existing business into smaller units or expansion through the establishment of separate units.

**decreasing annuity**   Payments made on an evenly spaced periodic basis that are decreasing in amount. Also called declining annuity.

**dedication**   A voluntary transfer of privately owned property for some public use.

**deed**   A written, legal instrument by which an estate or ownership interest in real property is conveyed by a grantor to a grantee when the deed is executed and delivered. Many different types of deeds exist. The main difference is the covenant made by the grantor, e.g., warranty deed, grant deed, executor's deed, quitclaim deed.

**deed of trust**   A legal instrument, similar to a mortgage, that conveys title to property to a third-party trustee and secures an obligation owed by the borrower to the lender.

**deed restriction**   A clause in the deed of a property that limits its type of use or intensity of use; usually passes with the land regardless of the owner.

**default ratio**   *See* break-even ratio.

**deferred annuity**   A series of cash flows in which payments occur at regular intervals and the first payment does not begin until some time in the future.

**deferred assets**   In accounting, that portion of expense items that has already been paid but that is applicable to the period(s) subsequent to the reporting date. Deferred charges or deferred expenses are the preferred usages.

**deferred maintenance**   Items that are in need of repair because upkeep and repairs have been delayed, the result of which is physical depreciation or loss in value of a building; a type of physical deterioration that is usually curable. *See* curable physical deterioration.

**deficiency**   An inadequate feature in a structure or one of its components. *See* functional obsolescence.

**deflation**   A state of the economy that occurs when general price levels are decreasing and the purchasing power of money is increasing.

**degrees of freedom**   In statistics, the sample size minus the number of independent variables used in an equation minus one. This term is a measure of the t-distribution and is used to estimate the standard deviation of the parent population. *See also* regression analysis, t-distribution.

**delta (△)**   A symbol used as a variable in yield capitalization formulas that represents an expected percentage change (either positive or negative) in property value over a holding period. Originally,

Ellwood used the symbol "app" for appreciation and "dep" for depreciation. *See also* yield capitalization formulas, yield capitalization.

**demand**    The quantity of real property desired at a certain price or rent at a specific time in a market area and/or market segment.

**demand unit**    In economics, an individual component capable of expressing demand for a product.

**demographic data**    Information about the human population, especially in reference to changes in size, density, distribution and characteristics of the population in a specific area.

**demography**    The study of human populations, especially in reference to size, density, distribution, characteristics and changes in those variables. Used particularly in the valuation of commercial properties.

**demolition costs**    The expenses required to tear down and remove an improvement; may be used in highest and best use analysis.

**density of land development**    The ratio of building units or occupants divided by a unit of land area (acre, square mile). An allowable density is commonly specified in zoning ordinances, e.g., buildings per acre.

**depletion**    A reduction in the value of an asset caused by the removal of an exhaustible material or resource, for example, the removal of minerals from a mine or oil from a well. *See also* wasting asset, Hoskold premise.

**depletion rate**    The rate at which an exhaustible material or resource is removed from an asset; equals the amount of recoverable reserves divided by the total volume of production expected. May be expressed in dollar amounts.

**depreciable life**    The total time period over which the depreciation of an asset may be allocated. The depreciable life for tax purposes may be different than the actual estimated service life.

**depreciable real property**    Property that is subject to wear and tear and is used in a trade or business or held for the production of income. Land and personal residences are not depreciable.

**depreciated cost**    Cost new less accrued depreciation as of the valuation date. *See also* accrued depreciation.

**depreciation**    The loss in property value due to age, wear and tear, any negative functional superadequacy or deficiencies and/or external forces. Also called cost recovery. *See also* accumulated depreciation, accrued depreciation.

**depreciation accrual rate** The periodic amount or percentage at which it is judged that decrease in property value occurs; the percentage at which amounts are computed to be set aside as accruals for anticipated decrease in asset or property value due to depreciation.

**depreciation allowance** *See* allowance for replacements.

**depreciation recapture** In taxation before the 1986 tax law changes, an amount of the capital gain upon sale of a property that is treated as ordinary income rather than capital gains income. When accelerated depreciation was used, depending on the type of property, some of the capital gain could be taxed as ordinary income. After the 1986 tax law changes, all of the capital gain is treated as ordinary income.

**depth influence** The incremental increase or decrease in the value of a lot that is a different depth than the standard.

**depth tables** Uniform percentage tables that indicate the proportion of site value attributable to each additional amount of depth in the lot. Depth tables are typically used in urban areas in which lot depths are often similar.

**descend** The transfer of real property to heirs of an estate when there is no will. *See also* devise.

**design** The architectural arrangement of a property. If not up to current standards, design may cause functional obsolescence.

**designated appraiser** A person who has been awarded formal professional recognition by a designation-granting appraisal organization. Typically, it is expected that the designation is awarded as the result of passing prescribed examinations at the conclusion of technical training courses, presenting acceptable demonstration appraisal reports and completing a prescribed period of appropriate appraisal field experience. However, some designating organizations do not require any continuing education or tests. A designated appraiser is not necessarily a licensed or certified appraiser. *See also* certified appraiser, licensed appraiser.

**deterioration** *See* curable physical deterioration, incurable physical deterioration.

**developer** One who organizes and supervises the construction of improvements in an attempt to put land to its most profitable use.

**developer's profit** The sum of money a developer expects to receive in addition to costs for the time and effort, coordination and risk-bearing necessary to develop real estate. That portion associated with creation of the real estate by a developer is referred to as developer's profit. *See also* entrepreneurial profit.

**development cost**   The cost to create a project including direct costs of labor and materials, contractor's overhead and profit plus indirect costs such as taxes and development loan interest.

**development feasibility**   The ease with which building permits for a project may be obtained, as well as the proposed project's ability to meet other regulatory requirements.

**development loan**   A loan used to cover the development costs of a project that is typically paid off from the proceeds for lot or unit sales. *See also* temporary financing.

**development method**   *See* subdivision analysis.

**development rights**   The right to build on or improve a property. Development rights may be sold separate from the land, e.g., when the land will be leased.

**devise**   A gift or transfer of real property through a will. The donor is called a devisor, and the recipient is called a devisee. *See also* descend.

**differential shift**   *See* shift/share analysis.

**dining room**   A room, usually measuring at least 100 square feet, used as a formal dining area in residential properties. Construction after the 1950s has placed less emphasis on the dining room, which in many newer homes is part of another room. *See also* building description, house zone.

**direct capitalization**   The capitalization method whereby forecasted first-year net operating income is divided by an estimated overall capitalization rate in order to arrive at a value estimate for the total property. *See also* income capitalization approach, yield capitalization.

For example, a property produces a first-year NOI of $20,000. The market indicates an overall capitalization rate of 0.09. The indicated value would be $222,222 ($20,000/0.09).

**direct costs**   Expenditures necessary for the labor and materials used in the construction of a new improvement, including contractor's overhead and profit. Also called hard costs. *See also* indirect costs.

**direct reduction mortgage**   A mortgage in which both parts of the principal and interest on the unpaid balance are paid in periodic, usually equal, installments adequate for amortization over the loan's term; an amortizing mortgage.

**direct sales comparison approach**   One of the three traditional appraisal approaches to estimating value. Value is estimated by comparing to the subject property similar properties that have sold recently. Formerly referred to as the "market approach." *See also* adjustments, appraisal, comparables, paired data analysis, sales adjustment grid, subject property, land.

**disaggregation** A differentiation of the subject property from other properties by subclassification into smaller groups with differing physical and locational characteristics.

**disclaimer** A denial or disavowal of any interest in or claim to the subject of an action, such as renunciation of any title, claim, interest, estate or trust.

**discount** A fee paid at the beginning of a time period for use of capital during an insuring period.

**discount point** *See* point.

**discount rate** A general term representing a compound interest rate used to convert expected future cash flow into a present value estimate. In appraisal practice, the discount rate is the competitive rate of return applicable to the interest and cash flows analyzed and is identified by adding a descriptor to the rate. For example, the mortgage interest rate is the mortgage discount rate. *See also* yield rate (Y).

**discount-anchored shopping center** A retail development in which a discount store is the major tenant in the development, with additional retail space usually consisting of smaller retail tenants. *See also* shopping center.

**discounted cash flow analysis (DCF)** In appraisal, any method whereby an appraiser prepares a cash flow forecast (including income from operations and resale) for the interests appraised, selects a discount rate that reflects the return expected for the interest and uses the rate to calculate the present value of each of the cash flows. The total present value of the cash becomes the value estimate for that interest. Sometimes the cash flow forecast is based on an assumed pattern of change, e.g., compound growth. Also referred to as discounted cash flow. *See also* income capitalization approach, internal rate of return (IRR), net present value (NPV), present value (PV), profitability index (PI), yield capitalization.

**discounting** The process of converting future income to a present value by mathematically reducing future cash flow by the implied interest that would have been earned assuming an initial investment, an interest rate and a specified period (possibly divided into shorter equal periodic increments). *See also* future value, income capitalization approach, present value (PV).

**discovery** (1) The process whereby the assessor identifies all taxable property in a jurisdiction and ensures that it is included on the assessment roll. (2) In law, the process by which the lawyers for the opposing sides prepare their causes for trial, through requiring, with court authority, the witnesses for the opposing sides to answer a number of written questions.

**disguised questioning procedure**  A study in which the objective of the study is not made known to the respondent.

**dispersion**  In statistics, the degree of scatter of values in a set of observations, usually measured from a central value, e.g., a mean or median. *See also* decentralization, variance, standard deviation.

**disposable income**  The personal earnings remaining after payments to the government, including income taxes, are deducted.

**distribution**  *See* apportionment to intrastate jurisdiction.

**district**  A type of neighborhood that represents homogeneous land use, e.g., residential, industrial agricultural. *See also* tax district.

**divided interest**  A partial interest in a property, e.g., a lessor's interest.

**dominant estate**  The estate that derives benefit from the servient estate in an easement. For example, an easement road passes over an owner's land (servient estate) to another parcel of land (dominant estate).

**dormer**  In construction, a projection containing a window, which is built upright from the slope of a roof.

**down payment**  An initial sum of money paid by a buyer to purchase a property. The remaining value is usually financed through debt. Down payment is not synonymous with the term earnest money. *See also* earnest money.

**downspout**  A pipe that carries rainwater from a gutter along the roof to the ground or sewer system.

**drawing power**  The relative ability of one retail establishment versus another to attract and retain a customer's patronage.

**drop ceiling**  A ceiling that is suspended below the joists above by hangers so that space exists between the ceiling and floor or slab above it.

**drywall**  In construction, an interior wallboard made of a material other than plaster, e.g., gypsum board, plasterboard, plywood or wood paneling.

**duct**  A passageway made of sheet metal or other suitable material used for conveying air or other gases at low pressures.

**due-on-sale clause**  In a mortgage contract, a provision that states that the outstanding loan balance is due upon sale or transfer of the mortgaged property. A due-on-sale clause precludes a new buyer from assuming the mortgage.

**dwelling**  A structure designed for occupancy as living quarters by one or more households. A dwelling is usually equipped with cooking, bathing and heating facilities. Dwellings do not include structures used on a transient basis, such as hotels or motels.

**dwelling unit**    A room or rooms containing a single kitchen, constituting an independent unit for living space of a single family. Dwelling units do not include hotel or motel rooms.

**early occupancy**  A situation in which the buyer is allowed to take possession of a property before closing of the sale. Additional risks may be incurred in this situation.

**earnest money**  A cash sum paid by a prospective buyer as evidence of good-faith intention to complete the sales transaction. The deposit is usually held in a trust or escrow account until the transaction is completed, at which time it is credited toward the down payment. Also called bargain money, caution money, hand money, or (in some states) a binder.

**easement**  A legal interest in real property that conveys use or enjoyment but not ownership of the property. *See also* avigation easement, easement appurtenant, easement in gross, perpetual easement, preservation easement, dominant estate, servient estate.

**easement appurtenant**  An easement attached to the dominant estate. An easement appurtenant is passed with the conveyance of the dominant estate and continues to burden the servient estate. *See also* easement.

**easement in gross**  A limited right of one person to use another's property when the right is not created for the benefit of land owned by the owner of the easement. An easement in gross is not attached to any particular estate or land, nor is it transferred through the conveyance of title. Examples include pipelines and telephone lines. *See also* easement.

**eaves**  In construction, the overhang of a roof that extends beyond the face of an exterior wall.

**economic age-life method**  A method used to estimate accrued depreciation by multiplying the reproduction or replacement cost by the ratio of effective age divided by total economic life. Curable and short-lived items are not estimated separately. *See also* accrued depreciation.

For example, a building has a total economic life of 60 years and an effective age of 20 years. The reproduction cost of the building is $900,000. The accrued depreciation can be found as follows:

$$\text{Accrued depreciation} = (20/60) \times \$900,000 = \$300,000$$

**economic base**    The industry in a geographic area that provides employment opportunities and allows it to attract income from outside its boundaries.

**economic base analysis**    A study that analyzes the economic activity of a community; used to predict population, income and other variables that affect real estate values or land utilization based on the relationship between basic and non-basic employment. *See also* input-output analysis.

**economic base multiplier**    The ratio of total employment to basic employment in an economic area; used to project increases in total employment when basic employment is expected to increase. For example, if basic employment is projected to increase by 3,000 jobs due to a new plant opening, and the economic base multiplier is 3, then total employment should increase by $3 \times 3,000 = 9,000$ jobs.

**economic depreciation**    *See* external obsolescence.

**economic feasibility**    *See* economically feasible.

**economic forces**    In appraisal theory, one type of force that affects property value. Includes effects on value such as supply and demand, employment, wage levels, industrial expansion and availability of mortgage credit. *See also* forces.

**economic good**    Any obtainable good involving elements of utility and scarcity that create a desire (demand) for the good. An economic good commands a price in market exchange whereas a free good, such as air or sunshine, does not.

**economic impact study**    A systematic analysis based on scientific methodology that seeks to identify and measure any effect on economic activity or market indicators resulting from the location, introduction or change of a major land-use activity within the market area. Examples are a proposed overhead high-voltage electric transmission line traversing the area or the sudden availability of unexpected information about a major employer or land user in the area.

**economic life**    The estimated time period during which an improvement yields a return over the economic rent attributable to the land itself; the estimated time period over which an improved property has value in excess of its salvage value. The economic life of an improvement is usually shorter than its actual physical life. *See also* remaining economic life, actual age, effective age.

**economic obsolescence** A type of external obsolescence in which value loss is caused by an occurrence or situation that adversely affects the employment, quality of life or economics of an area, e.g., loss of a major employer, a high tax base or changes in zoning. *See also* external obsolescence.

**economic rent** *See* market rent.

**economic study** Any analysis involving economic variables, hence it is so general that other studies could be considered a particular type of economic study. This type of study is designed to analyze the entire economy. Several approaches can be employed in making an economic study, classifying all of the economic activities carried out in the area into a number of categories that are then utilized in the detailed analysis. The most complex classification occurs in the input-output approach. *See also* economic base analysis, input-output analysis, local economic analysis.

**economically feasible** Refers to a real estate project that is able to meet defined financial investment objectives, the ability of a project to produce sufficient cash flows to repay all of the expenses involved in creating and marketing the project plus provide a competitive return to the owner/developer. A criterion of highest and best use analysis. *See also* highest and best use (HBU).

**economics** The study of the allocation of scarce resources among competing and relatively unlimited desires in such a way as to maximize human satisfactions.

**ED** *See* enumeration district (ED).

**effective age** The age of an improvement determined by its current condition and utility based on its design, location and current competitive market conditions. The effective age may be greater than or less than the actual age. *See also* actual age, economic life, remaining economic life.

**effective annual rate** The annual interest rate equivalent to a nominal rate that is compounded more frequently than annually. For example, if the nominal rate is 10% compounded monthly, the effective annual rate is $(1 + (.10/12))^{12} - 1 = 10.47\%$.

**effective demand** The desire to buy coupled with the ability to pay. When the word *demand* is used in economic writings, effective demand is usually assumed.

**effective gross income (EGI)** The anticipated income from the operation of a project after adjustment for vacancy and credit loss. The effective income can be further classified as actual, market and/or economic effective gross income depending on which rent levels were considered when making the calculation. *See also* effective gross income multiplier (EGIM), potential gross income (PGI).

For example, a property has 100,000 square feet of leasable space. Current rental rates are $12 per square foot. Vacancy is expected at 15%, and a collection loss of $20,000 is expected. The effective gross income is calculated as follows:

$$100,000 \text{ sq. ft} \times \$12/\text{sq. ft} = \$1,200,000$$
$$\$1,200,000 \times (1 - .15) = \$1,020,000$$
$$\$1,020,000 - \$20,000 = \$1,000,000 = \text{EGI}$$

**effective gross income multiplier (EGIM)**   The ratio of the sales price, after adjustment for non-realty interests and favorable financing divided by the projected first-year effective gross income. For income-producing properties, the EGIM can be derived from comparable sales as one method of estimating a property value in the direct sales comparison approach. *See also* effective gross income (EGI), potential gross income multiplier (PGIM), direct sales comparison approach.

For example, the value of an apartment building that produces an annual effective gross income of $400,000 is being estimated. The EGIMs of comparable apartment buildings range from 3.24 to 4.1. The indicated value range for the subject property would then be $1,296,000 to $1,640,000. ($400,000 × 3.24 = $1,296,000, $400,000 × 4.1 = $1,640,000)

**effective interest rate**   *See* effective rate.

**effective rate**   The true rate of return after consideration of all upfront costs, concessions, prepayment penalties, etc. *See also* annual percentage rate (APR).

For example, a 25-year term mortgage for $80,000 with monthly payments of $726.96 at 10% interest and 2 points has an effective rate of 10.26%. The effective rate is higher than the stated rate because points are charged to the loan, i.e., the borrower receives only $78,400 but makes payments based on $80,000. The effective rate is calculated by finding the internal rate of return that equates $78,400 with monthly payments of $726.96 for 25 years, as shown below.

$78,400 = \$726.96 \times a_{\overline{n}|(x\%, \ 25 \text{ yrs.})}$
x% = 10.26% using the monthly compound interest tables or a financial calculator

**effective rent**   The amount of periodic rent that is equivalent to the amount specified in a lease after considering rent concessions such as free rent. For example, if a 5-year lease calls for payment of $10,000 per year for the next 4 years with no rent during the first year, the effective rent is approximately ($10,000 × 4)/5, or $8,000 per year. A more precise answer would result by considering the time value of money. Using the above example and a 6% discount rate, the present value of the lease payments is $32,690. This is equivalent (in present value) to $7,760 per year for 5 years. *See also* rent.

**effective tax rate**   The ratio between a property's annual property tax and its market value; the tax rate times the assessed value divided by the market value; the official tax rate times the assessment ratio.

**effective yield**   *See* effective annual rate.

**efficiency (apartment)**   An apartment comprised of one room that is divided into kitchen, living and sleeping areas.

**efficiency ratio**   The ratio of net leasable area of a building divided by the gross area.

**EGI**   *See* effective gross income (EGI).

**EGIM**   *See* effective gross income multiplier (EGIM).

**egress**   The path by which one exits a property; the opposite of ingress.

**EIS**   *See* environmental impact study (EIS).

**elasticity**   In economics, refers to the ability of a product to maintain a quantity level of supply or demand as the price of that product changes. Elasticity is measured as the percent change in quantity supplied or demanded divided by the associated percent change in price. In a highly elastic product, a small change in price is associated with a large change in quantity. A good with many substitutes will be more elastic than a good with few substitutes.

**electrical system**   The wiring, circuit breakers, fuses, distribution box, wall switches, lighting fixtures and such necessary to provide sufficient electrical service to power all the electrical equipment in a building. Most wiring is armored cable. However, plastic-coated wire and knob-and-tube wiring have also been used. Wire is typically made of copper, but aluminum wire was used frequently after the 1940s. Because of its lower resistance to fire, aluminum use is now prohibited in some areas.

**elements of comparison**   A categorization of property characteristics that causes real estate prices to vary, e.g., property rights, financing terms, conditions of sale, date of sale (or market conditions), location and physical characteristics. *See also* direct sales comparison approach.

**elevator**   (1) A platform that raises and lowers on tracks in a shaft between the floors of a building to transport passengers and freight. (2) A storage building for commodities, such as grain, on agricultural properties.

**Ellwood formula**   An algebraic formula used to calculate an overall rate that is based on the mortgage equity analysis concept that allows for cash flow forecasts including the impact of financing. The formula allows for a direct solution for value even though the loan amount is entered as a percentage of value and any change in value (either appreciation or depreciation) may be entered as a percentage of value. The formula is as follows:

$$R_O = Y_E - M(Y_E + (P \times 1/S_{\overline{n}}) - R_M) - (\triangle_O \times 1/S_{\overline{n}})$$

where M equals the loan-to-value ratio, P equals the percent of loan paid off (from loan tables), $1/S_{\overline{n}}$ equals the sinking fund factor and $\triangle_O$ equals the total change in property value.

For example, an investor requires a 15% equity yield rate. The net operating income of a property is $10,000 per year for a 5-year holding period. The value of the property will increase by 20% over 5 years, and the loan on the property equals 75% of value, with a 12% rate, 15-year term and monthly payments. *See also* Akerson format, J factor, K factor, yield capitalization formulas. The value of the equity and property can be calculated as follows:

$$R_O = .15 - .75(.15 + .16348(.14832) - .14402) - .2(.14832)$$
$$R_O = .09767, \text{ or } 9.767\%$$
$$V = NOI/R_O = \$10,000/0.09767 = \$102,390$$

**Ellwood graph**    A graph depicting the relationship among value, potential yield rates and changes in cash flow over a holding period.

**Ellwood techniques**    Algebraic formulas used in yield capitalization that consider future cash flows and the effects of financing to find the overall capitalization rate and property value. *See also* Ellwood formula, J factor, K factor, yield capitalization, yield capitalization formulas.

**emblement**    A growing crop that is produced annually and is considered personal property.

**eminent domain**    The governmental right to take private property for public use upon the payment of just compensation. *See also* acquisition appraisal, before-and-after method, benefits, condemnation, consequential damages, damages, general benefits, partial taking, proximity damages, special benefits, value after the taking, value before the taking.

**employment base**    The number of people in a community who are gainfully employed.

**employment by job site**    Employment data obtained from businesses and firms and reported on the basis of the firm's location. These data are collected and reported by the Department of Labor in each state.

**employment by residence site** Employment data obtained from individuals and reported on the basis of their residence site. These data are collected by the Bureau of the Census.

**encroachment** A part of real estate that physically intrudes upon, overlaps or trespasses the property of another.

**encumbered property** A property that has attached to it a lien, claim, liability or charge. For example, mortgages, taxes, and easements cause a property to be encumbered.

**encumbrance** Any lien, claim, liability or charge attached to and binding on real property that may decrease (or increase) its value or that may burden, obstruct or restrict the use of a property but does not necessarily prevent conveyance by the owner; a right or interest in a property held by a person other than the legal owner of the property.

**energy efficiency** The extent to which a building or appliance can produce a given effect by using a minimum amount of energy. Energy efficient buildings are typically better insulated and weatherproofed or contain special features to minimize the costs of heating and cooling.

**entrepreneur** A manager, owner or developer who assumes the risk and management of a business or enterprise; a promoter, in the sense of one who undertakes to develop.

**entrepreneurial profit** The sum of money an entrepreneur expects to receive in addition to costs for the time and effort, coordination and risk bearing necessary to create a project. The portion associated with creation of the real estate by a developer is referred to as developer's profit. Properties that also include an operating business may include additional entrepreneurial profit that is reflected in the going-concern value of the property. *See also* going-concern value.

**enumeration district (ED)** A geographic area that contains approximately 800 persons or 250 housing units. EDs are revised each census for operational reasons. In urbanized areas, the ED counterpart is the block group (BG) that contains approximately 1,000 persons. The BG is composed of census "blocks" that conform to the common use of the word—a physical or geographic area that is rectangular or square.

**environment** The climate, topography, natural barriers, transportation systems and other factors of location that affect the value of a property.

**environmental deficiency** Environmental forces surrounding a property that cause deterioration of value, e.g., overcrowding, incompatible uses or inadequate utilities.

**environmental forces**  In appraisal theory, one of four categories of forces that affect property value; environmental forces include effects on value such as climate, location, topography, natural barriers and transportation systems. *See also* forces.

**environmental impact study (EIS)**  An analysis of the impact of a proposed land use on its environment, including the direct and indirect effects of the project during all phases of use and their long-run implications.

**Environmental Protection Agency (EPA)**  An independent agency of the executive branch of the federal government, created in 1970 with the responsibility of preventing and controlling water, air, and noise pollution and the nation's environment in general. The EPA sets standards, establishes timetables for these standards, enforces environmental laws, conducts research programs and provides help to other local and regional governmental control agencies.

**environmental regulations**  Standards set by the Environmental Protection Agency to control air, water and noise pollution and other environmental conditions.

**EPA**  *See* Environmental Protection Agency (EPA).

**equity**  The owner's capital investment in a property; the property value less the balance of any debt as of a particular point in time. Equity is equal to the property value if there is no debt on the property. For example, a property is purchased for $100,000. A loan equal to $70,000 is used to purchase the property. The remaining balance, $30,000, is provided by the buyer. The equity in the property then equals $30,000.

**equity build-up**  The periodic addition to equity caused by the gradual reduction in the mortgage balance as a result of periodic principal repayment provided for in a loan repayment contract.

**equity capitalization rate ($R_E$)**  The capitalization rate that reflects the relationship between a single year's before-tax cash flow and the equity investment in the property. The before-tax cash flow in this instance is the net operating income less the annual debt service payment, and the equity is the property value less any outstanding loan balance. The equity capitalization rate, when divided into the before-tax cash flows, gives an indication of the value of the equity. Also called cash flow rate, cash on cash rate, or equity dividend rate.

For example, a property produces a net operating income of $20,000 and has an annual mortgage payment of $16,400. The property was purchased for $200,000 with a $170,000 loan. The equity capitalization rate can be calculated as follows:

$$(\$20,000 - \$16,400)/(\$200,000 - \$170,000) = 12\%$$

**equity dividend**   *See* before-tax cash flow (BTCF).

**equity dividend rate**   *See* equity capitalization rate ($R_E$).

**equity kicker**   An equity interest in a property given to the mortgage lender.

**equity participation**   An agreement by which a lender receives some share of the income and/or cash flow of a property based on the performance of that property. The participation might be based on a percentage of the net operating income, cash flow from operations and/or the gain from sale of the property. The equity participation results in an additional return to the lender above the interest rate charged on the loan. For example, the loan might have an interest rate of 8% and provide for the lender to receive 30% of any net operating income in excess of $100,000 in any year plus 30% of the cash received when the property is sold (sales price less the loan balance).

**equity ratio**   The equity interest of a property divided by the total value; the percentage of an investment that is unencumbered by debt.

**equity residual technique**   An appraisal technique for solving for value by which the first year's before-tax cash flow (net operating income minus annual debt service) is capitalized by the equity capitalization rate (equity dividend) to arrive at an estimate of the equity value. The equity value is then added to the loan balance to arrive at an estimate for the total property.

For example, a property has attached to it a mortgage of $500,000 with annual payments of $54,500. The annual net operating income equals $68,000 and the equity cap rate equals 0.08. The property value is determined as follows:

| | |
|---|---:|
| Net operating income | $68,000 |
| Annual debt service | − 54,500 |
| Residual income to equity | $13,500 |
| Equity value capitalized: $13,500/0.08 = | $168,750 |
| Total property value: $168,750 + $500,000 = | $668,750 |

**equity yield rate ($Y_E$)**   A rate of return on the equity capital; the equity investor's internal rate of return based on expected before-tax cash flows and the investor's original equity; used as the discount rate in a discounted cash flow analysis to estimate the present value of the before-tax cash flows (from operation and resale) to arrive at a value estimate for the equity. The equity yield rate reflects the effect of financing on the investor's rate of return. *See also* after-tax equity yield rate ($Y_t$), before-tax equity yield rate, yield capitalization.

**erosion**   The gradual loss of surface land caused by acts of nature such as running water or wind.

**escalation clause**   *See* escalator clause.

**escalation costs**   Specific provisions in construction contracts to accommodate for any increase in the cost or prices of equipment, material, labor or supplies over those specified in the contract, due to price-level changes over time.

**escalator clause**   A clause appearing in a contract that provides for an adjustment in rent or sales price (either up or down) based on some event or index. An escalator clause is used to help offset increases in operating expenses.

**escape clause**   In a lease, a provision that allows a tenant to cancel a lease under conditions that would not ordinarily justify lease cancellation.

**escheat**   The government right to transfer property ownership to the state when the owner dies without a will or any ascertainable heirs.

**escrow**   Money, securities, instruments or other property or evidences of property deposited by two or more persons with a third person, to be delivered on a certain contingency or on the happening of a certain event.

**estate**   The degree, nature, or extent of interest or rights a person has in a property. *See also* fee simple estate, leased fee estate, leasehold estate, life estate, sandwich leasehold estate, subleasehold estate.

**evaluation**   An analysis of a property and its attributes in which a value estimate is not required. The study may consider any aspect of the property including the nature, quality and utility of an interest in the real estate. *See also* appraisal, valuation.

**excavation**   In construction, a process in which trenches are dug to provide undisturbed earth for the foundation to rest on, to accommodate footings for piers and chimneys, and to install water, electricity, septic and sewer lines.

**excess income**   *See* excess rent.

**excess land**   On an unimproved site, land that is not needed to accommodate a site's highest and best use. On an improved site, excess land is the surplus land that is not needed to serve or support the existing improvement.

**excess rent**   The amount by which contract rent exceeds market rent due to unfavorable lease terms. The additional rent could be a result of market changes, sales overage clauses and/or poor negotiating skills on the part of the tenant. For example, a retail tenant's sales increased markedly due to a new advertising campaign, and the tenant now pays $10.00 per square foot in base rent and $4.00 per square foot in overage rent. Similar spaces are renting for approximately $12.00 per square foot. The excess rent equals ($10.00 psf + $4.00 psf) − $12.00 psf = $2.00 psf. When valuing a property, that portion of income due to excess rent is usually considered riskier than that from the market rent.

**exclusionary zoning** A type of zoning that excludes racial minorities and low-income people from an area. Exclusionary zoning may be intentional or unintentional, e.g., specification of a minimum structure size.

**exculpatory clause** A clause that limits the recourse of one party against another in the event of default. In a mortgage, an exculpatory clause limits recovery to the property only.

**expected completion date** An indicator or measure of investor or management confidence expressed as the formal and official anticipated date of completion of a construction project. This date is generally forecast at the onset of planning for the project and may be revised as construction proceeds.

**expense ratio** *See* operating expense ratio (OER).

**expense stop** In a lease, a dollar amount (usually expressed on a per square foot basis) above which the tenant agrees to pay operating expenses. An expense stop is used to help protect the lessor from unexpected increases in expenses from inflation or other factors. The amount paid by the tenant is said to "pass through" to the tenant.

**expenses** *See* operating expenses.

**expert testimony** Testimony of persons who are skilled in some art, science, profession, or business, that skill or knowledge is not common to others, and that has come to such experts by reason of special study and experience in such art, science, profession, or business. (Culver v. Prudential Ins. Co., 6 W.W. Harr. 582,179 A. 400.)

**expert witness** One qualified to render expert testimony.

**exponential growth** *See* compound growth.

**export base theory** A model formulated to analyze the growth of a local economy. The theory recognizes that firms in the business sector of the local economy sell to both non-local and local consumers but non-local sales generate actual economic growth.

**exterior door** A door separating the inside of a building from the outside and made of solid wood, metal or glass. A hollow exterior door may signify poor quality construction.

**exterior wall** In construction, any outer wall, except a common wall, that encloses a building.

**external obsolescence**   A loss in property value resulting from negative influence outside the property itself. An element of accrued depreciation. External obsolescence is generally incurable and can be further defined as either economic obsolescence or locational obsolescence. Economic obsolescence is caused by a negative economic force that affects an entire area whereas locational obsolescence is caused by environmental or social forces that negatively affect a specific property due to its location. In the cost approach, the total loss in value from external obsolescence is distributed between the land and the improvements. External obsolescence can be measured by either capitalizing the income loss due to the negative influence or by comparing sales of similar properties that are subject to the negative influence and similar properties that are not subject to the negative influence. *See also* accrued depreciation, economic obsolescence, locational obsolescence.

For example, several retail stores in an urban center have moved to the suburbs, leaving a large percentage of vacant spaces in the center. A retail space in this center currently produces a net operating income (NOI) of $14,000 after physical and functional accrued depreciation are cured. Comparable stores in other leased-up centers in the same market area indicate that the NOI on the subject property would equal $18,000 after physical and functional accrued depreciation are cured if the center was more fully leased. An overall capitalization rate of 12.5% is estimated, and the overall loss attributable is 50% to the building and 50% to the land. The external obsolescence attributable to the building is calculated as follows:

| | |
|---|---:|
| Estimated NOI with no external obsolescence | $18,000 |
| NOI with external obsolescence | − 14,000 |
| Estimated annual NOI loss ($18,000 − $14,000) | $ 4,000 |
| Capitalized NOI loss ($4,000/.125) | $32,000 |
| Loss attributable to building ($32,000/2) | $16,000 |

**externalities**   An appraisal concept that states that economies or diseconomies outside a property's boundaries may have a positive or negative effect on its value.

**extraction method**   *See* allocation.

**extrapolation**   The process of forecasting future trends based on current and past data patterns and relationships. Extrapolation assumes that the same economic factors that affected past trends are likely to continue over the forecasting period.

# F

**facade**  The outer front wall of a building.

**face amount**  *See* face value.

**face value**  The value of a security as set forth in the document itself; the par value as shown on the document as opposed to the real value or market value that may differ if interest rates have changed. Also called face amount.

**facility**  Another term for complex or plant.

**factory**  An establishment for the manufacture of goods, including the necessary building and machinery; a manufacturing plant.

**fair market rent**  *See* market rent.

**fair market value**  An outdated appraisal term used synonymously with currently acceptable term market value.

**fair rental**  *See* market rent.

**fair value**  A specific value definition used by accountants when classifying loan losses. The definition is as follows:
"The fair value of the assets transferred is the amount that the debtor could reasonably expect to receive for them in a current sale between a willing buyer and a willing seller, that is, other than in a forced or liquidation sale. Fair value of assets shall be measured by their market value if an active market for them exists. If no active market exists for the assets transferred but exists for similar assets, the selling prices in that market may be helpful in estimating the fair value of the assets transferred. If no market price is available, a forecast of expected cash flows may aid in estimating the fair value of assets transferred, provided the expected cash flows are discounted at a rate commensurate with the risk involved."

SOURCE: Financial Accounting Standards Board, "Statement of Financing Accounting Standards No. 15: Accounting by Debtors and

Creditors for Troubled Debt Restructuring" (Stamford, Connecticut Financial Accounting Standards Board, 1987), p. 6.

**family room**   An informal room used for relaxation and entertainment, usually measuring at least 180 square feet and located near the kitchen. Family rooms evolved after World War II. Also called a recreation room. *See also* building description, house zone, living room.

**Fannie Mae**   *See* Federal National Mortgage Association (FNMA).

**fatigue**   In construction, cracking failure of a material resulting from repeated cyclic stress below the normal tensile strength.

**favorable leverage**   *See* positive leverage.

**feasibility**   The ability of a real estate project to satisfy the explicit objectives of an investor.

**feasibility analysis**   According to the Uniform Standards of Professional Appraisal Practice, a study of the cost-benefit relationship of an economic endeavor. *See also* absorption analysis, marketability study, market analysis, risk analysis, sensitivity analysis.

**feasibility rent**   The level of rent that would have to be achieved before it would become feasible to construct a new building in a market that has an excess of supply over demand and therefore has effective market rents (net of concessions) that are below the levels needed to support new construction. This number is used to calculate the loss in value due to the imbalance that may result in permanent or temporary external obsolescence.

**feasibility study**   *See* feasibility analysis.

**Federal Fair Housing Laws**   Enacted as part of the Civil Rights Act of 1968, this law makes discrimination on the basis of race, color, sex, religion or national origin illegal in the sale or rental of housing properties. The Act does not affect commercial or industrial properties. In 1988 the Act was amended to include families with children and handicapped people as additional protected clauses.

**federal funds rate**   The interest rate charged on loans made by banks to other banks. A signal of changes in the national economy.

**Federal Home Loan Mortgage Corporation (FHLMC)**   An agency directed by the Federal Home Loan Bank Board for the purpose of increasing the availability of mortgage funds and providing greater flexibility for mortgage investors. The FHLMC purchases single-family and condominium mortgages from approved financial institutions and resells its mortgage inventories. Also called Freddie Mac.

**federal income taxes**   Taxes imposed by the federal government on ordinary income. Depending on current tax laws, cash flows from operating and selling a property may be taxable, to some extent, at the federal income tax rate. *See also* tax liability.

**Federal National Mortgage Association (FNMA)**   An independent agency that purchases mortgages from the primary markets and issues long-term debentures and short-term discount notes. Also called Fannie Mae.

**Federal Reserve System**   The central banking system of the United States that regulates money supply and its member banks. The Federal Reserve System consists of 12 Federal Reserve Banks and their branches and banks that are members of the system.

**federal rule**   In an eminent domain proceeding, a rule followed by some states that specifies how an owner will be compensated in a partial taking. The federal rule defines just compensation as the value immediately before the taking minus the value immediately after the taking; any enhancement in the value of the remainder offsets the value of the taken property. *See also* eminent domain, remainder, state rule.

For example, a site of land is valued at $100,000. Part of the land is taken through an eminent domain proceeding. The value of the portion taken is $20,000. Off-site improvements installed by the government result in $8,000 in benefits to the remainder, making the value of the remainder after the taking equal to $88,000. Through the federal rule, the owner would be entitled to a just compensation of $12,000, e.g., $100,000 value before the taking minus $88,000 value after the taking.

If instead, part of the remainder is not usable after the partial taking and the value of the remainder after the taking is $72,000 ($8,000 in damages), the owner would be entitled to a just compensation of $28,000 ($100,000 value before the taking minus $72,000 value after the taking).

**federally related transaction**   As specified in the Financial Institutions Reform, Recovery and Enforcement Act of 1989, any sales transaction of real property that ultimately involves a federal agency. For example, the property may involve a loan that is made by a federally regulated or federally insured agency. Or, the lender may want to sell the mortgage in the secondary market. *See also* Financial Institutions Reform, Recovery and Enforcement Act (FIRREA).

**fee**   *See* fee simple estate.

**fee appraiser**   A person who charges a fee for estimating the value of real estate. *See also* appraiser.

**fee simple**   *See* fee simple estate.

**fee simple absolute**   *See* fee simple estate.

**fee simple defeasible**    A fee simple estate that is subject to end upon the happening of a specified condition. There are two types of fee simple defeasible: fee simple determinable and fee simple subject to a condition subsequent. The duration of a fee simple determinable estate is specified in the deed. The duration of a fee simple subject to a condition subsequent is specified by the grantor and is typically contingent on a specified use or condition. Also called qualified fee or defeasible fee.

**fee simple determinable**    *See* fee simple defeasible.

**fee simple estate**    Absolute ownership of real estate that is unencumbered by any other interest or estate and is subject to the limitations of eminent domain, escheat, police power and taxation. A fee simple estate can be valued by the present value of market rents. *See also* leased fee estate, leasehold estate, sandwich leasehold estate, subleasehold estate.

For example, suppose a building produces a net operating income of $500,000 at market rents. This income will increase at 3% per year over a 5-year holding period. With leases at the market rate as indicated above, the property value (fee simple) will also increase 3% per year. Assuming a 13% discount rate, the value of the fee simple estate (V) can be calculated as follows:

| Year | NOI (increase of 3%/yr.) | Resale |
|------|--------------------------|--------|
| 1 | 500,000 | |
| 2 | 515,000 | |
| 3 | 530,450 | |
| 4 | 546,364 | |
| 5 | 562,754 | $(1.03)^5 \times V$ |

$$V = \frac{500,000}{1.13} + \frac{515,000}{(1.13)^2} + \frac{530,450}{(1.13)^3} + \frac{546,364}{(1.13)^4} + \frac{562,754}{(1.13)^5} + \frac{(1.03)^5 \times V}{(1.13)^5}$$

$$V = 442,478 + 403,321 + 367,628 + 335,095 + 305,441 + (0.629207 \times V)$$

$$V = 1,853,962 + (0.629207 \times V)$$

$$V - (0.629207 \times V) = 1,853,962$$

$$0.370792 \times V = 1,853,962$$

$$V = 5,000,000$$

Now that we know the value (V), we can calculate the resale price after 5 years as follows:

$$\text{Resale price} = \$5,000,000 \times (1.03)^5 = \$5,796,370$$

The value of this fee simple estate could also be calculated by another method: Because income and value are increasing at the *same* compound rate, the going-in cap rate is equal to the discount rate $(Y_O)$ minus the compound growth rate $(g)$. The value can be calculated as follows:

$$V = \frac{NOI_1}{Y_O - g}$$

$$V = \frac{500,000}{.13 - .03}$$

$$V = \$5,000,000$$

**fee simple interest** *See* fee simple estate.

**FHLMC** *See* Federal Home Loan Mortgage Corporation (FHLMC).

**final value estimate** A range of values or a single dollar amount given at the end of an appraisal report that has been derived from the reconciliation of the different methods of valuation used in the report.

**finance charges** Costs incurred by a borrower either directly or indirectly and payable to a creditor. Includes costs such as mortgage service charges and origination fees.

**Financial Institutions Reform, Recovery and Enforcement Act (FIRREA)** A law passed in 1989 to provide guidelines for the regulation of financial institutions. One part of the law specifies that appraisers must become state-certified or licensed by July 1, 1991, to be able to appraise property involving a federally insured or regulated agency. Certified appraisers must be used in federally related transactions involving property valued at $1 million or more. Certified or licensed appraisers may appraise properties with a value of less than $1 million unless they are complex properties. *See also* certified appraiser, federally related transaction, licensed appraiser.

**financial leverage** *See* leverage, positive leverage, negative leverage, zero leverage.

**financial management rate of return (FMRR)** Similar in concept to the adjusted internal rate of return. Negative cash flows are discounted at a safe rate, and positive cash flows are compounded forward to the end of the holding period at a reinvestment rate. If negative cash flows occur after a positive cash flow, the negative cash flow is discounted back and netted against the positive cash flow. The net remaining is either discounted back (if negative) or compounded forward (if positive).

For example, a property was purchased for $90,000 and produces the following cash flows during a 5-year holding period: 5,000, −5,000, 10,000, 10,000, 12,000. The property is sold in year 5 for $95,000. The risk-free, or safe, rate is 7%, and the reinvestment rate is 9%. The financial management rate of return can be calculated as follows:

| Year | Cash Flow |
|------|-----------|
| 0 | (90,000) |
| 1 | 5,000 |
| 2 | (5,000) |
| 3 | 10,000 |
| 4 | 10,000 |
| 5 | 107,000 |

To find the FMRR, follow the steps below:
1. Discount negative cash flows back 1 year at the safe rate.
   Year 2 cash flow is discounted to year 1: $5,000/1.07 = 4,672.90$
2. Sum new cash flows. If still negative, discount back 1 year.
   Year 1 cash flow $= 5,000 - 4,672.90 = 327.10$
3. Compound positive cash flows forward at the reinvestment rate.

| Year | Cash Flow | Present Value | Future Value |
|------|-----------|---------------|--------------|
| 0 | (90,000) | (90,000) | |
| 1 | 327.10 | | 462 |
| 2 | 0 | | |
| 3 | 10,000 | | 11,881 |
| 4 | 10,000 | | 10,900 |
| 5 | 107,000 | | 107,000 |
| | | (90,000) | 130,243 |

4. Find the internal rate of return that equates the present value with the future value.

$$90,000 \times S^n_{(x\%, \ 5 \ years)} = 130,243$$
$$S^n_{(x\%, \ 5 \ years)} = 1.4471$$
$x\%$ (or FMRR) $= 7.67\%$, using annual compound
interest tables or a financial calculator

**financial risk**   Uncertainty caused by the method of financing an investment. *See also* risk.

**financial statement**   A formal record of the economic status of an individual or entity as of a specific date which usually classifies assets, liabilities, income, expenses and/or cash flows.

**financially feasible**   A requirement of highest and best use; refers to a project that satisfies the economic objectives of the investor.

**financing**   The use of debt to fund a portion of a real estate purchase. *See also* leverage.

**financing costs**   The expense incurred to acquire capital to finance a project. In mortgages, financing costs are often charged up front in the form of points. *See also* point.

**financing premium**   An incremental amount paid for a property purchased with favorable financing, for example, assumption of a below-market interest rate loan. *See also* cash equivalency adjustment.

**fire insurance**   A form of property insurance that covers losses due to fire and possibly other types of hazards such as smoke or storms.

**fire-resistive**   Properties or designs made to resist the effects of any fire to which a material or structure may be expected to be subjected. Fire-resistive materials or assemblies of materials are noncombustible, but noncombustible materials are not necessarily fire-resistive. Fire-resistive implies a higher degree of fire resistance than noncombustible. Fire-resistive construction is defined in terms of specified fire resistance as measured by the standard time-temperature curve.

**FIRREA**   *See* Financial Institutions Reform, Recovery, and Enforcement Act (FIRREA).

**first mortgage**   A mortgage that is given priority over all other liens on a property. In cases of foreclosure, the first mortgage will be repaid plus legal expenses before other mortgages are satisfied. *See also* senior mortgage.

**fixed assets**   Assets not readily convertible into cash. Fixed assets are characterized as having a remaining life longer than 1 year. They denote a firmness of purpose or intent by the owner to continue use or possession. "Fixed" does not refer to the immobility of an asset. Land, buildings and affixed machinery and equipment are fixed assets.

**fixed capital**   Capital invested in fixed property or assets that may be used many times in production. Assets that are considered long term in character, as land or buildings; ordinarily, but not necessarily, tangible assets.

**fixed capital costs**   *See* construction cost.

**fixed expense**   An operating expense that does not vary with the occupancy level of a property, e.g., property taxes, insurance, repairs and maintenance, advertising and promotions. *See also* variable expense.

**fixed liabilities**   Long-term obligations or debts; debts payable more than 1 year hence as distinguished from current liabilities.

**fixed operating expense**   *See* fixed expense.

**fixed rate mortgage**   A loan in which the interest rate is constant over the term of the loan. *See also* adjustable rate mortgage (ARM).

**fixity of location**   The unique immobility of real estate as compared to other investments, which makes it susceptible to and inescapable from the influence of the surrounding environment.

**fixture**   Personal property that becomes real property after it is attached to the land or building in a permanent manner. To determine if an item can be considered a fixture, it must meet 3 criteria: (1) it must be able to be removed without serious injury to itself or the real estate; (2) the character of the item must be such that it is specifically constructed for or carries out the purpose for which the building was built; (3) it must be the intention of the party that attached the item to leave it attached on a permanent basis. Examples of fixtures include built-in dishwashers, furnaces, garage door openers. Trade fixtures are not considered real property. *See also* trade fixture.

**flashing**   In construction, strips of sheet metal or other material used in roof and wall construction to protect structural angles and joints from water seepage.

**flat lease**   A lease in which payments are made at set intervals in equal amounts throughout the life of the loan.

**flat rental**   A rent specified in a lease that remains constant throughout the lease term.

**floating foundation**   In construction, a type of slab on ground foundation made of a mat, raft, or rigid foundation consisting of concrete slabs that are 4 to 8 feet thick and are heavily reinforced with steel. Floating foundations are used in soils with low load-bearing capacity. *See also* footing, foundation, pile.

**flood plain**   A geographic area close to a river or stream that is subject to flooding. In some areas, flood plains are mapped by the Federal Emergency Management Agency so that they may be covered by the National Flood Insurance Plan.

**floor area**   Total horizontal surface of a specific floor, or the total area of all floors in a multistory building, computed from the outside building dimensions of each floor. Balcony and mezzanine floor areas are computed separately and added to the total floor area.

**floor area ratio**   Floor area of a building divided by its lot size. A floor area ratio is often specified in zoning ordinances to regulate land use. For example, a building with 100,000 square feet of floor area is located on 10 acres (435,600 square feet) of land. The floor area ratio is $100,000/435,600 = 0.23$.

**floor load**  The live weight-supporting capabilities of a floor, measured in pounds per square foot; the weight, in pounds per square foot, that can be safely placed on the floor of a building if the weight is uniformly distributed.

**flue**  In construction, the enclosed passage in a chimney, usually made of fireclay or terra-cotta pipe, that allows for transmittal of smoke from the building. *See also* chimney.

**FMRR**  *See* financial management rate of return (FMRR).

**FNMA**  *See* Federal National Mortgage Association (FNMA).

**footing**  In construction, the base of a foundation wall, chimney or column that usually rests on solid ground and is wider than the structure being supported to distribute the weight of the structure over the ground.

**forced sale**  A sale that occurs because the mortgagor is unable or unwilling to make payments on the loan. A forced sale may occur under bankruptcy proceedings or to satisfy other outstanding liens. The value brought at a forced sale may not represent a true market value.

**forces**  In appraisal theory, any of 4 dynamic and changing powers and their interactions that affect the value of real property. Includes social forces (population trends), economic forces (employment, wage levels, supply and demand), governmental forces (zoning, fiscal policies, legislation) and environmental forces (climate, topography, transportation). *See also* economic forces, environmental forces, governmental forces, social forces.

**forecasting**  The process of assimilating past information and compiling the data for the purpose of drawing conclusions about the probable happenings or conditions in the future.

**foreclosure**  A legal process in which a default in payment (or other terms) of the mortgage note by the mortgagor causes the property used as security for the mortgage to be sold by the mortgagee in order to satisfy the debt.

**form report**  A specific format for presenting an appraisal report. Typically required by financial institutions, insurance companies, and government agencies. *See also* report.

**formal architecture**  Architectural styles identified by common attributes that meet aesthetic and functional criteria of people trained in architectural history. Styles are frequently named in reference to a geographic region, time period, or cultural group. *See also* vernacular architecture.

**foundation**    The base on which something is built; the part of a structure on which the superstructure is erected; the part of a building that is below the surface of the ground and on which the superstructure rests. Includes all construction that transmits the loads of the superstructure to the earth. *See also* floating foundation, slab on ground foundation, pier and beam foundation, basement, crawl space.

**foundation area**    The total ground or land area covered by the foundation of a structure, measured from the outside dimensions. Also called land coverage or site coverage.

**fraction rate capitalization**    *See* split rate capitalization.

**fractional appraisal**    (1) An appraisal of one of the component parts of a property, for example, the land disregarding the building or the building ignoring the land; also the appraisal of a lessee's or a lessor's interest. (2) An appraisal of a unit in itself, whether with or without regard to the effect of its separation from the whole of which it is a part.

**fractional interest**    *See* partial interest.

**frame**    The load-bearing skeleton of a building. *See also* framing.

**frame error**    A deviation that occurs in a study when the list that the analyst generates to represent the population omits certain individuals, whose opinions, attitudes, or other characteristics are not represented.

**framing**    A system of joining structural members that provides lateral, longitudinal, transverse and vertical support for a building. *See also* balloon framing, frame, platform framing, post and beam framing.

**Freddie Mac**    *See* Federal Home Loan Mortgage Corporation (FHLMC).

**free and clear title**    Title to real property that is free of any liens, mortgages or other encumbrances.

**free rent**    A rent concession that grants occupancy for a certain amount of time with no cost to the tenant. Free rent is used to initially sign a new tenant to a lease. *See also* concessions.

**freehold**    An ownership interest in real property in which the time period of ownership is unknown or undeterminable (life estate) or in which the ownership period is potentially indefinite or unpredictable (fee simple estate). Non-freehold estates last for a definite period of time such as leased fee or leasehold estates. In the Old English court system, only an owner of freehold property could bring a real action to court, and thus only freehold estates were regarded as real property.

**freestanding office location**   An independent office use, relatively un-constrained by other adjacent or nearby land uses.

**freestanding stores**   Retail stores not located in a planned shopping center or in association with a major business district.

**frictional vacancy**   The voluntary vacancy that occurs because of market imperfections, administered pricing policies and inventory holdings.

**front foot**   A measurement of land that abuts the street line or other landmark such as a river or lake. A front foot measurement is typi-cally used for lots in urban areas of near-uniform depth.

**frontage**   The length of a property that abuts the street line or other landmark such as a body of water. Frontage differs from width, which may vary from the front of the lot to the back.

**fully amortized mortgage**   A loan with equal periodic payments that al-low for both principal and interest to be recovered over the term of the loan. *See also* mortgage.

**function**   (1) In relation to a building, the intended use, activity or pur-pose for which a building was designated or altered. (2) In appraisal, the intended use or uses of an appraisal report by the client or a third party.

**functional depreciation**   *See* functional obsolescence.

**functional integration**   Refers to the important economic links that exist between the different political-geographic subareas in a local econ-omy. Functional integration is a concept that is used in the definition of a Metropolitan Statistical Area.

**functional inutility**   An impairment of the functional capacity or effi-ciency of a property or building according to market tastes and standards. Functional inutility is equivalent to functional obsoles-cence because the ongoing change makes layouts and features ob-solete.

**functional obsolescence**   A loss in the value of real estate improve-ments due to functional inadequacies or subadequacies due to poor design and/or change in market standards or requirements for building components. *See also* curable functional obsolescence, in-curable functional obsolescence.

**functional utility**   The extent to which a property is able to be used for the purpose that it was intended. Functional utility includes factors such as current trends in tastes and styles, architectural style, de-sign and layout, and traffic patterns.

**future benefits**   In appraisal, anticipated positive cash flows or appreci-ation in property value. A premise of the income approach.

**future value**   The worth of a property at some later date. *See also* future value of $1 ($S^n$), future value annuity of $1 per period ($S_{\overline{n}|}$).

**future value annuity of $1 per period ($S_{\overline{n}|}$)**   A compound interest factor that represents the sum to which a constant periodic investment of $1 per period will grow assuming compound growth at a specific rate of return for a specific number of compounding periods. It is shown in column 2 of the compound interest tables in Appendix B. In an appraisal, these payments are generally assumed to be made at the end of each period. The factor can be calculated through the following formula:

$$\frac{(1+i)^n - 1}{i}$$

where i equals the periodic interest rate and n equals the number of periods.

Also called amount of $1 per period and future value interest factor-annuity. *See also* six functions of $1.

**future value interest factor (FVIF)**   *See* future value of $1 ($S^n$).

**future value interest factor-annuity (FVIFA)**   *See* future value annuity of $1 per period ($S_{\overline{n}|}$).

**future value of $1 ($S^n$)**   The amount to which an investment of $1 grows with compound interest after a specified number of years at a specified interest rate. See column 1 of the compound interest tables in Appendix B. The factor is arrived at by adding $1 to the interest per period (i) and taking this to the exponent of the number of years (n), i.e., $(1+i)^n$. Also called the amount of $1, future value interest factor, and future worth of $1.

**FVIF (future value interest factor)**   *See* future value of $1 ($S^n$).

**FVIFA (future value interest factor-annuity)**   *See* future value annuity of $1 per period ($S_{\overline{n}|}$).

# G

**gable**   In construction, the triangular area above the eaves between two sloping rooflines.

**gap analysis**   A comparison of demand and supply to determine the existence of present and future excess demand or excess supply in a market. Another way of expressing the same thing is through the use of the phrase "unmet demand or supply shortages." *See* market gap analysis, spatial gap analysis.

**GBA**   *See* gross building area (GBA).

**general benefits**   In an eminent domain proceeding, the betterment gained by the general community from property adjacent to or near property that was taken from private use for a public improvement. *See also* benefits, condemnation, eminent domain, special benefits.

**general data**   Information that is not specific to a certain property, e.g., interest rates, employment rates and census information. *See also* data.

**general office space**   Functionally designed office space that houses a wide variety of office operations to support business operations located elsewhere.

**general partnership**   An organizational form of real estate ownership in which income, gains, losses, deductions and credits are passed through to individual partners who pay tax on their own income. A general partnership usually ensures that the death or bankruptcy of one partner will not force a termination of the business or cloud the title of the partnership property. However, partners share full liability for debts and obligations of the partnership and can be held responsible for actions of other partners. This form of ownership is not typically used for a large group of investors.

**general purpose industrial building**   An industrial building that can serve a variety of functions or alternate uses without major alteration or expenditure. This type of property appeals to a wide segment of the market for industrial property. A general purpose industrial building is usually found in most industrial parks and includes many light manufacturing buildings, warehouses and distribution facilities.

**generating plant**    A facility at which one or more electrical or mechanical machinery components, either under construction or in service or both, are designed to generate electricity.

**generative business**    A retail operation that has such strong market appeal that it is a primary destination for customers in a specific location. Department stores, well-known specialty stores, supermarkets and other anchor stores are examples of this type of market.

**gentrification**    A process in which neighborhood properties are purchased and renovated or rehabilitated. This process is not part of the normal neighborhood life cycle. *See also* neighborhood life cycle.

**geodetic survey system**    The United States Coast and Geodetic Survey System; a legal description of land used to map large areas in which the entire country is marked by a network of benchmarks located by latitude and longitude. Base lines, principal meridians and township lines as used in the rectangular survey system are shown with topographical features in detailed maps called quadrangles. The geodetic survey system is a variation of the rectangular survey system, which considers the topographical features of the earth's surface. *See also* land, rectangular survey system.

**GIM**    *See* gross income multiplier (GIM).

**Ginnie Mae**    *See* Government National Mortgage Association (GNMA).

**girder**    A principal horizontal structural member or beam that supports lesser beams, joists or walls.

**GLA**    *See* gross leasable area (GLA).

**GNMA**    *See* Government National Mortgage Association (GNMA).

**going-concern value**    The value of a property which includes the value due to a successful operating business enterprise which is expected to continue. Going-concern value results from the process of assembling the land, building, labor, equipment, and marketing operation and includes consideration of the efficiency of plant, the know-how of management, and the sufficiency of capital. The portion of going-concern value that exceeds that of the real property and tangible personal property is an intangible value that is referred to as business value. *See also* business value.

**going-in capitalization rate**    The overall capitalization rate found by dividing first year's net operating income by the present value of the property. When the term capitalization rate is used alone, it is assumed to be a going-in capitalization rate. For example, a property produces a net operating income (NOI) of $10,000 during the first year of operation. The value of the property is estimated to be $100,000. Therefore, the going-in capitalization rate would equal 10% ($10,000/$100,000). A second comparable property may produce a first-year NOI of $9,000. If other comparable properties also indicate going-in cap rates of 10%, the value of the second property could be estimated at $90,000 ($9,000/.10). *See also* capitalization rate, terminal capitalization rate.

**going-out capitalization rate**   *See* terminal capitalization rate.

**Government National Mortgage Association (GNMA)**   A government agency that purchases mortgages through its secondary mortgage market operations and issues mortgage-backed, federally insured securities called Collateralized Mortgage Obligations (CMOs). Also called Ginnie Mae.

**government survey method**   *See* rectangular survey method.

**governmental forces**   In appraisal theory, one of four forces thought to affect real estate value, e.g., government controls and regulations, public services, fiscal policies, and zoning and building codes. *See also* forces.

**grade**   (1) The slope of a surface expressed as a percentage of horizontal distance, e.g., a 2% upgrade indicates a rise of 2 feet for each 100 feet of horizontal distance. (2) The level or elevation of a lot. Rough grade is the surface on which topsoil will be spread. Finish grade is the final level after topsoil has been added.

**grading**   A process that takes place after construction in which excavated land is pushed back in place by the foundation to form the final level or slope of the land.

**graduated payment mortgage (GPM)**   A loan in which payments start low and increase over the term of the loan. The graduated payment mortgage is designed to help borrowers match payments with projected increases in income. *See also* mortgage.

**graduated rental lease**   A lease in which rent graduates (usually increases) periodically during a lease term based on changes specified in the lease. Also called step-up lease.

**grantee**   A person who receives property transferred by deed or who is granted property rights by a trust instrument or other document.

**grantor**   A person who transfers property to another by deed, or grants property rights to another through a trust instrument or other document.

**grantor-grantee index**    Public record books in a recorder's office that list all recorded instruments and a reference for finding the complete document. The books are separated for grantors and grantees and are stored by date and alphabetical order. Information such as name of grantor or grantee, type and date of instrument, book, page and date of recording, and a description are given.

**graphic analysis**    A method of analyzing comparable sales using Ellwood Graphic Analysis whereby a range of expectation with regard to the relationship between expected yield rates and associated changes in cash flow forecasts are projected using sensitivity analysis that, if required by an investor, would have resulted in the price paid for the comparable property. The technique is used to support the inputs in a discounted cash flow approach. *See also* rate analysis, discounted cash flow analysis (DCF), yield capitalization, Ellwood formula.

**GRM**    *See* gross rent multiplier (GRM).

**gross building area (GBA)**    The total floor area of a building measured in square feet from the external walls, excluding unenclosed areas. Unlike gross living area measurements, GBA does include basement areas. *See also* gross leasable area (GLA), gross living area.

**gross income**    Total income generated by an income-producing real estate property. *See* effective gross income (EGI), potential gross income (PGI).

**gross income multiplier (GIM)**    The ratio of the sales price or value divided by the annual potential gross income or effective gross income. The income used in the calculation may include income other than rent income. For example, a property with effective gross income of $450,000 per year is being appraised. The following three comparable properties have recently sold:

|  | Comp #1 | Comp #2 | Comp #3 |
|---|---|---|---|
| Adjusted sales price | $2,000,000 | $2,440,000 | $2,900,000 |
| Effective gross income | $400,000 | $473,000 | $549,000 |

A market value for the subject property can be roughly estimated by calculating the gross income multipliers of the above properties and then applying a weighted average to the gross income of the subject property. By calculating the GIMs of the above properties (comp #1  GIM = $2,000,000/$400,000 = 5.0,  comp #2  GIM = $2,440,000/$473,000 = 5.16,  comp #3  GIM = $2,900,000/$549,000 = 5.28), we see a range of multipliers from 5.0 to 5.28. Assuming that comp #3 and comp #2 are most similar to the subject, we might give more weight to these two multipliers and use a multiplier for the subject property of 5.20. By multiplying the multiplier of 5.20 by the subject's gross income of $450,000, we find an estimated value of $2,340,000 for the subject. This number can be used to compare the value calculated through the income and cost approaches to value.

Note that the effective gross income was used both to calculate the multipliers of the comparables and to find the estimated value of the subject property. Although both the effective gross income and potential gross income can be used to calculate an income multiplier, the type of income used must be kept consistent throughout the analysis. For example, in the above analysis, we could not use the subject property's potential gross income to estimate value because we used a multiplier based on the effective gross income. *See* effective gross income multiplier (EGIM), potential gross income multiplier (PGIM), gross rent multiplier (GRM).

**gross leasable area (GLA)**   The total floor area of a building that is designed for the occupancy of tenants. GLA does not include common areas but does include basements. *See also* gross building area (GBA), gross living area, net leasable area.

**gross lease**   A lease that specifies that the landlord is responsible for the payment of all operating expenses. The lease, however, may contain expense increase passthrough provisions. *See also* expense stop, net lease.

**gross living area**   Residential space measured by finished and habitable above-grade areas, excluding finished basements or attic areas. Gross living area is measured by the outside perimeter of the building. *See also* gross building area (GBA), gross leasable area (GLA).

**gross migration**   Number of migrants moving into or out of an area.

**gross rent**   Total rent generated by a residential real estate property that is leased. *See also* gross income.

**gross rent multiplier (GRM)**   The ratio of sales price or value divided by the potential or effective gross rent; a measure similar to the gross income multiplier but used exclusively for residential properties that receive rent only and no other types of income. *See* gross income multiplier (GIM).

The gross rent multiplier can be used in appraising to give a rough estimate of value. For example, a small rental house is being appraised. Two other similar rental properties have recently sold in the same neighborhood. The sales can be summarized as follows:

|  | Comp #1 | Comp #2 |
| --- | --- | --- |
| Adjusted sales price | $100,000 | $115,000 |
| Gross rent | $ 11,500 | $ 13,500 |
| GRM | 8.70 | 8.52 |

If the subject property rents for $12,000 per year, the value of the property indicated by the comparable sales would be $102,240 to $104,400.

$$\$12,000 \times 8.70 = \$104,400$$
$$\$12,000 \times 8.52 = \$102,240$$

**gross sales**   Total sales before subtracting returns, allowances and such.

**ground area**   The area of a building computed from the exterior dimensions of the ground floor.

**ground coverage area**   A ratio of the first floor area of a building divided by the land area.

**ground lease**   A lease for the use and occupancy of land only. Also called land lease.

**ground rent**   Rent paid for the right to use and occupy land; a percentage of total rent designated for land use and occupancy.

**ground rent capitalization**   A method of estimating land value by either dividing a first-year land lease payment by an appropriate land capitalization rate or by discounting a series of land lease payments by an appropriate land discount rate. For example, a parcel of land is leased for $2,400 per year. Sales of similar parcels of land indicate a land capitalization rate of 7%. The indicated land value would equal $2,400/0.07 = \$34,286$. *See also* land.

**groundwater**   All water that has seeped down beneath the surface of the ground or in the subsoil; water from springs or wells.

**grout**   A fluid mixture of sand and cement that is used to fill joints and small spaces in masonry work.

**gutter**   (1) A ridge on the shoulder of a road or along the point where a street meets a raised sidewalk that allows for the flowage of rainwater. (2) A trough running the length of a building along the roof that allows for the passage of rainwater off the building, usually through a downspout.

**hard costs**  *See* direct costs.

**hard goods**  That class of merchandise, sometimes referred to as hard-lines, composed primarily of durable items such as hardware, machines, heavy appliances, electrical and plumbing fixtures, and farming machinery and supplies.

**HBU**  *See* highest and best use (HBU).

**heating system**  A furnace or burner and the necessary ducts, registers, fans, pipes, radiators and such that are necessary to provide heat in a building. Several different types of systems can be used, e.g., warm or hot air, hot water, steam or electrical. Heating system fuels include coal, fuel oil, natural gas and electricity.

**heating, ventilation and air-conditioning system (HVAC)**  A system that provides consistent regulation and distribution of heat and fresh air throughout a building.

**highest and best use (HBU)**  The reasonable and probable use that results in the highest present value of the land after considering all legally permissible, physically possible and economically feasible uses. Capitalization rates or discount rates for each feasible use should reflect typical returns expected in the market. Highest and best use is usually determined under two different premises: as if the site was vacant and could be improved in the optimal manner or as the site is currently improved.

   In the latter premise, the highest and best use of the site will either be to keep the existing building or to demolish the building and develop a building that is the highest and best use. In general, it is not feasible to demolish an existing building as long as it contributes to the value of the site.

**high-rise apartment building**  (1) An apartment building, usually more than four stories high and equipped with an elevator and other modern conveniences. (2) An apartment building that is considered tall in relation to the structures surrounding it.

**historic district**   A zoning classification referring to a geographic area that has been recognized as having historical significance.

**historical age**   *See* actual age.

**historical cost**   *See* construction cost.

**holdback**   (1) The portion of a loan commitment that will not be funded until some additional requirement has been attained, such as pre-sale or rental of 70% of the units or completion of all building work. (2) In construction or interim financing, a percentage of the contractor's draw held back until satisfactory completion of the contractor's work and assurance of no mechanic's or materialman's liens.

**holding period**   The term of ownership or expected ownership of an investment. In appraisal, the holding period used reflects the appraiser's estimate as to what the typical expected holding period would be for a particular property.

**holdover tenant**   An occupant who remains at a property after his or her lease expires. The occupant generally has no rights whatsoever to the property and may be evicted or allowed to remain on the property by the landlord.

**home loan**   A loan secured by a residence for less than 4 families under either a mortgage or a deed of trust.

**Homeowner's Association**   An organization of condominium owners that is responsible for maintaining common areas of the condominium complex.

**homestead**   The farmhouse, auxiliary buildings and their lot found on a farm property.

**homestead exemption**   A release from assessment of a portion of the value of the property declared as a homestead.

**homestead site**   The amount of land on which the homestead is located.

**homogeneous**   Similar or like property types or neighborhoods in which inhabitants have similar cultural, social and economic backgrounds. Property values in a homogeneous neighborhood are thought to be more stabilized.

**Hoskold capitalization rate**   A factor derived by adding a speculative rate to a sinking fund factor for a safe rate and based on the premise that a portion of the net operating income (NOI) is reinvested at a "safe rate" in order to periodically replace the asset. The Hoskold cap rate has historically been used to capitalize the income produced by a wasting asset and should not be confused with the concept of a modified internal rate of return (IRR) or financial management rate of return (FMRR) that applies a reinvestment rate to all the cash flow received by the investor. *See also* Hoskold premise.

**Hoskold premise**    An appraisal theory that was designed to value the income stream of a wasting asset. Two separate interest rates are used: a speculative rate, representing a fair rate of return on capital, and a safe rate for a sinking fund designed to return all the invested capital in a lump sum at the termination of the investment. The Hoskold premise assumes that a portion of the net operating income (NOI) is reinvested at a safe rate to replace the investment. For example, a $10,000 per year annuity is discounted for 5 years at 10% but has a recapture of capital at 5%. Note that the sinking fund factor $1/S_{\overline{n}|}$ is at 5%.

$$R_O = Y_O + 1/S_{\overline{n}|} = (.10 + .180975 = 0.280975)$$
$$\$10,000/0.280975 = \$35,590$$

This value is lower than it would have been if the recapture rate was equal to 10%. A portion of the NOI had to be set aside at 5% to have $35,590 after 5 years.

$$\text{NOI} - \text{Sinking Fund} = \text{Balance} = \$10,000 - \$6,441 = \$3,559$$

The future value of $6,441 per year at 5% for 5 years is $35,590 (rounded), which replaces the investment. The balance of the NOI of $3,559 is like a perpetuity, and at 10% is worth $35,590. *See also* Ellwood techniques, Hoskold capitalization rate, yield capitalization.

**hotel**    A facility that offers temporary lodging and a few other services such as food, recreation and sometimes retail shops. It is not considered a residential property.

**hot-water system**    A furnace or hot-water heater that provides hot water. Electricity, gas or oil may be used to power the system. The size of the tank needed is determined by the number of inhabitants and the recovery rate of the unit.

**house zone**    Any of 3 different types of space in a house, characterized by the type of use for that area. For example, the private-sleeping zone includes the bedrooms, bathrooms and dressing rooms; the living-social zone includes the living room, dining room, family or recreation room, den and any enclosed porches; the working-service zone includes the kitchen, laundry, pantry and other work areas. Halls, stairways and entrances are considered circulation areas. *See also* building description.

**household**    The total number of persons who occupy a dwelling, including people not related to the householder, non-family occupants and single-person occupancy.

**household size**    The average size of a household, which is calculated by dividing the number of people residing in households by the number of households.

**housing inventory method**    An updating technique that uses population and household size figures from the previous census, local area data on building permits, demolitions, conversions and vacancies since the last census to estimate the current number of households.

**housing starts**    Housing units that are actually under construction. The actual number of housing starts may differ from the number of building permits issued. The number of housing starts is often used as an economic measure.

**housing submarket**    The product of disaggregation, defines a relatively homogeneous supply of housing units that tend to be occupied by a relatively homogeneous group of households. For example, the submarket of 3-bedroom split-level houses selling for $60,000 to $75,000 tends to be occupied by persons with similar economic, social and demographic characteristics.

**housing unit**    The area a housing consumer occupies (sleeping, eating, bathing, etc.) The term housing unit generally implies exclusive control by the occupant over the sleeping quarters but does not necessarily imply exclusive occupancy of kitchen, bathroom and living areas. Technically, the term dwelling unit refers to a housing unit that contains private kitchen and bathroom facilities, as well as private sleeping and living areas that are exclusively occupied by the household. *See also* dwelling, dwelling unit.

**Hoyt's sector theory**    *See* sector model (theory).

**Huff's Probability Formulation**    An extension, but substantial modification, of Reilly's Law of Retail Gravitation, which establishes the probability that a consumer located at a given point of origin will travel and shop at a specific shopping center or retail district.

**HVAC**    *See* heating, ventilation and air-conditioning system.

**hybrid mortgage**    A mortgage that allows the lender to participate in income produced from the property or attain some other type of equity interest. *See also* equity participation, mortgage.

**hyper-mall**    A shopping center that provides anchor stores and other stores that serve the whole spectrum of consumer desires and purchasing power. The mall contains discount stores at one end or in one area and upscale department stores at one end or in another area. Typically these areas are separated in some way. In addition, the mall can also contain stores that are not typically found in the existing shopping malls such as home improvement, hardware stores or auto parts stores. *See also* shopping center.

**impact fees**  A charge levied against developers of new residential, industrial or commercial properties by a municipal government to help pay for the added costs of public services generated by the new construction, for example, charges for hook-up costs for water and sewer lines, road improvements, and extra needs for school, fire and police services.

**import**  The influx of consumer dollars from beyond the designated trading area of a retail facility, usually from an area of limited retail activity.

**improved land**  A parcel of land that has been modified or developed for use in constructing improvements, for example, land that has been graded, drained or installed with utilities. *See also* unimproved land.

**improved site**  *See* improved land.

**improvement**  A structure or building that is permanently attached to the land. *See also* leasehold improvements.

**improvement ratio**  A ratio of the value of the improvements divided by the total value of the property.

**impulse good**  A product that is purchased without a prior decision to shop for it.

**income**  Cash flows or other benefits received. *See also* income capitalization approach, net operating income (NOI), taxable income.

**income and expense report**  In real estate, a monthly financial report that displays property operating income and expenses and distributions to the owner. *See also* income statement.

**income approach**  *See* income capitalization approach.

**income capitalization**  *See* direct capitalization, yield capitalization.

**income capitalization approach**   One of the three traditional appraisal approaches to estimating value. In this approach, value is based on the present value of future benefits of property ownership. In direct capitalization, a single year's income is converted to a value indication using a capitalization rate. In yield capitalization, future cash flows are estimated and discounted to a present value using a discount rate. *See also* appraisal, discount rate, capitalization rate, direct capitalization, yield capitalization.

**income participation**   *See* equity participation.

**income property**   A real estate property that is typically rented.

**income statement**   A record of the income and expenses incurred by a business during a specified time period. Also called profit and loss statement. *See also* balance sheet, income and expense report.

**income stream**   A consistent flow of money or benefits generated by an investment or property. *See also* annuity.

**income tax liability**   *See* tax liability.

**income-producing property**   *See* income property.

**increasing and decreasing returns, principle of**   An economic principle that states that the addition of more factors of production will increase the output at an increasing rate until a maximum is reached (the asset's maximum value). Then as more input factors are added, income will increase at a decreasing rate, producing an output value that is less than the cost of the added factor.

**increasing annuity**   Payments made on an evenly spaced periodic basis that are increasing in amount. *See also* annuity.

**incubator building**   An industrial property that is subdivided into space and leased to fledgling business or manufacturing firms in the hope that they will grow and require additional space.

**incurable depreciation**   *See* incurable functional obsolescence, incurable physical deterioration.

**incurable functional obsolescence**   A defect caused by a deficiency or superadequacy in the structure, materials or design of a structure. The defect is deemed incurable if the cost to cure the defect is greater than the anticipated increase in value after the defect is cured. A component of accrued depreciation. Incurable functional obsolescence due to a deficiency is measured as the net income loss attributable to the deficiency in comparison with otherwise competitive properties. The net income loss can be divided by the overall cap rate to find the amount of the obsolescence. For example, the estimated net income loss due to an incurable deficiency is estimated to be $1,000 per year. The overall cap rate is 10%. The estimated incurable functional obsolescence due to the deficiency would equal $1,000 ÷ 10% = $10,000.

Incurable functional obsolescence due to a superadequacy based on the *reproduction* cost is measured as the current reproduction cost of the superadequacy minus any physical deterioration already charged plus the present value of the added cost of ownership due to the superadequacy. For example, the current reproduction cost of a superadequacy is $2,000. Physical deterioration already charged equals $200. The cost of ownership of the superadequacy (additional taxes, insurance, maintenance and utility charges) equals $50 per year (with a present value of $500). The estimated amount of the incurable functional obsolescence equals:

| | |
|---|---|
| Current *reproduction* cost of superadequacy | $2,000 |
| Less physical deterioration | 200 |
| Plus present value cost of ownership | 500 |
| Total incurable functional obsolescence | $2,300 |

Incurable functional obsolescence due to a superadequacy based on the *replacement* cost does not consider physical deterioration, because the replacement cost does not include the cost to construct a superadequacy. For example, the replacement cost of a superadequacy equals $1,500. The present value of the additional cost of ownership due to the superadequacy equals $400. The estimated amount of the incurable functional obsolescence equals:

| | |
|---|---|
| Current *replacement* cost of superadequacy | $1,500 |
| Plus present value cost of ownership | 400 |
| Total incurable functional obsolescence | $1,900 |

Sometimes a superadequacy will cause the rent for the property to be higher than that of an equivalent property but not enough to justify the capital requirements of the item's cost. In this instance, the obsolescence is measured as the capitalized rent plus the superadequate item's current cost minus the physical deterioration plus the present value of the added cost of ownership. *See also* accrued depreciation, breakdown method, deficiency, superadequacy.

**incurable obsolescence**    *See* incurable functional obsolescence, incurable physical deterioration.

**incurable physical deterioration**    A defect caused by physical wear and tear on the building that is unreasonable or uneconomical to correct. An element of accrued depreciation. Incurable physical deterioration can be further classified as long-lived or short-lived. Long-lived items are expected to have a remaining economic life that equals the remaining economic life of the structure. Short-lived items are expected to have a remaining economic life that is less than the remaining economic life of the structure. Both types of incurable physical deterioration are measured by the physical age-life method, which calculates depreciation by multiplying the ratio of effective age divided by the total physical life of the item by the reproduction or replacement cost of the item minus any curable physical deterioration already charged. Incurable physical deterioration for short-lived items is calculated first and subtracted from the reproduction or replacement cost before the depreciation for long-lived items is calculated. *See also* accrued depreciation, breakdown method, physical age-life method.

For example, the roof and plumbing on a building each have an effective age of 10 years. The roof has a total physical life of 20 years, and the plumbing has a total physical life of 25 years. Outdoor paint was applied 5 years ago and has a total physical life of 10 years. The reproduction cost after curable physical depreciation was subtracted for the roof, plumbing and paint are $20,000, $12,000 and $6,000 respectively. The short-lived incurable physical deterioration can be estimated as follows:

| | Reproduction Cost Remaining | Effective Age | Total Physical Life | Ratio | Short-lived Incurable Physical Depreciation |
|---|---|---|---|---|---|
| Roof | $20,000 | 10 | 20 | 0.50 | $10,000 |
| Plumbing | $12,000 | 10 | 25 | 0.40 | $ 4,800 |
| Paint | $ 6,000 | 1 | 10 | 0.10 | $   600 |
| Total short-lived incurable physical depreciation | | | | | $15,400 |

Assume that the above building's reproduction cost of long-lived items equals $350,000. Depreciation due to curable physical deterioration and short-lived incurable deterioration equals $20,000. The building has an effective age of 10 years and has a total physical life of 50 years. The amount of incurable physical deterioration for long-lived items can be estimated as follows: Reproduction cost = $350,000 − $20,000 = $330,000.

| Reproduction Cost Remaining | Effective Age | Total Physical Life | Ratio | Long-lived Incurable Physical Depreciation |
|---|---|---|---|---|
| $330,000 | 10 | 50 | 0.20 | $66,000 |

**index lease**   A lease that specifies that rent adjustments in any year are based on changes in a specifically identified cost-of-living adjustment. *See also* lease.

**index rate**    The interest rate of a security or other index on which the interest rate of an adjustable rate mortgage is based, for example, interest rates on U.S. Treasury securities or inflation rates based on the consumer price index (CPI). *See also* adjustable rate mortgage (ARM).

**indirect costs**    Construction expenses for items other than labor and materials, e.g., financing costs, taxes, administrative costs, contractor's overhead and profit, legal fees, interest payments, insurance costs during construction and lease-up costs. Also called soft costs. *See also* direct costs.

**industrial park**    A cluster of buildings designed as a unit to be used for manufacturing, processing, assembly and storage of products or natural resources. Appurtenances such as public utilities, streets, railroad sidings, and water and sewage facilities are provided in the park.

**industrial plant**    A single location where industrial operations are performed, including all structures on the site.

**industrial property**    Land and buildings used for manufacturing, processing, assembly and storage of products or natural resources, e.g., warehouses, factories, oil wells.

**inflation index**    A time series trend that tracks the erosion of the purchasing power of currency.

**infrastructure**    (1) Facilities that are constructed in an urban area to support the majority of the population, e.g., roads, sewage and drainage systems. (2) The core of development in a building or complex, which serves as the source of utilities and support services.

**ingress**    The path by which one accesses or enters a property; the opposite of egress.

**input linkage**    For a business or firm, the costs of maintaining spatial relationships with the providers or suppliers of the inputs into the business or productive activity. The inputs can be labor services, materials, financial services, information, etc. *See also* linkage.

**input-output analysis**    A study of the internal relationships in the business sector. This analysis is an alternative to the circular flow of income as a descriptive technique for an economy. *See also* economic base analysis, local economic analysis.

**inside lot**    A lot located between the corner lots on a specific block. *See also* corner influence.

**installment contract**    A contract that specifies that a sale is paid through partial payments over a period of time. The title to property is not usually transferred until all payments under the contract are made.

**installment note**   A promissory note that specifies that payment of the principal is paid in partial payments at stated times.

**installment to amortize $1 (1/a$_{\overline{n}|}$)**   The periodic payment necessary to repay a $1 loan with interest paid at a specified rate and over a specified time on the outstanding balance, the reciprocal of the present value of an ordinary annuity. See column 6 of the compound interest tables in Appendix B and below.

$$\frac{i}{1 - [1/(1 + i)^n]}$$

where i equals the periodic interest rate and n equals the number of periods. Also called partial payment. *See also* six functions of $1.

**insulation**   In construction, material such as plasterboard, asbestos, compressed wood-wool or fiberboard placed between inner and outer surfaces that reduces the transfer of heat, cold or sound by dissipating air currents.

**insurable value**   The value of the destructible parts of a property. This value is used to determine the amount of insurance carried on the property.

**insured mortgage**   A mortgage in which payment is ensured by a party other than the borrower in case of default. The insurer usually requires a premium payment, e.g., FHA-insured mortgages, private mortgage insurance (PMI).

**intangible property**   In real estate, a non-material right, agreement or action that results in an exclusive or preferred position in the marketplace. For example, the right to use a franchise name such as Hilton for a hotel. *See also* intangible value.

**intangible value**   The worth of a non-material right, agreement or action that results in an exclusive or preferred position in the marketplace, the excess value attributable to an above-market lease. *See also* business value, going-concern value, goodwill.

**intercept locations**   Those competitive locations that are first encountered and first seen by potential users of the subject site and that, by virtue of their favorable exposure, may divert activity or capture part of the market being sought by the subject site.

**interest**   Money paid for the use of money over time; a return on capital. Interest payments are deductible for income tax purposes, although payments of principal are not. *See also* amortization schedule, effective annual rate, effective rate.

**interest expense**   The periodic cost incurred through a debt.

**interest in property**   The legal portion of a property that is owned, which may be a full or partial ownership interest, e.g., fee simple interest, leased fee interest, leasehold interest, subleasehold interest.

**interest rate**   The ratio of the cost of using money divided by the money advanced. *See also* interest.

**interest rate cap**   The maximum interest rate charge allowed on an adjustable rate mortgage. A cap may be set for a particular adjustment period or for the entire life of the loan. *See also* adjustable rate mortgage (ARM).

**interest rate risk**   The uncertainty caused by a variation in interest rates. *See also* risk.

**interest-only loan**   A nonamortizing loan in which payments of interest are made at specified times throughout the life of the loan and the principal is paid in a lump sum at the maturity of the loan.

**interim financing**   *See* temporary financing.

**interim use**   A temporary use for a property when the highest and best use of the property is different from the highest and best use of the land as if vacant.

**interior door**   A door within a building, often with a hollow core, but sometimes made of solid wood in older homes. The quality of the door often indicates the overall quality of construction for the building. Door types include louver, French, accordion and batten.

**interior wall**   In construction, any wall contained in the inner space of a building. Interior walls are typically made with wood studs covered by drywall materials, but ranging from simple wire partitions to solid masonry walls that provide fire protection.

**internal economies to scale**   *See* agglomeration economies.

**internal rate of return (IRR)**   A rate of return that discounts all expected future cash flows to a present value that is equal to the original investment. An IRR can be calculated for any defined cash flows, for example, for the whole property or for just the equity position. Also called yield rate. *See also* adjusted internal rate of return (AIRR), discounted cash flow analysis (DCF), multiple internal rates of return.

For example, a property is purchased for $100,000 and produces cash flows of $10,000 for 5 years, at which time it is sold for $110,000. The internal rate of return can be calculated as follows:

$$\$100,000 = \$10,000 \times a_{\overline{n}|(x\%,\ 5\ \text{yrs.})} + \$110,000 \times 1/S_{\overline{n}|(x\%,\ 5\ \text{yrs.})}$$
x% = 11.59% using an annual compound interest table
    or a financial calculator
Therefore, the internal rate of return equals 11.59%.

**interpolation**   The estimation of a value that falls within the range of available data on which the estimation is based. Interpolation is sometimes necessary when using financial tables because the factors are only calculated for a range of interest rates.

**interval ownership**   *See* time-sharing.

**invested capital**   *See* equity.

**investment**   Money or capital used to purchase an interest in a property, usually with the intention of receiving some sort of cash flow or profit from the property plus a recovery of the initial outlay of funds. An investment is usually considered a more long-term use, as distinguished from speculation. *See also* equity.

**investment analysis**   According to the Uniform Standards of Professional Appraisal Practice, a study that reflects the relationship between acquisition price and anticipated future benefits of a real estate investment.

**investment interest**   The amount of interest incurred to purchase or carry investment property, not including interest paid on a personal residence or passive-activity interest. Investment property includes property that produces income defined as interest, dividends, annuities or royalties and any trade or business in which the taxpayer does not materially participate, so long as that activity is not treated as a passive activity. Investment interest is deductible to the amount of the investment income.

**investment property**   Property or an interest in property that is purchased for the purpose of receiving a profit.

**investment value**   The value of a property to a particular investor. *See also* investment analysis.

**investment yield**   *See* internal rate of return (IRR).

**Inwood annuity factor**   *See* present value ordinary annuity $1 per period $(a_{\overline{n}|})$.

**Inwood premise**   An appraisal theory used to value an income stream of equal payments in which the present value of the income stream is based on a single discount figure; the basis for the present value of an ordinary annuity factor in compound interest tables. *See* present value ordinary annuity $1 per period $(a_{\overline{n}|})$.

**IRR**   *See* internal rate of return (IRR).

**J factor** A constant used to transform a variable income stream into its level equivalent annuity based on the equity yield rate. A way to stabilize income. The J factor represents a change in net operating income over a specified holding period with the pattern of change reflecting the change in a sinking fund based on growth determined by the equity yield rate. *See also* Ellwood formula, Ellwood techniques, K factor. The J factor can be calculated by the following formula:

$$J = 1/S_{\overline{n}} \times \left[ \frac{n}{1 - 1/(1 + Y_E)^n} - \frac{1}{Y_E} \right]$$

where $1/S_{\overline{n}}$ equals the sinking fund factor at the equity yield rate, n equals the holding period and Y equals the equity yield rate. When used with the Ellwood formula the equation becomes:

$$R_O = \frac{Y_E - M(Y_E + P \ 1/S_{\overline{n}} - R_M) - \triangle_O 1/S_{\overline{n}}}{1 + \triangle_I J}$$

where $R_O$ equals the overall capitalization rate, M equals the loan to value ratio, $Y_E$ equals the equity yield rate, P equals the percentage of loan paid off, $1/S_{\overline{n}}$ equals the sinking fund factor at the equity yield rate, $R_M$ equals the mortgage capitalization rate, $\triangle_O$ equals the change in total property value, $\triangle_I$ equals the total ratio change in income and J equals the J factor.

For example, a property is purchased with a 75% loan at a 10% interest rate, monthly payments and 20-year loan term. The property is held for 5 years and produces a net operating income (NOI) of $20,000. At the end of the 5 years the property value and NOI have increased by 5%. The equity investor expects a 12% yield. $P = 0.1020$. (From the annual compound interest tables in Appendix B, $1/S_{\overline{n}} = 0.1638$.) The overall cap rate can be determined as follows:

$$J = 0.1638 \times \left[ \frac{5}{1 - 1/(1+.12)^5} - \frac{1}{.12} \right] = 0.5283$$

$$R_O = \frac{.12 - .75(.12 + .1020 \times (.1638) - .1158) - .05(.1638)}{1 + (.05 \times .5283)} = 0.0937$$

The property value is $20,000/.0937 = $213,447.17

**joint tenancy**   Joint ownership by two or more persons with right of survivorship in which each person has an identical interest and right of possession. *See also* tenancy.

**joist**   In construction, the smaller horizontal timbers laid edgewise to which the boards of a floor or lath of a ceiling are nailed; $2 \times 4$ boards that support the floor.

**judgment**   The ability to formulate an opinion, estimate or conclusion about an issue or problem, given the data or evidence available. In appraising, the ability to render an estimate of value, usually depending on the knowledge, experience and analytical ability of the appraiser.

**judgment sampling**   (1) A nonprobability sampling technique in which a sample is selected according to someone's personal judgment. While such samples may be biased, they are often less costly than probability samples and, in certain instances, may be superior, as in small-scale surveys, in pilot studies or in constructing index numbers. (2) A nonprobability sampling technique in which the sample is drawn based on the interviewer's or the analyst's prior knowledge or expectations about individuals who will give a response.

**junior department store**   A store that in both size and selection of merchandise can be classified as being between a full-time department store and a variety store. *See also* shopping center.

**junior lien**   A lien placed on a property that has less priority than another lien on the same property.

**junior mortgage**   A mortgage that has less right or lien priority than another mortgage on the same property, for example, a second or third mortgage. A junior mortgage typically carries a higher interest rate because it contains more risk than a senior mortgage. *See also* second mortgage, senior mortgage.

**just compensation**   Fair and reasonable compensation to a private owner of property when property is taken for public use through condemnation. *See also* condemnation, eminent domain.

**K factor**   A factor that can be used to convert a stream of income that changes at a constant ratio (compound rate) into a level payment equivalent. A way of stabilizing income. Sometimes used in conjunction with the Ellwood formula. *See also* Ellwood formula, Ellwood techniques, J factor. The K factor can be calculated by the following formula:

$$K = \frac{1 - [(1 + C)^n / S^n]}{(Y_E - C)a_{\overline{n}|}}$$

where C equals the constant-ratio change in income, $S^n$ equals the future value factor, $Y_E$ equals the equity yield rate and $a_{\overline{n}|}$ equals the present value factor for an ordinary level annuity.

The K factor can then be used to find the overall capitalization rate for the property:

$$R_O = \frac{[Y_E - M(Y_E + P\ 1/S_{\overline{n}|} - R_M) - \triangle_O 1/S_{\overline{n}|}]}{K}$$

where $R_O$ equals the overall capitalization rate, M equals the loan to value ratio, $Y_E$ equals the equity yield rate, P equals the percentage of loan paid off, $1/S_{\overline{n}|}$ equals the sinking fund factor at the equity yield rate, $R_M$ equals the mortgage capitalization rate, $\triangle_O$ equals the change in total property value and K equals the K factor.

For example, a property is purchased with a 75% loan at a 10% interest rate, monthly payments and 20-year loan term. The property is held for 5 years and produces a net operating income (NOI) of $20,000. The NOI increases at 2% per year compounded. At the end of the 5 years, the property value will have increased by 5%. The equity investor expects a 12% yield. (From the annual compound interest tables in Appendix B, $S^n = 1.762342$, $a_{\overline{n}|} = 3.604776$, $P = 0.1020$, $1/S_{\overline{n}|} = 0.1638$.) The overall cap rate can be determined as follows:

$$K = [1 - ((1 + 0.02)^5 / 1.762342)] / [(0.12 - 0.02) \times 3.604776] = 1.0362$$

$$R_O = \frac{.12 - .75(.12 + .1020 \times (.1638) - .1158) - .05(.1638)}{1.0362} = 0.0928$$

The value of the property is $20,000/.0928 = $215,517.24

**kickers**   *See* equity kicker, equity participation.

**kitchen**   A room, usually measuring at least 80 square feet, used in residential properties for food preparation and storage, eating and entertainment. Considered to be the most important room in the house, the kitchen serves more functions than any other room. Most kitchens are laid out in a work triangle that consists of a sink/food preparation area, a refrigerator and a cooking area. The kitchen area should also include good ventilation, lighting and sufficient electrical outlets. *See also* building description, house zone.

**L** *See* land ratio (L).

**land** The earth's surface including the solid surface of the earth, water and anything attached to it; natural resources in their original state, e.g., mineral deposits, timber, soil. In law, land is considered to be the solid surface of the earth and does not include water. Common methods used to provide legal descriptions of land include the metes and bounds system, rectangular survey (government survey) system, geodetic survey system and lot and block system. Land valuation techniques include the direct sales comparison approach, allocation, extraction, subdivision development, land residual, and ground rent capitalization.

**land/building ratio** The ratio of land area divided by gross building area.

**land capitalization rate ($R_L$)** The rate that reflects the first-year land lease payment divided by the value of the land. *See also* band of investment technique (land-building formula), building residual technique, land residual technique.

**land contract** An installment contract that calls for periodic payments of sales price, usually with interest added. Title does not change hands until the contract is fulfilled. Often used as a vehicle for seller financing.

**land coverage** *See* foundation area.

**land development** The addition of improvements to land (utilities, roads, grading and services) that makes the land suitable for resale as developable sites for housing or other purposes.

**land improvements** *See* improvement.

**land lease** *See* ground lease.

**land ratio (L)** The ratio of land value to total property value. *See also* band of investment technique (land-building formula), building residual technique, land residual technique.

**land residual technique**   A technique used to find the value of a property by subtracting income attributable to the building from the net operating income and valuing the residual land income, for example, by dividing the land income by a land capitalization rate to arrive at a land value indication. The land value is then added to the building value to arrive at an estimate of value for the total property. The land residual technique is one way of evaluating the highest and best use of a site. Under its highest and best use, the building value should equal its development cost and the highest land value will result for this use. *See also* land.

For example, a property's building is valued at $100,000. Net operating income (NOI) for the property equals $30,000. The land cap rate equals 10% and building cap rate equals 13%. The land value and property value can be calculated as follows:

| | | |
|---|---|---|
| Building value | $100,000 | |
| NOI | | $30,000 |
| Building value $\times R_B$ (100,000 $\times$ 0.13) | | $-13,000$ |
| Residual income to land | | 17,000 |
| Land value (17,000/0.10) | 170,000 | |
| Total property value | $270,000 | |

**land use**   The utilization of a site to produce revenue or other benefits.

**landlocked**   A parcel of land that is surrounded by land belonging to another.

**landlord**   One who leases a property to another; the lessor. The landlord retains a reversionary interest in the property so that when the lease ends, the property will revert to the landlord.

**land-use intensity**   Local zoning codes designed to regulate the density of development on land, including restrictions on the minimum and maximum amount of floor area per land area, and living space and recreation space requirements. Important in the development of planned unit developments.

**land utilization studies**   An analysis of the potential uses of a parcel of land and a determination of the highest and best use for that parcel; a complete inventory of the parcels in a given community or other area classified by type of use, plus (in some cases) an analysis of the spatial patterns of use revealed by this inventory. Land utilization studies do not embody the viewpoint of any particular investor nor do they focus on any one parcel. Furthermore, no consideration of markets and feasibility is normally included.

**lath**   In construction, material fastened to the rafters, ceiling joists or wall studs to form a base for plaster, slates, tiles or shingles, e.g., wood, gypsum, wire or metal lath.

**laundry areas**   An area that is ideally a separate room, but may be in a closet, and may be located in any of several accepted areas throughout the house. *See also* building description, house zone.

**law of retail gravitation**   *See* Reilly's Model of Retail Gravitation, Huff's Probability Formulation, Converse's modification.

**layout**   The floor plan of a building.

**lease**   A written contract between a building owner and a tenant that transfers the right to occupy a specific property to the tenant for a specific period of time in return for a specified rent. The lease may also establish other rules, conditions and terms regarding the use and occupancy of the property under which the lease will be valid. *See also* master lease, net-net-net lease, passthrough lease, proprietary lease, recreational lease, sandwich lease, ground lease, gross lease, net lease, flat lease, graduated rental lease, revaluation lease, index lease.

**lease interest**   A property interest that arises from the association of a lease with a property, e.g., a leased fee estate or leasehold estate.

**lease option**   A clause in a lease that gives the tenant the right to purchase the property under specified conditions.

**lease premium**   *See* excess rent.

**lease rollover**   The re-leasing of a space with the same tenant, after the expiration of a previous lease on the same space.

**leaseback**   *See* sale-leaseback.

**leased fee estate**   An ownership interest in the real estate held by a landlord who has transferred the right of occupancy to a property through the execution of a lease. The landlord retains the right to receive rental payment throughout the term of the lease and the right to possess the property at the termination of the lease. The leased fee estate can be valued as the present value of the lease income plus the right to the reversion at the end of the lease. The discount rate used to value the leased fee estate may be higher or lower than the discount rate used to value the fee simple estate, depending on the risk associated with the lease. Characteristics such as the creditworthiness of the tenants and terms of the lease should be considered. Care must also be taken when using the cost approach to value a leased fee estate. The cost approach *always* gives a fee simple value. *See also* fee simple estate, leasehold estate, sandwich leasehold estate, subleasehold estate.

For example, assume that a building is leased so that NOI is $400,000 per year for a holding period of 5 years, at which time the lease expires with no renewal option. The resale value at the end of the 5 years is estimated to be $5,796,370. Assume a discount rate of

12.5%. The value of the leased fee estate (V) can now be calculated as follows:

$$V = \frac{400{,}000}{1.125} + \frac{400{,}000}{(1.125)^2} + \frac{400{,}000}{(1.125)^3} + \frac{400{,}000}{(1.125)^4} + \frac{400{,}000}{(1.125)^5} + \frac{5{,}796{,}370}{(1.125)^5}$$

$$V = \$4{,}640{,}801$$

**leasehold estate**    An ownership interest in real estate held by a tenant during the term of a lease. The tenant is given the right to use and occupy a property for a time and based on the restrictions contained in the lease. The leasehold estate can be valued as the present value of the difference between the market rent and the rent specified by the lease. The value of the leasehold estate is not necessarily equal to the difference between the value of the fee simple estate and the leased fee estate. The leasehold estate may be more or less risky than the fee simple estate or the leased fee estate. Any change in market rent will have the most effect on the value of the leasehold estate. Therefore, the leasehold estate may be discounted at a higher or lower rate than the fee simple estate or leased fee estate. *See also* fee simple estate, leased fee estate, sandwich leasehold estate, sub-leasehold estate.

For example, assume that a building is leased at a rate of $400,000 per year for a holding period of 5 years, at which time the lease expires with no renewal option. Market rates for this property equal $500,000 in the first year, increasing at a rate of 3% per year. Assume a discount rate of 18%. The value of the leasehold estate (V) can now be calculated as follows:

| Year | 1 | 2 | 3 | 4 | 5 |
|---|---|---|---|---|---|
| Market rent | 500,000 | 515,000 | 530,450 | 546,364 | 562,754 |
| Actual rent | 400,000 | 400,000 | 400,000 | 400,000 | 400,000 |
| Difference | 100,000 | 115,000 | 130,450 | 146,364 | 162,754 |

$$V = \frac{100{,}000}{1.18} + \frac{115{,}000}{(1.18)^2} + \frac{130{,}450}{(1.18)^3} + \frac{146{,}364}{(1.18)^4} + \frac{162{,}754}{(1.18)^5}$$

$$V = \$393{,}367$$

**leasehold improvements**    Improvements or additions made to a leased property by the lessee.

**leasehold mortgage**    A mortgage on the lessee's interest in the leased premises.

**legal description**    A description of a parcel of land complete enough to allow a competent surveyor to locate the exact boundaries of the land. *See also* land.

**legally conforming use**  A property use that is permitted by current zoning, including use, building setback, parking requirements and such. *See also* legally nonconforming use.

**legally nonconforming use**  A use that was lawfully established and maintained but no longer conforms to the zoning in which it is located. A legally nonconforming use is usually caused by zoning changes and precludes any additions or changes that were made without municipal approval.

**legally permissible**  Required in highest and best use; that which is allowable by law. To be the highest and best use of a site, the use must be legally permissible. *See also* legally nonconforming use.

**lender**  One who advances funds typically with an interest rate; any institution that invests funds in mortgages; the mortgagee. Typical real estate lenders include savings and loan associations, commercial banks, life insurance companies and pension funds.

**lender participation**  *See* equity participation.

**lessee**  A person or entity that has been granted the right to use and occupy a property as the result of the execution of a lease agreement; a tenant. *See also* leasehold estate.

**lessee's interest**  *See* leasehold estate.

**lessor**  The owner of a property who transfers the right to use and occupy the property to a tenant as the result of the execution of a lease agreement; a landlord. *See also* leased fee estate.

**lessor's interest**  *See* leased fee estate.

**less-than-freehold estate**  The estate held by a person who rents or leases property. This classification includes an estate for years, periodic tenancy, estate at will and estate at sufferance. *See* freehold, leasehold estate.

**letter of transmittal**  A letter accompanying an appraisal report that formally presents the report to the person who requested it and may include information such as: address and description of the property, property interest being appraised, statement that property inspection and all necessary analyses were completed by the appraiser, date of appraisal, value estimate, any extraordinary assumptions or limiting conditions, appraiser's signature and reference to accompanying appraisal.

**letter report**  A shortened appraisal report that states the conclusions of the appraiser's investigation and analysis. A letter report typically contains an identification of the property, purpose of the appraisal, a description of the analysis, the date of valuation and limiting conditions. Much of the data and reasoning are omitted. *See also* report.

**level annuity**    A periodic income stream consisting of equal payments over a specified number of periods of equal length. *See also* annuity.

**level-payment mortgage**    A mortgage in which equal, periodic payments are made over the life of the loan that cover both interest and principal. Payments are credited first against interest on the declining balance and then against principal, so that the amount of money credited to principal gradually increases over the life of the loan, while the amount credited to interest gradually decreases. *See also* amortization schedule.

**leverage**    The use of borrowed funds in the purchase of an investment. If the addition of the mortgage increases the return to the equity (equity dividend rate or equity yield rate), the addition of the mortgage has resulted in positive leverage. If the addition of the mortgage decreases the return to the equity, the addition of the mortgage has resulted in negative leverage. *See also* negative leverage, positive leverage, zero leverage. Some examples follow:

If $R_O > R_M$ then $R_E > R_O$ and if $Y_O > Y_M$ then $Y_E > Y_O$ (positive leverage)
If $R_O = R_M$ then $R_E = R_O$ and if $Y_O = Y_M$ then $Y_E = Y_O$ (zero leverage)
If $R_O < R_M$ then $R_E < R_O$ and if $Y_O < Y_M$ then $Y_E < Y_O$ (negative leverage)

**license**    A formal agreement from a constituted authority that allows an activity to be conducted.

**licensed appraiser**    As specified in the Financial Institutions Reform, Recovery and Enforcement Act (FIRREA), an appraiser who has been licensed by the appropriate state to value property. The FIRREA states that either licensed or certified appraisers may appraise property valued at less than $1 million that involves a federal agency. Each federal agency decides whether a licensed or certified appraiser is required on properties valued at less than $1,000,000. Only certified appraisers may appraise property valued at $1 million or more. *See also* certified appraiser; Financial Institutions Reform, Recovery and Enforcement Act (FIRREA); federally related transaction.

**lien**    A charge created by agreement or law against a property in which the property serves as the security for a debt.

**life annuity**    An annuity that comes only during the lifetime of the recipient, as distinguished from an annuity certain, which continues for a specified period of time. *See also* annuity, life estate.

**life cycle**    *See* neighborhood life cycle.

**life estate**    An estate that is limited to the lifetime of a designated party and conveys the rights to use, occupy and control the property. *See also* life annuity, life tenant.

**life tenant**    One who owns an estate that is limited to the lifetime of a designated party. *See also* life estate.

**limited common elements**    Items in a multi-unit project that are available for use by one or more, but not all, units, e.g., parking stalls or storage units. *See also* common areas.

**limited partner**    A passive investor in a limited partnership whose liability is limited to the initial contribution of capital plus any unpaid contributions that must be made in the future. *See also* limited partnership.

**limited partnership**    An ownership arrangement in which general and limited partners are included as equity investors in a real estate project. General partners are responsible for the management of the partnership and have unlimited liability in regard to the ownership agreement. Limited partners' liability is limited to the initial contribution of capital plus any unpaid contributions that must be made in the future. Losses from the property are passed through to all partners and may be used to offset other passive income for tax purposes. *See also* general partnership.

**limited purpose industrial building**    An industrial building that is designed and built to serve a specific function or functions and that may not be easily adapted to serve other alternative uses. Such property appeals to a smaller segment of the market and consequently has reduced utility once there is no longer an economic need for its original purpose. Includes both special purpose industrial buildings and single purpose industrial buildings.

**limiting conditions**    Specifications in an appraisal report that restrict the assumptions in the report to certain situations, for example, date and use of the appraisal, definition of value, identification of real estate and property rights being valued, definition of surveys used or not used.

**line of credit**    An agreement between a lender and a borrower in which the borrower can borrow up to a certain maximum amount of money from the lender without a formal loan submission. The borrower then has available a quick loan service without the delay of a credit review (although the line of credit is usually periodically reviewed). Lines of credit are usually used by banks for their most reliable and creditworthy customers.

**linear regression**    In statistics, an analysis of the nature of the relationship between two variables. *See also* multiple regression, correlation.

**linkage**    The time-distance relationship between a property or neighborhood and other destinations or originations.

**liquidation value**   The price received when a property is sold as a quick sale. *See* quick sale.

**liquidity**   The ease with which an asset may be sold for cash at a price close to its true value.

**lis pendens**   A recorded legal notice of the filing of a suit in which the title to a property may be affected. If this property is purchased, the buyer is then subject to any judgment entered. The notice of filing is not a lien on the property but rather a notice of pending action.

**listing price**   The asking price at which a property is listed for sale. The listing price does not necessarily equal the market value or the sales price. Also called asking price.

**live-load floor capacity**   A moving or variable weight that can be safely supported by a structure, expressed in pounds per square foot; the weight of people, furniture and equipment that can be supported by the floor. *See also* dead-load.

**livestock ranch**   A business enterprise that depends primarily on range forage for production of livestock and related products. Primary considerations in appraising a livestock ranch are the land, relationship of the land and vegetation to the livestock, type of operation, grazing potential of the land and use of nonfee land through leases or permits.

**living area**   *See* gross living area.

**living room**   A formal room, usually measuring at least 170 square feet, used in residential properties for relaxing and entertainment. At one time considered the center of the house, the living room is now used less frequently for entertaining as rooms such as the family room or kitchen have been expanded and used more often. *See also* building description, family room, house zone.

**load**   (1) The weight supported by a structural part or member. (2) The power delivered by a motor, transformer, generator or power station. (3) The electrical current carried through a circuit.

**load factor**   The ratio of the average kilowatt demand during a specified time interval to the rated capacity of the equipment for a given power plant or electric utility company.

**loan**   The act of borrowing or lending money. The term *loan* is often used loosely to imply a mortgage loan. *See also* loan balance, mortgage, note.

**loan balance**   The amount of principal left to be paid on a loan at a specified period of time. The loan balance equals the present value of future payments discounted at the contract rate of the loan. For example, a loan for $550,000 has terms of 20 years, 11% interest and monthly payments of \$5,677.04. After 5 years, the loan balance can be calculated as follows:

$PV = 5,677.04 \times a_{\overline{n}|(11\%, \; 15 \; years)}$
$a_{\overline{n}|(11\%, \; 15 \; years)} = 87.9819$ using a monthly compound interest table
$PV = 5,677.04 \times 87.9819$
$PV = 499,476.64$

**loan commitment**   *See* commitment.

**loan constant**   *See* mortgage capitalization rate ($R_M$).

**loan fee**   *See* point.

**loan payment**   *See* mortgage payment (PMT).

**loan term**   The length of time over which a loan must be paid off, as specified in a loan contract.

**loan to value ratio (M)**   The ratio of the outstanding loan balance divided by the total property value. For example, a property is purchased for \$15,000,000 with an \$11,250,000 loan. The loan to value ratio could be calculated as follows: $M = 11,250,000/15,000,000 = 0.75$. *See also* band of investment technique (mortgage-equity formula), Ellwood techniques.

**local economic analysis**   A study of the fundamental determinants of the demand and supply for all real estate in the market. The analysis considers the factors basic to the demand for all types of real estate in a local economy. Population, households, employment and income are the principal variables on the demand side of local economic analysis. Past trends and forecasts of these basic demand determinants are made for a defined geographic area. Factors on the supply side of the local economy such as the amount of land available for specific land uses, construction costs, local infrastructure, etc. are also considered. Economic base analysis and input-output analysis are two techniques to describe the local economy. *See also* economic base analysis, input-output analysis.

**localization economies**   Also known as external economies to the firms that are internal to the industry. *See* agglomeration economies.

**location**   The time-distance relationship (linkage) between a property or neighborhood and all other origins and destinations.

**location analysis**   A thorough study of a location in terms of a specific use, environment, time and anticipated pattern of change.

**location quotient**   A ratio of the local economy's employment percentage in a given industry to a larger economy's employment percentage in that same industry. The location quotient is used to identify export industries. Typically a value greater than 1 occurs for a basic industry.

**locational obsolescence**    A type of external obsolescence in which value loss is caused by a negative influence outside the property due to its location, e.g., a corner location in a residential area, a health hazard close to the property, or a change of property use close to the property. *See also* external obsolescence.

**loft building**    A multistory building with an open floor design that is used for light manufacturing, warehousing and sometimes offices.

**long-lived item**    A component with an expected remaining economic life that is the same as the remaining economic life of the entire structure.

**lot**    Land within a set of defined boundaries. Also called a parcel, plot or tract. *See also* site.

**lot and block survey system**    A legal description of subdivided land that refers to the lot by lot and block numbers that appear on survey maps and plats of recorded subdivided land. *See also* land.

**lump sum payment**    *See* balloon payment.

# M

**M** *See* loan to value ratio (M).

**machinery and equipment** All tangible fixed assets (tools, tooling, conveyor and other personal property) other than real estate used in any way to facilitate any manufacturing, assembly or warehousing activity. Distinguished from fixed building equipment.

**main** A pipe, conduit or circuit leading to or from the branches of a utility system, carrying the combined flow of all the branches.

**maintenance** Procedures and expenditures necessary to keep a property in operating condition. *See also* repairs, renovation.

**maintenance fee** The payments made by the individual owners in a condominium to the homeowner's association for expenses incurred in the maintenance and upkeep of the common areas.

**major tenant** *See* anchor tenant.

**mall** A landscaped public area that is designated for pedestrian use only. A mall area is typically used in shopping centers but also created in downtown areas to revitalize existing businesses and sometimes used in suburban areas to generate new business. *See also* shopping center.

**management fee** A fee paid for the administration and supervision of a property, typically considered a variable operating expense.

**manufactured housing** Residential buildings that are partially assembled or completely assembled before being placed on a permanent site.

**marginal tax rate** The ordinary income tax rate charged on the last dollar of income; the tax rate used when making investment decisions.

**market** The interaction of buyers and sellers who exchange a specific product for cash or other assets.

**market analysis**    According to the Uniform Standards of Professional Appraisal Practice, a study of real estate market conditions for a specific type of property.

**market approach**    *See* direct sales comparison approach.

**market area**    A geographic area or political jurisdiction in which similar property types compete on an economic basis for potential buyers, users or patrons.

**market comparison approach**    *See* direct sales comparison approach.

**market conditions**    Characteristics of the market such as vacancy rates, interest rates, employment levels, etc.

**market data approach**    *See* direct sales comparison approach.

**market disaggregation**    The process of dividing a market into smaller, more homogeneous submarkets based on product characteristics. *See also* disaggregation.

**market gap analysis**    An analysis to determine whether there is or will be unmet or unfilled demand in the market. *See* gap analysis.

**market participants**    Individuals actively engaged in real estate transactions. Primary market participants are those who invest in real property or who use real estate, e.g., buyers, sellers, owners, lenders, tenants. Secondary market participants include those who advise or assist primary participants, e.g., advisors, brokers, counselors, underwriters, appraisers.

**market price**    The amount actually paid, or to be paid, for a property in a particular transaction. Market price differs from market value. Market price is an accomplished historical fact, whereas market value is and remains an estimate. Market price does *not* assume prudent conduct by the parties, appropriate information is available, absence of undue stimulus or of any other condition basic to the market value concept.

**market rent**    The rental income that a property would command if exposed for lease in a competitive market.

**market rent equivalency adjustment**    The adjustment that reflects the impact of any existing below-market leases on the market value of a property. A market rent equivalency adjustment represents the difference between the fee simple interest and the leased fee interest, unless the leased fee interest is greater than the fee simple interest. In that case, the difference would be a non-realty interest known as the rent premium.

**market research**    *See* market analysis.

**market sales comparison approach**    *See* direct sales comparison approach.

**market segmentation** The identification and analysis of submarkets within a larger market. *See also* market disaggregation.

**market standard** The quality and/or quantity of various physical, financial, locational and site feature characteristics that define the norm for a market as established by competitive sites that are existing, in process and not yet developed.

**market study** *See* market analysis.

**market survey** *See* market analysis.

**market value** According to the Uniform Standards of Professional Appraisal Practice, market value is the major focus of most real property appraisal assignments. Both economic and legal definitions of market value have been developed and refined. A current economic definition agreed upon by federal financial institutions in the United States is:

The most probable price which a property should bring in a competitive and open market under all conditions requisite to a fair sale, the buyer and seller each acting prudently and knowledgeably, and assuming the price is not affected by undue stimulus. Implicit in this definition is the consummation of a sale as of a specified date and the passing of title from seller to buyer under conditions whereby:

1. buyer and seller are typically motivated;
2. both parties are well-informed or well-advised, and acting in what they consider their best interests;
3. a reasonable time is allowed for exposure in the open market;
4. payment is made in terms of cash in United States dollars or in terms of financial arrangements comparable thereto; and
5. the price represents the normal consideration for the property sold unaffected by special or creative financing or sales concessions granted by anyone associated with the sale.

Substitution of another currency for United States dollars in the fourth condition is appropriate in other countries or in reports addressed to clients from other countries.

Persons performing appraisal services that may be subject to litigation are cautioned to seek the exact legal definition of market value in the jurisdiction in which the services are being performed.

**marketability** The ease with which a property can be absorbed, sold or leased.

**marketability study** A real estate analysis of a specific property that addresses the ability of the property to be absorbed, sold or leased under current and anticipated market conditions.

**marketing period**   The time period beginning when an owner decides to start actively selling a property to when the sale is actually closed. The marketing period is typically an observable fact. If a marketing period that is shorter than typical is assumed in an analysis, the value found would be considered a forced, or liquidation value rather than market value.

**mass appraisal**   According to the Uniform Standards of Professional Appraisal Practice, the process of valuing a universe of properties as of a given date, utilizing standard methodology, employing common data and allowing for statistical testing.

**mass appraisal model**   According to the Uniform Standards of Professional Appraisal Practice, a mathematical expression of how supply and demand factors interact in a market. *See also* mass appraisal.

**master lease**   The dominant lease in a building or development that contains a sublease.

**master limited partnership (MLP)**   A limited partnership in which the individual interests are issued to one limited partner who arranges the public trading of the shares. Also called a publicly traded limited partnership. *See also* limited partnership.

**mat and raft foundation**   *See* floating foundation.

**maturity (loan)**   The termination period of a loan. May differ from amortization term, in which case a balloon payment is due at maturity.

**maximally productive**   One of four criteria in highest and best use analysis which states that a use is the highest and best use if it produces the highest value or price. *See also* highest and best use (HBU).

**mean**   An average of a set of numbers; the sum of a group of values divided by the number of values in the group; a measure of the central tendency of data. The mean is affected by extreme values. For example, the mean of the set of numbers 1,4, and 500 is 168.33 [(1 + 4 + 500)/3]. The mean of the set of numbers 1,4, and 5 is 3.33 [(1 + 4 + 5)/3]. *See also* median, mode, weighted average.

**measurement error**   A deviation that arises when individuals who respond to questions in a survey give information that is not true.

**median**   The middle figure in a numerically ordered set of data having an equal number of values lying above and below the middle figure; a measure of the central tendency of data. If an even number of data points are present in the data set, then the median is the average of the middle two figures. The median is not affected by extreme values as is the mean. For example, the median of the set of numbers 1,4, and 500 is 4. The median of the set of numbers 1,4, and 5 is also 4. *See also* mean, mode.

**mercantilism** A theory of value popular in the eighteenth and nineteenth centuries that stated that wealth is associated with a nation's power. Mercantilism focused on maintaining a favorable balance of trade through strong economic controls to accumulate gold. *See also* appraisal theories.

**meridian** Used in the rectangular survey method of describing land, lines running north and south.

**metes and bounds method** A legal description of land in which land boundaries are referred to by a point of origin, metes and bounds. The point of origin is extended by a line in a specified direction (metes). The points at which these lines change direction are called bounds. This process continues until the line has returned to the point of origin. The metes and bounds method is the oldest known land survey method and the primary method of describing property in many states. *See also* land.

**Metropolitan Statistical Area (MSA)** A central city containing at least 50,000 people with a total metropolitan population of at least 100,000; replaces the term Standard Metropolitan Statistical Area (SMSA). *See also* Consolidated Metropolitan Statistical Area (CMSA), Primary Metropolitan Statistical Area (PMSA).

**mezzanine** An intermediate floor with less area than the regular floors.

**migrant** A person who moves to a residence in a different county.

**mill** A term often used in tax assessment calculations to indicate $1/10$ of a cent.

**mineral rights** The rights to use subsurface land and extract profits from that land. Mineral rights are normally passed with the conveyance of real property but can be separated from the conveyance of real property.

**mini-mall shopping center** A typical gross leasable area between 80,000 and 150,000 square feet on a corresponding site of 8 to 15 acres, emerging as an enclosed mall mostly adapted to community-type shopping facilities in areas of extreme climatic variations. Key tenants in the mini-mall are a junior department store, variety, food or drug store. The remaining tenants consist of specialty services. *See also* shopping center.

**minimum lot size** Specified by a zoning ordinance, the smallest dimensions of a lot allowed for construction of a building.

**minimum rent** *See* base rent.

**miniwarehouse** A storage structure ranging in size from 10 to 200 square feet, designed for individuals and small businesses.

**misplaced improvement**   An improvement located on a tract of land whose highest and best use does not match the highest and best use of the tract of land as if vacant.

**mixed-use property**   A property having multiple property uses, e.g., office, retail, etc.

**MLP**   *See* master limited partnership (MLP).

**mobility**   In real estate, the ease with which people can move from one location to another.

**mode**   The most frequent value in a set of numbers or most frequent response in a set of responses. The mode is not affected by extreme numbers. If the sample size is very small and no duplicate numbers exist, a mode does not exist. For example, in the set of numbers 1,3,4,4,2,2,6, and 4, the mode is 4. In the set of numbers 1,3,4, and 5, there is no mode. *See also* mean, median.

**modernization**   A type of renovation in which worn or outdated elements are replaced with their current counterparts.

**modified economic age-life method**   A method of estimating accrued depreciation in which the ratio of effective age to total economic life is multiplied by the reproduction or replacement cost minus curable physical and functional obsolescence to calculate the incurable accrued depreciation. *See also* accrued depreciation.

   For example, the reproduction cost of a building equals $80,000. Curable physical and functional obsolescence is estimated to be $800. The total economic life equals 40 years and the effective age equals 20 years. The indicated incurable accrued depreciation can be calculated as follows:

$$(20/40) \times (80,000 - 800) = 39,600$$

The indicated property value equals $80,000 - 800 - 39,600 = \$39,600$.

**modified internal rate of return**   *See* adjusted internal rate of return (AIRR).

**module**   A standard measure of any size used in construction and design to allow repetition and save material and labor costs.

**molding**   In construction, a finishing board used to cover a joint, for example, the point where a wall meets the ceiling.

**money market**   The interaction of buyers and sellers of short-term money instruments.

**monitor**   A raised structure on a roof with windows or louvers that ventilate or light the building. Monitors are usually found on factories or warehouses.

**monitor roof**   A type of framing, generally found in industrial buildings, that includes an elevated central section and provides better lighting and ventilation.

**monthly present value interest factor (MPVIF)**   The present value reversion of $1 calculated on a monthly basis. *See also* present value reversion of $1 ($1/S^n$).

**monthly present value interest factor-annuity (MPVIFA)**   The present value of ordinary annuity $1 per period calculated on a monthly basis. *See* present value ordinary annuity of $1 per period ($a_{\overline{n}|}$).

**monument**   A natural or artificial visible object that is fixed in place and used by surveyors to establish real estate boundaries.

**mortgage**   A legal document in which real estate is named under certain conditions as the security or collateral for the repayment of a loan. *See also* assumable mortgage, blanket mortgage, closed mortgage, closed-end mortgage, collateralized mortgage, constant amortization mortgage, convertible mortgage, conventional mortgage, fully amortized mortgage, graduated payment mortgage (GPM), hybrid mortgage, insured mortgage, level-payment mortgage, nonconventional mortgage, partially amortizing mortgage, participation mortgage, reverse annuity mortgage (RAM), shared appreciation mortgage, wraparound mortgage, note, loan.

**mortgage balance**   *See* loan balance.

**mortgage capitalization rate ($R_M$)**   The mortgage capitalization rate that is the ratio of the first-year debt payment divided by the beginning loan balance. In some instances, the ratio may be calculated using one month's payment but typically it is the total of the loan payment for an entire year. Also referred to as a mortgage loan constant. *See also* band of investment technique.

For example, a $100,000 loan has terms of 10% interest, monthly payments, and a 20-year term. Monthly payments equal $965.02. The mortgage capitalization rate can be calculated as follows:

$$R_M = \frac{\$965.02 \times 12}{\$100,000} = 0.116, \text{ or } 11.6\%$$

**mortgage coefficient (C)**   A multiplier used in the Ellwood formula to compute a capitalization rate; a function of the terms of the mortgage loan, the projected ownership period and the equity yield rate.

**mortgage constant**   *See* mortgage capitalization rate ($R_M$).

**mortgage discount**   *See* point.

**mortgage equity analysis**   A real estate analysis or valuation approach to estimating value for an income-producing property, where the influence of mortgage financing is considered and the investment returns to the equity position are given primary importance. *See also* Ellwood techniques.

**mortgage interest**   Money paid for the use of borrowed money through a mortgage. The rate can be fixed or variable.

**mortgage loan constant**   *See* mortgage capitalization rate ($R_M$).

**mortgage note**   *See* note.

**mortgage payment (PMT)**   Money paid to a lender to decrease the principal and/or interest on a mortgage. The amount of the mortgage payment varies depending on the type of loan. On a level-payment mortgage, the payment can be calculated as the annuity to pay the principal at the specified interest rate and mortgage term. *See also* amortization schedule.

For example, the payment on a $100,000 mortgage at 10% over a 15-year term with level monthly payments can be calculated as follows:

$$PMT = 100,000 \times 1/a_{\overline{n}|(10\%,\ 15\ years)}$$
$$1/a_{\overline{n}|(10\%,\ 15\ years)} = 0.010746 \text{ using a monthly compound}$$
$$\text{interest table or financial calculator}$$
$$PMT = 100,000 \times 0.010746$$
$$PMT = \$1,074.61$$

**mortgage release price**   A specific amount of money that must be paid to a lender so that the lien specified by the mortgage on a particular property will be released.

**mortgage residual technique**   An appraisal technique for solving for value when the amount of available equity is known but the mortgage value is unknown. The mortgage value is found by subtracting income to equity from the net operating income and capitalizing this amount by the mortgage capitalization rate. The mortgage value is then added to the equity value to find the total property value. *See also* residual techniques.

For example, available equity equals $20,000. The annual net operating income (NOI) equals $10,000. The equity cap rate equals 0.12, and the mortgage cap rate equals 0.10. The property value is determined as follows:

| | |
|---|---:|
| NOI | $10,000 |
| Equity $\times R_E$ ($20,000 $\times$ .12) | $-$ 2,400 |
| Residual income to mortgage | $ 7,600 |
| | |
| Mortgage value capitalized (7,600/0.10) = | $76,000 |
| Equity value | + 20,000 |
| Total property value (20,000 + 76,000) = | $96,000 |

**mortgage revenue bonds**   Bonds issued by state and local governments or state housing finance agencies to finance the sale, repair or construction of real estate. Interest on mortgage revenue bonds is tax exempt, therefore, they are sold at a lower interest rate.

**mortgage term**   The length of time, specified in a mortgage contract, over which a mortgage loan must be paid off.

**mortgage yield rate ($Y_M$)**   The discount rate that equates the present value of the loan payments with the principal borrowed. *See* effective rate, mortgage interest.

**mortgage-backed securities**   Bond-type securities that are secured by pools of mortgages or trust deeds and are generally not an obligation of the issuer. Mortgage-backed securities are used to transfer funds from securities markets to housing markets. For example, Ginnie Mae, Freddie Mac and Fannie Mae have mortgage-backed securities programs.

**mortgagee**   One who advances funds for a mortgage loan and receives and holds the mortgage as security for a debt; the lender.

**mortgagor**   One who gives a mortgage as security for a loan; one who puts up his or her property as security for a loan; the borrower.

**most probable selling price**   The most likely price at which a property would sell if exposed in a competitive market for a reasonable period of time, under the market conditions at the date of the appraisal. *See also* market value.

**most probable use**   The use to which a property most probably will be put, given existing improvements, existing use of the property and existing market conditions as of the date of the analysis. Highest and best use in the context of most probable selling price.

**most profitable use**   Highest and best use in the context of investment value.

**mover**   A person who changes residence. *See also* migrant.

**MPVIF**   *See* monthly present value interest factor (MPVIF).

**MPVIFA**   *See* monthly present value interest factor-annuity (MPVIFA).

**MSA**   *See* Metropolitan Statistical Area (MSA).

**multifamily structure**   A structure that is architecturally intended for habitation by more than one family.

**multiple internal rates of return**   An occurrence in which more than one internal rate of return can be calculated from the same cash flows of an investment because the sign of the cash flows changes more than once. In this case, it may be more useful to look at the net present value using the appropriate discount rate. *See also* internal rate of return (IRR).

**multiple listing service**   A program created for the purpose of circulating property listings for sale to different salespersons so that several different brokers can cooperate to find a buyer.

**multiple nuclei model**   A land development model that theorizes that a city grows by developing multiple nodes of economic activity that are distributed over space. The nodes can be places of employment, retail districts and office districts.

**multiple regression**   In statistics, an analysis that measures the nature of the simultaneous influence of two or more independent variables on one dependent variable. Often used in mass appraisal of single family residences, especially for mass appraisal for assessed value. *See also* correlation, coefficient of multiple determination ($R^2$), linear regression.

# N

**narrative report**   The most common and complete type of appraisal report. It includes an introduction, assumptions of the appraisal, presentation and analysis of data and addenda. *See also* report.

**natural increase and migration method**   Updating technique that uses information from the most recent Census of Population about the number of resident females in the primary childbearing years, the fertility rate of women in this age category, the number of annual births per thousand, the survival rate or its complement and the death rate by age category to estimate current population.

**near twin approach**   In trade area analysis, the use of the trade area for a comparable or similar establishment to estimate the trade area for the subject property. The characteristics that determine comparability are internal factors such as age/condition of the structure, floor plan and layout, structural design, cleanliness, attractiveness, etc., and external factors such as location of competition, the street network serving the property, traffic volume, curb cuts and turn lanes, time/distance to customer, and the economic, demographic and psychographic characteristics of the customers and their expenditure patterns and habits.

**negative amortization**   The difference between the loan payment and the amount of interest charged when the loan payment is less than the interest charged per period. In effect, the loan balance increases each period by the amount of interest unpaid. This generally occurs in mortgages with initially low payments that increase at some point in time. Mortgages with negative amortization usually require higher interest rates or larger down payments. *See also* amortization schedule.

For example, a $200,000 graduated payment mortgage requires initial payments of $1,500 per month with a higher payment after 2 years. Interest is calculated on a 10% interest rate for 15 years. The amortization table that follows shows negative amortization as the balance increases because payments do not cover interest. The larger payments required later in the loan will be great enough to cover both principal and interest, therefore reducing the balance.

| Month | Beginning Balance | Payment | Interest Paid | Principal Paid | Ending Balance |
|---|---|---|---|---|---|
| 0 | | | | | 200,000.00 |
| 1 | 200,000.00 | 1,500 | 1,666.67 | (166.67) | 200,166.67 |
| 2 | 200,166.67 | 1,500 | 1,668.06 | (168.06) | 200,334.73 |
| 3 | 200,334.73 | 1,500 | 1,669.46 | (169.46) | 200,504.19 |
| 4 | 200,504.19 | 1,500 | 1,670.87 | (170.87) | 200,675.06 |
| . | | | | | . |
| . | | | | | . |
| . | | | | | . |

**negative cash flow**  A circumstance occurring when either the operating expenses are greater than the total income generated by an investment or the operating expenses plus any annual debt service payment are greater than the income generated in any one year. *See also* after-tax cash flow (ATCF), before-tax cash flow (BTCF).

For example, a property produces an effective gross income of $60,000. Operating expenses equal $45,000, and the debt service equals $22,000. A negative cash flow results that can be calculated as follows:

| | |
|---|---|
| Effective gross income | $60,000 |
| Operating expenses | − 45,000 |
| Net operating income | 15,000 |
| Debt service | − 22,000 |
| Negative cash flow (before tax) | − $7,000 |

**negative externalities**  Forces from outside the property's boundaries that cause the property value to decrease. *See also* externalities, positive externalities.

**negative leverage**  A situation in which the rate paid on a mortgage is greater than the rate generated by an investment on an unlevered basis. *See also* leverage, positive leverage, zero leverage. For example:

If $R_O < R_M$ then $R_E < R_O$ and if $Y_O < Y_M$ then $Y_E < Y_O$ (negative leverage)

where $R_E$ = the equity dividend rate,
$R_O$ = the overall capitalization rate,
$R_M$ = the mortgage capitalization rate,
$Y_O$ = the overall yield rate,
$Y_M$ = the mortgage yield rate,
and $Y_E$ = the equity yield rate.

**neighborhood**     A geographical area delineated by geographical or political boundaries that is characterized by having complementary land uses.

**neighborhood analysis**     The objective analysis of observable and/or quantifiable data indicating discernible patterns of urban growth, structure and change that may detract from or enhance property values. *See also* neighborhood life cycle.

**neighborhood boundaries**     Borders that surround the area that influences the value of a subject property. Neighborhood boundaries may coincide with changes in prevailing land use, occupant characteristics or physical characteristics.

**neighborhood life cycle**     The changes that occur in a neighborhood over time. The cycle is defined by four stages: growth, stability, decline, and revitalization. Gentrification is not part of the natural neighborhood life cycle. *See also* gentrification.

**neighborhood shopping center**     A shopping center that measures approximately 30,000 to 100,000 square feet with 15 to 20 retail or convenience store spaces (e.g., barber shop, laundry) and is typically anchored by a supermarket. A neighborhood shopping center may consist of more than one building with a common parking area and management. *See also* community shopping center, regional shopping center, super-regional shopping center.

**neoclassical theory**     A theory of value popular in the late nineteenth and early twentieth centuries that stressed supply and demand as factors for determining value. *See also* appraisal theories.

**net after taxes**     *See* after-tax cash flow (ATCF).

**net book value**     *See* book value.

**net income**     *See* net operating income (NOI).

**net income before recapture**     *See* net operating income (NOI).

**net income multiplier (NIM)**     The ratio of the price or value of a property divided by its net operating income; the reciprocal of the overall rate. For example, a property is purchased for $12,000,000. The first-year net operating income equals $1,000,000. The net income multiplier equals $12,000,000/$1,000,000 = 12. The overall rate ($R_o$) would equal $1/12 = 0.083$.

**net income ratio (NIR)**     The ratio of net operating income divided by effective gross income. For example, a property produces an effective gross income of $75,000. The net operating income equals $50,000. The net income ratio would equal: $50,000/$75,000 = 0.67$. The complement of this ratio is the operating expense ratio, i.e., the operating expense ratio plus the net income ratio equals 1. In this example, the operating expense ratio would equal 0.33. *See also* operating expense ratio (OER).

**net leasable area**    Floor space that can be rented to tenants; the space that is available for rent. Net leasable area generally excludes common areas. *See also* gross leasable area (GLA), net rented area.

**net lease**    A lease in which the tenant pays expenses such as property taxes, insurance and maintenance. Sometimes referred to as a net-net-net lease. *See also* gross lease, lease.

**net migration**    The number of migrants into the county less the number of migrants out of the county.

**net occupied area**    The amount of space actually occupied by tenants.

**net operating income (NOI)**    The actual or anticipated income remaining during a year after deducting operating expenses from effective gross income but before any deductions for debt service payment or income taxes.

For example, an office building consists of 10,000 square feet that is rented at the rate of $12 per square foot. The vacancy rate equals 15%, and there is no collection loss. Operating expenses equal $6 per square foot. The net operating income can be calculated as follows:

| | |
|---|---:|
| Potential gross income: (10,000 sf × $12/sf) | $120,000 |
| Vacancy loss ($120,000 × 0.15) | − 18,000 |
| Effective gross income | 102,000 |
| Operating expenses (10,000 sf × $6/sf) | − 60,000 |
| Net operating income | $ 42,000 |

**net present value (NPV)**    The discounted value of all future cash flows minus the initial cash outlay. A net present value greater than or equal to zero is acceptable. *See also* discounted cash flow analysis (DCF), internal rate of return (IRR), present value (PV).

For example, a property is purchased for $200,000 and held for 3 years, at which time it sells for $206,000. The property produces a cash flow of $20,000 for each of the 3 years it is held. A discount rate of 9% is deemed appropriate. The net present value of the property can be calculated as follows:

$$NPV = \$20,000 \times a_{\overline{n}|(9\%,\ 3\ yrs.)} + \$206,000 \times 1/S_{\overline{n}|(9\%,\ 3\ yrs.)} - \$200,000$$
Using annual compound interest tables,
$$a_{\overline{n}|(9\%,\ 3\ yrs.)} = 2.531295,\ 1/S^n_{(9\%,\ 3\ yrs.)} = 0.772183$$
$$NPV = \$20,000 \times 2.531295 + \$206,000 \times 0.772183 - \$200,000$$
$$NPV = \$9,695.60$$

**net proceeds**    Cash received after all liens and expenses have been paid.

**net realizable value**  A specific value definition used by accountants when classifying loan losses. The definition is as follows:

" 'Estimated net realizable value' means the estimated sales price in cash or cash equivalent upon subsequent disposition reduced by the sum of the following estimates: (1) direct of title policy, and other expenses of disposition, (2) costs of completion or improvement and (3) direct holding costs including taxes, maintenance, insurance (net of rental or other income) and cost of all capital (debt and equity) during the period to be held. The FASB has recently issued an exposure draft of a proposed statement of financial accounting standards, 'Capitalization of Interest Costs' and any pronouncement ultimately issued is expected to be applicable to associations. Some of the important factors usually involved in determining estimated net realizable values of loans and real estate for savings and loan associations are discussed below:
1. Estimated sales price. Usually this price is determined (a) by reference to comparable sales for cash or cash equivalents of individual units in the same development at approximately the same time, (b) by current offering price, (c) by reference to appraisals or (d) by a combination of those approaches.
2. Projected date of disposition. The date of disposition is within the control of management and may be extended or shortened to recognize their anticipation of the future condition of the real estate market or to recognize the need to improve or to complete construction of a project.
3. Estimated costs of disposition.
4. Estimated costs of improvements or completion. These costs are typically involved in the disposition of unimproved or partially improved property and of property needing rehabilitation.
5. Estimated direct holding costs. In determining estimated net realizable value, the estimated future sales price should be reduced by a provision for the average cost of all capital (debt and equity), taxes, maintenance and other direct holding costs during the period to be held."

SOURCE: American Institute of Certified Public Accountants, *Audit and Accounting Guide: Savings and Loan Associations* (New York: American Institute of Certified Public Accountants, Inc., 4th revised edition, 1987), p. 41.

**net rentable area**  *See* net leasable area.

**net rented area**  The amount of space in the building(s) under legal lease to tenants, whether the space is utilized or not. Distinguished from net leasable area.

**net sales**    Gross sales minus returns and allowances, e.g., trade discounts, items returned.

**net-net-net lease**    A lease in which the tenant pays all operating expenses including taxes, insurance and maintenance. *See also* net lease, lease.

**NIM**    *See* net income multiplier (NIM).

**NIR**    *See* net income ratio (NIR).

**NOI**    *See* net operating income (NOI).

**nominal interest rate**    The stated rate of interest in a note or contract. The nominal interest rate does not necessarily equal the effective annual rate or effective rate of interest. *See also* effective annual rate, effective rate, real interest rate.

**nomogram**    A diagram, chart or arrangement of scales used for the graphic solution of problems with fixed numerical relationships.

**nonbasic industry**    A service or support industry in an area; the opposite of a basic industry that generates income from outside the area.

**nonconforming use**    *See* legally nonconforming use.

**nonconventional mortgage**    A mortgage that is insured or guaranteed by a government agency or private insurance company, e.g., Federal Housing Administration, Veterans Administration.

**non-realty interests**    Property rights that might be purchased with real estate, land, buildings and fixtures that are either tangible or intangible personal property such as furniture in a hotel or the franchise (business) value of the hotel.

**non-recourse loan**    A loan, often used in real estate syndications, in which the borrower is not held personally liable for the note. Thus, only the property itself is collateral security for the loan. This type of loan allows limited partners in a syndication to deduct depreciation or other losses for tax purposes by adding their proportionate share of the mortgage in the tax basis.

**non-residential property**    Property that is not used as a permanent dwelling, e.g., office, industrial, retail, hotel and special purpose properties.

**non-specialized office space**    Speculative space that has no special facilities and is suitable for general office tenants.

**non-speculative office space**    Space custom-designed and built for the exclusive occupancy of a particular office user.

**non-structured questionnaire**    A questionnaire with no fixed list of questions with an attempt made to develop a free interchange between the interviewer and the respondent about a specific problem or issue.

**normal curve**   In statistics, a symmetrical bell-shaped curve that represents a probability distribution of numbers in which 68.3% of the values in the distribution fall within plus or minus 1 standard deviation of the mean, 95.4% of the values fall within plus or minus 2 standard deviations of the mean, and 99.7% fall within plus or minus 3 standard deviations of the mean. The values in the distribution can be derived from a large sample of any type of population. *See also* mean, normal probability distribution, standard deviation.

**normal distribution**   *See* normal probability distribution, normal curve.

**normal probability distribution**   In statistics, a continuous symmetrical probability distribution that can assume any number between negative infinity and positive infinity and is described by the mean value and standard deviation of the numbers in the distribution. The normal probability distribution can be graphed as a bell-shaped curve. Many types of statistical analyses, including regression analysis, rely on some sort of assumption regarding a normal probability distribution. *See also* normal curve, linear regression, multiple regression.

**note**   A legal document that acknowledges a promise to pay a specified debt. *See also* loan, mortgage.

**NPV**   *See* net present value (NPV).

**nuisance**   A land use that is incompatible or that interferes with the surrounding land uses, for example, activities that produce excessive noise or pollution in a residential area, a junkyard in a residential or other highly visible area or activities that are not socially acceptable. A nuisance is avoided through private deed restrictions and zoning laws.

**observed depreciation**   The loss in utility, hence in value, of a building or component, as compared with a new building or component, that is identified from direct inspection of the premises, detailed estimates of accrued physical deterioration, studies of functional deficiencies or defects and other observable conditions affecting the property and its desirability to potential users and/or purchasers.

**obsolescence**   A loss in value resulting from defects in design or forces outside the boundaries of a property. May be either functional or external. *See also* accrued depreciation, curable functional obsolescence, external obsolescence, incurable functional obsolescence.

**occupancy cost**   The outlay of funds necessary to maintain occupancy in a property excluding expenses directly attributable to the operation of a business.

**occupancy rate**   The income received from rented units in a property divided by the income that could be received if all the units were occupied.

**OER**   *See* operating expense ratio (OER).

**office building**   A building used primarily by companies to conduct business.

**office classifications**   A method of describing office buildings based on the location, physical condition, and financial returns it offers.
    Class A: The property has an excellent location and access; the building is in good to excellent physical condition and meets or exceeds building code requirements; returns are competitive with new construction.
    Class B: The property has a good location, construction and physical condition are good and meet code, but the building suffers from some functional obsolescence and physical deterioration; rents are below new construction.

Class C: The property is an older building (15–25 years) and may not meet code; the building suffers physical deterioration and functional obsolescence but remains part of the active supply, with reasonable occupancy rates at generally lower rents than Class B buildings.

**Office of Thrift Supervision (OTS)**    Created as a result of the Financial Institutions Reform, Recovery and Enforcement Act of 1989, a government office that replaced the Federal Home Loan Bank Board as the regulator of the thrift industry. The OTS operates under the U.S. Department of the Treasury to charter, regulate and supervise thrifts. See also Financial Institutions Reform, Recovery and Enforcement Act (FIRREA).

**off-site improvements**    Physical improvements that affect the use and the value of a parcel of land but that are not directly located on the land, e.g., streets, curbs, traffic signals, and water and sewer mains. *See also* on-site improvements.

**100% location**    A specific area considered to be the prime location in a city.

**on-site improvements**    Physical improvements that are constructed within the boundaries of a parcel of land, for example, buildings, structures and other support facilities installed within the boundaries of the property. *See also* off-site improvements.

**open space**    Land that has not been improved with buildings. Such land is often left by a developer in a subdivision for recreational use and enjoyment by all the property owners.

**open steel construction**    A type of construction in which a rigidly connected steel frame that is unwrapped, or without fireproofing, carries all loads directly to the foundation and footings. In a multistory structure, the exterior walls are carried on this framework, usually at each level.

**open-end mortgage**    A mortgage that allows the mortgagor to borrow additional sums based on specified conditions such as minimum asset to debt ratios.

**operating costs**    *See* operating expenses.

**operating expense ratio (OER)**    The ratio of total operating expenses divided by effective gross income. For example, a 30,000 square foot property produces an effective gross income of $10 per square foot. Operating expenses equal $6 per square foot. The operating expense ratio can be calculated as follows:

$$\frac{10,000 \text{ sf} \times \$6/\text{sf}}{10,000 \text{ sf} \times \$10/\text{sf}} = 0.60$$

The complement of this ratio is the net income ratio, i.e., the operating expense ratio plus the net income ratio equals 1. In this example, the net income ratio would equal 0.40. *See also* net income ratio (NIR).

**operating expenses** Expenditures necessary to maintain the real property and continue the production of income. Includes both fixed expenses and variable expenses but does not include debt service, depreciation or capital expenditures. *See also* fixed expense, variable expense.

**operating income** *See* net operating income (NOI).

**operating statement** *See* balance sheet, income and expense report, income statement, pro-forma statement.

**opportunity cost** The cost of options forgone or opportunities that are not chosen.

**optimum** The best or most desirable under the circumstances.

**option** A legal contract that allows one to buy, sell or lease real property within a specified time limit under specified terms.

**option term** The time period specified in an option agreement over which an option can be executed.

**option to renew** In a lease, a clause that gives the tenant the right to lease the same property under specified conditions after the current lease has expired.

**oral report** A complete unwritten appraisal report that contains an introduction, assumptions of appraisal, presentation and analysis of data and addenda. An oral report must be based on the same facts and conclusions as a written report. *See also* report.

**orchard** A planting of uniformly spaced fruit-bearing or nut-bearing trees. Primary considerations in appraising an orchard include an in-depth knowledge of the particular variety of tree, its characteristics, stage of development, production and requirements.

**ordinary annuity** A series of level payments that are made at the end of a series of equal time periods; the type of annuity assumed in compound interest tables. *See also* annuity in advance.

**ordinary income** *See* taxable income.

**original cost** The actual cost of a property to its present owner. Original cost may differ from construction cost if the current owner did not construct the property. *See also* construction cost, development cost.

**other income**   In an operating statement, income received from sources other than the primary source of income such as vending and parking. Income received from rents is not included in other income.

**OTS**   *See* Office of Thrift Supervisor (OTS).

**outlet mall**   A shopping center or mall whose stores carry merchandise that is being sold at a discounted price. The discount can arise for a variety of reasons, but the principal reasons are excessive manufacturer's inventories, irregular or substandard merchandise, discontinued products or very low overhead costs due to sparse tenant fixtures and common area decor. *See also* shopping center.

**outparcel**   A parcel of land adjacent to a shopping center that is improved so that it can be used by a tenant. Typical users of outparcels include banks and fast-food franchises.

**outstanding balance (B)**   (1) *See* loan balance. (2) The loan balance divided by the original principal. *See also* percentage of loan paid off (P).

**overage**   *See* overage rent.

**overage rent**   A rent paid in addition to a fixed base rent and usually based on a variable figure such as a percent of sales or an index. Because overage rent is less certain than the fixed base rent, it is usually discounted at a higher rate. *See also* rent.

**overall capitalization rate ($R_0$)**   A single year's cash flow ratio that is calculated by dividing the net operating income (NOI) by the total value of the property. When calculated using NOI for the first year of operations, the overall capitalization rate is sometimes referred to as a "current yield." However, it is *not* a yield rate that considers NOI over the entire holding period, nor does it consider resale proceeds. Thus it should not be confused with an overall yield rate. Frequently used to find the value of a property by dividing the first year's net operating income by the overall capitalization rate. The inverse of the overall capitalization rate is the net income multiplier. Also called overall cap rate. *See also* band of investment technique, capitalization, yield capitalization formulas, capitalization rate, direct capitalization, income capitalization approach, net income multiplier (NIM), overall yield rate ($Y_0$).

   For example, a property is valued at $100,000. The net operating income equals $9,000. The overall capitalization rate would equal $9,000/$100,000 = 0.09. The net income multiplier would equal 1/0.09, or 11.11.

**overall rate**   *See* overall capitalization rate ($R_0$).

**overall yield rate ($Y_0$)**   The discount rate that equates the present value of the net operating income (NOI) and resale proceeds with the purchase price. Sometimes referred to as a free and clear yield because the overall yield rate does not consider financing. *See also* internal rate of return (IRR), equity yield rate ($Y_E$), discount rate.

For example, a property produces an annual net operating income of $200,000. The property was purchased for $1,800,000 and resold after 5 years for $2,000,000. The overall yield rate can be calculated as follows:

$$1,800,000 = \$200,000 \times a_{\overline{n}|(x\%,\ 5\ \text{yrs.})} + 2,000,000 \times 1/S_{\overline{n}|(x\%,\ 5\ \text{yrs.})}$$

$x\% = 12.83\%$ using annual financial tables
    or financial calculator
Therefore, the overall yield rate equals 12.83%.

**overhead**    *See* administrative expenses.

**overimprovement**    *See* superadequacy.

**ownership of real property**    Partial or full possession of real estate rights or interests. *See also* estate, interest, right.

# P-Q

**P** *See* percentage of loan paid off.

**paired data analysis** A procedure used in the direct sales comparison approach to estimate values of specific property characteristics in order to find a value of the subject property. Property sales are paired by similar property characteristics. Ideally the properties are exactly the same except for one characteristic. The difference in sales price can then be attributed to the difference in this characteristic. However, usually several adjustments must be made to paired sales to isolate the effect of one characteristic. *See also* sales adjustment grid.

For example, a house sold for $200,000. One year later, the same house sold for $210,000. There were no changes in the property or its environment during that time period. An adjustment for time (market conditions) of 5% can be derived from these two sales [(210,000 − 200,000)/200,000 = 0.05].

**paired sales technique** *See* paired data analysis.

**panel board** A single integral enclosed unit including cabinet fuses and automatic overcurrent protective devices, with or without manual or automatic control devices, for the control of electric circuits. Designed to be accessible only from the front.

**parameter** (1) A variable that may assume any of a given set of values. (2) A statistic that characterizes a population. Usually parameters are unknown and must be inferred.

**parcel** *See* lot.

**parking area** The area of a facility such as a shopping area, industrial plant or supermarket used to park automobiles of customers and/or employees.

**parking index** *See* parking ratio.

**parking ratio**  The number of parking spaces per 1,000 square feet of gross leasable area. The accepted index changes based on property type.

**parquet floor**  A floor that is laid in short pieces of hardwood arranged in various patterns such as rectangular or square patterns; i.e. no long strips are used.

**partial interest**  A single interest in the real estate that represents less than the full bundle of rights, e.g., leased fee interest, leasehold interest, subleasehold interest.

**partial payment**  *See* installment to amortize $1 $(1/a_{\overline{n}|})$.

**partial release**  A mortgage clause in a blanket mortgage in which the lender agrees to release certain parcels from the mortgage lien upon payment of a specified amount by the mortgagor. The partial release is frequently used in tract development construction loans.

**partial taking**  The exercise of the power of eminent domain by the government in which part of a private property is taken for public use upon payment of just compensation. *See also* before and after method, condemnation, eminent domain.

**partially amortizing mortgage**  A loan in which the periodic payments are less than the interest charged per period, therefore, the loan is not fully amortized at maturity and the outstanding balance must be repaid in one lump sum upon maturity. *See also* amortization schedule, negative amortization.

**participation**  *See* equity participation.

**participation mortgage**  A loan in which the lender shares part of the income or resale proceeds from a property in return for a reduction in periodic loan repayments. *See also* equity participation.

**participation rate**  Employment by residence site divided by population.

**partition**  The division of real property into separately owned parcels according to the owners' proportionate shares, usually pursuant to a judicial decree. A partition severs the unity of possession but does not create or transfer a new title or interest in property.

**partnership**  A business arrangement in which two or more persons co-own a business or real property. Profits, losses and liabilities are dispersed in a specified manner. *See also* general partnership, limited partnership.

**partnership interest**  An ownership interest in a partnership. *See also* general partnership, limited partnership.

**party wall**    A wall erected on a property line for use of both property owners.

**passthrough**    The tax advantage of a partnership or real estate investment trust that permits cash flows and deductions, especially depreciation, to "pass through" the legal structure of the partnership directly to the individual investors. The term *passthrough* could also refer to expenses charged to a tenant as a result of expense stop provisions in a lease.

**passthrough lease**    A lease that requires some expenses to be paid by tenants. For example, insurance, taxes and utilities or a percentage of insurance, taxes and utilities may be paid by the tenant. *See also* net lease.

**payback period**    The number of years required for cumulative income from an investment to equal the amount initially invested. The payback period does not consider the time value of money and, therefore, is not a discounted cash flow analysis technique. *See also* discounted cash flow analysis (DCF).

For example, both the projects below require an initial cash outlay of $100,000 and have a payback period of 9 years. However, cash flows from the second project do not come in until the end of the holding period. Although this may create greater risk and a different rate of return, it is not reflected in the payback period calculation.

| | Project 1 | | | Project 2 | |
| --- | --- | --- | --- | --- | --- |
| Year | Cash Flow | Cumulative Cash Flow | Year | Cash Flow | Cumulative Cash Flow |
| 1 | 10,000 | 10,000 | 1 | 0 | 0 |
| 2 | 10,000 | 20,000 | 2 | 0 | 0 |
| 3 | 10,000 | 30,000 | 3 | 0 | 0 |
| 4 | 10,000 | 40,000 | 4 | 0 | 0 |
| 5 | 10,000 | 50,000 | 5 | 0 | 0 |
| 6 | 15,000 | 65,000 | 6 | 20,000 | 20,000 |
| 7 | 15,000 | 80,000 | 7 | 20,000 | 40,000 |
| 8 | 15,000 | 95,000 | 8 | 30,000 | 70,000 |
| 9 | 15,000 | 110,000 | 9 | 30,000 | 100,000 |

Because it took 9 years to recover the initial investment of $100,000, the payback period for both projects equals 9 years.

**payment**    *See* mortgage payment (PMI).

**penetration rate**    *See* capture rate.

**penthouse**    A building on the roof of a structure that contains elevator machinery, ventilating equipment, etc.

**percent complete**    The total of man-hours of labor (by type) expended, materials and quantities installed, and equipment and machinery incorporated into total construction activity to date, expressed as a percentage of total labor man-hours, materials quantities, equipment and machinery forecasted or budgeted to be required to complete construction of a facility fully ready to operate. All estimates and calculations are made as of a given date (usually the valuation date).

**percent installed**    Total installed costs on a given date, expressed as a percentage of total booked costs (or CWIP) as of that same date.

**percentage adjustments**    The adjustment of the price of a comparable property when the amount of adjustment is based on a percentage of either the price of the subject property or a percentage of the price of the comparable property. For example, suppose the comparable property sold for $100,000. If the subject was 10% inferior to the comparable property, then the adjusted price would be $100,000 − $.10 \times 100,000$ or $.90 \times \$100,000 = \$90,000$. It should be noted that this is not the same as if the comparable property was stated as being 10% better than the subject. In this case, the adjustment would be $\$100,000/(1.10) = \$90,909$. The adjustment is slightly different because in this case the percentage adjustment (10%) is applied to the subject's price. That is, $\$90,909 + \$90,909 \times .10 = \$90,000 \times (1.10) = \$100,000$.

**percentage of loan paid off (P)**    The amount of principal on a loan that has been paid off divided by the original amount of principal as of a specific time. The measure is used in Ellwood formulas and can be calculated by different methods. The complement of the outstanding balance divided by the original principal (B) so that $1 - B = P$. Another method of calculating P is to calculate the ratio of the sinking fund factor for the full term $(1/S_{\overline{n}})$ divided by the sinking fund factor for the holding period $(1/S_{\overline{n}p})$ so that $(1/S_{\overline{n}})/(1/S_{\overline{n}p}) = P$. The sinking fund factors can be found in compound interest tables. *See also* Ellwood formula, J factor, K factor, outstanding balance (B).

**percentage rent**    A type of rent that is based on a percent of sales from the property, usually associated with a guaranteed base rent. *See also* base rent, overage rent, rent.

For example, a 4,000 square foot retail store is leased for $14 per square foot plus 6% of sales greater than $1,000,000. If annual sales were $1,120,000, the total rent would equal:

| | |
|---|---|
| $14/sf \times 4,000$ sf = | $56,000 base rent |
| $0.06 \times (\$1,120,000 - \$1,000,000) =$ | 7,200 percentage rent |
| | $63,200 total rent |

**percentage-of-completion method**   A system of recording construction contract income in which income is estimated by the percentage of construction completed. Performance is often measured by the amount of costs incurred.

**perceptual distance**   *See* subjective distance.

**percolation test**   A test conducted by a hydraulic engineer to determine the ability of soil to absorb and drain water. The test helps to determine the suitability of the site for certain types of development and septic tanks.

**permanent loan**   A long-term loan that is used to finance a completed structure. Proceeds from the permanent loan are often used to pay off a temporary loan such as a construction loan.

**perpetual easement**   An easement that lasts forever. *See also* easement.

**perpetuity**   (1) The state of existing forever. (2) An ordinary annuity that continues forever. *See also* capitalization in perpetuity.

**personal property**   According to the Uniform Standards of Professional Appraisal Practice, identifiable, portable, and tangible objects, which are considered by the general public as being personal, e.g., furnishings, artwork, antiques, gems and jewelry, collectibles, machinery and equipment. All property that is not classified as real estate.

**personalty**   *See* personal property.

**PGI**   *See* potential gross income (PGI).

**PGIM**   *See* potential gross income multiplier (PGIM).

**physical age**   *See* actual age.

**physical age-life method**   A method of estimating incurable physical deterioration in which the deterioration is calculated by multiplying the ratio of effective age divided by the total physical life of the item by the reproduction or replacement cost of the item minus any curable physical deterioration already charged. *See* incurable physical deterioration.

**physical characteristics**   The tangible aspects of real estate.

**physical data**   *See* physical characteristics.

**physical depreciation**   *See* physical deterioration.

**physical deterioration**   *See* curable physical deterioration, incurable physical deterioration.

**physical life**   The actual time period over which a structure is considered habitable, in contrast to economic life. *See also* actual age, economic life, effective age, remaining economic life.

**physically possible**   One of four criteria in highest and best use analysis. For a use to be the highest and best use, the size, shape and terrain of the property must be able to accommodate the use. *See also* highest and best use (HBU).

**physiocrat**   A theory of value popular in the mid-eighteenth century which stressed the use of land and agricultural productivity as the source of wealth. *See also* appraisal theories.

**PI**   *See* profitability index (PI).

**pier and beam foundation**   A type of foundation in which piers resting on footings support beams or girders, which in turn support the superstructure. A relatively inexpensive type of foundation often used for resort houses, porches and outbuildings, but rarely used for residential homes because of building code restrictions. *See also* foundation.

**pile**   A wood timber or other tube that is driven into the ground to support the foundation of a building or pier when the soil has a low load-bearing capacity.

**pipeline analysis**   An analysis of the amount of space or the number of units that are currently in the construction phase.

**pitch**   In construction, the slope of a roof measured as the vertical distance in inches (rise) divided by the horizontal distance in feet (span).

**PITI (principal, interest, taxes and insurance)**   The four major portions of a usual monthly payment on real property (especially residences).

**PITI ratio**   A residential real estate underwriting term referring to the maximum percentage of the borrower's income (either gross or net) that may be allocated to total PITI on the property.

**plank and beam framing**   *See* post and beam framing.

**planned unit development (PUD)**   A class of zoning for a subdivision that sets density limits for a development but allows for the units to be laid out in clusters in order to provide for common open space.

**plans and specifications**   Working papers used in construction. Plans include all drawings pertaining to the property under consideration, e.g., building drawings, mechanical drawings, electrical drawings. Specifications are written instructions to the builder that contain information pertaining to dimensions, materials, workmanship, style, fabrication, color and finishes. Specifications supplement the detail indicated on the working drawings.

**plant**   The tangible property used in conducting a manufacturing business, including land, buildings, fixtures, machinery, appliances, tools and everything in which capital is invested or by which the work is accomplished but not including the material used or produced.

**plat**   A map showing and identifying the location of land that has been subdivided into individual lots. Locations are identified by lots, blocks and sections. Also given may be details such as streets, public easements, monuments, floodplains and elevations. When subdividing land, the developer generally presents a preliminary plat to the appropriate officials for consideration, then files a final plat after improvements are made and approved.

**plat book**   A public record of maps that identifies the location, size and owner of individual parcels of land in a specified area.

**plat map**   *See* plat.

**platform framing**   In construction, a type of framing in which the building is constructed one story at a time. Studs are cut at the height of each story, horizontal plates are laid on top, then the next story studs are attached and so on, so that each story serves as a platform for the next. Platform framing is the most common type of framing. *See also* balloon framing, post and beam framing.

**plot**   *See* lot.

**plot plan**   A map that shows the arrangement of improvements on a lot and includes details such as location, size of improvements, parking areas and landscaping.

**plottage**   An increment of value that results when extra utility is created by combining two or more sites under a single ownership.

**plottage value**   *See* plottage.

**plumbing system**   The piping and fixtures necessary to carry water, wastes and other fluids to and from a building. Piping consists of a large part of the cost of the plumbing system and may or may not be constructed to last for the life of the building. Water is carried under pressure through pipes, whereas waste pipes depend on gravity.

**PMI**   *See* mortgage payment (PMI).

**PMSA**   *See* Primary Metropolitan Statistical Area (PMSA).

**PMT**   *See* mortgage payment.

**point**   A fee charged by a lender to issue a loan; one point equals 1 percent of the loan. For example, a borrower who wishes to borrow $100,000 but will be charged 2 points must actually borrow $102,041 [$100,000/(1 − 0.02)]. In this case, payments would be based on the full amount of the loan ($102,041), but the borrower will only receive

$100,000 and the lender will receive a fee of $2,041. The effect of points is to raise the effective rate of the loan. Also called discount point. *See also* effective rate.

**point-of-origin survey**   Customer survey designed to determine what the primary trading area of a retail facility is by asking customers their home address. These addresses are pinpointed on a street map, allowing the researcher to delineate the trading area of a retail facility. Generally speaking, a minimum sample size of 300 is required to obtain a reasonable degree of accuracy.

**police power**   The governmental right to regulate property for the purpose of protecting public safety, health and general welfare, e.g., condemnation, rent control, zoning.

**pollution control equipment**   Equipment required by regulations or standards established under federal and state laws to correct hazards to health and safety leading to the contamination of the physical environment (especially air and water) by smoke, smog, fumes, light, noise, effluent, hazardous radiation and other emissions, including those from nuclear or other electric generating plants.

**positive cash flow**   An annual cash flow in which either the operating expenses are less than the total income generated by an investment or the operating expenses plus any annual debt service are less than the income generated. *See also* after-tax cash flow (ATCF), before-tax cash flow (BTCF).

For example, a property produces an effective gross income of $60,000. Operating expenses equal $35,000 and debt service equals $22,000. A positive cash flow results that can be calculated as follows:

| | |
|---|---:|
| Effective gross income | $60,000 |
| Operating expenses | − 35,000 |
| Net operating income | 25,000 |
| Debt service | − 22,000 |
| Positive cash flow (before tax) | $ 3,000 |

**positive externalities**   Economies or diseconomies outside a property's boundaries that cause the property value to increase. *See also* externalities, negative externalities.

**positive leverage**   A situation in which the rate paid on a mortgage is less than the rate generated by an investment on an unlevered basis. *See also* leverage, negative leverage, zero leverage. Some examples follow:

If $R_O > R_M$ then $R_E > R_O$ and if $Y_O > Y_M$ then $Y_E > Y_O$ (positive leverage)

where $R_E$ = the equity dividend rate,
$R_O$ = the overall capitalization rate,
$R_M$ = the mortgage capitalization rate,
$Y_O$ = the overall yield rate,
$Y_M$ = the mortgage yield rate,
and $Y_E$ = the equity yield rate.

**post and beam framing** In construction, a type of framing in which beams are placed up to 8 feet apart and are supported by posts and exterior walls. Frame members are much heavier than in other types of framing. This type of framing is popular in colonial houses and barns and gained some popularity in the 1970s. *See also* balloon framing, platform framing.

**potential demand** The desire or need for real estate. Potential demand represents the quantity of real estate of a particular type that would be taken off the market by being purchased.

**potential gross income (PGI)** The amount of theoretical income a property could potentially generate assuming 100% occupancy at market rental rates. For example, an office building contains 20,000 square feet of leasable area. Market rates for this type of building are currently $11 per square foot. The potential gross income equals $220,000 (20,000 sf × $11/sf). *See also* after-tax cash flow (ATCF), before-tax cash flow (BTCF), effective gross income (EGI), net operating income (NOI).

**potential gross income multiplier (PGIM)** The ratio calculated by dividing the sales price of a property by its potential gross income. For example, a property that produces a potential gross income of $220,000 is sold for $1,000,000. The potential gross income multiplier equals 4.54 ($1,000,000/$220,000).

**power plant** A plant, within a structure or building, that generates power from coal, gas, oil or water for its own use or for commercial distribution to others. Includes engines, dynamos, etc.

**precision** Refers to replication of estimates. Estimates are precise if they are close together. If the analyst uses two or more techniques to measure the same value (i.e., population) and the estimates are close together, the estimates are precise.

**pre-engineered building** A building constructed of predesigned, manufactured and assembled units, for example, wall, framing, floor and roof panels that are erected at the construction site.

**prepaid interest** Interest that is paid before it is due.

**prepayment** Debt that is paid before it is due. If interest rates have risen, a mortgagor may be offered a discount to prepay the mortgage so that the lender can lend the balance at the current higher rate. Depending on tax laws, the mortgagor may have to recognize the discount as income.

**prepayment penalty** A fee charged by a lender to allow a loan to be paid before it is due. It is usually calculated as a percentage of the loan.

**prepayment privilege** A mortgage provision that allows the mortgagor to pay off part or all of the loan before it is due.

**presale** The sale of a property before it is constructed. Sometimes lenders require the presale of some percentage of units before funds will be loaned on a multi-unit project such as a condominium. In some states, the developer must obtain a preliminary public report before the presale is binding.

**prescription** The acquisition of a right to property through adverse possession for a continuous and uninterrupted period of time as specified by a state statute. For example, an easement or right of way may be gained. Use of a property if the owner has granted permission, if the user has paid for the use or if the user has admitted that the owner has a superior right in the property does not entitle the user to rights through prescription. Distinguished from adverse possession in which title to a property is acquired.

**present value (PV)** The current value of a payment or series of future payments found by discounting the expected payments by a desired rate of return in order to compensate for the time value of money. *See also* discounted cash flow analysis (DCF), internal rate of return (IRR), yield capitalization.

For example, cash flows of $120,000 are received for 4 years. The appropriate discount rate is 10%. The present value can be calculated as follows:

$$PV = \$120,000 \times a_{\overline{n}|(10\%, \ 4 \ yrs.)}$$
$$a_{\overline{n}|(10\%, \ 4 \ yrs.)} = 3.169865 \text{ using annual compound interest tables}$$
$$PV = \$120,000 \times 3.169865$$
$$PV = \$380,383.80$$

**present value interest factor (PVIF)** *See* present value of $1 ($1/S^n$).

**present value interest factor-annuity (PVIFA)** *See* present value ordinary annuity of $1 per period ($a_{\overline{n}|}$).

**present value of an annuity** *See* present value annuity of $1 per period ($a_{\overline{n}|}$).

**present value of one factor** *See* present value of $1 ($1/S^n$).

**present value annuity of $1 per period ($a_{\overline{n}}$)**   A compound interest factor typically calculated for an annual interest rate that is used to discount a series of equal future cash flows in order to arrive at a current present value of the total stream of income; see column 5 of the compound interest tables in Appendix B. The factor is calculated through the following formula:

$$\frac{1-[1/(1+i)^n]}{i}$$

where i equals the periodic interest rate and n equals the number of periods. Also called present value interest factor annuity, present value of an annuity, present worth of $1 per period. *See also* six functions of a dollar.

**present value of $1 ($1/S^n$)**   A compound interest factor typically calculated for an annual interest rate that is used to discount an expected future cash flow in order to arrive at its current present value; see column 4 of the compound interest tables in Appendix B. The formula for calculating the present value interest factor (PVIF) is: $1/(1+i)^n$; where i equals the appropriate discount rate and n equals the holding period. Also called present value of one dollar, present value of one factor, present value interest factor, present worth of $1. *See also* six functions of a dollar.

**present worth**   *See* present value (PV).

**present worth of $1**   *See* present value of $1 ($1/S^n$).

**present worth of $1 per period**   *See* present value annuity of $1 per period ($a_{\overline{n}}$).

**preservation easement**   An easement that prevents certain physical changes from being made in a historic property. It is usually based on the condition of the property at the time the easement is made or immediately after a proposed restoration. *See also* easement.

**pre-tax cash flow (PTCF)**   *See* before-tax cash flow (BTCF).

**price**   The amount of money paid or asked for in a specific transaction; the price may include non-realty items such as personal property or a financing premium. The price does not necessarily equal the market value.

**price elasticity**   *See* elasticity.

**primary data**   Information gathered by the appraiser that is not available in a published source. *See also* data, secondary data.

**primary members**   The main load-carrying members of a structural system, including the columns, end-wall posts, rafters or other main support members.

**Primary Metropolitan Statistical Area (PMSA)**   An area of more than 1 million people that consists of a large urbanized county or a cluster of counties with very strong internal economic and social links. It was designated under standards set in 1980 by the Federal Committee of MSAs. *See also* Consolidated Metropolitan Statistical Area (CMSA), Metropolitan Statistical Area (MSA).

**primary mortgage market**   The interaction of lenders who originate loans for borrowers, usually service the loans and bear the long-term financing risk. *See also* secondary mortgage market.

**primary trade area**   (1) The geographic area immediately adjacent to the property and extending out for a definite driving time. Different retail establishments have different maximum driving times to establish the primary trade area. (2) The geographic area immediately surrounding the subject property from which 60% to 70% of the retail establishments' total sales are derived.

**prime rate**   The interest rate charged by commercial banks on short-term loans to their most reliable and creditworthy customers.

**principal and interest payment (P&I)**   *See* mortgage payment (PMT).

**principal (loan)**   The amount of capital borrowed or remaining to be paid on an investment. Also refers to that portion of a loan payment that reduces the balance of the loan. *See also* loan balance.

**principle (appraisal)**   *See* appraisal principles.

**probability**   A percentage number that represents the likelihood that an event will occur.

**probability analysis**   A study of the outcomes occurring under different scenarios. *See* risk analysis.

**probability sampling**   Sampling procedures based on the principle that each element in the population has a known chance of being selected into the sample.

**probability sampling techniques**   A set of sampling techniques that ensures that each member of the population has an equal and random chance of being selected for inclusion in the sample, thereby permitting the use of probabilistic statistical inference methods to analyze the results. Simple, stratified and systematic random sampling are included.

**proceeds of resale**   *See* reversion.

**profit**   (1) The proceeds of a transaction minus the cost of the transaction. (2) In economics, the residual that accrues to an entrepreneur after interest for capital, rent for land, and wages for labor and management are paid.

**profit and loss statement**    *See* income statement.

**profitability index (PI)**    The ratio of the present value of future cash flows at a specified discount rate divided by the initial cash outlay. Similar to the net present value except that the initial cash outlay is divided into the present value of future cash flows instead of subtracted from the present value of future cash flows. A profitability index greater than 1 is acceptable. *See also* net present value (NPV), discounted cash flow analysis (DCF).

For example, a property is purchased for $300,000 and sold 10 years later for $390,000. The net operating income (NOI) equals $28,000 per year. A discount rate of 9% is used. The profitability index can be calculated as follows:

First the present value of future cash flows is found:
$PV = \$28,000 \times a_{\overline{n}|(9\%,\ 10\ yrs.)} + \$390,000 \times 1/S^{n}_{(9\%,\ 10\ yrs.)}$
$a_{\overline{n}|(9\%,\ 10\ yrs.)} = 6.417658,$
$1/S^{n}_{(9\%,\ 10\ yrs.)} = 0.422411$ using annual compound interest tables
$PV = \$28,000 \times 6.417658 + \$390,000 \times 0.422411$
$PV = \$344,434.71$

The profitability index then equals the present value of future cash flows divided by the original cash outlay:
$PI = \$344,434.71/\$300,000.00 = 1.15$
The net present value would equal
$\$344,434.71 - \$300,000.00 = \$44,434.71$

**pro-forma statement**    A financial statement that contains forecasts of income and expenses from the operation of a real estate property based on a certain set of assumptions.

**progression**    An appraisal concept that states that the value of an inferior property is increased when it is associated with a superior property of the same type; opposite of regression.

**project cost**    The total cash outlay needed to complete a project, including costs such as those needed to obtain construction, land, equipment, financing and professional compensation.

**projected income**    The amount of net cash flow forecasted for a future period. Projected income may be used in the income approach.

**projection**    A mathematical process of extending historical trends into the future using either straight-line or curvilinear formula solutions.

**projection period**    *See* holding period.

**promissory note**    *See* note.

**property**    The right held by an entity to possess, to use, to encumber, to transfer and to exclude an item. The item may be tangible or intangible and be classified as real, personal or non-real.

**property characteristics**    Physical and functional features of the property including the site and structural characteristics that underlie the demand for the property or the space on the property.

**property insurance**    Protection by an owner/user against the risk of a certain loss or disastrous event.

**property line**    *See* boundaries.

**property management**    The process of overseeing the financial, physical and administrative aspects of property operations.

**property residual technique**    An outdated term applied to an appraisal technique used to find the value of a total property by discounting all expected future cash flows from operation and resale using a property discount rate. It is not really a residual technique because no residual income is found. Rather, it is an application of discounted cash flow analysis. *See also* residual techniques, discounted cash flow analysis (DCF).

For example, a property produces cash flows of $235,000 per year. The property is held for 8 years. The reversion value at this time is $2,000,000. The appropriate discount rate is 11%. The property value can be estimated as follows:

$$PV = \$235,000 \times a_{\overline{n}|(11\%,\ 8\ \text{yrs.})} + \$2,000,000 \times 1/S^n_{(11\%,\ 8\ \text{yrs.})}$$
$$a_{\overline{n}|(11\%,\ 8\ \text{yrs.})} = 5.146123,\ 1/S^n PVIF_{(11\%,\ 8\ \text{yrs.})} =$$
0.433926 using annual compound interest tables
$$PV = \$235,000 \times 5.146123 + \$2,000,000 \times 0.433926$$
$$PV = \$2,077,191$$

Therefore, the property value is approximately $2,077,191.

**property rights**    The privileges associated with the ownership of real estate, including rights such as the right to sell, lease, occupy or use. Property rights may be divided separately of the real estate itself.

**property tax**    An ad valorem tax issued by the government based on the assessed value of property; a government levy based on the assessed value of privately owned property. For example, a tax of $0.60 per $100 of value would result in a tax of $300 for a $50,000 home ($50,000/$100 × 0.60). *See also* tax liability.

**property tax assessment**    *See* assessment.

**property tax base**    *See* assessment base.

**property value (V)**    The monetary worth of interests held in real estate arising from property ownership. A property may have several different values depending on the interest or use involved. Common methods of estimating property value include the cost approach, direct sales comparison approach and income approach. *See also* value.

**property yield rate**    *See* overall yield rate ($Y_O$).

**proportional shift**   *See* shift/share analysis.

**proprietary lease**   In a multi-unit building, the lease a corporation provides to the stockholders, which allows them to use a specific unit under the conditions specified.

**proximity damage**   In an eminent domain proceeding, the damage to the remainder caused by its nearness to the public improvement being constructed or by its nearness to unfavorable characteristics of the public improvement such as noise, dust and such. *See also* condemnation, eminent domain, damages, consequential damages.

**psychographic characteristics**   Characteristics of potential buyers and tenants, including their attitudes, habits, lifestyle, tastes and preferences.

**PTCF (pre-tax cash flow)**   *See* before-tax cash flow (BTCF).

**public restrictions**   *See* zoning.

**PUD**   *See* planned unit development (PUD).

**purchase money**   The outlay of funds, either equity or debt, used to obtain a property.

**purchase option**   A provision in a lease that gives the lessee an option to purchase the property.

**purchase-money mortgage**   A mortgage taken back by a seller in lieu of cash from a buyer.

**purchasing power**   (1) The ability and willingness to pay for an economic good. (2) The appropriate multiplication of an income level by the number of customers. If households are the consuming unit, then mean household income should be used in conjunction with number of households to form the purchasing power variable. If individuals are the consuming unit, then per capita income should be used in conjunction with population to form the purchasing power variable.

**purpose of an appraisal**   The question for which the appraisal client seeks an answer, for example, the market value as of a specific date, the value of a particular property interest as of a stated date.

**PV**   *See* present value (PV).

**PVIF (present value interest factor)**   *See* present value of $1 ($1/S^n$).

**PVIFA (present value interest factor-annuity)**   *See* present value annuity of $1 per period ($a_{\overline{n}|}$).

**pyramid zoning**   A type of zoning in which higher-zoned uses are allowed in lower-zoned areas. For example, light industrial properties would be allowed in a lower classification of heavy industrial. *See also* zoning.

**quality (of construction)**　The character of the workmanship and materials used in the construction of a building. *See also* condition (of construction).

**quantity survey method**　The most comprehensive method of estimating building construction or reproduction costs in which the quantity and quality of all materials and labor are estimated on a current unit cost basis to arrive at a total cost estimate. The method duplicates the contractor's method of developing a bid. Also called builder's breakdown method, price take-off method. *See also* building cost.

**quick sale**　A property sale that was made with the primary intention of selling in a short amount of time. A quick sale may not represent a market value for the property. *See also* market value.

**quitclaim deed**　A legal instrument by which an estate or ownership interest in real property is conveyed by a grantor to a grantee without warranty of title.

**quota sample**　The initial steps in the quota sampling procedure are similar to the stratified random sampling procedure. However, in the final stage of the quota sampling procedure, a convenience sample is chosen instead of a random sample.

**r** (1) In appraisal, *see* basic rate (r). (2) In statistics, *see* coefficient of correlation (r).

**R$_B$** *See* building capitalization rate (R$_B$).

**R$_E$** *See* equity capitalization rate (R$_E$).

**R$_L$** *See* land capitalization rate (R$_L$).

**R$_M$** *See* mortgage capitalization rate (R$_M$).

**R$_O$** *See* overall capitalization rate (R$_O$).

**R$^2$** *See* coefficient of multiple determination (R$^2$).

**R-value** A method of rating the insulating ability or heat conductivity of material. Materials with higher R-values are better able to insulate from heat transfer.

**RAM** *See* reverse annuity mortgage.

**rafters** In construction, the structural members of a roof that support the roof load.

**random** Without uniformity of dimension or design. For example, in construction, masonry wall with stones placed irregularly, not in a straight course. Random flooring. *See also* random sample.

**random sample** In statistics, selection of an item in a population or group to be sampled by chance. *See also* simple random sample, cluster sampling, convenience sample.

**range** An interval in numbers ordered sequentially from the lowest to the highest number.

**range lines** In the rectangular survey system, a north-south line spaced 6 miles apart, used to define a township. *See also* rectangular survey method.

**range of value**    In an appraisal report, the confidence interval in which the final estimate of a property's value may lie.

**rate analysis**    A study of the validity of value estimations reached by using an overall capitalization rate in an appraisal report. The study analyzes the relationship of estimated resale prices to different yield levels, the sensitivity of the equity yield rate to fluctuations in value, and the inference of equity yield rates from market-derived overall capitalization rates. *See also* graphic analysis.

**rate extraction**    *See* graphic analysis.

**rate of capitalization**    *See* capitalization rate.

**rate of interest**    *See* interest rate.

**rate of performance**    In utility accounting and analysis, the actual income or rate of return earned on an investment, in contrast to a rate of return allowed or permitted but not necessarily accomplished.

**rate of return**    *See* internal rate of return (IRR).

**ratio analysis (technique)**    An updating technique used in the absence of complete information that determines from past data the ratio between two known data elements, only one of which is currently known, adjusts it for intervening trends and subsequently multiplies it by the currently known value to derive the unknown element.
    For example, a survey shows that the number of persons per household in a city is currently 3.5. However, the trend is decreasing due to increasing divorces and children moving away from home. The ratio is expected to average 3.2 for the next 5 years. Population is projected to increase by 6,400. Thus the number of households should increase by 6,400/3.2, or 2,000.

**raw land**    *See* unimproved land.

**real estate**    According to the Uniform Standards of Professional Appraisal Practice, an identified parcel or tract of land, including improvements if any. *See also* real property.

**real estate market**    The interaction of buyers and sellers who exchange real property rights for cash or other assets. *See also* secondary market.

**real estate taxes**    *See* property tax.

**real interest rate**    In financial theory, an interest rate that does not include a premium for anticipated inflation. For example, if the nominal interest rate for a mortgage loan is currently 12% and inflation is expected to be 3%, then the real interest rate is 9%. *See also* nominal interest rate.

**real property**    According to the Uniform Standards of Professional Appraisal Practice, the interests, benefits, and rights inherent in the ownership of real estate.

Comment: In some jurisdictions, the terms *real estate* and *real property* have the same legal meaning. The separate definitions recognize the traditional distinction between the two concepts in appraisal theory. *See also* personal property.

**realty**    *See* real property.

**reappraisal lease**    *See* revaluation lease.

**reassessment**    The revaluation of real property to assign new assessed values for tax purposes, based on appraisals by local government officials.

**recapture**    Depending on current tax laws, if capital gains are not taxed at the ordinary tax rate, any excess depreciation taken over the amount allowed under a straight-line method is taxed at the ordinary tax rate. Recapture prevents the taxpayer from taking advantage of both accelerated depreciation and capital gain treatment.

**reconciliation**    In the appraisal process, the analysis of value indications from different appraisal approaches to arrive at a final value estimate. *See also* report, approaches to value.

**reconstructed operating statement**    A document that states estimated future income and expenses of a property in the proper format for calculating net operating income (NOI). Statements prepared for the property owner often have to be reconstructed because they include items for accounting purposes such as tax depreciation.

**recording**    The process of filing a legal document with the appropriate government agency so that a public record is created. Recording of the document protects the parties involved and gives constructive notice to the public.

**recourse loan**    A loan for which a borrower is personally liable. *See also* non-recourse loan.

**recreation room**    *See* family room.

**recreational lease**    A written contract between a building owner and a tenant in which the right to occupy a property used for entertainment purposes (health clubs, tennis courts) is transferred to the tenant for a specific period of time in return for a specified rent. This type of lease is used primarily in residential condominium projects and is often a long-term net lease tied to the consumer price index (CPI).

**recreational property**    An improvement constructed for entertainment purposes.

**rectangular survey method**    A method initially used by the federal government of legally describing land by east-west lines (base lines) and north-south lines (principal meridians). Further lines are drawn located 6 miles apart. These east-west lines are called township lines and north-south lines are called range lines. The location within the township and range lines are called townships (measuring 36 square miles). Townships are further divided into 36 sections that measure 1 square mile. To account for the curvature of the earth, guide meridians are drawn every 24 miles east and west of the principal meridian and standard parallels are drawn every 24 miles north and south of the base line. Also called the government survey method. *See also* land.

**refinance**    To pay off one loan with the proceeds of a new, sometimes larger loan. Refinancing is used to produce extra funds from a property and sometimes used after interest rates have dropped to receive a lower interest rate; however, a penalty may be incurred. *See also* wraparound mortgage.

**regional shopping center**    A shopping center that measures approximately 300,000 to 750,000 square feet with 70 or more retail stores including general merchandise, apparel, furniture and other service and recreational facilities. A regional shopping center is typically near one or more full department stores of at least 100,000 square feet each. Located in populations in excess of 250,000. *See also* community shopping center, neighborhood shopping center, shopping center, super-regional shopping center.

**regression**    An appraisal concept that states that the value of a superior property is decreased when it is associated with an inferior property of the same type; opposite of progression. *See also* regression analysis.

**regression analysis**    A statistical technique used to measure the nature of the relationship between one or more independent variables and a dependent variable. *See* linear regression, multiple regression.

**regulations**    *See* area regulations.

**regulatory lag**    The time intervening between the initiation of a proceeding before a regulatory commission or agency and the effective date of the final decision or disposition of the case, as in a request by an electric utility for a rate increase or for a revision of allowable return on equity.

**rehabilitation costs**    Expenses to improve or transform an existing property into one having greater utility.

**Reilly's Model of Retail Gravitation**   An economic model which states that under normal conditions two cities draw retail trade from a smaller town. The ability to draw retail trade from the smaller city is in direct proportion to the population of the two larger cities and in an inverse proportion to the distance of the two cities to the smaller city.

**reinforced concrete construction**   Construction in which reinforced concrete is used for foundation, frames, floors, roofs and other structural members.

**reinvestment rate**   An interest rate used to modify interim cash flows in a cash flow analysis to arrive at a future value estimate when calculating an adjusted rate of return. *See* adjusted internal rate of return (AIRR), financial management rate of return (FMRR).

**relative per capita sales (RPCS)**   A measure of relative sales potential for a given product or retail category. RPCS is calculated by the following formula:

RPCS = local per capita sales/U.S. per capita sales

Instead of the U.S. as the benchmark, the state or the region can be used.

**release clause**   Used in contracts such as a blanket mortgage, a provision that removes the lien from a particular property upon payment of a specified amount of money.

**reliability**   *See* precision.

**remainder**   A future possessory interest in real estate that becomes effective upon the termination of another estate in that property.

**remaining economic life**   The time period over which an improvement is expected to add value above the value of the land as if vacant and valued at its highest and best use. *See also* actual age, effective age, economic life, physical life, remaining physical life.

**remaining physical life**   The estimated time period over which a building or structure is expected to remain in existence, given normal maintenance. *See also* actual age, effective age, economic life, remaining economic life, physical life.

**remodeling**   A type of renovation that changes property use by changing property design.

**renewal option**   A lease clause that allows the lessee to extend the lease under specified terms for a certain period of time.

**renovation**   The remodeling, restoration or modernization of a building.

**renovation costs**   *See* rehabilitation costs.

**rent**    The amount paid for the use of space or property as stated in a lease agreement. *See also* base rent, effective rent, excess rent, market rent, overage rent, percentage rent.

**rent concession**    *See* concessions.

**rent control**    Legal regulation by a state or local government that specifies a maximum rent that is allowed to be collected by landlords from their tenants for specific properties. An exercise of the government's police power.

**rent escalation**    *See* escalator clause.

**rent premium**    Any portion of the price paid for a property above the fee simple value created by lease payments above market levels.

**rent roll**    A report prepared periodically that lists units occupied, the tenant occupying each space, the rent paid for each space and possibly other terms of each lease contract such as term of lease and specifications for overage rents. A rent roll is sometimes required by lenders.

**rentable area**    *See* gross leasable area (GLA).

**rental**    *See* rental rate.

**rental agreement**    *See* lease.

**rental concession**    *See* concessions.

**rental rate**    A periodic expense paid by a tenant in exchange for use of a property. The rental rate may include a payment for tangible and intangible personal property in addition to real estate. The time period and rental unit vary by property type, for example, the rental rate for a retail space in a shopping center might be stated as $14.00 per square foot per year or the rental rate for a house might be stated as $600 per month.

**rental requirement**    In a commitment letter, a provision that states that a certain percentage of space must be leased before the full loan amount will be released.

**rental value**    *See* market rent.

**rent-up period**    The time period during which an income property is expected to lease up to a level of stabilized occupancy. Stabilized occupancy assumes rental achievement at market levels as well as physical occupancy at stabilized levels.

**repairs**    Current expenditures for minor alterations required to keep a building in operating condition. The term repairs does not include replacement or renovation of substantial parts of the building or a change in material or form of a building. *See also* maintenance, renovation.

**replacement allowance**   *See* allowance for replacements.

**replacement cost**   The cost of constructing a building today with a structure having the same functional utility as a structure being appraised. The cost includes construction using modern materials and modern techniques. *See also* reproduction cost, building cost.

**replacement model**   A hypothetical building or structure believed or intended to represent the optimum facility, in terms of current production technology, structural design and layout, and currently available materials. Used to replace the function of an existing building or structure under study. Also sometimes called ideal replacement model.

**replacement reserves**   *See* allowance for replacements.

**report**   According to the Uniform Standards of Professional Appraisal Practice, any communication, written or oral, of an appraisal, review or analysis; the document that is transmitted to the client upon completion of an assignment. *See also* appraisal, letter of transmittal, letter report.

Comment: Most reports are written, and most clients mandate written reports. Oral report guidelines (Standards Rule 2-4) and restrictions (Ethics Provision: Record Keeping) are included to cover court testimony and other oral communications of an appraisal, review or consulting service.

**reproduction cost**   The cost of constructing a building today with an exact duplicate or replica of a structure being appraised including all deficiencies, superadequacies and obsolescence that are in the current building. *See also* replacement cost, building cost.

**resale**   Sale of a property at the termination of the holding period. The resale price can be estimated by a growth rate or by a terminal cap rate applied to the net operating income (NOI) occurring the year following the holding period.

**reserve for replacement**   *See* allowance for replacements.

**residential area**   Part of a city or region in which land is primarily used for dwelling purposes.

**residential property**   Vacant sites or land improved with buildings devoted to or available for use for human habitation, e.g., single-family houses, rental apartments, residential condominium units, rooming houses. Hotels or motels are not considered residential property.

**residual**    Value or income attributable to a component such as financial, physical or legal estate components, after deducting an amount necessary to meet a required return on the other component. Residuals are used in capitalization procedures to determine a property value. *See also* residual income, residual techniques.

**residual income**    Income attributable to a component after the known income from other components is deducted from the total income. *See also* residual techniques.

**residual techniques**    Valuation techniques where one component of value (e.g., land or mortgage) is assumed to be known. Income is estimated for the known component and subtracted from net operating income to estimate values for the unknown component. *See also* building residual technique, equity residual technique, land residual technique, mortgage residual technique, property residual technique.

**Resolution Trust Corporation (RTC)**    A federal government agency created by the Financial Institutions Reform, Recovery and Enforcement Act of 1989 for the purpose of selling troubled savings and loans and their assets. *See also* Financial Institutions Reform, Recovery and Enforcement Act (FIRREA).

**restoration**    Extensive repairs and renovations needed to resume the layout, appearance and condition of a property as it was first built.

**restrictive covenant**    A private agreement that restricts the use or occupancy of real property and may involve control of lot size, placement of buildings, architecture or other such specifications. Typically contained in a deed or lease, a restrictive covenant is binding on all subsequent purchasers unless an expiration date is specified or a quitclaim deed is received from all previous holders.

**retail**    Use of a property characterized by the sale of merchandise, e.g., shopping areas.

**retrofit**    A modification of a building or equipment to incorporate changes made in later production of similar items. Retrofit may be done in the factory or field. Derived from retroactive refit.

**return of capital**    The recovery of the original investment either through operating income cash flows or proceeds from resale. Also called capital recovery.

**return on capital**    An annual rate of return that results when income received is greater than the invested capital.

**return on equity (ROE)**    *See* equity capitalization rate ($R_E$).

**reuse appraisal**    An appraisal that estimates the value of property in an urban renewal project area. Reuse appraisal is subject to the regulations specified in the renewal plan for the area and in the National Housing Act of 1949 and its amendments. *See also* appraisal.

**revaluation**    *See* reassessment.

**revaluation lease**    A lease in which rent is adjusted periodically, according to the revaluation of the real estate.

**reverse annuity mortgage (RAM)**    A mortgage, typically used by elderly people who have built up a significant amount of equity, in which the lender pays the homeowner periodic payments based on the accumulated equity in the real estate. Payments can be made directly or through an annuity purchase through an insurance company and are not necessarily equal in amount. The loan becomes due at a specific date or occurrence of an event such as sale of the property or death of the borrower. *See also* mortgage.

**reverse leverage**    *See* negative leverage.

**reversion**    The lump sum payment received by an investor at resale of the investment. *See also* after-tax cash flow (ATCF), before-tax cash flow (BTCF).

**reversion factor**    *See* present value reversion of \$1 ($1/S^n$).

**reversionary right**    The right to resume full occupancy and ownership of a property after the termination of a lease, easement or interest or after certain other conditions are met; the abandonment of an easement; the end of a lease.

**reversionary value**    The value of a property at resale. *See also* resale.

**review**    According to the Uniform Standards of Professional Appraisal Practice, the act or process of critically studying a report prepared by another.

**review appraiser**    An appraiser who inspects the reports of other appraisers to determine the validity of the conclusions and data given in the report. *See also* appraiser.

**rezoning**    A change or amendment to a zoning map.

**right**    A legal stake in the title or interest of real property.

**riparian rights**    A right of use (usufructuary right), held in common with other riparian owners, to use water on, under, adjacent to, or abutting on one's land, e.g., rights of boating, swimming and irrigation.

**risk**    Uncertainty arising from the probability that events will not occur as expected. *See also* business risk, financial risk, interest rate risk, risk analysis.

**risk analysis**    The study of real estate returns under different scenarios that represent different risk possibilities. Most commonly used in association with investment analysis. Different methods are used to analyze risk. One method of analyzing risk changes one input variable and recalculates the investment measures and/or values for different changes in this variable. For example, the net operating income (NOI) produced by a property could be changed in increments of plus or minus 5%, and measures such as the value, return or debt coverage ratio can then be calculated for each different value of NOI. The results tell how sensitive each output (value, return, etc.) is to a change in the input (NOI). If the output values change drastically or quickly reach a negative value with a small change in the input, the property may be more risky. In a second method of measuring risk, several input variables are changed in pessimistic, most likely and optimistic scenarios. An expected return or value and standard deviation of return or value can then be determined as a measure of risk.

For example, a property is expected to produce a return of 10% if the economy remains stable. Optimistically, if the economy improves, an expected return of 11% is estimated and in a pessimistic scenario, if the economy declines, an expected return of 8% is estimated. There is a 10% chance that the economy will improve, a 60% chance that the economy will remain stable and a 30% chance that the economy will decline. The expected return can be calculated as follows:

| Scenario | Return | Probability of Return | Probability × Return |
|----------|--------|-----------------------|----------------------|
| Pessimistic | 0.08 | 0.30 | 0.024 |
| Most likely | 0.10 | 0.60 | 0.06 |
| Optimistic | 0.11 | 0.10 | 0.011 |
| Expected return | | | 0.095 |

The standard deviation can now be calculated as:

$$(0.08 - 0.095)^2 + (0.10 - 0.095)^2 + (0.11 - 0.095)^2 = 0.0005$$

The square root of $0.0005 = 0.0218$ (the standard deviation)

Assuming a normal distribution, a 95% probability exists that the actual return on the property will fall between the expected return plus or minus 2 standard deviations, i.e., there is a 95% chance that the actual return will fall between 0.051 and 0.139. If the standard deviation had been higher, such as 5%, then the actual return would fall between $-0.05$ and 0.19 with a 95% probability. Because we now risk the chance of a negative return on the property, it is obvious that a higher standard deviation implies a higher risk. A property with an expected return of 9.5% and a standard deviation of 2% is preferred to a property with an expected return of 9.5% and a standard deviation of 5% because a higher risk is implied without a higher expected rate of return. However, a property with an expected return of 9.5% and a standard deviation of 2% is not necessarily better than a property with an expected return of 10.5% and a standard deviation of 5% because a higher expected rate of return is also associated with the higher risk. The judgment would be up to the risk level tolerated by the investor. *See also* sensitivity analysis, standard deviation.

**risk factor**   *See* risk premium.

**risk premium**   The amount of return on an investment above and beyond that which is available on a risk-free investment; the portion of a rate of return on investment that is assumed to cover the risk associated with that investment.

**risk rate**   The annual rate of return required to attract investment capital to an investment. This rate is higher than a "safe rate" at which cash flows from the investment are assumed to be reinvested when calculating an adjusted internal rate of return (AIRR). *See also* adjusted internal rate of return (AIRR).

**ROE (return on equity)**   *See* equity capitalization rate ($R_E$).

**roof**   The top of a structure. The frame of the roof is designed to support its own roof and is determined by the type of roof being built. Common roof types include: flat, gable, gambrel, hip, mansard, shed and salt box.

**roof surfacing**   A layer of waterproofing bitumen installed on the top surface of the membrane as a wearing surface. Additional protection may be provided by the addition of aggregates. In elastomeric systems, the ballasting aggregate.

**roofing system**   All components of the roofing assembly above the roof deck.

**RTC**   *See* Resolution Trust Corporation (RTC).

$S_{\overline{n}|}$    *See* accumulation of \$1 per period ($S_{\overline{n}|}$).

$1/S_{\overline{n}|}$    *See* sinking fund factor ($1/S_{\overline{n}|}$).

$S^n$    *See* amount of \$1 at compound interest ($S^n$).

$1/S^n$    *See* present value reversion of \$1 ($1/S^n$).

**safe rate**    The rate of return that can be obtained on a risk-free or relatively risk-free investment, for example, the rate on U.S. treasury bills.

**sale-leaseback**    A financing technique by which the owner sells a property and subsequently rents it from the buyer for continued use.

**sales adjustment grid**    A grid used in the direct sales comparison approach, in which the elements of comparison are listed by line for the subject property and comparable properties. A sales adjustment grid allows comparison of different properties for adjustment to find the value of the subject property. A condensed version of a residential sales adjustment grid might look something like the one illustrated below for a property being appraised as of 1/2/91:

|  | Subject | Comp #1 | Comp #2 | Comp $3 |
|---|---|---|---|---|
| Address | 100 Smith | 203 E. Main | 216 Second St. | 405 Maple St. |
| Total sq. ft. | 1,000 | 900 | 1,100 | 1,070 |
| Style | ranch | ranch | ranch | ranch |
| Age | 34 | 30 | 42 | 35 |
| Exterior | brick | stone | brick/vinyl | brick |
| Garage | 1 car | 1 car | 2 car det. | none |
| Lot size (sf) | 7,000 | 6,250 | 8,200 | 4,500 |
| Sales price | — | \$67,000 | \$75,000 | \$68,000 |
| Sale date | — | 12/28/90 | 6/15/90 | 1/10/90 |

|                          | Comp #1  | Comp #2  | Comp #3  |
|--------------------------|----------|----------|----------|
| Sales price              | $67,000  | $75,000  | $68,000  |
| Time                     | 0        | +   1%   | +   2%   |
| Adjusted price per sf    | $67,000  | $75,750  | $69,360  |
| Size                     | + 4,000  | − 4,000  | − 2,800  |
| Lot size                 | + 2,000  | − 3,000  | + 4,000  |
| Age                      | − 2,000  | + 4,000  | 0        |
| Quality                  | —        | —        | —        |
| Garage                   | 0        | − 1,500  | + 2,000  |
| Total adjustments        | + 4,000  | − 4,500  | + 3,200  |
| Adjusted price           | $71,000  | $71,250  | $72,560  |

**sales area**   In retail stores, rentable area minus storage space. The proportion of rentable store area devoted to sales varies among store types and among stores of the same type, so that calculations of sales or rent are more uniform if made on the basis of total store area.

**sales commission**   A charge paid to a broker or salesperson who sold the property. The sales commission is typically calculated as a percentage of the sales price, and paid by the seller.

**sales comparison approach**   *See* direct sales comparison approach.

**sales comparison grid**   *See* sales adjustment grid.

**sales per square foot**   Calculated by dividing the gross annual sales revenue by the square feet of floor area used to generate the revenue.

**sales potential**   Total retail spending by trade area residents, usually stated in terms of store type. This potential is the product of the multiplication of population and per capita expenditures. The sales potential provides the support base for the planned new facilities as well as for existing competitive facilities both within and beyond the trade area.

**sales price**   *See* price.

**sales price per square foot of building area**   The sales price of the property divided by the total square foot area (living or usable area) of the structure.

**sales price per square foot of ground floor area**   The sales price of the property divided by the total square foot area (living or usable area) of the first floor of the structure.

**sales ratio analysis**   A study that compares the assessed values to the sales prices of properties in a taxing jurisdiction. The analysis is used to determine the fairness or accurateness of assessed values.

**salvage value**   The value of any improvements, assuming they are moved from the site and sold for scrap.

**sampling error**   In statistics, the difference between a number derived from a portion of a population as compared to what the number would be if derived from the entire population.

**sandwich estate**   *See* sandwich leasehold estate.

**sandwich lease**   A lease created when an existing tenant sublets a space to another tenant.

**sandwich leasehold estate**   An estate that arises from a sandwich lease. The value of the sandwich leasehold can be estimated as the present value of the difference between the income from the sublease and the income from the lease. *See also* fee simple estate, leased fee estate, leasehold estate, subleasehold estate.

For example, suppose a property is currently leased at a below market rate of $400,000 per year. The lessee then subleases the property for the next 5 years at $500,000 per year (flat rental with a net lease). Assume a discount rate of 15%. The value of the sandwich leasehold can be estimated as follows:

| Year | 1 | 2 | 3 | 4 | 5 |
|------|-----|-----|-----|-----|-----|
|  | 500,000 | 500,000 | 500,000 | 500,000 | 500,000 |
|  | 400,000 | 400,000 | 400,000 | 400,000 | 400,000 |
|  | 100,000 | 100,000 | 100,000 | 100,000 | 100,000 |

Discounting at 15% ($100,000 $\times$ $a_{\overline{n}|15\%,\ 5\ \text{yrs.}}$) = $335,215

**sandwich leaseholder**   The lessor under a sandwich lease.

**sanitary sewer**   A sewer that carries only sewage, not storm water runoff.

**satellite city**   Places within the metropolitan statistical area that are places of employment and centers of commerce as well as having status as a separate political entity.

**satellite tenant**   A smaller tenant in a shopping center that is dependent on a larger tenant to attract business to the center, e.g., a candy store or specialty apparel store.

**sawtooth roof**   A roof consisting of a series of single-pitch roofs, usually found on factory buildings, garages or similar structures, and allows abundant light and ventilation.

**scarcity**   An environment in which demand is greater than supply for a particular product and an increase in value for the good typically results.

**scheduled rent**   The actual rent income required through a lease.

**scrap value**   The price expected for a part of a property that is old and removed from the premises to reclaim the value of the material of which it is made, for example, plumbing fixtures sold for their metal content.

**seasonality**   The fluctuation of supply and/or demand for a product that occurs with a high degree of regularity at certain times throughout the year.

**second mortgage**   A mortgage that is subordinate to the first mortgage. A type of junior mortgage.

**secondary data**   Data obtained from published sources that have not been collected by the appraiser, e.g., census information, demographic information and published interest rates. *See also* data, primary data.

**secondary mortgage market**   The interaction of buyers and sellers of existing mortgages. Created by government and private agencies, the secondary mortgage market provides greater liquidity for the mortgage market. *See also* Federal Home Loan Mortgage Corporation (FHLMC), Federal National Mortgage Association (FNMA), Government National Mortgage Association (GNMA).

**secondary trade area**   (1) The geographic area that is adjacent to the primary trade area and extends away from the site for a predetermined driving-time interval. (2) The geographic area from which the retail establishment is able to obtain an additional 20% of its total sales.

**section**   In the rectangular survey method of legally describing land, a section equals 640 acres, 1 square mile, or 1/36 of a township.

**sector model (theory)**   A theory of land use development in which a city expands outward in sectors that exist around the central business district (CBD). Each sector contains a particular land use, and new growth occurs at the outer fringe of that sector. Also called Hoyt's sector theory.

**secular trend**   The longtime growth or decline occurring within the data. Ordinarily, the period covered should include not less than 10 years.

**segmentation**   (1) The process of classifying consumers or buyers into relatively homogeneous groups based on their economic, demographic and/or psychographic characteristics (such as attitudes, habits, and lifestyles). (2) Differentiates the potential users of the subject property from the general population, according to defined consumer characteristics.

**segregated cost method**   *See* unit-in-place method.

**seller financing**   A method of financing a purchase of real estate in which the seller takes back a secured note and provides the buyer with financing for the property.

**selling costs**   *See* closing costs.

**senior mortgage**   A mortgage that is given precedence over another mortgage. In case of foreclosure, the senior mortgage will be fulfilled first. A senior mortgage is considered to be less risky than a junior mortgage. *See also* junior mortgage.

**sensitivity analysis**   The process of calculating investment returns for multiple sets of assumptions in order to assess the impact that changing the inputs has on the measures of return. Sensitivity analysis can be easily computed on a computer spreadsheet or software package and is commonly used in investment analyses. *See also* risk analysis.

   For example, when analyzing an income-producing property, the future net operating income (NOI) may have to be estimated. A table can be set up that shows the internal rate of return of the investment for different NOI growth rates.

| NOI Growth Rate | IRR |
|---|---|
| 0.00 | 0.147 |
| 0.02 | 0.154 |
| 0.04 | 0.171 |
| 0.06 | 0.182 |
| 0.08 | 0.200 |

The relative change in the IRR as compared to the change in the NOI growth rate tells how sensitive the IRR is to the change in the NOI.

**septic tank**   A tank in which sewage is held until it decomposes and flows into a septic field. Typically used in areas in which municipal sewage systems are not provided. *See also* sewer.

**sequence bias**   A distortion that occurs when a questionnaire suggests or induces an idea or an opinion in the mind of the respondent as a direct consequence of questions on the questionnaire.

**sequence of adjustments**   In the direct sales comparison approach, adjustments to comparable characteristics are sometimes preferred to be made in the following order to find the appropriate value of the subject property: property rights, financing terms, conditions of sale, market conditions, location and physical characteristics. If all the adjustments are on either a percentage basis or if all the adjustments are on a dollar basis, then the sequence does not matter. However, the sequence could matter when mixing dollar and percentage adjustments.

For example, suppose the comparable property sold for $100,000. Due to favorable financing, the comparable price included a $10,000 financing premium. Furthermore, the appraiser believes that the location of the subject is 10% better than that of the comparable. The price of the comparable should first be reduced by the $10,000 cash equivalency adjustment to remove the financing premium and obtain an indicated value of the real estate of $90,000. Then the cash equivalent price would be increased by 10% to obtain an adjusted price of $99,000. Note that this is not the same as first increasing the price (including the financing premium) by 10% to obtain $110,000 and then subtracting the $10,000 financing premium to obtain $100,000. This procedure is incorrect because only the real property is worth more at the better location. *See also* direct sales comparison approach.

**servient estate**    The estate that provides a benefit to another estate (dominant estate) in an easement. For example, an easement road passes over an owner's land (servient estate) to another parcel of land (dominant estate).

**set-off rule**    The rule followed by states in an eminent domain proceeding that specifies how special benefits are determined. Federal courts and some state courts allow benefits to be based on both the value of the land taken and the damages to the remainder. Other courts allow damages to be based on the remainder only. *See also* benefits, condemnation, eminent domain, remainder, special benefits.

**severance damage**    In an eminent domain proceeding in which part of a real property interest is taken for public use, severance damage is a loss in market value of the remainder that arises as a result of the taking. Severance damage is compensable to the owner. *See also* condemnation.

**sewer**    An underground system of pipes or conduits that carries sewage and/or rainwater from a point of reception to a point of disposal. *See also* septic tank.

**shared appreciation mortgage**    A participation mortgage in which the lender receives part of the increase in property value at the time of resale. *See also* mortgage.

**shared business**    Market appeal that is based upon the cumulative attraction of generative and complementary retail operations at a particular location. The individual business may not have sufficient drawing power but the combination of goods and services available attracts customers to the general vicinity where the appeal of individual establishments can be offered.

**share-of-the-market analysis**   An analytical technique in which it is assumed that strong stores, capably and aggressively merchandised, will obtain their representative share of the total market in that category, notwithstanding the existence of competing units. Stores that have an identifiable name appeal and impact on shopping habits, such as department stores, are strong enough to attract a certain share of total business, under normal operating conditions.

**shift/share analysis**   An analytical technique that measures the following relationships for a local economy:

share analysis—Employment in each industrial sector as a percentage of total employment in the local economy divided by employment in each industrial sector as a percentage of total employment in a geographically larger region such as the nation. Share analysis is the same as the location quotient.

differential shift—Compares the local change in employment (growth or decline) of each industrial sector to the national change of that industrial sector to determine whether the industry is changing locally at a different rate from the nation. Differential shift compares the rate of change in the local industry's employment level to the rate of change in the same industry's employment at the national level.

**shoppers' goods (or high order goods)**   Durable commodities that are relatively expensive and purchased infrequently when the desire or the need arises. Consequently, the consumer usually undertakes comparative shopping to investigate the quality and design differences, as well as price differences, of the various similar products on the market.

**shopping center**   A building that contains several retail stores, typically with one or more large department, discount or grocery store and a common parking area. *See also* community shopping center, hypermall, mall, mini-mall shopping center, neighborhood shopping center, outlet mall, regional shopping center, specialty shopping center, strip shopping center, super-regional shopping center.

**short-lived item**   A structural component with an expected remaining economic or useful life that is shorter than the remaining economic life of the structure as a whole. *See also* curable physical deterioration, incurable physical deterioration.

**short-term capital gain**   A term used prior to the 1986 tax law for a gain from the sale or exchange of a capital asset held one year or less. Short-term capital gains were taxed at the ordinary income tax rate. After the 1986 tax law, all gains were taxed at the ordinary income tax rate.

**SIC**   *See* standard industrial classification code (SIC).

**sill**    (1) The horizontal piece directly under a window or door, usually slanted downward to allow water to run off. (2) The lumber resting on and around a foundation that provides a level surface for the exterior wall studs and ends of floor joists to be fastened.

**simple interest**    Interest that is based only on the principal amount and not on accrued interest. For example, simple interest is paid on a loan of $100,000 for 2 years at 10% per year. The total interest paid after 2 years would equal $20,000 ($2 \times (\$100,000 \times 0.10)$). *See also* compound interest.

**simple random sample**    Selection of an item from a population by chance in such a way that each item in that population has an equal and known chance of being selected.

**single family structure**    A structure intended and used for occupancy by one family.

**single purpose industrial building**    An industrial building that is designed and built to serve a specific function so specialized and limited that it cannot be economically converted to an alternate use. Also sometimes called single use industrial building.

**single purpose property**    A property whose highest and best use is unique to that site. Land value in this case is based on the highest and best use of the property, regardless of the most-likely use.

**sinking fund**    An account created into which periodic payments are made that when compounded at a rate of return will grow to a target lump sum value as of a specific date in the future.

**sinking fund factor (1/S$_{\overline{n}}$)**    A compound interest factor that represents the level payment percentage required to be periodically invested and compounded at a specific interest rate in order to grow to an amount equal to $1 over a specified time period. See column 3 of the compound interest tables in Appendix B. The factor is calculated through the following formula:

$$\frac{i}{(1+i)^n - 1}$$

where i equals the periodic interest rate and n equals the number of periods. *See also* six functions of $1.

**site**    A plot of land improved for a specific purpose.

**site analysis**    *See* land.

**site coverage**    *See* foundation area.

**site description**    *See* land.

**site development cost**    Direct and indirect costs incurred to prepare a site for use such as clearing, grading, installing utilities, etc.

**site improvements**   *See* on-site improvements.

**site orientation**   The relationship between a structure and its surroundings.

**site plan**   A drawing showing the layout of a development, including the location of the buildings and site improvements.

**siting factor**   The origin of settlement in a city. The siting factor may relate to locational, climatic, commercial, political or defensive reasons. For example, cities near river ports were often established as trade centers or river crossings. *See* also city growth.

**six functions of $1**   The six compound interest factors that are used in the mathematics of finance in order to adjust present or future payments for the time value of money. Includes future value of $1 ($S^n$), future value annuity of $1 per period ($S_{\overline{n}}$), sinking fund factor ($1/S_{\overline{n}}$), present value of $1 ($1/S^n$), present value annuity of $1 per period ($a_{\overline{n}}$), and the installment to amortize $1 ($1/a_{\overline{n}}$).

**skewness**   In statistics, the degree to which more data points lie on one end of a spectrum than another.

**skin**   A covering, outer coating or surface layer. In construction, the covering of a structure.

**skin wall**   An external wall covering of aluminum, porcelain, enamel, steel or other material.

**slab**   In construction, any flat horizontal area made of reinforced concrete wood or stone. Usually refers to the interior floor of a building but can also refer to an exterior or roof area. A floor or foundation of concrete, either on the ground or supported above it.

**slab on ground foundation**   A permanent foundation built on footings, or a floating foundation made of concrete slabs reinforced with steel. The foundation is laid on a layer of sand or gravel and consists of a layer of insulation and reinforcing mesh covered by poured concrete. *See also* foundation.

**SMSA**   *See* Standard Metropolitan Statistical Area (SMSA).

**social characteristics**   *See* social forces.

**social forces**   In appraisal theory, one of four forces thought to influence property value. Refers to population characteristics such as population age and distribution. *See also* forces.

**soffit**   The underside of a stairway, beam, arch or other building member.

**soft costs**   *See* indirect costs.

**soft goods**   Merchandise, also known as softlines, of nondurable character such as wearing apparel and domestics (including linen and towels, bedding and yard goods).

**spatial gap analysis**    An analysis to determine if there is unsatisfied, unfulfilled or unmet demand that the proposed site could satisfy. *See* gap analysis.

**special assessment**    A tax imposed only against those parcels of realty that will benefit from a proposed public improvement. *See also* assessment.

**special benefits**    In an eminent domain proceeding, the betterment gained by the remaining property after a partial taking. *See also* benefits, condemnation, eminent domain, general benefits.

**special purpose industrial building**    A type of limited purpose industrial building that may be economically adapted to a limited range of alternate uses. In some jurisdictions, courts have specifically defined this term.

**special purpose property**    A property that is appropriate for only one use or a very limited number of uses. Its highest and best use will probably be continued at the current use or the building will be demolished so the property can be used for another use.

**specialty goods**    Items that shoppers will take more care and spend greater effort to purchase. *See also* specialty shopping center.

**specialty shopping center**    Centers that range from 40,000 to over 300,000 square feet, are developed around a special theme, and do not have major retail anchors. *See also* shopping center.

**specifications**    Construction details that supplement working drawings used by a builder to construct a property, including details such as materials to be used, dimensions and colors.

**speculative use**    Property that is held primarily for future sale. Value is based on the future highest and best use.

**split financing**    A method of financing the purchase of real estate in which land and improvements are financed separately. Split financing is used by developers to obtain more financing than would otherwise be available through conventional financing.

**split rate capitalization**    A method of capitalizing cash flows to find property value in which different capitalization rates are used for different types of cash flows, for example, a higher capitalization rate may be used for overage rents than for base rents because a higher degree of uncertainty and shorter duration associated with overage rents. Also called fractional rate capitalization.

**spot zoning**    A type of zoning that is specific to a small area or particular parcel of land, which is different and often incompatible with the surrounding land, for example, a commercial zoning for a parcel of land in a residentially zoned area. Spot zoning is generally not allowed by law.

**sprinkler system**   A fire protection system installed in buildings that consists of an overhead system of pipes containing pressurized water and are fitted with valves, or sprinkler heads, that open automatically at certain temperatures.

**square foot cost**   The cost of 1 square foot of an improvement that is obtained by dividing the actual or estimated cost of a building by its gross floor area, or by the actual or estimated cost of a land improvement by its square foot area. The square foot cost can also be multiplied by the number of square feet in a building or land improvement to produce the actual or estimated cost.

**stabilized income**   Estimated future cash inflows that may change but have been adjusted to an equal amount per year.

**stack**   A vertical vent pipe that extends above the roof or a vertical waste pipe.

**stake out**   A process that takes place before construction begins, in which a surveyor marks site and building lines, marking elevations and building corner lines on stakes and batter boards. The process helps to ensure that building corners will be square and that building lines will conform to setback requirements.

**standard deviation**   In statistics, the square root of the arithmetic mean of the squares of the deviations from the arithmetic mean of the frequency distribution. The standard deviation measures the extent of variability in a frequency distribution and it is often used as a measure of risk. *See also* mean, normal probability distribution, risk analysis, variance.

For example, the standard deviation of the set of numbers 3, 4, 6, 8, 10, and 5 can be calculated as follows:

the mean of the distribution $= (3 + 4 + 6 + 8 + 10 + 5)/6 = 6$
the variance $=$
  $[(3 - 6)^2 + (4 - 6)^2 + (6 - 6)^2 + (8 - 6)^2 + (10 - 6)^2 + (5 - 6)^2]/6 = 5.67$
the square root of $5.67 = 2.38$ (standard deviation)

**standard error**   In statistics, a measure of the error caused when a sample is used to draw conclusions for a population. Different types of standard errors can be measured, including the standard error of estimate, standard error of forecast, standard error of mean and standard error of regression coefficient.

**standard error of the estimate**   In statistics, a measure of the unexplained variation occurring in a sample of numbers; a measure of the goodness of fit in a regression line. *See also* linear regression, multiple regression.

**standard industrial classification code (SIC)**   Industry groups defined by the U.S. Government. This very detailed classification system lists the types of major industries such as construction, manufacturing (durable), manufacturing (nondurable), retail trade, wholesale trade, etc. Each of these 1-digit SIC codes is further subclassified by identifying the various types of other groupings in each major category. For example, manufacturing (durable) is broken down into subgroups such as primary metals, fabricated metals, machinery, transportation equipment, etc. Further subclassification also occurs as each of these 2-digit categories and 3-digit categories are subdivided into 4-digit categories.

**Standard Metropolitan Statistical Area (SMSA)**   An outdated term for Metropolitan Statistical Area (MSA).

**standard of living**   The minimum of the necessities or luxuries of life to which a person or a group may be accustomed or to which they aspire.

**standing stock**   The amount of real estate that has already been built. Standing stock is one indication of the supply of real estate.

**state rule**   In an eminent domain proceeding, a rule followed by some states that specifies how an owner will be compensated in a partial taking. The state rule defines just compensation as the sum of the value of the part taken plus any net damages to the remainder; benefits may offset damages to the remaining property, but may not offset the value of the property taken. The rule may vary slightly among and within states. *See also* damages, eminent domain, federal rule.

For example, a site of land is valued at $100,000. Part of the land is taken through an eminent domain proceeding. Off-site improvements installed by the government result in $8,000 in benefits to the remainder, making the value of the remainder after the taking equal to $88,000. (Before the taking, the part not taken is valued at $80,000 and the part taken is valued at $20,000.) Through the state rule, the owner would be entitled to a just compensation of $20,000 ($20,000 for the part taken; benefits on the remainder do not offset the value of the part taken.)

If instead, part of the remainder is not usable after the partial taking and the value of the remainder after the taking is valued at $72,000 ($8,000 in damages), the owner would be entitled to a just compensation of $28,000 ($20,000 for the part taken plus damages of $8,000 on the remainder.)

**statistical inference**   The process of drawing a conclusion from a sample and applying it to the entire population from which the sample was drawn.

**statistics** (1) A branch of mathematics that collects and evaluates data or samples of data. (2) A set of data.

**steel construction** A rigidly connected frame of steel that carries all external and internal loads and stresses to the foundations. Enclosing walls are supported by this frame, usually at floor levels. If the steel frame has no fireproofing, it is known as unprotected metal construction.

**step-down annuity** A type of annuity, typically resulting from a lease, in which a level series of payments decreases by a specified amount at a specific time and then remains level until the next adjustment. *See also* annuity.

**step-up annuity** A type of annuity, typically resulting from a lease, in which a level series of payments increases by a specified amount at a specific time and then remains level until the next adjustment. *See also* annuity.

**step-up lease** *See* graduated rental lease.

**storm sewer** A sewer that carries rainwater and sometimes industrial wastes.

**story** A horizontal division of a structure; the portion between one floor and the floor above or below it.

**straight-line capitalization** *See* yield capitalization formulas.

**straight-line recapture** A method of calculating recapture of wasting assets in which the recapture is deducted in an equal amount each year. It is typically calculated by dividing the asset value minus salvage value by the allowable useful life. *See also* accrued depreciation.

**stratification** The division of the market for urban real estate into many submarkets.

**stratified** (1) In geology, soil composed of or arranged in strata, or layers such as stratified aluminum. Those layers in soils that are produced by the process of soil formation are called horizons, while those inherited from the parent material are called strata. (2) In statistics, *see* stratified random sample.

**stratified random sample** A statistical sample in which the population is divided into fairly uniform groups, or strata, and then a random sample is drawn from each selected stratum.

**strip shopping center** A commercial use of real estate, such as a neighborhood shopping center, in which the buildings are adjoining and narrow in depth relative to their width. *See also* shopping center.

**structure** An edifice or building; an improvement, e.g., buildings, fences, kiosks, sheds and gazebos.

**structured questionnaire**  Structured questioning procedure that focuses upon a fixed list of predetermined questions. These questions are then asked, and there is no deviation from either the list of questions or the wording within those questions.

**stud**  In construction, the vertical metal or wood framing members to which horizontal pieces are attached; the supporting elements in walls and partitions that serve as the main support for the roof and/or second floor.

**stumpage value**  On timberlands, the contributory value of the merchantable timber as it stands in the forest to the total value of the real estate. *See also* timberland.

**subdivision**  A tract of land that has been improved with site improvements including streets, amenities, utilities, signage, etc. and divided into lots for sale as either residential, commercial or industrial sites.

**subdivision analysis**  A method of valuing residential, industrial or recreational land to be used for subdivision development. The analysis is typically used in feasibility studies and when comparable sales are scarce. The number and size of lots that can be economically, legally and physically created is first analyzed. Then comparable sales of finished lots are used to develop an absorption rate, development period, and total estimated sales price. Next, income and expenses are forecast. Finally the net cash flows are discounted to a present value in order to estimate the value of the land. Also called anticipated use method, cost of development method, development method, subdivision method. *See also* land. An example of a subdivision cash flow analysis follows:

Subdivision Cash Flow Analysis

| Time period | 1 | 2 | 3 | 4 | Total |
|---|---|---|---|---|---|
| Unit sales | 10 | 20 | 20 | 10 | 60 |
| Unit price | $ 50,000 | $ 52,500 | $ 55,000 | $ 57,500 | |
| Total income | $500,000 | $1,050,000 | $1,100,000 | $575,000 | $3,225,000 |
| Less: | | | | | |
| Development costs | $350,000 | $ 150,000 | 0 | 0 | $ 500,000 |
| Selling costs | 30,000 | 63,000 | 66,000 | 34,500 | 193,000 |
| Overhead | 50,000 | 50,000 | 30,000 | 30,000 | 160,000 |
| Developer profit | 50,000 | 105,000 | 110,000 | 57,500 | 322,500 |
| Net cash flow | $ 20,000 | $ 682,000 | $ 894,000 | $453,000 | $2,049,000 |
| PV factor @ 20% | .8333 | .6944 | .5787 | .4823 | |
| Present value | $ 16,666 | $ 473,581 | $ 517,358 | $218,482 | $1,226,087 |

Land value = $1,226,087 rounded to $1,226,000, assuming a 20% discount rate.

**subdivision regulations** A local ordinance that establishes minimum standards that must be met before a subdivision will be approved for development. Regulations include width of streets, size of lots and drainage requirements.

**subflooring** In construction, the floor directly connected to the floor joists but below the finish floor. Subflooring can be made of boards, plywood or concrete.

**subject building** In appraisal, the building being appraised. *See also* comparables, sales adjustment grid.

**subject property** In appraisal, the property being appraised. *See also* comparables, sales adjustment grid.

**subjective distance** A concept that focuses on consumer perceptions about distance and travel from one site to another. Consumers perceive the distance or time to be different from its actual figures. Pleasant circumstances can make subjective distance shorter than actual distance and time. Unpleasant circumstances have the opposite effect.

**sublease** An agreement in which the tenant (lessee) leases the property or part of the property to a third party, thus becoming a lessor. *See also* sandwich leasehold estate, sandwich lease, estate, subleasehold estate.

**subleasehold estate** The property interest associated with a sublease. The value of the subleasehold can be estimated as the present value of the difference between the market rent and the sublease rent. *See also* fee simple estate, leased fee estate, leasehold estate, sandwich leasehold estate.

For example, suppose a property is currently leased at a below-market rate of $400,000 per year. The lessee then subleases the property for the next 5 years at $500,000 per year. There are now two leaseholds: a sandwich leasehold and a subleasehold. Assuming a discount rate of 15%, the value of the sandwich leasehold can first be estimated as follows:

| Year | 1 | 2 | 3 | 4 | 5 |
|------|---|---|---|---|---|
|  | 500,000 | 500,000 | 500,000 | 500,000 | 500,000 |
|  | 400,000 | 400,000 | 400,000 | 400,000 | 400,000 |
|  | 100,000 | 100,000 | 100,000 | 100,000 | 100,000 |

Discounting at 15% ($100,000 $\times$ a$_{\overline{n}|15\%,\ 5\ yrs.}$) = $335,215

Assume that the market rate is $500,000 in year 1 and increases by 3% per year. We can now calculate the value of the subleasehold estate as follows:

| Year | 1 | 2 | 3 | 4 | 5 |
|------|---|---|---|---|---|
|  | 500,000 | 515,000 | 530,450 | 546,364 | 562,754 |
|  | 500,000 | 500,000 | 500,000 | 500,000 | 500,000 |
|  | 0 | 15,000 | 30,450 | 46,364 | 62,754 |

Discounting at 18% (A higher discount rate is used to adjust for risk. The subleasehold estate is riskier than the sandwich leasehold.) The value of the leasehold estate equals:

$$V = (15,000 \div 1.18)^2 + (30,450 \div 1.18)^3$$
$$+ (46,364 \div 1.18)^4 + 62,754 \div 1.18)^5$$
$$V = \$80,650$$

If we assume that it is reasonable to sum the values of the sandwich leasehold and the subleasehold to find the value of the lease-hold, the value of the leasehold can now be calculated as $335,215 + $80,650 = $415,865. The leasehold value may not be equal to the subleasehold value plus the sandwich leasehold depending on the relationship between the discount rates applicable for each interest.

**sublessee**    A tenant who leases space from another tenant and enjoys use of the property. *See also* sandwich leasehold estate, subleasehold estate.

**sublessor**    A tenant who leases space to another tenant.

**submarket**    A portion of a total market that is differentiated by buyers and sellers who have similar preferences.

**subordinate**    That which is of less precedence than another.

**subordinated mortgage**    A mortgage that is of less precedence (junior) to another loan.

**subordination clause**    An agreement in a contract by which a party with superior rights agrees to make its rights junior, or subordinate, to another party's rights.

**substitution**    The appraisal principle that states that a buyer will pay no more for a property than the cost of obtaining an equally desirable substitute. If several similar goods are supplied, the good with the lowest price will produce the greatest demand and quantity sold. Substitution is one of the key principles for both the direct sales comparison approach and the cost approach to appraisal. *See also* appraisal principles.

**substructure**    In construction, the foundation structure of a building located below or at ground level that provides the support base for the building. For example, footings, piles, columns, piers, beams and slabs are part of the substructure. Components such as parking garages that are not habitable may be considered as part of the substructure even though they are aboveground. *See also* infrastructure, superstructure.

**subsurface rights**   The right to the use and profit from the land that lies below the surface of a property, for example, the right to extract minerals or construct and maintain underground sewers and lines.

**suburb**   A community that contains relatively few places of employment in relation to the large amount of residential areas. Its residents typically work in other portions of the region such as the urbanized area or the central city.

**summation approach**   *See* cost approach.

**superadequacy**   A type of functional obsolescence that is caused by a structural component that is too large or of a higher quality than what is needed for the highest and best use of the property; an item in which its cost exceeds its value; an overimprovement (e.g., high ceilings in an office, built-in bookshelves in a building to be used as a restaurant). *See also* curable functional obsolescence, incurable functional obsolescence.

**superadequate features**   *See* superadequacy.

**supermarket**   A large retail store built on one level and in which goods are conveniently and conspicuously displayed so the customers may select what they want without the help of a clerk. Purchases are paid for at a checkout counter. The most common types of merchandise sold are food products and household supplies, but a wide variety of consumer goods can be offered. Most supermarkets are units of large chain store corporations.

**super-regional shopping center**   A shopping center that measures approximately 750,000 to greater than 1,000,000 square feet and contains a variety of general merchandise, apparel, furnishing, service and entertainment stores. Typically anchored by 3 or more major department stores of at least 100,000 square feet each. *See also* community shopping center, neighborhood shopping center, regional shopping center, shopping center.

**superstructure**   In construction, the part of a building that is above grade. For example, aboveground framing, insulation, ventilation, walls, doors, windows and such are considered as part of the superstructure. *See also* infrastructure, substructure.

**supply**   The quantity of a product available on the market at a particular time as a function of different prices. *See also* demand, supply and demand.

**supply and demand**   An appraisal principle that states that the value of a property depends on the quantity and price of the property type available in the market, and on the number of market participants and the price that they are willing to pay. *See also* appraisal principles, demand, supply.

**supply and demand study**    An analysis of the availability and desire for a specific type of property.

**surplus productivity**    The net income remaining after the costs of labor, capital and coordination have been deducted from total income.

**survey**    (1) The process by which the boundaries and area of a parcel of land is measured. Information such as the location of improvements, physical features of the land, easements, encroachments and lines of ownership are typically specified. (2) A map or plan that illustrates the results of the survey.

**survey of competition**    Identification of the properties in a market or trade area that have similar characteristics and attract the same potential buyers or space users. Also called competition analysis.

**suscipient business**    Market appeal from an independent source, such as a major public transportation facility, that attracts customers into an area where the retail operation can position itself and offer its goods or services. This type of market is parasitic or dependent on an external source and is subject to the peculiarities of that particular market, such as a retail business dependent on a "captive market" in an office center that closes on Saturday when most employees do not come to work.

**syndication**    A group of investors who have combined their financial resources with the expertise of a real estate professional for the common purpose of acquiring, developing, managing, operating or marketing real estate. Syndication may take any type of business form, e.g., corporation, joint ownership, joint venture or partnership. *See also* partnership.

**system**    An integrated operation of units that may be related entities or may be property elements such as machinery, buildings, land and other property used in the performance of services or the manufacture of products.

**systematic random sample**    A random sample drawn in such a way that a predetermined but random sequence of selection is established. For example, a sample can be drawn from a population that is accurately represented by a telephone directory when a random number from 1 through 10 is drawn to start the process (e.g., 6 for page 6), a random number is drawn to represent the successive pages to sample (such as 4 to establish the series 6, 10, 14, 18, etc.), and a random number or numbers are drawn to represent the listing(s) on each of the selected pages (if there are 180 names per page, the numbers 36, 83, and 121 could be drawn).

# T

**tangible property**  Property that has a physical presence. It can be real property such as buildings or personal property such as furniture and equipment. *See also* intangible property.

**targeting analysis**  A study that defines the demographics and other characteristics of a user population to see who they are and what can be sold to them.

**tax**  *See* property tax.

**tax abatement**  An exemption or reduction of taxes granted by a local government for a particular project over a specific time period.

**tax assessment**  *See* assessment.

**tax base**  *See* assessment base.

**tax book**  *See* tax roll.

**tax depreciation**  The loss in value of a building due to wear and tear that is allowed under tax law to be subtracted from income and sale proceeds.

**tax district**  The area under the authority of a taxing entity. The tax district may be part of one or several assessment districts. *See also* assessment district.

**tax exemption**  The state of not having to pay some or all of a government tax which is granted to homesteads in some states and to some nonprofit organizations.

**tax liability**  The dollar amount of taxes owed for a specific time period. The tax liability from operations equals the taxable income multiplied by the appropriate marginal ordinary income tax rate. The tax liability from sale of a property equals the capital gain multiplied by the appropriate marginal ordinary income tax rate. *See also* after-tax cash flow (ATCF), taxable income, capital gain, adjusted basis.

For example, a property is purchased for $800,000. The property produces a net operating income of $90,000, with annual interest and depreciation expenses of $55,000 and $25,000 respectively. An additional $50,000 is invested in the property. At the end of the holding period, the property is sold for $970,000. Accumulated depreciation at this time equals $110,000. Assume a tax rate of 28%. The tax liability from operations can be calculated as follows:

| | |
|---|---:|
| Net operating income | $90,000 |
| Interest | − 55,000 |
| Depreciation | − 25,000 |
| Taxable income | $10,000 |

Tax liability = taxable income × tax rate
Tax liability = $10,000 × 0.28 = $2,800

The tax liability from sale can then be calculated as follows:

The tax basis is calculated.

| | |
|---|---:|
| Original cost | $800,000 |
| Capital investment | 50,000 |
| Accumulated depreciation | − 110,000 |
| Basis | $740,000 |

The capital gain is then calculated as the selling price ($970,000) minus the basis ($740,000) to equal $230,000. The tax liability from resale thus equals:

Tax liability = capital gain × tax rate
Tax liability = $230,000 × 0.28
Tax liability = $64,400

**tax lien**   A lien attached to a property for property taxes that have not been paid.

**tax map**   A map that shows parcels of land in an assessment district. Also called assessment map or cadastral map.

**tax rate**   An amount, usually expressed in dollars per $100 of assessed value, that is used to calculate the property tax. The tax rate is derived by dividing the total amount of tax levy by the total assessed value of all properties in the assessment district. For example, if the tax rate is $0.60 per $100, the total tax levied on a $80,000 house is $480 ($80,000 × 0.60/100). *See also* tax liability.

**tax roll**   The official list of all taxpayers subject to property tax, the amounts of their assessments and the amounts of taxes due.

**tax sale**   The sale of a property to collect taxes that are due and have not been paid within the statutory period.

**tax shelter**     Attributes of an investment that decrease taxes by providing non-cash deductions for depreciation and interest or provide other opportunities to claim deductions from taxable income. For example, a property is purchased that produces a net operating income of $300,000. Interest paid on the property equals $225,000, and the depreciation deduction equals $135,000. The taxable income can be calculated as follows:

| | |
|---|---|
| Net operating income | $300,000 |
| Interest | − 225,000 |
| Depreciation | − 135,000 |
| Taxable income (loss) | ($60,000) |

Depreciation and interest reduce the income, thereby shielding some of the income from being taxed. Although the property may produce an actual positive before-tax cash flow, no taxes will be paid because the taxable income is negative. Depending on the character of the investor's other income, some of the $60,000 taxable loss may be used to offset other passive income and further reduce the tax burden. *See also* taxable income.

**tax status date**     *See* date of appraisal.

**tax stop**     In a lease, a provision that requires the lessee to pay property taxes above a certain level.

**taxable income**     Income that is taxable by law; calculated as the net operating income minus interest and depreciation. Taxable income from sale of a property equals the capital gain. Should not be confused with after-tax income or before-tax cash flow. *See also* net operating income (NOI), tax liability.

For example, a property produces a net operating income of $90,000. Annual mortgage interest equals $55,000, and depreciation on the property equals $25,000. The taxable income can be calculated as follows:

| | |
|---|---|
| Net operating income | $90,000 |
| Interest | − 55,000 |
| Depreciation | − 25,000 |
| Taxable income | $10,000 |

**taxable value**     *See* assessed value.

**taxation**     A government right to raise income for use of public property and projects by assessing goods and services.

**tax-free exchange**     A trade but not a sale of one property for another; capital gains can be deferred through a tax-free exchange.

**tax-free income**     Income that is not taxed as specified in federal income tax laws. Income sheltered by losses is not tax free. *See also* tax shelter.

**t-distribution**   In statistics, a continuous, symmetric probability distribution in which the standard deviation for the population is not or cannot be determined. The t-distribution is not a normal distribution and depends on the size of the sample, thus it is described by the degrees of freedom. The smaller the sample, the flatter the distribution curve is. The t-distribution is typically used for samples with fewer than 30 degrees of freedom, although it can be used for any size sample. *See also* linear regression, multiple regression.

**temporary financing**   Any of several different methods of short-term financing. *See also* bridge loan, bullet loan, construction loan, development loan.

**tenancy**   (1) The ownership of property by a title. (2) As conveyed in a lease, the right to use and occupy a space. *See also* joint tenancy, tenancy at will, tenancy by the entireties, tenancy in common, tenancy in severalty.

**tenancy at will**   An estate that has no fixed term and may be cancelled at any time. *See also* tenancy.

**tenancy by the entireties**   An equal, indivisible estate held by a husband and wife in which neither has a disposable interest in the property during the lifetime of the other, except by joint action. The property passes to the survivor upon death of one spouse. *See also* tenancy.

**tenancy in common**   An indivisible estate held by two or more persons that may be equal or unequal interests. The property passes to the heirs, not the survivor(s), on the death of one. *See also* tenancy.

**tenancy in severalty**   An estate held by one owner. *See also* tenancy.

**tenant**   The occupant of a building who has been given the right to possess the building or tenant space through the execution of a lease; the lessee.

**tenant alteration costs**   *See* tenant improvements.

**tenant contributions**   Costs paid by a tenant in excess of rent specified in a lease, e.g., utilities, common area maintenance.

**tenant improvements**   The interior finished components of a tenant space that may be installed either by the lessor or lessee.

**tenant mix**   The type and location of tenants, especially in regard to buildings such as shopping centers, that are leased to businesses dependent on one another to draw a maximum consumer base to the center.

**tenant turnover**   The frequency with which a space is leased to new tenants.

**tenement** (1) Appurtenances affixed to the land; items of a permanent nature that are affixed to the land and pass with conveyance of the land, e.g., buildings and improvements. (2) Older apartment buildings in an urban area that have not been well-kept.

**term** (1) A length of time over which a cash flow or other event occurs, for example, a mortgage term may be 15 years. (2) A contractual clause or provision.

**terminal capitalization rate** An overall capitalization rate used to forecast a reversionary value in a discounted cash flow analysis. Calculated by dividing the projected net operating income (NOI) for the year of sale by the selected rate. Sometimes the projected NOI for the year *after* the sale is used because this is the NOI that the buyer will receive for the first year. The terminal capitalization rate is typically forecast to be higher than the going-in cap rate due to a higher risk associated with estimating NOI at the time of the sale. *See also* capitalization rate, going-in capitalization rate.

For example, suppose an investor wants to estimate the resale price, assuming the property will be sold in year 10. NOI for year 11 is estimated to be $150,000. Current capitalization rates for similar properties are about 10%. The appraiser adds a risk premium of 50 basis points to obtain a terminal capitalization rate of 10.5%. Thus the estimated resale price is $150,000/.105 = $1,428,571.

**terminal value** *See* reversion.

**test boring** A process that takes place before construction begins in which engineers drill into the soil of a site to determine the character of the subsoil and the location of bedrock. The process helps ensure that the soil is sufficient to prevent tilting, sinking, or buckling of the building foundation after it is constructed.

**theory** A statement setting forth an apparent relationship among observed facts that have been substantiated to a degree. *See also* appraisal theories.

**timberland** Agricultural property that periodically produces merchantable timber. Timber crops are typically harvested every 20, 50, or 80 years, depending on the species and growing conditions. *See also* stumpage value.

**time series** A graphic presentation of a statistic as it changes through time which is used to analyze cyclical, random and other variations over time.

**time value of money** A financial principle based on the assumption that a positive interest can be earned on an investment and, therefore, money received today is more valuable than money received in the future. *See also* discounted cash flow analysis (DCF).

**time-price differential**  The difference between a property's purchase price and the higher total price the same property would cost if purchased on an installment basis (including finance charges). Under the Truth-in-Lending laws, a lender must disclose the time-price differential, as well as all finance charges of any kind in an installment contract.

**time-series chart**  A graphic representation of statistical data in which the independent variable (plotted along the horizontal axis) is time, and the values of the dependent variable (plotted along the vertical axis) are shown at various intervals of time. These values are connected by straight lines to form a continuous curve extending over the entire period covered by the chart. Also called temporal distribution.

**time-share ownership plan (TSO)**  A type of time-sharing in which owners receive a title to use the property for a specified time each year. Under an interval ownership plan, ownership terms last for a specified number of years, after which time, owners are free to enter into a new agreement. *See also* time-sharing.

**time-sharing**  A sale of limited, undivided ownership interests in a property in which each purchaser receives a deed conveying title to the unit for a specific period of time. *See also* time-share ownership plan (TSO).

**times interest earned**  The ratio of earnings of a business, before deducting interest expense, to that interest expense. The ratio is used in identifying and measuring risk by purchasers of debt issues (especially bonds or notes) of a company. Generally, the lower the ratio the greater the risk to the bond or note holder. Times interest earned may be the ratio of earnings before interest and income taxes to interest expense. Also called interest coverage.

**title**  The bundle of rights possessed by an owner; the rights or ownership of a property. Title may be held individually, jointly or by a corporation. *See also* abstract of title.

**Title XI**  Real Estate Appraisal Reform Amendments that are included in the Financial Institutions Reform, Recovery and Enforcement Act (FIRREA) of 1989 that provide for state licensing and certification of appraisers.

**topographic map**  A map that identifies locations by the features and contour of the land, e.g., rivers, land elevations and lakes.

**topography**  The features and contour of the land.

**total cost of construction**  *See* construction cost.

**township**    (1) In the rectangular survey system of legally describing land, an area 6 miles square containing 36 sections and 23,040 acres. *See also* rectangular survey method. (2) In some states, a political subdivision similar to a county.

**township lines**    In the rectangular survey system, lines spaced 6 miles apart that run east and west to define a township. *See also* rectangular survey method, township.

**tract**    A lot; often refers to a lot that will be subdivided into smaller parcels. *See also* lot.

**trade area**    A defined geographic area from which a business attracts the majority of its customers.

**trade fixture**    A type of personal property that is owned and attached to a rented space by the tenant and is used in conducting business. Differentiated from a regular fixture that is part of the real estate by the manner in which it is affixed, the character of the item and the intention of the tenant who attached the item. Whereas regular fixtures are real property, trade fixtures remain personal property. *See also* fixture.

**traffic**    The movement of people, vehicles and such along a way or past a point; the people and vehicles so moving along the way.

**traffic count**    A count of the number of people and/or vehicles moving past a location during a period of time; the number of pedestrians passing a retail location as a measure of its potential sales volume. Traffic counts are used to determine the volume of vehicular traffic past a proposed service station site. Counts may be made to determine the composition of the traffic, as the number of men or women or the number of private automobiles in contrast to number of trucks, buses, etc. Traffic counts may be made to reflect traffic conditions on certain days of the week or year and at certain hours of the day.

**traffic density**    The number of vehicles occupying a unit length of the moving lanes of roadway at a given instant. Usually expressed in vehicles per mile.

**traffic survey**    A survey made to obtain information such as data on the quantity and composition of traffic, origin and destination of people, purpose of trip or means of transportation, usually in relation to some specific time, as a certain day of the week.

**transaction price**    *See* price.

**transfer costs**    The inherent costs incurred by users of a site to travel to and from that site to other sites of interest such as home, school, doctor, etc., including monetary costs such as fuel, maintenance, repairs, tolls and parking, and nonmonetary costs such as the value of time spent in transportation.

**transfer economies**   *See* agglomeration economies.

**transferable development right**   *See* development rights.

**transition**   A period of time in which the use of an area changes, e.g., agricultural to residential.

**transition property**   A property, most typically an improved property, whose highest and best use as vacant exceeds its highest and best use as improved but not by enough to cover the costs of demolition and clearing. The property will contain an interim use until the difference in highest and best use values is sufficiently large to make the change.

**trend**   An arrangement of statistical data in accordance with its time of occurrence, usually over a period of years. A series of related changes that may be identified and projected into a probable future pattern. The application of cost or price indexes to translate purchasing power of one period to that of another period is called trending as in trended historical cost of construction.

**trend analysis**   A study of changes in the environment of a property. Used particularly in the income approach to help forecast future changes in property income, sales price and occupancy rates.

**trended cost**   An estimate of current cost to produce or construct a building or facility, obtained by adjusting historical or original cost in each construction period (usually a year) in terms of the construction cost index applicable to each period.

   Specifically, the ratio of the construction cost index for the current period to each earlier period's cost index is calculated, and that ratio is taken as the earlier period's multiplier. Each period's historical or original cost is multiplied by the applicable multiplier so calculated. The sum of these periodic products is the current cost to produce the structure (often used as an indicator of reproduction cost new).

**triple net lease**   *See* net-net-net lease.

**truss**   One of the various structural frames composed of three or more members creating a triangular structure that, as a whole, acts as a beam. A truss is used when the span or load is too great for the use of a single beam.

**trust**   A fiduciary arrangement in which the title to and control of property is placed in the hands of a third party (trustee) for the benefit of another person (trustor). It may be of a temporary or permanent nature.

**trustee**   A third party who holds property in trust for another and controls legal title to property under a trust agreement.

**trustor**   One for whom property is held under a trust agreement.

**TSO**   *See* time-share ownership plan (TSO).

**turnover**   The frequency with which property is sold or leased to a new owner or tenant.

**UCIAR**  *See* Uniform Commercial-Industrial Appraisal Report (UCIAR).

**underimproved land**  Land that does not generate the maximum amount of income that could be generated because it is not being used under its highest and best use.

**underimprovement**  An improvement whose highest and best use does not match the highest and best use of the land as if vacant or whose size is not optimal for the site size.

**undivided interest**  An interest held by a co-owner for an entire property.

**unencumbered property**  A property that does not have attached to it a lien, claim, liability or other unpaid charge; a property that is "free and clear." For example, mortgages, taxes and easements cause a property to be encumbered.

**unfavorable leverage**  *See* negative leverage.

**Uniform Commercial-Industrial Appraisal Report (UCIAR)**  An appraisal form developed to provide a consistent report of the value of commercial and industrial properties.

**Uniform Residential Appraisal Report (URAR)**  An appraisal form requested by many federal agencies to value residential properties in a consistent manner.

**Uniform Standards of Professional Appraisal Practice (USPAP)**  A set of standards originally developed by a committee of 9 appraisal associations to provide guidelines for the development of appraisal reports. Updates to the standards are currently the responsibility of the Appraisal Standards Board of The Appraisal Foundation. All appraisal members of the Foundation have adopted the standards. *See also* Appraisal Foundation, The.

**uniformity** In assessment, the equal distribution of assessed values as compared to market values. Fairness in the levying of property tax is implied.

**unimproved land** Land that is vacant or has not been developed to a useful state. Also called raw land. *See also* improved land.

**unit cost** The price of a number of similar items divided by the total number of items, for example, price per square foot. When multiplied by the total number of items, the unit cost will give the total price. Also called unit price.

**unit costs method of valuation** *See* unit-in-place method.

**unit (unitary) method of valuation** A technique of valuing a group of property items as one thing or as integrated parts of a system. In particular, the assessment or valuation of the combined properties of public utilities, railroads, pipeline companies and others that span several assessment or taxation districts, by valuing the operating property of the utility or other enterprise as a single unit or on the basis of the business enterprise as a whole. The value of non-operating assets or property is excluded.

Three techniques are used in unit valuation: a cost approach (sometimes limited to book costs); a sales comparison, or market, approach (the stock and debt approach); and an income approach (where it is important to distinguish between the capitalization rate used to value the enterprise and/or its property and the rate of return the utility is allowed to receive on its invested capital). The unit value thus derived is then apportioned and allocated among the state and local governmental taxing jurisdictions involved. Distinguished from situs valuation. *See also* central assessment, allocation to states, apportionment to intrastate jurisdiction.

**unit value** The market value of an entire property divided by a unit of measurement, e.g., value per square foot.

**unit-in-place method** A method of estimating building costs in which total building cost is estimated by summing prices for various building components as installed, based on specific units of use such as square footage or cubic footage. Also called the segregated cost method, unit costs method. *See also* building cost.

**units of comparison** A physical or economic measure that can be divided into the property's price to provide a more standardized comparison of the properties. The measure should be one that accounts for differences in the price typically paid for the properties such as price per square foot (office building), price per seat (theater) or price per gallon of gas pumped (gas station). Income can also be a unit of comparison such as when price is divided by effective gross income to obtain an effective gross income multiplier.

**URAR**   *See* Uniform Residential Appraisal Report (URAR).

**urban area**   Typically defined as any incorporated settlement that contains a population of 2,500 or more. Can also refer to an unincorporated place of 2,500 or more people located away from a city, or a settled area, whether incorporated or not, located in proximity to a city of 50,000 or more.

**urbanization economies**   Also known as external economies to the firms that are also external to the industry. *See* agglomeration economies.

**urbanized area**   (1) A geographic area that includes a central city plus the surrounding and densely populated areas that consist of: (a) contiguous incorporated places of 2,500 or more inhabitants, or urban areas; (b) incorporated places with fewer than 2,500 inhabitants, providing each has a closely settled area of 100 dwelling units or more; (c) adjacent unincorporated areas with a population density of 1,000 or more inhabitants per square mile; (d) other adjacent areas with a lower population density but serve to link together otherwise separate densely populated areas. (2) A central city plus the surrounding densely populated area. (3) The developed or built-up area of an urban region. It is the area in need of urban services provided by municipal agencies such as police, fire, water, sewer and solid waste departments.

**usable area**   The gross area minus common areas and lobbies. Stairwells, elevators, public corridors and washrooms, and maintenance rooms are not included in usable area.

**use classification**   The type of use to which a property is put, e.g., agricultural, commercial, industrial, residential.

**use value**   *See* value in use.

**use value assessment**   An assessment based on the value of property as it is currently used, not on its market value considering alternative uses. Use value assessment may be used where legislation has been enacted to preserve farmland, timberland or other open space land on urban fringes.

**useful life**   *See* economic life.

**user value**   The value of a property or space to a specific user. Sometimes more particularly the value of a property designed or adapted to fit the specific requirements of the user. In the latter case, such value often applies to the classification of special purpose property. Also called value in use.

**USPAP**   *See* Uniform Standards of Professional Appraisal Practice (USPAP).

**usual selling price**   *See* market value.

**utilities**   The operating services required by a developed area and provided by a public utility company, e.g., electricity, telephone, water and gas.

**utility**   In economics, the enjoyment gained from a good in relationship to its risk and return.

# V

**V** *See* property value (V).

**vacancies** Unoccupied space available for rent.

**vacancy allowance** In the income approach, a deduction from potential income for current or expected future space not rented due to tenant turnover. *See also* potential gross income (PGI), effective gross income (EGI).

**vacancy analysis** A study of the current and past vacancy levels and/or rates for a particular type of real estate, leading to a forecast into the near future.

**vacancy and collection loss** *See* vacancy allowance, collection loss.

**vacancy rate** (1) The ratio of the area of space that is not rented divided by the total leasable area. (2) The ratio of the rent that could be collected from vacant space if it was rented divided by the total rent the building is capable of generating.

**valuation** The process of estimating value for a specific set of interests as of a specific point in time for a real estate property. *See also* appraisal, evaluation.

**valuation date** *See* date of appraisal.

**value** The monetary worth of an entity or object. *See* market value, investment value, insurable value, assessed value, going-concern value, value in place, value in use, value after the taking, value before the taking, business value.

**value added** The anticipated increase in property value expected from correcting, or curling, a condition causing accrued depreciation.

**value after the taking** In a partial taking through a condemnation proceeding, the market value of the remaining property not taken in the condemnation. *See also* before-and-after method, condemnation.

**value before the taking**    In a partial taking through a condemnation proceeding, the market value of the entire property affected by the condemnation. *See also* before-and-after method, condemnation.

**value in exchange**    *See* market value.

**value in place**    The value of an item in place based on the use it contributes to the whole, e.g., equipment.

**value in use**    See user value

**variability**    In statistics, a measure of the dispersion of data points from the measure of central tendency, e.g., range, standard deviation, variance.

**variable**    A quantity that may take any one of a specified set of values.

**variable annuity**    A series of cash flows in which payments occur at regular intervals but in differing amounts. *See also* annuity.

**variable expense**    An operating expense that varies with the occupancy level or intensity of use of a property, e.g., utilities, management and maintenance. *See also* fixed expense.

**variable interest rate**    An interest rate on a mortgage that changes throughout the term of the mortgage and is usually tied to an index, e.g., treasury bills, prime rate.

**variable operating expenses**    *See* variable expense.

**variable rate mortgage**    *See* adjustable rate mortgage (ARM).

**variance**    (1) In statistics, the arithmetic mean of the squares of the deviations from the arithmetic mean of the frequency distribution. The variance measures the extent of variability in a frequency distribution. The square root of the variance equals the standard deviation. *See also* mean, risk analysis, standard deviation, normal probability distribution.

   For example, the variance of the set of numbers 3, 4, 6, 8, 10 and 5 can be calculated as follows:

the mean of the distribution $= (3+4+6+8+10+5)/6 = 6$
the variance $=$
   $((3-6)^2+(4-6)^2+(6-6)^2+(8-6)^2+(10-6)^2+(5-6)^2)/6 = 5.67$

(2) In zoning, a specific violation of the current zoning laws that is granted through permission of the zoning authority. It may involve use or structure of the real estate, for example, apartments in a single family residential area or a building that is too large or of a different style than that allowed through the current zoning.

**veneer** An ornamental or protective material used as an exterior to cover a less attractive or less expensive surface, for example, oak or mahogany over a less valuable wood, or brick over a frame exterior.

**vent** An opening or pipe that allows for the passage of air or gas to the outside of a building, for example, an opening in the attic to allow air circulation or a vent pipe from plumbing fixtures to a vent stack on the roof to allow sewer gases to escape.

**ventilation** The process of supplying or removing air by natural or mechanical means to or from a space.

**vernacular architecture** Architectural design without reference to specific aesthetic and functional criteria of formal styles; styles that are not formally studied by architectural historians, for example, traditional barns and mass-produced homes in modern subdivisions. *See also* formal architecture.

**vertical division** The separation of real property into air, ground and subsurface rights.

**vested interest** A right or estate that grants possession and use of a property at some later date but does not grant current use of the property. The vested interest, however, may be currently conveyed to another party.

**vineyard** A planting of uniformly spaced grapevines to produce income. Primary considerations in appraising a vineyard include an in-depth knowledge of the particular variety of vine, its characteristics, stage of development, production and requirements.

**visibility analysis** A process examining those elements that provide potential site users with the required information about the activities and conditions available on the site that result in a continued decision to use it. The study concentrates specifically on such areas as effective views of the full spectrum of the site's principal and supporting uses, specific activities and points from which visibility must be effective, signs and information about such activities, and information regarding access conditions and internal site connections.

**visitation rate** In retail trade analysis, the frequency of trips to the property per week, month or other appropriate time period.

**visual rights** The right to maintain a clear space so that a property may be seen, for example, the right to prevent a sign or billboard from being constructed that would constrict the view of a property from a road.

**volitional fallacy** A misconception occurring when an analyst becomes overly optimistic about a project. Occurs when the analyst is swayed by the client's enthusiasm for the product and begins to believe that the project is unjustifiably unique in character.

**volume of new construction**   The amount of property that has recently been built. The volume of new construction is one indication of the supply of real estate.

# W-Z

**wainscot**   Wall material used in the lower portion of a wall that is different from the material in the rest of the wall.

**wall covering**   The exterior wall skin, consisting of panels or sheets and their attachments, trim fascia and weather sealants.

**wall-bearing construction**   Construction in which the roof and floors are carried directly by exterior walls of plain brick, plastered brick or other masonry. Posts and columns are used only when the length of the interior span requires intermediate support for a roof or floor.

**warehouse**   A structure that is designed and used for the storage of wares, goods and merchandise, usually classified as industrial.

**warranty deed**   A deed that conveys to the grantee title to the property free and clear of all encumbrances, except those specifically set forth in the document.

**wasting asset**   (1) A substance that is depleted through drilling, mining or exploitation, e.g., timber, oil, interest. *See also* Hoskold premise. (2) Rights that have a limited term, e.g., patent rights, franchises.

**watershed**   A watercourse that parts and ultimately drains into a bordering body of water, for example, the drainage basin of the Mississippi River. Also called drainage basin.

**wear and tear**   Physical deterioration of property due to weathering, aging and use. *See also* curable physical deterioration, incurable physical deterioration.

**weighted average**   The mean of a set of numbers that is calculated by applying a weight factor to each component, representing its size compared to the whole. For example, as used in a band of investment technique to find an overall capitalization rate, the weighted average of the land and building capitalization rates is calculated by multiplying each by its percentage value as compared to the whole value. *See also* mean, band of investment technique.

   For example, the weighted average of an 8% land cap rate and an 11% building cap rate, when the building value equals $100,000 and the total property value equals $340,000 is:

weighted average =
$(100,000/340,000) \times 0.11 + (1 - (100,000/340,000)) \times 0.08 = 0.089 = R_O$

**window type**   Window types vary widely. Most are constructed with wood, aluminum or steel. Some types include fixed, sliding, double-single hung, casement, awning, hopper, center pivot, and jalousie. The window type, material and manufacturer should be noted in an appraisal. Storm windows are often added to provide extra insulation.

**work letter**   An addition to a lease that specifies what services, equipment and interior finishes will be provided by the landlord to the tenant and what will be provided by the tenant.

**working capital**   In accounting, current assets minus current liabilities; the liquid assets a company uses to conduct business.

**wraparound mortgage**   A mortgage in which the lender takes over payments of a previous mortgage and in turn provides a mortgage in the amount of the previous mortgage plus an additional amount. A wraparound mortgage is subordinate to the previous loan.

**Y**   *See* yield rate (Y).

**$Y_E$**   *See* equity yield rate ($Y_E$).

**$Y_M$**   *See* mortgage yield rate ($Y_M$).

**$Y_O$**   *See* overall yield rate ($Y_O$).

**$Y_t$**   *See* after-tax equity yield rate ($Y_t$).

**yield**   *See* internal rate of return (IRR).

**yield analysis**   *See* graphic analysis.

**yield capitalization**   A method of estimating property value by discounting all expected future cash flows to a present value by a rate typical for investors in the marketplace for the interest being valued. The approach may or may not explicitly include financing. Algebraic formulas have been developed to discount future cash flows; however, these are no longer needed with the availability of computer spreadsheets. *See also* yield capitalization formulas, Hoskold premise, Inwood premise, Ellwood formula, Akerson format, J factor, K factor, discounted cash flow analysis (DCF).

   For example, a property produces cash flows of $235,000 per year. The property is held for 8 years. The reversion value at this time is $2,000,000. The appropriate discount rate is 11%. The property value can be estimated as follows:

$$PV = 235{,}000 \times a_{\overline{n}|(11\%,\ 8\ yrs.)} + \$2{,}000{,}000 \times 1/S^n_{(11\%,\ 8\ yrs.)}$$
$$a_{\overline{n}|(11\%,\ 8\ yrs.)} = 5.146123, \quad 1/S^n_{(11\%,\ 8\ yrs.)} = 0.433926$$

using annual compound interest tables

$$PV = 235{,}000 \times 5.146123 + \$2{,}000{,}000 \times 0.433926$$
$$PV = \$2{,}077{,}191$$

Therefore, the property value is approximately \$2,077,191.

**yield capitalization formulas**   Yield capitalization formulas are formulas that are used to calculate an overall rate ($R_O$) for a property. These formulas were developed as shortcut techniques for estimating value with a discounted cash flow analysis based on the yield rate ($Y_O$) for the property. These formulas express the overall rate as being equal to the yield rate plus or minus a term, which accounts for assumptions about how the property's income and value are projected to change over the holding period. This term will differ for different income patterns.

In general, yield capitalization formulas can be written as $R_O = Y_O - \triangle_O a$, where $\triangle_O$ is the total change in property value over the holding period and a is referred to as an annualizer. The calculation of a depends on the particular assumptions about how the income pattern changes over time. The most common situations are shown below:

*Level Income:* $R_O = Y_O - \triangle_O\ 1/S_{\overline{n}|}$, where $\triangle_O$ equals the change in property value over the holding period, and $1/S_{\overline{n}|}$ equals the sinking fund factor for a particular discount rate and holding period. (In this case, $1/S_{\overline{n}|}$ is the annualizer.)

For example, a property produces a net operating income (NOI) of \$10,000 per year for 5 years. The value of the property will increase 20% total over the 5 years. The discount rate is 10%. The value can be calculated by the above formula, where $Y_O = 10\%$, $\triangle_O = 20\%$ and $1/S_{\overline{n}|}$ is .163797 (from tables at 10%).

$$R_O = .10 - (.20 \times .163797) = .067241$$
$$Value = NOI/R_O = \$10{,}000/.067241 = \$148{,}720$$

The problem can also be solved by an algebraic equation, using present value factors as follows:

$$Value = annuity \times a_{\overline{n}|} + [(1 + total\ growth) \times Value \times 1/S^n]$$
$$V = (10{,}000 \times 3.7908) + (1.2 \times V \times .620921) = \$148{,}720$$

*Straight-line (constant amount) Growth:* $R_O = Y_O - \triangle_O\ 1/n$, where n equals the holding period, $1/n$ is the annualizer, $\triangle_O$ equals the total change in value over the holding period, and $\triangle_O\ 1/n$ equals the percentage drop in value for the first year. In this case, value is assumed to decline by the same dollar amount each year.

For example: A property produces a first year net operating income (NOI) of \$16,000. The property value will decrease 20% total over a 5-year holding period, and the discount rate is 12%. The value can be calculated as follows:

$$\triangle_O \ 1/n = -0.20/5 = -0.04$$
$$R_O = .12 - (-.04) = .16$$
$$V = NOI/R_O = \$16,000/.16 = \$100,000$$

The solution can be verified using present value factors as follows: We can calculate the implied change in NOI as follows:

$$\triangle_I = V \times \triangle \ 1/n \times Y_O,$$
where $\triangle_I$ equals the first year change in income
$$\triangle_I = \$100,000 \times -.04 \times .12 = -\$480$$

Thus the NOI for the 5-year holding period can be calculated by subtracting $480 from each year's NOI as follows: $16,000, $15,520, $15,040, $14,560, and $14,080. The resale price after 5-years would equal $100,000 \times (1 - 0.2) = \$80,000$. Thus, the total cash flows for the 5 year period equal: $16,000, $15,520, $15,040, $14,560, $14,080. The present value of these cash flows at 12% is $100,000 as we calculated with the straight-line capitalization formula above.

*Compound (exponential curve or constant ratio) Growth:* $R_O = Y_O -$ CR, where CR equals the compound rate of change in property value. In this case the growth rate is already expressed on an annual basis, thus there is no need for an annualizer applied to the total change in value.

For example, a property produces a first year net operating income (NOI) of $10,000. Property value will increase 4% over a 5-year holding period, and income will also increase 4% per year. The discount rate is 14%. The value can be calculated as follows:

$$R_O = 0.14 - 0.04 = 0.10$$
$$V = \$10,000/0.10 = \$100,000$$

The problem can also be verified, using present value factors as follows:

The NOI each year can be calculated by multiplying each year's NOI by 1 plus the growth rate:
$10,000 \times 1.04 = \$10,400$ and so on.
So NOIs over the 5-year holding period equal $10,000, $10,400, $10,816, $11,249, $11,699.
The resale price equals $100,000 \times (1.04)^5 = \$121,665$.
Thus, the total cash flows over the 5-year period equal: $10,000, $10,400, $10,816, $11,249, $133,364.

The present value of the income and resale at 14% is $100,000, as we calculated using the compound growth capitalization formula above.

**yield rate (Y)**   The return on an investment, which considers income received over time; the discount rate that equates the present value of future cash flows with the initial investment. Same as internal rate of return. *See also* equity yield rate ($Y_E$), overall yield rate ($Y_O$).

**yield to maturity**   *See* yield rate.

**zero leverage**   The use of borrowed funds at a rate equal to the equity yield rate. *See also* leverage. Some examples follow:

If $R_O = R_M$ then $R_E = R_O$ and if $Y_O = Y_M$ then $Y_E = Y_O$ (zero leverage)

$$\text{where } R_E = \text{the equity dividend rate,}$$
$$R_O = \text{the overall capitalization rate,}$$
$$R_M = \text{the mortgage capitalization rate,}$$
$$Y_O = \text{the overall yield rate,}$$
$$Y_M = \text{the mortgage yield rate,}$$
$$\text{and } Y_E = \text{the equity yield rate.}$$

**zero lot line**   An improved property in which one or more sides of the building are located directly on a boundary line of the lot. This type of land use may be restricted by zoning ordinances.

**zip code area**   A geographic area established by the postal service. The boundaries are not stable, and the areas do not represent demographic and economic homogeneity.

**zoning**   An application of police power by a local government that provides a legal mechanism for the government to regulate land use and density of development for privately owned real property. Zoning establishes areas with uniform restrictions regarding property characteristics such as property use (residential, commercial, etc.), improvement height, specifications for signs and billboards, and density of development. *See also* area regulations, buffer zone, building codes, building restrictions, exclusionary zoning, police power, pyramid zoning, spot zoning.

**zoning map**   A map of a community that visually specifies the types of zoning in different areas of a community.

**zoning ordinance**   A legal statute passed by a government that restricts the use of real property to protect health, safety and the general welfare of the public; an application of police power. *See also* zoning.

**zoning restrictions**   *See* zoning.

**zoning variance**   A legal modification in a zoning ordinance that allows a property to be of a different nature than that specified in the ordinance. A zoning variance is not a change in or exception from the zoning. *See also* legally nonconforming use.

# Appendix A

## Symbols, Acronyms and Abbreviations

| | |
|---|---|
| **a** | annualizer |
| **$a_{\overline{n}}$** | present value annuity of $1 per period |
| **$1/a_{\overline{n}}$** | installment to amortize $1 |
| **AIRR** | adjusted internal rate of return |
| **APR** | annual percentage rate |
| **ARM** | adjustable rate mortgage |
| **ATCF** | after-tax cash flow |
| **ATIRR** | after-tax internal rate of return |
| **B** | 1. building ratio<br>2. outstanding balance |
| **BG** | block group |
| **BPI** | buying power index |
| **BTCF** | before-tax cash flow |
| **BTIRR** | before-tax internal rate of return |
| **BTU** | British Thermal Unit |
| **C** | mortgage coefficient |
| **CAM** | common area maintenance |
| **CBD** | central business district |
| **CCD** | census county division |
| **CMO** | collateralized mortgage obligation |
| **CMSA** | Consolidated Metropolitan Statistical Area |
| **CPI** | consumer price index |
| **CRV** | certificate of reasonable value |
| **CTS** | Class, Type, Style |
| **CWIP** | construction work in progress |

| | |
|---|---|
| **DCF** | discounted cash flow analysis |
| **DCR** | debt coverage ratio |
| $\triangle_o$ | change in property value |
| $\triangle_I$ | change in income |
| **ED** | enumeration district |
| **EGI** | effective gross income |
| **EGIM** | effective gross income multiplier |
| **EIS** | environmental impact study |
| **EPA** | Environmental Protection Agency |
| **FASB** | Financial Accounting Standards Board |
| **FHLMC** | Federal Home Loan Mortgage Corporation |
| **FIRREA** | Financial Institutions Reform, Recovery and Enforcement Act |
| **FLHBB** | Federal Home Loan Bank Board |
| **FMRR** | financial management rate of return |
| **FNMA** | Federal National Mortgage Association |
| **FVIF** | future value interest factor |
| **FVIFA** | future value interest factor-annuity |
| **GBA** | gross building area |
| **GIM** | gross income multiplier |
| **GLA** | gross leasable area |
| **GNMA** | Government National Mortgage Association |
| **GPM** | graduated payment mortgage |
| **GRM** | gross rent multiplier |
| **HBU** | highest and best use |
| **HVAC** | heating, ventilating and air-conditioning |
| **i** | nominal rate of interest |
| **IRR** | internal rate of return |
| **L** | land to value ratio |
| **M** | loan to value ratio |
| **MLP** | master limited partnership |
| **MSA** | Metropolitan Statistical Area |

| | |
|---|---|
| **NIM** | net income multiplier |
| **NIR** | net income ratio |
| **NOI** | net operating income |
| **NPV** | net present value |
| **OER** | operating expense ratio |
| **P** | percentage of loan paid off |
| **PGI** | potential gross income |
| **PGIM** | potential gross income multiplier |
| **PI** | profitability index |
| **P&I** | principal and interest payment |
| **PITI** | principal, interest, taxes and insurance |
| **PMI** | private mortgage insurance |
| **PMT** | mortgage payment |
| **PMSA** | Primary Metropolitan Statistical Area |
| **PTCF** | pre-tax cash flow |
| **PUD** | planned unit development |
| **PV** | present value |
| **PVIF** | present value interest factor |
| **PVIFA** | present value interest factor-annuity |
| **r** | 1. In appraisal, basic capitalization rate<br>2. In statistics, coefficient of correlation |
| $R_B$ | building capitalization rate |
| $R_E$ | equity capitalization rate |
| $R_L$ | land capitalization rate |
| $R_M$ | mortgage capitalization rate |
| $R_O$ | overall capitalization rate |
| $R^2$ | coefficient of multiple determination |
| **RAM** | reverse annuity mortgage |
| **ROE** | return on equity |
| **RTC** | Resolution Trust Corporation |
| $S_{\overline{n}\rvert}$ | future value annuity of \$1 per period |
| $1/S_{\overline{n}\rvert}$ | sinking fund factor |

| | |
|---|---|
| $S^n$ | future value of $1 |
| $1/S^n$ | present value of $1 |
| SIC | standard industrial classification |
| SMSA | Standard Metropolitan Statistical Area |
| TSO | time-share ownership plan |
| UCIAR | Uniform Commercial-Industrial Appraisal Report |
| URAR | Uniform Residential Appraisal Report |
| USPAP | Uniform Standards of Professional Appraisal Practice |
| V | property value |
| $V_B$ | building value |
| $V_E$ | equity value |
| $V_L$ | land value |
| $V_M$ | mortgage value |
| $V_R$ | reversionary value |
| Y | yield rate |
| $Y_E$ | equity yield rate |
| $Y_M$ | mortgage yield rate |
| $Y_O$ | overall yield rate |
| $Y_t$ | after-tax equity yield rate |

# Appendix B
# Monthly Compound
# Interest Tables

6.00% ANNUAL INTEREST RATE          0.5000% MONTHLY EFFECTIVE INTEREST RATE

| | 1 Future Value of $1 | 2 Future Value Annuity of $1 per Month | 3 Sinking Fund Factor | 4 Present Value of $1 (Reversion) | 5 Present Value Annuity of $1 per Month | 6 Installment to Amortize $1 | |
|---|---|---|---|---|---|---|---|
| Months | | | | | | | Months |
| 1 | 1.005000 | 1.000000 | 1.000000 | 0.995025 | 0.995025 | 1.005000 | 1 |
| 2 | 1.010025 | 2.005000 | 0.498753 | 0.990075 | 1.985099 | 0.503753 | 2 |
| 3 | 1.015075 | 3.015025 | 0.331672 | 0.985149 | 2.970248 | 0.336672 | 3 |
| 4 | 1.020151 | 4.030100 | 0.248133 | 0.980248 | 3.950496 | 0.253133 | 4 |
| 5 | 1.025251 | 5.050251 | 0.198010 | 0.975371 | 4.925866 | 0.203010 | 5 |
| 6 | 1.030378 | 6.075502 | 0.164595 | 0.970518 | 5.896384 | 0.169595 | 6 |
| 7 | 1.035529 | 7.105879 | 0.140729 | 0.965690 | 6.862074 | 0.145729 | 7 |
| 8 | 1.040707 | 8.141409 | 0.122829 | 0.960885 | 7.822959 | 0.127829 | 8 |
| 9 | 1.045911 | 9.182116 | 0.108907 | 0.956105 | 8.779064 | 0.113907 | 9 |
| 10 | 1.051140 | 10.228026 | 0.097771 | 0.951348 | 9.730412 | 0.102771 | 10 |
| 11 | 1.056396 | 11.279167 | 0.088659 | 0.946615 | 10.677027 | 0.093659 | 11 |
| 12 | 1.061678 | 12.335562 | 0.081066 | 0.941905 | 11.618932 | 0.086066 | 12 |
| Years | | | | | | | Months |
| 1 | 1.061678 | 12.335562 | 0.081066 | 0.941905 | 11.618932 | 0.086066 | 12 |
| 2 | 1.127160 | 25.431955 | 0.039321 | 0.887186 | 22.562866 | 0.044321 | 24 |
| 3 | 1.196681 | 39.336105 | 0.025422 | 0.835645 | 32.871016 | 0.030422 | 36 |
| 4 | 1.270489 | 54.097832 | 0.018485 | 0.787098 | 42.580318 | 0.023485 | 48 |
| 5 | 1.348850 | 69.770031 | 0.014333 | 0.741372 | 51.725561 | 0.019333 | 60 |
| 6 | 1.432044 | 86.408856 | 0.011573 | 0.698302 | 60.339514 | 0.016573 | 72 |
| 7 | 1.520370 | 104.073927 | 0.009609 | 0.657735 | 68.453042 | 0.014609 | 84 |
| 8 | 1.614143 | 122.828542 | 0.008141 | 0.619524 | 76.095218 | 0.013141 | 96 |
| 9 | 1.713699 | 142.739900 | 0.007006 | 0.583533 | 83.293424 | 0.012006 | 108 |
| 10 | 1.819397 | 163.879347 | 0.006102 | 0.549633 | 90.073453 | 0.011102 | 120 |
| 11 | 1.931613 | 186.322629 | 0.005367 | 0.517702 | 96.459599 | 0.010367 | 132 |
| 12 | 2.050751 | 210.150163 | 0.004759 | 0.487626 | 102.474743 | 0.009759 | 144 |
| 13 | 2.177237 | 235.447328 | 0.004247 | 0.459298 | 108.140440 | 0.009247 | 156 |
| 14 | 2.311524 | 262.304766 | 0.003812 | 0.432615 | 113.476990 | 0.008812 | 168 |
| 15 | 2.454094 | 290.818712 | 0.003439 | 0.407482 | 118.503515 | 0.008439 | 180 |
| 16 | 2.605457 | 321.091337 | 0.003114 | 0.383810 | 123.238025 | 0.008114 | 192 |
| 17 | 2.766156 | 353.231110 | 0.002831 | 0.361513 | 127.697486 | 0.007831 | 204 |
| 18 | 2.936766 | 387.353194 | 0.002582 | 0.340511 | 131.897876 | 0.007582 | 216 |
| 19 | 3.117899 | 423.579854 | 0.002361 | 0.320729 | 135.854246 | 0.007361 | 228 |
| 20 | 3.310204 | 462.040895 | 0.002164 | 0.302096 | 139.580772 | 0.007164 | 240 |
| 21 | 3.514371 | 502.874129 | 0.001989 | 0.284546 | 143.090806 | 0.006989 | 252 |
| 22 | 3.731129 | 546.225867 | 0.001831 | 0.268015 | 146.396927 | 0.006831 | 264 |
| 23 | 3.961257 | 592.251446 | 0.001688 | 0.252445 | 149.510979 | 0.006688 | 276 |
| 24 | 4.205579 | 641.115782 | 0.001560 | 0.237779 | 152.444121 | 0.006560 | 288 |
| 25 | 4.464970 | 692.993962 | 0.001443 | 0.223966 | 155.206864 | 0.006443 | 300 |
| 26 | 4.740359 | 748.071876 | 0.001337 | 0.210954 | 157.809106 | 0.006337 | 312 |
| 27 | 5.032734 | 806.546875 | 0.001240 | 0.198699 | 160.260172 | 0.006240 | 324 |
| 28 | 5.343142 | 868.628484 | 0.001151 | 0.187156 | 162.568844 | 0.006151 | 336 |
| 29 | 5.672696 | 934.539150 | 0.001070 | 0.176283 | 164.743394 | 0.006070 | 348 |
| 30 | 6.022575 | 1004.515042 | 0.000996 | 0.166042 | 166.791614 | 0.005996 | 360 |
| 31 | 6.394034 | 1078.806895 | 0.000927 | 0.156396 | 168.720844 | 0.005927 | 372 |
| 32 | 6.788405 | 1157.680906 | 0.000864 | 0.147310 | 170.537996 | 0.005864 | 384 |
| 33 | 7.207098 | 1241.419693 | 0.000806 | 0.138752 | 172.249581 | 0.005806 | 396 |
| 34 | 7.651617 | 1330.323306 | 0.000752 | 0.130691 | 173.861732 | 0.005752 | 408 |
| 35 | 8.123551 | 1424.710299 | 0.000702 | 0.123099 | 175.380226 | 0.005702 | 420 |
| 36 | 8.624594 | 1524.918875 | 0.000656 | 0.115947 | 176.810504 | 0.005656 | 432 |
| 37 | 9.156540 | 1631.308097 | 0.000613 | 0.109212 | 178.157690 | 0.005613 | 444 |
| 38 | 9.721296 | 1744.259173 | 0.000573 | 0.102867 | 179.426611 | 0.005573 | 456 |
| 39 | 10.320884 | 1864.176824 | 0.000536 | 0.096891 | 180.621815 | 0.005536 | 468 |
| 40 | 10.957454 | 1991.490734 | 0.000502 | 0.091262 | 181.747584 | 0.005502 | 480 |

6.50% ANNUAL INTEREST RATE          0.5417% MONTHLY EFFECTIVE INTEREST RATE

| | 1<br>Future Value<br>of $1 | 2<br>Future Value<br>Annuity of<br>$1 per Month | 3<br>Sinking<br>Fund<br>Factor | 4<br>Present Value<br>of $1<br>(Reversion) | 5<br>Present Value<br>Annuity of<br>$1 per Month | 6<br>Installment<br>to<br>Amortize $1 | |
|---|---|---|---|---|---|---|---|
| Months | | | | | | | Months |
| 1 | 1.005417 | 1.000000 | 1.000000 | 0.994613 | 0.994613 | 1.005417 | 1 |
| 2 | 1.010863 | 2.005417 | 0.498649 | 0.989254 | 1.983867 | 0.504066 | 2 |
| 3 | 1.016338 | 3.016279 | 0.331534 | 0.983924 | 2.967791 | 0.336951 | 3 |
| 4 | 1.021843 | 4.032618 | 0.247978 | 0.978624 | 3.946415 | 0.253395 | 4 |
| 5 | 1.027378 | 5.054461 | 0.197845 | 0.973351 | 4.919766 | 0.203262 | 5 |
| 6 | 1.032943 | 6.081839 | 0.164424 | 0.968107 | 5.887873 | 0.169841 | 6 |
| 7 | 1.038538 | 7.114782 | 0.140552 | 0.962892 | 6.850765 | 0.145969 | 7 |
| 8 | 1.044164 | 8.153321 | 0.122649 | 0.957704 | 7.808469 | 0.128066 | 8 |
| 9 | 1.049820 | 9.197485 | 0.108725 | 0.952545 | 8.761014 | 0.114142 | 9 |
| 10 | 1.055506 | 10.247304 | 0.097587 | 0.947413 | 9.708426 | 0.103003 | 10 |
| 11 | 1.061224 | 11.302811 | 0.088474 | 0.942309 | 10.650735 | 0.093890 | 11 |
| 12 | 1.066972 | 12.364034 | 0.080880 | 0.937232 | 11.587967 | 0.086296 | 12 |
| Years | | | | | | | Months |
| 1 | 1.066972 | 12.364034 | 0.080880 | 0.937232 | 11.587967 | 0.086296 | 12 |
| 2 | 1.138429 | 25.556111 | 0.039130 | 0.878404 | 22.448578 | 0.044546 | 24 |
| 3 | 1.214672 | 39.631685 | 0.025232 | 0.823268 | 32.627489 | 0.030649 | 36 |
| 4 | 1.296020 | 54.649927 | 0.018298 | 0.771593 | 42.167488 | 0.023715 | 48 |
| 5 | 1.382817 | 70.673968 | 0.014149 | 0.723161 | 51.108680 | 0.019566 | 60 |
| 6 | 1.475427 | 87.771168 | 0.011393 | 0.677770 | 59.488649 | 0.016810 | 72 |
| 7 | 1.574239 | 106.013400 | 0.009433 | 0.635227 | 67.342623 | 0.014849 | 84 |
| 8 | 1.679669 | 125.477348 | 0.007970 | 0.595355 | 74.703617 | 0.013386 | 96 |
| 9 | 1.792160 | 146.244833 | 0.006838 | 0.557986 | 81.602576 | 0.012255 | 108 |
| 10 | 1.912184 | 168.403154 | 0.005938 | 0.522962 | 88.068500 | 0.011355 | 120 |
| 11 | 2.040246 | 192.045460 | 0.005207 | 0.490137 | 94.128569 | 0.010624 | 132 |
| 12 | 2.176885 | 217.271134 | 0.004603 | 0.459372 | 99.808260 | 0.010019 | 144 |
| 13 | 2.322675 | 244.186218 | 0.004095 | 0.430538 | 105.131446 | 0.009512 | 156 |
| 14 | 2.478229 | 272.903856 | 0.003664 | 0.403514 | 110.120506 | 0.009081 | 168 |
| 15 | 2.644201 | 303.544767 | 0.003294 | 0.378186 | 114.796412 | 0.008711 | 180 |
| 16 | 2.821288 | 336.237756 | 0.002974 | 0.354448 | 119.178820 | 0.008391 | 192 |
| 17 | 3.010235 | 371.120256 | 0.002695 | 0.332200 | 123.286152 | 0.008111 | 204 |
| 18 | 3.211836 | 408.338901 | 0.002449 | 0.311348 | 127.135675 | 0.007866 | 216 |
| 19 | 3.426938 | 448.050147 | 0.002232 | 0.291806 | 130.743570 | 0.007649 | 228 |
| 20 | 3.656447 | 490.420930 | 0.002039 | 0.273490 | 134.125004 | 0.007456 | 240 |
| 21 | 3.901326 | 535.629362 | 0.001867 | 0.256323 | 137.294192 | 0.007284 | 252 |
| 22 | 4.162605 | 583.865486 | 0.001713 | 0.240234 | 140.264456 | 0.007129 | 264 |
| 23 | 4.441382 | 635.332073 | 0.001574 | 0.225155 | 143.048282 | 0.006991 | 276 |
| 24 | 4.738830 | 690.245473 | 0.001449 | 0.211023 | 145.657372 | 0.006865 | 288 |
| 25 | 5.056198 | 748.836525 | 0.001335 | 0.197777 | 148.102695 | 0.006752 | 300 |
| 26 | 5.394821 | 811.351528 | 0.001233 | 0.185363 | 150.394529 | 0.006649 | 312 |
| 27 | 5.756122 | 878.053277 | 0.001139 | 0.173728 | 152.542509 | 0.006556 | 324 |
| 28 | 6.141620 | 949.222165 | 0.001053 | 0.162823 | 154.555664 | 0.006470 | 336 |
| 29 | 6.552936 | 1025.157366 | 0.000975 | 0.152603 | 156.442457 | 0.006392 | 348 |
| 30 | 6.991798 | 1106.178087 | 0.000904 | 0.143025 | 158.210820 | 0.006321 | 360 |
| 31 | 7.460052 | 1192.624917 | 0.000838 | 0.134047 | 159.868185 | 0.006255 | 372 |
| 32 | 7.959665 | 1284.861251 | 0.000778 | 0.125633 | 161.421521 | 0.006195 | 384 |
| 33 | 8.492739 | 1383.274822 | 0.000723 | 0.117748 | 162.877357 | 0.006140 | 396 |
| 34 | 9.061513 | 1488.279333 | 0.000672 | 0.110357 | 164.241813 | 0.006089 | 408 |
| 35 | 9.668379 | 1600.316191 | 0.000625 | 0.103430 | 165.520625 | 0.006042 | 420 |
| 36 | 10.315889 | 1719.856364 | 0.000581 | 0.096938 | 166.719167 | 0.005998 | 432 |
| 37 | 11.006763 | 1847.402364 | 0.000541 | 0.090853 | 167.842480 | 0.005958 | 444 |
| 38 | 11.743906 | 1983.490356 | 0.000504 | 0.085151 | 168.895284 | 0.005921 | 456 |
| 39 | 12.530417 | 2128.692413 | 0.000470 | 0.079806 | 169.882006 | 0.005886 | 468 |
| 40 | 13.369602 | 2283.618920 | 0.000438 | 0.074797 | 170.806793 | 0.005855 | 480 |

7.00% ANNUAL INTEREST RATE          0.5833% MONTHLY EFFECTIVE INTEREST RATE

| | 1<br>Future Value<br>of $1 | 2<br>Future Value<br>Annuity of<br>$1 per Month | 3<br>Sinking<br>Fund<br>Factor | 4<br>Present Value<br>of $1<br>(Reversion) | 5<br>Present Value<br>Annuity of<br>$1 per Month | 6<br>Installment<br>to<br>Amortize $1 | |
|---|---|---|---|---|---|---|---|
| Months | | | | | | | Months |
| 1 | 1.005833 | 1.000000 | 1.000000 | 0.994200 | 0.994200 | 1.005833 | 1 |
| 2 | 1.011701 | 2.005833 | 0.498546 | 0.988435 | 1.982635 | 0.504379 | 2 |
| 3 | 1.017602 | 3.017534 | 0.331396 | 0.982702 | 2.965337 | 0.337230 | 3 |
| 4 | 1.023538 | 4.035136 | 0.247823 | 0.977003 | 3.942340 | 0.253656 | 4 |
| 5 | 1.029509 | 5.058675 | 0.197680 | 0.971337 | 4.913677 | 0.203514 | 5 |
| 6 | 1.035514 | 6.088184 | 0.164253 | 0.965704 | 5.879381 | 0.170086 | 6 |
| 7 | 1.041555 | 7.123698 | 0.140377 | 0.960103 | 6.839484 | 0.146210 | 7 |
| 8 | 1.047631 | 8.165253 | 0.122470 | 0.954535 | 7.794019 | 0.128304 | 8 |
| 9 | 1.053742 | 9.212883 | 0.108544 | 0.948999 | 8.743018 | 0.114377 | 9 |
| 10 | 1.059889 | 10.266625 | 0.097403 | 0.943495 | 9.686513 | 0.103236 | 10 |
| 11 | 1.066071 | 11.326514 | 0.088288 | 0.938024 | 10.624537 | 0.094122 | 11 |
| 12 | 1.072290 | 12.392585 | 0.080693 | 0.932583 | 11.557120 | 0.086527 | 12 |
| Years | | | | | | | Months |
| 1 | 1.072290 | 12.392585 | 0.080693 | 0.932583 | 11.557120 | 0.086527 | 12 |
| 2 | 1.149806 | 25.681032 | 0.038939 | 0.869712 | 22.335099 | 0.044773 | 24 |
| 3 | 1.232926 | 39.930101 | 0.025044 | 0.811079 | 32.386464 | 0.030877 | 36 |
| 4 | 1.322054 | 55.209236 | 0.018113 | 0.756399 | 41.760201 | 0.023946 | 48 |
| 5 | 1.417625 | 71.592902 | 0.013968 | 0.705405 | 50.501994 | 0.019801 | 60 |
| 6 | 1.520106 | 89.160944 | 0.011216 | 0.657849 | 58.654444 | 0.017049 | 72 |
| 7 | 1.629994 | 107.998981 | 0.009259 | 0.613499 | 66.257285 | 0.015093 | 84 |
| 8 | 1.747826 | 128.198821 | 0.007800 | 0.572139 | 73.347569 | 0.013634 | 96 |
| 9 | 1.874177 | 149.858909 | 0.006673 | 0.533568 | 79.959850 | 0.012506 | 108 |
| 10 | 2.009661 | 173.084807 | 0.005778 | 0.497596 | 86.126354 | 0.011611 | 120 |
| 11 | 2.154940 | 197.989707 | 0.005051 | 0.464050 | 91.877134 | 0.010884 | 132 |
| 12 | 2.310721 | 224.694985 | 0.004450 | 0.432765 | 97.240216 | 0.010284 | 144 |
| 13 | 2.477763 | 253.330789 | 0.003947 | 0.403590 | 102.241738 | 0.009781 | 156 |
| 14 | 2.656881 | 284.036677 | 0.003521 | 0.376381 | 106.906074 | 0.009354 | 168 |
| 15 | 2.848947 | 316.962297 | 0.003155 | 0.351007 | 111.255958 | 0.008988 | 180 |
| 16 | 3.054897 | 352.268112 | 0.002839 | 0.327343 | 115.312587 | 0.008672 | 192 |
| 17 | 3.275736 | 390.126188 | 0.002563 | 0.305275 | 119.095732 | 0.008397 | 204 |
| 18 | 3.512539 | 430.721027 | 0.002322 | 0.284694 | 122.623831 | 0.008155 | 216 |
| 19 | 3.766461 | 474.250470 | 0.002109 | 0.265501 | 125.914077 | 0.007942 | 228 |
| 20 | 4.038739 | 520.926660 | 0.001920 | 0.247602 | 128.982506 | 0.007753 | 240 |
| 21 | 4.330700 | 570.977075 | 0.001751 | 0.230910 | 131.844073 | 0.007585 | 252 |
| 22 | 4.643766 | 624.645640 | 0.001601 | 0.215342 | 134.512723 | 0.007434 | 264 |
| 23 | 4.979464 | 682.193009 | 0.001466 | 0.200825 | 137.001461 | 0.007299 | 276 |
| 24 | 5.339430 | 743.902347 | 0.001344 | 0.187286 | 139.322418 | 0.007178 | 288 |
| 25 | 5.725418 | 810.071693 | 0.001234 | 0.174660 | 141.486903 | 0.007068 | 300 |
| 26 | 6.139309 | 881.024427 | 0.001135 | 0.162885 | 143.505467 | 0.006968 | 312 |
| 27 | 6.583120 | 957.106339 | 0.001045 | 0.151904 | 145.387946 | 0.006878 | 324 |
| 28 | 7.059015 | 1038.688219 | 0.000963 | 0.141663 | 147.143515 | 0.006796 | 336 |
| 29 | 7.569311 | 1126.167659 | 0.000888 | 0.132112 | 148.780729 | 0.006721 | 348 |
| 30 | 8.116497 | 1219.970996 | 0.000820 | 0.123206 | 150.307568 | 0.006653 | 360 |
| 31 | 8.703240 | 1320.555383 | 0.000757 | 0.114900 | 151.731473 | 0.006591 | 372 |
| 32 | 9.332398 | 1428.411024 | 0.000700 | 0.107154 | 153.059383 | 0.006533 | 384 |
| 33 | 10.007037 | 1544.063557 | 0.000648 | 0.099930 | 154.297770 | 0.006481 | 396 |
| 34 | 10.730447 | 1668.076622 | 0.000599 | 0.093193 | 155.452669 | 0.006433 | 408 |
| 35 | 11.506152 | 1801.054601 | 0.000555 | 0.086910 | 156.529709 | 0.006389 | 420 |
| 36 | 12.337932 | 1943.645569 | 0.000514 | 0.081051 | 157.534139 | 0.006348 | 432 |
| 37 | 13.229843 | 2096.544450 | 0.000477 | 0.075587 | 158.470853 | 0.006310 | 444 |
| 38 | 14.186229 | 2260.496403 | 0.000442 | 0.070491 | 159.344418 | 0.006276 | 456 |
| 39 | 15.211753 | 2436.300456 | 0.000410 | 0.065739 | 160.159090 | 0.006244 | 468 |
| 40 | 16.311411 | 2624.813398 | 0.000381 | 0.061307 | 160.918839 | 0.006214 | 480 |

7.50% ANNUAL INTEREST RATE          0.6250% MONTHLY EFFECTIVE INTEREST RATE

| | 1<br>Future Value<br>of $1 | 2<br>Future Value<br>Annuity of<br>$1 per Month | 3<br>Sinking<br>Fund<br>Factor | 4<br>Present Value<br>of $1<br>(Reversion) | 5<br>Present Value<br>Annuity of<br>$1 per Month | 6<br>Installment<br>to<br>Amortize $1 | |
|---|---|---|---|---|---|---|---|
| Months | | | | | | | Months |
| 1 | 1.006250 | 1.000000 | 1.000000 | 0.993789 | 0.993789 | 1.006250 | 1 |
| 2 | 1.012539 | 2.006250 | 0.498442 | 0.987616 | 1.981405 | 0.504692 | 2 |
| 3 | 1.018867 | 3.018789 | 0.331259 | 0.981482 | 2.962887 | 0.337509 | 3 |
| 4 | 1.025235 | 4.037656 | 0.247668 | 0.975386 | 3.938273 | 0.253918 | 4 |
| 5 | 1.031643 | 5.062892 | 0.197516 | 0.969327 | 4.907600 | 0.203766 | 5 |
| 6 | 1.038091 | 6.094535 | 0.164081 | 0.963307 | 5.870907 | 0.170331 | 6 |
| 7 | 1.044579 | 7.132626 | 0.140201 | 0.957324 | 6.828231 | 0.146451 | 7 |
| 8 | 1.051108 | 8.177205 | 0.122291 | 0.951377 | 7.779608 | 0.128541 | 8 |
| 9 | 1.057677 | 9.228312 | 0.108362 | 0.945468 | 8.725076 | 0.114612 | 9 |
| 10 | 1.064287 | 10.285989 | 0.097220 | 0.939596 | 9.664672 | 0.103470 | 10 |
| 11 | 1.070939 | 11.350277 | 0.088104 | 0.933760 | 10.598432 | 0.094354 | 11 |
| 12 | 1.077633 | 12.421216 | 0.080507 | 0.927960 | 11.526392 | 0.086757 | 12 |
| Years | | | | | | | Months |
| 1 | 1.077633 | 12.421216 | 0.080507 | 0.927960 | 11.526392 | 0.086757 | 12 |
| 2 | 1.161292 | 25.806723 | 0.038750 | 0.861110 | 22.222423 | 0.045000 | 24 |
| 3 | 1.251446 | 40.231382 | 0.024856 | 0.799076 | 32.147913 | 0.031106 | 36 |
| 4 | 1.348599 | 55.775864 | 0.017929 | 0.741510 | 41.358371 | 0.024179 | 48 |
| 5 | 1.453294 | 72.527105 | 0.013788 | 0.688092 | 49.905308 | 0.020038 | 60 |
| 6 | 1.566117 | 90.578789 | 0.011040 | 0.638522 | 57.836524 | 0.017290 | 72 |
| 7 | 1.687699 | 110.031871 | 0.009088 | 0.592523 | 65.196376 | 0.015338 | 84 |
| 8 | 1.818720 | 130.995147 | 0.007634 | 0.549837 | 72.026024 | 0.013884 | 96 |
| 9 | 1.959912 | 153.585857 | 0.006511 | 0.510227 | 78.363665 | 0.012761 | 108 |
| 10 | 2.112065 | 177.930342 | 0.005620 | 0.473470 | 84.244743 | 0.011870 | 120 |
| 11 | 2.276030 | 204.164753 | 0.004898 | 0.439362 | 89.702148 | 0.011148 | 132 |
| 12 | 2.452724 | 232.435809 | 0.004302 | 0.407710 | 94.766401 | 0.010552 | 144 |
| 13 | 2.643135 | 262.901620 | 0.003804 | 0.378339 | 99.465827 | 0.010054 | 156 |
| 14 | 2.848329 | 295.732572 | 0.003381 | 0.351083 | 103.826706 | 0.009631 | 168 |
| 15 | 3.069452 | 331.112276 | 0.003020 | 0.325791 | 107.873427 | 0.009270 | 180 |
| 16 | 3.307741 | 369.238599 | 0.002708 | 0.302321 | 111.628623 | 0.008958 | 192 |
| 17 | 3.564530 | 410.324767 | 0.002437 | 0.280542 | 115.113294 | 0.008687 | 204 |
| 18 | 3.841254 | 454.600560 | 0.002200 | 0.260332 | 118.346930 | 0.008450 | 216 |
| 19 | 4.139460 | 502.313599 | 0.001991 | 0.241577 | 121.347615 | 0.008241 | 228 |
| 20 | 4.460817 | 553.730725 | 0.001806 | 0.224174 | 124.132131 | 0.008056 | 240 |
| 21 | 4.807122 | 609.139496 | 0.001642 | 0.208025 | 126.716051 | 0.007892 | 252 |
| 22 | 5.180311 | 668.849794 | 0.001495 | 0.193039 | 129.113825 | 0.007745 | 264 |
| 23 | 5.582472 | 733.195558 | 0.001364 | 0.179132 | 131.338863 | 0.007614 | 276 |
| 24 | 6.015854 | 802.536650 | 0.001246 | 0.166227 | 133.403610 | 0.007496 | 288 |
| 25 | 6.482880 | 877.260872 | 0.001140 | 0.154252 | 135.319613 | 0.007390 | 300 |
| 26 | 6.986163 | 957.786129 | 0.001044 | 0.143140 | 137.097587 | 0.007294 | 312 |
| 27 | 7.528517 | 1044.562771 | 0.000957 | 0.132828 | 138.747475 | 0.007207 | 324 |
| 28 | 8.112976 | 1138.076109 | 0.000879 | 0.123259 | 140.278506 | 0.007129 | 336 |
| 29 | 8.742807 | 1238.849131 | 0.000807 | 0.114380 | 141.699242 | 0.007057 | 348 |
| 30 | 9.421534 | 1347.445425 | 0.000742 | 0.106140 | 143.017627 | 0.006992 | 360 |
| 31 | 10.152952 | 1464.472331 | 0.000683 | 0.098494 | 144.241037 | 0.006933 | 372 |
| 32 | 10.941152 | 1590.584340 | 0.000629 | 0.091398 | 145.376312 | 0.006879 | 384 |
| 33 | 11.790542 | 1726.486751 | 0.000579 | 0.084814 | 146.429801 | 0.006829 | 396 |
| 34 | 12.705873 | 1872.939621 | 0.000534 | 0.078704 | 147.407398 | 0.006784 | 408 |
| 35 | 13.692263 | 2030.762007 | 0.000492 | 0.073034 | 148.314568 | 0.006742 | 420 |
| 36 | 14.755228 | 2200.836555 | 0.000454 | 0.067773 | 149.156386 | 0.006704 | 432 |
| 37 | 15.900715 | 2384.114432 | 0.000419 | 0.062890 | 149.937560 | 0.006669 | 444 |
| 38 | 17.135129 | 2581.620647 | 0.000387 | 0.058360 | 150.662457 | 0.006637 | 456 |
| 39 | 18.465374 | 2794.459783 | 0.000358 | 0.054155 | 151.335133 | 0.006608 | 468 |
| 40 | 19.898889 | 3023.822174 | 0.000331 | 0.050254 | 151.959350 | 0.006581 | 480 |

8.00% ANNUAL INTEREST RATE                    0.6667% MONTHLY EFFECTIVE INTEREST RATE

| | 1<br>Future Value<br>of $1 | 2<br>Future Value<br>Annuity of<br>$1 per Month | 3<br>Sinking<br>Fund<br>Factor | 4<br>Present Value<br>of $1<br>(Reversion) | 5<br>Present Value<br>Annuity of<br>$1 per Month | 6<br>Installment<br>to<br>Amortize $1 | |
|---|---|---|---|---|---|---|---|
| Months | | | | | | | Months |
| 1 | 1.006667 | 1.000000 | 1.000000 | 0.993377 | 0.993377 | 1.006667 | 1 |
| 2 | 1.013378 | 2.006667 | 0.498339 | 0.986799 | 1.980176 | 0.505006 | 2 |
| 3 | 1.020134 | 3.020044 | 0.331121 | 0.980264 | 2.960440 | 0.337788 | 3 |
| 4 | 1.026935 | 4.040178 | 0.247514 | 0.973772 | 3.934212 | 0.254181 | 4 |
| 5 | 1.033781 | 5.067113 | 0.197351 | 0.967323 | 4.901535 | 0.204018 | 5 |
| 6 | 1.040673 | 6.100893 | 0.163910 | 0.960917 | 5.862452 | 0.170577 | 6 |
| 7 | 1.047610 | 7.141566 | 0.140025 | 0.954553 | 6.817005 | 0.146692 | 7 |
| 8 | 1.054595 | 8.189176 | 0.122112 | 0.948232 | 7.765237 | 0.128779 | 8 |
| 9 | 1.061625 | 9.243771 | 0.108181 | 0.941952 | 8.707189 | 0.114848 | 9 |
| 10 | 1.068703 | 10.305396 | 0.097037 | 0.935714 | 9.642903 | 0.103703 | 10 |
| 11 | 1.075827 | 11.374099 | 0.087919 | 0.929517 | 10.572420 | 0.094586 | 11 |
| 12 | 1.083000 | 12.449926 | 0.080322 | 0.923361 | 11.495782 | 0.086988 | 12 |
| Years | | | | | | | Months |
| 1 | 1.083000 | 12.449926 | 0.080322 | 0.923361 | 11.495782 | 0.086988 | 12 |
| 2 | 1.172888 | 25.933190 | 0.038561 | 0.852596 | 22.110544 | 0.045227 | 24 |
| 3 | 1.270237 | 40.535558 | 0.024670 | 0.787255 | 31.911806 | 0.031336 | 36 |
| 4 | 1.375666 | 56.349915 | 0.017746 | 0.726921 | 40.961913 | 0.024413 | 48 |
| 5 | 1.489846 | 73.476856 | 0.013610 | 0.671210 | 49.318433 | 0.020276 | 60 |
| 6 | 1.613502 | 92.025325 | 0.010867 | 0.619770 | 57.034522 | 0.017533 | 72 |
| 7 | 1.747422 | 112.113308 | 0.008920 | 0.572272 | 64.159261 | 0.015586 | 84 |
| 8 | 1.892457 | 133.868583 | 0.007470 | 0.528414 | 70.737970 | 0.014137 | 96 |
| 9 | 2.049530 | 157.429535 | 0.006352 | 0.487917 | 76.812497 | 0.013019 | 108 |
| 10 | 2.219640 | 182.946035 | 0.005466 | 0.450523 | 82.421481 | 0.012133 | 120 |
| 11 | 2.403869 | 210.580392 | 0.004749 | 0.415996 | 87.600600 | 0.011415 | 132 |
| 12 | 2.603389 | 240.508387 | 0.004158 | 0.384115 | 92.382800 | 0.010825 | 144 |
| 13 | 2.819469 | 272.920390 | 0.003664 | 0.354677 | 96.798498 | 0.010331 | 156 |
| 14 | 3.053484 | 308.022574 | 0.003247 | 0.327495 | 100.875784 | 0.009913 | 168 |
| 15 | 3.306921 | 346.038222 | 0.002890 | 0.302396 | 104.640592 | 0.009557 | 180 |
| 16 | 3.581394 | 387.209149 | 0.002583 | 0.279221 | 108.116871 | 0.009249 | 192 |
| 17 | 3.878648 | 431.797244 | 0.002316 | 0.257822 | 111.326733 | 0.008983 | 204 |
| 18 | 4.200574 | 480.086128 | 0.002083 | 0.238063 | 114.290596 | 0.008750 | 216 |
| 19 | 4.549220 | 532.382966 | 0.001878 | 0.219818 | 117.027313 | 0.008545 | 228 |
| 20 | 4.926803 | 589.020416 | 0.001698 | 0.202971 | 119.554292 | 0.008364 | 240 |
| 21 | 5.335725 | 650.358746 | 0.001538 | 0.187416 | 121.887606 | 0.008204 | 252 |
| 22 | 5.778588 | 716.788127 | 0.001395 | 0.173053 | 124.042099 | 0.008062 | 264 |
| 23 | 6.258207 | 788.731114 | 0.001268 | 0.159790 | 126.031475 | 0.007935 | 276 |
| 24 | 6.777636 | 866.645333 | 0.001154 | 0.147544 | 127.868388 | 0.007821 | 288 |
| 25 | 7.340176 | 951.026395 | 0.001051 | 0.136237 | 129.564523 | 0.007718 | 300 |
| 26 | 7.949407 | 1042.411042 | 0.000959 | 0.125796 | 131.130668 | 0.007626 | 312 |
| 27 | 8.609204 | 1141.380571 | 0.000876 | 0.116155 | 132.576786 | 0.007543 | 324 |
| 28 | 9.323763 | 1248.564521 | 0.000801 | 0.107253 | 133.912076 | 0.007468 | 336 |
| 29 | 10.097631 | 1364.644687 | 0.000733 | 0.099033 | 135.145031 | 0.007399 | 348 |
| 30 | 10.935730 | 1490.359449 | 0.000671 | 0.091443 | 136.283494 | 0.007338 | 360 |
| 31 | 11.843390 | 1626.508474 | 0.000615 | 0.084435 | 137.334707 | 0.007281 | 372 |
| 32 | 12.826385 | 1773.957801 | 0.000564 | 0.077964 | 138.305357 | 0.007230 | 384 |
| 33 | 13.890969 | 1933.645350 | 0.000517 | 0.071989 | 139.201617 | 0.007184 | 396 |
| 34 | 15.043913 | 2106.586886 | 0.000475 | 0.066472 | 140.029190 | 0.007141 | 408 |
| 35 | 16.292550 | 2293.882485 | 0.000436 | 0.061378 | 140.793338 | 0.007103 | 420 |
| 36 | 17.644824 | 2496.723526 | 0.000401 | 0.056674 | 141.498923 | 0.007067 | 432 |
| 37 | 19.109335 | 2716.400273 | 0.000368 | 0.052330 | 142.150433 | 0.007035 | 444 |
| 38 | 20.695401 | 2954.310082 | 0.000338 | 0.048320 | 142.752013 | 0.007005 | 456 |
| 39 | 22.413109 | 3211.966288 | 0.000311 | 0.044617 | 143.307488 | 0.006978 | 468 |
| 40 | 24.273386 | 3491.007831 | 0.000286 | 0.041197 | 143.820392 | 0.006953 | 480 |

8.50% ANNUAL INTEREST RATE          0.7083% MONTHLY EFFECTIVE INTEREST RATE

| | 1 | 2 | 3 | 4 | 5 | 6 | |
|---|---|---|---|---|---|---|---|
| | Future Value of $1 | Future Value Annuity of $1 per Month | Sinking Fund Factor | Present Value of $1 (Reversion) | Present Value Annuity of $1 per Month | Installment to Amortize $1 | |
| Months | | | | | | | Months |
| 1 | 1.007083 | 1.000000 | 1.000000 | 0.992966 | 0.992966 | 1.007083 | 1 |
| 2 | 1.014217 | 2.007083 | 0.498235 | 0.985982 | 1.978949 | 0.505319 | 2 |
| 3 | 1.021401 | 3.021300 | 0.330983 | 0.979048 | 2.957996 | 0.338067 | 3 |
| 4 | 1.028636 | 4.042701 | 0.247359 | 0.972161 | 3.930158 | 0.254443 | 4 |
| 5 | 1.035922 | 5.071337 | 0.197187 | 0.965324 | 4.895482 | 0.204270 | 5 |
| 6 | 1.043260 | 6.107259 | 0.163740 | 0.958534 | 5.854016 | 0.170823 | 6 |
| 7 | 1.050650 | 7.150519 | 0.139850 | 0.951792 | 6.805808 | 0.146933 | 7 |
| 8 | 1.058092 | 8.201168 | 0.121934 | 0.945098 | 7.750906 | 0.129017 | 8 |
| 9 | 1.065586 | 9.259260 | 0.108000 | 0.938450 | 8.689356 | 0.115083 | 9 |
| 10 | 1.073134 | 10.324846 | 0.096854 | 0.931850 | 9.621206 | 0.103937 | 10 |
| 11 | 1.080736 | 11.397980 | 0.087735 | 0.925296 | 10.546501 | 0.094818 | 11 |
| 12 | 1.088391 | 12.478716 | 0.080136 | 0.918788 | 11.465289 | 0.087220 | 12 |
| Years | | | | | | | Months |
| 1 | 1.088391 | 12.478716 | 0.080136 | 0.918788 | 11.465289 | 0.087220 | 12 |
| 2 | 1.184595 | 26.060437 | 0.038372 | 0.844171 | 21.999453 | 0.045456 | 24 |
| 3 | 1.289302 | 40.842659 | 0.024484 | 0.775613 | 31.678112 | 0.031568 | 36 |
| 4 | 1.403265 | 56.931495 | 0.017565 | 0.712624 | 40.570744 | 0.024648 | 48 |
| 5 | 1.527301 | 74.442437 | 0.013433 | 0.654750 | 48.741183 | 0.020517 | 60 |
| 6 | 1.662300 | 93.501188 | 0.010695 | 0.601576 | 56.248080 | 0.017778 | 72 |
| 7 | 1.809232 | 114.244559 | 0.008753 | 0.552721 | 63.145324 | 0.015836 | 84 |
| 8 | 1.969152 | 136.821455 | 0.007309 | 0.507833 | 69.482425 | 0.014392 | 96 |
| 9 | 2.143207 | 161.393943 | 0.006196 | 0.466590 | 75.304875 | 0.013279 | 108 |
| 10 | 2.332647 | 188.138416 | 0.005315 | 0.428698 | 80.654470 | 0.012399 | 120 |
| 11 | 2.538832 | 217.246858 | 0.004603 | 0.393882 | 85.569611 | 0.011686 | 132 |
| 12 | 2.763242 | 248.928220 | 0.004017 | 0.361894 | 90.085581 | 0.011101 | 144 |
| 13 | 3.007487 | 283.409927 | 0.003528 | 0.332504 | 94.234798 | 0.010612 | 156 |
| 14 | 3.273321 | 320.939504 | 0.003116 | 0.305500 | 98.047046 | 0.010199 | 168 |
| 15 | 3.562653 | 361.786353 | 0.002764 | 0.280690 | 101.549693 | 0.009847 | 180 |
| 16 | 3.877559 | 406.243693 | 0.002462 | 0.257894 | 104.767881 | 0.009545 | 192 |
| 17 | 4.220300 | 454.630657 | 0.002200 | 0.236950 | 107.724713 | 0.009283 | 204 |
| 18 | 4.593337 | 507.294589 | 0.001971 | 0.217707 | 110.441412 | 0.009055 | 216 |
| 19 | 4.999346 | 564.613533 | 0.001771 | 0.200026 | 112.937482 | 0.008854 | 228 |
| 20 | 5.441243 | 626.998951 | 0.001595 | 0.183782 | 115.230840 | 0.008678 | 240 |
| 21 | 5.922199 | 694.898672 | 0.001439 | 0.168856 | 117.337948 | 0.008522 | 252 |
| 22 | 6.445667 | 768.800112 | 0.001301 | 0.155143 | 119.273933 | 0.008384 | 264 |
| 23 | 7.015406 | 849.233766 | 0.001178 | 0.142543 | 121.052692 | 0.008261 | 276 |
| 24 | 7.635504 | 936.777024 | 0.001067 | 0.130967 | 122.686994 | 0.008151 | 288 |
| 25 | 8.310413 | 1032.058310 | 0.000969 | 0.120331 | 124.188570 | 0.008052 | 300 |
| 26 | 9.044978 | 1135.761595 | 0.000880 | 0.110559 | 125.568199 | 0.007964 | 312 |
| 27 | 9.844472 | 1248.631307 | 0.000801 | 0.101580 | 126.835785 | 0.007884 | 324 |
| 28 | 10.714634 | 1371.477676 | 0.000729 | 0.093330 | 128.000428 | 0.007812 | 336 |
| 29 | 11.661710 | 1505.182546 | 0.000664 | 0.085751 | 129.070487 | 0.007748 | 348 |
| 30 | 12.692499 | 1650.705711 | 0.000606 | 0.078787 | 130.053643 | 0.007689 | 360 |
| 31 | 13.814400 | 1809.091800 | 0.000553 | 0.072388 | 130.956956 | 0.007636 | 372 |
| 32 | 15.035468 | 1981.477780 | 0.000505 | 0.066509 | 131.786908 | 0.007588 | 384 |
| 33 | 16.364466 | 2169.101112 | 0.000461 | 0.061108 | 132.549457 | 0.007544 | 396 |
| 34 | 17.810936 | 2373.308640 | 0.000421 | 0.056145 | 133.250078 | 0.007505 | 408 |
| 35 | 19.385261 | 2595.566257 | 0.000385 | 0.051586 | 133.893800 | 0.007469 | 420 |
| 36 | 21.098742 | 2837.469426 | 0.000352 | 0.047396 | 134.485244 | 0.007436 | 432 |
| 37 | 22.963679 | 3100.754635 | 0.000323 | 0.043547 | 135.028655 | 0.007406 | 444 |
| 38 | 24.993459 | 3387.311862 | 0.000295 | 0.040010 | 135.527934 | 0.007379 | 456 |
| 39 | 27.202654 | 3699.198142 | 0.000270 | 0.036761 | 135.986665 | 0.007354 | 468 |
| 40 | 29.607121 | 4038.652333 | 0.000248 | 0.033776 | 136.408142 | 0.007331 | 480 |

9.00% ANNUAL INTEREST RATE              0.7500% MONTHLY EFFECTIVE INTEREST RATE

| | 1 | 2 | 3 | 4 | 5 | 6 | |
|---|---|---|---|---|---|---|---|
| | Future Value of $1 | Future Value Annuity of $1 per Month | Sinking Fund Factor | Present Value of $1 (Reversion) | Present Value Annuity of $1 per Month | Installment to Amortize $1 | |
| Months | | | | | | | Months |
| 1 | 1.007500 | 1.000000 | 1.000000 | 0.992556 | 0.992556 | 1.007500 | 1 |
| 2 | 1.015056 | 2.007500 | 0.498132 | 0.985167 | 1.977723 | 0.505632 | 2 |
| 3 | 1.022669 | 3.022556 | 0.330846 | 0.977833 | 2.955556 | 0.338346 | 3 |
| 4 | 1.030339 | 4.045225 | 0.247205 | 0.970554 | 3.926110 | 0.254705 | 4 |
| 5 | 1.038067 | 5.075565 | 0.197022 | 0.963329 | 4.889440 | 0.204522 | 5 |
| 6 | 1.045852 | 6.113631 | 0.163569 | 0.956158 | 5.845598 | 0.171069 | 6 |
| 7 | 1.053696 | 7.159484 | 0.139675 | 0.949040 | 6.794638 | 0.147175 | 7 |
| 8 | 1.061599 | 8.213180 | 0.121756 | 0.941975 | 7.736613 | 0.129256 | 8 |
| 9 | 1.069561 | 9.274779 | 0.107819 | 0.934963 | 8.671576 | 0.115319 | 9 |
| 10 | 1.077583 | 10.344339 | 0.096671 | 0.928003 | 9.599580 | 0.104171 | 10 |
| 11 | 1.085664 | 11.421922 | 0.087551 | 0.921095 | 10.520675 | 0.095051 | 11 |
| 12 | 1.093807 | 12.507586 | 0.079951 | 0.914238 | 11.434913 | 0.087451 | 12 |
| Years | | | | | | | Months |
| 1 | 1.093807 | 12.507586 | 0.079951 | 0.914238 | 11.434913 | 0.087451 | 12 |
| 2 | 1.196414 | 26.188471 | 0.038185 | 0.835831 | 21.889146 | 0.045685 | 24 |
| 3 | 1.308645 | 41.152716 | 0.024300 | 0.764149 | 31.446805 | 0.031800 | 36 |
| 4 | 1.431405 | 57.520711 | 0.017385 | 0.698614 | 40.184782 | 0.024885 | 48 |
| 5 | 1.565681 | 75.424137 | 0.013258 | 0.638700 | 48.173374 | 0.020758 | 60 |
| 6 | 1.712553 | 95.007028 | 0.010526 | 0.583924 | 55.476849 | 0.018026 | 72 |
| 7 | 1.873202 | 116.426928 | 0.008589 | 0.533845 | 62.153965 | 0.016089 | 84 |
| 8 | 2.048921 | 139.856164 | 0.007150 | 0.488062 | 68.258439 | 0.014650 | 96 |
| 9 | 2.241124 | 165.483223 | 0.006043 | 0.446205 | 73.839382 | 0.013543 | 108 |
| 10 | 2.451357 | 193.514277 | 0.005168 | 0.407937 | 78.941693 | 0.012668 | 120 |
| 11 | 2.681311 | 224.174837 | 0.004461 | 0.372952 | 83.606420 | 0.011961 | 132 |
| 12 | 2.932837 | 257.711570 | 0.003880 | 0.340967 | 87.871092 | 0.011380 | 144 |
| 13 | 3.207957 | 294.394279 | 0.003397 | 0.311725 | 91.770018 | 0.010897 | 156 |
| 14 | 3.508886 | 334.518079 | 0.002989 | 0.284991 | 95.334564 | 0.010489 | 168 |
| 15 | 3.838043 | 378.405769 | 0.002643 | 0.260549 | 98.593409 | 0.010143 | 180 |
| 16 | 4.198078 | 426.410427 | 0.002345 | 0.238204 | 101.572769 | 0.009845 | 192 |
| 17 | 4.591887 | 478.918252 | 0.002088 | 0.217775 | 104.296613 | 0.009588 | 204 |
| 18 | 5.022638 | 536.351674 | 0.001864 | 0.199099 | 106.786856 | 0.009364 | 216 |
| 19 | 5.493796 | 599.172747 | 0.001669 | 0.182024 | 109.063531 | 0.009169 | 228 |
| 20 | 6.009152 | 667.886870 | 0.001497 | 0.166413 | 111.144954 | 0.008997 | 240 |
| 21 | 6.572851 | 743.046852 | 0.001346 | 0.152141 | 113.047870 | 0.008846 | 252 |
| 22 | 7.189430 | 825.257358 | 0.001212 | 0.139093 | 114.787589 | 0.008712 | 264 |
| 23 | 7.863848 | 915.179777 | 0.001093 | 0.127164 | 116.378106 | 0.008593 | 276 |
| 24 | 8.601532 | 1013.537539 | 0.000987 | 0.116258 | 117.832218 | 0.008487 | 288 |
| 25 | 9.408415 | 1121.121937 | 0.000892 | 0.106288 | 119.161622 | 0.008392 | 300 |
| 26 | 10.290989 | 1238.798495 | 0.000807 | 0.097172 | 120.377014 | 0.008307 | 312 |
| 27 | 11.256354 | 1367.513924 | 0.000731 | 0.088839 | 121.488172 | 0.008231 | 324 |
| 28 | 12.312278 | 1508.303750 | 0.000663 | 0.081220 | 122.504035 | 0.008163 | 336 |
| 29 | 13.467255 | 1662.300631 | 0.000602 | 0.074254 | 123.432776 | 0.008102 | 348 |
| 30 | 14.730576 | 1830.743483 | 0.000546 | 0.067886 | 124.281866 | 0.008046 | 360 |
| 31 | 16.112406 | 2014.987436 | 0.000496 | 0.062064 | 125.058136 | 0.007996 | 372 |
| 32 | 17.623861 | 2216.514743 | 0.000451 | 0.056741 | 125.767832 | 0.007951 | 384 |
| 33 | 19.277100 | 2436.946701 | 0.000410 | 0.051875 | 126.416664 | 0.007910 | 396 |
| 34 | 21.085425 | 2678.056697 | 0.000373 | 0.047426 | 127.009850 | 0.007873 | 408 |
| 35 | 23.063384 | 2941.784474 | 0.000340 | 0.043359 | 127.552164 | 0.007840 | 420 |
| 36 | 25.226888 | 3230.251735 | 0.000310 | 0.039640 | 128.047967 | 0.007810 | 432 |
| 37 | 27.593344 | 3545.779215 | 0.000282 | 0.036241 | 128.501250 | 0.007782 | 444 |
| 38 | 30.181790 | 3890.905350 | 0.000257 | 0.033133 | 128.915659 | 0.007757 | 456 |
| 39 | 33.013050 | 4268.406696 | 0.000234 | 0.030291 | 129.294526 | 0.007734 | 468 |
| 40 | 36.109902 | 4681.320273 | 0.000214 | 0.027693 | 129.640902 | 0.007714 | 480 |

9.50% ANNUAL INTEREST RATE          0.7917% MONTHLY EFFECTIVE INTEREST RATE

| | 1<br>Future Value<br>of $1 | 2<br>Future Value<br>Annuity of<br>$1 per Month | 3<br>Sinking<br>Fund<br>Factor | 4<br>Present Value<br>of $1<br>(Reversion) | 5<br>Present Value<br>Annuity of<br>$1 per Month | 6<br>Installment<br>to<br>Amortize $1 | |
|---|---|---|---|---|---|---|---|
| Months | | | | | | | Months |
| 1 | 1.007917 | 1.000000 | 1.000000 | 0.992146 | 0.992146 | 1.007917 | 1 |
| 2 | 1.015896 | 2.007917 | 0.498029 | 0.984353 | 1.976498 | 0.505945 | 2 |
| 3 | 1.023939 | 3.023813 | 0.330708 | 0.976621 | 2.953119 | 0.338625 | 3 |
| 4 | 1.032045 | 4.047751 | 0.247051 | 0.968950 | 3.922070 | 0.254967 | 4 |
| 5 | 1.040215 | 5.079796 | 0.196858 | 0.961340 | 4.883409 | 0.204775 | 5 |
| 6 | 1.048450 | 6.120011 | 0.163398 | 0.953789 | 5.837198 | 0.171315 | 6 |
| 7 | 1.056750 | 7.168461 | 0.139500 | 0.946297 | 6.783496 | 0.147417 | 7 |
| 8 | 1.065116 | 8.225211 | 0.121577 | 0.938865 | 7.722360 | 0.129494 | 8 |
| 9 | 1.073548 | 9.290328 | 0.107639 | 0.931490 | 8.653851 | 0.115555 | 9 |
| 10 | 1.082047 | 10.363876 | 0.096489 | 0.924174 | 9.578024 | 0.104406 | 10 |
| 11 | 1.090614 | 11.445923 | 0.087367 | 0.916915 | 10.494940 | 0.095284 | 11 |
| 12 | 1.099248 | 12.536537 | 0.079767 | 0.909713 | 11.404653 | 0.087684 | 12 |
| Years | | | | | | | Months |
| 1 | 1.099248 | 12.536537 | 0.079767 | 0.909713 | 11.404653 | 0.087684 | 12 |
| 2 | 1.208345 | 26.317295 | 0.037998 | 0.827578 | 21.779615 | 0.045914 | 24 |
| 3 | 1.328271 | 41.465760 | 0.024116 | 0.752859 | 31.217856 | 0.032033 | 36 |
| 4 | 1.460098 | 58.117673 | 0.017206 | 0.684885 | 39.803947 | 0.025123 | 48 |
| 5 | 1.605009 | 76.422249 | 0.013085 | 0.623049 | 47.614827 | 0.021002 | 60 |
| 6 | 1.764303 | 96.543509 | 0.010358 | 0.566796 | 54.720488 | 0.018275 | 72 |
| 7 | 1.939406 | 118.661756 | 0.008427 | 0.515622 | 61.184601 | 0.016344 | 84 |
| 8 | 2.131887 | 142.975186 | 0.006994 | 0.469068 | 67.065090 | 0.014911 | 96 |
| 9 | 2.343472 | 169.701665 | 0.005893 | 0.426717 | 72.414648 | 0.013809 | 108 |
| 10 | 2.576055 | 199.080682 | 0.005023 | 0.388190 | 77.281211 | 0.012940 | 120 |
| 11 | 2.831723 | 231.375495 | 0.004322 | 0.353142 | 81.708388 | 0.012239 | 132 |
| 12 | 3.112764 | 266.875491 | 0.003747 | 0.321258 | 85.735849 | 0.011664 | 144 |
| 13 | 3.421699 | 305.898776 | 0.003269 | 0.292253 | 89.399684 | 0.011186 | 156 |
| 14 | 3.761294 | 348.795027 | 0.002867 | 0.265866 | 92.732722 | 0.010784 | 168 |
| 15 | 4.134593 | 395.948628 | 0.002526 | 0.241862 | 95.764831 | 0.010442 | 180 |
| 16 | 4.544942 | 447.782110 | 0.002233 | 0.220025 | 98.523180 | 0.010150 | 192 |
| 17 | 4.996016 | 504.759939 | 0.001981 | 0.200159 | 101.032487 | 0.009898 | 204 |
| 18 | 5.491859 | 567.392681 | 0.001762 | 0.182088 | 103.315236 | 0.009679 | 216 |
| 19 | 6.036912 | 636.241570 | 0.001572 | 0.165648 | 105.391883 | 0.009488 | 228 |
| 20 | 6.636061 | 711.923546 | 0.001405 | 0.150692 | 107.281037 | 0.009321 | 240 |
| 21 | 7.294674 | 795.116775 | 0.001258 | 0.137086 | 108.999624 | 0.009174 | 252 |
| 22 | 8.018653 | 886.566731 | 0.001128 | 0.124709 | 110.563046 | 0.009045 | 264 |
| 23 | 8.814485 | 987.092874 | 0.001013 | 0.113450 | 111.985311 | 0.008930 | 276 |
| 24 | 9.689302 | 1097.595994 | 0.000911 | 0.103207 | 113.279165 | 0.008828 | 288 |
| 25 | 10.650941 | 1219.066282 | 0.000820 | 0.093888 | 114.456200 | 0.008737 | 300 |
| 26 | 11.708022 | 1352.592202 | 0.000739 | 0.085412 | 115.526965 | 0.008656 | 312 |
| 27 | 12.870014 | 1499.370247 | 0.000667 | 0.077700 | 116.501054 | 0.008584 | 324 |
| 28 | 14.147332 | 1660.715659 | 0.000602 | 0.070685 | 117.387195 | 0.008519 | 336 |
| 29 | 15.551421 | 1838.074212 | 0.000544 | 0.064303 | 118.193330 | 0.008461 | 348 |
| 30 | 17.094862 | 2033.035174 | 0.000492 | 0.058497 | 118.926681 | 0.008409 | 360 |
| 31 | 18.791486 | 2247.345541 | 0.000445 | 0.053216 | 119.593820 | 0.008362 | 372 |
| 32 | 20.656495 | 2482.925693 | 0.000403 | 0.048411 | 120.200725 | 0.008319 | 384 |
| 33 | 22.706602 | 2741.886607 | 0.000365 | 0.044040 | 120.752835 | 0.008281 | 396 |
| 34 | 24.960178 | 3026.548765 | 0.000330 | 0.040064 | 121.255097 | 0.008247 | 408 |
| 35 | 27.437415 | 3339.462955 | 0.000299 | 0.036447 | 121.712011 | 0.008216 | 420 |
| 36 | 30.160512 | 3683.433122 | 0.000271 | 0.033156 | 122.127671 | 0.008188 | 432 |
| 37 | 33.153870 | 4061.541498 | 0.000246 | 0.030162 | 122.505803 | 0.008163 | 444 |
| 38 | 36.444312 | 4477.176216 | 0.000223 | 0.027439 | 122.849795 | 0.008140 | 456 |
| 39 | 40.061322 | 4934.061676 | 0.000203 | 0.024962 | 123.162729 | 0.008119 | 468 |
| 40 | 44.037311 | 5436.291914 | 0.000184 | 0.022708 | 123.447408 | 0.008101 | 480 |

10.00% ANNUAL INTEREST RATE          0.8333% MONTHLY EFFECTIVE INTEREST RATE

| | 1<br>Future Value<br>of $1 | 2<br>Future Value<br>Annuity of<br>$1 per Month | 3<br>Sinking<br>Fund<br>Factor | 4<br>Present Value<br>of $1<br>(Reversion) | 5<br>Present Value<br>Annuity of<br>$1 per Month | 6<br>Installment<br>to<br>Amortize $1 | |
|---|---|---|---|---|---|---|---|
| Months | | | | | | | Months |
| 1 | 1.008333 | 1.000000 | 1.000000 | 0.991736 | 0.991736 | 1.008333 | 1 |
| 2 | 1.016736 | 2.008333 | 0.497925 | 0.983539 | 1.975275 | 0.506259 | 2 |
| 3 | 1.025209 | 3.025069 | 0.330571 | 0.975411 | 2.950686 | 0.338904 | 3 |
| 4 | 1.033752 | 4.050278 | 0.246897 | 0.967350 | 3.918036 | 0.255230 | 4 |
| 5 | 1.042367 | 5.084031 | 0.196694 | 0.959355 | 4.877391 | 0.205028 | 5 |
| 6 | 1.051053 | 6.126398 | 0.163228 | 0.951427 | 5.828817 | 0.171561 | 6 |
| 7 | 1.059812 | 7.177451 | 0.139325 | 0.943563 | 6.772381 | 0.147659 | 7 |
| 8 | 1.068644 | 8.237263 | 0.121400 | 0.935765 | 7.708146 | 0.129733 | 8 |
| 9 | 1.077549 | 9.305907 | 0.107459 | 0.928032 | 8.636178 | 0.115792 | 9 |
| 10 | 1.086529 | 10.383456 | 0.096307 | 0.920362 | 9.556540 | 0.104640 | 10 |
| 11 | 1.095583 | 11.469985 | 0.087184 | 0.912756 | 10.469296 | 0.095517 | 11 |
| 12 | 1.104713 | 12.565568 | 0.079583 | 0.905212 | 11.374508 | 0.087916 | 12 |
| Years | | | | | | | Months |
| 1 | 1.104713 | 12.565568 | 0.079583 | 0.905212 | 11.374508 | 0.087916 | 12 |
| 2 | 1.220391 | 26.446915 | 0.037812 | 0.819410 | 21.670855 | 0.046145 | 24 |
| 3 | 1.348182 | 41.781821 | 0.023934 | 0.741740 | 30.991236 | 0.032267 | 36 |
| 4 | 1.489354 | 58.722492 | 0.017029 | 0.671432 | 39.428160 | 0.025363 | 48 |
| 5 | 1.645309 | 77.437072 | 0.012914 | 0.607789 | 47.065369 | 0.021247 | 60 |
| 6 | 1.817594 | 98.111314 | 0.010193 | 0.550178 | 53.978665 | 0.018526 | 72 |
| 7 | 2.007920 | 120.950418 | 0.008268 | 0.498028 | 60.236667 | 0.016601 | 84 |
| 8 | 2.218176 | 146.181076 | 0.006841 | 0.450821 | 65.901488 | 0.015174 | 96 |
| 9 | 2.450448 | 174.053713 | 0.005745 | 0.408089 | 71.029355 | 0.014079 | 108 |
| 10 | 2.707041 | 204.844979 | 0.004882 | 0.369407 | 75.671163 | 0.013215 | 120 |
| 11 | 2.990504 | 238.860493 | 0.004187 | 0.334392 | 79.872986 | 0.012520 | 132 |
| 12 | 3.303649 | 276.437876 | 0.003617 | 0.302696 | 83.676528 | 0.011951 | 144 |
| 13 | 3.649584 | 317.950102 | 0.003145 | 0.274004 | 87.119542 | 0.011478 | 156 |
| 14 | 4.031743 | 363.809201 | 0.002749 | 0.248032 | 90.236201 | 0.011082 | 168 |
| 15 | 4.453920 | 414.470346 | 0.002413 | 0.224521 | 93.057439 | 0.010746 | 180 |
| 16 | 4.920303 | 470.436376 | 0.002126 | 0.203240 | 95.611259 | 0.010459 | 192 |
| 17 | 5.435523 | 532.262780 | 0.001879 | 0.183975 | 97.923008 | 0.010212 | 204 |
| 18 | 6.004693 | 600.563216 | 0.001665 | 0.166536 | 100.015633 | 0.009998 | 216 |
| 19 | 6.633463 | 676.015601 | 0.001479 | 0.150751 | 101.909902 | 0.009813 | 228 |
| 20 | 7.328074 | 759.368836 | 0.001317 | 0.136462 | 103.624619 | 0.009650 | 240 |
| 21 | 8.095419 | 851.450244 | 0.001174 | 0.123527 | 105.176801 | 0.009508 | 252 |
| 22 | 8.943115 | 953.173779 | 0.001049 | 0.111818 | 106.581856 | 0.009382 | 264 |
| 23 | 9.879576 | 1065.549097 | 0.000938 | 0.101219 | 107.853730 | 0.009272 | 276 |
| 24 | 10.914097 | 1189.691580 | 0.000841 | 0.091625 | 109.005045 | 0.009174 | 288 |
| 25 | 12.056945 | 1326.833403 | 0.000754 | 0.082940 | 110.047230 | 0.009087 | 300 |
| 26 | 13.319465 | 1478.335767 | 0.000676 | 0.075078 | 110.990629 | 0.009010 | 312 |
| 27 | 14.714187 | 1645.702407 | 0.000608 | 0.067962 | 111.844605 | 0.008941 | 324 |
| 28 | 16.254954 | 1830.594523 | 0.000546 | 0.061520 | 112.617635 | 0.008880 | 336 |
| 29 | 17.957060 | 2034.847258 | 0.000491 | 0.055688 | 113.317392 | 0.008825 | 348 |
| 30 | 19.837399 | 2260.487925 | 0.000442 | 0.050410 | 113.950820 | 0.008776 | 360 |
| 31 | 21.914634 | 2509.756117 | 0.000398 | 0.045632 | 114.524207 | 0.008732 | 372 |
| 32 | 24.209383 | 2785.125947 | 0.000359 | 0.041306 | 115.043244 | 0.008692 | 384 |
| 33 | 26.744422 | 3089.330596 | 0.000324 | 0.037391 | 115.513083 | 0.008657 | 396 |
| 34 | 29.544912 | 3425.389447 | 0.000292 | 0.033847 | 115.938387 | 0.008625 | 408 |
| 35 | 32.638650 | 3796.638052 | 0.000263 | 0.030639 | 116.323377 | 0.008597 | 420 |
| 36 | 36.056344 | 4206.761236 | 0.000238 | 0.027734 | 116.671876 | 0.008571 | 432 |
| 37 | 39.831914 | 4659.829677 | 0.000215 | 0.025105 | 116.987340 | 0.008548 | 444 |
| 38 | 44.002836 | 5160.340305 | 0.000194 | 0.022726 | 117.272903 | 0.008527 | 456 |
| 39 | 48.610508 | 5713.260935 | 0.000175 | 0.020572 | 117.531398 | 0.008508 | 468 |
| 40 | 53.700663 | 6324.079581 | 0.000158 | 0.018622 | 117.765391 | 0.008491 | 480 |

10.50% ANNUAL INTEREST RATE          0.8750% MONTHLY EFFECTIVE INTEREST RATE

| | 1<br>Future Value<br>of $1 | 2<br>Future Value<br>Annuity of<br>$1 per Month | 3<br>Sinking<br>Fund<br>Factor | 4<br>Present Value<br>of $1<br>(Reversion) | 5<br>Present Value<br>Annuity of<br>$1 per Month | 6<br>Installment<br>to<br>Amortize $1 | |
|---|---|---|---|---|---|---|---|
| Months | | | | | | | Months |
| 1 | 1.008750 | 1.000000 | 1.000000 | 0.991326 | 0.991326 | 1.008750 | 1 |
| 2 | 1.017577 | 2.008750 | 0.497822 | 0.982727 | 1.974053 | 0.506572 | 2 |
| 3 | 1.026480 | 3.026327 | 0.330434 | 0.974203 | 2.948256 | 0.339184 | 3 |
| 4 | 1.035462 | 4.052807 | 0.246743 | 0.965752 | 3.914008 | 0.255493 | 4 |
| 5 | 1.044522 | 5.088269 | 0.196530 | 0.957375 | 4.871384 | 0.205280 | 5 |
| 6 | 1.053662 | 6.132791 | 0.163058 | 0.949071 | 5.820455 | 0.171808 | 6 |
| 7 | 1.062881 | 7.186453 | 0.139151 | 0.940839 | 6.761293 | 0.147901 | 7 |
| 8 | 1.072182 | 8.249335 | 0.121222 | 0.932678 | 7.693971 | 0.129972 | 8 |
| 9 | 1.081563 | 9.321516 | 0.107279 | 0.924588 | 8.618559 | 0.116029 | 9 |
| 10 | 1.091027 | 10.403080 | 0.096125 | 0.916568 | 9.535126 | 0.104875 | 10 |
| 11 | 1.100573 | 11.494107 | 0.087001 | 0.908617 | 10.443743 | 0.095751 | 11 |
| 12 | 1.110203 | 12.594680 | 0.079399 | 0.900736 | 11.344479 | 0.088149 | 12 |
| Years | | | | | | | Months |
| 1 | 1.110203 | 12.594680 | 0.079399 | 0.900736 | 11.344479 | 0.088149 | 12 |
| 2 | 1.232552 | 26.577337 | 0.037626 | 0.811325 | 21.562858 | 0.046376 | 24 |
| 3 | 1.368383 | 42.100932 | 0.023752 | 0.730789 | 30.766918 | 0.032502 | 36 |
| 4 | 1.519184 | 59.335280 | 0.016853 | 0.658248 | 39.057344 | 0.025603 | 48 |
| 5 | 1.686603 | 78.468912 | 0.012744 | 0.592908 | 46.524827 | 0.021494 | 60 |
| 6 | 1.872472 | 99.711137 | 0.010029 | 0.534053 | 53.251057 | 0.018779 | 72 |
| 7 | 2.078825 | 123.294329 | 0.008111 | 0.481041 | 59.309613 | 0.016861 | 84 |
| 8 | 2.307919 | 149.476469 | 0.006690 | 0.433291 | 64.766771 | 0.015440 | 96 |
| 9 | 2.562260 | 178.543972 | 0.005601 | 0.390280 | 69.682229 | 0.014351 | 108 |
| 10 | 2.844630 | 210.814814 | 0.004743 | 0.351540 | 74.109758 | 0.013493 | 120 |
| 11 | 3.158118 | 246.642013 | 0.004054 | 0.316644 | 78.097792 | 0.012804 | 132 |
| 12 | 3.506153 | 286.417494 | 0.003491 | 0.285213 | 81.689957 | 0.012241 | 144 |
| 13 | 3.892543 | 330.576371 | 0.003025 | 0.256901 | 84.925549 | 0.011775 | 156 |
| 14 | 4.321515 | 379.601707 | 0.002634 | 0.231400 | 87.839962 | 0.011384 | 168 |
| 15 | 4.797761 | 434.029805 | 0.002304 | 0.208431 | 90.465078 | 0.011054 | 180 |
| 16 | 5.326491 | 494.456068 | 0.002022 | 0.187741 | 92.829614 | 0.010772 | 192 |
| 17 | 5.913488 | 561.541512 | 0.001781 | 0.169105 | 94.959437 | 0.010531 | 204 |
| 18 | 6.565175 | 636.020005 | 0.001572 | 0.152319 | 96.877844 | 0.010322 | 216 |
| 19 | 7.288680 | 718.706284 | 0.001391 | 0.137199 | 98.605822 | 0.010141 | 228 |
| 20 | 8.091918 | 810.504876 | 0.001234 | 0.123580 | 100.162274 | 0.009984 | 240 |
| 21 | 8.983675 | 912.419990 | 0.001096 | 0.111313 | 101.564226 | 0.009846 | 252 |
| 22 | 9.973707 | 1025.566501 | 0.000975 | 0.100264 | 102.827014 | 0.009725 | 264 |
| 23 | 11.072844 | 1151.182148 | 0.000869 | 0.090311 | 103.964453 | 0.009619 | 276 |
| 24 | 12.293109 | 1290.641073 | 0.000775 | 0.081346 | 104.988985 | 0.009525 | 288 |
| 25 | 13.647852 | 1445.468853 | 0.000692 | 0.073272 | 105.911817 | 0.009442 | 300 |
| 26 | 15.151893 | 1617.359188 | 0.000618 | 0.065998 | 106.743045 | 0.009368 | 312 |
| 27 | 16.821684 | 1808.192431 | 0.000553 | 0.059447 | 107.491762 | 0.009303 | 324 |
| 28 | 18.675491 | 2020.056156 | 0.000495 | 0.053546 | 108.166158 | 0.009245 | 336 |
| 29 | 20.733595 | 2255.267995 | 0.000443 | 0.048231 | 108.773611 | 0.009193 | 348 |
| 30 | 23.018509 | 2516.400990 | 0.000397 | 0.043443 | 109.320766 | 0.009147 | 360 |
| 31 | 25.555228 | 2806.311742 | 0.000356 | 0.039131 | 109.813607 | 0.009106 | 372 |
| 32 | 28.371502 | 3128.171659 | 0.000320 | 0.035247 | 110.257527 | 0.009070 | 384 |
| 33 | 31.498139 | 3485.501649 | 0.000287 | 0.031748 | 110.657382 | 0.009037 | 396 |
| 34 | 34.969343 | 3882.210638 | 0.000258 | 0.028596 | 111.017546 | 0.009008 | 408 |
| 35 | 38.823085 | 4322.638325 | 0.000231 | 0.025758 | 111.341958 | 0.008981 | 420 |
| 36 | 43.101523 | 4811.602664 | 0.000208 | 0.023201 | 111.634167 | 0.008958 | 432 |
| 37 | 47.851460 | 5354.452560 | 0.000187 | 0.020898 | 111.897371 | 0.008937 | 444 |
| 38 | 53.124856 | 5957.126387 | 0.000168 | 0.018824 | 112.134448 | 0.008918 | 456 |
| 39 | 58.979398 | 6626.216950 | 0.000151 | 0.016955 | 112.347992 | 0.008901 | 468 |
| 40 | 65.479132 | 7369.043601 | 0.000136 | 0.015272 | 112.540338 | 0.008886 | 480 |

11.00% ANNUAL INTEREST RATE                    0.9167% MONTHLY EFFECTIVE INTEREST RATE

| | 1 Future Value of $1 | 2 Future Value Annuity of $1 per Month | 3 Sinking Fund Factor | 4 Present Value of $1 (Reversion) | 5 Present Value Annuity of $1 per Month | 6 Installment to Amortize $1 | |
|---|---|---|---|---|---|---|---|
| Months | | | | | | | Months |
| 1 | 1.009167 | 1.000000 | 1.000000 | 0.990917 | 0.990917 | 1.009167 | 1 |
| 2 | 1.018417 | 2.009167 | 0.497719 | 0.981916 | 1.972832 | 0.506885 | 2 |
| 3 | 1.027753 | 3.027584 | 0.330296 | 0.972997 | 2.945829 | 0.339463 | 3 |
| 4 | 1.037174 | 4.055337 | 0.246589 | 0.964158 | 3.909987 | 0.255755 | 4 |
| 5 | 1.046681 | 5.092511 | 0.196367 | 0.955401 | 4.865388 | 0.205533 | 5 |
| 6 | 1.056276 | 6.139192 | 0.162888 | 0.946722 | 5.812110 | 0.172055 | 6 |
| 7 | 1.065958 | 7.195468 | 0.138976 | 0.938123 | 6.750233 | 0.148143 | 7 |
| 8 | 1.075730 | 8.261427 | 0.121044 | 0.929602 | 7.679835 | 0.130211 | 8 |
| 9 | 1.085591 | 9.337156 | 0.107099 | 0.921158 | 8.600992 | 0.116266 | 9 |
| 10 | 1.095542 | 10.422747 | 0.095944 | 0.912790 | 9.513783 | 0.105111 | 10 |
| 11 | 1.105584 | 11.518289 | 0.086818 | 0.904499 | 10.418282 | 0.095985 | 11 |
| 12 | 1.115719 | 12.623873 | 0.079215 | 0.896283 | 11.314565 | 0.088382 | 12 |
| Years | | | | | | | Months |
| 1 | 1.115719 | 12.623873 | 0.079215 | 0.896283 | 11.314565 | 0.088382 | 12 |
| 2 | 1.244829 | 26.708566 | 0.037441 | 0.803323 | 21.455619 | 0.046608 | 24 |
| 3 | 1.388879 | 42.423123 | 0.023572 | 0.720005 | 30.544874 | 0.032739 | 36 |
| 4 | 1.549598 | 59.956151 | 0.016679 | 0.645329 | 38.691421 | 0.025846 | 48 |
| 5 | 1.728916 | 79.518080 | 0.012576 | 0.578397 | 45.993034 | 0.021742 | 60 |
| 6 | 1.928984 | 101.343692 | 0.009867 | 0.518408 | 52.537346 | 0.019034 | 72 |
| 7 | 2.152204 | 125.694940 | 0.007956 | 0.464640 | 58.402903 | 0.017122 | 84 |
| 8 | 2.401254 | 152.864085 | 0.006542 | 0.416449 | 63.660103 | 0.015708 | 96 |
| 9 | 2.679124 | 183.177212 | 0.005459 | 0.373256 | 68.372043 | 0.014626 | 108 |
| 10 | 2.989150 | 216.998139 | 0.004608 | 0.334543 | 72.595275 | 0.013775 | 120 |
| 11 | 3.335051 | 254.732784 | 0.003926 | 0.299846 | 76.380487 | 0.013092 | 132 |
| 12 | 3.720979 | 296.834038 | 0.003369 | 0.268747 | 79.773109 | 0.012536 | 144 |
| 13 | 4.151566 | 343.807200 | 0.002909 | 0.240873 | 82.813859 | 0.012075 | 156 |
| 14 | 4.631980 | 396.216042 | 0.002524 | 0.215890 | 85.539231 | 0.011691 | 168 |
| 15 | 5.167988 | 454.689575 | 0.002199 | 0.193499 | 87.981937 | 0.011366 | 180 |
| 16 | 5.766021 | 519.929596 | 0.001923 | 0.173430 | 90.171293 | 0.011090 | 192 |
| 17 | 6.433259 | 592.719117 | 0.001687 | 0.155442 | 92.133576 | 0.010854 | 204 |
| 18 | 7.177708 | 673.931757 | 0.001484 | 0.139320 | 93.892337 | 0.010650 | 216 |
| 19 | 8.008304 | 764.542228 | 0.001308 | 0.124870 | 95.468685 | 0.010475 | 228 |
| 20 | 8.935015 | 865.638038 | 0.001155 | 0.111919 | 96.881539 | 0.010322 | 240 |
| 21 | 9.968965 | 978.432537 | 0.001022 | 0.100311 | 98.147856 | 0.010189 | 252 |
| 22 | 11.122562 | 1104.279485 | 0.000906 | 0.089907 | 99.282835 | 0.010072 | 264 |
| 23 | 12.409652 | 1244.689295 | 0.000803 | 0.080582 | 100.300098 | 0.009970 | 276 |
| 24 | 13.845682 | 1401.347165 | 0.000714 | 0.072225 | 101.211853 | 0.009880 | 288 |
| 25 | 15.447889 | 1576.133301 | 0.000634 | 0.064734 | 102.029044 | 0.009801 | 300 |
| 26 | 17.235500 | 1771.145485 | 0.000565 | 0.058020 | 102.761478 | 0.009731 | 312 |
| 27 | 19.229972 | 1988.724252 | 0.000503 | 0.052002 | 103.417947 | 0.009670 | 324 |
| 28 | 21.455242 | 2231.480981 | 0.000448 | 0.046609 | 104.006328 | 0.009615 | 336 |
| 29 | 23.938018 | 2502.329236 | 0.000400 | 0.041775 | 104.533685 | 0.009566 | 348 |
| 30 | 26.708098 | 2804.519736 | 0.000357 | 0.037442 | 105.006346 | 0.009523 | 360 |
| 31 | 29.798728 | 3141.679369 | 0.000318 | 0.033558 | 105.429984 | 0.009485 | 372 |
| 32 | 33.247002 | 3517.854723 | 0.000284 | 0.030078 | 105.809684 | 0.009451 | 384 |
| 33 | 37.094306 | 3937.560650 | 0.000254 | 0.026958 | 106.150002 | 0.009421 | 396 |
| 34 | 41.386816 | 4405.834459 | 0.000227 | 0.024162 | 106.455024 | 0.009394 | 408 |
| 35 | 46.176050 | 4928.296368 | 0.000203 | 0.021656 | 106.728409 | 0.009370 | 420 |
| 36 | 51.519489 | 5511.216962 | 0.000181 | 0.019410 | 106.973440 | 0.009348 | 432 |
| 37 | 57.481264 | 6161.592447 | 0.000162 | 0.017397 | 107.193057 | 0.009329 | 444 |
| 38 | 64.132929 | 6887.228628 | 0.000145 | 0.015593 | 107.389897 | 0.009312 | 456 |
| 39 | 71.554317 | 7696.834582 | 0.000130 | 0.013975 | 107.566320 | 0.009297 | 468 |
| 40 | 79.834499 | 8600.127195 | 0.000116 | 0.012526 | 107.724446 | 0.009283 | 480 |

11.50% ANNUAL INTEREST RATE          0.9583% MONTHLY EFFECTIVE INTEREST RATE

| | 1<br>Future Value<br>of $1 | 2<br>Future Value<br>Annuity of<br>$1 per Month | 3<br>Sinking<br>Fund<br>Factor | 4<br>Present Value<br>of $1<br>(Reversion) | 5<br>Present Value<br>Annuity of<br>$1 per Month | 6<br>Installment<br>to<br>Amortize $1 | |
|---|---|---|---|---|---|---|---|
| Months | | | | | | | Months |
| 1 | 1.009583 | 1.000000 | 1.000000 | 0.990508 | 0.990508 | 1.009583 | 1 |
| 2 | 1.019259 | 2.009583 | 0.497616 | 0.981105 | 1.971613 | 0.507199 | 2 |
| 3 | 1.029026 | 3.028842 | 0.330159 | 0.971792 | 2.943405 | 0.339743 | 3 |
| 4 | 1.038888 | 4.057868 | 0.246435 | 0.962568 | 3.905973 | 0.256018 | 4 |
| 5 | 1.048844 | 5.096756 | 0.196203 | 0.953431 | 4.859404 | 0.205787 | 5 |
| 6 | 1.058895 | 6.145600 | 0.162718 | 0.944380 | 5.803784 | 0.172301 | 6 |
| 7 | 1.069043 | 7.204495 | 0.138802 | 0.935416 | 6.739200 | 0.148386 | 7 |
| 8 | 1.079288 | 8.273538 | 0.120867 | 0.926537 | 7.665737 | 0.130451 | 8 |
| 9 | 1.089631 | 9.352827 | 0.106920 | 0.917742 | 8.583479 | 0.116503 | 9 |
| 10 | 1.100074 | 10.442458 | 0.095763 | 0.909030 | 9.492509 | 0.105346 | 10 |
| 11 | 1.110616 | 11.542531 | 0.086636 | 0.900401 | 10.392910 | 0.096219 | 11 |
| 12 | 1.121259 | 12.653147 | 0.079032 | 0.891854 | 11.284764 | 0.088615 | 12 |
| Years | | | | | | | Months |
| 1 | 1.121259 | 12.653147 | 0.079032 | 0.891854 | 11.284764 | 0.088615 | 12 |
| 2 | 1.257222 | 26.840607 | 0.037257 | 0.795404 | 21.349130 | 0.046840 | 24 |
| 3 | 1.409672 | 42.748428 | 0.023393 | 0.709385 | 30.325079 | 0.032976 | 36 |
| 4 | 1.580608 | 60.585221 | 0.016506 | 0.632668 | 38.330318 | 0.026089 | 48 |
| 5 | 1.772272 | 80.584891 | 0.012409 | 0.564248 | 45.469825 | 0.021993 | 60 |
| 6 | 1.987176 | 103.009708 | 0.009708 | 0.503227 | 51.837225 | 0.019291 | 72 |
| 7 | 2.228140 | 128.153744 | 0.007803 | 0.448805 | 57.516018 | 0.017386 | 84 |
| 8 | 2.498323 | 156.346728 | 0.006396 | 0.400269 | 62.580675 | 0.015979 | 96 |
| 9 | 2.801268 | 187.958374 | 0.005320 | 0.356981 | 67.097611 | 0.014904 | 108 |
| 10 | 3.140948 | 223.403228 | 0.004476 | 0.318375 | 71.126060 | 0.014060 | 120 |
| 11 | 3.521817 | 263.146100 | 0.003800 | 0.283944 | 74.718850 | 0.013384 | 132 |
| 12 | 3.948870 | 307.708167 | 0.003250 | 0.253237 | 77.923095 | 0.012833 | 144 |
| 13 | 4.427707 | 357.673800 | 0.002796 | 0.225851 | 80.780815 | 0.012379 | 156 |
| 14 | 4.964608 | 413.698232 | 0.002417 | 0.201426 | 83.329485 | 0.012001 | 168 |
| 15 | 5.566613 | 476.516149 | 0.002099 | 0.179642 | 85.602527 | 0.011682 | 180 |
| 16 | 6.241617 | 546.951324 | 0.001828 | 0.160215 | 87.629750 | 0.011412 | 192 |
| 17 | 6.998471 | 625.927421 | 0.001598 | 0.142888 | 89.437737 | 0.011181 | 204 |
| 18 | 7.847101 | 714.480107 | 0.001400 | 0.127436 | 91.050199 | 0.010983 | 216 |
| 19 | 8.798635 | 813.770632 | 0.001229 | 0.113654 | 92.488279 | 0.010812 | 228 |
| 20 | 9.865552 | 925.101060 | 0.001081 | 0.101363 | 93.770838 | 0.010664 | 240 |
| 21 | 11.061842 | 1049.931340 | 0.000952 | 0.090401 | 94.914693 | 0.010536 | 252 |
| 22 | 12.403194 | 1189.898456 | 0.000840 | 0.080624 | 95.934846 | 0.010424 | 264 |
| 23 | 13.907196 | 1346.837891 | 0.000742 | 0.071905 | 96.844673 | 0.010326 | 276 |
| 24 | 15.593574 | 1522.807696 | 0.000657 | 0.064129 | 97.656106 | 0.010240 | 288 |
| 25 | 17.484440 | 1720.115481 | 0.000581 | 0.057194 | 98.379787 | 0.010165 | 300 |
| 26 | 19.604591 | 1941.348676 | 0.000515 | 0.051008 | 99.025204 | 0.010098 | 312 |
| 27 | 21.981831 | 2189.408459 | 0.000457 | 0.045492 | 99.600823 | 0.010040 | 324 |
| 28 | 24.647333 | 2467.547806 | 0.000405 | 0.040572 | 100.114191 | 0.009989 | 336 |
| 29 | 27.636052 | 2779.414142 | 0.000360 | 0.036185 | 100.572040 | 0.009943 | 348 |
| 30 | 30.987181 | 3129.097181 | 0.000320 | 0.032271 | 100.980375 | 0.009903 | 360 |
| 31 | 34.744666 | 3521.182550 | 0.000284 | 0.028781 | 101.344550 | 0.009867 | 372 |
| 32 | 38.957781 | 3960.811927 | 0.000252 | 0.025669 | 101.669341 | 0.009836 | 384 |
| 33 | 43.681775 | 4453.750468 | 0.000225 | 0.022893 | 101.959008 | 0.009808 | 396 |
| 34 | 48.978598 | 5006.462404 | 0.000200 | 0.020417 | 102.217348 | 0.009783 | 408 |
| 35 | 54.917710 | 5626.195819 | 0.000178 | 0.018209 | 102.447750 | 0.009761 | 420 |
| 36 | 61.576995 | 6321.077691 | 0.000158 | 0.016240 | 102.653235 | 0.009742 | 432 |
| 37 | 69.043780 | 7100.220473 | 0.000141 | 0.014484 | 102.836498 | 0.009724 | 444 |
| 38 | 77.415982 | 7973.841584 | 0.000125 | 0.012917 | 102.999941 | 0.009709 | 456 |
| 39 | 86.803392 | 8953.397405 | 0.000112 | 0.011520 | 103.145709 | 0.009695 | 468 |
| 40 | 97.329113 | 10051.733506 | 0.000099 | 0.010274 | 103.275713 | 0.009683 | 480 |

12.00% ANNUAL INTEREST RATE          1.0000% MONTHLY EFFECTIVE INTEREST RATE

| | 1<br>Future Value<br>of $1 | 2<br>Future Value<br>Annuity of<br>$1 per Month | 3<br>Sinking<br>Fund<br>Factor | 4<br>Present Value<br>of $1<br>(Reversion) | 5<br>Present Value<br>Annuity of<br>$1 per Month | 6<br>Installment<br>to<br>Amortize $1 | |
|---|---|---|---|---|---|---|---|
| Months | | | | | | | Months |
| 1 | 1.010000 | 1.000000 | 1.000000 | 0.990099 | 0.990099 | 1.010000 | 1 |
| 2 | 1.020100 | 2.010000 | 0.497512 | 0.980296 | 1.970395 | 0.507512 | 2 |
| 3 | 1.030301 | 3.030100 | 0.330022 | 0.970590 | 2.940985 | 0.340022 | 3 |
| 4 | 1.040604 | 4.060401 | 0.246281 | 0.960980 | 3.901966 | 0.256281 | 4 |
| 5 | 1.051010 | 5.101005 | 0.196040 | 0.951466 | 4.853431 | 0.206040 | 5 |
| 6 | 1.061520 | 6.152015 | 0.162548 | 0.942045 | 5.795476 | 0.172548 | 6 |
| 7 | 1.072135 | 7.213535 | 0.138628 | 0.932718 | 6.728195 | 0.148628 | 7 |
| 8 | 1.082857 | 8.285671 | 0.120690 | 0.923483 | 7.651678 | 0.130690 | 8 |
| 9 | 1.093685 | 9.368527 | 0.106740 | 0.914340 | 8.566018 | 0.116740 | 9 |
| 10 | 1.104622 | 10.462213 | 0.095582 | 0.905287 | 9.471305 | 0.105582 | 10 |
| 11 | 1.115668 | 11.566835 | 0.086454 | 0.896324 | 10.367628 | 0.096454 | 11 |
| 12 | 1.126825 | 12.682503 | 0.078849 | 0.887449 | 11.255077 | 0.088849 | 12 |
| Years | | | | | | | Months |
| 1 | 1.126825 | 12.682503 | 0.078849 | 0.887449 | 11.255077 | 0.088849 | 12 |
| 2 | 1.269735 | 26.973465 | 0.037073 | 0.787566 | 21.243387 | 0.047073 | 24 |
| 3 | 1.430769 | 43.076878 | 0.023214 | 0.698925 | 30.107505 | 0.033214 | 36 |
| 4 | 1.612226 | 61.222608 | 0.016334 | 0.620260 | 37.973959 | 0.026334 | 48 |
| 5 | 1.816697 | 81.669670 | 0.012244 | 0.550450 | 44.955038 | 0.022244 | 60 |
| 6 | 2.047099 | 104.709931 | 0.009550 | 0.488496 | 51.150391 | 0.019550 | 72 |
| 7 | 2.306723 | 130.672274 | 0.007653 | 0.433515 | 56.648453 | 0.017653 | 84 |
| 8 | 2.599273 | 159.927293 | 0.006253 | 0.384723 | 61.527703 | 0.016253 | 96 |
| 9 | 2.928926 | 192.892579 | 0.005184 | 0.341422 | 65.857790 | 0.015184 | 108 |
| 10 | 3.300387 | 230.038689 | 0.004347 | 0.302995 | 69.700522 | 0.014347 | 120 |
| 11 | 3.718959 | 271.895856 | 0.003678 | 0.268892 | 73.110752 | 0.013678 | 132 |
| 12 | 4.190616 | 319.061559 | 0.003134 | 0.238628 | 76.137157 | 0.013134 | 144 |
| 13 | 4.722091 | 372.209054 | 0.002687 | 0.211771 | 78.822939 | 0.012687 | 156 |
| 14 | 5.320970 | 432.096982 | 0.002314 | 0.187936 | 81.206434 | 0.012314 | 168 |
| 15 | 5.995802 | 499.580198 | 0.002002 | 0.166783 | 83.321664 | 0.012002 | 180 |
| 16 | 6.756220 | 575.621974 | 0.001737 | 0.148012 | 85.198824 | 0.011737 | 192 |
| 17 | 7.613078 | 661.307751 | 0.001512 | 0.131353 | 86.864707 | 0.011512 | 204 |
| 18 | 8.578606 | 757.860630 | 0.001320 | 0.116569 | 88.343095 | 0.011320 | 216 |
| 19 | 9.666588 | 866.658830 | 0.001154 | 0.103449 | 89.655089 | 0.011154 | 228 |
| 20 | 10.892554 | 989.255365 | 0.001011 | 0.091806 | 90.819416 | 0.011011 | 240 |
| 21 | 12.274002 | 1127.400210 | 0.000887 | 0.081473 | 91.852698 | 0.010887 | 252 |
| 22 | 13.830653 | 1283.065279 | 0.000779 | 0.072303 | 92.769683 | 0.010779 | 264 |
| 23 | 15.584726 | 1458.472574 | 0.000686 | 0.064165 | 93.583461 | 0.010686 | 276 |
| 24 | 17.561259 | 1656.125905 | 0.000604 | 0.056944 | 94.305647 | 0.010604 | 288 |
| 25 | 19.788466 | 1878.846626 | 0.000532 | 0.050534 | 94.946551 | 0.010532 | 300 |
| 26 | 22.298139 | 2129.813909 | 0.000470 | 0.044847 | 95.515321 | 0.010470 | 312 |
| 27 | 25.126101 | 2412.610125 | 0.000414 | 0.039799 | 96.020075 | 0.010414 | 324 |
| 28 | 28.312720 | 2731.271980 | 0.000366 | 0.035320 | 96.468019 | 0.010366 | 336 |
| 29 | 31.903481 | 3090.348134 | 0.000324 | 0.031345 | 96.865546 | 0.010324 | 348 |
| 30 | 35.949641 | 3494.964133 | 0.000286 | 0.027817 | 97.218331 | 0.010286 | 360 |
| 31 | 40.508956 | 3950.895567 | 0.000253 | 0.024686 | 97.531410 | 0.010253 | 372 |
| 32 | 45.646505 | 4464.650520 | 0.000224 | 0.021907 | 97.809252 | 0.010224 | 384 |
| 33 | 51.435625 | 5043.562459 | 0.000198 | 0.019442 | 98.055822 | 0.010198 | 396 |
| 34 | 57.958949 | 5695.894923 | 0.000176 | 0.017254 | 98.274641 | 0.010176 | 408 |
| 35 | 65.309595 | 6430.959471 | 0.000155 | 0.015312 | 98.468831 | 0.010155 | 420 |
| 36 | 73.592486 | 7259.248603 | 0.000138 | 0.013588 | 98.641166 | 0.010138 | 432 |
| 37 | 82.925855 | 8192.585529 | 0.000122 | 0.012059 | 98.794103 | 0.010122 | 444 |
| 38 | 93.442929 | 9244.292939 | 0.000108 | 0.010702 | 98.929828 | 0.010108 | 456 |
| 39 | 105.293832 | 10429.383172 | 0.000096 | 0.009497 | 99.050277 | 0.010096 | 468 |
| 40 | 118.647725 | 11764.772510 | 0.000085 | 0.008428 | 99.157169 | 0.010085 | 480 |

12.50% ANNUAL INTEREST RATE      1.0417% MONTHLY EFFECTIVE INTEREST RATE

| | 1<br>Future Value<br>of $1 | 2<br>Future Value<br>Annuity of<br>$1 per Month | 3<br>Sinking<br>Fund<br>Factor | 4<br>Present Value<br>of $1<br>(Reversion) | 5<br>Present Value<br>Annuity of<br>$1 per Month | 6<br>Installment<br>to<br>Amortize $1 | |
|---|---|---|---|---|---|---|---|
| Months | | | | | | | Months |
| 1 | 1.010417 | 1.000000 | 1.000000 | 0.989691 | 0.989691 | 1.010417 | 1 |
| 2 | 1.020942 | 2.010417 | 0.497409 | 0.979488 | 1.969178 | 0.507826 | 2 |
| 3 | 1.031577 | 3.031359 | 0.329885 | 0.969390 | 2.938568 | 0.340302 | 3 |
| 4 | 1.042322 | 4.062935 | 0.246127 | 0.959396 | 3.897965 | 0.256544 | 4 |
| 5 | 1.053180 | 5.105257 | 0.195877 | 0.949506 | 4.847470 | 0.206293 | 5 |
| 6 | 1.064150 | 6.158437 | 0.162379 | 0.939717 | 5.787187 | 0.172796 | 6 |
| 7 | 1.075235 | 7.222588 | 0.138455 | 0.930029 | 6.717216 | 0.148871 | 7 |
| 8 | 1.086436 | 8.297823 | 0.120514 | 0.920441 | 7.637657 | 0.130930 | 8 |
| 9 | 1.097753 | 9.384258 | 0.106561 | 0.910952 | 8.548609 | 0.116978 | 9 |
| 10 | 1.109188 | 10.482011 | 0.095402 | 0.901561 | 9.450170 | 0.105818 | 10 |
| 11 | 1.120742 | 11.591199 | 0.086272 | 0.892266 | 10.342436 | 0.096689 | 11 |
| 12 | 1.132416 | 12.711940 | 0.078666 | 0.883068 | 11.225504 | 0.089083 | 12 |
| Years | | | | | | | Months |
| 1 | 1.132416 | 12.711940 | 0.078666 | 0.883068 | 11.225504 | 0.089083 | 12 |
| 2 | 1.282366 | 27.107146 | 0.036891 | 0.779809 | 21.138383 | 0.047307 | 24 |
| 3 | 1.452172 | 43.408507 | 0.023037 | 0.688624 | 29.892126 | 0.033454 | 36 |
| 4 | 1.644463 | 61.868431 | 0.016163 | 0.608101 | 37.622274 | 0.026580 | 48 |
| 5 | 1.862216 | 82.772744 | 0.012081 | 0.536995 | 44.448517 | 0.022498 | 60 |
| 6 | 2.108803 | 106.445124 | 0.009395 | 0.474203 | 50.476552 | 0.019811 | 72 |
| 7 | 2.388043 | 133.252107 | 0.007505 | 0.418753 | 55.799715 | 0.017921 | 84 |
| 8 | 2.704258 | 163.608765 | 0.006112 | 0.369787 | 60.500428 | 0.016529 | 96 |
| 9 | 3.062345 | 197.985131 | 0.005051 | 0.326547 | 64.651476 | 0.015468 | 108 |
| 10 | 3.467849 | 236.913480 | 0.004221 | 0.288363 | 68.317132 | 0.014638 | 120 |
| 11 | 3.927048 | 280.996567 | 0.003559 | 0.254644 | 71.554154 | 0.013975 | 132 |
| 12 | 4.447052 | 330.916961 | 0.003022 | 0.224868 | 74.412664 | 0.013439 | 144 |
| 13 | 5.035913 | 387.447618 | 0.002581 | 0.198574 | 76.936921 | 0.012998 | 156 |
| 14 | 5.702748 | 451.463840 | 0.002215 | 0.175354 | 79.166011 | 0.012632 | 168 |
| 15 | 6.457884 | 523.956837 | 0.001909 | 0.154849 | 81.134449 | 0.012325 | 180 |
| 16 | 7.313011 | 606.049070 | 0.001650 | 0.136743 | 82.872712 | 0.012067 | 192 |
| 17 | 8.281371 | 699.011633 | 0.001431 | 0.120753 | 84.407717 | 0.011847 | 204 |
| 18 | 9.377958 | 804.283930 | 0.001243 | 0.106633 | 85.763229 | 0.011660 | 216 |
| 19 | 10.619750 | 923.495968 | 0.001083 | 0.094164 | 86.960239 | 0.011500 | 228 |
| 20 | 12.025975 | 1058.493594 | 0.000945 | 0.083153 | 88.017279 | 0.011361 | 240 |
| 21 | 13.618407 | 1211.367071 | 0.000826 | 0.073430 | 88.950717 | 0.011242 | 252 |
| 22 | 15.421703 | 1384.483450 | 0.000722 | 0.064844 | 89.775006 | 0.011139 | 264 |
| 23 | 17.463783 | 1580.523215 | 0.000633 | 0.057261 | 90.502909 | 0.011049 | 276 |
| 24 | 19.776269 | 1802.521791 | 0.000555 | 0.050566 | 91.145697 | 0.010971 | 288 |
| 25 | 22.394964 | 2053.916541 | 0.000487 | 0.044653 | 91.713322 | 0.010904 | 300 |
| 26 | 25.360417 | 2338.599989 | 0.000428 | 0.039432 | 92.214573 | 0.010844 | 312 |
| 27 | 28.718543 | 2660.980094 | 0.000376 | 0.034821 | 92.657212 | 0.010792 | 324 |
| 28 | 32.521339 | 3026.048499 | 0.000330 | 0.030749 | 93.048092 | 0.010747 | 336 |
| 29 | 36.827686 | 3439.457817 | 0.000291 | 0.027153 | 93.393265 | 0.010707 | 348 |
| 30 | 41.704262 | 3907.609164 | 0.000256 | 0.023978 | 93.698077 | 0.010673 | 360 |
| 31 | 47.226576 | 4437.751261 | 0.000225 | 0.021175 | 93.967246 | 0.010642 | 372 |
| 32 | 53.480132 | 5038.092678 | 0.000198 | 0.018699 | 94.204941 | 0.010615 | 384 |
| 33 | 60.561760 | 5717.928933 | 0.000175 | 0.016512 | 94.414841 | 0.010592 | 396 |
| 34 | 68.581108 | 6487.786416 | 0.000154 | 0.014581 | 94.600198 | 0.010571 | 408 |
| 35 | 77.662348 | 7359.585384 | 0.000136 | 0.012876 | 94.763880 | 0.010553 | 420 |
| 36 | 87.946089 | 8346.824524 | 0.000120 | 0.011371 | 94.908422 | 0.010536 | 432 |
| 37 | 99.591562 | 9464.789968 | 0.000106 | 0.010041 | 95.036063 | 0.010522 | 444 |
| 38 | 112.779083 | 10730.791976 | 0.000093 | 0.008867 | 95.148778 | 0.010510 | 456 |
| 39 | 127.712843 | 12164.432965 | 0.000082 | 0.007830 | 95.248314 | 0.010499 | 468 |
| 40 | 144.624073 | 13787.911025 | 0.000073 | 0.006914 | 95.336210 | 0.010489 | 480 |

13.00% ANNUAL INTEREST RATE          1.0833% MONTHLY EFFECTIVE INTEREST RATE

| | 1<br>Future Value<br>of $1 | 2<br>Future Value<br>Annuity of<br>$1 per Month | 3<br>Sinking<br>Fund<br>Factor | 4<br>Present Value<br>of $1<br>(Reversion) | 5<br>Present Value<br>Annuity of<br>$1 per Month | 6<br>Installment<br>to<br>Amortize $1 | |
|---|---|---|---|---|---|---|---|
| Months | | | | | | | Months |
| 1 | 1.010833 | 1.000000 | 1.000000 | 0.989283 | 0.989283 | 1.010833 | 1 |
| 2 | 1.021784 | 2.010833 | 0.497306 | 0.978680 | 1.967963 | 0.508140 | 2 |
| 3 | 1.032853 | 3.032617 | 0.329748 | 0.968192 | 2.936155 | 0.340581 | 3 |
| 4 | 1.044043 | 4.065471 | 0.245974 | 0.957815 | 3.893970 | 0.256807 | 4 |
| 5 | 1.055353 | 5.109513 | 0.195713 | 0.947550 | 4.841520 | 0.206547 | 5 |
| 6 | 1.066786 | 6.164866 | 0.162210 | 0.937395 | 5.778915 | 0.173043 | 6 |
| 7 | 1.078343 | 7.231652 | 0.138281 | 0.927349 | 6.706264 | 0.149114 | 7 |
| 8 | 1.090025 | 8.309995 | 0.120337 | 0.917410 | 7.623674 | 0.131170 | 8 |
| 9 | 1.101834 | 9.400020 | 0.106383 | 0.907578 | 8.531253 | 0.117216 | 9 |
| 10 | 1.113770 | 10.501854 | 0.095221 | 0.897851 | 9.429104 | 0.106055 | 10 |
| 11 | 1.125836 | 11.615624 | 0.086091 | 0.888229 | 10.317333 | 0.096924 | 11 |
| 12 | 1.138032 | 12.741460 | 0.078484 | 0.878710 | 11.196042 | 0.089317 | 12 |
| Years | | | | | | | Months |
| 1 | 1.138032 | 12.741460 | 0.078484 | 0.878710 | 11.196042 | 0.089317 | 12 |
| 2 | 1.295118 | 27.241655 | 0.036708 | 0.772130 | 21.034112 | 0.047542 | 24 |
| 3 | 1.473886 | 43.743348 | 0.022861 | 0.678478 | 29.678917 | 0.033694 | 36 |
| 4 | 1.677330 | 62.522811 | 0.015994 | 0.596185 | 37.275190 | 0.026827 | 48 |
| 5 | 1.908857 | 83.894449 | 0.011920 | 0.523874 | 43.950107 | 0.022753 | 60 |
| 6 | 2.172341 | 108.216068 | 0.009241 | 0.460333 | 49.815421 | 0.020074 | 72 |
| 7 | 2.472194 | 135.894861 | 0.007359 | 0.404499 | 54.969328 | 0.018192 | 84 |
| 8 | 2.813437 | 167.394225 | 0.005974 | 0.355437 | 59.498115 | 0.016807 | 96 |
| 9 | 3.201783 | 203.241525 | 0.004920 | 0.312326 | 63.477604 | 0.015754 | 108 |
| 10 | 3.643733 | 244.036917 | 0.004098 | 0.274444 | 66.974419 | 0.014931 | 120 |
| 11 | 4.146687 | 290.463399 | 0.003443 | 0.241156 | 70.047103 | 0.014276 | 132 |
| 12 | 4.719064 | 343.298242 | 0.002913 | 0.211906 | 72.747100 | 0.013746 | 144 |
| 13 | 5.370448 | 403.426010 | 0.002479 | 0.186204 | 75.119613 | 0.013312 | 156 |
| 14 | 6.111745 | 471.853363 | 0.002119 | 0.163619 | 77.204363 | 0.012953 | 168 |
| 15 | 6.955364 | 549.725914 | 0.001819 | 0.143774 | 79.036253 | 0.012652 | 180 |
| 16 | 7.915430 | 638.347406 | 0.001567 | 0.126336 | 80.645952 | 0.012400 | 192 |
| 17 | 9.008017 | 739.201542 | 0.001353 | 0.111012 | 82.060410 | 0.012186 | 204 |
| 18 | 10.251416 | 853.976825 | 0.001171 | 0.097548 | 83.303307 | 0.012004 | 216 |
| 19 | 11.666444 | 984.594826 | 0.001016 | 0.085716 | 84.395453 | 0.011849 | 228 |
| 20 | 13.276792 | 1133.242353 | 0.000882 | 0.075319 | 85.355132 | 0.011716 | 240 |
| 21 | 15.109421 | 1302.408067 | 0.000768 | 0.066184 | 86.198412 | 0.011601 | 252 |
| 22 | 17.195012 | 1494.924144 | 0.000669 | 0.058156 | 86.939409 | 0.011502 | 264 |
| 23 | 19.568482 | 1714.013694 | 0.000583 | 0.051103 | 87.590531 | 0.011417 | 276 |
| 24 | 22.269568 | 1963.344717 | 0.000509 | 0.044904 | 88.162677 | 0.011343 | 288 |
| 25 | 25.343491 | 2247.091520 | 0.000445 | 0.039458 | 88.665428 | 0.011278 | 300 |
| 26 | 28.841716 | 2570.004599 | 0.000389 | 0.034672 | 89.107200 | 0.011222 | 312 |
| 27 | 32.822810 | 2937.490172 | 0.000340 | 0.030467 | 89.495389 | 0.011174 | 324 |
| 28 | 37.353424 | 3355.700690 | 0.000298 | 0.026771 | 89.836495 | 0.011131 | 336 |
| 29 | 42.509410 | 3831.637843 | 0.000261 | 0.023524 | 90.136227 | 0.011094 | 348 |
| 30 | 48.377089 | 4373.269783 | 0.000229 | 0.020671 | 90.399605 | 0.011062 | 360 |
| 31 | 55.054699 | 4989.664524 | 0.000200 | 0.018164 | 90.631038 | 0.011034 | 372 |
| 32 | 62.654036 | 5691.141761 | 0.000176 | 0.015961 | 90.834400 | 0.011009 | 384 |
| 33 | 71.302328 | 6489.445641 | 0.000154 | 0.014025 | 91.013097 | 0.010987 | 396 |
| 34 | 81.144365 | 7397.941387 | 0.000135 | 0.012324 | 91.170119 | 0.010969 | 408 |
| 35 | 92.344923 | 8431.839055 | 0.000119 | 0.010829 | 91.308095 | 0.010952 | 420 |
| 36 | 105.091522 | 9608.448184 | 0.000104 | 0.009516 | 91.429337 | 0.010937 | 432 |
| 37 | 119.597566 | 10947.467591 | 0.000091 | 0.008361 | 91.535873 | 0.010925 | 444 |
| 38 | 136.105914 | 12471.315170 | 0.000080 | 0.007347 | 91.629487 | 0.010914 | 456 |
| 39 | 154.892951 | 14205.503212 | 0.000070 | 0.006456 | 91.711747 | 0.010904 | 468 |
| 40 | 176.273210 | 16179.065533 | 0.000062 | 0.005673 | 91.784030 | 0.010895 | 480 |

13.50% ANNUAL INTEREST RATE  1.1250% MONTHLY EFFECTIVE INTEREST RATE

| | 1<br>Future Value<br>of $1 | 2<br>Future Value<br>Annuity of<br>$1 per Month | 3<br>Sinking<br>Fund<br>Factor | 4<br>Present Value<br>of $1<br>(Reversion) | 5<br>Present Value<br>Annuity of<br>$1 per Month | 6<br>Installment<br>to<br>Amortize $1 | |
|---|---|---|---|---|---|---|---|
| Months | | | | | | | Months |
| 1 | 1.011250 | 1.000000 | 1.000000 | 0.988875 | 0.988875 | 1.011250 | 1 |
| 2 | 1.022627 | 2.011250 | 0.497203 | 0.977874 | 1.966749 | 0.508453 | 2 |
| 3 | 1.034131 | 3.033877 | 0.329611 | 0.966995 | 2.933745 | 0.340861 | 3 |
| 4 | 1.045765 | 4.068008 | 0.245821 | 0.956238 | 3.889982 | 0.257071 | 4 |
| 5 | 1.057530 | 5.113773 | 0.195550 | 0.945600 | 4.835582 | 0.206800 | 5 |
| 6 | 1.069427 | 6.171303 | 0.162040 | 0.935080 | 5.770662 | 0.173290 | 6 |
| 7 | 1.081458 | 7.240730 | 0.138108 | 0.924677 | 6.695339 | 0.149358 | 7 |
| 8 | 1.093625 | 8.322188 | 0.120161 | 0.914391 | 7.609730 | 0.131411 | 8 |
| 9 | 1.105928 | 9.415813 | 0.106204 | 0.904218 | 8.513948 | 0.117454 | 9 |
| 10 | 1.118370 | 10.521741 | 0.095041 | 0.894159 | 9.408107 | 0.106291 | 10 |
| 11 | 1.130951 | 11.640110 | 0.085910 | 0.884211 | 10.292318 | 0.097160 | 11 |
| 12 | 1.143674 | 12.771061 | 0.078302 | 0.874375 | 11.166693 | 0.089552 | 12 |
| Years | | | | | | | Months |
| 1 | 1.143674 | 12.771061 | 0.078302 | 0.874375 | 11.166693 | 0.089552 | 12 |
| 2 | 1.307991 | 27.376998 | 0.036527 | 0.764531 | 20.930567 | 0.047777 | 24 |
| 3 | 1.495916 | 44.081434 | 0.022685 | 0.668487 | 29.467851 | 0.033935 | 36 |
| 4 | 1.710841 | 63.185871 | 0.015826 | 0.584508 | 36.932637 | 0.027076 | 48 |
| 5 | 1.956645 | 85.035127 | 0.011760 | 0.511079 | 43.459656 | 0.023010 | 60 |
| 6 | 2.237765 | 110.023563 | 0.009089 | 0.446874 | 49.166717 | 0.020339 | 72 |
| 7 | 2.559275 | 138.602198 | 0.007215 | 0.390736 | 54.156827 | 0.018465 | 84 |
| 8 | 2.926977 | 171.286853 | 0.005838 | 0.341649 | 58.520052 | 0.017088 | 96 |
| 9 | 3.347509 | 208.667457 | 0.004792 | 0.298730 | 62.335146 | 0.016042 | 108 |
| 10 | 3.828460 | 251.418698 | 0.003977 | 0.261202 | 65.670968 | 0.015227 | 120 |
| 11 | 4.378512 | 300.312201 | 0.003330 | 0.228388 | 68.587726 | 0.014580 | 132 |
| 12 | 5.007593 | 356.230450 | 0.002807 | 0.199697 | 71.138066 | 0.014057 | 144 |
| 13 | 5.727056 | 420.182722 | 0.002380 | 0.174610 | 73.368018 | 0.013630 | 156 |
| 14 | 6.549887 | 493.323301 | 0.002027 | 0.152674 | 75.317832 | 0.013277 | 168 |
| 15 | 7.490939 | 576.972311 | 0.001733 | 0.133495 | 77.022700 | 0.012983 | 180 |
| 16 | 8.567195 | 672.639547 | 0.001487 | 0.116724 | 78.513394 | 0.012737 | 192 |
| 17 | 9.798082 | 782.051719 | 0.001279 | 0.102061 | 79.816818 | 0.012529 | 204 |
| 18 | 11.205816 | 907.183624 | 0.001102 | 0.089239 | 80.956500 | 0.012352 | 216 |
| 19 | 12.815805 | 1050.293785 | 0.000952 | 0.078029 | 81.953009 | 0.012202 | 228 |
| 20 | 14.657109 | 1213.965218 | 0.000824 | 0.068226 | 82.824331 | 0.012074 | 240 |
| 21 | 16.762961 | 1401.152054 | 0.000714 | 0.059655 | 83.586193 | 0.011964 | 252 |
| 22 | 19.171370 | 1615.232853 | 0.000619 | 0.052161 | 84.252345 | 0.011869 | 264 |
| 23 | 21.925805 | 1860.071591 | 0.000538 | 0.045608 | 84.834813 | 0.011788 | 276 |
| 24 | 25.075983 | 2140.087398 | 0.000467 | 0.039879 | 85.344107 | 0.011717 | 288 |
| 25 | 28.678761 | 2460.334319 | 0.000406 | 0.034869 | 85.789421 | 0.011656 | 300 |
| 26 | 32.799166 | 2826.592538 | 0.000354 | 0.030489 | 86.178793 | 0.011604 | 312 |
| 27 | 37.511568 | 3245.472702 | 0.000308 | 0.026658 | 86.519249 | 0.011558 | 324 |
| 28 | 42.901021 | 3724.535238 | 0.000268 | 0.023309 | 86.816936 | 0.011518 | 336 |
| 29 | 49.064802 | 4272.426817 | 0.000234 | 0.020381 | 87.077226 | 0.011484 | 348 |
| 30 | 56.114160 | 4899.036412 | 0.000204 | 0.017821 | 87.304817 | 0.011454 | 360 |
| 31 | 64.176330 | 5615.673790 | 0.000178 | 0.015582 | 87.503816 | 0.011428 | 372 |
| 32 | 73.396828 | 6435.273643 | 0.000155 | 0.013625 | 87.677816 | 0.011405 | 384 |
| 33 | 83.942077 | 7372.629046 | 0.000136 | 0.011913 | 87.829958 | 0.011386 | 396 |
| 34 | 96.002408 | 8444.658462 | 0.000118 | 0.010416 | 87.962986 | 0.011368 | 408 |
| 35 | 109.795500 | 9670.711105 | 0.000103 | 0.009108 | 88.079303 | 0.011353 | 420 |
| 36 | 125.570307 | 11072.916176 | 0.000090 | 0.007964 | 88.181007 | 0.011340 | 432 |
| 37 | 143.611551 | 12676.582277 | 0.000079 | 0.006963 | 88.269935 | 0.011329 | 444 |
| 38 | 164.244860 | 14510.654207 | 0.000069 | 0.006088 | 88.347692 | 0.011319 | 456 |
| 39 | 187.842648 | 16608.235397 | 0.000060 | 0.005324 | 88.415680 | 0.011310 | 468 |
| 40 | 214.830836 | 19007.185391 | 0.000053 | 0.004655 | 88.475127 | 0.011303 | 480 |

14.00% ANNUAL INTEREST RATE                    1.1667% MONTHLY EFFECTIVE INTEREST RATE

| | 1<br>Future Value<br>of $1 | 2<br>Future Value<br>Annuity of<br>$1 per Month | 3<br>Sinking<br>Fund<br>Factor | 4<br>Present Value<br>of $1<br>(Reversion) | 5<br>Present Value<br>Annuity of<br>$1 per Month | 6<br>Installment<br>to<br>Amortize $1 | |
|---|---|---|---|---|---|---|---|
| Months | | | | | | | Months |
| 1 | 1.011667 | 1.000000 | 1.000000 | 0.988468 | 0.988468 | 1.011667 | 1 |
| 2 | 1.023469 | 2.011667 | 0.497100 | 0.977069 | 1.965537 | 0.508767 | 2 |
| 3 | 1.035410 | 3.035136 | 0.329475 | 0.965801 | 2.931338 | 0.341141 | 3 |
| 4 | 1.047490 | 4.070546 | 0.245667 | 0.954663 | 3.886001 | 0.257334 | 4 |
| 5 | 1.059710 | 5.118036 | 0.195387 | 0.943654 | 4.829655 | 0.207054 | 5 |
| 6 | 1.072074 | 6.177746 | 0.161871 | 0.932772 | 5.762427 | 0.173538 | 6 |
| 7 | 1.084581 | 7.249820 | 0.137934 | 0.922015 | 6.684442 | 0.149601 | 7 |
| 8 | 1.097235 | 8.334401 | 0.119985 | 0.911382 | 7.595824 | 0.131651 | 8 |
| 9 | 1.110036 | 9.431636 | 0.106026 | 0.900872 | 8.496696 | 0.117693 | 9 |
| 10 | 1.122986 | 10.541672 | 0.094862 | 0.890483 | 9.387178 | 0.106528 | 10 |
| 11 | 1.136088 | 11.664658 | 0.085729 | 0.880214 | 10.267392 | 0.097396 | 11 |
| 12 | 1.149342 | 12.800745 | 0.078120 | 0.870063 | 11.137455 | 0.089787 | 12 |
| Years | | | | | | | Months |
| 1 | 1.149342 | 12.800745 | 0.078120 | 0.870063 | 11.137455 | 0.089787 | 12 |
| 2 | 1.320987 | 27.513180 | 0.036346 | 0.757010 | 20.827743 | 0.048013 | 24 |
| 3 | 1.518266 | 44.422800 | 0.022511 | 0.658646 | 29.258904 | 0.034178 | 36 |
| 4 | 1.745007 | 63.857736 | 0.015660 | 0.573064 | 36.594546 | 0.027326 | 48 |
| 5 | 2.005610 | 86.195125 | 0.011602 | 0.498601 | 42.977016 | 0.023268 | 60 |
| 6 | 2.305132 | 111.868425 | 0.008939 | 0.433815 | 48.530168 | 0.020606 | 72 |
| 7 | 2.649385 | 141.375828 | 0.007073 | 0.377446 | 53.361760 | 0.018740 | 84 |
| 8 | 3.045049 | 175.289927 | 0.005705 | 0.328402 | 57.565549 | 0.017372 | 96 |
| 9 | 3.499803 | 214.268826 | 0.004667 | 0.285730 | 61.223111 | 0.016334 | 108 |
| 10 | 4.022471 | 259.068912 | 0.003860 | 0.248603 | 64.405420 | 0.015527 | 120 |
| 11 | 4.623195 | 310.559534 | 0.003220 | 0.216301 | 67.174230 | 0.014887 | 132 |
| 12 | 5.313632 | 369.739871 | 0.002705 | 0.188195 | 69.583269 | 0.014371 | 144 |
| 13 | 6.107180 | 437.758319 | 0.002284 | 0.163742 | 71.679284 | 0.013951 | 156 |
| 14 | 7.019239 | 515.934780 | 0.001938 | 0.142466 | 73.502950 | 0.013605 | 168 |
| 15 | 8.067507 | 605.786272 | 0.001651 | 0.123954 | 75.089654 | 0.013317 | 180 |
| 16 | 9.272324 | 709.056369 | 0.001410 | 0.107848 | 76.470187 | 0.013077 | 192 |
| 17 | 10.657072 | 827.749031 | 0.001208 | 0.093834 | 77.671337 | 0.012875 | 204 |
| 18 | 12.248621 | 964.167496 | 0.001037 | 0.081642 | 78.716413 | 0.012704 | 216 |
| 19 | 14.077855 | 1120.958972 | 0.000892 | 0.071034 | 79.625696 | 0.012559 | 228 |
| 20 | 16.180270 | 1301.166005 | 0.000769 | 0.061804 | 80.416829 | 0.012435 | 240 |
| 21 | 18.596664 | 1508.285522 | 0.000663 | 0.053773 | 81.105164 | 0.012330 | 252 |
| 22 | 21.373928 | 1746.336688 | 0.000573 | 0.046786 | 81.704060 | 0.012239 | 264 |
| 23 | 24.565954 | 2019.938898 | 0.000495 | 0.040707 | 82.225136 | 0.012162 | 276 |
| 24 | 28.234683 | 2334.401417 | 0.000428 | 0.035417 | 82.678506 | 0.012095 | 288 |
| 25 | 32.451308 | 2695.826407 | 0.000371 | 0.030815 | 83.072966 | 0.012038 | 300 |
| 26 | 37.297652 | 3111.227338 | 0.000321 | 0.026811 | 83.416171 | 0.011988 | 312 |
| 27 | 42.867759 | 3588.665088 | 0.000279 | 0.023328 | 83.714781 | 0.011945 | 324 |
| 28 | 49.269718 | 4137.404359 | 0.000242 | 0.020296 | 83.974591 | 0.011908 | 336 |
| 29 | 56.627757 | 4768.093467 | 0.000210 | 0.017659 | 84.200641 | 0.011876 | 348 |
| 30 | 65.084661 | 5492.970967 | 0.000182 | 0.015365 | 84.397320 | 0.011849 | 360 |
| 31 | 74.804537 | 6326.103143 | 0.000158 | 0.013368 | 84.568442 | 0.011825 | 372 |
| 32 | 85.975998 | 7283.656968 | 0.000137 | 0.011631 | 84.717330 | 0.011804 | 384 |
| 33 | 98.815828 | 8384.213825 | 0.000119 | 0.010120 | 84.846871 | 0.011786 | 396 |
| 34 | 113.573184 | 9649.130077 | 0.000104 | 0.008805 | 84.959580 | 0.011770 | 408 |
| 35 | 130.534434 | 11102.951488 | 0.000090 | 0.007661 | 85.057645 | 0.011757 | 420 |
| 36 | 150.028711 | 12773.889538 | 0.000078 | 0.006665 | 85.142966 | 0.011745 | 432 |
| 37 | 172.434303 | 14694.368868 | 0.000068 | 0.005799 | 85.217202 | 0.011735 | 444 |
| 38 | 198.185992 | 16901.656478 | 0.000059 | 0.005046 | 85.281792 | 0.011726 | 456 |
| 39 | 227.783490 | 19438.584899 | 0.000051 | 0.004390 | 85.337989 | 0.011718 | 468 |
| 40 | 261.801139 | 22354.383358 | 0.000045 | 0.003820 | 85.386883 | 0.011711 | 480 |

14.50% ANNUAL INTEREST RATE      1.2083% MONTHLY EFFECTIVE INTEREST RATE

| | 1<br>Future Value<br>of $1 | 2<br>Future Value<br>Annuity of<br>$1 per Month | 3<br>Sinking<br>Fund<br>Factor | 4<br>Present Value<br>of $1<br>(Reversion) | 5<br>Present Value<br>Annuity of<br>$1 per Month | 6<br>Installment<br>to<br>Amortize $1 | |
|---|---|---|---|---|---|---|---|
| Months | | | | | | | Months |
| 1 | 1.012083 | 1.000000 | 1.000000 | 0.988061 | 0.988061 | 1.012083 | 1 |
| 2 | 1.024313 | 2.012083 | 0.496997 | 0.976264 | 1.964325 | 0.509081 | 2 |
| 3 | 1.036690 | 3.036396 | 0.329338 | 0.964609 | 2.928934 | 0.341421 | 3 |
| 4 | 1.049216 | 4.073086 | 0.245514 | 0.953092 | 3.882026 | 0.257597 | 4 |
| 5 | 1.061894 | 5.122302 | 0.195225 | 0.941713 | 4.823739 | 0.207308 | 5 |
| 6 | 1.074726 | 6.184197 | 0.161702 | 0.930470 | 5.754209 | 0.173786 | 6 |
| 7 | 1.087712 | 7.258922 | 0.137761 | 0.919361 | 6.673570 | 0.149845 | 7 |
| 8 | 1.100855 | 8.346634 | 0.119809 | 0.908385 | 7.581955 | 0.131892 | 8 |
| 9 | 1.114157 | 9.447490 | 0.105848 | 0.897539 | 8.479495 | 0.117932 | 9 |
| 10 | 1.127620 | 10.561647 | 0.094682 | 0.886824 | 9.366318 | 0.106766 | 10 |
| 11 | 1.141245 | 11.689267 | 0.085549 | 0.876236 | 10.242554 | 0.097632 | 11 |
| 12 | 1.155035 | 12.830512 | 0.077939 | 0.865774 | 11.108328 | 0.090023 | 12 |
| Years | | | | | | | Months |
| 1 | 1.155035 | 12.830512 | 0.077939 | 0.865774 | 11.108328 | 0.090023 | 12 |
| 2 | 1.334107 | 27.650207 | 0.036166 | 0.749565 | 20.725634 | 0.048249 | 24 |
| 3 | 1.540940 | 44.767478 | 0.022338 | 0.648954 | 29.052051 | 0.034421 | 36 |
| 4 | 1.779841 | 64.538532 | 0.015495 | 0.561848 | 36.260850 | 0.027578 | 48 |
| 5 | 2.055779 | 87.374798 | 0.011445 | 0.486434 | 42.502042 | 0.023528 | 60 |
| 6 | 2.374497 | 113.751493 | 0.008791 | 0.421142 | 47.905507 | 0.020874 | 72 |
| 7 | 2.742628 | 144.217508 | 0.006934 | 0.364614 | 52.583688 | 0.019017 | 84 |
| 8 | 3.167833 | 179.406832 | 0.005574 | 0.315673 | 56.633938 | 0.017657 | 96 |
| 9 | 3.658959 | 220.051745 | 0.004544 | 0.273302 | 60.140540 | 0.016628 | 108 |
| 10 | 4.226227 | 266.998057 | 0.003745 | 0.236618 | 63.176466 | 0.015829 | 120 |
| 11 | 4.881441 | 321.222707 | 0.003113 | 0.204858 | 65.804893 | 0.015196 | 132 |
| 12 | 5.638237 | 383.854095 | 0.002605 | 0.177360 | 68.080518 | 0.014688 | 144 |
| 13 | 6.512363 | 456.195562 | 0.002192 | 0.153554 | 70.050696 | 0.014275 | 156 |
| 14 | 7.522010 | 539.752513 | 0.001853 | 0.132943 | 71.756425 | 0.013936 | 168 |
| 15 | 8.688187 | 636.263747 | 0.001572 | 0.115099 | 73.233202 | 0.013655 | 180 |
| 16 | 10.035163 | 747.737633 | 0.001337 | 0.099650 | 74.511757 | 0.013421 | 192 |
| 17 | 11.590968 | 876.493913 | 0.001141 | 0.086274 | 75.618698 | 0.013224 | 204 |
| 18 | 13.387978 | 1025.211968 | 0.000975 | 0.074694 | 76.577058 | 0.013059 | 216 |
| 19 | 15.463588 | 1196.986579 | 0.000835 | 0.064668 | 77.406782 | 0.012919 | 228 |
| 20 | 17.860991 | 1395.392327 | 0.000717 | 0.055988 | 78.125136 | 0.012800 | 240 |
| 21 | 20.630076 | 1624.557981 | 0.000616 | 0.048473 | 78.747069 | 0.012699 | 252 |
| 22 | 23.828467 | 1889.252413 | 0.000529 | 0.041967 | 79.285522 | 0.012613 | 264 |
| 23 | 27.522721 | 2194.983839 | 0.000456 | 0.036334 | 79.751701 | 0.012539 | 276 |
| 24 | 31.789716 | 2548.114445 | 0.000392 | 0.031457 | 80.155306 | 0.012476 | 288 |
| 25 | 36.718246 | 2955.992779 | 0.000338 | 0.027234 | 80.504738 | 0.012422 | 300 |
| 26 | 42.410872 | 3427.106674 | 0.000292 | 0.023579 | 80.807267 | 0.012375 | 312 |
| 27 | 48.986057 | 3971.259878 | 0.000252 | 0.020414 | 81.069189 | 0.012335 | 324 |
| 28 | 56.580627 | 4599.776067 | 0.000217 | 0.017674 | 81.295954 | 0.012301 | 336 |
| 29 | 65.352625 | 5325.734484 | 0.000188 | 0.015302 | 81.492281 | 0.012271 | 348 |
| 30 | 75.484592 | 6164.242121 | 0.000162 | 0.013248 | 81.662256 | 0.012246 | 360 |
| 31 | 87.187373 | 7132.748085 | 0.000140 | 0.011470 | 81.809416 | 0.012224 | 372 |
| 32 | 100.704498 | 8251.406712 | 0.000121 | 0.009930 | 81.936824 | 0.012205 | 384 |
| 33 | 116.317255 | 9543.496975 | 0.000105 | 0.008597 | 82.047130 | 0.012188 | 396 |
| 34 | 134.350542 | 11035.906907 | 0.000091 | 0.007443 | 82.142630 | 0.012174 | 408 |
| 35 | 155.179625 | 12759.693140 | 0.000078 | 0.006444 | 82.225312 | 0.012162 | 420 |
| 36 | 179.237953 | 14750.727180 | 0.000068 | 0.005579 | 82.296896 | 0.012151 | 432 |
| 37 | 207.026173 | 17050.441884 | 0.000059 | 0.004830 | 82.358871 | 0.012142 | 444 |
| 38 | 239.122549 | 19706.693669 | 0.000051 | 0.004182 | 82.412528 | 0.012134 | 456 |
| 39 | 276.194997 | 22774.758387 | 0.000044 | 0.003621 | 82.458982 | 0.012127 | 468 |
| 40 | 319.014986 | 26318.481600 | 0.000038 | 0.003135 | 82.499201 | 0.012121 | 480 |

230    **Appendix B**

15.00% ANNUAL INTEREST RATE        1.2500% MONTHLY EFFECTIVE INTEREST RATE

| | 1<br>Future Value<br>of $1 | 2<br>Future Value<br>Annuity of<br>$1 per Month | 3<br>Sinking<br>Fund<br>Factor | 4<br>Present Value<br>of $1<br>(Reversion) | 5<br>Present Value<br>Annuity of<br>$1 per Month | 6<br>Installment<br>to<br>Amortize $1 | |
|---|---|---|---|---|---|---|---|
| Months | | | | | | | Months |
| 1 | 1.012500 | 1.000000 | 1.000000 | 0.987654 | 0.987654 | 1.012500 | 1 |
| 2 | 1.025156 | 2.012500 | 0.496894 | 0.975461 | 1.963115 | 0.509394 | 2 |
| 3 | 1.037971 | 3.037656 | 0.329201 | 0.963418 | 2.926534 | 0.341701 | 3 |
| 4 | 1.050945 | 4.075627 | 0.245361 | 0.951524 | 3.878058 | 0.257861 | 4 |
| 5 | 1.064082 | 5.126572 | 0.195062 | 0.939777 | 4.817835 | 0.207562 | 5 |
| 6 | 1.077383 | 6.190654 | 0.161534 | 0.928175 | 5.746010 | 0.174034 | 6 |
| 7 | 1.090850 | 7.268038 | 0.137589 | 0.916716 | 6.662726 | 0.150089 | 7 |
| 8 | 1.104486 | 8.358888 | 0.119633 | 0.905398 | 7.568124 | 0.132133 | 8 |
| 9 | 1.118292 | 9.463374 | 0.105671 | 0.894221 | 8.462345 | 0.118171 | 9 |
| 10 | 1.132271 | 10.581666 | 0.094503 | 0.883181 | 9.345526 | 0.107003 | 10 |
| 11 | 1.146424 | 11.713937 | 0.085368 | 0.872277 | 10.217803 | 0.097868 | 11 |
| 12 | 1.160755 | 12.860361 | 0.077758 | 0.861509 | 11.079312 | 0.090258 | 12 |
| Years | | | | | | | Months |
| 1 | 1.160755 | 12.860361 | 0.077758 | 0.861509 | 11.079312 | 0.090258 | 12 |
| 2 | 1.347351 | 27.788084 | 0.035987 | 0.742197 | 20.624235 | 0.048487 | 24 |
| 3 | 1.563944 | 45.115505 | 0.022165 | 0.639409 | 28.847267 | 0.034665 | 36 |
| 4 | 1.815355 | 65.228388 | 0.015331 | 0.550856 | 35.931481 | 0.027831 | 48 |
| 5 | 2.107181 | 88.574508 | 0.011290 | 0.474568 | 42.034592 | 0.023790 | 60 |
| 6 | 2.445920 | 115.673621 | 0.008645 | 0.408844 | 47.292474 | 0.021145 | 72 |
| 7 | 2.839113 | 147.129040 | 0.006797 | 0.352223 | 51.822185 | 0.019297 | 84 |
| 8 | 3.295513 | 183.641059 | 0.005445 | 0.303443 | 55.724570 | 0.017945 | 96 |
| 9 | 3.825282 | 226.022551 | 0.004424 | 0.261419 | 59.086509 | 0.016924 | 108 |
| 10 | 4.440213 | 275.217058 | 0.003633 | 0.225214 | 61.982847 | 0.016133 | 120 |
| 11 | 5.153998 | 332.319805 | 0.003009 | 0.194024 | 64.478068 | 0.015509 | 132 |
| 12 | 5.982526 | 398.602077 | 0.002509 | 0.167153 | 66.627722 | 0.015009 | 144 |
| 13 | 6.944244 | 475.539523 | 0.002103 | 0.144004 | 68.479668 | 0.014603 | 156 |
| 14 | 8.060563 | 564.845011 | 0.001770 | 0.124061 | 70.075134 | 0.014270 | 168 |
| 15 | 9.356334 | 668.506759 | 0.001496 | 0.106879 | 71.449643 | 0.013996 | 180 |
| 16 | 10.860408 | 788.832603 | 0.001268 | 0.092078 | 72.633794 | 0.013768 | 192 |
| 17 | 12.606267 | 928.501369 | 0.001077 | 0.079326 | 73.653950 | 0.013577 | 204 |
| 18 | 14.632781 | 1090.622520 | 0.000917 | 0.068340 | 74.532823 | 0.013417 | 216 |
| 19 | 16.985067 | 1278.805378 | 0.000782 | 0.058875 | 75.289980 | 0.013282 | 228 |
| 20 | 19.715494 | 1497.239481 | 0.000668 | 0.050722 | 75.942278 | 0.013168 | 240 |
| 21 | 22.884848 | 1750.787854 | 0.000571 | 0.043697 | 76.504237 | 0.013071 | 252 |
| 22 | 26.563691 | 2045.095272 | 0.000489 | 0.037645 | 76.988370 | 0.012989 | 264 |
| 23 | 30.833924 | 2386.713938 | 0.000419 | 0.032432 | 77.405455 | 0.012919 | 276 |
| 24 | 35.790617 | 2783.249347 | 0.000359 | 0.027940 | 77.764777 | 0.012859 | 288 |
| 25 | 41.544120 | 3243.529615 | 0.000308 | 0.024071 | 78.074336 | 0.012808 | 300 |
| 26 | 48.222525 | 3777.802015 | 0.000265 | 0.020737 | 78.341024 | 0.012765 | 312 |
| 27 | 55.974514 | 4397.961118 | 0.000227 | 0.017865 | 78.570778 | 0.012727 | 324 |
| 28 | 64.972670 | 5117.813598 | 0.000195 | 0.015391 | 78.768713 | 0.012695 | 336 |
| 29 | 75.417320 | 5953.385616 | 0.000168 | 0.013260 | 78.939236 | 0.012668 | 348 |
| 30 | 87.540995 | 6923.279611 | 0.000144 | 0.011423 | 79.086142 | 0.012644 | 360 |
| 31 | 101.613606 | 8049.088447 | 0.000124 | 0.009841 | 79.212704 | 0.012624 | 372 |
| 32 | 117.948452 | 9355.876140 | 0.000107 | 0.008478 | 79.321738 | 0.012607 | 384 |
| 33 | 136.909198 | 10872.735858 | 0.000092 | 0.007304 | 79.415671 | 0.012592 | 396 |
| 34 | 158.917970 | 12633.437629 | 0.000079 | 0.006293 | 79.496596 | 0.012579 | 408 |
| 35 | 184.464752 | 14677.180163 | 0.000068 | 0.005421 | 79.566313 | 0.012568 | 420 |
| 36 | 214.118294 | 17049.463544 | 0.000059 | 0.004670 | 79.626375 | 0.012559 | 432 |
| 37 | 248.538777 | 19803.102194 | 0.000050 | 0.004024 | 79.678119 | 0.012550 | 444 |
| 38 | 288.492509 | 22999.400699 | 0.000043 | 0.003466 | 79.722696 | 0.012543 | 456 |
| 39 | 334.868983 | 26709.518627 | 0.000037 | 0.002986 | 79.761101 | 0.012537 | 468 |
| 40 | 388.700685 | 31016.054774 | 0.000032 | 0.002573 | 79.794186 | 0.012532 | 480 |

15.50% ANNUAL INTEREST RATE          1.2917% MONTHLY EFFECTIVE INTEREST RATE

| | 1<br>Future Value<br>of $1 | 2<br>Future Value<br>Annuity of<br>$1 per Month | 3<br>Sinking<br>Fund<br>Factor | 4<br>Present Value<br>of $1<br>(Reversion) | 5<br>Present Value<br>Annuity of<br>$1 per Month | 6<br>Installment<br>to<br>Amortize $1 | |
|---|---|---|---|---|---|---|---|
| Months | | | | | | | Months |
| 1 | 1.012917 | 1.000000 | 1.000000 | 0.987248 | 0.987248 | 1.012917 | 1 |
| 2 | 1.026000 | 2.012917 | 0.496792 | 0.974659 | 1.961907 | 0.509708 | 2 |
| 3 | 1.039253 | 3.038917 | 0.329065 | 0.962230 | 2.924137 | 0.341981 | 3 |
| 4 | 1.052676 | 4.078170 | 0.245208 | 0.949960 | 3.874096 | 0.258125 | 4 |
| 5 | 1.066273 | 5.130846 | 0.194900 | 0.937846 | 4.811942 | 0.207816 | 5 |
| 6 | 1.080046 | 6.197119 | 0.161365 | 0.925886 | 5.737828 | 0.174282 | 6 |
| 7 | 1.093997 | 7.277165 | 0.137416 | 0.914080 | 6.651908 | 0.150333 | 7 |
| 8 | 1.108128 | 8.371162 | 0.119458 | 0.902423 | 7.554331 | 0.132374 | 8 |
| 9 | 1.122441 | 9.479290 | 0.105493 | 0.890916 | 8.445247 | 0.118410 | 9 |
| 10 | 1.136939 | 10.601730 | 0.094324 | 0.879555 | 9.324801 | 0.107241 | 10 |
| 11 | 1.151624 | 11.738669 | 0.085189 | 0.868339 | 10.193140 | 0.098105 | 11 |
| 12 | 1.166500 | 12.890294 | 0.077578 | 0.857266 | 11.050406 | 0.090494 | 12 |
| Years | | | | | | | Months |
| 1 | 1.166500 | 12.890294 | 0.077578 | 0.857266 | 11.050406 | 0.090494 | 12 |
| 2 | 1.360721 | 27.926817 | 0.035808 | 0.734904 | 20.523538 | 0.048725 | 24 |
| 3 | 1.587281 | 45.466916 | 0.021994 | 0.630008 | 28.644529 | 0.034911 | 36 |
| 4 | 1.851563 | 65.927435 | 0.015168 | 0.540084 | 35.606374 | 0.028085 | 48 |
| 5 | 2.159847 | 89.794622 | 0.011137 | 0.462996 | 41.574525 | 0.024053 | 60 |
| 6 | 2.519461 | 117.635687 | 0.008501 | 0.396910 | 46.690816 | 0.021417 | 72 |
| 7 | 2.938950 | 150.112280 | 0.006662 | 0.340258 | 51.076835 | 0.019578 | 84 |
| 8 | 3.428284 | 187.996213 | 0.005319 | 0.291691 | 54.836819 | 0.018236 | 96 |
| 9 | 3.999093 | 232.187807 | 0.004307 | 0.250057 | 58.060124 | 0.017224 | 108 |
| 10 | 4.664940 | 283.737285 | 0.003524 | 0.214365 | 60.823352 | 0.016441 | 120 |
| 11 | 5.441651 | 343.869732 | 0.002908 | 0.183768 | 63.192173 | 0.015825 | 132 |
| 12 | 6.347684 | 414.014209 | 0.002415 | 0.157538 | 65.222881 | 0.015332 | 144 |
| 13 | 7.404571 | 495.837716 | 0.002017 | 0.135052 | 66.963738 | 0.014933 | 156 |
| 14 | 8.637429 | 591.284807 | 0.001691 | 0.115775 | 68.456114 | 0.014608 | 168 |
| 15 | 10.075557 | 702.623803 | 0.001423 | 0.099250 | 69.735477 | 0.014340 | 180 |
| 16 | 11.753134 | 832.500700 | 0.001201 | 0.085084 | 70.832231 | 0.014118 | 192 |
| 17 | 13.710027 | 984.002053 | 0.001016 | 0.072939 | 71.772440 | 0.013933 | 204 |
| 18 | 15.992741 | 1160.728325 | 0.000862 | 0.062528 | 72.578449 | 0.013778 | 216 |
| 19 | 18.655526 | 1366.879457 | 0.000732 | 0.053603 | 73.269413 | 0.013648 | 228 |
| 20 | 21.761665 | 1607.354675 | 0.000622 | 0.045952 | 73.861752 | 0.013539 | 240 |
| 21 | 25.384974 | 1887.868929 | 0.000530 | 0.039393 | 74.369545 | 0.013446 | 252 |
| 22 | 29.611562 | 2215.088702 | 0.000451 | 0.033771 | 74.804857 | 0.013368 | 264 |
| 23 | 34.541877 | 2596.790447 | 0.000385 | 0.028950 | 75.178036 | 0.013302 | 276 |
| 24 | 40.293086 | 3042.045391 | 0.000329 | 0.024818 | 75.497949 | 0.013245 | 288 |
| 25 | 47.001870 | 3561.435118 | 0.000281 | 0.021276 | 75.772200 | 0.013197 | 300 |
| 26 | 54.827664 | 4167.303044 | 0.000240 | 0.018239 | 76.007306 | 0.013157 | 312 |
| 27 | 63.956450 | 4874.047755 | 0.000205 | 0.015636 | 76.208854 | 0.013122 | 324 |
| 28 | 74.605175 | 5698.465199 | 0.000175 | 0.013404 | 76.381634 | 0.013092 | 336 |
| 29 | 87.026910 | 6660.147843 | 0.000150 | 0.011491 | 76.529752 | 0.013067 | 348 |
| 30 | 101.516858 | 7781.950293 | 0.000129 | 0.009851 | 76.656729 | 0.013045 | 360 |
| 31 | 118.419377 | 9090.532435 | 0.000110 | 0.008445 | 76.765582 | 0.013027 | 372 |
| 32 | 138.136160 | 10616.993021 | 0.000094 | 0.007239 | 76.858898 | 0.013011 | 384 |
| 33 | 161.135779 | 12397.608731 | 0.000081 | 0.006206 | 76.938894 | 0.012997 | 396 |
| 34 | 187.964827 | 14474.696298 | 0.000069 | 0.005320 | 77.007473 | 0.012986 | 408 |
| 35 | 219.260901 | 16897.618178 | 0.000059 | 0.004561 | 77.066262 | 0.012976 | 420 |
| 36 | 255.767761 | 19723.955656 | 0.000051 | 0.003910 | 77.116661 | 0.012967 | 432 |
| 37 | 298.352998 | 23020.877279 | 0.000043 | 0.003352 | 77.159866 | 0.012960 | 444 |
| 38 | 348.028662 | 26866.735135 | 0.000037 | 0.002873 | 77.196904 | 0.012954 | 456 |
| 39 | 405.975306 | 31352.926903 | 0.000032 | 0.002463 | 77.228655 | 0.012949 | 468 |
| 40 | 473.570044 | 36586.067943 | 0.000027 | 0.002112 | 77.255875 | 0.012944 | 480 |

## 232    Appendix B

16.00% ANNUAL INTEREST RATE          1.3333% MONTHLY EFFECTIVE INTEREST RATE

| | 1<br>Future Value<br>of $1 | 2<br>Future Value<br>Annuity of<br>$1 per Month | 3<br>Sinking<br>Fund<br>Factor | 4<br>Present Value<br>of $1<br>(Reversion) | 5<br>Present Value<br>Annuity of<br>$1 per Month | 6<br>Installment<br>to<br>Amortize $1 | |
|---|---|---|---|---|---|---|---|
| Months | | | | | | | Months |
| 1 | 1.013333 | 1.000000 | 1.000000 | 0.986842 | 0.986842 | 1.013333 | 1 |
| 2 | 1.026844 | 2.013333 | 0.496689 | 0.973857 | 1.960699 | 0.510022 | 2 |
| 3 | 1.040536 | 3.040178 | 0.328928 | 0.961043 | 2.921743 | 0.342261 | 3 |
| 4 | 1.054410 | 4.080713 | 0.245055 | 0.948398 | 3.870141 | 0.258389 | 4 |
| 5 | 1.068468 | 5.135123 | 0.194737 | 0.935919 | 4.806060 | 0.208071 | 5 |
| 6 | 1.082715 | 6.203591 | 0.161197 | 0.923604 | 5.729665 | 0.174530 | 6 |
| 7 | 1.097151 | 7.286306 | 0.137244 | 0.911452 | 6.641116 | 0.150577 | 7 |
| 8 | 1.111779 | 8.383457 | 0.119283 | 0.899459 | 7.540575 | 0.132616 | 8 |
| 9 | 1.126603 | 9.495236 | 0.105316 | 0.887624 | 8.428199 | 0.118649 | 9 |
| 10 | 1.141625 | 10.621839 | 0.094146 | 0.875945 | 9.304144 | 0.107479 | 10 |
| 11 | 1.156846 | 11.763464 | 0.085009 | 0.864419 | 10.168563 | 0.098342 | 11 |
| 12 | 1.172271 | 12.920310 | 0.077398 | 0.853045 | 11.021609 | 0.090731 | 12 |
| Years | | | | | | | Months |
| 1 | 1.172271 | 12.920310 | 0.077398 | 0.853045 | 11.021609 | 0.090731 | 12 |
| 2 | 1.374219 | 28.066412 | 0.035630 | 0.727686 | 20.423539 | 0.048963 | 24 |
| 3 | 1.610957 | 45.821745 | 0.021824 | 0.620749 | 28.443811 | 0.035157 | 36 |
| 4 | 1.888477 | 66.635803 | 0.015007 | 0.529527 | 35.285465 | 0.028340 | 48 |
| 5 | 2.213807 | 91.035516 | 0.010985 | 0.451711 | 41.121706 | 0.024318 | 60 |
| 6 | 2.595181 | 119.638587 | 0.008359 | 0.385330 | 46.100283 | 0.021692 | 72 |
| 7 | 3.042255 | 153.169132 | 0.006529 | 0.328704 | 50.347235 | 0.019862 | 84 |
| 8 | 3.566347 | 192.476010 | 0.005195 | 0.280399 | 53.970077 | 0.018529 | 96 |
| 9 | 4.180724 | 238.554316 | 0.004192 | 0.239193 | 57.060524 | 0.017525 | 108 |
| 10 | 4.900941 | 292.570569 | 0.003418 | 0.204042 | 59.696816 | 0.016751 | 120 |
| 11 | 5.745230 | 355.892244 | 0.002810 | 0.174057 | 61.945692 | 0.016143 | 132 |
| 12 | 6.734965 | 430.122395 | 0.002325 | 0.148479 | 63.864085 | 0.015658 | 144 |
| 13 | 7.895203 | 517.140233 | 0.001934 | 0.126659 | 65.500561 | 0.015267 | 156 |
| 14 | 9.255316 | 619.148703 | 0.001615 | 0.108046 | 66.896549 | 0.014948 | 168 |
| 15 | 10.849737 | 738.730255 | 0.001354 | 0.092168 | 68.087390 | 0.014687 | 180 |
| 16 | 12.718830 | 878.912215 | 0.001138 | 0.078624 | 69.103231 | 0.014471 | 192 |
| 17 | 14.909912 | 1043.243434 | 0.000959 | 0.067069 | 69.969789 | 0.014292 | 204 |
| 18 | 17.478455 | 1235.884123 | 0.000809 | 0.057213 | 70.709003 | 0.014142 | 216 |
| 19 | 20.489482 | 1461.711177 | 0.000684 | 0.048806 | 71.339585 | 0.014017 | 228 |
| 20 | 24.019222 | 1726.441638 | 0.000579 | 0.041633 | 71.877501 | 0.013913 | 240 |
| 21 | 28.157032 | 2036.777427 | 0.000491 | 0.035515 | 72.336367 | 0.013824 | 252 |
| 22 | 33.007667 | 2400.575011 | 0.000417 | 0.030296 | 72.727801 | 0.013750 | 264 |
| 23 | 38.693924 | 2827.044294 | 0.000354 | 0.025844 | 73.061711 | 0.013687 | 276 |
| 24 | 45.359757 | 3326.981781 | 0.000301 | 0.022046 | 73.346552 | 0.013634 | 288 |
| 25 | 53.173919 | 3913.043898 | 0.000256 | 0.018806 | 73.589534 | 0.013589 | 300 |
| 26 | 62.334232 | 4600.067404 | 0.000217 | 0.016043 | 73.796809 | 0.013551 | 312 |
| 27 | 73.072600 | 5405.444997 | 0.000185 | 0.013685 | 73.973623 | 0.013518 | 324 |
| 28 | 85.660875 | 6349.565632 | 0.000157 | 0.011674 | 74.124454 | 0.013491 | 336 |
| 29 | 100.417742 | 7456.330682 | 0.000134 | 0.009958 | 74.253120 | 0.013467 | 348 |
| 30 | 117.716787 | 8753.759030 | 0.000114 | 0.008495 | 74.362878 | 0.013448 | 360 |
| 31 | 137.995952 | 10274.696396 | 0.000097 | 0.007247 | 74.456506 | 0.013431 | 372 |
| 32 | 161.768625 | 12057.646856 | 0.000083 | 0.006182 | 74.536375 | 0.013416 | 384 |
| 33 | 189.636635 | 14147.747615 | 0.000071 | 0.005273 | 74.604507 | 0.013404 | 396 |
| 34 | 222.305489 | 16597.911700 | 0.000060 | 0.004498 | 74.662626 | 0.013394 | 408 |
| 35 | 260.602233 | 19470.167508 | 0.000051 | 0.003837 | 74.712205 | 0.013385 | 420 |
| 36 | 305.496388 | 22837.229116 | 0.000044 | 0.003273 | 74.754498 | 0.013377 | 432 |
| 37 | 358.124495 | 26784.337116 | 0.000037 | 0.002792 | 74.790576 | 0.013371 | 444 |
| 38 | 419.818887 | 31411.416562 | 0.000032 | 0.002382 | 74.821352 | 0.013365 | 456 |
| 39 | 492.141422 | 36835.606677 | 0.000027 | 0.002032 | 74.847605 | 0.013360 | 468 |
| 40 | 576.923018 | 43194.226353 | 0.000023 | 0.001733 | 74.870000 | 0.013356 | 480 |

16.50% ANNUAL INTEREST RATE        1.3750% MONTHLY EFFECTIVE INTEREST RATE

| | 1 | 2 | 3 | 4 | 5 | 6 | |
|---|---|---|---|---|---|---|---|
| | Future Value of $1 | Future Value Annuity of $1 per Month | Sinking Fund Factor | Present Value of $1 (Reversion) | Present Value Annuity of $1 per Month | Installment to Amortize $1 | |
| Months | | | | | | | Months |
| 1 | 1.013750 | 1.000000 | 1.000000 | 0.986436 | 0.986436 | 1.013750 | 1 |
| 2 | 1.027689 | 2.013750 | 0.496586 | 0.973057 | 1.959493 | 0.510336 | 2 |
| 3 | 1.041820 | 3.041439 | 0.328792 | 0.959859 | 2.919352 | 0.342542 | 3 |
| 4 | 1.056145 | 4.083259 | 0.244902 | 0.946840 | 3.866192 | 0.258652 | 4 |
| 5 | 1.070667 | 5.139404 | 0.194575 | 0.933997 | 4.800190 | 0.208325 | 5 |
| 6 | 1.085388 | 6.210070 | 0.161029 | 0.921329 | 5.721519 | 0.174779 | 6 |
| 7 | 1.100313 | 7.295459 | 0.137072 | 0.908833 | 6.630351 | 0.150822 | 7 |
| 8 | 1.115442 | 8.395771 | 0.119108 | 0.896506 | 7.526857 | 0.132858 | 8 |
| 9 | 1.130779 | 9.511213 | 0.105139 | 0.884346 | 8.411203 | 0.118889 | 9 |
| 10 | 1.146327 | 10.641993 | 0.093967 | 0.872351 | 9.283554 | 0.107717 | 10 |
| 11 | 1.162089 | 11.788320 | 0.084830 | 0.860519 | 10.144073 | 0.098580 | 11 |
| 12 | 1.178068 | 12.950409 | 0.077218 | 0.848847 | 10.992921 | 0.090968 | 12 |
| Years | | | | | | | Months |
| 1 | 1.178068 | 12.950409 | 0.077218 | 0.848847 | 10.992921 | 0.090968 | 12 |
| 2 | 1.387845 | 28.206874 | 0.035452 | 0.720542 | 20.324232 | 0.049202 | 24 |
| 3 | 1.634975 | 46.180028 | 0.021654 | 0.611630 | 28.245091 | 0.035404 | 36 |
| 4 | 1.926112 | 67.353629 | 0.014847 | 0.519181 | 34.968691 | 0.028597 | 48 |
| 5 | 2.269092 | 92.297573 | 0.010835 | 0.440705 | 40.676001 | 0.024585 | 60 |
| 6 | 2.673145 | 121.683238 | 0.008218 | 0.374091 | 45.520636 | 0.021968 | 72 |
| 7 | 3.149146 | 156.301554 | 0.006398 | 0.317546 | 49.632991 | 0.020148 | 84 |
| 8 | 3.709909 | 197.084288 | 0.005074 | 0.269548 | 53.123753 | 0.018824 | 96 |
| 9 | 4.370526 | 245.129128 | 0.004079 | 0.228805 | 56.086877 | 0.017829 | 108 |
| 10 | 5.148777 | 301.729222 | 0.003314 | 0.194221 | 58.602117 | 0.017064 | 120 |
| 11 | 6.065610 | 368.407990 | 0.002714 | 0.164864 | 60.737172 | 0.016464 | 132 |
| 12 | 7.145702 | 446.960120 | 0.002237 | 0.139944 | 62.549508 | 0.015987 | 144 |
| 13 | 8.418123 | 539.499881 | 0.001854 | 0.118791 | 64.087904 | 0.015604 | 156 |
| 14 | 9.917123 | 648.518025 | 0.001542 | 0.100836 | 65.393767 | 0.015292 | 168 |
| 15 | 11.683046 | 776.948825 | 0.001287 | 0.085594 | 66.502246 | 0.015037 | 180 |
| 16 | 13.763425 | 928.249057 | 0.001077 | 0.072656 | 67.443176 | 0.014827 | 192 |
| 17 | 16.214252 | 1106.491039 | 0.000904 | 0.061674 | 68.241881 | 0.014654 | 204 |
| 18 | 19.101493 | 1316.472236 | 0.000760 | 0.052352 | 68.919860 | 0.014510 | 216 |
| 19 | 22.502860 | 1563.844393 | 0.000639 | 0.044439 | 69.495360 | 0.014389 | 228 |
| 20 | 26.509903 | 1855.265646 | 0.000539 | 0.037722 | 69.983873 | 0.014289 | 240 |
| 21 | 31.230471 | 2198.579736 | 0.000455 | 0.032020 | 70.398545 | 0.014205 | 252 |
| 22 | 36.791623 | 2603.027124 | 0.000384 | 0.027180 | 70.750538 | 0.014134 | 264 |
| 23 | 43.343038 | 3079.493701 | 0.000325 | 0.023072 | 71.049327 | 0.014075 | 276 |
| 24 | 51.061052 | 3640.803789 | 0.000275 | 0.019584 | 71.302953 | 0.014025 | 288 |
| 25 | 60.153398 | 4302.065315 | 0.000232 | 0.016624 | 71.518243 | 0.013982 | 300 |
| 26 | 70.864801 | 5081.076442 | 0.000197 | 0.014111 | 71.700991 | 0.013947 | 312 |
| 27 | 83.483564 | 5998.804623 | 0.000167 | 0.011978 | 71.856116 | 0.013917 | 324 |
| 28 | 98.349326 | 7079.950943 | 0.000141 | 0.010168 | 71.987794 | 0.013891 | 336 |
| 29 | 115.862206 | 8353.614965 | 0.000120 | 0.008631 | 72.099568 | 0.013870 | 348 |
| 30 | 136.493572 | 9854.077955 | 0.000101 | 0.007326 | 72.194447 | 0.013851 | 360 |
| 31 | 160.798727 | 11621.725581 | 0.000086 | 0.006219 | 72.274985 | 0.013836 | 372 |
| 32 | 189.431855 | 13704.134912 | 0.000073 | 0.005279 | 72.343350 | 0.013823 | 384 |
| 33 | 223.163631 | 16157.354974 | 0.000062 | 0.004481 | 72.401381 | 0.013812 | 396 |
| 34 | 262.901961 | 19047.415341 | 0.000053 | 0.003804 | 72.450640 | 0.013803 | 408 |
| 35 | 309.716421 | 22452.103348 | 0.000045 | 0.003229 | 72.492454 | 0.013795 | 420 |
| 36 | 364.867044 | 26463.057775 | 0.000038 | 0.002741 | 72.527947 | 0.013788 | 432 |
| 37 | 429.838236 | 31188.235349 | 0.000032 | 0.002326 | 72.558076 | 0.013782 | 444 |
| 38 | 506.378726 | 36754.816450 | 0.000027 | 0.001975 | 72.583650 | 0.013777 | 456 |
| 39 | 596.548638 | 43312.628228 | 0.000023 | 0.001676 | 72.605359 | 0.013773 | 468 |
| 40 | 702.774938 | 51038.177275 | 0.000020 | 0.001423 | 72.623787 | 0.013770 | 480 |

17.00% ANNUAL INTEREST RATE          1.4167% MONTHLY EFFECTIVE INTEREST RATE

| | 1<br>Future Value<br>of $1 | 2<br>Future Value<br>Annuity of<br>$1 per Month | 3<br>Sinking<br>Fund<br>Factor | 4<br>Present Value<br>of $1<br>(Reversion) | 5<br>Present Value<br>Annuity of<br>$1 per Month | 6<br>Installment<br>to<br>Amortize $1 | |
|---|---|---|---|---|---|---|---|
| Months | | | | | | | Months |
| 1 | 1.014167 | 1.000000 | 1.000000 | 0.986031 | 0.986031 | 1.014167 | 1 |
| 2 | 1.028534 | 2.014167 | 0.496483 | 0.972258 | 1.958289 | 0.510650 | 2 |
| 3 | 1.043105 | 3.042701 | 0.328655 | 0.958676 | 2.916965 | 0.342822 | 3 |
| 4 | 1.057882 | 4.085806 | 0.244750 | 0.945285 | 3.862250 | 0.258916 | 4 |
| 5 | 1.072869 | 5.143688 | 0.194413 | 0.932080 | 4.794330 | 0.208580 | 5 |
| 6 | 1.088068 | 6.216557 | 0.160861 | 0.919060 | 5.713391 | 0.175027 | 6 |
| 7 | 1.103482 | 7.304625 | 0.136900 | 0.906222 | 6.619613 | 0.151066 | 7 |
| 8 | 1.119115 | 8.408107 | 0.118933 | 0.893563 | 7.513176 | 0.133100 | 8 |
| 9 | 1.134969 | 9.527222 | 0.104962 | 0.881081 | 8.394257 | 0.119129 | 9 |
| 10 | 1.151048 | 10.662191 | 0.093789 | 0.868774 | 9.263031 | 0.107956 | 10 |
| 11 | 1.167354 | 11.813238 | 0.084651 | 0.856638 | 10.119669 | 0.098817 | 11 |
| 12 | 1.183892 | 12.980593 | 0.077038 | 0.844672 | 10.964341 | 0.091205 | 12 |
| Years | | | | | | | Months |
| 1 | 1.183892 | 12.980593 | 0.077038 | 0.844672 | 10.964341 | 0.091205 | 12 |
| 2 | 1.401600 | 28.348209 | 0.035276 | 0.713471 | 20.225611 | 0.049442 | 24 |
| 3 | 1.659342 | 46.541802 | 0.021486 | 0.602648 | 28.048345 | 0.035653 | 36 |
| 4 | 1.964482 | 68.081048 | 0.014688 | 0.509040 | 34.655988 | 0.028855 | 48 |
| 5 | 2.325733 | 93.581182 | 0.010686 | 0.429972 | 40.237278 | 0.024853 | 60 |
| 6 | 2.753417 | 123.770579 | 0.008079 | 0.363185 | 44.951636 | 0.022246 | 72 |
| 7 | 3.259747 | 159.511558 | 0.006269 | 0.306772 | 48.933722 | 0.020436 | 84 |
| 8 | 3.859188 | 201.825006 | 0.004955 | 0.259122 | 52.297278 | 0.019121 | 96 |
| 9 | 4.568860 | 251.919548 | 0.003970 | 0.218873 | 55.138379 | 0.018136 | 108 |
| 10 | 5.409036 | 311.226062 | 0.003213 | 0.184876 | 57.538177 | 0.017380 | 120 |
| 11 | 6.403713 | 381.438553 | 0.002622 | 0.156159 | 59.565218 | 0.016788 | 132 |
| 12 | 7.581303 | 464.562540 | 0.002153 | 0.131903 | 61.277403 | 0.016319 | 144 |
| 13 | 8.975441 | 562.972341 | 0.001776 | 0.111415 | 62.723638 | 0.015943 | 156 |
| 14 | 10.625951 | 679.478890 | 0.001472 | 0.094109 | 63.945231 | 0.015638 | 168 |
| 15 | 12.579975 | 817.410030 | 0.001223 | 0.079491 | 64.977077 | 0.015390 | 180 |
| 16 | 14.893329 | 980.705566 | 0.001020 | 0.067144 | 65.848648 | 0.015186 | 192 |
| 17 | 17.632089 | 1174.029800 | 0.000852 | 0.056715 | 66.584839 | 0.015018 | 204 |
| 18 | 20.874484 | 1402.904761 | 0.000713 | 0.047905 | 67.206679 | 0.014879 | 216 |
| 19 | 24.713129 | 1673.867935 | 0.000597 | 0.040464 | 67.731930 | 0.014764 | 228 |
| 20 | 29.257669 | 1994.658995 | 0.000501 | 0.034179 | 68.175595 | 0.014668 | 240 |
| 21 | 34.637912 | 2374.440878 | 0.000421 | 0.028870 | 68.550346 | 0.014588 | 252 |
| 22 | 41.007538 | 2824.061507 | 0.000354 | 0.024386 | 68.866887 | 0.014521 | 264 |
| 23 | 48.548485 | 3356.363651 | 0.000298 | 0.020598 | 69.134261 | 0.014465 | 276 |
| 24 | 57.476150 | 3986.551756 | 0.000251 | 0.017399 | 69.360104 | 0.014418 | 288 |
| 25 | 68.045538 | 4732.626240 | 0.000211 | 0.014696 | 69.550868 | 0.014378 | 300 |
| 26 | 80.558550 | 5615.897651 | 0.000178 | 0.012413 | 69.712000 | 0.014345 | 312 |
| 27 | 95.372601 | 6661.595368 | 0.000150 | 0.010485 | 69.848104 | 0.014317 | 324 |
| 28 | 112.910833 | 7899.588246 | 0.000127 | 0.008857 | 69.963067 | 0.014293 | 336 |
| 29 | 133.674202 | 9365.237774 | 0.000107 | 0.007481 | 70.060174 | 0.014273 | 348 |
| 30 | 158.255782 | 11100.408126 | 0.000090 | 0.006319 | 70.142196 | 0.014257 | 360 |
| 31 | 187.357711 | 13154.661953 | 0.000076 | 0.005337 | 70.211479 | 0.014243 | 372 |
| 32 | 221.811244 | 15586.676066 | 0.000064 | 0.004508 | 70.270000 | 0.014231 | 384 |
| 33 | 262.600497 | 18465.917458 | 0.000054 | 0.003808 | 70.319431 | 0.014221 | 396 |
| 34 | 310.890557 | 21874.627526 | 0.000046 | 0.003217 | 70.361184 | 0.014212 | 408 |
| 35 | 368.060758 | 25910.171179 | 0.000039 | 0.002717 | 70.396451 | 0.014205 | 420 |
| 36 | 435.744087 | 30687.817929 | 0.000033 | 0.002295 | 70.426241 | 0.014199 | 432 |
| 37 | 515.873821 | 36344.034396 | 0.000028 | 0.001938 | 70.451403 | 0.014194 | 444 |
| 38 | 610.738749 | 43040.382285 | 0.000023 | 0.001637 | 70.472657 | 0.014190 | 456 |
| 39 | 723.048553 | 50968.133160 | 0.000020 | 0.001383 | 70.490609 | 0.014186 | 468 |
| 40 | 856.011201 | 60353.731845 | 0.000017 | 0.001168 | 70.505773 | 0.014183 | 480 |

17.50% ANNUAL INTEREST RATE          1.4583% MONTHLY EFFECTIVE INTEREST RATE

| | 1<br>Future Value<br>of $1 | 2<br>Future Value<br>Annuity of<br>$1 per Month | 3<br>Sinking<br>Fund<br>Factor | 4<br>Present Value<br>of $1<br>(Reversion) | 5<br>Present Value<br>Annuity of<br>$1 per Month | 6<br>Installment<br>to<br>Amortize $1 | |
|---|---|---|---|---|---|---|---|
| Months | | | | | | | Months |
| 1 | 1.014583 | 1.000000 | 1.000000 | 0.985626 | 0.985626 | 1.014583 | 1 |
| 2 | 1.029379 | 2.014583 | 0.496381 | 0.971459 | 1.957085 | 0.510964 | 2 |
| 3 | 1.044391 | 3.043963 | 0.328519 | 0.957496 | 2.914581 | 0.343102 | 3 |
| 4 | 1.059622 | 4.088354 | 0.244597 | 0.943733 | 3.858314 | 0.259181 | 4 |
| 5 | 1.075075 | 5.147976 | 0.194251 | 0.930168 | 4.788482 | 0.208834 | 5 |
| 6 | 1.090753 | 6.223050 | 0.160693 | 0.916798 | 5.705280 | 0.175276 | 6 |
| 7 | 1.106660 | 7.313950 | 0.136728 | 0.903620 | 6.608900 | 0.151311 | 7 |
| 8 | 1.122798 | 8.420463 | 0.118758 | 0.890632 | 7.499532 | 0.133342 | 8 |
| 9 | 1.139173 | 9.543261 | 0.104786 | 0.877830 | 8.377362 | 0.119369 | 9 |
| 10 | 1.155785 | 10.682434 | 0.093612 | 0.865212 | 9.242575 | 0.108195 | 10 |
| 11 | 1.172641 | 11.838219 | 0.084472 | 0.852776 | 10.095351 | 0.099055 | 11 |
| 12 | 1.189742 | 13.010860 | 0.076859 | 0.840519 | 10.935869 | 0.091442 | 12 |
| Years | | | | | | | Months |
| 1 | 1.189742 | 13.010860 | 0.076859 | 0.840519 | 10.935869 | 0.091442 | 12 |
| 2 | 1.415485 | 28.490422 | 0.035100 | 0.706471 | 20.127671 | 0.049683 | 24 |
| 3 | 1.684062 | 46.907104 | 0.021319 | 0.593802 | 27.853550 | 0.035902 | 36 |
| 4 | 2.003599 | 68.818198 | 0.014531 | 0.499102 | 34.347296 | 0.029114 | 48 |
| 5 | 2.383765 | 94.886740 | 0.010539 | 0.419504 | 39.805409 | 0.025122 | 60 |
| 6 | 2.836065 | 125.901571 | 0.007943 | 0.352601 | 44.393055 | 0.022526 | 72 |
| 7 | 3.374184 | 162.801210 | 0.006142 | 0.296368 | 48.249057 | 0.020726 | 84 |
| 8 | 4.014408 | 206.702250 | 0.004838 | 0.249103 | 51.490098 | 0.019421 | 96 |
| 9 | 4.776108 | 258.933147 | 0.003862 | 0.209375 | 54.214253 | 0.018445 | 108 |
| 10 | 5.682335 | 321.074424 | 0.003115 | 0.175984 | 56.503956 | 0.017698 | 120 |
| 11 | 6.760511 | 395.006493 | 0.002532 | 0.147918 | 58.428493 | 0.017115 | 132 |
| 12 | 8.043262 | 482.966559 | 0.002071 | 0.124328 | 60.046103 | 0.016654 | 144 |
| 13 | 9.569405 | 587.616318 | 0.001702 | 0.104500 | 61.405734 | 0.016285 | 156 |
| 14 | 11.385120 | 712.122501 | 0.001404 | 0.087834 | 62.548529 | 0.015988 | 168 |
| 15 | 13.545352 | 860.252699 | 0.001162 | 0.073826 | 63.509070 | 0.015746 | 180 |
| 16 | 16.115470 | 1036.489374 | 0.000965 | 0.062052 | 64.316422 | 0.015548 | 192 |
| 17 | 19.173247 | 1246.165497 | 0.000802 | 0.052156 | 64.995017 | 0.015386 | 204 |
| 18 | 22.811211 | 1495.625924 | 0.000669 | 0.043838 | 65.565388 | 0.015252 | 216 |
| 19 | 27.139450 | 1792.419399 | 0.000558 | 0.036847 | 66.044796 | 0.015141 | 228 |
| 20 | 32.288935 | 2145.526975 | 0.000466 | 0.030970 | 66.447747 | 0.015049 | 240 |
| 21 | 38.415493 | 2565.633784 | 0.000390 | 0.026031 | 66.786434 | 0.014973 | 252 |
| 22 | 45.704514 | 3065.452376 | 0.000326 | 0.021880 | 67.071108 | 0.014910 | 264 |
| 23 | 54.376566 | 3660.107401 | 0.000273 | 0.018390 | 67.310381 | 0.014857 | 276 |
| 24 | 64.694069 | 4367.593285 | 0.000229 | 0.015457 | 67.511495 | 0.014812 | 288 |
| 25 | 76.969232 | 5209.318748 | 0.000192 | 0.012992 | 67.680535 | 0.014775 | 300 |
| 26 | 91.573505 | 6210.754636 | 0.000161 | 0.010920 | 67.822616 | 0.014744 | 312 |
| 27 | 108.948818 | 7402.204679 | 0.000135 | 0.009179 | 67.942037 | 0.014718 | 324 |
| 28 | 129.620953 | 8819.722487 | 0.000113 | 0.007715 | 68.042414 | 0.014697 | 336 |
| 29 | 154.215454 | 10506.202542 | 0.000095 | 0.006484 | 68.126782 | 0.014679 | 348 |
| 30 | 183.476557 | 12512.678200 | 0.000080 | 0.005450 | 68.197695 | 0.014663 | 360 |
| 31 | 218.289712 | 14899.865974 | 0.000067 | 0.004581 | 68.257298 | 0.014650 | 372 |
| 32 | 259.708375 | 17740.002830 | 0.000056 | 0.003850 | 68.307396 | 0.014640 | 384 |
| 33 | 308.985885 | 21119.032099 | 0.000047 | 0.003236 | 68.349504 | 0.014631 | 396 |
| 34 | 367.613394 | 25139.204149 | 0.000040 | 0.002720 | 68.384897 | 0.014623 | 408 |
| 35 | 437.364986 | 29922.170503 | 0.000033 | 0.002286 | 68.414645 | 0.014617 | 420 |
| 36 | 520.351365 | 35612.665055 | 0.000028 | 0.001922 | 68.439649 | 0.014611 | 432 |
| 37 | 619.083721 | 42382.883753 | 0.000024 | 0.001615 | 68.460666 | 0.014607 | 444 |
| 38 | 736.549723 | 50437.695301 | 0.000020 | 0.001358 | 68.478330 | 0.014603 | 456 |
| 39 | 876.303925 | 60020.840537 | 0.000017 | 0.001141 | 68.493178 | 0.014600 | 468 |
| 40 | 1042.575327 | 71422.308104 | 0.000014 | 0.000959 | 68.505657 | 0.014597 | 480 |

236    **Appendix B**

18.00% ANNUAL INTEREST RATE          1.5000% MONTHLY EFFECTIVE INTEREST RATE

| | 1 | 2 | 3 | 4 | 5 | 6 | |
|---|---|---|---|---|---|---|---|
| | Future Value of $1 | Future Value Annuity of $1 per Month | Sinking Fund Factor | Present Value of $1 (Reversion) | Present Value Annuity of $1 per Month | Installment to Amortize $1 | |
| Months | | | | | | | Months |
| 1 | 1.015000 | 1.000000 | 1.000000 | 0.985222 | 0.985222 | 1.015000 | 1 |
| 2 | 1.030225 | 2.015000 | 0.496278 | 0.970662 | 1.955883 | 0.511278 | 2 |
| 3 | 1.045678 | 3.045225 | 0.328383 | 0.956317 | 2.912200 | 0.343383 | 3 |
| 4 | 1.061364 | 4.090903 | 0.244445 | 0.942184 | 3.854385 | 0.259445 | 4 |
| 5 | 1.077284 | 5.152267 | 0.194089 | 0.928260 | 4.782645 | 0.209089 | 5 |
| 6 | 1.093443 | 6.229551 | 0.160525 | 0.914542 | 5.697187 | 0.175525 | 6 |
| 7 | 1.109845 | 7.322994 | 0.136556 | 0.901027 | 6.598214 | 0.151556 | 7 |
| 8 | 1.126493 | 8.432839 | 0.118584 | 0.887711 | 7.485925 | 0.133584 | 8 |
| 9 | 1.143390 | 9.559332 | 0.104610 | 0.874592 | 8.360517 | 0.119610 | 9 |
| 10 | 1.160541 | 10.702722 | 0.093434 | 0.861667 | 9.222185 | 0.108434 | 10 |
| 11 | 1.177949 | 11.863262 | 0.084294 | 0.848933 | 10.071118 | 0.099294 | 11 |
| 12 | 1.195618 | 13.041211 | 0.076680 | 0.836387 | 10.907505 | 0.091680 | 12 |
| Years | | | | | | | Months |
| 1 | 1.195618 | 13.041211 | 0.076680 | 0.836387 | 10.907505 | 0.091680 | 12 |
| 2 | 1.429503 | 28.633521 | 0.034924 | 0.699544 | 20.030405 | 0.049924 | 24 |
| 3 | 1.709140 | 47.275969 | 0.021152 | 0.585090 | 27.660684 | 0.036152 | 36 |
| 4 | 2.043478 | 69.565219 | 0.014375 | 0.489362 | 34.042554 | 0.029375 | 48 |
| 5 | 2.443220 | 96.214652 | 0.010393 | 0.409296 | 39.380269 | 0.025393 | 60 |
| 6 | 2.921158 | 128.077197 | 0.007808 | 0.342330 | 43.844667 | 0.022808 | 72 |
| 7 | 3.492590 | 166.172636 | 0.006018 | 0.286321 | 47.578633 | 0.021018 | 84 |
| 8 | 4.175804 | 211.720235 | 0.004723 | 0.239475 | 50.701675 | 0.019723 | 96 |
| 9 | 4.992667 | 266.177771 | 0.003757 | 0.200294 | 53.313749 | 0.018757 | 108 |
| 10 | 5.969323 | 331.288191 | 0.003019 | 0.167523 | 55.498454 | 0.018019 | 120 |
| 11 | 7.137031 | 409.135393 | 0.002444 | 0.140114 | 57.325714 | 0.017444 | 132 |
| 12 | 8.533164 | 502.210922 | 0.001991 | 0.117190 | 58.854011 | 0.016991 | 144 |
| 13 | 10.202406 | 613.493716 | 0.001630 | 0.098016 | 60.132260 | 0.016630 | 156 |
| 14 | 12.198182 | 746.545446 | 0.001340 | 0.081979 | 61.201371 | 0.016340 | 168 |
| 15 | 14.584368 | 905.624513 | 0.001104 | 0.068567 | 62.095562 | 0.016104 | 180 |
| 16 | 17.437335 | 1095.822335 | 0.000913 | 0.057348 | 62.843452 | 0.015913 | 192 |
| 17 | 20.848395 | 1323.226308 | 0.000756 | 0.047965 | 63.468978 | 0.015756 | 204 |
| 18 | 24.926719 | 1595.114630 | 0.000627 | 0.040118 | 63.992160 | 0.015627 | 216 |
| 19 | 29.802839 | 1920.189249 | 0.000521 | 0.033554 | 64.429743 | 0.015521 | 228 |
| 20 | 35.632816 | 2308.854370 | 0.000433 | 0.028064 | 64.795732 | 0.015433 | 240 |
| 21 | 42.603242 | 2773.549452 | 0.000361 | 0.023472 | 65.101841 | 0.015361 | 252 |
| 22 | 50.937210 | 3329.147335 | 0.000300 | 0.019632 | 65.357866 | 0.015300 | 264 |
| 23 | 60.901454 | 3993.430261 | 0.000250 | 0.016420 | 65.572002 | 0.015250 | 276 |
| 24 | 72.814885 | 4787.658998 | 0.000209 | 0.013733 | 65.751103 | 0.015209 | 288 |
| 25 | 87.058800 | 5737.253308 | 0.000174 | 0.011486 | 65.900901 | 0.015174 | 300 |
| 26 | 104.089083 | 6872.605521 | 0.000146 | 0.009607 | 66.026190 | 0.015146 | 312 |
| 27 | 124.450799 | 8230.053258 | 0.000122 | 0.008035 | 66.130980 | 0.015122 | 324 |
| 28 | 148.795637 | 9853.042439 | 0.000101 | 0.006721 | 66.218625 | 0.015101 | 336 |
| 29 | 177.902767 | 11793.517795 | 0.000085 | 0.005621 | 66.291930 | 0.015085 | 348 |
| 30 | 212.703781 | 14113.585393 | 0.000071 | 0.004701 | 66.353242 | 0.015071 | 360 |
| 31 | 254.312506 | 16887.500372 | 0.000059 | 0.003932 | 66.404522 | 0.015059 | 372 |
| 32 | 304.060653 | 20204.043526 | 0.000049 | 0.003289 | 66.447412 | 0.015049 | 384 |
| 33 | 363.540442 | 24169.362788 | 0.000041 | 0.002751 | 66.483285 | 0.015041 | 396 |
| 34 | 434.655558 | 28910.370554 | 0.000035 | 0.002301 | 66.513289 | 0.015035 | 408 |
| 35 | 519.682084 | 34578.805589 | 0.000029 | 0.001924 | 66.538383 | 0.015029 | 420 |
| 36 | 621.341343 | 41356.089521 | 0.000024 | 0.001609 | 66.559372 | 0.015024 | 432 |
| 37 | 742.887000 | 49459.133344 | 0.000020 | 0.001346 | 66.576927 | 0.015020 | 444 |
| 38 | 888.209197 | 59147.279782 | 0.000017 | 0.001126 | 66.591609 | 0.015017 | 456 |
| 39 | 1061.959056 | 70730.603711 | 0.000014 | 0.000942 | 66.603890 | 0.015014 | 468 |
| 40 | 1269.697544 | 84579.836287 | 0.000012 | 0.000788 | 66.614161 | 0.015012 | 480 |

18.50% ANNUAL INTEREST RATE          1.5417% MONTHLY EFFECTIVE INTEREST RATE

| | 1<br>Future Value<br>of $1 | 2<br>Future Value<br>Annuity of<br>$1 per Month | 3<br>Sinking<br>Fund<br>Factor | 4<br>Present Value<br>of $1<br>(Reversion) | 5<br>Present Value<br>Annuity of<br>$1 per Month | 6<br>Installment<br>to<br>Amortize $1 | |
|---|---|---|---|---|---|---|---|
| Months | | | | | | | Months |
| 1 | 1.015417 | 1.000000 | 1.000000 | 0.984817 | 0.984817 | 1.015417 | 1 |
| 2 | 1.031071 | 2.015417 | 0.496175 | 0.969865 | 1.954683 | 0.511592 | 2 |
| 3 | 1.046967 | 3.046488 | 0.328247 | 0.955140 | 2.909823 | 0.343664 | 3 |
| 4 | 1.063107 | 4.093454 | 0.244292 | 0.940639 | 3.850462 | 0.259709 | 4 |
| 5 | 1.079497 | 5.156562 | 0.193928 | 0.926357 | 4.776819 | 0.209344 | 5 |
| 6 | 1.096139 | 6.236059 | 0.160358 | 0.912293 | 5.689112 | 0.175774 | 6 |
| 7 | 1.113038 | 7.332198 | 0.136385 | 0.898442 | 6.587554 | 0.151801 | 7 |
| 8 | 1.130197 | 8.445236 | 0.118410 | 0.884801 | 7.472355 | 0.133827 | 8 |
| 9 | 1.147621 | 9.575433 | 0.104434 | 0.871368 | 8.343723 | 0.119851 | 9 |
| 10 | 1.165314 | 10.723055 | 0.093257 | 0.858138 | 9.201861 | 0.108674 | 10 |
| 11 | 1.183279 | 11.888368 | 0.084116 | 0.845109 | 10.046970 | 0.099532 | 11 |
| 12 | 1.201521 | 13.071647 | 0.076501 | 0.832278 | 10.879248 | 0.091918 | 12 |
| Years | | | | | | | Months |
| 1 | 1.201521 | 13.071647 | 0.076501 | 0.832278 | 10.879248 | 0.091918 | 12 |
| 2 | 1.443653 | 28.777510 | 0.034749 | 0.692687 | 19.933810 | 0.050166 | 24 |
| 3 | 1.734580 | 47.648436 | 0.020987 | 0.576508 | 27.469724 | 0.036404 | 36 |
| 4 | 2.084135 | 70.322255 | 0.014220 | 0.479815 | 33.741702 | 0.029637 | 48 |
| 5 | 2.504132 | 97.565330 | 0.010250 | 0.399340 | 38.961733 | 0.025666 | 60 |
| 6 | 3.008768 | 130.298463 | 0.007675 | 0.332362 | 43.306252 | 0.023091 | 72 |
| 7 | 3.615099 | 169.628018 | 0.005895 | 0.276618 | 46.922100 | 0.021312 | 84 |
| 8 | 4.343618 | 216.883312 | 0.004611 | 0.230223 | 49.931492 | 0.020027 | 96 |
| 9 | 5.218949 | 273.661552 | 0.003654 | 0.191609 | 52.436143 | 0.019071 | 108 |
| 10 | 6.270678 | 341.881813 | 0.002925 | 0.159472 | 54.520710 | 0.018342 | 120 |
| 11 | 7.534353 | 423.849905 | 0.002359 | 0.132725 | 56.255650 | 0.017776 | 132 |
| 12 | 9.052685 | 522.336307 | 0.001914 | 0.110464 | 57.699602 | 0.017331 | 144 |
| 13 | 10.876993 | 640.669811 | 0.001561 | 0.091937 | 58.901372 | 0.016978 | 156 |
| 14 | 13.068938 | 782.850028 | 0.001277 | 0.076517 | 59.901580 | 0.016694 | 168 |
| 15 | 15.702606 | 953.682578 | 0.001049 | 0.063684 | 60.734031 | 0.016465 | 180 |
| 16 | 18.867015 | 1158.941514 | 0.000863 | 0.053003 | 61.426861 | 0.016280 | 192 |
| 17 | 22.669119 | 1405.564483 | 0.000711 | 0.044113 | 62.003489 | 0.016128 | 204 |
| 18 | 27.237428 | 1701.887217 | 0.000588 | 0.036714 | 62.483404 | 0.016004 | 216 |
| 19 | 32.726348 | 2057.925274 | 0.000486 | 0.030556 | 62.882827 | 0.015903 | 228 |
| 20 | 39.321402 | 2485.712559 | 0.000402 | 0.025431 | 63.215258 | 0.015819 | 240 |
| 21 | 47.245499 | 2999.708064 | 0.000333 | 0.021166 | 63.491933 | 0.015750 | 252 |
| 22 | 56.766471 | 3617.284577 | 0.000276 | 0.017616 | 63.722203 | 0.015693 | 264 |
| 23 | 68.206120 | 4359.315869 | 0.000229 | 0.014661 | 63.913852 | 0.015646 | 276 |
| 24 | 81.951101 | 5250.882223 | 0.000190 | 0.012202 | 64.073358 | 0.015607 | 288 |
| 25 | 98.465988 | 6322.118126 | 0.000158 | 0.010156 | 64.206111 | 0.015575 | 300 |
| 26 | 118.308975 | 7609.230808 | 0.000131 | 0.008452 | 64.316598 | 0.015548 | 312 |
| 27 | 142.150745 | 9155.724025 | 0.000109 | 0.007035 | 64.408554 | 0.015526 | 324 |
| 28 | 170.797139 | 11013.868459 | 0.000091 | 0.005855 | 64.485088 | 0.015507 | 336 |
| 29 | 205.216389 | 13246.468450 | 0.000075 | 0.004873 | 64.548785 | 0.015492 | 348 |
| 30 | 246.571848 | 15928.984743 | 0.000063 | 0.004056 | 64.601798 | 0.015479 | 360 |
| 31 | 296.261311 | 19152.085024 | 0.000052 | 0.003375 | 64.645920 | 0.015469 | 372 |
| 32 | 355.964255 | 23024.708445 | 0.000043 | 0.002809 | 64.682642 | 0.015460 | 384 |
| 33 | 427.698611 | 27677.747710 | 0.000036 | 0.002338 | 64.713205 | 0.015453 | 396 |
| 34 | 513.888962 | 33268.473181 | 0.000030 | 0.001946 | 64.738641 | 0.015447 | 408 |
| 35 | 617.448498 | 39985.848538 | 0.000025 | 0.001620 | 64.759812 | 0.015442 | 420 |
| 36 | 741.877481 | 48056.917654 | 0.000021 | 0.001348 | 64.777431 | 0.015437 | 432 |
| 37 | 891.381545 | 57754.478565 | 0.000017 | 0.001122 | 64.792096 | 0.015434 | 444 |
| 38 | 1071.013852 | 69406.303899 | 0.000014 | 0.000934 | 64.804301 | 0.015431 | 456 |
| 39 | 1286.845883 | 83406.219432 | 0.000012 | 0.000777 | 64.814459 | 0.015429 | 468 |
| 40 | 1546.172651 | 100227.415195 | 0.000010 | 0.000647 | 64.822913 | 0.015427 | 480 |

19.00% ANNUAL INTEREST RATE          1.5833% MONTHLY EFFECTIVE INTEREST RATE

| | 1 | 2 | 3 | 4 | 5 | 6 | |
|---|---|---|---|---|---|---|---|
| | Future Value of $1 | Future Value Annuity of $1 per Month | Sinking Fund Factor | Present Value of $1 (Reversion) | Present Value Annuity of $1 per Month | Installment to Amortize $1 | |
| Months | | | | | | | Months |
| 1 | 1.015833 | 1.000000 | 1.000000 | 0.984413 | 0.984413 | 1.015833 | 1 |
| 2 | 1.031917 | 2.015833 | 0.496073 | 0.969070 | 1.953483 | 0.511906 | 2 |
| 3 | 1.048256 | 3.047751 | 0.328111 | 0.953965 | 2.907449 | 0.343944 | 3 |
| 4 | 1.064853 | 4.096007 | 0.244140 | 0.939096 | 3.846545 | 0.259974 | 4 |
| 5 | 1.081714 | 5.160860 | 0.193766 | 0.924459 | 4.771004 | 0.209599 | 5 |
| 6 | 1.098841 | 6.242574 | 0.160190 | 0.910050 | 5.681054 | 0.176024 | 6 |
| 7 | 1.116239 | 7.341415 | 0.136214 | 0.895865 | 6.576920 | 0.152047 | 7 |
| 8 | 1.133913 | 8.457654 | 0.118236 | 0.881902 | 7.458822 | 0.134069 | 8 |
| 9 | 1.151866 | 9.591566 | 0.104258 | 0.868156 | 8.326978 | 0.120092 | 9 |
| 10 | 1.170104 | 10.743433 | 0.093080 | 0.854625 | 9.181602 | 0.108913 | 10 |
| 11 | 1.188631 | 11.913537 | 0.083938 | 0.841304 | 10.022906 | 0.099771 | 11 |
| 12 | 1.207451 | 13.102168 | 0.076323 | 0.828191 | 10.851097 | 0.092157 | 12 |
| Years | | | | | | | Months |
| 1 | 1.207451 | 13.102168 | 0.076323 | 0.828191 | 10.851097 | 0.092157 | 12 |
| 2 | 1.457938 | 28.922394 | 0.034575 | 0.685900 | 19.837878 | 0.050409 | 24 |
| 3 | 1.760389 | 48.024542 | 0.020823 | 0.568056 | 27.280649 | 0.036656 | 36 |
| 4 | 2.125583 | 71.089450 | 0.014067 | 0.470459 | 33.444684 | 0.029900 | 48 |
| 5 | 2.566537 | 98.939196 | 0.010107 | 0.389630 | 38.549682 | 0.025941 | 60 |
| 6 | 3.098968 | 132.566399 | 0.007543 | 0.322688 | 42.777596 | 0.023377 | 72 |
| 7 | 3.741852 | 173.169599 | 0.005775 | 0.267247 | 46.279115 | 0.021608 | 84 |
| 8 | 4.518103 | 222.195973 | 0.004501 | 0.221332 | 49.179042 | 0.020334 | 96 |
| 9 | 5.455388 | 281.392918 | 0.003554 | 0.183305 | 51.580735 | 0.019387 | 108 |
| 10 | 6.587114 | 352.870328 | 0.002834 | 0.151812 | 53.569796 | 0.018667 | 120 |
| 11 | 7.953617 | 439.175798 | 0.002277 | 0.125729 | 55.217118 | 0.018110 | 132 |
| 12 | 9.603603 | 543.385424 | 0.001840 | 0.104128 | 56.581415 | 0.017674 | 144 |
| 13 | 11.595879 | 669.213441 | 0.001494 | 0.086238 | 57.711314 | 0.017328 | 156 |
| 14 | 14.001456 | 821.144606 | 0.001218 | 0.071421 | 58.647086 | 0.017051 | 168 |
| 15 | 16.906072 | 1004.594042 | 0.000995 | 0.059150 | 59.422084 | 0.016829 | 180 |
| 16 | 20.413254 | 1226.100247 | 0.000816 | 0.048988 | 60.063930 | 0.016649 | 192 |
| 17 | 24.648004 | 1493.558135 | 0.000670 | 0.040571 | 60.595501 | 0.016503 | 204 |
| 18 | 29.761257 | 1816.500430 | 0.000551 | 0.033601 | 61.035743 | 0.016384 | 216 |
| 19 | 35.935259 | 2206.437425 | 0.000453 | 0.027828 | 61.400348 | 0.016287 | 228 |
| 20 | 43.390065 | 2677.267240 | 0.000374 | 0.023047 | 61.702310 | 0.016207 | 240 |
| 21 | 52.391377 | 3245.771169 | 0.000308 | 0.019087 | 61.952393 | 0.016141 | 252 |
| 22 | 63.260020 | 3932.211806 | 0.000254 | 0.015808 | 62.159509 | 0.016088 | 264 |
| 23 | 76.383375 | 4761.055238 | 0.000210 | 0.013092 | 62.331041 | 0.016043 | 276 |
| 24 | 92.229182 | 5761.843068 | 0.000174 | 0.010843 | 62.473102 | 0.016007 | 288 |
| 25 | 111.362218 | 6970.245332 | 0.000143 | 0.008980 | 62.590755 | 0.015977 | 300 |
| 26 | 134.464421 | 8429.331851 | 0.000119 | 0.007437 | 62.688195 | 0.015952 | 312 |
| 27 | 162.359199 | 10191.107326 | 0.000098 | 0.006159 | 62.768894 | 0.015931 | 324 |
| 28 | 196.040777 | 12318.364881 | 0.000081 | 0.005101 | 62.835728 | 0.015915 | 336 |
| 29 | 236.709632 | 14886.924139 | 0.000067 | 0.004225 | 62.891079 | 0.015901 | 348 |
| 30 | 285.815282 | 17988.333579 | 0.000056 | 0.003499 | 62.936920 | 0.015889 | 360 |
| 31 | 345.107947 | 21733.133503 | 0.000046 | 0.002898 | 62.974886 | 0.015879 | 372 |
| 32 | 416.700935 | 26254.795909 | 0.000038 | 0.002400 | 63.006328 | 0.015871 | 384 |
| 33 | 503.145960 | 31714.481694 | 0.000032 | 0.001987 | 63.032369 | 0.015865 | 396 |
| 34 | 607.524092 | 38306.784745 | 0.000026 | 0.001646 | 63.053935 | 0.015859 | 408 |
| 35 | 733.555571 | 46266.667644 | 0.000022 | 0.001363 | 63.071796 | 0.015855 | 420 |
| 36 | 885.732406 | 55877.836195 | 0.000018 | 0.001129 | 63.086589 | 0.015851 | 432 |
| 37 | 1069.478478 | 67482.851256 | 0.000015 | 0.000935 | 63.098840 | 0.015848 | 444 |
| 38 | 1291.342856 | 81495.338274 | 0.000012 | 0.000774 | 63.108986 | 0.015846 | 456 |
| 39 | 1559.233220 | 98414.729710 | 0.000010 | 0.000641 | 63.117389 | 0.015843 | 468 |
| 40 | 1882.697708 | 118844.065787 | 0.000008 | 0.000531 | 63.124348 | 0.015842 | 480 |

19.50% ANNUAL INTEREST RATE          1.6250% MONTHLY EFFECTIVE INTEREST RATE

| | 1 | 2 | 3 | 4 | 5 | 6 | |
|---|---|---|---|---|---|---|---|
| | Future Value of $1 | Future Value Annuity of $1 per Month | Sinking Fund Factor | Present Value of $1 (Reversion) | Present Value Annuity of $1 per Month | Installment to Amortize $1 | |
| Months | | | | | | | Months |
| 1 | 1.016250 | 1.000000 | 1.000000 | 0.984010 | 0.984010 | 1.016250 | 1 |
| 2 | 1.032764 | 2.016250 | 0.495970 | 0.968275 | 1.952285 | 0.512220 | 2 |
| 3 | 1.049546 | 3.049014 | 0.327975 | 0.952792 | 2.905078 | 0.344225 | 3 |
| 4 | 1.066602 | 4.098561 | 0.243988 | 0.937557 | 3.842635 | 0.260238 | 4 |
| 5 | 1.083934 | 5.165162 | 0.193605 | 0.922565 | 4.765200 | 0.209855 | 5 |
| 6 | 1.101548 | 6.249096 | 0.160023 | 0.907814 | 5.673014 | 0.176273 | 6 |
| 7 | 1.119448 | 7.350644 | 0.136043 | 0.893297 | 6.566311 | 0.152293 | 7 |
| 8 | 1.137639 | 8.470092 | 0.118062 | 0.879013 | 7.445325 | 0.134312 | 8 |
| 9 | 1.156126 | 9.607731 | 0.104083 | 0.864958 | 8.310283 | 0.120333 | 9 |
| 10 | 1.174913 | 10.763856 | 0.092904 | 0.851127 | 9.161410 | 0.109154 | 10 |
| 11 | 1.194005 | 11.938769 | 0.083761 | 0.837517 | 9.998927 | 0.100011 | 11 |
| 12 | 1.213408 | 13.132774 | 0.076145 | 0.824125 | 10.823053 | 0.092395 | 12 |
| Years | | | | | | | Months |
| 1 | 1.213408 | 13.132774 | 0.076145 | 0.824125 | 10.823053 | 0.092395 | 12 |
| 2 | 1.472358 | 29.068182 | 0.034402 | 0.679183 | 19.742605 | 0.050652 | 24 |
| 3 | 1.786570 | 48.404326 | 0.020659 | 0.559732 | 27.093435 | 0.036909 | 36 |
| 4 | 2.167838 | 71.866950 | 0.013915 | 0.461289 | 33.151440 | 0.030165 | 48 |
| 5 | 2.630471 | 100.336676 | 0.009966 | 0.380160 | 38.143997 | 0.026216 | 60 |
| 6 | 3.191833 | 134.882057 | 0.007414 | 0.313300 | 42.258489 | 0.023664 | 72 |
| 7 | 3.872995 | 176.799685 | 0.005656 | 0.258198 | 45.649346 | 0.021906 | 84 |
| 8 | 4.699521 | 227.662852 | 0.004392 | 0.212788 | 48.443838 | 0.020642 | 96 |
| 9 | 5.702435 | 289.380604 | 0.003456 | 0.175364 | 50.746850 | 0.019706 | 108 |
| 10 | 6.919378 | 364.269392 | 0.002745 | 0.144522 | 52.644820 | 0.018995 | 120 |
| 11 | 8.396025 | 455.140015 | 0.002197 | 0.119104 | 54.208986 | 0.018447 | 132 |
| 12 | 10.187801 | 565.403117 | 0.001769 | 0.098157 | 55.498055 | 0.018019 | 144 |
| 13 | 12.361955 | 699.197202 | 0.001430 | 0.080893 | 56.560409 | 0.017680 | 156 |
| 14 | 15.000089 | 861.543958 | 0.001161 | 0.066666 | 57.435922 | 0.017411 | 168 |
| 15 | 18.201222 | 1058.536743 | 0.000945 | 0.054941 | 58.157454 | 0.017195 | 180 |
| 16 | 22.085501 | 1297.569280 | 0.000771 | 0.045279 | 58.752088 | 0.017021 | 192 |
| 17 | 26.798714 | 1587.613173 | 0.000630 | 0.037315 | 59.242140 | 0.016880 | 204 |
| 18 | 32.517763 | 1939.554631 | 0.000516 | 0.030752 | 59.646005 | 0.016766 | 216 |
| 19 | 39.457300 | 2366.603063 | 0.000423 | 0.025344 | 59.978840 | 0.016673 | 228 |
| 20 | 47.877787 | 2884.786867 | 0.000347 | 0.020887 | 60.253138 | 0.016597 | 240 |
| 21 | 58.095269 | 3513.555022 | 0.000285 | 0.017213 | 60.479194 | 0.016535 | 252 |
| 22 | 70.493240 | 4276.507066 | 0.000234 | 0.014186 | 60.665492 | 0.016484 | 264 |
| 23 | 85.537031 | 5202.278860 | 0.000192 | 0.011691 | 60.819025 | 0.016442 | 276 |
| 24 | 103.791282 | 6325.617371 | 0.000158 | 0.009635 | 60.945556 | 0.016408 | 288 |
| 25 | 125.941129 | 7688.684833 | 0.000130 | 0.007940 | 61.049833 | 0.016380 | 300 |
| 26 | 152.817920 | 9342.641223 | 0.000107 | 0.006544 | 61.135770 | 0.016357 | 312 |
| 27 | 185.430422 | 11349.564442 | 0.000088 | 0.005393 | 61.206593 | 0.016338 | 324 |
| 28 | 225.002680 | 13784.780285 | 0.000073 | 0.004444 | 61.264961 | 0.016323 | 336 |
| 29 | 273.019957 | 16739.689647 | 0.000060 | 0.003663 | 61.313062 | 0.016310 | 348 |
| 30 | 331.284485 | 20325.199061 | 0.000049 | 0.003019 | 61.352704 | 0.016299 | 360 |
| 31 | 401.983105 | 24675.883358 | 0.000041 | 0.002488 | 61.385374 | 0.016291 | 372 |
| 32 | 487.769346 | 29955.036659 | 0.000033 | 0.002050 | 61.412299 | 0.016283 | 384 |
| 33 | 591.863021 | 36360.801284 | 0.000028 | 0.001690 | 61.434487 | 0.016278 | 396 |
| 34 | 718.171075 | 44133.604629 | 0.000023 | 0.001392 | 61.452774 | 0.016273 | 408 |
| 35 | 871.434226 | 53565.183118 | 0.000019 | 0.001148 | 61.467844 | 0.016269 | 420 |
| 36 | 1057.404894 | 65009.531938 | 0.000015 | 0.000946 | 61.480264 | 0.016265 | 432 |
| 37 | 1283.063112 | 78896.191532 | 0.000013 | 0.000779 | 61.490499 | 0.016263 | 444 |
| 38 | 1556.878505 | 95746.369530 | 0.000010 | 0.000642 | 61.498935 | 0.016260 | 456 |
| 39 | 1889.128177 | 116192.503219 | 0.000009 | 0.000529 | 61.505886 | 0.016259 | 468 |
| 40 | 2292.282448 | 141001.996799 | 0.000007 | 0.000436 | 61.511616 | 0.016257 | 480 |

20.00% ANNUAL INTEREST RATE          1.6667% MONTHLY EFFECTIVE INTEREST RATE

| | 1<br>Future Value<br>of $1 | 2<br>Future Value<br>Annuity of<br>$1 per Month | 3<br>Sinking<br>Fund<br>Factor | 4<br>Present Value<br>of $1<br>(Reversion) | 5<br>Present Value<br>Annuity of<br>$1 per Month | 6<br>Installment<br>to<br>Amortize $1 | |
|---|---|---|---|---|---|---|---|
| Months | | | | | | | Months |
| 1 | 1.016667 | 1.000000 | 1.000000 | 0.983607 | 0.983607 | 1.016667 | 1 |
| 2 | 1.033611 | 2.016667 | 0.495868 | 0.967482 | 1.951088 | 0.512534 | 2 |
| 3 | 1.050838 | 3.050278 | 0.327839 | 0.951622 | 2.902710 | 0.344506 | 3 |
| 4 | 1.068352 | 4.101116 | 0.243836 | 0.936021 | 3.838731 | 0.260503 | 4 |
| 5 | 1.086158 | 5.169468 | 0.193444 | 0.920677 | 4.759408 | 0.210110 | 5 |
| 6 | 1.104260 | 6.255625 | 0.159856 | 0.905583 | 5.664991 | 0.176523 | 6 |
| 7 | 1.122665 | 7.359886 | 0.135872 | 0.890738 | 6.555729 | 0.152538 | 7 |
| 8 | 1.141376 | 8.482551 | 0.117889 | 0.876136 | 7.431865 | 0.134556 | 8 |
| 9 | 1.160399 | 9.623926 | 0.103908 | 0.861773 | 8.293637 | 0.120574 | 9 |
| 10 | 1.179739 | 10.784325 | 0.092727 | 0.847645 | 9.141283 | 0.109394 | 10 |
| 11 | 1.199401 | 11.964064 | 0.083584 | 0.833749 | 9.975032 | 0.100250 | 11 |
| 12 | 1.219391 | 13.163465 | 0.075968 | 0.820081 | 10.795113 | 0.092635 | 12 |
| Years | | | | | | | Months |
| 1 | 1.219391 | 13.163465 | 0.075968 | 0.820081 | 10.795113 | 0.092635 | 12 |
| 2 | 1.486915 | 29.214877 | 0.034229 | 0.672534 | 19.647986 | 0.050896 | 24 |
| 3 | 1.813130 | 48.787826 | 0.020497 | 0.551532 | 26.908062 | 0.037164 | 36 |
| 4 | 2.210915 | 72.654905 | 0.013764 | 0.452301 | 32.861916 | 0.030430 | 48 |
| 5 | 2.695970 | 101.758208 | 0.009827 | 0.370924 | 37.744561 | 0.026494 | 60 |
| 6 | 3.287442 | 137.246517 | 0.007286 | 0.304188 | 41.748727 | 0.023953 | 72 |
| 7 | 4.008677 | 180.520645 | 0.005540 | 0.249459 | 45.032470 | 0.022206 | 84 |
| 8 | 4.888145 | 233.288730 | 0.004287 | 0.204577 | 47.725406 | 0.020953 | 96 |
| 9 | 5.960561 | 297.633662 | 0.003360 | 0.167769 | 49.933833 | 0.020027 | 108 |
| 10 | 7.268255 | 376.095300 | 0.002659 | 0.137585 | 51.744924 | 0.019326 | 120 |
| 11 | 8.862845 | 471.770720 | 0.002120 | 0.112831 | 53.230165 | 0.018786 | 132 |
| 12 | 10.807275 | 588.436476 | 0.001699 | 0.092530 | 54.448184 | 0.018366 | 144 |
| 13 | 13.178294 | 730.697658 | 0.001369 | 0.075882 | 55.447059 | 0.018035 | 156 |
| 14 | 16.069495 | 904.169675 | 0.001106 | 0.062230 | 56.266217 | 0.017773 | 168 |
| 15 | 19.594998 | 1115.699905 | 0.000896 | 0.051033 | 56.937994 | 0.017563 | 180 |
| 16 | 23.893966 | 1373.637983 | 0.000728 | 0.041852 | 57.488906 | 0.017395 | 192 |
| 17 | 29.136090 | 1688.165376 | 0.000592 | 0.034322 | 57.940698 | 0.017259 | 204 |
| 18 | 35.528288 | 2071.697274 | 0.000483 | 0.028147 | 58.311205 | 0.017149 | 216 |
| 19 | 43.322878 | 2539.372652 | 0.000394 | 0.023082 | 58.615050 | 0.017060 | 228 |
| 20 | 52.827531 | 3109.651838 | 0.000322 | 0.018930 | 58.864229 | 0.016988 | 240 |
| 21 | 64.417420 | 3805.045193 | 0.000263 | 0.015524 | 59.068575 | 0.016929 | 252 |
| 22 | 78.550028 | 4653.001652 | 0.000215 | 0.012731 | 59.236156 | 0.016882 | 264 |
| 23 | 95.783203 | 5686.992197 | 0.000176 | 0.010440 | 59.373585 | 0.016843 | 276 |
| 24 | 116.797184 | 6947.831050 | 0.000144 | 0.008562 | 59.486289 | 0.016811 | 288 |
| 25 | 142.421445 | 8485.286707 | 0.000118 | 0.007021 | 59.578715 | 0.016785 | 300 |
| 26 | 173.667440 | 10360.046428 | 0.000097 | 0.005758 | 59.654512 | 0.016763 | 312 |
| 27 | 211.768529 | 12646.111719 | 0.000079 | 0.004722 | 59.716672 | 0.016746 | 324 |
| 28 | 258.228656 | 15433.719354 | 0.000065 | 0.003873 | 59.767648 | 0.016731 | 336 |
| 29 | 314.881721 | 18832.903252 | 0.000053 | 0.003176 | 59.809452 | 0.016720 | 348 |
| 30 | 383.963963 | 22977.837794 | 0.000044 | 0.002604 | 59.843735 | 0.016710 | 360 |
| 31 | 468.202234 | 28032.134021 | 0.000036 | 0.002136 | 59.871850 | 0.016702 | 372 |
| 32 | 570.921630 | 34195.297782 | 0.000029 | 0.001752 | 59.894907 | 0.016696 | 384 |
| 33 | 696.176745 | 41710.604726 | 0.000024 | 0.001436 | 59.913815 | 0.016691 | 396 |
| 34 | 848.911717 | 50874.703014 | 0.000020 | 0.001178 | 59.929321 | 0.016686 | 408 |
| 35 | 1035.155379 | 62049.322767 | 0.000016 | 0.000966 | 59.942038 | 0.016683 | 420 |
| 36 | 1262.259241 | 75675.554472 | 0.000013 | 0.000792 | 59.952466 | 0.016680 | 432 |
| 37 | 1539.187666 | 92291.259933 | 0.000011 | 0.000650 | 59.961018 | 0.016678 | 444 |
| 38 | 1876.871717 | 112552.303043 | 0.000009 | 0.000533 | 59.968032 | 0.016676 | 456 |
| 39 | 2288.640640 | 137258.438381 | 0.000007 | 0.000437 | 59.973784 | 0.016674 | 468 |
| 40 | 2790.747993 | 167384.879555 | 0.000006 | 0.000358 | 59.978500 | 0.016673 | 480 |

20.50% ANNUAL INTEREST RATE　　　　1.7083% MONTHLY EFFECTIVE INTEREST RATE

| | 1<br>Future Value<br>of $1 | 2<br>Future Value<br>Annuity of<br>$1 per Month | 3<br>Sinking<br>Fund<br>Factor | 4<br>Present Value<br>of $1<br>(Reversion) | 5<br>Present Value<br>Annuity of<br>$1 per Month | 6<br>Installment<br>to<br>Amortize $1 | |
|---|---|---|---|---|---|---|---|
| Months | | | | | | | Months |
| 1 | 1.017083 | 1.000000 | 1.000000 | 0.983204 | 0.983204 | 1.017083 | 1 |
| 2 | 1.034459 | 2.017083 | 0.495765 | 0.966689 | 1.949893 | 0.512849 | 2 |
| 3 | 1.052131 | 3.051542 | 0.327703 | 0.950452 | 2.900345 | 0.344787 | 3 |
| 4 | 1.070104 | 4.103672 | 0.243684 | 0.934488 | 3.834834 | 0.260768 | 4 |
| 5 | 1.088385 | 5.173777 | 0.193282 | 0.918792 | 4.753626 | 0.210366 | 5 |
| 6 | 1.106979 | 6.262162 | 0.159689 | 0.903360 | 5.656986 | 0.176773 | 6 |
| 7 | 1.125889 | 7.369141 | 0.135701 | 0.888187 | 6.545172 | 0.152784 | 7 |
| 8 | 1.145123 | 8.495030 | 0.117716 | 0.873268 | 7.418441 | 0.134799 | 8 |
| 9 | 1.164686 | 9.640154 | 0.103733 | 0.858601 | 8.277041 | 0.120816 | 9 |
| 10 | 1.184583 | 10.804840 | 0.092551 | 0.844179 | 9.121220 | 0.109634 | 10 |
| 11 | 1.204819 | 11.989422 | 0.083407 | 0.830000 | 9.951220 | 0.100490 | 11 |
| 12 | 1.225402 | 13.194242 | 0.075791 | 0.816059 | 10.767279 | 0.092874 | 12 |
| Years | | | | | | | Months |
| 1 | 1.225402 | 13.194242 | 0.075791 | 0.816059 | 10.767279 | 0.092874 | 12 |
| 2 | 1.501609 | 29.362487 | 0.034057 | 0.665952 | 19.554014 | 0.051140 | 24 |
| 3 | 1.840074 | 49.175080 | 0.020336 | 0.543456 | 26.724508 | 0.037419 | 36 |
| 4 | 2.254830 | 73.453465 | 0.013614 | 0.443492 | 32.576054 | 0.030697 | 48 |
| 5 | 2.763072 | 103.204237 | 0.009690 | 0.361916 | 37.351261 | 0.026773 | 60 |
| 6 | 3.385873 | 139.660882 | 0.007160 | 0.295345 | 41.248111 | 0.024244 | 72 |
| 7 | 4.149055 | 184.334913 | 0.005425 | 0.241019 | 44.428171 | 0.022508 | 84 |
| 8 | 5.084258 | 239.078544 | 0.004183 | 0.196686 | 47.023287 | 0.021266 | 96 |
| 9 | 6.230259 | 306.161478 | 0.003266 | 0.160507 | 49.141055 | 0.020350 | 108 |
| 10 | 7.634569 | 388.365015 | 0.002575 | 0.130983 | 50.869278 | 0.019658 | 120 |
| 11 | 9.355413 | 489.097362 | 0.002045 | 0.106890 | 52.279611 | 0.019128 | 132 |
| 12 | 11.464139 | 612.534945 | 0.001633 | 0.087229 | 53.430525 | 0.018716 | 144 |
| 13 | 14.048174 | 763.795559 | 0.001309 | 0.071184 | 54.369739 | 0.018393 | 156 |
| 14 | 17.214655 | 949.150562 | 0.001054 | 0.058090 | 55.136193 | 0.018137 | 168 |
| 15 | 21.094867 | 1176.284885 | 0.000850 | 0.047405 | 55.761665 | 0.017933 | 180 |
| 16 | 25.849684 | 1454.615652 | 0.000687 | 0.038685 | 56.272086 | 0.017771 | 192 |
| 17 | 31.676245 | 1795.682628 | 0.000557 | 0.031569 | 56.688621 | 0.017640 | 204 |
| 18 | 38.816122 | 2213.626655 | 0.000452 | 0.025762 | 57.028537 | 0.017535 | 216 |
| 19 | 47.565339 | 2725.775945 | 0.000367 | 0.021024 | 57.305929 | 0.017450 | 228 |
| 20 | 58.286644 | 3353.364518 | 0.000298 | 0.017157 | 57.532297 | 0.017382 | 240 |
| 21 | 71.424548 | 4122.412577 | 0.000243 | 0.014001 | 57.717027 | 0.017326 | 252 |
| 22 | 87.523758 | 5064.805318 | 0.000197 | 0.011425 | 57.867777 | 0.017281 | 264 |
| 23 | 107.251755 | 6219.614917 | 0.000161 | 0.009324 | 57.990799 | 0.017244 | 276 |
| 24 | 131.426475 | 7634.720477 | 0.000131 | 0.007609 | 58.091191 | 0.017214 | 288 |
| 25 | 161.050216 | 9368.793133 | 0.000107 | 0.006209 | 58.173117 | 0.017190 | 300 |
| 26 | 197.351197 | 11493.728585 | 0.000087 | 0.005067 | 58.239974 | 0.017170 | 312 |
| 27 | 241.834477 | 14097.627945 | 0.000071 | 0.004135 | 58.294533 | 0.017154 | 324 |
| 28 | 296.344362 | 17288.450456 | 0.000058 | 0.003374 | 58.339056 | 0.017141 | 336 |
| 29 | 363.140863 | 21198.489552 | 0.000047 | 0.002754 | 58.375390 | 0.017131 | 348 |
| 30 | 444.993404 | 25989.857819 | 0.000038 | 0.002247 | 58.405041 | 0.017122 | 360 |
| 31 | 545.295642 | 31861.208287 | 0.000031 | 0.001834 | 58.429237 | 0.017115 | 372 |
| 32 | 668.206166 | 39055.970701 | 0.000026 | 0.001497 | 58.448983 | 0.017109 | 384 |
| 33 | 818.820923 | 47872.444265 | 0.000021 | 0.001221 | 58.465096 | 0.017104 | 396 |
| 34 | 1003.384491 | 58676.165312 | 0.000017 | 0.000997 | 58.478246 | 0.017100 | 408 |
| 35 | 1229.548987 | 71915.062655 | 0.000014 | 0.000813 | 58.488977 | 0.017097 | 420 |
| 36 | 1506.691329 | 88138.028994 | 0.000011 | 0.000664 | 58.497734 | 0.017095 | 432 |
| 37 | 1846.302005 | 108017.678332 | 0.000009 | 0.000542 | 58.504881 | 0.017093 | 444 |
| 38 | 2262.461480 | 132378.232968 | 0.000008 | 0.000442 | 58.510712 | 0.017091 | 456 |
| 39 | 2772.423977 | 162229.696242 | 0.000006 | 0.000361 | 58.515472 | 0.017089 | 468 |
| 40 | 3397.332852 | 198809.727894 | 0.000005 | 0.000294 | 58.519355 | 0.017088 | 480 |

21.00% ANNUAL INTEREST RATE                    1.7500% MONTHLY EFFECTIVE INTEREST RATE

| | 1<br>Future Value<br>of $1 | 2<br>Future Value<br>Annuity of<br>$1 per Month | 3<br>Sinking<br>Fund<br>Factor | 4<br>Present Value<br>of $1<br>(Reversion) | 5<br>Present Value<br>Annuity of<br>$1 per Month | 6<br>Installment<br>to<br>Amortize $1 | |
|---|---|---|---|---|---|---|---|
| Months | | | | | | | Months |
| 1 | 1.017500 | 1.000000 | 1.000000 | 0.982801 | 0.982801 | 1.017500 | 1 |
| 2 | 1.035306 | 2.017500 | 0.495663 | 0.965898 | 1.948699 | 0.513163 | 2 |
| 3 | 1.053424 | 3.052806 | 0.327567 | 0.949285 | 2.897984 | 0.345067 | 3 |
| 4 | 1.071859 | 4.106230 | 0.243532 | 0.932959 | 3.830943 | 0.261032 | 4 |
| 5 | 1.090617 | 5.178089 | 0.193121 | 0.916913 | 4.747855 | 0.210621 | 5 |
| 6 | 1.109702 | 6.268706 | 0.159523 | 0.901143 | 5.648998 | 0.177023 | 6 |
| 7 | 1.129122 | 7.378408 | 0.135531 | 0.885644 | 6.534641 | 0.153031 | 7 |
| 8 | 1.148882 | 8.507530 | 0.117543 | 0.870412 | 7.405053 | 0.135043 | 8 |
| 9 | 1.168987 | 9.656412 | 0.103558 | 0.855441 | 8.260494 | 0.121058 | 9 |
| 10 | 1.189444 | 10.825399 | 0.092375 | 0.840729 | 9.101223 | 0.109875 | 10 |
| 11 | 1.210260 | 12.014844 | 0.083230 | 0.826269 | 9.927492 | 0.100730 | 11 |
| 12 | 1.231439 | 13.225104 | 0.075614 | 0.812058 | 10.739550 | 0.093114 | 12 |
| Years | | | | | | | Months |
| 1 | 1.231439 | 13.225104 | 0.075614 | 0.812058 | 10.739550 | 0.093114 | 12 |
| 2 | 1.516443 | 29.511016 | 0.033886 | 0.659438 | 19.460686 | 0.051386 | 24 |
| 3 | 1.867407 | 49.566129 | 0.020175 | 0.535502 | 26.542753 | 0.037675 | 36 |
| 4 | 2.299599 | 74.262784 | 0.013466 | 0.434858 | 32.293801 | 0.030966 | 48 |
| 5 | 2.831816 | 104.675216 | 0.009553 | 0.353130 | 36.963986 | 0.027053 | 60 |
| 6 | 3.487210 | 142.126280 | 0.007036 | 0.286762 | 40.756445 | 0.024536 | 72 |
| 7 | 4.294287 | 188.244992 | 0.005312 | 0.232868 | 43.836142 | 0.022812 | 84 |
| 8 | 5.288154 | 245.037388 | 0.004081 | 0.189102 | 46.337035 | 0.021581 | 96 |
| 9 | 6.512041 | 314.973777 | 0.003175 | 0.153562 | 48.367904 | 0.020675 | 108 |
| 10 | 8.019183 | 401.096196 | 0.002493 | 0.124701 | 50.017087 | 0.019993 | 120 |
| 11 | 9.875138 | 507.150729 | 0.001972 | 0.101264 | 51.356319 | 0.019472 | 132 |
| 12 | 12.160633 | 637.750450 | 0.001568 | 0.082233 | 52.443854 | 0.019068 | 144 |
| 13 | 14.975081 | 798.576080 | 0.001252 | 0.066778 | 53.326994 | 0.018752 | 156 |
| 14 | 18.440904 | 996.623085 | 0.001003 | 0.054227 | 54.044156 | 0.018503 | 168 |
| 15 | 22.708854 | 1240.505953 | 0.000806 | 0.044036 | 54.626532 | 0.018306 | 180 |
| 16 | 27.964576 | 1540.832905 | 0.000649 | 0.035760 | 55.099456 | 0.018149 | 192 |
| 17 | 34.436678 | 1910.667320 | 0.000523 | 0.029039 | 55.483497 | 0.018023 | 204 |
| 18 | 42.406679 | 2366.095959 | 0.000423 | 0.023581 | 55.795361 | 0.017923 | 216 |
| 19 | 52.221252 | 2926.928691 | 0.000342 | 0.019149 | 56.048612 | 0.017842 | 228 |
| 20 | 64.307303 | 3617.560166 | 0.000276 | 0.015550 | 56.254267 | 0.017776 | 240 |
| 21 | 79.190541 | 4468.030916 | 0.000224 | 0.012628 | 56.421270 | 0.017724 | 252 |
| 22 | 97.518346 | 5515.334034 | 0.000181 | 0.010254 | 56.556887 | 0.017681 | 264 |
| 23 | 120.087925 | 6805.024269 | 0.000147 | 0.008327 | 56.667015 | 0.017647 | 276 |
| 24 | 147.880992 | 8393.199527 | 0.000119 | 0.006762 | 56.756446 | 0.017619 | 288 |
| 25 | 182.106467 | 10348.940980 | 0.000097 | 0.005491 | 56.829069 | 0.017597 | 300 |
| 26 | 224.253063 | 12757.317895 | 0.000078 | 0.004459 | 56.888043 | 0.017578 | 312 |
| 27 | 276.154038 | 15723.087912 | 0.000064 | 0.003621 | 56.935933 | 0.017564 | 324 |
| 28 | 340.066940 | 19375.253711 | 0.000052 | 0.002941 | 56.974823 | 0.017552 | 336 |
| 29 | 418.771800 | 23872.674261 | 0.000042 | 0.002388 | 57.006404 | 0.017542 | 348 |
| 30 | 515.692058 | 29410.974741 | 0.000034 | 0.001939 | 57.032049 | 0.017534 | 360 |
| 31 | 635.043475 | 36231.055691 | 0.000028 | 0.001575 | 57.052875 | 0.017528 | 372 |
| 32 | 782.017501 | 44629.571504 | 0.000022 | 0.001279 | 57.069786 | 0.017522 | 384 |
| 33 | 963.007096 | 54971.834062 | 0.000018 | 0.001038 | 57.083519 | 0.017518 | 396 |
| 34 | 1185.884799 | 67707.702783 | 0.000015 | 0.000843 | 57.094671 | 0.017515 | 408 |
| 35 | 1460.345164 | 83391.152235 | 0.000012 | 0.000685 | 57.103727 | 0.017512 | 420 |
| 36 | 1798.326448 | 102704.368485 | 0.000010 | 0.000556 | 57.111082 | 0.017510 | 432 |
| 37 | 2214.529890 | 126487.422272 | 0.000008 | 0.000452 | 57.117054 | 0.017508 | 444 |
| 38 | 2727.059170 | 155754.809736 | 0.000006 | 0.000367 | 57.121903 | 0.017506 | 456 |
| 39 | 3358.207877 | 191840.450090 | 0.000005 | 0.000298 | 57.125841 | 0.017505 | 468 |
| 40 | 4135.429207 | 236253.097541 | 0.000004 | 0.000242 | 57.129039 | 0.017504 | 480 |

21.50% ANNUAL INTEREST RATE       1.7917% MONTHLY EFFECTIVE INTEREST RATE

| | 1<br>Future Value<br>of $1 | 2<br>Future Value<br>Annuity of<br>$1 per Month | 3<br>Sinking<br>Fund<br>Factor | 4<br>Present Value<br>of $1<br>(Reversion) | 5<br>Present Value<br>Annuity of<br>$1 per Month | 6<br>Installment<br>to<br>Amortize $1 | |
|---|---|---|---|---|---|---|---|
| Months | | | | | | | Months |
| 1 | 1.017917 | 1.000000 | 1.000000 | 0.982399 | 0.982399 | 1.017917 | 1 |
| 2 | 1.036154 | 2.017917 | 0.495561 | 0.965107 | 1.947506 | 0.513477 | 2 |
| 3 | 1.054719 | 3.054071 | 0.327432 | 0.948120 | 2.895626 | 0.345348 | 3 |
| 4 | 1.073616 | 4.108790 | 0.243381 | 0.931432 | 3.827058 | 0.261297 | 4 |
| 5 | 1.092851 | 5.182406 | 0.192961 | 0.915037 | 4.742095 | 0.210877 | 5 |
| 6 | 1.112432 | 6.275257 | 0.159356 | 0.898932 | 5.641027 | 0.177273 | 6 |
| 7 | 1.132363 | 7.387689 | 0.135360 | 0.883109 | 6.524136 | 0.153277 | 7 |
| 8 | 1.152651 | 8.520051 | 0.117370 | 0.867565 | 7.391701 | 0.135287 | 8 |
| 9 | 1.173303 | 9.672702 | 0.103384 | 0.852295 | 8.243996 | 0.121300 | 9 |
| 10 | 1.194324 | 10.846005 | 0.092200 | 0.837294 | 9.081290 | 0.110117 | 10 |
| 11 | 1.215723 | 12.040329 | 0.083054 | 0.822556 | 9.903846 | 0.100971 | 11 |
| 12 | 1.237504 | 13.256052 | 0.075437 | 0.808078 | 10.711924 | 0.093354 | 12 |
| Years | | | | | | | Months |
| 1 | 1.237504 | 13.256052 | 0.075437 | 0.808078 | 10.711924 | 0.093354 | 12 |
| 2 | 1.531417 | 29.660472 | 0.033715 | 0.652990 | 19.367995 | 0.051632 | 24 |
| 3 | 1.895135 | 49.961013 | 0.020016 | 0.527667 | 26.362775 | 0.037932 | 36 |
| 4 | 2.345237 | 75.083018 | 0.013319 | 0.426396 | 32.015103 | 0.031235 | 48 |
| 5 | 2.902241 | 106.171607 | 0.009419 | 0.344561 | 36.582626 | 0.027335 | 60 |
| 6 | 3.591536 | 144.643867 | 0.006914 | 0.278432 | 40.273540 | 0.024830 | 72 |
| 7 | 4.444541 | 192.253454 | 0.005201 | 0.224995 | 43.256087 | 0.023118 | 84 |
| 8 | 5.500138 | 251.170521 | 0.003981 | 0.181814 | 45.666217 | 0.021898 | 96 |
| 9 | 6.806445 | 324.080641 | 0.003086 | 0.146920 | 47.613791 | 0.021002 | 108 |
| 10 | 8.423004 | 414.307227 | 0.002414 | 0.118722 | 49.187582 | 0.020330 | 120 |
| 11 | 10.423504 | 525.963010 | 0.001901 | 0.095937 | 50.459329 | 0.019818 | 132 |
| 12 | 12.899131 | 664.137518 | 0.001506 | 0.077525 | 51.486999 | 0.019422 | 144 |
| 13 | 15.962729 | 835.129061 | 0.001197 | 0.062646 | 52.317436 | 0.019114 | 156 |
| 14 | 19.753945 | 1046.731823 | 0.000955 | 0.050623 | 52.988495 | 0.018872 | 168 |
| 15 | 24.445591 | 1308.591144 | 0.000764 | 0.040907 | 53.530763 | 0.018681 | 180 |
| 16 | 30.251523 | 1632.643169 | 0.000613 | 0.033056 | 53.968957 | 0.018529 | 192 |
| 17 | 37.436389 | 2033.658931 | 0.000492 | 0.026712 | 54.323052 | 0.018408 | 204 |
| 18 | 46.327691 | 2529.917645 | 0.000395 | 0.021585 | 54.609189 | 0.018312 | 216 |
| 19 | 57.330715 | 3144.039919 | 0.000318 | 0.017443 | 54.840410 | 0.018235 | 228 |
| 20 | 70.947004 | 3904.018849 | 0.000256 | 0.014095 | 55.027254 | 0.018173 | 240 |
| 21 | 87.797220 | 4844.496015 | 0.000206 | 0.011390 | 55.178239 | 0.018123 | 252 |
| 22 | 108.649434 | 6008.340515 | 0.000166 | 0.009204 | 55.300247 | 0.018083 | 264 |
| 23 | 134.454138 | 7448.603043 | 0.000134 | 0.007437 | 55.398838 | 0.018051 | 276 |
| 24 | 166.387569 | 9230.934059 | 0.000108 | 0.006010 | 55.478508 | 0.018025 | 288 |
| 25 | 205.905325 | 11436.576288 | 0.000087 | 0.004857 | 55.542887 | 0.018004 | 300 |
| 26 | 254.808717 | 14166.067944 | 0.000071 | 0.003925 | 55.594911 | 0.017987 | 312 |
| 27 | 315.326874 | 17543.825501 | 0.000057 | 0.003171 | 55.636950 | 0.017974 | 324 |
| 28 | 390.218350 | 21723.814872 | 0.000046 | 0.002563 | 55.670921 | 0.017963 | 336 |
| 29 | 482.896871 | 26896.569531 | 0.000037 | 0.002071 | 55.698372 | 0.017954 | 348 |
| 30 | 597.586935 | 33297.875465 | 0.000030 | 0.001673 | 55.720555 | 0.017947 | 360 |
| 31 | 739.516379 | 41219.518837 | 0.000024 | 0.001352 | 55.738480 | 0.017941 | 372 |
| 32 | 915.154671 | 51022.586268 | 0.000020 | 0.001093 | 55.752965 | 0.017936 | 384 |
| 33 | 1132.507805 | 63153.923989 | 0.000016 | 0.000883 | 55.764670 | 0.017933 | 396 |
| 34 | 1401.483235 | 78166.506116 | 0.000013 | 0.000714 | 55.774129 | 0.017929 | 408 |
| 35 | 1734.341475 | 96744.640475 | 0.000010 | 0.000577 | 55.781772 | 0.017927 | 420 |
| 36 | 2146.254966 | 119735.160913 | 0.000008 | 0.000466 | 55.787948 | 0.017925 | 432 |
| 37 | 2655.999667 | 148186.027928 | 0.000007 | 0.000377 | 55.792939 | 0.017923 | 444 |
| 38 | 3286.810906 | 183394.097102 | 0.000005 | 0.000304 | 55.796972 | 0.017922 | 456 |
| 39 | 4067.442503 | 226964.232742 | 0.000004 | 0.000246 | 55.800231 | 0.017921 | 468 |
| 40 | 5033.477431 | 280882.461270 | 0.000004 | 0.000199 | 55.802865 | 0.017920 | 480 |

22.00% ANNUAL INTEREST RATE          1.8333% MONTHLY EFFECTIVE INTEREST RATE

| | 1<br>Future Value<br>of $1 | 2<br>Future Value<br>Annuity of<br>$1 per Month | 3<br>Sinking<br>Fund<br>Factor | 4<br>Present Value<br>of $1<br>(Reversion) | 5<br>Present Value<br>Annuity of<br>$1 per Month | 6<br>Installment<br>to<br>Amortize $1 | |
|---|---|---|---|---|---|---|---|
| Months | | | | | | | Months |
| 1 | 1.018333 | 1.000000 | 1.000000 | 0.981997 | 0.981997 | 1.018333 | 1 |
| 2 | 1.037003 | 2.018333 | 0.495458 | 0.964318 | 1.946314 | 0.513792 | 2 |
| 3 | 1.056014 | 3.055336 | 0.327296 | 0.946957 | 2.893271 | 0.345630 | 3 |
| 4 | 1.075375 | 4.111351 | 0.243229 | 0.929908 | 3.823179 | 0.261562 | 4 |
| 5 | 1.095090 | 5.186725 | 0.192800 | 0.913167 | 4.736346 | 0.211133 | 5 |
| 6 | 1.115167 | 6.281815 | 0.159190 | 0.896727 | 5.633073 | 0.177523 | 6 |
| 7 | 1.135611 | 7.396982 | 0.135190 | 0.880583 | 6.513656 | 0.153524 | 7 |
| 8 | 1.156431 | 8.532593 | 0.117198 | 0.864730 | 7.378386 | 0.135531 | 8 |
| 9 | 1.177632 | 9.689024 | 0.103210 | 0.849162 | 8.227548 | 0.121543 | 9 |
| 10 | 1.199222 | 10.866656 | 0.092025 | 0.833874 | 9.061421 | 0.110358 | 10 |
| 11 | 1.221208 | 12.065878 | 0.082878 | 0.818861 | 9.880283 | 0.101212 | 11 |
| 12 | 1.243597 | 13.287086 | 0.075261 | 0.804119 | 10.684402 | 0.093594 | 12 |
| Years | | | | | | | Months |
| 1 | 1.243597 | 13.287086 | 0.075261 | 0.804119 | 10.684402 | 0.093594 | 12 |
| 2 | 1.546532 | 29.810861 | 0.033545 | 0.646608 | 19.275936 | 0.051878 | 24 |
| 3 | 1.923262 | 50.359771 | 0.019857 | 0.519950 | 26.184554 | 0.038190 | 36 |
| 4 | 2.391763 | 75.914324 | 0.013173 | 0.418102 | 31.739908 | 0.031506 | 48 |
| 5 | 2.974388 | 107.693880 | 0.009286 | 0.336204 | 36.207074 | 0.027619 | 60 |
| 6 | 3.698938 | 147.214827 | 0.006793 | 0.270348 | 39.799209 | 0.025126 | 72 |
| 7 | 4.599987 | 196.362941 | 0.005093 | 0.217392 | 42.687714 | 0.023426 | 84 |
| 8 | 5.720528 | 257.483368 | 0.003884 | 0.174809 | 45.010417 | 0.022217 | 96 |
| 9 | 7.114030 | 333.492521 | 0.002999 | 0.140567 | 46.878147 | 0.021332 | 108 |
| 10 | 8.846983 | 428.017244 | 0.002336 | 0.113033 | 48.380024 | 0.020670 | 120 |
| 11 | 11.002078 | 545.567866 | 0.001833 | 0.090892 | 49.587713 | 0.020166 | 132 |
| 12 | 13.682146 | 691.753417 | 0.001446 | 0.073088 | 50.558839 | 0.019779 | 144 |
| 13 | 17.015070 | 873.549268 | 0.001145 | 0.058771 | 51.339740 | 0.019478 | 156 |
| 14 | 21.159883 | 1099.629967 | 0.000909 | 0.047259 | 51.967678 | 0.019243 | 168 |
| 15 | 26.314358 | 1380.783150 | 0.000724 | 0.038002 | 52.472614 | 0.019058 | 180 |
| 16 | 32.724445 | 1730.424286 | 0.000578 | 0.030558 | 52.878644 | 0.018911 | 192 |
| 17 | 40.696008 | 2165.236806 | 0.000462 | 0.024572 | 53.205140 | 0.018795 | 204 |
| 18 | 50.609416 | 2705.968169 | 0.000370 | 0.019759 | 53.467682 | 0.018703 | 216 |
| 19 | 62.937697 | 3378.419841 | 0.000296 | 0.015889 | 53.678797 | 0.018629 | 228 |
| 20 | 78.269105 | 4214.678439 | 0.000237 | 0.012776 | 53.848558 | 0.018571 | 240 |
| 21 | 97.335191 | 5254.646770 | 0.000190 | 0.010274 | 53.985067 | 0.018524 | 252 |
| 22 | 121.045710 | 6547.947827 | 0.000153 | 0.008261 | 54.094836 | 0.018486 | 264 |
| 23 | 150.532031 | 8156.292597 | 0.000123 | 0.006643 | 54.183103 | 0.018456 | 276 |
| 24 | 187.201119 | 10156.424648 | 0.000098 | 0.005342 | 54.254081 | 0.018432 | 288 |
| 25 | 232.802670 | 12643.782022 | 0.000079 | 0.004295 | 54.311155 | 0.018412 | 300 |
| 26 | 289.512604 | 15737.051142 | 0.000064 | 0.003454 | 54.357050 | 0.018397 | 312 |
| 27 | 360.036884 | 19583.830033 | 0.000051 | 0.002777 | 54.393955 | 0.018384 | 324 |
| 28 | 447.740637 | 24367.671098 | 0.000041 | 0.002233 | 54.423631 | 0.018374 | 336 |
| 29 | 556.808724 | 30316.839476 | 0.000033 | 0.001796 | 54.447494 | 0.018366 | 348 |
| 30 | 692.445423 | 37715.204912 | 0.000027 | 0.001444 | 54.466682 | 0.018360 | 360 |
| 31 | 861.122759 | 46915.786851 | 0.000021 | 0.001161 | 54.482112 | 0.018355 | 372 |
| 32 | 1070.889316 | 58357.599066 | 0.000017 | 0.000934 | 54.494520 | 0.018350 | 384 |
| 33 | 1331.754289 | 72586.597581 | 0.000014 | 0.000751 | 54.504497 | 0.018347 | 396 |
| 34 | 1656.165076 | 90281.731443 | 0.000011 | 0.000604 | 54.512520 | 0.018344 | 408 |
| 35 | 2059.601222 | 112287.339359 | 0.000009 | 0.000486 | 54.518971 | 0.018342 | 420 |
| 36 | 2561.313031 | 139653.438060 | 0.000007 | 0.000390 | 54.524159 | 0.018340 | 432 |
| 37 | 3185.240121 | 173685.824755 | 0.000006 | 0.000314 | 54.528330 | 0.018339 | 444 |
| 38 | 3961.153714 | 216008.384389 | 0.000005 | 0.000252 | 54.531684 | 0.018338 | 456 |
| 39 | 4926.077203 | 268640.574719 | 0.000004 | 0.000203 | 54.534382 | 0.018337 | 468 |
| 40 | 6126.052753 | 334093.786504 | 0.000003 | 0.000163 | 54.536551 | 0.018336 | 480 |

22.50% ANNUAL INTEREST RATE      1.8750% MONTHLY EFFECTIVE INTEREST RATE

| | 1<br>Future Value<br>of $1 | 2<br>Future Value<br>Annuity of<br>$1 per Month | 3<br>Sinking<br>Fund<br>Factor | 4<br>Present Value<br>of $1<br>(Reversion) | 5<br>Present Value<br>Annuity of<br>$1 per Month | 6<br>Installment<br>to<br>Amortize $1 | |
|---|---|---|---|---|---|---|---|
| Months | | | | | | | Months |
| 1 | 1.018750 | 1.000000 | 1.000000 | 0.981595 | 0.981595 | 1.018750 | 1 |
| 2 | 1.037852 | 2.018750 | 0.495356 | 0.963529 | 1.945124 | 0.514106 | 2 |
| 3 | 1.057311 | 3.056602 | 0.327161 | 0.945795 | 2.890919 | 0.345911 | 3 |
| 4 | 1.077136 | 4.113913 | 0.243078 | 0.928388 | 3.819307 | 0.261828 | 4 |
| 5 | 1.097332 | 5.191049 | 0.192639 | 0.911301 | 4.730608 | 0.211389 | 5 |
| 6 | 1.117907 | 6.288381 | 0.159023 | 0.894529 | 5.625137 | 0.177773 | 6 |
| 7 | 1.138868 | 7.406288 | 0.135020 | 0.878065 | 6.503202 | 0.153770 | 7 |
| 8 | 1.160222 | 8.545156 | 0.117025 | 0.861904 | 7.365106 | 0.135775 | 8 |
| 9 | 1.181976 | 9.705378 | 0.103036 | 0.846041 | 8.211147 | 0.121786 | 9 |
| 10 | 1.204138 | 10.887353 | 0.091850 | 0.830470 | 9.041617 | 0.110600 | 10 |
| 11 | 1.226715 | 12.091491 | 0.082703 | 0.815185 | 9.856802 | 0.101453 | 11 |
| 12 | 1.249716 | 13.318207 | 0.075085 | 0.800182 | 10.656983 | 0.093835 | 12 |
| Years | | | | | | | Months |
| 1 | 1.249716 | 13.318207 | 0.075085 | 0.800182 | 10.656983 | 0.093835 | 12 |
| 2 | 1.561791 | 29.962188 | 0.033375 | 0.640291 | 19.184505 | 0.052125 | 24 |
| 3 | 1.951796 | 50.762444 | 0.019700 | 0.512349 | 26.008071 | 0.038450 | 36 |
| 4 | 2.439191 | 76.756864 | 0.013028 | 0.409972 | 31.468162 | 0.031778 | 48 |
| 5 | 3.048297 | 109.242516 | 0.009154 | 0.328052 | 35.837226 | 0.027904 | 60 |
| 6 | 3.809507 | 149.840369 | 0.006674 | 0.262501 | 39.333271 | 0.025424 | 72 |
| 7 | 4.760803 | 200.576169 | 0.004986 | 0.210049 | 42.130742 | 0.023736 | 84 |
| 8 | 5.949654 | 263.981530 | 0.003788 | 0.168077 | 44.369226 | 0.022538 | 96 |
| 9 | 7.435380 | 343.220248 | 0.002914 | 0.134492 | 46.160420 | 0.021664 | 108 |
| 10 | 9.292116 | 442.246172 | 0.002261 | 0.107618 | 47.593700 | 0.021011 | 120 |
| 11 | 11.612509 | 566.000490 | 0.001767 | 0.086114 | 48.740585 | 0.020517 | 132 |
| 12 | 14.512343 | 720.658289 | 0.001388 | 0.068907 | 49.658301 | 0.020138 | 144 |
| 13 | 18.136313 | 913.936672 | 0.001094 | 0.055138 | 50.392640 | 0.019844 | 156 |
| 14 | 22.665247 | 1155.479833 | 0.000865 | 0.044120 | 50.980245 | 0.019615 | 168 |
| 15 | 28.325130 | 1457.340277 | 0.000686 | 0.035304 | 51.450435 | 0.019436 | 180 |
| 16 | 35.398379 | 1834.580217 | 0.000545 | 0.028250 | 51.826673 | 0.019295 | 192 |
| 17 | 44.237934 | 2306.023148 | 0.000434 | 0.022605 | 52.127732 | 0.019184 | 204 |
| 18 | 55.284871 | 2895.193100 | 0.000345 | 0.018088 | 52.368633 | 0.019095 | 216 |
| 19 | 69.090408 | 3631.488437 | 0.000275 | 0.014474 | 52.561398 | 0.019025 | 228 |
| 20 | 86.343415 | 4551.648778 | 0.000220 | 0.011582 | 52.715645 | 0.018970 | 240 |
| 21 | 107.904779 | 5701.588225 | 0.000175 | 0.009267 | 52.839070 | 0.018925 | 252 |
| 22 | 134.850370 | 7138.686385 | 0.000140 | 0.007416 | 52.937833 | 0.018890 | 264 |
| 23 | 168.524715 | 8934.651489 | 0.000112 | 0.005934 | 53.016861 | 0.018862 | 276 |
| 24 | 210.608097 | 11179.098493 | 0.000089 | 0.004748 | 53.080098 | 0.018839 | 288 |
| 25 | 263.200388 | 13984.020669 | 0.000072 | 0.003799 | 53.130699 | 0.018822 | 300 |
| 26 | 328.925835 | 17489.377848 | 0.000057 | 0.003040 | 53.171189 | 0.018807 | 312 |
| 27 | 411.064002 | 21870.080120 | 0.000046 | 0.002433 | 53.203589 | 0.018796 | 324 |
| 28 | 513.713415 | 27344.715492 | 0.000037 | 0.001947 | 53.229514 | 0.018787 | 336 |
| 29 | 641.996068 | 34186.456971 | 0.000029 | 0.001558 | 53.250259 | 0.018779 | 348 |
| 30 | 802.313000 | 42736.693342 | 0.000023 | 0.001246 | 53.266859 | 0.018773 | 360 |
| 31 | 1002.663695 | 53422.063760 | 0.000019 | 0.000997 | 53.280142 | 0.018769 | 372 |
| 32 | 1253.045241 | 66775.746161 | 0.000015 | 0.000798 | 53.290770 | 0.018765 | 384 |
| 33 | 1565.951158 | 83464.061746 | 0.000012 | 0.000639 | 53.299275 | 0.018762 | 396 |
| 34 | 1956.994807 | 104319.723031 | 0.000010 | 0.000511 | 53.306081 | 0.018760 | 408 |
| 35 | 2445.688459 | 130383.384485 | 0.000008 | 0.000409 | 53.311526 | 0.018758 | 420 |
| 36 | 3056.416919 | 162955.569038 | 0.000006 | 0.000327 | 53.315884 | 0.018756 | 432 |
| 37 | 3819.654278 | 203661.561497 | 0.000005 | 0.000262 | 53.319370 | 0.018755 | 444 |
| 38 | 4773.484504 | 254532.506901 | 0.000004 | 0.000209 | 53.322161 | 0.018754 | 456 |
| 39 | 5965.501759 | 318106.760466 | 0.000003 | 0.000168 | 53.324393 | 0.018753 | 468 |
| 40 | 7455.185243 | 397556.546279 | 0.000003 | 0.000134 | 53.326179 | 0.018753 | 480 |

23.00% ANNUAL INTEREST RATE    1.9167% MONTHLY EFFECTIVE INTEREST RATE

| | 1 | 2 | 3 | 4 | 5 | 6 | |
|---|---|---|---|---|---|---|---|
| | Future Value of $1 | Future Value Annuity of $1 per Month | Sinking Fund Factor | Present Value of $1 (Reversion) | Present Value Annuity of $1 per Month | Installment to Amortize $1 | |
| Months | | | | | | | Months |
| 1 | 1.019167 | 1.000000 | 1.000000 | 0.981194 | 0.981194 | 1.019167 | 1 |
| 2 | 1.038701 | 2.019167 | 0.495254 | 0.962741 | 1.943935 | 0.514420 | 2 |
| 3 | 1.058609 | 3.057867 | 0.327025 | 0.944636 | 2.888571 | 0.346192 | 3 |
| 4 | 1.078899 | 4.116476 | 0.242926 | 0.926871 | 3.815441 | 0.262093 | 4 |
| 5 | 1.099578 | 5.195376 | 0.192479 | 0.909440 | 4.724881 | 0.211646 | 5 |
| 6 | 1.120653 | 6.294954 | 0.158857 | 0.892337 | 5.617218 | 0.178024 | 6 |
| 7 | 1.142132 | 7.415607 | 0.134851 | 0.875555 | 6.492773 | 0.154017 | 7 |
| 8 | 1.164023 | 8.557739 | 0.116853 | 0.859089 | 7.351862 | 0.136020 | 8 |
| 9 | 1.186334 | 9.721763 | 0.102862 | 0.842933 | 8.194795 | 0.122029 | 9 |
| 10 | 1.209072 | 10.908097 | 0.091675 | 0.827081 | 9.021876 | 0.110842 | 10 |
| 11 | 1.232246 | 12.117168 | 0.082528 | 0.811526 | 9.833403 | 0.101694 | 11 |
| 12 | 1.255864 | 13.349414 | 0.074910 | 0.796265 | 10.629667 | 0.094076 | 12 |
| Years | | | | | | | Months |
| 1 | 1.255864 | 13.349414 | 0.074910 | 0.796265 | 10.629667 | 0.094076 | 12 |
| 2 | 1.577194 | 30.114460 | 0.033207 | 0.634037 | 19.093696 | 0.052373 | 24 |
| 3 | 1.980741 | 51.169073 | 0.019543 | 0.504862 | 25.833304 | 0.038710 | 36 |
| 4 | 2.487540 | 77.610799 | 0.012885 | 0.402004 | 31.199816 | 0.032051 | 48 |
| 5 | 3.124012 | 110.818005 | 0.009024 | 0.320101 | 35.472979 | 0.028190 | 60 |
| 6 | 3.923333 | 152.521731 | 0.006556 | 0.254885 | 38.875549 | 0.025723 | 72 |
| 7 | 4.927172 | 204.895930 | 0.004881 | 0.202956 | 41.584895 | 0.024047 | 84 |
| 8 | 6.187857 | 270.670790 | 0.003695 | 0.161607 | 43.742252 | 0.022861 | 96 |
| 9 | 7.771105 | 353.275053 | 0.002831 | 0.128682 | 45.460079 | 0.021997 | 108 |
| 10 | 9.759449 | 457.014754 | 0.002188 | 0.102465 | 46.827924 | 0.021355 | 120 |
| 11 | 12.256539 | 587.297686 | 0.001703 | 0.081589 | 47.917090 | 0.020869 | 132 |
| 12 | 15.392543 | 750.915300 | 0.001332 | 0.064967 | 48.784355 | 0.020498 | 144 |
| 13 | 19.330937 | 956.396733 | 0.001046 | 0.051731 | 49.474928 | 0.020212 | 156 |
| 14 | 24.277024 | 1214.453422 | 0.000823 | 0.041191 | 50.024806 | 0.019990 | 168 |
| 15 | 30.488635 | 1538.537467 | 0.000650 | 0.032799 | 50.462655 | 0.019817 | 180 |
| 16 | 38.289572 | 1945.542878 | 0.000514 | 0.026117 | 50.811299 | 0.019681 | 192 |
| 17 | 48.086486 | 2456.686228 | 0.000407 | 0.020796 | 51.088911 | 0.019574 | 204 |
| 18 | 60.390076 | 3098.612642 | 0.000323 | 0.016559 | 51.309965 | 0.019489 | 216 |
| 19 | 75.841708 | 3904.784769 | 0.000256 | 0.013185 | 51.485981 | 0.019423 | 228 |
| 20 | 95.246853 | 4917.227136 | 0.000203 | 0.010499 | 51.626137 | 0.019370 | 240 |
| 21 | 119.617072 | 6188.716824 | 0.000162 | 0.008360 | 51.737739 | 0.019328 | 252 |
| 22 | 150.222748 | 7785.534657 | 0.000128 | 0.006657 | 51.826603 | 0.019295 | 264 |
| 23 | 188.659306 | 9790.920321 | 0.000102 | 0.005301 | 51.897362 | 0.019269 | 276 |
| 24 | 236.930388 | 12309.411522 | 0.000081 | 0.004221 | 51.953705 | 0.019248 | 288 |
| 25 | 297.552290 | 15472.293377 | 0.000065 | 0.003361 | 51.998569 | 0.019231 | 300 |
| 26 | 373.685140 | 19444.442108 | 0.000051 | 0.002676 | 52.034293 | 0.019218 | 312 |
| 27 | 469.297629 | 24432.919789 | 0.000041 | 0.002131 | 52.062739 | 0.019208 | 324 |
| 28 | 589.373890 | 30697.768177 | 0.000033 | 0.001697 | 52.085389 | 0.019199 | 336 |
| 29 | 740.173316 | 38565.564293 | 0.000026 | 0.001351 | 52.103424 | 0.019193 | 348 |
| 30 | 929.556851 | 48446.444386 | 0.000021 | 0.001076 | 52.117785 | 0.019187 | 360 |
| 31 | 1167.396771 | 60855.483712 | 0.000016 | 0.000857 | 52.129221 | 0.019183 | 372 |
| 32 | 1466.091310 | 76439.546625 | 0.000013 | 0.000682 | 52.138326 | 0.019180 | 384 |
| 33 | 1841.210960 | 96011.006630 | 0.000010 | 0.000543 | 52.145576 | 0.019177 | 396 |
| 34 | 2312.310138 | 120590.094180 | 0.000008 | 0.000432 | 52.151349 | 0.019175 | 408 |
| 35 | 2903.946528 | 151458.079737 | 0.000007 | 0.000344 | 52.155946 | 0.019173 | 420 |
| 36 | 3646.961235 | 190224.064457 | 0.000005 | 0.000274 | 52.159607 | 0.019172 | 432 |
| 37 | 4580.086487 | 238908.860183 | 0.000004 | 0.000218 | 52.162522 | 0.019171 | 444 |
| 38 | 5751.964683 | 300050.331294 | 0.000003 | 0.000174 | 52.164842 | 0.019170 | 456 |
| 39 | 7223.684053 | 376835.689717 | 0.000003 | 0.000138 | 52.166690 | 0.019169 | 468 |
| 40 | 9071.963089 | 473267.639441 | 0.000002 | 0.000110 | 52.168162 | 0.019169 | 480 |

23.50% ANNUAL INTEREST RATE           1.9583% MONTHLY EFFECTIVE INTEREST RATE

| | 1<br>Future Value<br>of $1 | 2<br>Future Value<br>Annuity of<br>$1 per Month | 3<br>Sinking<br>Fund<br>Factor | 4<br>Present Value<br>of $1<br>(Reversion) | 5<br>Present Value<br>Annuity of<br>$1 per Month | 6<br>Installment<br>to<br>Amortize $1 | |
|---|---|---|---|---|---|---|---|
| Months | | | | | | | Months |
| 1 | 1.019583 | 1.000000 | 1.000000 | 0.980793 | 0.980793 | 1.019583 | 1 |
| 2 | 1.039550 | 2.019583 | 0.495152 | 0.961955 | 1.942747 | 0.514735 | 2 |
| 3 | 1.059908 | 3.059134 | 0.326890 | 0.943478 | 2.886225 | 0.346473 | 3 |
| 4 | 1.080665 | 4.119042 | 0.242775 | 0.925357 | 3.811582 | 0.262358 | 4 |
| 5 | 1.101828 | 5.199706 | 0.192319 | 0.907583 | 4.719165 | 0.211902 | 5 |
| 6 | 1.123405 | 6.301534 | 0.158692 | 0.890151 | 5.609316 | 0.178275 | 6 |
| 7 | 1.145405 | 7.424939 | 0.134681 | 0.873054 | 6.482369 | 0.154265 | 7 |
| 8 | 1.167836 | 8.570344 | 0.116681 | 0.856285 | 7.338654 | 0.136265 | 8 |
| 9 | 1.190706 | 9.738180 | 0.102689 | 0.839838 | 8.178492 | 0.122272 | 9 |
| 10 | 1.214024 | 10.928886 | 0.091501 | 0.823707 | 9.002199 | 0.111084 | 10 |
| 11 | 1.237799 | 12.142910 | 0.082353 | 0.807886 | 9.810085 | 0.101936 | 11 |
| 12 | 1.262039 | 13.380708 | 0.074734 | 0.792369 | 10.602453 | 0.094318 | 12 |
| Years | | | | | | | Months |
| 1 | 1.262039 | 13.380708 | 0.074734 | 0.792369 | 10.602453 | 0.094318 | 12 |
| 2 | 1.592742 | 30.267682 | 0.033039 | 0.627848 | 19.003505 | 0.052622 | 24 |
| 3 | 2.010102 | 51.579700 | 0.019387 | 0.497487 | 25.660234 | 0.038971 | 36 |
| 4 | 2.536827 | 78.476295 | 0.012743 | 0.394193 | 30.934818 | 0.032326 | 48 |
| 5 | 3.201575 | 112.420843 | 0.008895 | 0.312346 | 35.114232 | 0.028478 | 60 |
| 6 | 4.040512 | 155.260182 | 0.006441 | 0.247493 | 38.425869 | 0.026024 | 72 |
| 7 | 5.099283 | 209.325093 | 0.004777 | 0.196106 | 41.049906 | 0.024361 | 84 |
| 8 | 6.435493 | 277.557113 | 0.003603 | 0.155388 | 43.129111 | 0.023186 | 96 |
| 9 | 8.121843 | 363.668574 | 0.002750 | 0.123125 | 44.776608 | 0.022333 | 108 |
| 10 | 10.250081 | 472.344585 | 0.002117 | 0.097560 | 46.082032 | 0.021700 | 120 |
| 11 | 12.936001 | 609.497936 | 0.001641 | 0.077304 | 47.116410 | 0.021224 | 132 |
| 12 | 16.325736 | 782.590795 | 0.001278 | 0.061253 | 47.936018 | 0.020861 | 144 |
| 13 | 20.603714 | 1001.040713 | 0.000999 | 0.048535 | 48.585450 | 0.020582 | 156 |
| 14 | 26.002688 | 1276.733000 | 0.000783 | 0.038458 | 49.100039 | 0.020367 | 168 |
| 15 | 32.816403 | 1624.667383 | 0.000616 | 0.030473 | 49.507784 | 0.020199 | 180 |
| 16 | 41.415576 | 2063.774099 | 0.000485 | 0.024146 | 49.830868 | 0.020068 | 192 |
| 17 | 52.268067 | 2617.943844 | 0.000382 | 0.019132 | 50.086869 | 0.019965 | 204 |
| 18 | 65.964332 | 3317.327603 | 0.000301 | 0.015160 | 50.289717 | 0.019885 | 216 |
| 19 | 83.249551 | 4199.977093 | 0.000238 | 0.012012 | 50.450447 | 0.019821 | 228 |
| 20 | 105.064170 | 5313.915060 | 0.000188 | 0.009518 | 50.577805 | 0.019772 | 240 |
| 21 | 132.595066 | 6719.748075 | 0.000149 | 0.007542 | 50.678719 | 0.019732 | 252 |
| 22 | 167.340128 | 8493.963986 | 0.000118 | 0.005976 | 50.758680 | 0.019701 | 264 |
| 23 | 211.189746 | 10733.093433 | 0.000093 | 0.004735 | 50.822039 | 0.019677 | 276 |
| 24 | 266.529669 | 13558.961834 | 0.000074 | 0.003752 | 50.872242 | 0.019657 | 288 |
| 25 | 336.370803 | 17125.317603 | 0.000058 | 0.002973 | 50.912022 | 0.019642 | 300 |
| 26 | 424.513029 | 21626.197213 | 0.000046 | 0.002356 | 50.943542 | 0.019630 | 312 |
| 27 | 535.751944 | 27306.482237 | 0.000037 | 0.001867 | 50.968517 | 0.019620 | 324 |
| 28 | 676.139779 | 34475.222740 | 0.000029 | 0.001479 | 50.988307 | 0.019612 | 336 |
| 29 | 853.314683 | 43522.451915 | 0.000023 | 0.001172 | 51.003988 | 0.019606 | 348 |
| 30 | 1076.916300 | 54940.406816 | 0.000018 | 0.000929 | 51.016413 | 0.019602 | 360 |
| 31 | 1359.110232 | 69350.309735 | 0.000014 | 0.000736 | 51.026258 | 0.019598 | 372 |
| 32 | 1715.249944 | 87536.167355 | 0.000011 | 0.000583 | 51.034059 | 0.019595 | 384 |
| 33 | 2164.712104 | 110487.426587 | 0.000009 | 0.000462 | 51.040241 | 0.019592 | 396 |
| 34 | 2731.950821 | 139452.807892 | 0.000007 | 0.000366 | 51.045138 | 0.019591 | 408 |
| 35 | 3447.828132 | 176008.245030 | 0.000006 | 0.000290 | 51.049019 | 0.019589 | 420 |
| 36 | 4351.293125 | 222142.627669 | 0.000005 | 0.000230 | 51.052094 | 0.019588 | 432 |
| 37 | 5491.501066 | 280366.011881 | 0.000004 | 0.000182 | 51.054531 | 0.019587 | 444 |
| 38 | 6930.487809 | 353846.185995 | 0.000003 | 0.000144 | 51.056462 | 0.019586 | 456 |
| 39 | 8746.545015 | 446581.022024 | 0.000002 | 0.000114 | 51.057992 | 0.019586 | 468 |
| 40 | 11038.479801 | 563615.989849 | 0.000002 | 0.000091 | 51.059204 | 0.019585 | 480 |

24.00% ANNUAL INTEREST RATE        2.0000% MONTHLY EFFECTIVE INTEREST RATE

| | 1 | 2 | 3 | 4 | 5 | 6 | |
|---|---|---|---|---|---|---|---|
| | Future Value of $1 | Future Value Annuity of $1 per Month | Sinking Fund Factor | Present Value of $1 (Reversion) | Present Value Annuity of $1 per Month | Installment to Amortize $1 | |
| Months | | | | | | | Months |
| 1 | 1.120000 | 1.000000 | 1.000000 | 0.980392 | 0.980392 | 1.020000 | 1 |
| 2 | 1.040400 | 2.020000 | 0.495050 | 0.961169 | 1.941561 | 0.515050 | 2 |
| 3 | 1.061208 | 3.060400 | 0.326755 | 0.942322 | 2.883883 | 0.346755 | 3 |
| 4 | 1.082432 | 4.121608 | 0.242624 | 0.923845 | 3.807729 | 0.262624 | 4 |
| 5 | 1.104081 | 5.204040 | 0.192158 | 0.905731 | 4.713460 | 0.212158 | 5 |
| 6 | 1.126162 | 6.308121 | 0.158526 | 0.887971 | 5.601431 | 0.178526 | 6 |
| 7 | 1.148686 | 7.434283 | 0.134512 | 0.870560 | 6.471991 | 0.154512 | 7 |
| 8 | 1.171659 | 8.582969 | 0.116510 | 0.853490 | 7.325481 | 0.136510 | 8 |
| 9 | 1.195093 | 9.754628 | 0.102515 | 0.836755 | 8.162237 | 0.122515 | 9 |
| 10 | 1.218994 | 10.949721 | 0.091327 | 0.820348 | 8.982585 | 0.111327 | 10 |
| 11 | 1.243374 | 12.168715 | 0.082178 | 0.804263 | 9.786848 | 0.102178 | 11 |
| 12 | 1.268242 | 13.412090 | 0.074560 | 0.788493 | 10.575341 | 0.094560 | 12 |
| Years | | | | | | | Months |
| 1 | 1.268242 | 13.412090 | 0.074560 | 0.788493 | 10.575341 | 0.094560 | 12 |
| 2 | 1.608437 | 30.421862 | 0.032871 | 0.621721 | 18.913926 | 0.052871 | 24 |
| 3 | 2.039887 | 51.994367 | 0.019233 | 0.490223 | 25.488842 | 0.039233 | 36 |
| 4 | 2.587070 | 79.353519 | 0.012602 | 0.386538 | 30.673120 | 0.032602 | 48 |
| 5 | 3.281031 | 114.051539 | 0.008768 | 0.304782 | 34.760887 | 0.028768 | 60 |
| 6 | 4.161140 | 158.057019 | 0.006327 | 0.240319 | 37.984063 | 0.026327 | 72 |
| 7 | 5.277332 | 213.866607 | 0.004676 | 0.189490 | 40.525516 | 0.024676 | 84 |
| 8 | 6.692933 | 284.646659 | 0.003513 | 0.149411 | 42.529434 | 0.023513 | 96 |
| 9 | 8.488258 | 374.412879 | 0.002671 | 0.117810 | 44.109510 | 0.022671 | 108 |
| 10 | 10.765163 | 488.258152 | 0.002048 | 0.092892 | 45.355389 | 0.022048 | 120 |
| 11 | 13.652830 | 632.641484 | 0.001581 | 0.073245 | 46.337756 | 0.021581 | 132 |
| 12 | 17.315089 | 815.754461 | 0.001226 | 0.057753 | 47.112345 | 0.021226 | 144 |
| 13 | 21.959720 | 1047.985991 | 0.000954 | 0.045538 | 47.723104 | 0.020954 | 156 |
| 14 | 27.850234 | 1342.511724 | 0.000745 | 0.035906 | 48.204683 | 0.020745 | 168 |
| 15 | 35.320831 | 1716.041568 | 0.000583 | 0.028312 | 48.584405 | 0.020583 | 180 |
| 16 | 44.795355 | 2189.767727 | 0.000457 | 0.022324 | 48.883813 | 0.020457 | 192 |
| 17 | 56.811341 | 2790.567042 | 0.000358 | 0.017602 | 49.119894 | 0.020358 | 204 |
| 18 | 72.050517 | 3552.525843 | 0.000281 | 0.013879 | 49.306042 | 0.020281 | 216 |
| 19 | 91.377477 | 4518.873840 | 0.000221 | 0.010944 | 49.452819 | 0.020221 | 228 |
| 20 | 115.888735 | 5744.436758 | 0.000174 | 0.008629 | 49.568552 | 0.020174 | 240 |
| 21 | 146.974937 | 7298.746872 | 0.000137 | 0.006804 | 49.659806 | 0.020137 | 252 |
| 22 | 186.399758 | 9269.987921 | 0.000108 | 0.005365 | 49.731759 | 0.020108 | 264 |
| 23 | 236.399964 | 11769.998206 | 0.000085 | 0.004230 | 49.788494 | 0.020085 | 276 |
| 24 | 299.812315 | 14940.615736 | 0.000067 | 0.003335 | 49.833229 | 0.020067 | 288 |
| 25 | 380.234508 | 18961.725403 | 0.000053 | 0.002630 | 49.868502 | 0.020053 | 300 |
| 26 | 482.229295 | 24061.464743 | 0.000042 | 0.002074 | 49.896315 | 0.020042 | 312 |
| 27 | 611.583346 | 30529.167315 | 0.000033 | 0.001635 | 49.918245 | 0.020033 | 324 |
| 28 | 775.635561 | 38731.778032 | 0.000026 | 0.001289 | 49.935537 | 0.020026 | 336 |
| 29 | 983.693435 | 49134.671768 | 0.000020 | 0.001017 | 49.949171 | 0.020020 | 348 |
| 30 | 1247.561128 | 62328.056387 | 0.000016 | 0.000802 | 49.959922 | 0.020016 | 360 |
| 31 | 1582.209163 | 79060.458174 | 0.000013 | 0.000632 | 49.968399 | 0.020013 | 372 |
| 32 | 2006.623789 | 100281.189443 | 0.000010 | 0.000498 | 49.975083 | 0.020010 | 384 |
| 33 | 2544.884155 | 127194.207750 | 0.000008 | 0.000393 | 49.980353 | 0.020008 | 396 |
| 34 | 3227.528448 | 161326.422385 | 0.000006 | 0.000310 | 49.984508 | 0.020006 | 408 |
| 35 | 4093.286471 | 204614.323526 | 0.000005 | 0.000244 | 49.987785 | 0.020005 | 420 |
| 36 | 5191.276979 | 259513.848951 | 0.000004 | 0.000193 | 49.990368 | 0.020004 | 432 |
| 37 | 6583.794432 | 329139.721597 | 0.000003 | 0.000152 | 49.992406 | 0.020003 | 444 |
| 38 | 8349.843265 | 417442.163270 | 0.000002 | 0.000120 | 49.994012 | 0.020002 | 456 |
| 39 | 10589.620207 | 529431.010361 | 0.000002 | 0.000094 | 49.995278 | 0.020002 | 468 |
| 40 | 13430.198935 | 671459.946767 | 0.000001 | 0.000074 | 49.996277 | 0.020001 | 480 |

24.50% ANNUAL INTEREST RATE  2.0417% MONTHLY EFFECTIVE INTEREST RATE

| | 1 Future Value of $1 | 2 Future Value Annuity of $1 per Month | 3 Sinking Fund Factor | 4 Present Value of $1 (Reversion) | 5 Present Value Annuity of $1 per Month | 6 Installment to Amortize $1 | |
|---|---|---|---|---|---|---|---|
| Months | | | | | | | Months |
| 1 | 1.020417 | 1.000000 | 1.000000 | 0.979992 | 0.979992 | 1.020417 | 1 |
| 2 | 1.041250 | 2.020417 | 0.494947 | 0.960384 | 1.940376 | 0.515364 | 2 |
| 3 | 1.062509 | 3.061667 | 0.326619 | 0.941168 | 2.881544 | 0.347036 | 3 |
| 4 | 1.084202 | 4.124176 | 0.242473 | 0.922337 | 3.803882 | 0.262889 | 4 |
| 5 | 1.106338 | 5.208378 | 0.191998 | 0.903883 | 4.707765 | 0.212415 | 5 |
| 6 | 1.128925 | 6.314716 | 0.158360 | 0.885798 | 5.593563 | 0.178777 | 6 |
| 7 | 1.151974 | 7.443641 | 0.134343 | 0.868075 | 6.461638 | 0.154760 | 7 |
| 8 | 1.175494 | 8.595615 | 0.116338 | 0.850706 | 7.312344 | 0.136755 | 8 |
| 9 | 1.199493 | 9.771109 | 0.102343 | 0.833685 | 8.146029 | 0.122759 | 9 |
| 10 | 1.223983 | 10.970603 | 0.091153 | 0.817005 | 8.963034 | 0.111569 | 10 |
| 11 | 1.248973 | 12.194586 | 0.082004 | 0.800658 | 9.763692 | 0.102420 | 11 |
| 12 | 1.274473 | 13.443559 | 0.074385 | 0.784638 | 10.548330 | 0.094802 | 12 |
| Years | | | | | | | Months |
| 1 | 1.274473 | 13.443559 | 0.074385 | 0.784638 | 10.548330 | 0.094802 | 12 |
| 2 | 1.624281 | 30.577006 | 0.032704 | 0.615657 | 18.824954 | 0.053121 | 24 |
| 3 | 2.070101 | 52.413117 | 0.019079 | 0.483068 | 25.319109 | 0.039464 | 36 |
| 4 | 2.638287 | 80.242642 | 0.012462 | 0.379034 | 30.414672 | 0.032879 | 48 |
| 5 | 3.362425 | 115.710612 | 0.008642 | 0.297404 | 34.412846 | 0.029059 | 60 |
| 6 | 4.285319 | 160.913569 | 0.006215 | 0.233355 | 37.549965 | 0.026631 | 72 |
| 7 | 5.461521 | 218.523501 | 0.004576 | 0.183099 | 40.011470 | 0.024993 | 84 |
| 8 | 6.960560 | 291.945785 | 0.003425 | 0.143667 | 41.942860 | 0.023842 | 96 |
| 9 | 8.871043 | 385.520478 | 0.002594 | 0.112726 | 43.458303 | 0.023011 | 108 |
| 10 | 11.305902 | 504.778864 | 0.001981 | 0.088449 | 44.647377 | 0.022398 | 120 |
| 11 | 14.409063 | 656.770417 | 0.001523 | 0.069401 | 45.580371 | 0.021939 | 132 |
| 12 | 18.363956 | 850.479494 | 0.001176 | 0.054454 | 46.312433 | 0.021592 | 144 |
| 13 | 23.404360 | 1097.356415 | 0.000911 | 0.042727 | 46.886837 | 0.021328 | 156 |
| 14 | 29.828217 | 1411.994300 | 0.000708 | 0.033525 | 47.337536 | 0.021125 | 168 |
| 15 | 38.015247 | 1812.991680 | 0.000552 | 0.026305 | 47.691172 | 0.020968 | 180 |
| 16 | 48.449392 | 2324.051875 | 0.000430 | 0.020640 | 47.968648 | 0.020847 | 192 |
| 17 | 61.747426 | 2975.384116 | 0.000336 | 0.016195 | 48.186367 | 0.020753 | 204 |
| 18 | 78.695405 | 3805.489246 | 0.000263 | 0.012707 | 48.357197 | 0.020679 | 216 |
| 19 | 100.295142 | 4863.435533 | 0.000206 | 0.009971 | 48.491237 | 0.020622 | 228 |
| 20 | 127.823416 | 6211.759144 | 0.000161 | 0.007823 | 48.596410 | 0.020578 | 240 |
| 21 | 162.907448 | 7930.160714 | 0.000126 | 0.006138 | 48.678933 | 0.020543 | 252 |
| 22 | 207.621087 | 10120.216520 | 0.000099 | 0.004816 | 48.743683 | 0.020515 | 264 |
| 23 | 264.607398 | 12911.382754 | 0.000077 | 0.003779 | 48.794489 | 0.020494 | 276 |
| 24 | 337.234892 | 16468.647788 | 0.000061 | 0.002965 | 48.834353 | 0.020477 | 288 |
| 25 | 429.796648 | 21002.284792 | 0.000048 | 0.002327 | 48.865632 | 0.020464 | 300 |
| 26 | 547.764074 | 26780.281172 | 0.000037 | 0.001826 | 48.890175 | 0.020454 | 312 |
| 27 | 698.110332 | 34144.179547 | 0.000029 | 0.001432 | 48.909432 | 0.020446 | 324 |
| 28 | 889.722527 | 43529.266642 | 0.000023 | 0.001124 | 48.924541 | 0.020440 | 336 |
| 29 | 1133.927030 | 55490.303490 | 0.000018 | 0.000882 | 48.936397 | 0.020435 | 348 |
| 30 | 1445.158989 | 70734.317851 | 0.000014 | 0.000692 | 48.945700 | 0.020431 | 360 |
| 31 | 1841.815611 | 90162.397274 | 0.000011 | 0.000543 | 48.952999 | 0.020428 | 372 |
| 32 | 2347.343628 | 114922.953193 | 0.000009 | 0.000426 | 48.958726 | 0.020425 | 384 |
| 33 | 2991.625260 | 146479.604581 | 0.000007 | 0.000334 | 48.963220 | 0.020423 | 396 |
| 34 | 3812.744581 | 186697.693788 | 0.000005 | 0.000262 | 48.966746 | 0.020422 | 408 |
| 35 | 4859.238701 | 237954.548629 | 0.000004 | 0.000206 | 48.969512 | 0.020421 | 420 |
| 36 | 6192.966838 | 303280.008392 | 0.000003 | 0.000161 | 48.971683 | 0.020420 | 432 |
| 37 | 7892.766875 | 386535.520391 | 0.000003 | 0.000127 | 48.973386 | 0.020419 | 444 |
| 38 | 10059.115537 | 492642.393626 | 0.000002 | 0.000099 | 48.974723 | 0.020419 | 456 |
| 39 | 12820.067663 | 627872.701838 | 0.000002 | 0.000078 | 48.975771 | 0.020418 | 468 |
| 40 | 16338.825643 | 800220.031482 | 0.000001 | 0.000061 | 48.976594 | 0.020418 | 480 |

25.00% ANNUAL INTEREST RATE          2.0833% MONTHLY EFFECTIVE INTEREST RATE

| | 1<br>Future Value<br>of $1 | 2<br>Future Value<br>Annuity of<br>$1 per Month | 3<br>Sinking<br>Fund<br>Factor | 4<br>Present Value<br>of $1<br>(Reversion) | 5<br>Present Value<br>Annuity of<br>$1 per Month | 6<br>Installment<br>to<br>Amortize $1 | |
|---|---|---|---|---|---|---|---|
| Months | | | | | | | Months |
| 1 | 1.020833 | 1.000000 | 1.000000 | 0.979592 | 0.979592 | 1.020833 | 1 |
| 2 | 1.042101 | 2.020833 | 0.494845 | 0.959600 | 1.939192 | 0.515679 | 2 |
| 3 | 1.063811 | 3.062934 | 0.326484 | 0.940016 | 2.879208 | 0.347318 | 3 |
| 4 | 1.085974 | 4.126745 | 0.242322 | 0.920832 | 3.800041 | 0.263155 | 4 |
| 5 | 1.108598 | 5.212719 | 0.191838 | 0.902040 | 4.702081 | 0.212672 | 5 |
| 6 | 1.131694 | 6.321317 | 0.158195 | 0.883631 | 5.585712 | 0.179028 | 6 |
| 7 | 1.155271 | 7.453011 | 0.134174 | 0.865598 | 6.451310 | 0.155007 | 7 |
| 8 | 1.179339 | 8.608283 | 0.116167 | 0.847932 | 7.299242 | 0.137001 | 8 |
| 9 | 1.203909 | 9.787622 | 0.102107 | 0.830628 | 8.129870 | 0.123003 | 9 |
| 10 | 1.228990 | 10.991531 | 0.090979 | 0.813676 | 8.943546 | 0.111812 | 10 |
| 11 | 1.254594 | 12.220521 | 0.081830 | 0.797070 | 9.740616 | 0.102663 | 11 |
| 12 | 1.280732 | 13.475115 | 0.074211 | 0.780804 | 10.521420 | 0.095044 | 12 |
| Years | | | | | | | Months |
| 1 | 1.280732 | 13.475115 | 0.074211 | 0.780804 | 10.521420 | 0.095044 | 12 |
| 2 | 1.640273 | 30.733120 | 0.032538 | 0.609654 | 18.736585 | 0.053372 | 24 |
| 3 | 2.100750 | 52.835991 | 0.018926 | 0.476021 | 25.151016 | 0.039760 | 36 |
| 4 | 2.690497 | 81.143837 | 0.012324 | 0.371679 | 30.159427 | 0.033157 | 48 |
| 5 | 3.445804 | 117.398588 | 0.008518 | 0.290208 | 34.070014 | 0.029351 | 60 |
| 6 | 4.413150 | 163.831191 | 0.006104 | 0.226596 | 37.123415 | 0.026937 | 72 |
| 7 | 5.652060 | 223.298892 | 0.004478 | 0.176927 | 39.507522 | 0.025312 | 84 |
| 8 | 7.238772 | 299.461053 | 0.003339 | 0.138145 | 41.369041 | 0.024173 | 96 |
| 9 | 9.270924 | 397.004337 | 0.002519 | 0.107864 | 42.822522 | 0.023352 | 108 |
| 10 | 11.873565 | 521.931099 | 0.001916 | 0.084221 | 43.957406 | 0.022749 | 120 |
| 11 | 15.206849 | 681.928746 | 0.001466 | 0.065760 | 44.843528 | 0.022300 | 132 |
| 12 | 19.475891 | 886.842783 | 0.001128 | 0.051346 | 45.535414 | 0.021961 | 144 |
| 13 | 24.943389 | 1149.282656 | 0.000870 | 0.040091 | 46.075642 | 0.021703 | 156 |
| 14 | 31.945785 | 1485.397684 | 0.000673 | 0.031303 | 46.497454 | 0.021507 | 168 |
| 15 | 40.913975 | 1915.870809 | 0.000522 | 0.024442 | 46.826807 | 0.021355 | 180 |
| 16 | 52.399819 | 2467.191327 | 0.000405 | 0.019084 | 47.083966 | 0.021239 | 192 |
| 17 | 67.110102 | 3173.284913 | 0.000315 | 0.014901 | 47.284757 | 0.021148 | 204 |
| 18 | 85.950026 | 4077.601254 | 0.000245 | 0.011635 | 47.441536 | 0.021079 | 216 |
| 19 | 110.078911 | 5235.787733 | 0.000191 | 0.009084 | 47.563949 | 0.021024 | 228 |
| 20 | 140.981536 | 6719.113709 | 0.000149 | 0.007093 | 47.659530 | 0.020982 | 240 |
| 21 | 180.559502 | 8618.856102 | 0.000116 | 0.005538 | 47.734160 | 0.020949 | 252 |
| 22 | 231.248253 | 11051.916141 | 0.000090 | 0.004324 | 47.792431 | 0.020924 | 264 |
| 23 | 296.166936 | 14168.012923 | 0.000071 | 0.003376 | 47.837929 | 0.020904 | 276 |
| 24 | 379.310342 | 18158.896417 | 0.000055 | 0.002636 | 47.873455 | 0.020888 | 288 |
| 25 | 485.794726 | 23270.146863 | 0.000043 | 0.002058 | 47.901193 | 0.020876 | 300 |
| 26 | 622.172638 | 29816.286623 | 0.000034 | 0.001607 | 47.922851 | 0.020867 | 312 |
| 27 | 796.836134 | 38200.134415 | 0.000026 | 0.001255 | 47.939762 | 0.020860 | 324 |
| 28 | 1020.533185 | 48937.592881 | 0.000020 | 0.000980 | 47.952966 | 0.020854 | 336 |
| 29 | 1307.029059 | 62689.394820 | 0.000016 | 0.000765 | 47.963275 | 0.020849 | 348 |
| 30 | 1673.953366 | 80301.761580 | 0.000012 | 0.000597 | 47.971325 | 0.020846 | 360 |
| 31 | 2143.884907 | 102858.475547 | 0.000010 | 0.000466 | 47.977611 | 0.020843 | 372 |
| 32 | 2745.741063 | 131747.571029 | 0.000008 | 0.000364 | 47.982518 | 0.020841 | 384 |
| 33 | 3516.557237 | 168746.747371 | 0.000006 | 0.000284 | 47.986350 | 0.020839 | 396 |
| 34 | 4503.765838 | 216132.760232 | 0.000005 | 0.000222 | 47.989342 | 0.020838 | 408 |
| 35 | 5768.115051 | 276821.522435 | 0.000004 | 0.000173 | 47.991678 | 0.020837 | 420 |
| 36 | 7387.406991 | 354547.535567 | 0.000003 | 0.000135 | 47.993502 | 0.020836 | 432 |
| 37 | 9461.285285 | 454093.693669 | 0.000002 | 0.000106 | 47.994927 | 0.020836 | 444 |
| 38 | 12117.366669 | 581585.600092 | 0.000002 | 0.000083 | 47.996039 | 0.020835 | 456 |
| 39 | 15519.093925 | 744868.508377 | 0.000001 | 0.000064 | 47.996907 | 0.020835 | 468 |
| 40 | 19875.793382 | 953990.082332 | 0.000001 | 0.000050 | 47.997585 | 0.020834 | 480 |

# Appendix C
# Annual Compound
# Interest Tables

6.00% ANNUAL INTEREST RATE

| | 1 Future Value of $1 | 2 Future Value Annuity of $1 per Year | 3 Sinking Fund Factor | 4 Present Value of $1 (Reversion) | 5 Present Value Annuity of $1 per Year | 6 Installment to Amortize $1 | |
|---|---|---|---|---|---|---|---|
| Years | | | | | | | Years |
| 1 | 1.060000 | 1.000000 | 1.000000 | 0.943396 | 0.943396 | 1.060000 | 1 |
| 2 | 1.123600 | 2.060000 | 0.485437 | 0.889996 | 1.833393 | 0.545437 | 2 |
| 3 | 1.191016 | 3.183600 | 0.314110 | 0.839619 | 2.673012 | 0.374110 | 3 |
| 4 | 1.262477 | 4.374616 | 0.228591 | 0.792094 | 3.465106 | 0.288591 | 4 |
| 5 | 1.338226 | 5.637093 | 0.177396 | 0.747258 | 4.212364 | 0.237396 | 5 |
| 6 | 1.418519 | 6.975319 | 0.143363 | 0.704961 | 4.917324 | 0.203363 | 6 |
| 7 | 1.503630 | 8.393838 | 0.119135 | 0.665057 | 5.582381 | 0.179135 | 7 |
| 8 | 1.593848 | 9.897468 | 0.101036 | 0.627412 | 6.209794 | 0.161036 | 8 |
| 9 | 1.689479 | 11.491316 | 0.087022 | 0.591898 | 6.801692 | 0.147022 | 9 |
| 10 | 1.790848 | 13.180795 | 0.075868 | 0.558395 | 7.360087 | 0.135868 | 10 |
| 11 | 1.898299 | 14.971643 | 0.066793 | 0.526788 | 7.886875 | 0.126793 | 11 |
| 12 | 2.012196 | 16.869941 | 0.059277 | 0.496969 | 8.383844 | 0.119277 | 12 |
| 13 | 2.132928 | 18.882138 | 0.052960 | 0.468839 | 8.852683 | 0.112960 | 13 |
| 14 | 2.260904 | 21.015066 | 0.047585 | 0.442301 | 9.294984 | 0.107585 | 14 |
| 15 | 2.396558 | 23.275970 | 0.042963 | 0.417265 | 9.712249 | 0.102963 | 15 |
| 16 | 2.540352 | 25.672528 | 0.038952 | 0.393646 | 10.105895 | 0.098952 | 16 |
| 17 | 2.692773 | 28.212880 | 0.035445 | 0.371364 | 10.477260 | 0.095445 | 17 |
| 18 | 2.854339 | 30.905653 | 0.032357 | 0.350344 | 10.827603 | 0.092357 | 18 |
| 19 | 3.025600 | 33.759992 | 0.029621 | 0.330513 | 11.158116 | 0.089621 | 19 |
| 20 | 3.207135 | 36.785591 | 0.027185 | 0.311805 | 11.469921 | 0.087185 | 20 |
| 21 | 3.399564 | 39.992727 | 0.025005 | 0.294155 | 11.764077 | 0.085005 | 21 |
| 22 | 3.603537 | 43.392290 | 0.023046 | 0.277505 | 12.041582 | 0.083046 | 22 |
| 23 | 3.819750 | 46.995828 | 0.021278 | 0.261797 | 12.303379 | 0.081278 | 23 |
| 24 | 4.048935 | 50.815577 | 0.019679 | 0.246979 | 12.550358 | 0.079679 | 24 |
| 25 | 4.291871 | 54.864512 | 0.018227 | 0.232999 | 12.783356 | 0.078227 | 25 |
| 26 | 4.549383 | 59.156383 | 0.016904 | 0.219810 | 13.003166 | 0.076904 | 26 |
| 27 | 4.822346 | 63.705766 | 0.015697 | 0.207368 | 13.210534 | 0.075697 | 27 |
| 28 | 5.111687 | 68.528112 | 0.014593 | 0.195630 | 13.406164 | 0.074593 | 28 |
| 29 | 5.418388 | 73.639798 | 0.013580 | 0.184557 | 13.590721 | 0.073580 | 29 |
| 30 | 5.743491 | 79.058186 | 0.012649 | 0.174110 | 13.764831 | 0.072649 | 30 |
| 31 | 6.088101 | 84.801677 | 0.011792 | 0.164255 | 13.929086 | 0.071792 | 31 |
| 32 | 6.453387 | 90.889778 | 0.011002 | 0.154957 | 14.084043 | 0.071002 | 32 |
| 33 | 6.840590 | 97.343165 | 0.010273 | 0.146186 | 14.230230 | 0.070273 | 33 |
| 34 | 7.251025 | 104.183755 | 0.009598 | 0.137912 | 14.368141 | 0.069598 | 34 |
| 35 | 7.686087 | 111.434780 | 0.008974 | 0.130105 | 14.498246 | 0.068974 | 35 |
| 36 | 8.147252 | 119.120867 | 0.008395 | 0.122741 | 14.620987 | 0.068395 | 36 |
| 37 | 8.636087 | 127.268119 | 0.007857 | 0.115793 | 14.736780 | 0.067857 | 37 |
| 38 | 9.154252 | 135.904206 | 0.007358 | 0.109239 | 14.846019 | 0.067358 | 38 |
| 39 | 9.703507 | 145.058458 | 0.006894 | 0.103056 | 14.949075 | 0.066894 | 39 |
| 40 | 10.285718 | 154.761966 | 0.006462 | 0.097222 | 15.046297 | 0.066462 | 40 |
| 41 | 10.902861 | 165.047684 | 0.006059 | 0.091719 | 15.138016 | 0.066059 | 41 |
| 42 | 11.557033 | 175.950545 | 0.005683 | 0.086527 | 15.224543 | 0.065683 | 42 |
| 43 | 12.250455 | 187.507577 | 0.005333 | 0.081630 | 15.306173 | 0.065333 | 43 |
| 44 | 12.985482 | 199.758032 | 0.005006 | 0.077009 | 15.383182 | 0.065006 | 44 |
| 45 | 13.764611 | 212.743514 | 0.004700 | 0.072650 | 15.455832 | 0.064700 | 45 |
| 46 | 14.590487 | 226.508125 | 0.004415 | 0.068538 | 15.524370 | 0.064415 | 46 |
| 47 | 15.465917 | 241.098612 | 0.004148 | 0.064658 | 15.589028 | 0.064148 | 47 |
| 48 | 16.393872 | 256.564529 | 0.003898 | 0.060998 | 15.650027 | 0.063898 | 48 |
| 49 | 17.377504 | 272.958401 | 0.003664 | 0.057546 | 15.707572 | 0.063664 | 49 |
| 50 | 18.420154 | 290.335905 | 0.003444 | 0.054288 | 15.761861 | 0.063444 | 50 |

6.50% ANNUAL INTEREST RATE

| | 1<br>Future Value<br>of $1 | 2<br>Future Value<br>Annuity of<br>$1 per Year | 3<br>Sinking<br>Fund<br>Factor | 4<br>Present Value<br>of $1<br>(Reversion) | 5<br>Present Value<br>Annuity of<br>$1 per Year | 6<br>Installment<br>to<br>Amortize $1 | |
|---|---|---|---|---|---|---|---|
| Years | | | | | | | Years |
| 1 | 1.065000 | 1.000000 | 1.000000 | 0.938967 | 0.938967 | 1.065000 | 1 |
| 2 | 1.134225 | 2.065000 | 0.484262 | 0.881659 | 1.820626 | 0.549262 | 2 |
| 3 | 1.207950 | 3.199225 | 0.312576 | 0.827849 | 2.648476 | 0.377576 | 3 |
| 4 | 1.286466 | 4.407175 | 0.226903 | 0.777323 | 3.425799 | 0.291903 | 4 |
| 5 | 1.370087 | 5.693641 | 0.175635 | 0.729881 | 4.155679 | 0.240635 | 5 |
| 6 | 1.459142 | 7.063728 | 0.141568 | 0.685334 | 4.841014 | 0.206568 | 6 |
| 7 | 1.553987 | 8.522870 | 0.117331 | 0.643506 | 5.484520 | 0.182331 | 7 |
| 8 | 1.654996 | 10.076856 | 0.099237 | 0.604231 | 6.088751 | 0.164237 | 8 |
| 9 | 1.762570 | 11.731852 | 0.085238 | 0.567353 | 6.656104 | 0.150238 | 9 |
| 10 | 1.877137 | 13.494423 | 0.074105 | 0.532726 | 7.188830 | 0.139105 | 10 |
| 11 | 1.999151 | 15.371560 | 0.065055 | 0.500212 | 7.689042 | 0.130055 | 11 |
| 12 | 2.129096 | 17.370711 | 0.057568 | 0.469683 | 8.158725 | 0.122568 | 12 |
| 13 | 2.267487 | 19.499808 | 0.051283 | 0.441017 | 8.599742 | 0.116283 | 13 |
| 14 | 2.414874 | 21.767295 | 0.045940 | 0.414100 | 9.013842 | 0.110940 | 14 |
| 15 | 2.571841 | 24.182169 | 0.041353 | 0.388827 | 9.402669 | 0.106353 | 15 |
| 16 | 2.739011 | 26.754010 | 0.037378 | 0.365095 | 9.767764 | 0.102378 | 16 |
| 17 | 2.917046 | 29.493021 | 0.033906 | 0.342813 | 10.110577 | 0.098906 | 17 |
| 18 | 3.106654 | 32.410067 | 0.030855 | 0.321890 | 10.432466 | 0.095855 | 18 |
| 19 | 3.308587 | 35.516722 | 0.028156 | 0.302244 | 10.734710 | 0.093156 | 19 |
| 20 | 3.523645 | 38.825309 | 0.025756 | 0.283797 | 11.018507 | 0.090756 | 20 |
| 21 | 3.752682 | 42.348954 | 0.023613 | 0.266476 | 11.284983 | 0.088613 | 21 |
| 22 | 3.996606 | 46.101636 | 0.021691 | 0.250212 | 11.535196 | 0.086691 | 22 |
| 23 | 4.256386 | 50.098242 | 0.019961 | 0.234941 | 11.770137 | 0.084961 | 23 |
| 24 | 4.533051 | 54.354628 | 0.018398 | 0.220602 | 11.990739 | 0.083398 | 24 |
| 25 | 4.827699 | 58.887679 | 0.016981 | 0.207138 | 12.197877 | 0.081981 | 25 |
| 26 | 5.141500 | 63.715378 | 0.015695 | 0.194496 | 12.392373 | 0.080695 | 26 |
| 27 | 5.475697 | 68.856877 | 0.014523 | 0.182625 | 12.574998 | 0.079523 | 27 |
| 28 | 5.831617 | 74.332574 | 0.013453 | 0.171479 | 12.746477 | 0.078453 | 28 |
| 29 | 6.210672 | 80.164192 | 0.012474 | 0.161013 | 12.907490 | 0.077474 | 29 |
| 30 | 6.614366 | 86.374864 | 0.011577 | 0.151186 | 13.058676 | 0.076577 | 30 |
| 31 | 7.044300 | 92.989230 | 0.010754 | 0.141959 | 13.200635 | 0.075754 | 31 |
| 32 | 7.502179 | 100.033530 | 0.009997 | 0.133295 | 13.333929 | 0.074997 | 32 |
| 33 | 7.989821 | 107.535710 | 0.009299 | 0.125159 | 13.459088 | 0.074299 | 33 |
| 34 | 8.509159 | 115.525531 | 0.008656 | 0.117520 | 13.576609 | 0.073656 | 34 |
| 35 | 9.062255 | 124.034690 | 0.008062 | 0.110348 | 13.686957 | 0.073062 | 35 |
| 36 | 9.651301 | 133.096945 | 0.007513 | 0.103613 | 13.790570 | 0.072513 | 36 |
| 37 | 10.278636 | 142.748247 | 0.007005 | 0.097289 | 13.887859 | 0.072005 | 37 |
| 38 | 10.946747 | 153.026883 | 0.006535 | 0.091351 | 13.979210 | 0.071535 | 38 |
| 39 | 11.658286 | 163.973630 | 0.006099 | 0.085776 | 14.064986 | 0.071099 | 39 |
| 40 | 12.416075 | 175.631916 | 0.005694 | 0.080541 | 14.145527 | 0.070694 | 40 |
| 41 | 13.223119 | 188.047990 | 0.005318 | 0.075625 | 14.221152 | 0.070318 | 41 |
| 42 | 14.082622 | 201.271110 | 0.004968 | 0.071010 | 14.292161 | 0.069968 | 42 |
| 43 | 14.997993 | 215.353732 | 0.004644 | 0.066676 | 14.358837 | 0.069644 | 43 |
| 44 | 15.972862 | 230.351725 | 0.004341 | 0.062606 | 14.421443 | 0.069341 | 44 |
| 45 | 17.011098 | 246.324587 | 0.004060 | 0.058785 | 14.480228 | 0.069060 | 45 |
| 46 | 18.116820 | 263.335685 | 0.003797 | 0.055197 | 14.535426 | 0.068797 | 46 |
| 47 | 19.294413 | 281.452504 | 0.003553 | 0.051828 | 14.587254 | 0.068553 | 47 |
| 48 | 20.548550 | 300.746917 | 0.003325 | 0.048665 | 14.635919 | 0.068325 | 48 |
| 49 | 21.884205 | 321.295467 | 0.003112 | 0.045695 | 14.681615 | 0.068112 | 49 |
| 50 | 23.306679 | 343.179672 | 0.002914 | 0.042906 | 14.724521 | 0.067914 | 50 |

7.00% ANNUAL INTEREST RATE

| | 1<br>Future Value<br>of $1 | 2<br>Future Value<br>Annuity of<br>$1 per Year | 3<br>Sinking<br>Fund<br>Factor | 4<br>Present Value<br>of $1<br>(Reversion) | 5<br>Present Value<br>Annuity of<br>$1 per Year | 6<br>Installment<br>to<br>Amortize $1 | |
|---|---|---|---|---|---|---|---|
| Years | | | | | | | Years |
| 1 | 1.070000 | 1.000000 | 1.000000 | 0.934579 | 0.934579 | 1.070000 | 1 |
| 2 | 1.144900 | 2.070000 | 0.483092 | 0.873439 | 1.808018 | 0.553092 | 2 |
| 3 | 1.225043 | 3.214900 | 0.311052 | 0.816298 | 2.624316 | 0.381052 | 3 |
| 4 | 1.310796 | 4.439943 | 0.225228 | 0.762895 | 3.387211 | 0.295228 | 4 |
| 5 | 1.402552 | 5.750739 | 0.173891 | 0.712986 | 4.100197 | 0.243891 | 5 |
| 6 | 1.500730 | 7.153291 | 0.139796 | 0.666342 | 4.766540 | 0.209796 | 6 |
| 7 | 1.605781 | 8.654021 | 0.115553 | 0.622750 | 5.389289 | 0.185553 | 7 |
| 8 | 1.718186 | 10.259803 | 0.097468 | 0.582009 | 5.971299 | 0.167468 | 8 |
| 9 | 1.838459 | 11.977989 | 0.083486 | 0.543934 | 6.515232 | 0.153486 | 9 |
| 10 | 1.967151 | 13.816448 | 0.072378 | 0.508349 | 7.023582 | 0.142378 | 10 |
| 11 | 2.104852 | 15.783599 | 0.063357 | 0.475093 | 7.498674 | 0.133357 | 11 |
| 12 | 2.252192 | 17.888451 | 0.055902 | 0.444012 | 7.942686 | 0.125902 | 12 |
| 13 | 2.409845 | 20.140643 | 0.049651 | 0.414964 | 8.357651 | 0.119651 | 13 |
| 14 | 2.578534 | 22.550488 | 0.044345 | 0.387817 | 8.745468 | 0.114345 | 14 |
| 15 | 2.759032 | 25.129022 | 0.039795 | 0.362446 | 9.107914 | 0.109795 | 15 |
| 16 | 2.952164 | 27.888054 | 0.035858 | 0.338735 | 9.446649 | 0.105858 | 16 |
| 17 | 3.158815 | 30.840217 | 0.032425 | 0.316574 | 9.763223 | 0.102425 | 17 |
| 18 | 3.379932 | 33.999033 | 0.029413 | 0.295864 | 10.059087 | 0.099413 | 18 |
| 19 | 3.616528 | 37.378965 | 0.026753 | 0.276508 | 10.335595 | 0.096753 | 19 |
| 20 | 3.869684 | 40.995492 | 0.024393 | 0.258419 | 10.594014 | 0.094393 | 20 |
| 21 | 4.140562 | 44.865177 | 0.022289 | 0.241513 | 10.835527 | 0.092289 | 21 |
| 22 | 4.430402 | 49.005739 | 0.020406 | 0.225713 | 11.061240 | 0.090406 | 22 |
| 23 | 4.740530 | 53.436141 | 0.018714 | 0.210947 | 11.272187 | 0.088714 | 23 |
| 24 | 5.072367 | 58.176671 | 0.017189 | 0.197147 | 11.469334 | 0.087189 | 24 |
| 25 | 5.427433 | 63.249038 | 0.015811 | 0.184249 | 11.653583 | 0.085811 | 25 |
| 26 | 5.807353 | 68.676470 | 0.014561 | 0.172195 | 11.825779 | 0.084561 | 26 |
| 27 | 6.213868 | 74.483823 | 0.013426 | 0.160930 | 11.986709 | 0.083426 | 27 |
| 28 | 6.648838 | 80.697691 | 0.012392 | 0.150402 | 12.137111 | 0.082392 | 28 |
| 29 | 7.114257 | 87.346529 | 0.011449 | 0.140563 | 12.277674 | 0.081449 | 29 |
| 30 | 7.612255 | 94.460786 | 0.010586 | 0.131367 | 12.409041 | 0.080586 | 30 |
| 31 | 8.145113 | 102.073041 | 0.009797 | 0.122773 | 12.531814 | 0.079797 | 31 |
| 32 | 8.715271 | 110.218154 | 0.009073 | 0.114741 | 12.646555 | 0.079073 | 32 |
| 33 | 9.325340 | 118.933425 | 0.008408 | 0.107235 | 12.753790 | 0.078408 | 33 |
| 34 | 9.978114 | 128.258765 | 0.007797 | 0.100219 | 12.854009 | 0.077797 | 34 |
| 35 | 10.676581 | 138.236878 | 0.007234 | 0.093663 | 12.947672 | 0.077234 | 35 |
| 36 | 11.423942 | 148.913460 | 0.006715 | 0.087535 | 13.035208 | 0.076715 | 36 |
| 37 | 12.223618 | 160.337402 | 0.006237 | 0.081809 | 13.117017 | 0.076237 | 37 |
| 38 | 13.079271 | 172.561020 | 0.005795 | 0.076457 | 13.193473 | 0.075795 | 38 |
| 39 | 13.994820 | 185.640292 | 0.005387 | 0.071455 | 13.264928 | 0.075387 | 39 |
| 40 | 14.974458 | 199.635112 | 0.005009 | 0.066780 | 13.331709 | 0.075009 | 40 |
| 41 | 16.022670 | 214.609570 | 0.004660 | 0.062412 | 13.394120 | 0.074660 | 41 |
| 42 | 17.144257 | 230.632240 | 0.004336 | 0.058329 | 13.452449 | 0.074336 | 42 |
| 43 | 18.344355 | 247.776496 | 0.004036 | 0.054513 | 13.506962 | 0.074036 | 43 |
| 44 | 19.628460 | 266.120851 | 0.003758 | 0.050946 | 13.557908 | 0.073758 | 44 |
| 45 | 21.002452 | 285.749311 | 0.003500 | 0.047613 | 13.605522 | 0.073500 | 45 |
| 46 | 22.472623 | 306.751763 | 0.003260 | 0.044499 | 13.650020 | 0.073260 | 46 |
| 47 | 24.045707 | 329.224386 | 0.003037 | 0.041587 | 13.691608 | 0.073037 | 47 |
| 48 | 25.728901 | 353.270093 | 0.002831 | 0.038867 | 13.730474 | 0.072831 | 48 |
| 49 | 27.529930 | 378.999000 | 0.002639 | 0.036324 | 13.766799 | 0.072639 | 49 |
| 50 | 29.457025 | 406.528929 | 0.002460 | 0.033948 | 13.800746 | 0.072460 | 50 |

7.50% ANNUAL INTEREST RATE

| | 1<br>Future Value<br>of $1 | 2<br>Future Value<br>Annuity of<br>$1 per Year | 3<br>Sinking<br>Fund<br>Factor | 4<br>Present Value<br>of $1<br>(Reversion) | 5<br>Present Value<br>Annuity of<br>$1 per Year | 6<br>Installment<br>to<br>Amortize $1 | |
|---|---|---|---|---|---|---|---|
| Years | | | | | | | Years |
| 1 | 1.075000 | 1.000000 | 1.000000 | 0.930233 | 0.930233 | 1.075000 | 1 |
| 2 | 1.155625 | 2.075000 | 0.481928 | 0.865333 | 1.795565 | 0.556928 | 2 |
| 3 | 1.242297 | 3.230625 | 0.309538 | 0.804961 | 2.600526 | 0.384538 | 3 |
| 4 | 1.335469 | 4.472922 | 0.223568 | 0.748801 | 3.349326 | 0.298568 | 4 |
| 5 | 1.435629 | 5.808391 | 0.172165 | 0.696559 | 4.045885 | 0.247165 | 5 |
| 6 | 1.543302 | 7.244020 | 0.138045 | 0.647962 | 4.693846 | 0.213045 | 6 |
| 7 | 1.659049 | 8.787322 | 0.113800 | 0.602755 | 5.296601 | 0.188800 | 7 |
| 8 | 1.783478 | 10.446371 | 0.095727 | 0.560702 | 5.857304 | 0.170727 | 8 |
| 9 | 1.917239 | 12.229849 | 0.081767 | 0.521583 | 6.378887 | 0.156767 | 9 |
| 10 | 2.061032 | 14.147087 | 0.070686 | 0.485194 | 6.864081 | 0.145686 | 10 |
| 11 | 2.215609 | 16.208119 | 0.061697 | 0.451343 | 7.315424 | 0.136697 | 11 |
| 12 | 2.381780 | 18.423728 | 0.054278 | 0.419854 | 7.735278 | 0.129278 | 12 |
| 13 | 2.560413 | 20.805508 | 0.048064 | 0.390562 | 8.125840 | 0.123064 | 13 |
| 14 | 2.752444 | 23.365921 | 0.042797 | 0.363313 | 8.489154 | 0.117797 | 14 |
| 15 | 2.958877 | 26.118365 | 0.038287 | 0.337966 | 8.827120 | 0.113287 | 15 |
| 16 | 3.180793 | 29.077242 | 0.034391 | 0.314387 | 9.141507 | 0.109391 | 16 |
| 17 | 3.419353 | 32.258035 | 0.031000 | 0.292453 | 9.433960 | 0.106000 | 17 |
| 18 | 3.675804 | 35.677388 | 0.028029 | 0.272049 | 9.706009 | 0.103029 | 18 |
| 19 | 3.951489 | 39.353192 | 0.025411 | 0.253069 | 9.959078 | 0.100411 | 19 |
| 20 | 4.247851 | 43.304681 | 0.023092 | 0.235413 | 10.194491 | 0.098092 | 20 |
| 21 | 4.566440 | 47.552532 | 0.021029 | 0.218989 | 10.413480 | 0.096029 | 21 |
| 22 | 4.908923 | 52.118972 | 0.019187 | 0.203711 | 10.617191 | 0.094187 | 22 |
| 23 | 5.277092 | 57.027895 | 0.017535 | 0.189498 | 10.806689 | 0.092535 | 23 |
| 24 | 5.672874 | 62.304987 | 0.016050 | 0.176277 | 10.982967 | 0.091050 | 24 |
| 25 | 6.098340 | 67.977862 | 0.014711 | 0.163979 | 11.146946 | 0.089711 | 25 |
| 26 | 6.555715 | 74.076201 | 0.013500 | 0.152539 | 11.299485 | 0.088500 | 26 |
| 27 | 7.047394 | 80.631916 | 0.012402 | 0.141896 | 11.441381 | 0.087402 | 27 |
| 28 | 7.575948 | 87.679310 | 0.011405 | 0.131997 | 11.573378 | 0.086405 | 28 |
| 29 | 8.144144 | 95.255258 | 0.010498 | 0.122788 | 11.696165 | 0.085498 | 29 |
| 30 | 8.754955 | 103.399403 | 0.009671 | 0.114221 | 11.810386 | 0.084671 | 30 |
| 31 | 9.411577 | 112.154358 | 0.008916 | 0.106252 | 11.916638 | 0.083916 | 31 |
| 32 | 10.117445 | 121.565935 | 0.008226 | 0.098839 | 12.015478 | 0.083226 | 32 |
| 33 | 10.876253 | 131.683380 | 0.007594 | 0.091943 | 12.107421 | 0.082594 | 33 |
| 34 | 11.691972 | 142.559633 | 0.007015 | 0.085529 | 12.192950 | 0.082015 | 34 |
| 35 | 12.568870 | 154.251606 | 0.006483 | 0.079562 | 12.272511 | 0.081483 | 35 |
| 36 | 13.511536 | 166.820476 | 0.005994 | 0.074011 | 12.346522 | 0.080994 | 36 |
| 37 | 14.524901 | 180.332012 | 0.005545 | 0.068847 | 12.415370 | 0.080545 | 37 |
| 38 | 15.614268 | 194.856913 | 0.005132 | 0.064044 | 12.479414 | 0.080132 | 38 |
| 39 | 16.785339 | 210.471181 | 0.004751 | 0.059576 | 12.538989 | 0.079751 | 39 |
| 40 | 18.044239 | 227.256520 | 0.004400 | 0.055419 | 12.594409 | 0.079400 | 40 |
| 41 | 19.397557 | 245.300759 | 0.004077 | 0.051553 | 12.645962 | 0.079077 | 41 |
| 42 | 20.852374 | 264.698315 | 0.003778 | 0.047956 | 12.693918 | 0.078778 | 42 |
| 43 | 22.416302 | 285.550689 | 0.003502 | 0.044610 | 12.738528 | 0.078502 | 43 |
| 44 | 24.097524 | 307.966991 | 0.003247 | 0.041498 | 12.780026 | 0.078247 | 44 |
| 45 | 25.904839 | 332.064515 | 0.003011 | 0.038603 | 12.818629 | 0.078011 | 45 |
| 46 | 27.847702 | 357.969354 | 0.002794 | 0.035910 | 12.854539 | 0.077794 | 46 |
| 47 | 29.936279 | 385.817055 | 0.002592 | 0.033404 | 12.887943 | 0.077592 | 47 |
| 48 | 32.181500 | 415.753334 | 0.002405 | 0.031074 | 12.919017 | 0.077405 | 48 |
| 49 | 34.595113 | 447.934835 | 0.002232 | 0.028906 | 12.947922 | 0.077232 | 49 |
| 50 | 37.189746 | 482.529947 | 0.002072 | 0.026889 | 12.974812 | 0.077072 | 50 |

8.00% ANNUAL INTEREST RATE

| | 1<br>Future Value<br>of $1 | 2<br>Future Value<br>Annuity of<br>$1 per Year | 3<br>Sinking<br>Fund<br>Factor | 4<br>Present Value<br>of $1<br>(Reversion) | 5<br>Present Value<br>Annuity of<br>$1 per Year | 6<br>Installment<br>to<br>Amortize $1 | |
|---|---|---|---|---|---|---|---|
| Years | | | | | | | Years |
| 1 | 1.080000 | 1.000000 | 1.000000 | 0.925926 | 0.925926 | 1.080000 | 1 |
| 2 | 1.166400 | 2.080000 | 0.480769 | 0.857339 | 1.783265 | 0.560769 | 2 |
| 3 | 1.259712 | 3.246400 | 0.308034 | 0.793832 | 2.577097 | 0.388034 | 3 |
| 4 | 1.360489 | 4.506112 | 0.221921 | 0.735030 | 3.312127 | 0.301921 | 4 |
| 5 | 1.469328 | 5.866601 | 0.170456 | 0.680583 | 3.992710 | 0.250456 | 5 |
| 6 | 1.586874 | 7.335929 | 0.136315 | 0.630170 | 4.622880 | 0.216315 | 6 |
| 7 | 1.713824 | 8.922803 | 0.112072 | 0.583490 | 5.206370 | 0.192072 | 7 |
| 8 | 1.850930 | 10.636628 | 0.094015 | 0.540269 | 5.746639 | 0.174015 | 8 |
| 9 | 1.999005 | 12.487558 | 0.080080 | 0.500249 | 6.246888 | 0.160080 | 9 |
| 10 | 2.158925 | 14.486562 | 0.069029 | 0.463193 | 6.710081 | 0.149029 | 10 |
| 11 | 2.331639 | 16.645487 | 0.060076 | 0.428883 | 7.138964 | 0.140076 | 11 |
| 12 | 2.518170 | 18.977126 | 0.052695 | 0.397114 | 7.536078 | 0.132695 | 12 |
| 13 | 2.719624 | 21.495297 | 0.046522 | 0.367698 | 7.903776 | 0.126522 | 13 |
| 14 | 2.937194 | 24.214920 | 0.041297 | 0.340461 | 8.244237 | 0.121297 | 14 |
| 15 | 3.172169 | 27.152114 | 0.036830 | 0.315242 | 8.559479 | 0.116830 | 15 |
| 16 | 3.425943 | 30.324283 | 0.032977 | 0.291890 | 8.851369 | 0.112977 | 16 |
| 17 | 3.700018 | 33.750226 | 0.029629 | 0.270269 | 9.121638 | 0.109629 | 17 |
| 18 | 3.996019 | 37.450244 | 0.026702 | 0.250249 | 9.371887 | 0.106702 | 18 |
| 19 | 4.315701 | 41.446263 | 0.024128 | 0.231712 | 9.603599 | 0.104128 | 19 |
| 20 | 4.660957 | 45.761964 | 0.021852 | 0.214548 | 9.818147 | 0.101852 | 20 |
| 21 | 5.033834 | 50.422921 | 0.019832 | 0.198656 | 10.016803 | 0.099832 | 21 |
| 22 | 5.436540 | 55.456755 | 0.018032 | 0.183941 | 10.200744 | 0.098032 | 22 |
| 23 | 5.871464 | 60.893296 | 0.016422 | 0.170315 | 10.371059 | 0.096422 | 23 |
| 24 | 6.341181 | 66.764759 | 0.014978 | 0.157699 | 10.528758 | 0.094978 | 24 |
| 25 | 6.848475 | 73.105940 | 0.013679 | 0.146018 | 10.674776 | 0.093679 | 25 |
| 26 | 7.396353 | 79.954415 | 0.012507 | 0.135202 | 10.809978 | 0.092507 | 26 |
| 27 | 7.988061 | 87.350768 | 0.011448 | 0.125187 | 10.935165 | 0.091448 | 27 |
| 28 | 8.627106 | 95.338830 | 0.010489 | 0.115914 | 11.051078 | 0.090489 | 28 |
| 29 | 9.317275 | 103.965936 | 0.009619 | 0.107328 | 11.158406 | 0.089619 | 29 |
| 30 | 10.062657 | 113.283211 | 0.008827 | 0.099377 | 11.257783 | 0.088827 | 30 |
| 31 | 10.867669 | 123.345868 | 0.008107 | 0.092016 | 11.349799 | 0.088107 | 31 |
| 32 | 11.737083 | 134.213537 | 0.007451 | 0.085200 | 11.434999 | 0.087451 | 32 |
| 33 | 12.676050 | 145.950620 | 0.006852 | 0.078889 | 11.513888 | 0.086852 | 33 |
| 34 | 13.690134 | 158.626670 | 0.006304 | 0.073045 | 11.586934 | 0.086304 | 34 |
| 35 | 14.785344 | 172.316804 | 0.005803 | 0.067635 | 11.654568 | 0.085803 | 35 |
| 36 | 15.968172 | 187.102148 | 0.005345 | 0.062625 | 11.717193 | 0.085345 | 36 |
| 37 | 17.245626 | 203.070320 | 0.004924 | 0.057986 | 11.775179 | 0.084924 | 37 |
| 38 | 18.625276 | 220.315945 | 0.004539 | 0.053690 | 11.828869 | 0.084539 | 38 |
| 39 | 20.115298 | 238.941221 | 0.004185 | 0.049713 | 11.878582 | 0.084185 | 39 |
| 40 | 21.724521 | 259.056519 | 0.003860 | 0.046031 | 11.924613 | 0.083860 | 40 |
| 41 | 23.462483 | 280.781040 | 0.003561 | 0.042621 | 11.967235 | 0.083561 | 41 |
| 42 | 25.339482 | 304.243523 | 0.003287 | 0.039464 | 12.006699 | 0.083287 | 42 |
| 43 | 27.366640 | 329.583005 | 0.003034 | 0.036541 | 12.043240 | 0.083034 | 43 |
| 44 | 29.555972 | 356.949646 | 0.002802 | 0.033834 | 12.077074 | 0.082802 | 44 |
| 45 | 31.920449 | 386.505617 | 0.002587 | 0.031328 | 12.108402 | 0.082587 | 45 |
| 46 | 34.474085 | 418.426067 | 0.002390 | 0.029007 | 12.137409 | 0.082390 | 46 |
| 47 | 37.232012 | 452.900152 | 0.002208 | 0.026859 | 12.164267 | 0.082208 | 47 |
| 48 | 40.210573 | 490.132164 | 0.002040 | 0.024869 | 12.189136 | 0.082040 | 48 |
| 49 | 43.427419 | 530.342737 | 0.001886 | 0.023027 | 12.212163 | 0.081886 | 49 |
| 50 | 46.901613 | 573.770156 | 0.001743 | 0.021321 | 12.233485 | 0.081743 | 50 |

8.50% ANNUAL INTEREST RATE

| | 1<br>Future Value<br>of $1 | 2<br>Future Value<br>Annuity of<br>$1 per Year | 3<br>Sinking<br>Fund<br>Factor | 4<br>Present Value<br>of $1<br>(Reversion) | 5<br>Present Value<br>Annuity of<br>$1 per Year | 6<br>Installment<br>to<br>Amortize $1 | |
|---|---|---|---|---|---|---|---|
| Years | | | | | | | Years |
| 1 | 1.085000 | 1.000000 | 1.000000 | 0.921659 | 0.921659 | 1.085000 | 1 |
| 2 | 1.177225 | 2.085000 | 0.479616 | 0.849455 | 1.771114 | 0.564616 | 2 |
| 3 | 1.277289 | 3.262225 | 0.306539 | 0.782908 | 2.554022 | 0.391539 | 3 |
| 4 | 1.385859 | 4.539514 | 0.220288 | 0.721574 | 3.275597 | 0.305288 | 4 |
| 5 | 1.503657 | 5.925373 | 0.168766 | 0.665045 | 3.940642 | 0.253766 | 5 |
| 6 | 1.631468 | 7.429030 | 0.134607 | 0.612945 | 4.553587 | 0.219607 | 6 |
| 7 | 1.770142 | 9.060497 | 0.110369 | 0.564926 | 5.118514 | 0.195369 | 7 |
| 8 | 1.920604 | 10.830639 | 0.092331 | 0.520669 | 5.639183 | 0.177331 | 8 |
| 9 | 2.083856 | 12.751244 | 0.078424 | 0.479880 | 6.119063 | 0.163424 | 9 |
| 10 | 2.260983 | 14.835099 | 0.067408 | 0.442285 | 6.561348 | 0.152408 | 10 |
| 11 | 2.453167 | 17.096083 | 0.058493 | 0.407636 | 6.968984 | 0.143493 | 11 |
| 12 | 2.661686 | 19.549250 | 0.051153 | 0.375702 | 7.344686 | 0.136153 | 12 |
| 13 | 2.887930 | 22.210936 | 0.045023 | 0.346269 | 7.690955 | 0.130023 | 13 |
| 14 | 3.133404 | 25.098866 | 0.039842 | 0.319142 | 8.010097 | 0.124842 | 14 |
| 15 | 3.399743 | 28.232269 | 0.035420 | 0.294140 | 8.304237 | 0.120420 | 15 |
| 16 | 3.688721 | 31.632012 | 0.031614 | 0.271097 | 8.575333 | 0.116614 | 16 |
| 17 | 4.002262 | 35.320733 | 0.028312 | 0.249859 | 8.825192 | 0.113312 | 17 |
| 18 | 4.342455 | 39.322995 | 0.025430 | 0.230285 | 9.055476 | 0.110430 | 18 |
| 19 | 4.711563 | 43.665450 | 0.022901 | 0.212244 | 9.267720 | 0.107901 | 19 |
| 20 | 5.112046 | 48.377013 | 0.020671 | 0.195616 | 9.463337 | 0.105671 | 20 |
| 21 | 5.546570 | 53.489059 | 0.018695 | 0.180292 | 9.643628 | 0.103695 | 21 |
| 22 | 6.018028 | 59.035629 | 0.016939 | 0.166167 | 9.809796 | 0.101939 | 22 |
| 23 | 6.529561 | 65.053658 | 0.015372 | 0.153150 | 9.962945 | 0.100372 | 23 |
| 24 | 7.084574 | 71.583219 | 0.013970 | 0.141152 | 10.104097 | 0.098970 | 24 |
| 25 | 7.686762 | 78.667792 | 0.012712 | 0.130094 | 10.234191 | 0.097712 | 25 |
| 26 | 8.340137 | 86.354555 | 0.011580 | 0.119902 | 10.354093 | 0.096580 | 26 |
| 27 | 9.049049 | 94.694692 | 0.010560 | 0.110509 | 10.464602 | 0.095560 | 27 |
| 28 | 9.818218 | 103.743741 | 0.009639 | 0.101851 | 10.566453 | 0.094639 | 28 |
| 29 | 10.652766 | 113.561959 | 0.008806 | 0.093872 | 10.660326 | 0.093806 | 29 |
| 30 | 11.558252 | 124.214725 | 0.008051 | 0.086518 | 10.746844 | 0.093051 | 30 |
| 31 | 12.540703 | 135.772977 | 0.007365 | 0.079740 | 10.826584 | 0.092365 | 31 |
| 32 | 13.606663 | 148.313680 | 0.006742 | 0.073493 | 10.900078 | 0.091742 | 32 |
| 33 | 14.763229 | 161.920343 | 0.006176 | 0.067736 | 10.967813 | 0.091176 | 33 |
| 34 | 16.018104 | 176.683572 | 0.005660 | 0.062429 | 11.030243 | 0.090660 | 34 |
| 35 | 17.379642 | 192.701675 | 0.005189 | 0.057539 | 11.087781 | 0.090189 | 35 |
| 36 | 18.856912 | 210.081318 | 0.004760 | 0.053031 | 11.140812 | 0.089760 | 36 |
| 37 | 20.459750 | 228.938230 | 0.004368 | 0.048876 | 11.189689 | 0.089368 | 37 |
| 38 | 22.198828 | 249.397979 | 0.004010 | 0.045047 | 11.234736 | 0.089010 | 38 |
| 39 | 24.085729 | 271.596808 | 0.003682 | 0.041518 | 11.276255 | 0.088682 | 39 |
| 40 | 26.133016 | 295.682536 | 0.003382 | 0.038266 | 11.314520 | 0.088382 | 40 |
| 41 | 28.354322 | 321.815552 | 0.003107 | 0.035268 | 11.349788 | 0.088107 | 41 |
| 42 | 30.764439 | 350.169874 | 0.002856 | 0.032505 | 11.382293 | 0.087856 | 42 |
| 43 | 33.379417 | 380.934313 | 0.002625 | 0.029959 | 11.412252 | 0.087625 | 43 |
| 44 | 36.216667 | 414.313730 | 0.002414 | 0.027612 | 11.439864 | 0.087414 | 44 |
| 45 | 39.295084 | 450.530397 | 0.002220 | 0.025448 | 11.465312 | 0.087220 | 45 |
| 46 | 42.635166 | 489.825480 | 0.002042 | 0.023455 | 11.488767 | 0.087042 | 46 |
| 47 | 46.259155 | 532.460646 | 0.001878 | 0.021617 | 11.510384 | 0.086878 | 47 |
| 48 | 50.191183 | 578.719801 | 0.001728 | 0.019924 | 11.530308 | 0.086728 | 48 |
| 49 | 54.457434 | 628.910984 | 0.001590 | 0.018363 | 11.548671 | 0.086590 | 49 |
| 50 | 59.086316 | 683.368418 | 0.001463 | 0.016924 | 11.565595 | 0.086463 | 50 |

9.00% ANNUAL INTEREST RATE

| | 1 Future Value of $1 | 2 Future Value Annuity of $1 per Year | 3 Sinking Fund Factor | 4 Present Value of $1 (Reversion) | 5 Present Value Annuity of $1 per Year | 6 Installment to Amortize $1 | |
|---|---|---|---|---|---|---|---|
| Years | | | | | | | Years |
| 1 | 1.090000 | 1.000000 | 1.000000 | 0.917431 | 0.917431 | 1.090000 | 1 |
| 2 | 1.188100 | 2.090000 | 0.478469 | 0.841680 | 1.759111 | 0.568469 | 2 |
| 3 | 1.295029 | 3.278100 | 0.305055 | 0.772183 | 2.531295 | 0.395055 | 3 |
| 4 | 1.411582 | 4.573129 | 0.218669 | 0.708425 | 3.239720 | 0.308669 | 4 |
| 5 | 1.538624 | 5.984711 | 0.167092 | 0.649931 | 3.889651 | 0.257092 | 5 |
| 6 | 1.677100 | 7.523335 | 0.132920 | 0.596267 | 4.485919 | 0.222920 | 6 |
| 7 | 1.828039 | 9.200435 | 0.108691 | 0.547034 | 5.032953 | 0.198691 | 7 |
| 8 | 1.992563 | 11.028474 | 0.090674 | 0.501866 | 5.534819 | 0.180674 | 8 |
| 9 | 2.171893 | 13.021036 | 0.076799 | 0.460428 | 5.995247 | 0.166799 | 9 |
| 10 | 2.367364 | 15.192930 | 0.065820 | 0.422411 | 6.417658 | 0.155820 | 10 |
| 11 | 2.580426 | 17.560293 | 0.056947 | 0.387533 | 6.805191 | 0.146947 | 11 |
| 12 | 2.812665 | 20.140720 | 0.049651 | 0.355535 | 7.160725 | 0.139651 | 12 |
| 13 | 3.065805 | 22.953385 | 0.043567 | 0.326179 | 7.486904 | 0.133567 | 13 |
| 14 | 3.341727 | 26.019189 | 0.038433 | 0.299246 | 7.786150 | 0.128433 | 14 |
| 15 | 3.642482 | 29.360916 | 0.034059 | 0.274538 | 8.060688 | 0.124059 | 15 |
| 16 | 3.970306 | 33.003399 | 0.030300 | 0.251870 | 8.312558 | 0.120300 | 16 |
| 17 | 4.327633 | 36.973705 | 0.027046 | 0.231073 | 8.543631 | 0.117046 | 17 |
| 18 | 4.717120 | 41.301338 | 0.024212 | 0.211994 | 8.755625 | 0.114212 | 18 |
| 19 | 5.141661 | 46.018458 | 0.021730 | 0.194490 | 8.950115 | 0.111730 | 19 |
| 20 | 5.604411 | 51.160120 | 0.019546 | 0.178431 | 9.128546 | 0.109546 | 20 |
| 21 | 6.108808 | 56.764530 | 0.017617 | 0.163698 | 9.292244 | 0.107617 | 21 |
| 22 | 6.658600 | 62.873338 | 0.015905 | 0.150182 | 9.442425 | 0.105905 | 22 |
| 23 | 7.257874 | 69.531939 | 0.014382 | 0.137781 | 9.580207 | 0.104382 | 23 |
| 24 | 7.911083 | 76.789813 | 0.013023 | 0.126405 | 9.706612 | 0.103023 | 24 |
| 25 | 8.623081 | 84.700896 | 0.011806 | 0.115968 | 9.822580 | 0.101806 | 25 |
| 26 | 9.399158 | 93.323977 | 0.010715 | 0.106393 | 9.928972 | 0.100715 | 26 |
| 27 | 10.245082 | 102.723135 | 0.009735 | 0.097608 | 10.026580 | 0.099735 | 27 |
| 28 | 11.167140 | 112.968217 | 0.008852 | 0.089548 | 10.116128 | 0.098852 | 28 |
| 29 | 12.172182 | 124.135356 | 0.008056 | 0.082155 | 10.198283 | 0.098056 | 29 |
| 30 | 13.267678 | 136.307539 | 0.007336 | 0.075371 | 10.273654 | 0.097336 | 30 |
| 31 | 14.461770 | 149.575217 | 0.006686 | 0.069148 | 10.342802 | 0.096686 | 31 |
| 32 | 15.763329 | 164.036987 | 0.006096 | 0.063438 | 10.406240 | 0.096096 | 32 |
| 33 | 17.182028 | 179.800315 | 0.005562 | 0.058200 | 10.464441 | 0.095562 | 33 |
| 34 | 18.728411 | 196.982344 | 0.005077 | 0.053395 | 10.517835 | 0.095077 | 34 |
| 35 | 20.413968 | 215.710755 | 0.004636 | 0.048986 | 10.566821 | 0.094636 | 35 |
| 36 | 22.251225 | 236.124723 | 0.004235 | 0.044941 | 10.611763 | 0.094235 | 36 |
| 37 | 24.253835 | 258.375948 | 0.003870 | 0.041231 | 10.652993 | 0.093870 | 37 |
| 38 | 26.436680 | 282.629783 | 0.003538 | 0.037826 | 10.690820 | 0.093538 | 38 |
| 39 | 28.815982 | 309.066463 | 0.003236 | 0.034703 | 10.725523 | 0.093236 | 39 |
| 40 | 31.409420 | 337.882445 | 0.002960 | 0.031838 | 10.757360 | 0.092960 | 40 |
| 41 | 34.236268 | 369.291865 | 0.002708 | 0.029209 | 10.786569 | 0.092708 | 41 |
| 42 | 37.317532 | 403.528133 | 0.002478 | 0.026797 | 10.813366 | 0.092478 | 42 |
| 43 | 40.676110 | 440.845665 | 0.002268 | 0.024584 | 10.837950 | 0.092268 | 43 |
| 44 | 44.336960 | 481.521775 | 0.002077 | 0.022555 | 10.860505 | 0.092077 | 44 |
| 45 | 48.327286 | 525.858734 | 0.001902 | 0.020692 | 10.881197 | 0.091902 | 45 |
| 46 | 52.676742 | 574.186021 | 0.001742 | 0.018984 | 10.900181 | 0.091742 | 46 |
| 47 | 57.417649 | 626.862762 | 0.001595 | 0.017416 | 10.917597 | 0.091595 | 47 |
| 48 | 62.585237 | 684.280411 | 0.001461 | 0.015978 | 10.933575 | 0.091461 | 48 |
| 49 | 68.217908 | 746.865648 | 0.001339 | 0.014659 | 10.948234 | 0.091339 | 49 |
| 50 | 74.357520 | 815.083556 | 0.001227 | 0.013449 | 10.961683 | 0.091227 | 50 |

9.50% ANNUAL INTEREST RATE

| | 1<br>Future Value<br>of $1 | 2<br>Future Value<br>Annuity of<br>$1 per Year | 3<br>Sinking<br>Fund<br>Factor | 4<br>Present Value<br>of $1<br>(Reversion) | 5<br>Present Value<br>Annuity of<br>$1 per Year | 6<br>Installment<br>to<br>Amortize $1 | |
|---|---|---|---|---|---|---|---|
| Years | | | | | | | Years |
| 1 | 1.095000 | 1.000000 | 1.000000 | 0.913242 | 0.913242 | 1.095000 | 1 |
| 2 | 1.199025 | 2.095000 | 0.477327 | 0.834011 | 1.747253 | 0.572327 | 2 |
| 3 | 1.312932 | 3.294025 | 0.303580 | 0.761654 | 2.508907 | 0.398580 | 3 |
| 4 | 1.437661 | 4.606957 | 0.217063 | 0.695574 | 3.204481 | 0.312063 | 4 |
| 5 | 1.574239 | 6.044618 | 0.165436 | 0.635228 | 3.839709 | 0.260436 | 5 |
| 6 | 1.723791 | 7.618857 | 0.131253 | 0.580117 | 4.419825 | 0.226253 | 6 |
| 7 | 1.887552 | 9.342648 | 0.107036 | 0.529787 | 4.949612 | 0.202036 | 7 |
| 8 | 2.066869 | 11.230200 | 0.089046 | 0.483824 | 5.433436 | 0.184046 | 8 |
| 9 | 2.263222 | 13.297069 | 0.075205 | 0.441848 | 5.875284 | 0.170205 | 9 |
| 10 | 2.478228 | 15.560291 | 0.064266 | 0.403514 | 6.278798 | 0.159266 | 10 |
| 11 | 2.713659 | 18.038518 | 0.055437 | 0.368506 | 6.647304 | 0.150437 | 11 |
| 12 | 2.971457 | 20.752178 | 0.048188 | 0.336535 | 6.983839 | 0.143188 | 12 |
| 13 | 3.253745 | 23.723634 | 0.042152 | 0.307338 | 7.291178 | 0.137152 | 13 |
| 14 | 3.562851 | 26.977380 | 0.037068 | 0.280674 | 7.571852 | 0.132068 | 14 |
| 15 | 3.901322 | 30.540231 | 0.032744 | 0.256323 | 7.828175 | 0.127744 | 15 |
| 16 | 4.271948 | 34.441553 | 0.029035 | 0.234085 | 8.062260 | 0.124035 | 16 |
| 17 | 4.677783 | 38.713500 | 0.025831 | 0.213777 | 8.276037 | 0.120831 | 17 |
| 18 | 5.122172 | 43.391283 | 0.023046 | 0.195230 | 8.471266 | 0.118046 | 18 |
| 19 | 5.608778 | 48.513454 | 0.020613 | 0.178292 | 8.649558 | 0.115613 | 19 |
| 20 | 6.141612 | 54.122233 | 0.018477 | 0.162824 | 8.812382 | 0.113477 | 20 |
| 21 | 6.725065 | 60.263845 | 0.016594 | 0.148697 | 8.961080 | 0.111594 | 21 |
| 22 | 7.363946 | 66.988910 | 0.014928 | 0.135797 | 9.096876 | 0.109928 | 22 |
| 23 | 8.063521 | 74.352856 | 0.013449 | 0.124015 | 9.220892 | 0.108449 | 23 |
| 24 | 8.829556 | 82.416378 | 0.012134 | 0.113256 | 9.334148 | 0.107134 | 24 |
| 25 | 9.668364 | 91.245934 | 0.010959 | 0.103430 | 9.437578 | 0.105959 | 25 |
| 26 | 10.586858 | 100.914297 | 0.009909 | 0.094457 | 9.532034 | 0.104909 | 26 |
| 27 | 11.592610 | 111.501156 | 0.008969 | 0.086262 | 9.618296 | 0.103969 | 27 |
| 28 | 12.693908 | 123.093766 | 0.008124 | 0.078778 | 9.697074 | 0.103124 | 28 |
| 29 | 13.899829 | 135.787673 | 0.007364 | 0.071943 | 9.769018 | 0.102364 | 29 |
| 30 | 15.220313 | 149.687502 | 0.006681 | 0.065702 | 9.834719 | 0.101681 | 30 |
| 31 | 16.666242 | 164.907815 | 0.006064 | 0.060002 | 9.894721 | 0.101064 | 31 |
| 32 | 18.249535 | 181.574057 | 0.005507 | 0.054796 | 9.949517 | 0.100507 | 32 |
| 33 | 19.983241 | 199.823593 | 0.005004 | 0.050042 | 9.999559 | 0.100004 | 33 |
| 34 | 21.881649 | 219.806834 | 0.004549 | 0.045700 | 10.045259 | 0.099549 | 34 |
| 35 | 23.960406 | 241.688483 | 0.004138 | 0.041736 | 10.086995 | 0.099138 | 35 |
| 36 | 26.236644 | 265.648889 | 0.003764 | 0.038115 | 10.125109 | 0.098764 | 36 |
| 37 | 28.729126 | 291.885534 | 0.003426 | 0.034808 | 10.159917 | 0.098426 | 37 |
| 38 | 31.458393 | 320.614659 | 0.003119 | 0.031788 | 10.191705 | 0.098119 | 38 |
| 39 | 34.446940 | 352.073052 | 0.002840 | 0.029030 | 10.220735 | 0.097840 | 39 |
| 40 | 37.719399 | 386.519992 | 0.002587 | 0.026512 | 10.247247 | 0.097587 | 40 |
| 41 | 41.302742 | 424.239391 | 0.002357 | 0.024211 | 10.271458 | 0.097357 | 41 |
| 42 | 45.226503 | 465.542133 | 0.002148 | 0.022111 | 10.293569 | 0.097148 | 42 |
| 43 | 49.523020 | 510.768636 | 0.001958 | 0.020193 | 10.313762 | 0.096958 | 43 |
| 44 | 54.227707 | 560.291656 | 0.001785 | 0.018441 | 10.332203 | 0.096785 | 44 |
| 45 | 59.379340 | 614.519364 | 0.001627 | 0.016841 | 10.349043 | 0.096627 | 45 |
| 46 | 65.020377 | 673.898703 | 0.001484 | 0.015380 | 10.364423 | 0.096484 | 46 |
| 47 | 71.197313 | 738.919080 | 0.001353 | 0.014045 | 10.378469 | 0.096353 | 47 |
| 48 | 77.961057 | 810.116393 | 0.001234 | 0.012827 | 10.391296 | 0.096234 | 48 |
| 49 | 85.367358 | 888.077450 | 0.001126 | 0.011714 | 10.403010 | 0.096126 | 49 |
| 50 | 93.477257 | 973.444808 | 0.001027 | 0.010698 | 10.413707 | 0.096027 | 50 |

10.00% ANNUAL INTEREST RATE

| | 1<br>Future Value<br>of $1 | 2<br>Future Value<br>Annuity of<br>$1 per Year | 3<br>Sinking<br>Fund<br>Factor | 4<br>Present Value<br>of $1<br>(Reversion) | 5<br>Present Value<br>Annuity of<br>$1 per Year | 6<br>Installment<br>to<br>Amortize $1 | |
|---|---|---|---|---|---|---|---|
| Years | | | | | | | Years |
| 1 | 1.100000 | 1.000000 | 1.000000 | 0.909091 | 0.909091 | 1.100000 | 1 |
| 2 | 1.210000 | 2.100000 | 0.476190 | 0.826446 | 1.735537 | 0.576190 | 2 |
| 3 | 1.331000 | 3.310000 | 0.302115 | 0.751315 | 2.486852 | 0.402115 | 3 |
| 4 | 1.464100 | 4.641000 | 0.215471 | 0.683013 | 3.169865 | 0.315471 | 4 |
| 5 | 1.610510 | 6.105100 | 0.163797 | 0.620921 | 3.790787 | 0.263797 | 5 |
| 6 | 1.771561 | 7.715610 | 0.129607 | 0.564474 | 4.355261 | 0.229607 | 6 |
| 7 | 1.948717 | 9.487171 | 0.105405 | 0.513158 | 4.868419 | 0.205405 | 7 |
| 8 | 2.143589 | 11.435888 | 0.087444 | 0.466507 | 5.334926 | 0.187444 | 8 |
| 9 | 2.357948 | 13.579477 | 0.073641 | 0.424098 | 5.759024 | 0.173641 | 9 |
| 10 | 2.593742 | 15.937425 | 0.062745 | 0.385543 | 6.144567 | 0.162745 | 10 |
| 11 | 2.853117 | 18.531167 | 0.053963 | 0.350494 | 6.495061 | 0.153963 | 11 |
| 12 | 3.138428 | 21.384284 | 0.046763 | 0.318631 | 6.813692 | 0.146763 | 12 |
| 13 | 3.452271 | 24.522712 | 0.040779 | 0.289664 | 7.103356 | 0.140779 | 13 |
| 14 | 3.797498 | 27.974983 | 0.035746 | 0.263331 | 7.366687 | 0.135746 | 14 |
| 15 | 4.177248 | 31.772482 | 0.031474 | 0.239392 | 7.606080 | 0.131474 | 15 |
| 16 | 4.594973 | 35.949730 | 0.027817 | 0.217629 | 7.823709 | 0.127817 | 16 |
| 17 | 5.054470 | 40.544703 | 0.024664 | 0.197845 | 8.021553 | 0.124664 | 17 |
| 18 | 5.559917 | 45.599173 | 0.021930 | 0.179859 | 8.201412 | 0.121930 | 18 |
| 19 | 6.115909 | 51.159090 | 0.019547 | 0.163508 | 8.364920 | 0.119547 | 19 |
| 20 | 6.727500 | 57.274999 | 0.017460 | 0.148644 | 8.513564 | 0.117460 | 20 |
| 21 | 7.400250 | 64.002499 | 0.015624 | 0.135131 | 8.648694 | 0.115624 | 21 |
| 22 | 8.140275 | 71.402749 | 0.014005 | 0.122846 | 8.771540 | 0.114005 | 22 |
| 23 | 8.954302 | 79.543024 | 0.012572 | 0.111678 | 8.883218 | 0.112572 | 23 |
| 24 | 9.849733 | 88.497327 | 0.011300 | 0.101526 | 8.984744 | 0.111300 | 24 |
| 25 | 10.834706 | 98.347059 | 0.010168 | 0.092296 | 9.077040 | 0.110168 | 25 |
| 26 | 11.918177 | 109.181765 | 0.009159 | 0.083905 | 9.160945 | 0.109159 | 26 |
| 27 | 13.109994 | 121.099942 | 0.008258 | 0.076278 | 9.237223 | 0.108258 | 27 |
| 28 | 14.420994 | 134.209936 | 0.007451 | 0.069343 | 9.306567 | 0.107451 | 28 |
| 29 | 15.863093 | 148.630930 | 0.006728 | 0.063039 | 9.369606 | 0.106728 | 29 |
| 30 | 17.449402 | 164.494023 | 0.006079 | 0.057309 | 9.426914 | 0.106079 | 30 |
| 31 | 19.194342 | 181.943425 | 0.005496 | 0.052099 | 9.479013 | 0.105496 | 31 |
| 32 | 21.113777 | 201.137767 | 0.004972 | 0.047362 | 9.526376 | 0.104972 | 32 |
| 33 | 23.225154 | 222.251544 | 0.004499 | 0.043057 | 9.569432 | 0.104499 | 33 |
| 34 | 25.547670 | 245.476699 | 0.004074 | 0.039143 | 9.608575 | 0.104074 | 34 |
| 35 | 28.102437 | 271.024368 | 0.003690 | 0.035584 | 9.644159 | 0.103690 | 35 |
| 36 | 30.912681 | 299.126805 | 0.003343 | 0.032349 | 9.676508 | 0.103343 | 36 |
| 37 | 34.003949 | 330.039486 | 0.003030 | 0.029408 | 9.705917 | 0.103030 | 37 |
| 38 | 37.404343 | 364.043434 | 0.002747 | 0.026735 | 9.732651 | 0.102747 | 38 |
| 39 | 41.144778 | 401.447778 | 0.002491 | 0.024304 | 9.756956 | 0.102491 | 39 |
| 40 | 45.259256 | 442.592556 | 0.002259 | 0.022095 | 9.779051 | 0.102259 | 40 |
| 41 | 49.785181 | 487.851811 | 0.002050 | 0.020086 | 9.799137 | 0.102050 | 41 |
| 42 | 54.763699 | 537.636992 | 0.001860 | 0.018260 | 9.817397 | 0.101860 | 42 |
| 43 | 60.240069 | 592.400692 | 0.001688 | 0.016600 | 9.833998 | 0.101688 | 43 |
| 44 | 66.264076 | 652.640761 | 0.001532 | 0.015091 | 9.849089 | 0.101532 | 44 |
| 45 | 72.890484 | 718.904837 | 0.001391 | 0.013719 | 9.862808 | 0.101391 | 45 |
| 46 | 80.179532 | 791.795321 | 0.001263 | 0.012472 | 9.875280 | 0.101263 | 46 |
| 47 | 88.197485 | 871.974853 | 0.001147 | 0.011338 | 9.886618 | 0.101147 | 47 |
| 48 | 97.017234 | 960.172338 | 0.001041 | 0.010307 | 9.896926 | 0.101041 | 48 |
| 49 | 106.718957 | 1057.189572 | 0.000946 | 0.009370 | 9.906296 | 0.100946 | 49 |
| 50 | 117.390853 | 1163.908529 | 0.000859 | 0.008519 | 9.914814 | 0.100859 | 50 |

10.50% ANNUAL INTEREST RATE

| | 1<br>Future Value<br>of $1 | 2<br>Future Value<br>Annuity of<br>$1 per Year | 3<br>Sinking<br>Fund<br>Factor | 4<br>Present Value<br>of $1<br>(Reversion) | 5<br>Present Value<br>Annuity of<br>$1 per Year | 6<br>Installment<br>to<br>Amortize $1 | |
|---|---|---|---|---|---|---|---|
| Years | | | | | | | Years |
| 1 | 1.105000 | 1.000000 | 1.000000 | 0.904977 | 0.904977 | 1.105000 | 1 |
| 2 | 1.221025 | 2.105000 | 0.475059 | 0.818984 | 1.723961 | 0.580059 | 2 |
| 3 | 1.349233 | 3.326025 | 0.300659 | 0.741162 | 2.465123 | 0.405659 | 3 |
| 4 | 1.490902 | 4.675258 | 0.213892 | 0.670735 | 3.135858 | 0.318892 | 4 |
| 5 | 1.647447 | 6.166160 | 0.162175 | 0.607000 | 3.742858 | 0.267175 | 5 |
| 6 | 1.820429 | 7.813606 | 0.127982 | 0.549321 | 4.292179 | 0.232982 | 6 |
| 7 | 2.011574 | 9.634035 | 0.103799 | 0.497123 | 4.789303 | 0.208799 | 7 |
| 8 | 2.222789 | 11.645609 | 0.085869 | 0.449885 | 5.239188 | 0.190869 | 8 |
| 9 | 2.456182 | 13.868398 | 0.072106 | 0.407136 | 5.646324 | 0.177106 | 9 |
| 10 | 2.714081 | 16.324579 | 0.061257 | 0.368449 | 6.014773 | 0.166257 | 10 |
| 11 | 2.999059 | 19.038660 | 0.052525 | 0.333438 | 6.348211 | 0.157525 | 11 |
| 12 | 3.313961 | 22.037720 | 0.045377 | 0.301754 | 6.649964 | 0.150377 | 12 |
| 13 | 3.661926 | 25.351680 | 0.039445 | 0.273080 | 6.923045 | 0.144445 | 13 |
| 14 | 4.046429 | 29.013607 | 0.034467 | 0.247132 | 7.170176 | 0.139467 | 14 |
| 15 | 4.471304 | 33.060035 | 0.030248 | 0.223648 | 7.393825 | 0.135248 | 15 |
| 16 | 4.940791 | 37.531339 | 0.026644 | 0.202397 | 7.596221 | 0.131644 | 16 |
| 17 | 5.459574 | 42.472130 | 0.023545 | 0.183164 | 7.779386 | 0.128545 | 17 |
| 18 | 6.032829 | 47.931703 | 0.020863 | 0.165760 | 7.945146 | 0.125863 | 18 |
| 19 | 6.666276 | 53.964532 | 0.018531 | 0.150009 | 8.095154 | 0.123531 | 19 |
| 20 | 7.366235 | 60.630808 | 0.016493 | 0.135755 | 8.230909 | 0.121493 | 20 |
| 21 | 8.139690 | 67.997043 | 0.014707 | 0.122855 | 8.353764 | 0.119707 | 21 |
| 22 | 8.994357 | 76.136732 | 0.013134 | 0.111181 | 8.464945 | 0.118134 | 22 |
| 23 | 9.938764 | 85.131089 | 0.011747 | 0.100616 | 8.565561 | 0.116747 | 23 |
| 24 | 10.982335 | 95.069854 | 0.010519 | 0.091055 | 8.656616 | 0.115519 | 24 |
| 25 | 12.135480 | 106.052188 | 0.009429 | 0.082403 | 8.739019 | 0.114429 | 25 |
| 26 | 13.409705 | 118.187668 | 0.008461 | 0.074573 | 8.813592 | 0.113461 | 26 |
| 27 | 14.817724 | 131.597373 | 0.007599 | 0.067487 | 8.881079 | 0.112599 | 27 |
| 28 | 16.373585 | 146.415097 | 0.006830 | 0.061074 | 8.942153 | 0.111830 | 28 |
| 29 | 18.092812 | 162.788683 | 0.006143 | 0.055271 | 8.997423 | 0.111143 | 29 |
| 30 | 19.992557 | 180.881494 | 0.005528 | 0.050019 | 9.047442 | 0.110528 | 30 |
| 31 | 22.091775 | 200.874051 | 0.004978 | 0.045266 | 9.092707 | 0.109978 | 31 |
| 32 | 24.411412 | 222.965827 | 0.004485 | 0.040964 | 9.133672 | 0.109485 | 32 |
| 33 | 26.974610 | 247.377238 | 0.004042 | 0.037072 | 9.170744 | 0.109042 | 33 |
| 34 | 29.806944 | 274.351848 | 0.003645 | 0.033549 | 9.204293 | 0.108645 | 34 |
| 35 | 32.936673 | 304.158792 | 0.003288 | 0.030361 | 9.234654 | 0.108288 | 35 |
| 36 | 36.395024 | 337.095466 | 0.002967 | 0.027476 | 9.262131 | 0.107967 | 36 |
| 37 | 40.216501 | 373.490489 | 0.002677 | 0.024865 | 9.286996 | 0.107677 | 37 |
| 38 | 44.439234 | 413.706991 | 0.002417 | 0.022503 | 9.309499 | 0.107417 | 38 |
| 39 | 49.105354 | 458.146225 | 0.002183 | 0.020364 | 9.329863 | 0.107183 | 39 |
| 40 | 54.261416 | 507.251579 | 0.001971 | 0.018429 | 9.348292 | 0.106971 | 40 |
| 41 | 59.958864 | 561.512994 | 0.001781 | 0.016678 | 9.364970 | 0.106781 | 41 |
| 42 | 66.254545 | 621.471859 | 0.001609 | 0.015093 | 9.380064 | 0.106609 | 42 |
| 43 | 73.211272 | 687.726404 | 0.001454 | 0.013659 | 9.393723 | 0.106454 | 43 |
| 44 | 80.898456 | 760.937676 | 0.001314 | 0.012361 | 9.406084 | 0.106314 | 44 |
| 45 | 89.392794 | 841.836132 | 0.001188 | 0.011187 | 9.417271 | 0.106188 | 45 |
| 46 | 98.779037 | 931.228926 | 0.001074 | 0.010124 | 9.427394 | 0.106074 | 46 |
| 47 | 109.150836 | 1030.007963 | 0.000971 | 0.009162 | 9.436556 | 0.105971 | 47 |
| 48 | 120.611674 | 1139.158800 | 0.000878 | 0.008291 | 9.444847 | 0.105878 | 48 |
| 49 | 133.275900 | 1259.770473 | 0.000794 | 0.007503 | 9.452350 | 0.105794 | 49 |
| 50 | 147.269869 | 1393.046373 | 0.000718 | 0.006790 | 9.459140 | 0.105718 | 50 |

11.00% ANNUAL INTEREST RATE

| | 1 | 2 | 3 | 4 | 5 | 6 | |
|---|---|---|---|---|---|---|---|
| | Future Value of $1 | Future Value Annuity of $1 per Year | Sinking Fund Factor | Present Value of $1 (Reversion) | Present Value Annuity of $1 per Year | Installment to Amortize $1 | |
| Years | | | | | | | Years |
| 1 | 1.110000 | 1.000000 | 1.000000 | 0.900901 | 0.900901 | 1.110000 | 1 |
| 2 | 1.232100 | 2.110000 | 0.473934 | 0.811622 | 1.712523 | 0.583934 | 2 |
| 3 | 1.367631 | 3.342100 | 0.299213 | 0.731191 | 2.443715 | 0.409213 | 3 |
| 4 | 1.518070 | 4.709731 | 0.212326 | 0.658731 | 3.102446 | 0.322326 | 4 |
| 5 | 1.685058 | 6.227801 | 0.160570 | 0.593451 | 3.695897 | 0.270570 | 5 |
| 6 | 1.870415 | 7.912860 | 0.126377 | 0.534641 | 4.230538 | 0.236377 | 6 |
| 7 | 2.076160 | 9.783274 | 0.102215 | 0.481658 | 4.712196 | 0.212215 | 7 |
| 8 | 2.304538 | 11.859434 | 0.084321 | 0.433926 | 5.146123 | 0.194321 | 8 |
| 9 | 2.558037 | 14.163972 | 0.070602 | 0.390925 | 5.537048 | 0.180602 | 9 |
| 10 | 2.839421 | 16.722009 | 0.059801 | 0.352184 | 5.889232 | 0.169801 | 10 |
| 11 | 3.151757 | 19.561430 | 0.051121 | 0.317283 | 6.206515 | 0.161121 | 11 |
| 12 | 3.498451 | 22.713187 | 0.044027 | 0.285841 | 6.492356 | 0.154027 | 12 |
| 13 | 3.883280 | 26.211638 | 0.038151 | 0.257514 | 6.749870 | 0.148151 | 13 |
| 14 | 4.310441 | 30.094918 | 0.033228 | 0.231995 | 6.981865 | 0.143228 | 14 |
| 15 | 4.784589 | 34.405359 | 0.029065 | 0.209004 | 7.190870 | 0.139065 | 15 |
| 16 | 5.310894 | 39.189948 | 0.025517 | 0.188292 | 7.379162 | 0.135517 | 16 |
| 17 | 5.895093 | 44.500843 | 0.022471 | 0.169633 | 7.548794 | 0.132471 | 17 |
| 18 | 6.543553 | 50.395936 | 0.019843 | 0.152822 | 7.701617 | 0.129843 | 18 |
| 19 | 7.263344 | 56.939488 | 0.017563 | 0.137678 | 7.839294 | 0.127563 | 19 |
| 20 | 8.062312 | 64.202832 | 0.015576 | 0.124034 | 7.963328 | 0.125576 | 20 |
| 21 | 8.949166 | 72.265144 | 0.013838 | 0.111742 | 8.075070 | 0.123838 | 21 |
| 22 | 9.933574 | 81.214309 | 0.012313 | 0.100669 | 8.175739 | 0.122313 | 22 |
| 23 | 11.026267 | 91.147884 | 0.010971 | 0.090693 | 8.266432 | 0.120971 | 23 |
| 24 | 12.239157 | 102.174151 | 0.009787 | 0.081705 | 8.348137 | 0.119787 | 24 |
| 25 | 13.585464 | 114.413307 | 0.008740 | 0.073608 | 8.421745 | 0.118740 | 25 |
| 26 | 15.079865 | 127.998771 | 0.007813 | 0.066314 | 8.488058 | 0.117813 | 26 |
| 27 | 16.738650 | 143.078636 | 0.006989 | 0.059742 | 8.547800 | 0.116989 | 27 |
| 28 | 18.579901 | 159.817286 | 0.006257 | 0.053822 | 8.601622 | 0.116257 | 28 |
| 29 | 20.623691 | 178.397187 | 0.005605 | 0.048488 | 8.650110 | 0.115605 | 29 |
| 30 | 22.892297 | 199.020878 | 0.005025 | 0.043683 | 8.693793 | 0.115025 | 30 |
| 31 | 25.410449 | 221.913174 | 0.004506 | 0.039354 | 8.733146 | 0.114506 | 31 |
| 32 | 28.205599 | 247.323624 | 0.004043 | 0.035454 | 8.768600 | 0.114043 | 32 |
| 33 | 31.308214 | 275.529222 | 0.003629 | 0.031940 | 8.800541 | 0.113629 | 33 |
| 34 | 34.752118 | 306.837437 | 0.003259 | 0.028775 | 8.829316 | 0.113259 | 34 |
| 35 | 38.574851 | 341.589555 | 0.002927 | 0.025924 | 8.855240 | 0.112927 | 35 |
| 36 | 42.818085 | 380.164406 | 0.002630 | 0.023355 | 8.878594 | 0.112630 | 36 |
| 37 | 47.528074 | 422.982490 | 0.002364 | 0.021040 | 8.899635 | 0.112364 | 37 |
| 38 | 52.756162 | 470.510564 | 0.002125 | 0.018955 | 8.918590 | 0.112125 | 38 |
| 39 | 58.559340 | 523.266726 | 0.001911 | 0.017077 | 8.935666 | 0.111911 | 39 |
| 40 | 65.000867 | 581.826066 | 0.001719 | 0.015384 | 8.951051 | 0.111719 | 40 |
| 41 | 72.150963 | 646.826934 | 0.001546 | 0.013860 | 8.964911 | 0.111546 | 41 |
| 42 | 80.087569 | 718.977896 | 0.001391 | 0.012486 | 8.977397 | 0.111391 | 42 |
| 43 | 88.897201 | 799.065465 | 0.001251 | 0.011249 | 8.988646 | 0.111251 | 43 |
| 44 | 98.675893 | 887.962666 | 0.001126 | 0.010134 | 8.998780 | 0.111126 | 44 |
| 45 | 109.530242 | 986.638559 | 0.001014 | 0.009130 | 9.007910 | 0.111014 | 45 |
| 46 | 121.578568 | 1096.168801 | 0.000912 | 0.008225 | 9.016135 | 0.110912 | 46 |
| 47 | 134.952211 | 1217.747369 | 0.000821 | 0.007410 | 9.023545 | 0.110821 | 47 |
| 48 | 149.796954 | 1352.699580 | 0.000739 | 0.006676 | 9.030221 | 0.110739 | 48 |
| 49 | 166.274619 | 1502.496533 | 0.000666 | 0.006014 | 9.036235 | 0.110666 | 49 |
| 50 | 184.564827 | 1668.771152 | 0.000599 | 0.005418 | 9.041653 | 0.110599 | 50 |

11.50% ANNUAL INTEREST RATE

| | 1<br>Future Value<br>of $1 | 2<br>Future Value<br>Annuity of<br>$1 per Year | 3<br>Sinking<br>Fund<br>Factor | 4<br>Present Value<br>of $1<br>(Reversion) | 5<br>Present Value<br>Annuity of<br>$1 per Year | 6<br>Installment<br>to<br>Amortize $1 | |
|---|---|---|---|---|---|---|---|
| Years | | | | | | | Years |
| 1 | 1.115000 | 1.000000 | 1.000000 | 0.896861 | 0.896861 | 1.115000 | 1 |
| 2 | 1.243225 | 2.115000 | 0.472813 | 0.804360 | 1.701221 | 0.587813 | 2 |
| 3 | 1.386196 | 3.358225 | 0.297776 | 0.721399 | 2.422619 | 0.412776 | 3 |
| 4 | 1.545608 | 4.744421 | 0.210774 | 0.646994 | 3.069614 | 0.325774 | 4 |
| 5 | 1.723353 | 6.290029 | 0.158982 | 0.580264 | 3.649878 | 0.273982 | 5 |
| 6 | 1.921539 | 8.013383 | 0.124791 | 0.520416 | 4.170294 | 0.239791 | 6 |
| 7 | 2.142516 | 9.934922 | 0.100655 | 0.466741 | 4.637035 | 0.215655 | 7 |
| 8 | 2.388905 | 12.077438 | 0.082799 | 0.418602 | 5.055637 | 0.197799 | 8 |
| 9 | 2.663629 | 14.466343 | 0.069126 | 0.375428 | 5.431064 | 0.184126 | 9 |
| 10 | 2.969947 | 17.129972 | 0.058377 | 0.336706 | 5.767771 | 0.173377 | 10 |
| 11 | 3.311491 | 20.099919 | 0.049751 | 0.301979 | 6.069750 | 0.164751 | 11 |
| 12 | 3.692312 | 23.411410 | 0.042714 | 0.270833 | 6.340583 | 0.157714 | 12 |
| 13 | 4.116928 | 27.103722 | 0.036895 | 0.242900 | 6.583482 | 0.151895 | 13 |
| 14 | 4.590375 | 31.220650 | 0.032030 | 0.217847 | 6.801329 | 0.147030 | 14 |
| 15 | 5.118268 | 35.811025 | 0.027924 | 0.195379 | 6.996708 | 0.142924 | 15 |
| 16 | 5.706869 | 40.929293 | 0.024432 | 0.175227 | 7.171935 | 0.139432 | 16 |
| 17 | 6.363159 | 46.636161 | 0.021443 | 0.157155 | 7.329090 | 0.136443 | 17 |
| 18 | 7.094922 | 52.999320 | 0.018868 | 0.140946 | 7.470036 | 0.133868 | 18 |
| 19 | 7.910838 | 60.094242 | 0.016641 | 0.126409 | 7.596445 | 0.131641 | 19 |
| 20 | 8.820584 | 68.005080 | 0.014705 | 0.113371 | 7.709816 | 0.129705 | 20 |
| 21 | 9.834951 | 76.825664 | 0.013016 | 0.101678 | 7.811494 | 0.128016 | 21 |
| 22 | 10.965971 | 86.660615 | 0.011539 | 0.091191 | 7.902685 | 0.126539 | 22 |
| 23 | 12.227057 | 97.626586 | 0.010243 | 0.081786 | 7.984471 | 0.125243 | 23 |
| 24 | 13.633169 | 109.853643 | 0.009103 | 0.073351 | 8.057822 | 0.124103 | 24 |
| 25 | 15.200983 | 123.486812 | 0.008098 | 0.065785 | 8.123607 | 0.123098 | 25 |
| 26 | 16.949096 | 138.687796 | 0.007210 | 0.059000 | 8.182607 | 0.122210 | 26 |
| 27 | 18.898243 | 155.636892 | 0.006425 | 0.052915 | 8.235522 | 0.121425 | 27 |
| 28 | 21.071540 | 174.535135 | 0.005730 | 0.047457 | 8.282979 | 0.120730 | 28 |
| 29 | 23.494768 | 195.606675 | 0.005112 | 0.042563 | 8.325542 | 0.120112 | 29 |
| 30 | 26.196666 | 219.101443 | 0.004564 | 0.038173 | 8.363715 | 0.119564 | 30 |
| 31 | 29.209282 | 245.298109 | 0.004077 | 0.034236 | 8.397951 | 0.119077 | 31 |
| 32 | 32.568350 | 274.507391 | 0.003643 | 0.030705 | 8.428655 | 0.118643 | 32 |
| 33 | 36.313710 | 307.075741 | 0.003257 | 0.027538 | 8.456193 | 0.118257 | 33 |
| 34 | 40.489787 | 343.389451 | 0.002912 | 0.024698 | 8.480891 | 0.117912 | 34 |
| 35 | 45.146112 | 383.879238 | 0.002605 | 0.022150 | 8.503041 | 0.117605 | 35 |
| 36 | 50.337915 | 429.025351 | 0.002331 | 0.019866 | 8.522907 | 0.117331 | 36 |
| 37 | 56.126776 | 479.363266 | 0.002086 | 0.017817 | 8.540723 | 0.117086 | 37 |
| 38 | 62.581355 | 535.490042 | 0.001867 | 0.015979 | 8.556703 | 0.116867 | 38 |
| 39 | 69.778211 | 598.071396 | 0.001672 | 0.014331 | 8.571034 | 0.116672 | 39 |
| 40 | 77.802705 | 667.849607 | 0.001497 | 0.012853 | 8.583887 | 0.116497 | 40 |
| 41 | 86.750016 | 745.652312 | 0.001341 | 0.011527 | 8.595414 | 0.116341 | 41 |
| 42 | 96.726268 | 832.402327 | 0.001201 | 0.010338 | 8.605753 | 0.116201 | 42 |
| 43 | 107.849788 | 929.128595 | 0.001076 | 0.009272 | 8.615025 | 0.116076 | 43 |
| 44 | 120.252514 | 1036.978384 | 0.000964 | 0.008316 | 8.623341 | 0.115964 | 44 |
| 45 | 134.081553 | 1157.230898 | 0.000864 | 0.007458 | 8.630799 | 0.115864 | 45 |
| 46 | 149.500932 | 1291.312451 | 0.000774 | 0.006689 | 8.637488 | 0.115774 | 46 |
| 47 | 166.693539 | 1440.813383 | 0.000694 | 0.005999 | 8.643487 | 0.115694 | 47 |
| 48 | 185.863296 | 1607.506922 | 0.000622 | 0.005380 | 8.648867 | 0.115622 | 48 |
| 49 | 207.237575 | 1793.370218 | 0.000558 | 0.004825 | 8.653692 | 0.115558 | 49 |
| 50 | 231.069896 | 2000.607793 | 0.000500 | 0.004328 | 8.658020 | 0.115500 | 50 |

12.00% ANNUAL INTEREST RATE

| | 1<br>Future Value<br>of $1 | 2<br>Future Value<br>Annuity of<br>$1 per Year | 3<br>Sinking<br>Fund<br>Factor | 4<br>Present Value<br>of $1<br>(Reversion) | 5<br>Present Value<br>Annuity of<br>$1 per Year | 6<br>Installment<br>to<br>Amortize $1 | |
|---|---|---|---|---|---|---|---|
| Years | | | | | | | Years |
| 1 | 1.120000 | 1.000000 | 1.000000 | 0.892857 | 0.892857 | 1.120000 | 1 |
| 2 | 1.254400 | 2.120000 | 0.471698 | 0.797194 | 1.690051 | 0.591698 | 2 |
| 3 | 1.404928 | 3.374400 | 0.296349 | 0.711780 | 2.401831 | 0.416349 | 3 |
| 4 | 1.573519 | 4.779328 | 0.209234 | 0.635518 | 3.037349 | 0.329234 | 4 |
| 5 | 1.762342 | 6.352847 | 0.157410 | 0.567427 | 3.604776 | 0.277410 | 5 |
| 6 | 1.973823 | 8.115189 | 0.123226 | 0.506631 | 4.111407 | 0.243226 | 6 |
| 7 | 2.210681 | 10.089012 | 0.099118 | 0.452349 | 4.563757 | 0.219118 | 7 |
| 8 | 2.475963 | 12.299693 | 0.081303 | 0.403883 | 4.967640 | 0.201303 | 8 |
| 9 | 2.773079 | 14.775656 | 0.067679 | 0.360610 | 5.328250 | 0.187679 | 9 |
| 10 | 3.105848 | 17.548735 | 0.056984 | 0.321973 | 5.650223 | 0.176984 | 10 |
| 11 | 3.478550 | 20.654583 | 0.048415 | 0.287476 | 5.937699 | 0.168415 | 11 |
| 12 | 3.895976 | 24.133133 | 0.041437 | 0.256675 | 6.194374 | 0.161437 | 12 |
| 13 | 4.363493 | 28.029109 | 0.035677 | 0.229174 | 6.423548 | 0.155677 | 13 |
| 14 | 4.887112 | 32.392602 | 0.030871 | 0.204620 | 6.628168 | 0.150871 | 14 |
| 15 | 5.473566 | 37.279715 | 0.026824 | 0.182696 | 6.810864 | 0.146824 | 15 |
| 16 | 6.130394 | 42.753280 | 0.023390 | 0.163122 | 6.973986 | 0.143390 | 16 |
| 17 | 6.866041 | 48.883674 | 0.020457 | 0.145644 | 7.119630 | 0.140457 | 17 |
| 18 | 7.689966 | 55.749715 | 0.017937 | 0.130040 | 7.249670 | 0.137937 | 18 |
| 19 | 8.612762 | 63.439681 | 0.015763 | 0.116107 | 7.365777 | 0.135763 | 19 |
| 20 | 9.646293 | 72.052442 | 0.013879 | 0.103667 | 7.469444 | 0.133879 | 20 |
| 21 | 10.803848 | 81.698736 | 0.012240 | 0.092560 | 7.562003 | 0.132240 | 21 |
| 22 | 12.100310 | 92.502584 | 0.010811 | 0.082643 | 7.644646 | 0.130811 | 22 |
| 23 | 13.552347 | 104.602894 | 0.009560 | 0.073788 | 7.718434 | 0.129560 | 23 |
| 24 | 15.178629 | 118.155241 | 0.008463 | 0.065882 | 7.784316 | 0.128463 | 24 |
| 25 | 17.000064 | 133.333870 | 0.007500 | 0.058823 | 7.843139 | 0.127500 | 25 |
| 26 | 19.040072 | 150.333934 | 0.006652 | 0.052521 | 7.895660 | 0.126652 | 26 |
| 27 | 21.324881 | 169.374007 | 0.005904 | 0.046894 | 7.942554 | 0.125904 | 27 |
| 28 | 23.883866 | 190.698887 | 0.005244 | 0.041869 | 7.984423 | 0.125244 | 28 |
| 29 | 26.749930 | 214.582754 | 0.004660 | 0.037383 | 8.021806 | 0.124660 | 29 |
| 30 | 29.959922 | 241.332684 | 0.004144 | 0.033378 | 8.055184 | 0.124144 | 30 |
| 31 | 33.555113 | 271.292606 | 0.003686 | 0.029802 | 8.084986 | 0.123686 | 31 |
| 32 | 37.581726 | 304.847719 | 0.003280 | 0.026609 | 8.111594 | 0.123280 | 32 |
| 33 | 42.091533 | 342.429446 | 0.002920 | 0.023758 | 8.135352 | 0.122920 | 33 |
| 34 | 47.142517 | 384.520979 | 0.002601 | 0.021212 | 8.156564 | 0.122601 | 34 |
| 35 | 52.799620 | 431.663496 | 0.002317 | 0.018940 | 8.175504 | 0.122317 | 35 |
| 36 | 59.135574 | 484.463116 | 0.002064 | 0.016910 | 8.192414 | 0.122064 | 36 |
| 37 | 66.231843 | 543.598690 | 0.001840 | 0.015098 | 8.207513 | 0.121840 | 37 |
| 38 | 74.179664 | 609.830533 | 0.001640 | 0.013481 | 8.220993 | 0.121640 | 38 |
| 39 | 83.081224 | 684.010197 | 0.001462 | 0.012036 | 8.233030 | 0.121462 | 39 |
| 40 | 93.050970 | 767.091420 | 0.001304 | 0.010747 | 8.243777 | 0.121304 | 40 |
| 41 | 104.217087 | 860.142391 | 0.001163 | 0.009595 | 8.253372 | 0.121163 | 41 |
| 42 | 116.723137 | 964.359478 | 0.001037 | 0.008567 | 8.261939 | 0.121037 | 42 |
| 43 | 130.729914 | 1081.082615 | 0.000925 | 0.007649 | 8.269589 | 0.120925 | 43 |
| 44 | 146.417503 | 1211.812529 | 0.000825 | 0.006830 | 8.276418 | 0.120825 | 44 |
| 45 | 163.987604 | 1358.230032 | 0.000736 | 0.006098 | 8.282516 | 0.120736 | 45 |
| 46 | 183.666116 | 1522.217636 | 0.000657 | 0.005445 | 8.287961 | 0.120657 | 46 |
| 47 | 205.706050 | 1705.883752 | 0.000586 | 0.004861 | 8.292822 | 0.120586 | 47 |
| 48 | 230.390776 | 1911.589803 | 0.000523 | 0.004340 | 8.297163 | 0.120523 | 48 |
| 49 | 258.037669 | 2141.980579 | 0.000467 | 0.003875 | 8.301038 | 0.120467 | 49 |
| 50 | 289.002190 | 2400.018249 | 0.000417 | 0.003460 | 8.304498 | 0.120417 | 50 |

12.50% ANNUAL INTEREST RATE

| | 1<br>Future Value<br>of $1 | 2<br>Future Value<br>Annuity of<br>$1 per Year | 3<br>Sinking<br>Fund<br>Factor | 4<br>Present Value<br>of $1<br>(Reversion) | 5<br>Present Value<br>Annuity of<br>$1 per Year | 6<br>Installment<br>to<br>Amortize $1 | |
|---|---|---|---|---|---|---|---|
| Years | | | | | | | Years |
| 1 | 1.125000 | 1.000000 | 1.000000 | 0.888889 | 0.888889 | 1.125000 | 1 |
| 2 | 1.265625 | 2.125000 | 0.470588 | 0.790123 | 1.679012 | 0.595588 | 2 |
| 3 | 1.423828 | 3.390625 | 0.294931 | 0.702332 | 2.381344 | 0.419931 | 3 |
| 4 | 1.601807 | 4.814453 | 0.207708 | 0.624295 | 3.005639 | 0.332708 | 4 |
| 5 | 1.802032 | 6.416260 | 0.155854 | 0.554929 | 3.560568 | 0.280854 | 5 |
| 6 | 2.027287 | 8.218292 | 0.121680 | 0.493270 | 4.053839 | 0.246680 | 6 |
| 7 | 2.280697 | 10.245579 | 0.097603 | 0.438462 | 4.492301 | 0.222603 | 7 |
| 8 | 2.565785 | 12.526276 | 0.079832 | 0.389744 | 4.882045 | 0.204832 | 8 |
| 9 | 2.886508 | 15.092061 | 0.066260 | 0.346439 | 5.228485 | 0.191260 | 9 |
| 10 | 3.247321 | 17.978568 | 0.055622 | 0.307946 | 5.536431 | 0.180622 | 10 |
| 11 | 3.653236 | 21.225889 | 0.047112 | 0.273730 | 5.810161 | 0.172112 | 11 |
| 12 | 4.109891 | 24.879125 | 0.040194 | 0.243315 | 6.053476 | 0.165194 | 12 |
| 13 | 4.623627 | 28.989016 | 0.034496 | 0.216280 | 6.269757 | 0.159496 | 13 |
| 14 | 5.201580 | 33.612643 | 0.029751 | 0.192249 | 6.462006 | 0.154751 | 14 |
| 15 | 5.851778 | 38.814223 | 0.025764 | 0.170888 | 6.632894 | 0.150764 | 15 |
| 16 | 6.583250 | 44.666001 | 0.022388 | 0.151901 | 6.784795 | 0.147388 | 16 |
| 17 | 7.406156 | 51.249252 | 0.019512 | 0.135023 | 6.919818 | 0.144512 | 17 |
| 18 | 8.331926 | 58.655408 | 0.017049 | 0.120020 | 7.039838 | 0.142049 | 18 |
| 19 | 9.373417 | 66.987334 | 0.014928 | 0.106685 | 7.146523 | 0.139928 | 19 |
| 20 | 10.545094 | 76.360751 | 0.013096 | 0.094831 | 7.241353 | 0.138096 | 20 |
| 21 | 11.863231 | 86.905845 | 0.011507 | 0.084294 | 7.325647 | 0.136507 | 21 |
| 22 | 13.346134 | 98.769075 | 0.010125 | 0.074928 | 7.400575 | 0.135125 | 22 |
| 23 | 15.014401 | 112.115210 | 0.008919 | 0.066603 | 7.467178 | 0.133919 | 23 |
| 24 | 16.891201 | 127.129611 | 0.007866 | 0.059202 | 7.526381 | 0.132866 | 24 |
| 25 | 19.002602 | 144.020812 | 0.006943 | 0.052624 | 7.579005 | 0.131943 | 25 |
| 26 | 21.377927 | 163.023414 | 0.006134 | 0.046777 | 7.625782 | 0.131134 | 26 |
| 27 | 24.050168 | 184.401340 | 0.005423 | 0.041580 | 7.667362 | 0.130423 | 27 |
| 28 | 27.056438 | 208.451508 | 0.004797 | 0.036960 | 7.704322 | 0.129797 | 28 |
| 29 | 30.438493 | 235.507946 | 0.004246 | 0.032853 | 7.737175 | 0.129246 | 29 |
| 30 | 34.243305 | 265.946440 | 0.003760 | 0.029203 | 7.766378 | 0.128760 | 30 |
| 31 | 38.523718 | 300.189745 | 0.003331 | 0.025958 | 7.792336 | 0.128331 | 31 |
| 32 | 43.339183 | 338.713463 | 0.002952 | 0.023074 | 7.815410 | 0.127952 | 32 |
| 33 | 48.756581 | 382.052645 | 0.002617 | 0.020510 | 7.835920 | 0.127617 | 33 |
| 34 | 54.851153 | 430.809226 | 0.002321 | 0.018231 | 7.854151 | 0.127321 | 34 |
| 35 | 61.707547 | 485.660379 | 0.002059 | 0.016205 | 7.870356 | 0.127059 | 35 |
| 36 | 69.420991 | 547.367927 | 0.001827 | 0.014405 | 7.884761 | 0.126827 | 36 |
| 37 | 78.098615 | 616.788918 | 0.001621 | 0.012804 | 7.897565 | 0.126621 | 37 |
| 38 | 87.860942 | 694.887532 | 0.001439 | 0.011382 | 7.908947 | 0.126439 | 38 |
| 39 | 98.843559 | 782.748474 | 0.001278 | 0.010117 | 7.919064 | 0.126278 | 39 |
| 40 | 111.199004 | 881.592033 | 0.001134 | 0.008993 | 7.928057 | 0.126134 | 40 |
| 41 | 125.098880 | 992.791037 | 0.001007 | 0.007994 | 7.936051 | 0.126007 | 41 |
| 42 | 140.736240 | 1117.889917 | 0.000895 | 0.007105 | 7.943156 | 0.125895 | 42 |
| 43 | 158.328270 | 1258.626157 | 0.000795 | 0.006316 | 7.949472 | 0.125795 | 43 |
| 44 | 178.119303 | 1416.954426 | 0.000706 | 0.005614 | 7.955086 | 0.125706 | 44 |
| 45 | 200.384216 | 1595.073729 | 0.000627 | 0.004990 | 7.960077 | 0.125627 | 45 |
| 46 | 225.432243 | 1795.457946 | 0.000557 | 0.004436 | 7.964513 | 0.125557 | 46 |
| 47 | 253.611274 | 2020.890189 | 0.000495 | 0.003943 | 7.968456 | 0.125495 | 47 |
| 48 | 285.312683 | 2274.501462 | 0.000440 | 0.003505 | 7.971961 | 0.125440 | 48 |
| 49 | 320.976768 | 2559.814145 | 0.000391 | 0.003115 | 7.975076 | 0.125391 | 49 |
| 50 | 361.098864 | 2880.790913 | 0.000347 | 0.002769 | 7.977845 | 0.125347 | 50 |

13.00% ANNUAL INTEREST RATE

| | 1<br>Future Value<br>of $1 | 2<br>Future Value<br>Annuity of<br>$1 per Year | 3<br>Sinking<br>Fund<br>Factor | 4<br>Present Value<br>of $1<br>(Reversion) | 5<br>Present Value<br>Annuity of<br>$1 per Year | 6<br>Installment<br>to<br>Amortize $1 | |
|---|---|---|---|---|---|---|---|
| Years | | | | | | | Years |
| 1 | 1.130000 | 1.000000 | 1.000000 | 0.884956 | 0.884956 | 1.130000 | 1 |
| 2 | 1.276900 | 2.130000 | 0.469484 | 0.783147 | 1.668102 | 0.599484 | 2 |
| 3 | 1.442897 | 3.406900 | 0.293522 | 0.693050 | 2.361153 | 0.423522 | 3 |
| 4 | 1.630474 | 4.849797 | 0.206194 | 0.613319 | 2.974471 | 0.336194 | 4 |
| 5 | 1.842435 | 6.480271 | 0.154315 | 0.542760 | 3.517231 | 0.284315 | 5 |
| 6 | 2.081952 | 8.322706 | 0.120153 | 0.480319 | 3.997550 | 0.250153 | 6 |
| 7 | 2.352605 | 10.404658 | 0.096111 | 0.425061 | 4.422610 | 0.226111 | 7 |
| 8 | 2.658444 | 12.757263 | 0.078387 | 0.376160 | 4.798770 | 0.208387 | 8 |
| 9 | 3.004042 | 15.415707 | 0.064869 | 0.332885 | 5.131655 | 0.194869 | 9 |
| 10 | 3.394567 | 18.419749 | 0.054290 | 0.294588 | 5.426243 | 0.184290 | 10 |
| 11 | 3.835861 | 21.814317 | 0.045841 | 0.260698 | 5.686941 | 0.175841 | 11 |
| 12 | 4.334523 | 25.650178 | 0.038986 | 0.230706 | 5.917647 | 0.168986 | 12 |
| 13 | 4.898011 | 29.984701 | 0.033350 | 0.204165 | 6.121812 | 0.163350 | 13 |
| 14 | 5.534753 | 34.882712 | 0.028667 | 0.180677 | 6.302488 | 0.158667 | 14 |
| 15 | 6.254270 | 40.417464 | 0.024742 | 0.159891 | 6.462379 | 0.154742 | 15 |
| 16 | 7.067326 | 46.671735 | 0.021426 | 0.141496 | 6.603875 | 0.151426 | 16 |
| 17 | 7.986078 | 53.739060 | 0.018608 | 0.125218 | 6.729093 | 0.148608 | 17 |
| 18 | 9.024268 | 61.725138 | 0.016201 | 0.110812 | 6.839905 | 0.146201 | 18 |
| 19 | 10.197423 | 70.749406 | 0.014134 | 0.098064 | 6.937969 | 0.144134 | 19 |
| 20 | 11.523088 | 80.946829 | 0.012354 | 0.086782 | 7.024752 | 0.142354 | 20 |
| 21 | 13.021089 | 92.469917 | 0.010814 | 0.076798 | 7.101550 | 0.140814 | 21 |
| 22 | 14.713831 | 105.491006 | 0.009479 | 0.067963 | 7.169513 | 0.139479 | 22 |
| 23 | 16.626629 | 120.204837 | 0.008319 | 0.060144 | 7.229658 | 0.138319 | 23 |
| 24 | 18.788091 | 136.831465 | 0.007308 | 0.053225 | 7.282883 | 0.137308 | 24 |
| 25 | 21.230542 | 155.619556 | 0.006426 | 0.047102 | 7.329985 | 0.136426 | 25 |
| 26 | 23.990513 | 176.850098 | 0.005655 | 0.041683 | 7.371668 | 0.135655 | 26 |
| 27 | 27.109279 | 200.840611 | 0.004979 | 0.036888 | 7.408556 | 0.134979 | 27 |
| 28 | 30.633486 | 227.949890 | 0.004387 | 0.032644 | 7.441200 | 0.134387 | 28 |
| 29 | 34.615839 | 258.583376 | 0.003867 | 0.028889 | 7.470088 | 0.133867 | 29 |
| 30 | 39.115898 | 293.199215 | 0.003411 | 0.025565 | 7.495653 | 0.133411 | 30 |
| 31 | 44.200965 | 332.315113 | 0.003009 | 0.022624 | 7.518277 | 0.133009 | 31 |
| 32 | 49.947090 | 376.516078 | 0.002656 | 0.020021 | 7.538299 | 0.132656 | 32 |
| 33 | 56.440212 | 426.463168 | 0.002345 | 0.017718 | 7.556016 | 0.132345 | 33 |
| 34 | 63.777439 | 482.903380 | 0.002071 | 0.015680 | 7.571696 | 0.132071 | 34 |
| 35 | 72.068506 | 546.680819 | 0.001829 | 0.013876 | 7.585572 | 0.131829 | 35 |
| 36 | 81.437412 | 618.749325 | 0.001616 | 0.012279 | 7.597851 | 0.131616 | 36 |
| 37 | 92.024276 | 700.186738 | 0.001428 | 0.010867 | 7.608718 | 0.131428 | 37 |
| 38 | 103.987432 | 792.211014 | 0.001262 | 0.009617 | 7.618334 | 0.131262 | 38 |
| 39 | 117.505798 | 896.198445 | 0.001116 | 0.008510 | 7.626844 | 0.131116 | 39 |
| 40 | 132.781552 | 1013.704243 | 0.000986 | 0.007531 | 7.634376 | 0.130986 | 40 |
| 41 | 150.043153 | 1146.485795 | 0.000872 | 0.006665 | 7.641040 | 0.130872 | 41 |
| 42 | 169.548763 | 1296.528948 | 0.000771 | 0.005898 | 7.646938 | 0.130771 | 42 |
| 43 | 191.590103 | 1466.077712 | 0.000682 | 0.005219 | 7.652158 | 0.130682 | 43 |
| 44 | 216.496816 | 1657.667814 | 0.000603 | 0.004619 | 7.656777 | 0.130603 | 44 |
| 45 | 244.641402 | 1874.164630 | 0.000534 | 0.004088 | 7.660864 | 0.130534 | 45 |
| 46 | 276.444784 | 2118.806032 | 0.000472 | 0.003617 | 7.664482 | 0.130472 | 46 |
| 47 | 312.382606 | 2395.250816 | 0.000417 | 0.003201 | 7.667683 | 0.130417 | 47 |
| 48 | 352.992345 | 2707.633422 | 0.000369 | 0.002833 | 7.670516 | 0.130369 | 48 |
| 49 | 398.881350 | 3060.625767 | 0.000327 | 0.002507 | 7.673023 | 0.130327 | 49 |
| 50 | 450.735925 | 3459.507117 | 0.000289 | 0.002219 | 7.675242 | 0.130289 | 50 |

13.50% ANNUAL INTEREST RATE

| | 1<br>Future Value<br>of $1 | 2<br>Future Value<br>Annuity of<br>$1 per Year | 3<br>Sinking<br>Fund<br>Factor | 4<br>Present Value<br>of $1<br>(Reversion) | 5<br>Present Value<br>Annuity of<br>$1 per Year | 6<br>Installment<br>to<br>Amortize $1 | |
|---|---|---|---|---|---|---|---|
| Years | | | | | | | Years |
| 1 | 1.135000 | 1.000000 | 1.000000 | 0.881057 | 0.881057 | 1.135000 | 1 |
| 2 | 1.288225 | 2.135000 | 0.468384 | 0.776262 | 1.657319 | 0.603384 | 2 |
| 3 | 1.462135 | 3.423225 | 0.292122 | 0.683931 | 2.341250 | 0.427122 | 3 |
| 4 | 1.659524 | 4.885360 | 0.204693 | 0.602583 | 2.943833 | 0.339693 | 4 |
| 5 | 1.883559 | 6.544884 | 0.152791 | 0.530910 | 3.474743 | 0.287791 | 5 |
| 6 | 2.137840 | 8.428443 | 0.118646 | 0.467762 | 3.942505 | 0.253646 | 6 |
| 7 | 2.426448 | 10.566283 | 0.094641 | 0.412125 | 4.354630 | 0.229641 | 7 |
| 8 | 2.754019 | 12.992731 | 0.076966 | 0.363106 | 4.717735 | 0.211966 | 8 |
| 9 | 3.125811 | 15.746750 | 0.063505 | 0.319917 | 5.037652 | 0.198505 | 9 |
| 10 | 3.547796 | 18.872561 | 0.052987 | 0.281865 | 5.319517 | 0.187987 | 10 |
| 11 | 4.026748 | 22.420357 | 0.044602 | 0.248339 | 5.567857 | 0.179602 | 11 |
| 12 | 4.570359 | 26.447106 | 0.037811 | 0.218801 | 5.786658 | 0.172811 | 12 |
| 13 | 5.187358 | 31.017465 | 0.032240 | 0.192776 | 5.979434 | 0.167240 | 13 |
| 14 | 5.887651 | 36.204823 | 0.027621 | 0.169847 | 6.149281 | 0.162621 | 14 |
| 15 | 6.682484 | 42.092474 | 0.023757 | 0.149645 | 6.298926 | 0.158757 | 15 |
| 16 | 7.584619 | 48.774957 | 0.020502 | 0.131846 | 6.430772 | 0.155502 | 16 |
| 17 | 8.608543 | 56.359577 | 0.017743 | 0.116164 | 6.546936 | 0.152743 | 17 |
| 18 | 9.770696 | 64.968120 | 0.015392 | 0.102347 | 6.649283 | 0.150392 | 18 |
| 19 | 11.089740 | 74.738816 | 0.013380 | 0.090173 | 6.739456 | 0.148380 | 19 |
| 20 | 12.586855 | 85.828556 | 0.011651 | 0.079448 | 6.818904 | 0.146651 | 20 |
| 21 | 14.286080 | 98.415411 | 0.010161 | 0.069998 | 6.888902 | 0.145161 | 21 |
| 22 | 16.214701 | 112.701491 | 0.008873 | 0.061672 | 6.950575 | 0.143873 | 22 |
| 23 | 18.403686 | 128.916193 | 0.007757 | 0.054337 | 7.004912 | 0.142757 | 23 |
| 24 | 20.888184 | 147.319879 | 0.006788 | 0.047874 | 7.052786 | 0.141788 | 24 |
| 25 | 23.708088 | 168.208062 | 0.005945 | 0.042180 | 7.094965 | 0.140945 | 25 |
| 26 | 26.908680 | 191.916151 | 0.005211 | 0.037163 | 7.132128 | 0.140211 | 26 |
| 27 | 30.541352 | 218.824831 | 0.004570 | 0.032742 | 7.164870 | 0.139570 | 27 |
| 28 | 34.664435 | 249.366183 | 0.004010 | 0.028848 | 7.193718 | 0.139010 | 28 |
| 29 | 39.344133 | 284.030618 | 0.003521 | 0.025417 | 7.219135 | 0.138521 | 29 |
| 30 | 44.655591 | 323.374752 | 0.003092 | 0.022394 | 7.241529 | 0.138092 | 30 |
| 31 | 50.684096 | 368.030343 | 0.002717 | 0.019730 | 7.261259 | 0.137717 | 31 |
| 32 | 57.526449 | 418.714439 | 0.002388 | 0.017383 | 7.278642 | 0.137388 | 32 |
| 33 | 65.292520 | 476.240889 | 0.002100 | 0.015316 | 7.293958 | 0.137100 | 33 |
| 34 | 74.107010 | 541.533409 | 0.001847 | 0.013494 | 7.307452 | 0.136847 | 34 |
| 35 | 84.111457 | 615.640419 | 0.001624 | 0.011889 | 7.319341 | 0.136624 | 35 |
| 36 | 95.466503 | 699.751875 | 0.001429 | 0.010475 | 7.329816 | 0.136429 | 36 |
| 37 | 108.354481 | 795.218378 | 0.001258 | 0.009229 | 7.339045 | 0.136258 | 37 |
| 38 | 122.982336 | 903.572859 | 0.001107 | 0.008131 | 7.347176 | 0.136107 | 38 |
| 39 | 139.584951 | 1026.555195 | 0.000974 | 0.007164 | 7.354340 | 0.135974 | 39 |
| 40 | 158.428920 | 1166.140147 | 0.000858 | 0.006312 | 7.360652 | 0.135858 | 40 |
| 41 | 179.816824 | 1324.569067 | 0.000755 | 0.005561 | 7.366213 | 0.135755 | 41 |
| 42 | 204.092095 | 1504.385891 | 0.000665 | 0.004900 | 7.371113 | 0.135665 | 42 |
| 43 | 231.644528 | 1708.477986 | 0.000585 | 0.004317 | 7.375430 | 0.135585 | 43 |
| 44 | 262.916539 | 1940.122514 | 0.000515 | 0.003803 | 7.379233 | 0.135515 | 44 |
| 45 | 298.410272 | 2203.039053 | 0.000454 | 0.003351 | 7.382585 | 0.135454 | 45 |
| 46 | 338.695659 | 2501.449326 | 0.000400 | 0.002953 | 7.385537 | 0.135400 | 46 |
| 47 | 384.419573 | 2840.144984 | 0.000352 | 0.002601 | 7.388138 | 0.135352 | 47 |
| 48 | 436.316215 | 3224.564557 | 0.000310 | 0.002292 | 7.390430 | 0.135310 | 48 |
| 49 | 495.218904 | 3660.880773 | 0.000273 | 0.002019 | 7.392450 | 0.135273 | 49 |
| 50 | 562.073456 | 4156.099677 | 0.000241 | 0.001779 | 7.394229 | 0.135241 | 50 |

14.00% ANNUAL INTEREST RATE

| | 1<br>Future Value<br>of $1 | 2<br>Future Value<br>Annuity of<br>$1 per Year | 3<br>Sinking<br>Fund<br>Factor | 4<br>Present Value<br>of $1<br>(Reversion) | 5<br>Present Value<br>Annuity of<br>$1 per Year | 6<br>Installment<br>to<br>Amortize $1 | |
|---|---|---|---|---|---|---|---|
| Years | | | | | | | Years |
| 1 | 1.140000 | 1.000000 | 1.000000 | 0.877193 | 0.877193 | 1.140000 | 1 |
| 2 | 1.299600 | 2.140000 | 0.467290 | 0.769468 | 1.646661 | 0.607290 | 2 |
| 3 | 1.481544 | 3.439600 | 0.290731 | 0.674972 | 2.321632 | 0.430731 | 3 |
| 4 | 1.688960 | 4.921144 | 0.203205 | 0.592080 | 2.913712 | 0.343205 | 4 |
| 5 | 1.925415 | 6.610104 | 0.151284 | 0.519369 | 3.433081 | 0.291284 | 5 |
| 6 | 2.194973 | 8.535519 | 0.117157 | 0.455587 | 3.888668 | 0.257157 | 6 |
| 7 | 2.502269 | 10.730491 | 0.093192 | 0.399637 | 4.288305 | 0.233192 | 7 |
| 8 | 2.852586 | 13.232760 | 0.075570 | 0.350559 | 4.638864 | 0.215570 | 8 |
| 9 | 3.251949 | 16.085347 | 0.062168 | 0.307508 | 4.946372 | 0.202168 | 9 |
| 10 | 3.707221 | 19.337295 | 0.051714 | 0.269744 | 5.216116 | 0.191714 | 10 |
| 11 | 4.226232 | 23.044516 | 0.043394 | 0.236617 | 5.452733 | 0.183394 | 11 |
| 12 | 4.817905 | 27.270749 | 0.036669 | 0.207559 | 5.660292 | 0.176669 | 12 |
| 13 | 5.492411 | 32.088654 | 0.031164 | 0.182069 | 5.842362 | 0.171164 | 13 |
| 14 | 6.261349 | 37.581065 | 0.026609 | 0.159710 | 6.002072 | 0.166609 | 14 |
| 15 | 7.137938 | 43.842414 | 0.022809 | 0.140096 | 6.142168 | 0.162809 | 15 |
| 16 | 8.137249 | 50.980352 | 0.019615 | 0.122892 | 6.265060 | 0.159615 | 16 |
| 17 | 9.276464 | 59.117601 | 0.016915 | 0.107800 | 6.372859 | 0.156915 | 17 |
| 18 | 10.575169 | 68.394066 | 0.014621 | 0.094561 | 6.467420 | 0.154621 | 18 |
| 19 | 12.055693 | 78.969235 | 0.012663 | 0.082948 | 6.550369 | 0.152663 | 19 |
| 20 | 13.743490 | 91.024928 | 0.010986 | 0.072762 | 6.623131 | 0.150986 | 20 |
| 21 | 15.667578 | 104.768418 | 0.009545 | 0.063826 | 6.686957 | 0.149545 | 21 |
| 22 | 17.861039 | 120.435996 | 0.008303 | 0.055988 | 6.742944 | 0.148303 | 22 |
| 23 | 20.361585 | 138.297035 | 0.007231 | 0.049112 | 6.792056 | 0.147231 | 23 |
| 24 | 23.212207 | 158.658620 | 0.006303 | 0.043081 | 6.835137 | 0.146303 | 24 |
| 25 | 26.461916 | 181.870827 | 0.005498 | 0.037790 | 6.872927 | 0.145498 | 25 |
| 26 | 30.166584 | 208.332743 | 0.004800 | 0.033149 | 6.906077 | 0.144800 | 26 |
| 27 | 34.389906 | 238.499327 | 0.004193 | 0.029078 | 6.935155 | 0.144193 | 27 |
| 28 | 39.204493 | 272.889233 | 0.003664 | 0.025507 | 6.960662 | 0.143664 | 28 |
| 29 | 44.693122 | 312.093725 | 0.003204 | 0.022375 | 6.983037 | 0.143204 | 29 |
| 30 | 50.950159 | 356.786847 | 0.002803 | 0.019627 | 7.002664 | 0.142803 | 30 |
| 31 | 58.083181 | 407.737006 | 0.002453 | 0.017217 | 7.019881 | 0.142453 | 31 |
| 32 | 66.214826 | 465.820186 | 0.002147 | 0.015102 | 7.034983 | 0.142147 | 32 |
| 33 | 75.484902 | 532.035012 | 0.001880 | 0.013248 | 7.048231 | 0.141880 | 33 |
| 34 | 86.052788 | 607.519914 | 0.001646 | 0.011621 | 7.059852 | 0.141646 | 34 |
| 35 | 98.100178 | 693.572702 | 0.001442 | 0.010194 | 7.070045 | 0.141442 | 35 |
| 36 | 111.834203 | 791.672881 | 0.001263 | 0.008942 | 7.078987 | 0.141263 | 36 |
| 37 | 127.490992 | 903.507084 | 0.001107 | 0.007844 | 7.086831 | 0.141107 | 37 |
| 38 | 145.339731 | 1030.998076 | 0.000970 | 0.006880 | 7.093711 | 0.140970 | 38 |
| 39 | 165.687293 | 1176.337806 | 0.000850 | 0.006035 | 7.099747 | 0.140850 | 39 |
| 40 | 188.883514 | 1342.025099 | 0.000745 | 0.005294 | 7.105041 | 0.140745 | 40 |
| 41 | 215.327206 | 1530.908613 | 0.000653 | 0.004644 | 7.109685 | 0.140653 | 41 |
| 42 | 245.473015 | 1746.235819 | 0.000573 | 0.004074 | 7.113759 | 0.140573 | 42 |
| 43 | 279.839237 | 1991.708833 | 0.000502 | 0.003573 | 7.117332 | 0.140502 | 43 |
| 44 | 319.016730 | 2271.548070 | 0.000440 | 0.003135 | 7.120467 | 0.140440 | 44 |
| 45 | 363.679072 | 2590.564800 | 0.000386 | 0.002750 | 7.123217 | 0.140386 | 45 |
| 46 | 414.594142 | 2954.243872 | 0.000338 | 0.002412 | 7.125629 | 0.140338 | 46 |
| 47 | 472.637322 | 3368.838014 | 0.000297 | 0.002116 | 7.127744 | 0.140297 | 47 |
| 48 | 538.806547 | 3841.475336 | 0.000260 | 0.001856 | 7.129600 | 0.140260 | 48 |
| 49 | 614.239464 | 4380.281883 | 0.000228 | 0.001628 | 7.131228 | 0.140228 | 49 |
| 50 | 700.232988 | 4994.521346 | 0.000200 | 0.001428 | 7.132656 | 0.140200 | 50 |

14.50% ANNUAL INTEREST RATE

| | 1 Future Value of $1 | 2 Future Value Annuity of $1 per Year | 3 Sinking Fund Factor | 4 Present Value of $1 (Reversion) | 5 Present Value Annuity of $1 per Year | 6 Installment to Amortize $1 | |
|---|---|---|---|---|---|---|---|
| Years | | | | | | | Years |
| 1 | 1.145000 | 1.000000 | 1.000000 | 0.873362 | 0.873362 | 1.145000 | 1 |
| 2 | 1.311025 | 2.145000 | 0.466200 | 0.762762 | 1.636124 | 0.611200 | 2 |
| 3 | 1.501124 | 3.456025 | 0.289350 | 0.666168 | 2.302292 | 0.434350 | 3 |
| 4 | 1.718787 | 4.957149 | 0.201729 | 0.581806 | 2.884098 | 0.346729 | 4 |
| 5 | 1.968011 | 6.675935 | 0.149792 | 0.508127 | 3.392225 | 0.294792 | 5 |
| 6 | 2.253372 | 8.643946 | 0.115688 | 0.443779 | 3.836005 | 0.260688 | 6 |
| 7 | 2.580111 | 10.897318 | 0.091766 | 0.387580 | 4.223585 | 0.236766 | 7 |
| 8 | 2.954227 | 13.477429 | 0.074198 | 0.338498 | 4.562083 | 0.219198 | 8 |
| 9 | 3.382590 | 16.431656 | 0.060858 | 0.295631 | 4.857714 | 0.205858 | 9 |
| 10 | 3.873066 | 19.814246 | 0.050469 | 0.258193 | 5.115908 | 0.195469 | 10 |
| 11 | 4.434660 | 23.687312 | 0.042217 | 0.225496 | 5.341404 | 0.187217 | 11 |
| 12 | 5.077686 | 28.121972 | 0.035559 | 0.196940 | 5.538344 | 0.180559 | 12 |
| 13 | 5.813950 | 33.199658 | 0.030121 | 0.172000 | 5.710344 | 0.175121 | 13 |
| 14 | 6.656973 | 39.013609 | 0.025632 | 0.150218 | 5.860563 | 0.170632 | 14 |
| 15 | 7.622234 | 45.670582 | 0.021896 | 0.131195 | 5.991758 | 0.166896 | 15 |
| 16 | 8.727458 | 53.292816 | 0.018764 | 0.114581 | 6.106339 | 0.163764 | 16 |
| 17 | 9.992940 | 62.020275 | 0.016124 | 0.100071 | 6.206409 | 0.161124 | 17 |
| 18 | 11.441916 | 72.013215 | 0.013886 | 0.087398 | 6.293807 | 0.158886 | 18 |
| 19 | 13.100994 | 83.455131 | 0.011982 | 0.076330 | 6.370137 | 0.156982 | 19 |
| 20 | 15.000638 | 96.556125 | 0.010357 | 0.066664 | 6.436801 | 0.155357 | 20 |
| 21 | 17.175731 | 111.556763 | 0.008964 | 0.058222 | 6.495023 | 0.153964 | 21 |
| 22 | 19.666212 | 128.732494 | 0.007768 | 0.050849 | 6.545871 | 0.152768 | 22 |
| 23 | 22.517812 | 148.398705 | 0.006739 | 0.044409 | 6.590281 | 0.151739 | 23 |
| 24 | 25.782895 | 170.916517 | 0.005851 | 0.038785 | 6.629066 | 0.150851 | 24 |
| 25 | 29.521415 | 196.699412 | 0.005084 | 0.033874 | 6.662940 | 0.150084 | 25 |
| 26 | 33.802020 | 226.220827 | 0.004420 | 0.029584 | 6.692524 | 0.149420 | 26 |
| 27 | 38.703313 | 260.022847 | 0.003846 | 0.025838 | 6.718362 | 0.148846 | 27 |
| 28 | 44.315293 | 298.726160 | 0.003348 | 0.022566 | 6.740927 | 0.148348 | 28 |
| 29 | 50.741011 | 343.041453 | 0.002915 | 0.019708 | 6.760635 | 0.147915 | 29 |
| 30 | 58.098457 | 393.782464 | 0.002539 | 0.017212 | 6.777847 | 0.147539 | 30 |
| 31 | 66.522734 | 451.880921 | 0.002213 | 0.015032 | 6.792880 | 0.147213 | 31 |
| 32 | 76.168530 | 518.403655 | 0.001929 | 0.013129 | 6.806008 | 0.146929 | 32 |
| 33 | 87.212967 | 594.572185 | 0.001682 | 0.011466 | 6.817475 | 0.146682 | 33 |
| 34 | 99.858847 | 681.785151 | 0.001467 | 0.010014 | 6.827489 | 0.146467 | 34 |
| 35 | 114.338380 | 781.643998 | 0.001279 | 0.008746 | 6.836235 | 0.146279 | 35 |
| 36 | 130.917445 | 895.982378 | 0.001116 | 0.007638 | 6.843873 | 0.146116 | 36 |
| 37 | 149.900474 | 1026.899823 | 0.000974 | 0.006671 | 6.850544 | 0.145974 | 37 |
| 38 | 171.636043 | 1176.800297 | 0.000850 | 0.005826 | 6.856370 | 0.145850 | 38 |
| 39 | 196.523269 | 1348.436340 | 0.000742 | 0.005088 | 6.861459 | 0.145742 | 39 |
| 40 | 225.019143 | 1544.959609 | 0.000647 | 0.004444 | 6.865903 | 0.145647 | 40 |
| 41 | 257.646919 | 1769.978753 | 0.000565 | 0.003881 | 6.869784 | 0.145565 | 41 |
| 42 | 295.005722 | 2027.625672 | 0.000493 | 0.003390 | 6.873174 | 0.145493 | 42 |
| 43 | 337.781552 | 2322.631394 | 0.000431 | 0.002960 | 6.876135 | 0.145431 | 43 |
| 44 | 386.759877 | 2660.412947 | 0.000376 | 0.002586 | 6.878720 | 0.145376 | 44 |
| 45 | 442.840059 | 3047.172824 | 0.000328 | 0.002258 | 6.880978 | 0.145328 | 45 |
| 46 | 507.051868 | 3490.012883 | 0.000287 | 0.001972 | 6.882950 | 0.145287 | 46 |
| 47 | 580.574389 | 3997.064751 | 0.000250 | 0.001722 | 6.884673 | 0.145250 | 47 |
| 48 | 664.757675 | 4577.639140 | 0.000218 | 0.001504 | 6.886177 | 0.145218 | 48 |
| 49 | 761.147538 | 5242.396816 | 0.000191 | 0.001314 | 6.887491 | 0.145191 | 49 |
| 50 | 871.513931 | 6003.544354 | 0.000167 | 0.001147 | 6.888638 | 0.145167 | 50 |

15.00% ANNUAL INTEREST RATE

| | 1<br>Future Value<br>of $1 | 2<br>Future Value<br>Annuity of<br>$1 per Year | 3<br>Sinking<br>Fund<br>Factor | 4<br>Present Value<br>of $1<br>(Reversion) | 5<br>Present Value<br>Annuity of<br>$1 per Year | 6<br>Installment<br>to<br>Amortize $1 | |
|---|---|---|---|---|---|---|---|
| Years | | | | | | | Years |
| 1 | 1.150000 | 1.000000 | 1.000000 | 0.869565 | 0.869565 | 1.150000 | 1 |
| 2 | 1.322500 | 2.150000 | 0.465116 | 0.756144 | 1.625709 | 0.615116 | 2 |
| 3 | 1.520875 | 3.472500 | 0.287977 | 0.657516 | 2.283225 | 0.437977 | 3 |
| 4 | 1.749006 | 4.993375 | 0.200265 | 0.571753 | 2.854978 | 0.350265 | 4 |
| 5 | 2.011357 | 6.742381 | 0.148316 | 0.497177 | 3.352155 | 0.298316 | 5 |
| 6 | 2.313061 | 8.753738 | 0.114237 | 0.432328 | 3.784483 | 0.264237 | 6 |
| 7 | 2.660020 | 11.066799 | 0.090360 | 0.375937 | 4.160420 | 0.240360 | 7 |
| 8 | 3.059023 | 13.726819 | 0.072850 | 0.326902 | 4.487322 | 0.222850 | 8 |
| 9 | 3.517876 | 16.785842 | 0.059574 | 0.284262 | 4.771584 | 0.209574 | 9 |
| 10 | 4.045558 | 20.303718 | 0.049252 | 0.247185 | 5.018769 | 0.199252 | 10 |
| 11 | 4.652391 | 24.349276 | 0.041069 | 0.214943 | 5.233712 | 0.191069 | 11 |
| 12 | 5.350250 | 29.001667 | 0.034481 | 0.186907 | 5.420619 | 0.184481 | 12 |
| 13 | 6.152788 | 34.351917 | 0.029110 | 0.162528 | 5.583147 | 0.179110 | 13 |
| 14 | 7.075706 | 40.504705 | 0.024688 | 0.141329 | 5.724476 | 0.174688 | 14 |
| 15 | 8.137062 | 47.580411 | 0.021017 | 0.122894 | 5.847370 | 0.171017 | 15 |
| 16 | 9.357621 | 55.717472 | 0.017948 | 0.106865 | 5.954235 | 0.167948 | 16 |
| 17 | 10.761264 | 65.075093 | 0.015367 | 0.092926 | 6.047161 | 0.165367 | 17 |
| 18 | 12.375454 | 75.836357 | 0.013186 | 0.080805 | 6.127966 | 0.163186 | 18 |
| 19 | 14.231772 | 88.211811 | 0.011336 | 0.070265 | 6.198231 | 0.161336 | 19 |
| 20 | 16.366537 | 102.443583 | 0.009761 | 0.061100 | 6.259331 | 0.159761 | 20 |
| 21 | 18.821518 | 118.810120 | 0.008417 | 0.053131 | 6.312462 | 0.158417 | 21 |
| 22 | 21.644746 | 137.631638 | 0.007266 | 0.046201 | 6.358663 | 0.157266 | 22 |
| 23 | 24.891458 | 159.276384 | 0.006278 | 0.040174 | 6.398837 | 0.156278 | 23 |
| 24 | 28.625176 | 184.167841 | 0.005430 | 0.034934 | 6.433771 | 0.155430 | 24 |
| 25 | 32.918953 | 212.793017 | 0.004699 | 0.030378 | 6.464149 | 0.154699 | 25 |
| 26 | 37.856796 | 245.711970 | 0.004070 | 0.026415 | 6.490564 | 0.154070 | 26 |
| 27 | 43.535315 | 283.568766 | 0.003526 | 0.022970 | 6.513534 | 0.153526 | 27 |
| 28 | 50.065612 | 327.104080 | 0.003057 | 0.019974 | 6.533508 | 0.153057 | 28 |
| 29 | 57.575454 | 377.169693 | 0.002651 | 0.017369 | 6.550877 | 0.152651 | 29 |
| 30 | 66.211772 | 434.745146 | 0.002300 | 0.015103 | 6.565980 | 0.152300 | 30 |
| 31 | 76.143538 | 500.956918 | 0.001996 | 0.013133 | 6.579113 | 0.151996 | 31 |
| 32 | 87.565068 | 577.100456 | 0.001733 | 0.011420 | 6.590533 | 0.151733 | 32 |
| 33 | 100.699829 | 664.665524 | 0.001505 | 0.009931 | 6.600463 | 0.151505 | 33 |
| 34 | 115.804803 | 765.365353 | 0.001307 | 0.008635 | 6.609099 | 0.151307 | 34 |
| 35 | 133.175523 | 881.170156 | 0.001135 | 0.007509 | 6.616607 | 0.151135 | 35 |
| 36 | 153.151852 | 1014.345680 | 0.000986 | 0.006529 | 6.623137 | 0.150986 | 36 |
| 37 | 176.124630 | 1167.497532 | 0.000857 | 0.005678 | 6.628815 | 0.150857 | 37 |
| 38 | 202.543324 | 1343.622161 | 0.000744 | 0.004937 | 6.633752 | 0.150744 | 38 |
| 39 | 232.924823 | 1546.165485 | 0.000647 | 0.004293 | 6.638045 | 0.150647 | 39 |
| 40 | 267.863546 | 1779.090308 | 0.000562 | 0.003733 | 6.641778 | 0.150562 | 40 |
| 41 | 308.043078 | 2046.953854 | 0.000489 | 0.003246 | 6.645025 | 0.150489 | 41 |
| 42 | 354.249540 | 2354.996933 | 0.000425 | 0.002823 | 6.647848 | 0.150425 | 42 |
| 43 | 407.386971 | 2709.246473 | 0.000369 | 0.002455 | 6.650302 | 0.150369 | 43 |
| 44 | 468.495017 | 3116.633443 | 0.000321 | 0.002134 | 6.652437 | 0.150321 | 44 |
| 45 | 538.769269 | 3585.128460 | 0.000279 | 0.001856 | 6.654293 | 0.150279 | 45 |
| 46 | 619.584659 | 4123.897729 | 0.000242 | 0.001614 | 6.655907 | 0.150242 | 46 |
| 47 | 712.522358 | 4743.482388 | 0.000211 | 0.001403 | 6.657310 | 0.150211 | 47 |
| 48 | 819.400712 | 5456.004746 | 0.000183 | 0.001220 | 6.658531 | 0.150183 | 48 |
| 49 | 942.310819 | 6275.405458 | 0.000159 | 0.001061 | 6.659592 | 0.150159 | 49 |
| 50 | 1083.657442 | 7217.716277 | 0.000139 | 0.000923 | 6.660515 | 0.150139 | 50 |

15.50% ANNUAL INTEREST RATE

| Years | 1<br>Future Value<br>of $1 | 2<br>Future Value<br>Annuity of<br>$1 per Year | 3<br>Sinking<br>Fund<br>Factor | 4<br>Present Value<br>of $1<br>(Reversion) | 5<br>Present Value<br>Annuity of<br>$1 per Year | 6<br>Installment<br>to<br>Amortize $1 | Years |
|---|---|---|---|---|---|---|---|
| 1 | 1.155000 | 1.000000 | 1.000000 | 0.865801 | 0.865801 | 1.155000 | 1 |
| 2 | 1.334025 | 2.155000 | 0.464037 | 0.749611 | 1.615412 | 0.619037 | 2 |
| 3 | 1.540799 | 3.489025 | 0.286613 | 0.649014 | 2.264426 | 0.441613 | 3 |
| 4 | 1.779623 | 5.029824 | 0.198814 | 0.561917 | 2.826343 | 0.353814 | 4 |
| 5 | 2.055464 | 6.809447 | 0.146855 | 0.486508 | 3.312851 | 0.301855 | 5 |
| 6 | 2.374061 | 8.864911 | 0.112804 | 0.421219 | 3.734070 | 0.267804 | 6 |
| 7 | 2.742041 | 11.238972 | 0.088976 | 0.364692 | 4.098762 | 0.243976 | 7 |
| 8 | 3.167057 | 13.981013 | 0.071526 | 0.315751 | 4.414513 | 0.226526 | 8 |
| 9 | 3.657951 | 17.148070 | 0.058316 | 0.273377 | 4.687890 | 0.213316 | 9 |
| 10 | 4.224933 | 20.806020 | 0.048063 | 0.236690 | 4.924580 | 0.203063 | 10 |
| 11 | 4.879798 | 25.030954 | 0.039951 | 0.204927 | 5.129506 | 0.194951 | 11 |
| 12 | 5.636166 | 29.910751 | 0.033433 | 0.177426 | 5.306932 | 0.188433 | 12 |
| 13 | 6.509772 | 35.546918 | 0.028132 | 0.153615 | 5.460547 | 0.183132 | 13 |
| 14 | 7.518787 | 42.056690 | 0.023777 | 0.133000 | 5.593547 | 0.178777 | 14 |
| 15 | 8.684199 | 49.575477 | 0.020171 | 0.115152 | 5.708699 | 0.175171 | 15 |
| 16 | 10.030250 | 58.259676 | 0.017165 | 0.099698 | 5.808397 | 0.172165 | 16 |
| 17 | 11.584938 | 68.289926 | 0.014643 | 0.086319 | 5.894716 | 0.169643 | 17 |
| 18 | 13.380604 | 79.874864 | 0.012520 | 0.074735 | 5.969451 | 0.167520 | 18 |
| 19 | 15.454598 | 93.255468 | 0.010723 | 0.064706 | 6.034157 | 0.165723 | 19 |
| 20 | 17.850060 | 108.710066 | 0.009199 | 0.056022 | 6.090179 | 0.164199 | 20 |
| 21 | 20.616820 | 126.560126 | 0.007901 | 0.048504 | 6.138683 | 0.162901 | 21 |
| 22 | 23.812427 | 147.176945 | 0.006795 | 0.041995 | 6.180678 | 0.161795 | 22 |
| 23 | 27.503353 | 170.989372 | 0.005848 | 0.036359 | 6.217037 | 0.160848 | 23 |
| 24 | 31.766372 | 198.492725 | 0.005038 | 0.031480 | 6.248517 | 0.160038 | 24 |
| 25 | 36.690160 | 230.259097 | 0.004343 | 0.027255 | 6.275772 | 0.159343 | 25 |
| 26 | 42.377135 | 266.949257 | 0.003746 | 0.023598 | 6.299370 | 0.158746 | 26 |
| 27 | 48.945591 | 309.326392 | 0.003233 | 0.020431 | 6.319801 | 0.158233 | 27 |
| 28 | 56.532157 | 358.271982 | 0.002791 | 0.017689 | 6.337490 | 0.157791 | 28 |
| 29 | 65.294642 | 414.804140 | 0.002411 | 0.015315 | 6.352805 | 0.157411 | 29 |
| 30 | 75.415311 | 480.098781 | 0.002083 | 0.013260 | 6.366065 | 0.157083 | 30 |
| 31 | 87.104684 | 555.514092 | 0.001800 | 0.011480 | 6.377546 | 0.156800 | 31 |
| 32 | 100.605910 | 642.618777 | 0.001556 | 0.009940 | 6.387485 | 0.156556 | 32 |
| 33 | 116.199826 | 743.224687 | 0.001345 | 0.008606 | 6.396091 | 0.156345 | 33 |
| 34 | 134.210800 | 859.424513 | 0.001164 | 0.007451 | 6.403542 | 0.156164 | 34 |
| 35 | 155.013474 | 993.635313 | 0.001006 | 0.006451 | 6.409993 | 0.156006 | 35 |
| 36 | 179.040562 | 1148.648787 | 0.000871 | 0.005585 | 6.415579 | 0.155871 | 36 |
| 37 | 206.791849 | 1327.689348 | 0.000753 | 0.004836 | 6.420414 | 0.155753 | 37 |
| 38 | 238.844586 | 1534.481197 | 0.000652 | 0.004187 | 6.424601 | 0.155652 | 38 |
| 39 | 275.865496 | 1773.325783 | 0.000564 | 0.003625 | 6.428226 | 0.155564 | 39 |
| 40 | 318.624648 | 2049.191279 | 0.000488 | 0.003138 | 6.431365 | 0.155488 | 40 |
| 41 | 368.011469 | 2367.815928 | 0.000422 | 0.002717 | 6.434082 | 0.155422 | 41 |
| 42 | 425.053246 | 2735.827397 | 0.000366 | 0.002353 | 6.436435 | 0.155366 | 42 |
| 43 | 490.936500 | 3160.880643 | 0.000316 | 0.002037 | 6.438471 | 0.155316 | 43 |
| 44 | 567.031657 | 3651.817143 | 0.000274 | 0.001764 | 6.440235 | 0.155274 | 44 |
| 45 | 654.921564 | 4218.848800 | 0.000237 | 0.001527 | 6.441762 | 0.155237 | 45 |
| 46 | 756.434406 | 4873.770364 | 0.000205 | 0.001322 | 6.443084 | 0.155205 | 46 |
| 47 | 873.681739 | 5630.204770 | 0.000178 | 0.001145 | 6.444229 | 0.155178 | 47 |
| 48 | 1009.102409 | 6503.886510 | 0.000154 | 0.000991 | 6.445219 | 0.155154 | 48 |
| 49 | 1165.513282 | 7512.988919 | 0.000133 | 0.000858 | 6.446077 | 0.155133 | 49 |
| 50 | 1346.167841 | 8678.502201 | 0.000115 | 0.000743 | 6.446820 | 0.155115 | 50 |

16.00% ANNUAL INTEREST RATE

| | 1 Future Value of $1 | 2 Future Value Annuity of $1 per Year | 3 Sinking Fund Factor | 4 Present Value of $1 (Reversion) | 5 Present Value Annuity of $1 per Year | 6 Installment to Amortize $1 | |
|---|---|---|---|---|---|---|---|
| Years | | | | | | | Years |
| 1 | 1.160000 | 1.000000 | 1.000000 | 0.862069 | 0.862069 | 1.160000 | 1 |
| 2 | 1.345600 | 2.160000 | 0.462963 | 0.743163 | 1.605232 | 0.622963 | 2 |
| 3 | 1.560896 | 3.505600 | 0.285258 | 0.640658 | 2.245890 | 0.445258 | 3 |
| 4 | 1.810639 | 5.066496 | 0.197375 | 0.552291 | 2.798181 | 0.357375 | 4 |
| 5 | 2.100342 | 6.877135 | 0.145409 | 0.476113 | 3.274294 | 0.305409 | 5 |
| 6 | 2.436396 | 8.977477 | 0.111390 | 0.410442 | 3.684736 | 0.271390 | 6 |
| 7 | 2.826220 | 11.413873 | 0.087613 | 0.353830 | 4.038565 | 0.247613 | 7 |
| 8 | 3.278415 | 14.240093 | 0.070224 | 0.305025 | 4.343591 | 0.230224 | 8 |
| 9 | 3.802961 | 17.518508 | 0.057082 | 0.262953 | 4.606544 | 0.217082 | 9 |
| 10 | 4.411435 | 21.321469 | 0.046901 | 0.226684 | 4.833227 | 0.206901 | 10 |
| 11 | 5.117265 | 25.732904 | 0.038861 | 0.195417 | 5.028644 | 0.198861 | 11 |
| 12 | 5.936027 | 30.850169 | 0.032415 | 0.168463 | 5.197107 | 0.192415 | 12 |
| 13 | 6.885791 | 36.786196 | 0.027184 | 0.145227 | 5.342334 | 0.187184 | 13 |
| 14 | 7.987518 | 43.671987 | 0.022898 | 0.125195 | 5.467529 | 0.182898 | 14 |
| 15 | 9.265521 | 51.659505 | 0.019358 | 0.107927 | 5.575456 | 0.179358 | 15 |
| 16 | 10.748004 | 60.925026 | 0.016414 | 0.093041 | 5.668497 | 0.176414 | 16 |
| 17 | 12.467685 | 71.673030 | 0.013952 | 0.080207 | 5.748704 | 0.173952 | 17 |
| 18 | 14.462514 | 84.140715 | 0.011885 | 0.069144 | 5.817848 | 0.171885 | 18 |
| 19 | 16.776517 | 98.603230 | 0.010142 | 0.059607 | 5.877455 | 0.170142 | 19 |
| 20 | 19.460759 | 115.379747 | 0.008667 | 0.051385 | 5.928841 | 0.168667 | 20 |
| 21 | 22.574481 | 134.840506 | 0.007416 | 0.044298 | 5.973139 | 0.167416 | 21 |
| 22 | 26.186398 | 157.414987 | 0.006353 | 0.038188 | 6.011326 | 0.166353 | 22 |
| 23 | 30.376222 | 183.601385 | 0.005447 | 0.032920 | 6.044247 | 0.165447 | 23 |
| 24 | 35.236417 | 213.977607 | 0.004673 | 0.028380 | 6.072627 | 0.164673 | 24 |
| 25 | 40.874244 | 249.214024 | 0.004013 | 0.024465 | 6.097092 | 0.164013 | 25 |
| 26 | 47.414123 | 290.088267 | 0.003447 | 0.021091 | 6.118183 | 0.163447 | 26 |
| 27 | 55.000382 | 337.502390 | 0.002963 | 0.018182 | 6.136364 | 0.162963 | 27 |
| 28 | 63.800444 | 392.502773 | 0.002548 | 0.015674 | 6.152038 | 0.162548 | 28 |
| 29 | 74.008515 | 456.303216 | 0.002192 | 0.013512 | 6.165550 | 0.162192 | 29 |
| 30 | 85.849877 | 530.311731 | 0.001886 | 0.011648 | 6.177198 | 0.161886 | 30 |
| 31 | 99.585857 | 616.161608 | 0.001623 | 0.010042 | 6.187240 | 0.161623 | 31 |
| 32 | 115.519594 | 715.747465 | 0.001397 | 0.008657 | 6.195897 | 0.161397 | 32 |
| 33 | 134.002729 | 831.267059 | 0.001203 | 0.007463 | 6.203359 | 0.161203 | 33 |
| 34 | 155.443166 | 965.269789 | 0.001036 | 0.006433 | 6.209792 | 0.161036 | 34 |
| 35 | 180.314073 | 1120.712955 | 0.000892 | 0.005546 | 6.215338 | 0.160892 | 35 |
| 36 | 209.164324 | 1301.027028 | 0.000769 | 0.004781 | 6.220119 | 0.160769 | 36 |
| 37 | 242.630616 | 1510.191352 | 0.000662 | 0.004121 | 6.224241 | 0.160662 | 37 |
| 38 | 281.451515 | 1752.821968 | 0.000571 | 0.003553 | 6.227794 | 0.160571 | 38 |
| 39 | 326.483757 | 2034.273483 | 0.000492 | 0.003063 | 6.230857 | 0.160492 | 39 |
| 40 | 378.721158 | 2360.757241 | 0.000424 | 0.002640 | 6.233497 | 0.160424 | 40 |
| 41 | 439.316544 | 2739.478399 | 0.000365 | 0.002276 | 6.235773 | 0.160365 | 41 |
| 42 | 509.607191 | 3178.794943 | 0.000315 | 0.001962 | 6.237736 | 0.160315 | 42 |
| 43 | 591.144341 | 3688.402134 | 0.000271 | 0.001692 | 6.239427 | 0.160271 | 43 |
| 44 | 685.727436 | 4279.546475 | 0.000234 | 0.001458 | 6.240886 | 0.160234 | 44 |
| 45 | 795.443826 | 4965.273911 | 0.000201 | 0.001257 | 6.242143 | 0.160201 | 45 |
| 46 | 922.714838 | 5760.717737 | 0.000174 | 0.001084 | 6.243227 | 0.160174 | 46 |
| 47 | 1070.349212 | 6683.432575 | 0.000150 | 0.000934 | 6.244161 | 0.160150 | 47 |
| 48 | 1241.605086 | 7753.781787 | 0.000129 | 0.000805 | 6.244966 | 0.160129 | 48 |
| 49 | 1440.261900 | 8995.386873 | 0.000111 | 0.000694 | 6.245661 | 0.160111 | 49 |
| 50 | 1670.703804 | 10435.648773 | 0.000096 | 0.000599 | 6.246259 | 0.160096 | 50 |

16.50% ANNUAL INTEREST RATE

| | 1<br>Future Value<br>of $1 | 2<br>Future Value<br>Annuity of<br>$1 per Year | 3<br>Sinking<br>Fund<br>Factor | 4<br>Present Value<br>of $1<br>(Reversion) | 5<br>Present Value<br>Annuity of<br>$1 per Year | 6<br>Installment<br>to<br>Amortize $1 | |
|---|---|---|---|---|---|---|---|
| Years | | | | | | | Years |
| 1 | 1.165000 | 1.000000 | 1.000000 | 0.858369 | 0.858369 | 1.165000 | 1 |
| 2 | 1.357225 | 2.165000 | 0.461894 | 0.736798 | 1.595167 | 0.626894 | 2 |
| 3 | 1.581167 | 3.522225 | 0.283911 | 0.632444 | 2.227611 | 0.448911 | 3 |
| 4 | 1.842060 | 5.103392 | 0.195948 | 0.542871 | 2.770481 | 0.360948 | 4 |
| 5 | 2.146000 | 6.945452 | 0.143979 | 0.465983 | 3.236465 | 0.308979 | 5 |
| 6 | 2.500089 | 9.091451 | 0.109993 | 0.399986 | 3.636450 | 0.274993 | 6 |
| 7 | 2.912604 | 11.591541 | 0.086270 | 0.343335 | 3.979786 | 0.251270 | 7 |
| 8 | 3.393184 | 14.504145 | 0.068946 | 0.294708 | 4.274494 | 0.233946 | 8 |
| 9 | 3.953059 | 17.897329 | 0.055874 | 0.252969 | 4.527463 | 0.220874 | 9 |
| 10 | 4.605314 | 21.850388 | 0.045766 | 0.217140 | 4.744603 | 0.210766 | 10 |
| 11 | 5.365191 | 26.455702 | 0.037799 | 0.186387 | 4.930990 | 0.202799 | 11 |
| 12 | 6.250447 | 31.820893 | 0.031426 | 0.159989 | 5.090978 | 0.196426 | 12 |
| 13 | 7.281771 | 38.071341 | 0.026266 | 0.137329 | 5.228308 | 0.191266 | 13 |
| 14 | 8.483263 | 45.353112 | 0.022049 | 0.117879 | 5.346187 | 0.187049 | 14 |
| 15 | 9.883002 | 53.836375 | 0.018575 | 0.101184 | 5.447371 | 0.183575 | 15 |
| 16 | 11.513697 | 63.719377 | 0.015694 | 0.086853 | 5.534224 | 0.180694 | 16 |
| 17 | 13.413457 | 75.233075 | 0.013292 | 0.074552 | 5.608776 | 0.178292 | 17 |
| 18 | 15.626678 | 88.646532 | 0.011281 | 0.063993 | 5.672769 | 0.176281 | 18 |
| 19 | 18.205080 | 104.273210 | 0.009590 | 0.054930 | 5.727699 | 0.174590 | 19 |
| 20 | 21.208918 | 122.478289 | 0.008165 | 0.047150 | 5.774849 | 0.173165 | 20 |
| 21 | 24.708389 | 143.687207 | 0.006960 | 0.040472 | 5.815321 | 0.171960 | 21 |
| 22 | 28.785273 | 168.395596 | 0.005938 | 0.034740 | 5.850061 | 0.170938 | 22 |
| 23 | 33.534843 | 197.180869 | 0.005071 | 0.029820 | 5.879880 | 0.170071 | 23 |
| 24 | 39.068093 | 230.715713 | 0.004334 | 0.025596 | 5.905477 | 0.169334 | 24 |
| 25 | 45.514328 | 269.783805 | 0.003707 | 0.021971 | 5.927448 | 0.168707 | 25 |
| 26 | 53.024192 | 315.298133 | 0.003172 | 0.018859 | 5.946307 | 0.168172 | 26 |
| 27 | 61.773184 | 368.322325 | 0.002715 | 0.016188 | 5.962495 | 0.167715 | 27 |
| 28 | 71.965759 | 430.095509 | 0.002325 | 0.013895 | 5.976391 | 0.167325 | 28 |
| 29 | 83.840109 | 502.061268 | 0.001992 | 0.011927 | 5.988318 | 0.166992 | 29 |
| 30 | 97.673727 | 585.901377 | 0.001707 | 0.010238 | 5.998557 | 0.166707 | 30 |
| 31 | 113.789892 | 683.575105 | 0.001463 | 0.008788 | 6.007345 | 0.166463 | 31 |
| 32 | 132.565224 | 797.364997 | 0.001254 | 0.007543 | 6.014888 | 0.166254 | 32 |
| 33 | 154.436487 | 929.930221 | 0.001075 | 0.006475 | 6.021363 | 0.166075 | 33 |
| 34 | 179.920837 | 1084.368708 | 0.000922 | 0.005558 | 6.026921 | 0.165922 | 34 |
| 35 | 209.607775 | 1264.289545 | 0.000791 | 0.004771 | 6.031692 | 0.165791 | 35 |
| 36 | 244.193058 | 1473.897320 | 0.000678 | 0.004095 | 6.035787 | 0.165678 | 36 |
| 37 | 284.484912 | 1718.090377 | 0.000582 | 0.003515 | 6.039302 | 0.165582 | 37 |
| 38 | 331.424923 | 2002.575290 | 0.000499 | 0.003017 | 6.042320 | 0.165499 | 38 |
| 39 | 386.110035 | 2334.000212 | 0.000428 | 0.002590 | 6.044909 | 0.165428 | 39 |
| 40 | 449.818191 | 2720.110247 | 0.000368 | 0.002223 | 6.047133 | 0.165368 | 40 |
| 41 | 524.038192 | 3169.928438 | 0.000315 | 0.001908 | 6.049041 | 0.165315 | 41 |
| 42 | 610.504494 | 3693.966630 | 0.000271 | 0.001638 | 6.050679 | 0.165271 | 42 |
| 43 | 711.237736 | 4304.471124 | 0.000232 | 0.001406 | 6.052085 | 0.165232 | 43 |
| 44 | 828.591962 | 5015.708860 | 0.000199 | 0.001207 | 6.053292 | 0.165199 | 44 |
| 45 | 965.309636 | 5844.300822 | 0.000171 | 0.001036 | 6.054328 | 0.165171 | 45 |
| 46 | 1124.585725 | 6809.610458 | 0.000147 | 0.000889 | 6.055217 | 0.165147 | 46 |
| 47 | 1310.142370 | 7934.196183 | 0.000126 | 0.000763 | 6.055980 | 0.165126 | 47 |
| 48 | 1526.315861 | 9244.338553 | 0.000108 | 0.000655 | 6.056635 | 0.165108 | 48 |
| 49 | 1778.157978 | 10770.654414 | 0.000093 | 0.000562 | 6.057198 | 0.165093 | 49 |
| 50 | 2071.554045 | 12548.812393 | 0.000080 | 0.000483 | 6.057680 | 0.165080 | 50 |

17.00% ANNUAL INTEREST RATE

| | 1<br>Future Value<br>of $1 | 2<br>Future Value<br>Annuity of<br>$1 per Year | 3<br>Sinking<br>Fund<br>Factor | 4<br>Present Value<br>of $1<br>(Reversion) | 5<br>Present Value<br>Annuity of<br>$1 per Year | 6<br>Installment<br>to<br>Amortize $1 | |
|---|---|---|---|---|---|---|---|
| Years | | | | | | | Years |
| 1 | 1.170000 | 1.000000 | 1.000000 | 0.854701 | 0.854701 | 1.170000 | 1 |
| 2 | 1.368900 | 2.170000 | 0.460829 | 0.730514 | 1.585214 | 0.630829 | 2 |
| 3 | 1.601613 | 3.538900 | 0.282574 | 0.624371 | 2.209585 | 0.452574 | 3 |
| 4 | 1.873887 | 5.140513 | 0.194533 | 0.533650 | 2.743235 | 0.364533 | 4 |
| 5 | 2.192448 | 7.014400 | 0.142564 | 0.456111 | 3.199346 | 0.312564 | 5 |
| 6 | 2.565164 | 9.206848 | 0.108615 | 0.389839 | 3.589185 | 0.278615 | 6 |
| 7 | 3.001242 | 11.772012 | 0.084947 | 0.333195 | 3.922380 | 0.254947 | 7 |
| 8 | 3.511453 | 14.773255 | 0.067690 | 0.284782 | 4.207163 | 0.237690 | 8 |
| 9 | 4.108400 | 18.284708 | 0.054691 | 0.243404 | 4.450566 | 0.224691 | 9 |
| 10 | 4.806828 | 22.393108 | 0.044657 | 0.208037 | 4.658604 | 0.214657 | 10 |
| 11 | 5.623989 | 27.199937 | 0.036765 | 0.177810 | 4.836413 | 0.206765 | 11 |
| 12 | 6.580067 | 32.823926 | 0.030466 | 0.151974 | 4.988387 | 0.200466 | 12 |
| 13 | 7.698679 | 39.403993 | 0.025378 | 0.129892 | 5.118280 | 0.195378 | 13 |
| 14 | 9.007454 | 47.102672 | 0.021230 | 0.111019 | 5.229299 | 0.191230 | 14 |
| 15 | 10.538721 | 56.110126 | 0.017822 | 0.094888 | 5.324187 | 0.187822 | 15 |
| 16 | 12.330304 | 66.648848 | 0.015004 | 0.081101 | 5.405288 | 0.185004 | 16 |
| 17 | 14.426456 | 78.979152 | 0.012662 | 0.069317 | 5.474605 | 0.182662 | 17 |
| 18 | 16.878953 | 93.405608 | 0.010706 | 0.059245 | 5.533851 | 0.180706 | 18 |
| 19 | 19.748375 | 110.284561 | 0.009067 | 0.050637 | 5.584488 | 0.179067 | 19 |
| 20 | 23.105599 | 130.032936 | 0.007690 | 0.043280 | 5.627767 | 0.177690 | 20 |
| 21 | 27.033551 | 153.138535 | 0.006530 | 0.036991 | 5.664758 | 0.176530 | 21 |
| 22 | 31.629255 | 180.172086 | 0.005550 | 0.031616 | 5.696375 | 0.175550 | 22 |
| 23 | 37.006228 | 211.801341 | 0.004721 | 0.027022 | 5.723397 | 0.174721 | 23 |
| 24 | 43.297287 | 248.807569 | 0.004019 | 0.023096 | 5.746493 | 0.174019 | 24 |
| 25 | 50.657826 | 292.104856 | 0.003423 | 0.019740 | 5.766234 | 0.173423 | 25 |
| 26 | 59.269656 | 342.762681 | 0.002917 | 0.016872 | 5.783106 | 0.172917 | 26 |
| 27 | 69.345497 | 402.032337 | 0.002487 | 0.014421 | 5.797526 | 0.172487 | 27 |
| 28 | 81.134232 | 471.377835 | 0.002121 | 0.012325 | 5.809851 | 0.172121 | 28 |
| 29 | 94.927051 | 552.512066 | 0.001810 | 0.010534 | 5.820386 | 0.171810 | 29 |
| 30 | 111.064650 | 647.439118 | 0.001545 | 0.009004 | 5.829390 | 0.171545 | 30 |
| 31 | 129.945641 | 758.503768 | 0.001318 | 0.007696 | 5.837085 | 0.171318 | 31 |
| 32 | 152.036399 | 888.449408 | 0.001126 | 0.006577 | 5.843663 | 0.171126 | 32 |
| 33 | 177.882587 | 1040.485808 | 0.000961 | 0.005622 | 5.849284 | 0.170961 | 33 |
| 34 | 208.122627 | 1218.368395 | 0.000821 | 0.004805 | 5.854089 | 0.170821 | 34 |
| 35 | 243.503474 | 1426.491022 | 0.000701 | 0.004107 | 5.858196 | 0.170701 | 35 |
| 36 | 284.899064 | 1669.994496 | 0.000599 | 0.003510 | 5.861706 | 0.170599 | 36 |
| 37 | 333.331905 | 1954.893560 | 0.000512 | 0.003000 | 5.864706 | 0.170512 | 37 |
| 38 | 389.998329 | 2288.225465 | 0.000437 | 0.002564 | 5.867270 | 0.170437 | 38 |
| 39 | 456.298045 | 2678.223794 | 0.000373 | 0.002192 | 5.869461 | 0.170373 | 39 |
| 40 | 533.868713 | 3134.521839 | 0.000319 | 0.001873 | 5.871335 | 0.170319 | 40 |
| 41 | 624.626394 | 3668.390552 | 0.000273 | 0.001601 | 5.872936 | 0.170273 | 41 |
| 42 | 730.812881 | 4293.016946 | 0.000233 | 0.001368 | 5.874304 | 0.170233 | 42 |
| 43 | 855.051071 | 5023.829827 | 0.000199 | 0.001170 | 5.875473 | 0.170199 | 43 |
| 44 | 1000.409753 | 5878.880897 | 0.000170 | 0.001000 | 5.876473 | 0.170170 | 44 |
| 45 | 1170.479411 | 6879.290650 | 0.000145 | 0.000854 | 5.877327 | 0.170145 | 45 |
| 46 | 1369.460910 | 8049.770061 | 0.000124 | 0.000730 | 5.878058 | 0.170124 | 46 |
| 47 | 1602.269265 | 9419.230971 | 0.000106 | 0.000624 | 5.878682 | 0.170106 | 47 |
| 48 | 1874.655040 | 11021.500236 | 0.000091 | 0.000533 | 5.879215 | 0.170091 | 48 |
| 49 | 2193.346397 | 12896.155276 | 0.000078 | 0.000456 | 5.879671 | 0.170078 | 49 |
| 50 | 2566.215284 | 15089.501673 | 0.000066 | 0.000390 | 5.880061 | 0.170066 | 50 |

17.50% ANNUAL INTEREST RATE

| | 1<br>Future Value<br>of $1 | 2<br>Future Value<br>Annuity of<br>$1 per Year | 3<br>Sinking<br>Fund<br>Factor | 4<br>Present Value<br>of $1<br>(Reversion) | 5<br>Present Value<br>Annuity of<br>$1 per Year | 6<br>Installment<br>to<br>Amortize $1 | |
|---|---|---|---|---|---|---|---|
| Years | | | | | | | Years |
| 1 | 1.175000 | 1.000000 | 1.000000 | 0.851064 | 0.851064 | 1.175000 | 1 |
| 2 | 1.380625 | 2.175000 | 0.459770 | 0.724310 | 1.575373 | 0.634770 | 2 |
| 3 | 1.622234 | 3.555625 | 0.281245 | 0.616434 | 2.191807 | 0.456245 | 3 |
| 4 | 1.906125 | 5.177859 | 0.193130 | 0.524624 | 2.716432 | 0.368130 | 4 |
| 5 | 2.239697 | 7.083985 | 0.141163 | 0.446489 | 3.162921 | 0.316163 | 5 |
| 6 | 2.631644 | 9.323682 | 0.107254 | 0.379991 | 3.542911 | 0.282254 | 6 |
| 7 | 3.092182 | 11.955326 | 0.083645 | 0.323396 | 3.866307 | 0.258645 | 7 |
| 8 | 3.633314 | 15.047509 | 0.066456 | 0.275231 | 4.141538 | 0.241456 | 8 |
| 9 | 4.269144 | 18.680823 | 0.053531 | 0.234239 | 4.375777 | 0.228531 | 9 |
| 10 | 5.016244 | 22.949967 | 0.043573 | 0.199352 | 4.575129 | 0.218573 | 10 |
| 11 | 5.894087 | 27.966211 | 0.035757 | 0.169662 | 4.744791 | 0.210757 | 11 |
| 12 | 6.925552 | 33.860298 | 0.029533 | 0.144393 | 4.889184 | 0.204533 | 12 |
| 13 | 8.137524 | 40.785850 | 0.024518 | 0.122888 | 5.012071 | 0.199518 | 13 |
| 14 | 9.561590 | 48.923373 | 0.020440 | 0.104585 | 5.116657 | 0.195440 | 14 |
| 15 | 11.234869 | 58.484964 | 0.017098 | 0.089009 | 5.205665 | 0.192098 | 15 |
| 16 | 13.200971 | 69.719832 | 0.014343 | 0.075752 | 5.281417 | 0.189343 | 16 |
| 17 | 15.511141 | 82.920803 | 0.012060 | 0.064470 | 5.345887 | 0.187060 | 17 |
| 18 | 18.225590 | 98.431944 | 0.010159 | 0.054868 | 5.400755 | 0.185159 | 18 |
| 19 | 21.415068 | 116.657534 | 0.008572 | 0.046696 | 5.447451 | 0.183572 | 19 |
| 20 | 25.162705 | 138.072602 | 0.007243 | 0.039741 | 5.487192 | 0.182243 | 20 |
| 21 | 29.566179 | 163.235307 | 0.006126 | 0.033822 | 5.521015 | 0.181126 | 21 |
| 22 | 34.740260 | 192.801486 | 0.005187 | 0.028785 | 5.549800 | 0.180187 | 22 |
| 23 | 40.819806 | 227.541746 | 0.004395 | 0.024498 | 5.574298 | 0.179395 | 23 |
| 24 | 47.963272 | 268.361552 | 0.003726 | 0.020849 | 5.595147 | 0.178726 | 24 |
| 25 | 56.356844 | 316.324823 | 0.003161 | 0.017744 | 5.612891 | 0.178161 | 25 |
| 26 | 66.219292 | 372.681667 | 0.002683 | 0.015101 | 5.627992 | 0.177683 | 26 |
| 27 | 77.807668 | 438.900959 | 0.002278 | 0.012852 | 5.640845 | 0.177278 | 27 |
| 28 | 91.424010 | 516.708627 | 0.001935 | 0.010938 | 5.651783 | 0.176935 | 28 |
| 29 | 107.423211 | 608.132637 | 0.001644 | 0.009309 | 5.661092 | 0.176644 | 29 |
| 30 | 126.222273 | 715.555848 | 0.001398 | 0.007923 | 5.669014 | 0.176398 | 30 |
| 31 | 148.311171 | 841.778122 | 0.001188 | 0.006743 | 5.675757 | 0.176188 | 31 |
| 32 | 174.265626 | 990.089293 | 0.001010 | 0.005738 | 5.681495 | 0.176010 | 32 |
| 33 | 204.762111 | 1164.354919 | 0.000859 | 0.004884 | 5.686379 | 0.175859 | 33 |
| 34 | 240.595480 | 1369.117030 | 0.000730 | 0.004156 | 5.690535 | 0.175730 | 34 |
| 35 | 282.699689 | 1609.712511 | 0.000621 | 0.003537 | 5.694072 | 0.175621 | 35 |
| 36 | 332.172135 | 1892.412200 | 0.000528 | 0.003010 | 5.697083 | 0.175528 | 36 |
| 37 | 390.302259 | 2224.584335 | 0.000450 | 0.002562 | 5.699645 | 0.175450 | 37 |
| 38 | 458.605154 | 2614.886594 | 0.000382 | 0.002181 | 5.701826 | 0.175382 | 38 |
| 39 | 538.861056 | 3073.491747 | 0.000325 | 0.001856 | 5.703681 | 0.175325 | 39 |
| 40 | 633.161741 | 3612.352803 | 0.000277 | 0.001579 | 5.705261 | 0.175277 | 40 |
| 41 | 743.965045 | 4245.514544 | 0.000236 | 0.001344 | 5.706605 | 0.175236 | 41 |
| 42 | 874.158928 | 4989.479589 | 0.000200 | 0.001144 | 5.707749 | 0.175200 | 42 |
| 43 | 1027.136740 | 5863.638517 | 0.000171 | 0.000974 | 5.708722 | 0.175171 | 43 |
| 44 | 1206.885670 | 6890.775258 | 0.000145 | 0.000829 | 5.709551 | 0.175145 | 44 |
| 45 | 1418.090662 | 8097.660928 | 0.000123 | 0.000705 | 5.710256 | 0.175123 | 45 |
| 46 | 1666.256528 | 9515.751590 | 0.000105 | 0.000600 | 5.710856 | 0.175105 | 46 |
| 47 | 1957.851421 | 11182.008118 | 0.000089 | 0.000511 | 5.711367 | 0.175089 | 47 |
| 48 | 2300.475419 | 13139.859539 | 0.000076 | 0.000435 | 5.711802 | 0.175076 | 48 |
| 49 | 2703.058618 | 15440.334958 | 0.000065 | 0.000370 | 5.712172 | 0.175065 | 49 |
| 50 | 3176.093876 | 18143.393576 | 0.000055 | 0.000315 | 5.712487 | 0.175055 | 50 |

18.00% ANNUAL INTEREST RATE

| | 1<br>Future Value<br>of $1 | 2<br>Future Value<br>Annuity of<br>$1 per Year | 3<br>Sinking<br>Fund<br>Factor | 4<br>Present Value<br>of $1<br>(Reversion) | 5<br>Present Value<br>Annuity of<br>$1 per Year | 6<br>Installment<br>to<br>Amortize $1 | |
|---|---|---|---|---|---|---|---|
| Years | | | | | | | Years |
| 1 | 1.180000 | 1.000000 | 1.000000 | 0.847458 | 0.847458 | 1.180000 | 1 |
| 2 | 1.392400 | 2.180000 | 0.458716 | 0.718184 | 1.565642 | 0.638716 | 2 |
| 3 | 1.643032 | 3.572400 | 0.279924 | 0.608631 | 2.174273 | 0.459924 | 3 |
| 4 | 1.938778 | 5.215432 | 0.191739 | 0.515789 | 2.690062 | 0.371739 | 4 |
| 5 | 2.287758 | 7.154210 | 0.139778 | 0.437109 | 3.127171 | 0.319778 | 5 |
| 6 | 2.699554 | 9.441968 | 0.105910 | 0.370432 | 3.497603 | 0.285910 | 6 |
| 7 | 3.185474 | 12.141522 | 0.082362 | 0.313925 | 3.811528 | 0.262362 | 7 |
| 8 | 3.758859 | 15.326996 | 0.065244 | 0.266038 | 4.077566 | 0.245244 | 8 |
| 9 | 4.435454 | 19.085855 | 0.052395 | 0.225456 | 4.303022 | 0.232395 | 9 |
| 10 | 5.233836 | 23.521309 | 0.042515 | 0.191064 | 4.494086 | 0.222515 | 10 |
| 11 | 6.175926 | 28.755144 | 0.034776 | 0.161919 | 4.656005 | 0.214776 | 11 |
| 12 | 7.287593 | 34.931070 | 0.028628 | 0.137220 | 4.793225 | 0.208628 | 12 |
| 13 | 8.599359 | 42.218663 | 0.023686 | 0.116288 | 4.909513 | 0.203686 | 13 |
| 14 | 10.147244 | 50.818022 | 0.019678 | 0.098549 | 5.008062 | 0.199678 | 14 |
| 15 | 11.973748 | 60.965266 | 0.016403 | 0.083516 | 5.091578 | 0.196403 | 15 |
| 16 | 14.129023 | 72.939014 | 0.013710 | 0.070776 | 5.162354 | 0.193710 | 16 |
| 17 | 16.672247 | 87.068036 | 0.011485 | 0.059980 | 5.222334 | 0.191485 | 17 |
| 18 | 19.673251 | 103.740283 | 0.009639 | 0.050830 | 5.273164 | 0.189639 | 18 |
| 19 | 23.214436 | 123.413534 | 0.008103 | 0.043077 | 5.316241 | 0.188103 | 19 |
| 20 | 27.393035 | 146.627970 | 0.006820 | 0.036506 | 5.352746 | 0.186820 | 20 |
| 21 | 32.323781 | 174.021005 | 0.005746 | 0.030937 | 5.383683 | 0.185746 | 21 |
| 22 | 38.142061 | 206.344785 | 0.004846 | 0.026218 | 5.409901 | 0.184846 | 22 |
| 23 | 45.007632 | 244.486847 | 0.004090 | 0.022218 | 5.432120 | 0.184090 | 23 |
| 24 | 53.109006 | 289.494479 | 0.003454 | 0.018829 | 5.450949 | 0.183454 | 24 |
| 25 | 62.668627 | 342.603486 | 0.002919 | 0.015957 | 5.466906 | 0.182919 | 25 |
| 26 | 73.948980 | 405.272113 | 0.002467 | 0.013523 | 5.480429 | 0.182467 | 26 |
| 27 | 87.259797 | 479.221093 | 0.002087 | 0.011460 | 5.491889 | 0.182087 | 27 |
| 28 | 102.966560 | 566.480890 | 0.001765 | 0.009712 | 5.501601 | 0.181765 | 28 |
| 29 | 121.500541 | 669.447450 | 0.001494 | 0.008230 | 5.509831 | 0.181494 | 29 |
| 30 | 143.370638 | 790.947991 | 0.001264 | 0.006975 | 5.516806 | 0.181264 | 30 |
| 31 | 169.177353 | 934.318630 | 0.001070 | 0.005911 | 5.522717 | 0.181070 | 31 |
| 32 | 199.629277 | 1103.495983 | 0.000906 | 0.005009 | 5.527726 | 0.180906 | 32 |
| 33 | 235.562547 | 1303.125260 | 0.000767 | 0.004245 | 5.531971 | 0.180767 | 33 |
| 34 | 277.963805 | 1538.687807 | 0.000650 | 0.003598 | 5.535569 | 0.180650 | 34 |
| 35 | 327.997290 | 1816.651612 | 0.000550 | 0.003049 | 5.538618 | 0.180550 | 35 |
| 36 | 387.036802 | 2144.648902 | 0.000466 | 0.002584 | 5.541201 | 0.180466 | 36 |
| 37 | 456.703427 | 2531.685705 | 0.000395 | 0.002190 | 5.543391 | 0.180395 | 37 |
| 38 | 538.910044 | 2988.389132 | 0.000335 | 0.001856 | 5.545247 | 0.180335 | 38 |
| 39 | 635.913852 | 3527.299175 | 0.000284 | 0.001573 | 5.546819 | 0.180284 | 39 |
| 40 | 750.378345 | 4163.213027 | 0.000240 | 0.001333 | 5.548152 | 0.180240 | 40 |
| 41 | 885.446447 | 4913.591372 | 0.000204 | 0.001129 | 5.549281 | 0.180204 | 41 |
| 42 | 1044.826807 | 5799.037819 | 0.000172 | 0.000957 | 5.550238 | 0.180172 | 42 |
| 43 | 1232.895633 | 6843.864626 | 0.000146 | 0.000811 | 5.551049 | 0.180146 | 43 |
| 44 | 1454.816847 | 8076.760259 | 0.000124 | 0.000687 | 5.551737 | 0.180124 | 44 |
| 45 | 1716.683879 | 9531.577105 | 0.000105 | 0.000583 | 5.552319 | 0.180105 | 45 |
| 46 | 2025.686977 | 11248.260984 | 0.000089 | 0.000494 | 5.552813 | 0.180089 | 46 |
| 47 | 2390.310633 | 13273.947961 | 0.000075 | 0.000418 | 5.553231 | 0.180075 | 47 |
| 48 | 2820.566547 | 15664.258594 | 0.000064 | 0.000355 | 5.553586 | 0.180064 | 48 |
| 49 | 3328.268525 | 18484.825141 | 0.000054 | 0.000300 | 5.553886 | 0.180054 | 49 |
| 50 | 3927.356860 | 21813.093666 | 0.000046 | 0.000255 | 5.554141 | 0.180046 | 50 |

18.50% ANNUAL INTEREST RATE

| Years | 1<br>Future Value<br>of $1 | 2<br>Future Value<br>Annuity of<br>$1 per Year | 3<br>Sinking<br>Fund<br>Factor | 4<br>Present Value<br>of $1<br>(Reversion) | 5<br>Present Value<br>Annuity of<br>$1 per Year | 6<br>Installment<br>to<br>Amortize $1 | Years |
|---|---|---|---|---|---|---|---|
| 1 | 1.185000 | 1.000000 | 1.000000 | 0.843882 | 0.843882 | 1.185000 | 1 |
| 2 | 1.404225 | 2.185000 | 0.457666 | 0.712137 | 1.556018 | 0.642666 | 2 |
| 3 | 1.664007 | 3.589225 | 0.278612 | 0.600959 | 2.156978 | 0.463612 | 3 |
| 4 | 1.971848 | 5.253232 | 0.190359 | 0.507139 | 2.664116 | 0.375359 | 4 |
| 5 | 2.336640 | 7.225079 | 0.138407 | 0.427965 | 3.092081 | 0.323407 | 5 |
| 6 | 2.768918 | 9.561719 | 0.104584 | 0.361152 | 3.453233 | 0.289584 | 6 |
| 7 | 3.281168 | 12.330637 | 0.081099 | 0.304770 | 3.758003 | 0.266099 | 7 |
| 8 | 3.888184 | 15.611805 | 0.064054 | 0.257189 | 4.015192 | 0.249054 | 8 |
| 9 | 4.607498 | 19.499989 | 0.051282 | 0.217038 | 4.232230 | 0.236282 | 9 |
| 10 | 5.459885 | 24.107487 | 0.041481 | 0.183154 | 4.415384 | 0.226481 | 10 |
| 11 | 6.469964 | 29.567372 | 0.033821 | 0.154560 | 4.569944 | 0.218821 | 11 |
| 12 | 7.666907 | 36.037336 | 0.027749 | 0.130431 | 4.700375 | 0.212749 | 12 |
| 13 | 9.085285 | 43.704243 | 0.022881 | 0.110068 | 4.810443 | 0.207881 | 13 |
| 14 | 10.766063 | 52.789528 | 0.018943 | 0.092884 | 4.903327 | 0.203943 | 14 |
| 15 | 12.757784 | 63.555591 | 0.015734 | 0.078384 | 4.981711 | 0.200734 | 15 |
| 16 | 15.117974 | 76.313375 | 0.013104 | 0.066146 | 5.047857 | 0.198104 | 16 |
| 17 | 17.914800 | 91.431350 | 0.010937 | 0.055820 | 5.103677 | 0.195937 | 17 |
| 18 | 21.229038 | 109.346149 | 0.009145 | 0.047105 | 5.150782 | 0.194145 | 18 |
| 19 | 25.156410 | 130.575187 | 0.007658 | 0.039751 | 5.190534 | 0.192658 | 19 |
| 20 | 29.810345 | 155.731596 | 0.006421 | 0.033545 | 5.224079 | 0.191421 | 20 |
| 21 | 35.325259 | 185.541942 | 0.005390 | 0.028308 | 5.252387 | 0.190390 | 21 |
| 22 | 41.860432 | 220.867201 | 0.004528 | 0.023889 | 5.276276 | 0.189528 | 22 |
| 23 | 49.604612 | 262.727633 | 0.003806 | 0.020159 | 5.296436 | 0.188806 | 23 |
| 24 | 58.781465 | 312.332245 | 0.003202 | 0.017012 | 5.313448 | 0.188202 | 24 |
| 25 | 69.656036 | 371.113710 | 0.002695 | 0.014356 | 5.327804 | 0.187695 | 25 |
| 26 | 82.542403 | 440.769747 | 0.002269 | 0.012115 | 5.339919 | 0.187269 | 26 |
| 27 | 97.812748 | 523.312150 | 0.001911 | 0.010224 | 5.350143 | 0.186911 | 27 |
| 28 | 115.908106 | 621.124898 | 0.001610 | 0.008628 | 5.358770 | 0.186610 | 28 |
| 29 | 137.351106 | 737.033004 | 0.001357 | 0.007281 | 5.366051 | 0.186357 | 29 |
| 30 | 162.761060 | 874.384110 | 0.001144 | 0.006144 | 5.372195 | 0.186144 | 30 |
| 31 | 192.871856 | 1037.145170 | 0.000964 | 0.005185 | 5.377380 | 0.185964 | 31 |
| 32 | 228.553150 | 1230.017026 | 0.000813 | 0.004375 | 5.381755 | 0.185813 | 32 |
| 33 | 270.835483 | 1458.570176 | 0.000686 | 0.003692 | 5.385447 | 0.185686 | 33 |
| 34 | 320.940047 | 1729.405659 | 0.000578 | 0.003116 | 5.388563 | 0.185578 | 34 |
| 35 | 380.313956 | 2050.345706 | 0.000488 | 0.002629 | 5.391192 | 0.185488 | 35 |
| 36 | 450.672037 | 2430.659662 | 0.000411 | 0.002219 | 5.393411 | 0.185411 | 36 |
| 37 | 534.046364 | 2881.331699 | 0.000347 | 0.001872 | 5.395284 | 0.185347 | 37 |
| 38 | 632.844942 | 3415.378063 | 0.000293 | 0.001580 | 5.396864 | 0.185293 | 38 |
| 39 | 749.921256 | 4048.223005 | 0.000247 | 0.001333 | 5.398197 | 0.185247 | 39 |
| 40 | 888.656688 | 4798.144261 | 0.000208 | 0.001125 | 5.399323 | 0.185208 | 40 |
| 41 | 1053.058176 | 5686.800949 | 0.000176 | 0.000950 | 5.400272 | 0.185176 | 41 |
| 42 | 1247.873938 | 6739.859125 | 0.000148 | 0.000801 | 5.401074 | 0.185148 | 42 |
| 43 | 1478.730617 | 7987.733063 | 0.000125 | 0.000676 | 5.401750 | 0.185125 | 43 |
| 44 | 1752.295781 | 9466.463679 | 0.000106 | 0.000571 | 5.402321 | 0.185106 | 44 |
| 45 | 2076.470500 | 11218.759460 | 0.000089 | 0.000482 | 5.402802 | 0.185089 | 45 |
| 46 | 2460.617543 | 13295.229960 | 0.000075 | 0.000406 | 5.403209 | 0.185075 | 46 |
| 47 | 2915.831788 | 15755.847503 | 0.000063 | 0.000343 | 5.403552 | 0.185063 | 47 |
| 48 | 3455.260669 | 18671.679291 | 0.000054 | 0.000289 | 5.403841 | 0.185054 | 48 |
| 49 | 4094.483893 | 22126.939959 | 0.000045 | 0.000244 | 5.404085 | 0.185045 | 49 |
| 50 | 4851.963413 | 26221.423852 | 0.000038 | 0.000206 | 5.404291 | 0.185038 | 50 |

19.00% ANNUAL INTEREST RATE

| | 1<br>Future Value<br>of $1 | 2<br>Future Value<br>Annuity of<br>$1 per Year | 3<br>Sinking<br>Fund<br>Factor | 4<br>Present Value<br>of $1<br>(Reversion) | 5<br>Present Value<br>Annuity of<br>$1 per Year | 6<br>Installment<br>to<br>Amortize $1 | |
|---|---|---|---|---|---|---|---|
| Years | | | | | | | Years |
| 1 | 1.190000 | 1.000000 | 1.000000 | 0.840336 | 0.840336 | 1.190000 | 1 |
| 2 | 1.416100 | 2.190000 | 0.456621 | 0.706165 | 1.546501 | 0.646621 | 2 |
| 3 | 1.685159 | 3.606100 | 0.277308 | 0.593416 | 2.139917 | 0.467308 | 3 |
| 4 | 2.005339 | 5.291259 | 0.188991 | 0.498669 | 2.638586 | 0.378991 | 4 |
| 5 | 2.386354 | 7.296598 | 0.137050 | 0.419049 | 3.057635 | 0.327050 | 5 |
| 6 | 2.839761 | 9.682952 | 0.103274 | 0.352142 | 3.409777 | 0.293274 | 6 |
| 7 | 3.379315 | 12.522713 | 0.079855 | 0.295918 | 3.705695 | 0.269855 | 7 |
| 8 | 4.021385 | 15.902028 | 0.062885 | 0.248671 | 3.954366 | 0.252885 | 8 |
| 9 | 4.785449 | 19.923413 | 0.050192 | 0.208967 | 4.163332 | 0.240192 | 9 |
| 10 | 5.694684 | 24.708862 | 0.040471 | 0.175602 | 4.338935 | 0.230471 | 10 |
| 11 | 6.776674 | 30.403546 | 0.032891 | 0.147565 | 4.486500 | 0.222891 | 11 |
| 12 | 8.064242 | 37.180220 | 0.026896 | 0.124004 | 4.610504 | 0.216896 | 12 |
| 13 | 9.596448 | 45.244461 | 0.022102 | 0.104205 | 4.714709 | 0.212102 | 13 |
| 14 | 11.419773 | 54.840909 | 0.018235 | 0.087567 | 4.802277 | 0.208235 | 14 |
| 15 | 13.589530 | 66.260682 | 0.015092 | 0.073586 | 4.875863 | 0.205092 | 15 |
| 16 | 16.171540 | 79.850211 | 0.012523 | 0.061837 | 4.937700 | 0.202523 | 16 |
| 17 | 19.244133 | 96.021751 | 0.010414 | 0.051964 | 4.989664 | 0.200414 | 17 |
| 18 | 22.900518 | 115.265884 | 0.008676 | 0.043667 | 5.033331 | 0.198676 | 18 |
| 19 | 27.251616 | 138.166402 | 0.007238 | 0.036695 | 5.070026 | 0.197238 | 19 |
| 20 | 32.429423 | 165.418018 | 0.006045 | 0.030836 | 5.100862 | 0.196045 | 20 |
| 21 | 38.591014 | 197.847442 | 0.005054 | 0.025913 | 5.126775 | 0.195054 | 21 |
| 22 | 45.923307 | 236.438456 | 0.004229 | 0.021775 | 5.148550 | 0.194229 | 22 |
| 23 | 54.648735 | 282.361762 | 0.003542 | 0.018299 | 5.166849 | 0.193542 | 23 |
| 24 | 65.031994 | 337.010497 | 0.002967 | 0.015377 | 5.182226 | 0.192967 | 24 |
| 25 | 77.388073 | 402.042491 | 0.002487 | 0.012922 | 5.195148 | 0.192487 | 25 |
| 26 | 92.091807 | 479.430565 | 0.002086 | 0.010859 | 5.206007 | 0.192086 | 26 |
| 27 | 109.589251 | 571.522372 | 0.001750 | 0.009125 | 5.215132 | 0.191750 | 27 |
| 28 | 130.411208 | 681.111623 | 0.001468 | 0.007668 | 5.222800 | 0.191468 | 28 |
| 29 | 155.189338 | 811.522831 | 0.001232 | 0.006444 | 5.229243 | 0.191232 | 29 |
| 30 | 184.675312 | 966.712169 | 0.001034 | 0.005415 | 5.234658 | 0.191034 | 30 |
| 31 | 219.763621 | 1151.387481 | 0.000869 | 0.004550 | 5.239209 | 0.190869 | 31 |
| 32 | 261.518710 | 1371.151103 | 0.000729 | 0.003824 | 5.243033 | 0.190729 | 32 |
| 33 | 311.207264 | 1632.669812 | 0.000612 | 0.003213 | 5.246246 | 0.190612 | 33 |
| 34 | 370.336645 | 1943.877077 | 0.000514 | 0.002700 | 5.248946 | 0.190514 | 34 |
| 35 | 440.700607 | 2314.213721 | 0.000432 | 0.002269 | 5.251215 | 0.190432 | 35 |
| 36 | 524.433722 | 2754.914328 | 0.000363 | 0.001907 | 5.253122 | 0.190363 | 36 |
| 37 | 624.076130 | 3279.348051 | 0.000305 | 0.001602 | 5.254724 | 0.190305 | 37 |
| 38 | 742.650594 | 3903.424180 | 0.000256 | 0.001347 | 5.256071 | 0.190256 | 38 |
| 39 | 883.754207 | 4646.074775 | 0.000215 | 0.001132 | 5.257202 | 0.190215 | 39 |
| 40 | 1051.667507 | 5529.828982 | 0.000181 | 0.000951 | 5.258153 | 0.190181 | 40 |
| 41 | 1251.484333 | 6581.496488 | 0.000152 | 0.000799 | 5.258952 | 0.190152 | 41 |
| 42 | 1489.266356 | 7832.980821 | 0.000128 | 0.000671 | 5.259624 | 0.190128 | 42 |
| 43 | 1772.226964 | 9322.247177 | 0.000107 | 0.000564 | 5.260188 | 0.190107 | 43 |
| 44 | 2108.950087 | 11094.474141 | 0.000090 | 0.000474 | 5.260662 | 0.190090 | 44 |
| 45 | 2509.650603 | 13203.424228 | 0.000076 | 0.000398 | 5.261061 | 0.190076 | 45 |
| 46 | 2986.484218 | 15713.074831 | 0.000064 | 0.000335 | 5.261396 | 0.190064 | 46 |
| 47 | 3553.916219 | 18699.559049 | 0.000053 | 0.000281 | 5.261677 | 0.190053 | 47 |
| 48 | 4229.160301 | 22253.475268 | 0.000045 | 0.000236 | 5.261913 | 0.190045 | 48 |
| 49 | 5032.700758 | 26482.635569 | 0.000038 | 0.000199 | 5.262112 | 0.190038 | 49 |
| 50 | 5988.913902 | 31515.336327 | 0.000032 | 0.000167 | 5.262279 | 0.190032 | 50 |

19.50% ANNUAL INTEREST RATE

| | 1<br>Future Value<br>of $1 | 2<br>Future Value<br>Annuity of<br>$1 per Year | 3<br>Sinking<br>Fund<br>Factor | 4<br>Present Value<br>of $1<br>(Reversion) | 5<br>Present Value<br>Annuity of<br>$1 per Year | 6<br>Installment<br>to<br>Amortize $1 | |
|---|---|---|---|---|---|---|---|
| Years | | | | | | | Years |
| 1 | 1.195000 | 1.000000 | 1.000000 | 0.836820 | 0.836820 | 1.195000 | 1 |
| 2 | 1.428025 | 2.195000 | 0.455581 | 0.700268 | 1.537088 | 0.650581 | 2 |
| 3 | 1.706490 | 3.623025 | 0.276012 | 0.585998 | 2.123086 | 0.471012 | 3 |
| 4 | 2.039255 | 5.329515 | 0.187634 | 0.490375 | 2.613461 | 0.382634 | 4 |
| 5 | 2.436910 | 7.368770 | 0.135708 | 0.410356 | 3.023817 | 0.330708 | 5 |
| 6 | 2.912108 | 9.805680 | 0.101982 | 0.343394 | 3.367211 | 0.296982 | 6 |
| 7 | 3.479969 | 12.717788 | 0.078630 | 0.287359 | 3.654570 | 0.273630 | 7 |
| 8 | 4.158563 | 16.197757 | 0.061737 | 0.240468 | 3.895037 | 0.256737 | 8 |
| 9 | 4.969482 | 20.356319 | 0.049125 | 0.201228 | 4.096266 | 0.244125 | 9 |
| 10 | 5.938531 | 25.325802 | 0.039485 | 0.168392 | 4.264657 | 0.234485 | 10 |
| 11 | 7.096545 | 31.264333 | 0.031985 | 0.140914 | 4.405571 | 0.226985 | 11 |
| 12 | 8.480371 | 38.360878 | 0.026068 | 0.117919 | 4.523490 | 0.221068 | 12 |
| 13 | 10.134044 | 46.841249 | 0.021349 | 0.098677 | 4.622168 | 0.216349 | 13 |
| 14 | 12.110182 | 56.975293 | 0.017551 | 0.082575 | 4.704743 | 0.212551 | 14 |
| 15 | 14.471668 | 69.085475 | 0.014475 | 0.069101 | 4.773843 | 0.209475 | 15 |
| 16 | 17.293643 | 83.557143 | 0.011968 | 0.057825 | 4.831668 | 0.206968 | 16 |
| 17 | 20.665903 | 100.850785 | 0.009916 | 0.048389 | 4.880057 | 0.204916 | 17 |
| 18 | 24.695754 | 121.516689 | 0.008229 | 0.040493 | 4.920550 | 0.203229 | 18 |
| 19 | 29.511426 | 146.212443 | 0.006839 | 0.033885 | 4.954435 | 0.201839 | 19 |
| 20 | 35.266154 | 175.723869 | 0.005691 | 0.028356 | 4.982791 | 0.200691 | 20 |
| 21 | 42.143055 | 210.990024 | 0.004740 | 0.023729 | 5.006519 | 0.199740 | 21 |
| 22 | 50.360950 | 253.133078 | 0.003950 | 0.019857 | 5.026376 | 0.198950 | 22 |
| 23 | 60.181336 | 303.494029 | 0.003295 | 0.016616 | 5.042993 | 0.198295 | 23 |
| 24 | 71.916696 | 363.675364 | 0.002750 | 0.013905 | 5.056898 | 0.197750 | 24 |
| 25 | 85.940452 | 435.592060 | 0.002296 | 0.011636 | 5.068534 | 0.197296 | 25 |
| 26 | 102.698840 | 521.532512 | 0.001917 | 0.009737 | 5.078271 | 0.196917 | 26 |
| 27 | 122.725114 | 624.231352 | 0.001602 | 0.008148 | 5.086419 | 0.196602 | 27 |
| 28 | 146.656511 | 746.956465 | 0.001339 | 0.006819 | 5.093238 | 0.196339 | 28 |
| 29 | 175.254530 | 893.612976 | 0.001119 | 0.005706 | 5.098944 | 0.196119 | 29 |
| 30 | 209.429164 | 1068.867506 | 0.000936 | 0.004775 | 5.103719 | 0.195936 | 30 |
| 31 | 250.267851 | 1278.296670 | 0.000782 | 0.003996 | 5.107714 | 0.195782 | 31 |
| 32 | 299.070082 | 1528.564521 | 0.000654 | 0.003344 | 5.111058 | 0.195654 | 32 |
| 33 | 357.388747 | 1827.634602 | 0.000547 | 0.002798 | 5.113856 | 0.195547 | 33 |
| 34 | 427.079553 | 2185.023350 | 0.000458 | 0.002341 | 5.116198 | 0.195458 | 34 |
| 35 | 510.360066 | 2612.102903 | 0.000383 | 0.001959 | 5.118157 | 0.195383 | 35 |
| 36 | 609.880279 | 3122.462969 | 0.000320 | 0.001640 | 5.119797 | 0.195320 | 36 |
| 37 | 728.806933 | 3732.343248 | 0.000268 | 0.001372 | 5.121169 | 0.195268 | 37 |
| 38 | 870.924285 | 4461.150181 | 0.000224 | 0.001148 | 5.122317 | 0.195224 | 38 |
| 39 | 1040.754521 | 5332.074466 | 0.000188 | 0.000961 | 5.123278 | 0.195188 | 39 |
| 40 | 1243.701652 | 6372.828987 | 0.000157 | 0.000804 | 5.124082 | 0.195157 | 40 |
| 41 | 1486.223475 | 7616.530640 | 0.000131 | 0.000673 | 5.124755 | 0.195131 | 41 |
| 42 | 1776.037052 | 9102.754114 | 0.000110 | 0.000563 | 5.125318 | 0.195110 | 42 |
| 43 | 2122.364277 | 10878.791167 | 0.000092 | 0.000471 | 5.125789 | 0.195092 | 43 |
| 44 | 2536.225312 | 13001.155444 | 0.000077 | 0.000394 | 5.126183 | 0.195077 | 44 |
| 45 | 3030.789247 | 15537.380756 | 0.000064 | 0.000330 | 5.126513 | 0.195064 | 45 |
| 46 | 3621.793151 | 18568.170003 | 0.000054 | 0.000276 | 5.126789 | 0.195054 | 46 |
| 47 | 4328.042815 | 22189.963154 | 0.000045 | 0.000231 | 5.127020 | 0.195045 | 47 |
| 48 | 5172.011164 | 26518.005968 | 0.000038 | 0.000193 | 5.127214 | 0.195038 | 48 |
| 49 | 6180.553341 | 31690.017132 | 0.000032 | 0.000162 | 5.127375 | 0.195032 | 49 |
| 50 | 7385.761242 | 37870.570473 | 0.000026 | 0.000135 | 5.127511 | 0.195026 | 50 |

20.00% ANNUAL INTEREST RATE

| | 1 Future Value of $1 | 2 Future Value Annuity of $1 per Year | 3 Sinking Fund Factor | 4 Present Value of $1 (Reversion) | 5 Present Value Annuity of $1 per Year | 6 Installment to Amortize $1 | |
|---|---|---|---|---|---|---|---|
| Years | | | | | | | Years |
| 1 | 1.200000 | 1.000000 | 1.000000 | 0.833333 | 0.833333 | 1.200000 | 1 |
| 2 | 1.440000 | 2.200000 | 0.454545 | 0.694444 | 1.527778 | 0.654545 | 2 |
| 3 | 1.728000 | 3.640000 | 0.274725 | 0.578704 | 2.106481 | 0.474725 | 3 |
| 4 | 2.073600 | 5.368000 | 0.186289 | 0.482253 | 2.588735 | 0.386289 | 4 |
| 5 | 2.488320 | 7.441600 | 0.134380 | 0.401878 | 2.990612 | 0.334380 | 5 |
| 6 | 2.985984 | 9.929920 | 0.100706 | 0.334898 | 3.325510 | 0.300706 | 6 |
| 7 | 3.583181 | 12.915904 | 0.077424 | 0.279082 | 3.604592 | 0.277424 | 7 |
| 8 | 4.299817 | 16.499085 | 0.060609 | 0.232568 | 3.837160 | 0.260609 | 8 |
| 9 | 5.159780 | 20.798902 | 0.048079 | 0.193807 | 4.030967 | 0.248079 | 9 |
| 10 | 6.191736 | 25.958682 | 0.038523 | 0.161506 | 4.192472 | 0.238523 | 10 |
| 11 | 7.430084 | 32.150419 | 0.031104 | 0.134588 | 4.327060 | 0.231104 | 11 |
| 12 | 8.916100 | 39.580502 | 0.025265 | 0.112157 | 4.439217 | 0.225265 | 12 |
| 13 | 10.699321 | 48.496603 | 0.020620 | 0.093464 | 4.532681 | 0.220620 | 13 |
| 14 | 12.839185 | 59.195923 | 0.016893 | 0.077887 | 4.610567 | 0.216893 | 14 |
| 15 | 15.407022 | 72.035108 | 0.013882 | 0.064905 | 4.675473 | 0.213882 | 15 |
| 16 | 18.488426 | 87.442129 | 0.011436 | 0.054088 | 4.729561 | 0.211436 | 16 |
| 17 | 22.186111 | 105.930555 | 0.009440 | 0.045073 | 4.774634 | 0.209440 | 17 |
| 18 | 26.623333 | 128.116666 | 0.007805 | 0.037561 | 4.812195 | 0.207805 | 18 |
| 19 | 31.948000 | 154.740000 | 0.006462 | 0.031301 | 4.843496 | 0.206462 | 19 |
| 20 | 38.337600 | 186.688000 | 0.005357 | 0.026084 | 4.869580 | 0.205357 | 20 |
| 21 | 44.005120 | 225.025600 | 0.004444 | 0.021737 | 4.891316 | 0.204444 | 21 |
| 22 | 55.206144 | 271.030719 | 0.003690 | 0.018114 | 4.909430 | 0.203690 | 22 |
| 23 | 66.247373 | 326.236863 | 0.003065 | 0.015095 | 4.924525 | 0.203065 | 23 |
| 24 | 79.496847 | 392.484236 | 0.002548 | 0.012579 | 4.937104 | 0.202548 | 24 |
| 25 | 95.396217 | 471.981083 | 0.002119 | 0.010483 | 4.947587 | 0.202119 | 25 |
| 26 | 114.475460 | 567.377300 | 0.001762 | 0.008735 | 4.956323 | 0.201762 | 26 |
| 27 | 137.370552 | 681.852760 | 0.001467 | 0.007280 | 4.963602 | 0.201467 | 27 |
| 28 | 164.844662 | 819.223312 | 0.001221 | 0.006066 | 4.969668 | 0.201221 | 28 |
| 29 | 197.813595 | 984.067974 | 0.001016 | 0.005055 | 4.974724 | 0.201016 | 29 |
| 30 | 237.376314 | 1181.881569 | 0.000846 | 0.004213 | 4.978936 | 0.200846 | 30 |
| 31 | 284.851577 | 1419.257883 | 0.000705 | 0.003511 | 4.982447 | 0.200705 | 31 |
| 32 | 341.821892 | 1704.109459 | 0.000587 | 0.002926 | 4.985372 | 0.200587 | 32 |
| 33 | 410.186270 | 2045.931351 | 0.000489 | 0.002438 | 4.987810 | 0.200489 | 33 |
| 34 | 492.223524 | 2456.117621 | 0.000407 | 0.002032 | 4.989842 | 0.200407 | 34 |
| 35 | 590.668229 | 2948.341146 | 0.000339 | 0.001693 | 4.991535 | 0.200339 | 35 |
| 36 | 708.801875 | 3539.009375 | 0.000283 | 0.001411 | 4.992946 | 0.200283 | 36 |
| 37 | 850.562250 | 4247.811250 | 0.000235 | 0.001176 | 4.994122 | 0.200235 | 37 |
| 38 | 1020.674700 | 5098.373500 | 0.000196 | 0.000980 | 4.995101 | 0.200196 | 38 |
| 39 | 1224.809640 | 6119.048200 | 0.000163 | 0.000816 | 4.995918 | 0.200163 | 39 |
| 40 | 1469.771568 | 7343.857840 | 0.000136 | 0.000680 | 4.996598 | 0.200136 | 40 |
| 41 | 1763.725882 | 8813.629408 | 0.000113 | 0.000567 | 4.997165 | 0.200113 | 41 |
| 42 | 2116.471058 | 10577.355289 | 0.000095 | 0.000472 | 4.997638 | 0.200095 | 42 |
| 43 | 2539.765269 | 12693.826347 | 0.000079 | 0.000394 | 4.998031 | 0.200079 | 43 |
| 44 | 3047.718323 | 15233.591617 | 0.000066 | 0.000328 | 4.998359 | 0.200066 | 44 |
| 45 | 3657.261988 | 18281.309940 | 0.000055 | 0.000273 | 4.998633 | 0.200055 | 45 |
| 46 | 4388.714386 | 21938.571928 | 0.000046 | 0.000228 | 4.998861 | 0.200046 | 46 |
| 47 | 5266.457263 | 26327.286314 | 0.000038 | 0.000190 | 4.999051 | 0.200038 | 47 |
| 48 | 6319.748715 | 31593.743576 | 0.000032 | 0.000158 | 4.999209 | 0.200032 | 48 |
| 49 | 7583.698458 | 37913.492292 | 0.000026 | 0.000132 | 4.999341 | 0.200026 | 49 |
| 50 | 9100.438150 | 45497.190750 | 0.000022 | 0.000110 | 4.999451 | 0.200022 | 50 |

20.50% ANNUAL INTEREST RATE

| | 1<br>Future Value<br>of $1 | 2<br>Future Value<br>Annuity of<br>$1 per Year | 3<br>Sinking<br>Fund<br>Factor | 4<br>Present Value<br>of $1<br>(Reversion) | 5<br>Present Value<br>Annuity of<br>$1 per Year | 6<br>Installment<br>to<br>Amortize $1 | |
|---|---|---|---|---|---|---|---|
| Years | | | | | | | Years |
| 1 | 1.205000 | 1.000000 | 1.000000 | 0.829876 | 0.829876 | 1.205000 | 1 |
| 2 | 1.452025 | 2.205000 | 0.453515 | 0.688693 | 1.518569 | 0.658515 | 2 |
| 3 | 1.749690 | 3.657025 | 0.273446 | 0.571530 | 2.090099 | 0.478446 | 3 |
| 4 | 2.108377 | 5.406715 | 0.184955 | 0.474299 | 2.564397 | 0.389955 | 4 |
| 5 | 2.540594 | 7.515092 | 0.133066 | 0.393609 | 2.958006 | 0.338066 | 5 |
| 6 | 3.061416 | 10.055686 | 0.099446 | 0.326646 | 3.284652 | 0.304446 | 6 |
| 7 | 3.689006 | 13.117101 | 0.076236 | 0.271076 | 3.555728 | 0.281236 | 7 |
| 8 | 4.445252 | 16.806107 | 0.059502 | 0.224959 | 3.780687 | 0.264502 | 8 |
| 9 | 5.356529 | 21.251359 | 0.047056 | 0.186688 | 3.967375 | 0.252056 | 9 |
| 10 | 6.454617 | 26.607887 | 0.037583 | 0.154928 | 4.122303 | 0.242583 | 10 |
| 11 | 7.777813 | 33.062504 | 0.030246 | 0.128571 | 4.250874 | 0.235246 | 11 |
| 12 | 9.372265 | 40.840317 | 0.024486 | 0.106698 | 4.357572 | 0.229486 | 12 |
| 13 | 11.293579 | 50.212582 | 0.019915 | 0.088546 | 4.446118 | 0.224915 | 13 |
| 14 | 13.608763 | 61.506162 | 0.016259 | 0.073482 | 4.519600 | 0.221259 | 14 |
| 15 | 16.398560 | 75.114925 | 0.013313 | 0.060981 | 4.580581 | 0.218313 | 15 |
| 16 | 19.760264 | 91.513485 | 0.010927 | 0.050607 | 4.631187 | 0.215927 | 16 |
| 17 | 23.811119 | 111.273749 | 0.008987 | 0.041997 | 4.673184 | 0.213987 | 17 |
| 18 | 28.692398 | 135.084868 | 0.007403 | 0.034852 | 4.708037 | 0.212403 | 18 |
| 19 | 34.574339 | 163.777266 | 0.006106 | 0.028923 | 4.736960 | 0.211106 | 19 |
| 20 | 41.662079 | 198.351605 | 0.005042 | 0.024003 | 4.760963 | 0.210042 | 20 |
| 21 | 50.202805 | 240.013684 | 0.004166 | 0.019919 | 4.780882 | 0.209166 | 21 |
| 22 | 60.494380 | 290.216489 | 0.003446 | 0.016530 | 4.797412 | 0.208446 | 22 |
| 23 | 72.895728 | 350.710869 | 0.002851 | 0.013718 | 4.811131 | 0.207851 | 23 |
| 24 | 87.839353 | 423.606598 | 0.002361 | 0.011384 | 4.822515 | 0.207361 | 24 |
| 25 | 105.846420 | 511.445950 | 0.001955 | 0.009448 | 4.831963 | 0.206955 | 25 |
| 26 | 127.544936 | 617.292370 | 0.001620 | 0.007840 | 4.839803 | 0.206620 | 26 |
| 27 | 153.691648 | 744.837306 | 0.001343 | 0.006507 | 4.846310 | 0.206343 | 27 |
| 28 | 185.198435 | 898.528954 | 0.001113 | 0.005400 | 4.851709 | 0.206113 | 28 |
| 29 | 223.164115 | 1083.727389 | 0.000923 | 0.004481 | 4.856190 | 0.205923 | 29 |
| 30 | 268.912758 | 1306.891504 | 0.000765 | 0.003719 | 4.859909 | 0.205765 | 30 |
| 31 | 324.039874 | 1575.804262 | 0.000635 | 0.003086 | 4.862995 | 0.205635 | 31 |
| 32 | 390.468048 | 1899.844136 | 0.000526 | 0.002561 | 4.865556 | 0.205526 | 32 |
| 33 | 470.513998 | 2290.312184 | 0.000437 | 0.002125 | 4.867681 | 0.205437 | 33 |
| 34 | 566.969367 | 2760.826181 | 0.000362 | 0.001764 | 4.869445 | 0.205362 | 34 |
| 35 | 683.198087 | 3327.795548 | 0.000300 | 0.001464 | 4.870909 | 0.205300 | 35 |
| 36 | 823.253695 | 4010.993636 | 0.000249 | 0.001215 | 4.872123 | 0.205249 | 36 |
| 37 | 992.020703 | 4834.247331 | 0.000207 | 0.001008 | 4.873131 | 0.205207 | 37 |
| 38 | 1195.384947 | 5826.268034 | 0.000172 | 0.000837 | 4.873968 | 0.205172 | 38 |
| 39 | 1440.438861 | 7021.652981 | 0.000142 | 0.000694 | 4.874662 | 0.205142 | 39 |
| 40 | 1735.728828 | 8462.091842 | 0.000118 | 0.000576 | 4.875238 | 0.205118 | 40 |
| 41 | 2091.553237 | 10197.820669 | 0.000098 | 0.000478 | 4.875717 | 0.205098 | 41 |
| 42 | 2520.321651 | 12289.373907 | 0.000081 | 0.000397 | 4.876113 | 0.205081 | 42 |
| 43 | 3036.987589 | 14809.695557 | 0.000068 | 0.000329 | 4.876443 | 0.205068 | 43 |
| 44 | 3659.570045 | 17846.683147 | 0.000056 | 0.000273 | 4.876716 | 0.205056 | 44 |
| 45 | 4409.781904 | 21506.253192 | 0.000046 | 0.000227 | 4.876943 | 0.205046 | 45 |
| 46 | 5313.787195 | 25916.035096 | 0.000039 | 0.000188 | 4.877131 | 0.205039 | 46 |
| 47 | 6403.113570 | 31229.822291 | 0.000032 | 0.000156 | 4.877287 | 0.205032 | 47 |
| 48 | 7715.751851 | 37632.935861 | 0.000027 | 0.000130 | 4.877417 | 0.205027 | 48 |
| 49 | 9297.480981 | 45348.687712 | 0.000022 | 0.000108 | 4.877524 | 0.205022 | 49 |
| 50 | 11203.464582 | 54646.168693 | 0.000018 | 0.000089 | 4.877613 | 0.205018 | 50 |

21.00% ANNUAL INTEREST RATE

| | 1<br>Future Value<br>of $1 | 2<br>Future Value<br>Annuity of<br>$1 per Year | 3<br>Sinking<br>Fund<br>Factor | 4<br>Present Value<br>of $1<br>(Reversion) | 5<br>Present Value<br>Annuity of<br>$1 per Year | 6<br>Installment<br>to<br>Amortize $1 | |
|---|---|---|---|---|---|---|---|
| Years | | | | | | | Years |
| 1 | 1.210000 | 1.000000 | 1.000000 | 0.826446 | 0.826446 | 1.210000 | 1 |
| 2 | 1.464100 | 2.210000 | 0.452489 | 0.683013 | 1.509460 | 0.662489 | 2 |
| 3 | 1.771561 | 3.674100 | 0.272175 | 0.564474 | 2.073934 | 0.482175 | 3 |
| 4 | 2.143589 | 5.445661 | 0.183632 | 0.466507 | 2.540441 | 0.393632 | 4 |
| 5 | 2.593742 | 7.589250 | 0.131765 | 0.385543 | 2.925984 | 0.341765 | 5 |
| 6 | 3.138428 | 10.182992 | 0.098203 | 0.318631 | 3.244615 | 0.308203 | 6 |
| 7 | 3.797498 | 13.321421 | 0.075067 | 0.263331 | 3.507946 | 0.285067 | 7 |
| 8 | 4.594973 | 17.118919 | 0.058415 | 0.217629 | 3.725576 | 0.268415 | 8 |
| 9 | 5.559917 | 21.713892 | 0.046053 | 0.179859 | 3.905434 | 0.256053 | 9 |
| 10 | 6.727500 | 27.273809 | 0.036665 | 0.148644 | 4.054078 | 0.246665 | 10 |
| 11 | 8.140275 | 34.001309 | 0.029411 | 0.122846 | 4.176924 | 0.239411 | 11 |
| 12 | 9.849733 | 42.141584 | 0.023730 | 0.101526 | 4.278450 | 0.233730 | 12 |
| 13 | 11.918177 | 51.991317 | 0.019234 | 0.083905 | 4.362355 | 0.229234 | 13 |
| 14 | 14.420994 | 63.909493 | 0.015647 | 0.069343 | 4.431698 | 0.225647 | 14 |
| 15 | 17.449402 | 78.330487 | 0.012766 | 0.057309 | 4.489007 | 0.222766 | 15 |
| 16 | 21.113777 | 95.779889 | 0.010441 | 0.047362 | 4.536369 | 0.220441 | 16 |
| 17 | 25.547670 | 116.893666 | 0.008555 | 0.039143 | 4.575512 | 0.218555 | 17 |
| 18 | 30.912681 | 142.441336 | 0.007020 | 0.032349 | 4.607861 | 0.217020 | 18 |
| 19 | 37.404343 | 173.354016 | 0.005769 | 0.026735 | 4.634596 | 0.215769 | 19 |
| 20 | 45.259256 | 210.758360 | 0.004745 | 0.022095 | 4.656691 | 0.214745 | 20 |
| 21 | 54.763699 | 256.017615 | 0.003906 | 0.018260 | 4.674951 | 0.213906 | 21 |
| 22 | 66.264076 | 310.781315 | 0.003218 | 0.015091 | 4.690042 | 0.213218 | 22 |
| 23 | 80.179532 | 377.045391 | 0.002652 | 0.012472 | 4.702514 | 0.212652 | 23 |
| 24 | 97.017234 | 457.224923 | 0.002187 | 0.010307 | 4.712822 | 0.212187 | 24 |
| 25 | 117.390853 | 554.242157 | 0.001804 | 0.008519 | 4.721340 | 0.211804 | 25 |
| 26 | 142.042932 | 671.633009 | 0.001489 | 0.007040 | 4.728380 | 0.211489 | 26 |
| 27 | 171.871948 | 813.675941 | 0.001229 | 0.005818 | 4.734199 | 0.211229 | 27 |
| 28 | 207.965057 | 985.547889 | 0.001015 | 0.004809 | 4.739007 | 0.211015 | 28 |
| 29 | 251.637719 | 1193.512946 | 0.000838 | 0.003974 | 4.742981 | 0.210838 | 29 |
| 30 | 304.481640 | 1445.150664 | 0.000692 | 0.003284 | 4.746265 | 0.210692 | 30 |
| 31 | 368.422784 | 1749.632304 | 0.000572 | 0.002714 | 4.748980 | 0.210572 | 31 |
| 32 | 445.791568 | 2118.055088 | 0.000472 | 0.002243 | 4.751223 | 0.210472 | 32 |
| 33 | 539.407798 | 2563.846656 | 0.000390 | 0.001854 | 4.753077 | 0.210390 | 33 |
| 34 | 652.683435 | 3103.254454 | 0.000322 | 0.001532 | 4.754609 | 0.210322 | 34 |
| 35 | 789.746957 | 3755.937890 | 0.000266 | 0.001266 | 4.755875 | 0.210266 | 35 |
| 36 | 955.593818 | 4545.684846 | 0.000220 | 0.001046 | 4.756922 | 0.210220 | 36 |
| 37 | 1156.268519 | 5501.278664 | 0.000182 | 0.000865 | 4.757786 | 0.210182 | 37 |
| 38 | 1399.084909 | 6657.547183 | 0.000150 | 0.000715 | 4.758501 | 0.210150 | 38 |
| 39 | 1692.892739 | 8056.632092 | 0.000124 | 0.000591 | 4.759092 | 0.210124 | 39 |
| 40 | 2048.400215 | 9749.524831 | 0.000103 | 0.000488 | 4.759580 | 0.210103 | 40 |
| 41 | 2478.564260 | 11797.925046 | 0.000085 | 0.000403 | 4.759984 | 0.210085 | 41 |
| 42 | 2999.062754 | 14276.489306 | 0.000070 | 0.000333 | 4.760317 | 0.210070 | 42 |
| 43 | 3628.865933 | 17275.552060 | 0.000058 | 0.000276 | 4.760593 | 0.210058 | 43 |
| 44 | 4390.927778 | 20904.417992 | 0.000048 | 0.000228 | 4.760820 | 0.210048 | 44 |
| 45 | 5313.022612 | 25295.345771 | 0.000040 | 0.000188 | 4.761008 | 0.210040 | 45 |
| 46 | 6428.757360 | 30608.368383 | 0.000033 | 0.000156 | 4.761164 | 0.210033 | 46 |
| 47 | 7778.796406 | 37037.125743 | 0.000027 | 0.000129 | 4.761293 | 0.210027 | 47 |
| 48 | 9412.343651 | 44815.922149 | 0.000022 | 0.000106 | 4.761399 | 0.210022 | 48 |
| 49 | 11388.935818 | 54228.265800 | 0.000018 | 0.000088 | 4.761487 | 0.210018 | 49 |
| 50 | 13780.612340 | 65617.201618 | 0.000015 | 0.000073 | 4.761559 | 0.210015 | 50 |

21.50% ANNUAL INTEREST RATE

| | 1 | 2 | 3 | 4 | 5 | 6 | |
|---|---|---|---|---|---|---|---|
| | Future Value of $1 | Future Value Annuity of $1 per Year | Sinking Fund Factor | Present Value of $1 (Reversion) | Present Value Annuity of $1 per Year | Installment to Amortize $1 | |
| Years | | | | | | | Years |
| 1 | 1.215000 | 1.000000 | 1.000000 | 0.823045 | 0.823045 | 1.215000 | 1 |
| 2 | 1.476225 | 2.215000 | 0.451467 | 0.677404 | 1.500449 | 0.666467 | 2 |
| 3 | 1.793613 | 3.691225 | 0.270913 | 0.557534 | 2.057983 | 0.485913 | 3 |
| 4 | 2.179240 | 5.484838 | 0.182321 | 0.458876 | 2.516858 | 0.397321 | 4 |
| 5 | 2.647777 | 7.664079 | 0.130479 | 0.377675 | 2.894533 | 0.345479 | 5 |
| 6 | 3.217049 | 10.311856 | 0.096976 | 0.310844 | 3.205377 | 0.311976 | 6 |
| 7 | 3.908714 | 13.528904 | 0.073916 | 0.255839 | 3.461216 | 0.288916 | 7 |
| 8 | 4.749088 | 17.437619 | 0.057347 | 0.210567 | 3.671783 | 0.272347 | 8 |
| 9 | 5.770142 | 22.186707 | 0.045072 | 0.173306 | 3.845089 | 0.260072 | 9 |
| 10 | 7.010723 | 27.956849 | 0.035769 | 0.142639 | 3.987727 | 0.250769 | 10 |
| 11 | 8.518028 | 34.967572 | 0.028598 | 0.117398 | 4.105125 | 0.243598 | 11 |
| 12 | 10.349404 | 43.485599 | 0.022996 | 0.096624 | 4.201749 | 0.237996 | 12 |
| 13 | 12.574526 | 53.835003 | 0.018575 | 0.079526 | 4.281275 | 0.233575 | 13 |
| 14 | 15.278049 | 66.409529 | 0.015058 | 0.065453 | 4.346728 | 0.230058 | 14 |
| 15 | 18.562829 | 81.687578 | 0.012242 | 0.053871 | 4.400600 | 0.227242 | 15 |
| 16 | 22.553837 | 100.250407 | 0.009975 | 0.044338 | 4.444938 | 0.224975 | 16 |
| 17 | 27.402913 | 122.804244 | 0.008143 | 0.036492 | 4.481430 | 0.223143 | 17 |
| 18 | 33.294539 | 150.207157 | 0.006657 | 0.030035 | 4.511465 | 0.221657 | 18 |
| 19 | 40.452865 | 183.501696 | 0.005450 | 0.024720 | 4.536185 | 0.220450 | 19 |
| 20 | 49.150230 | 223.954560 | 0.004465 | 0.020346 | 4.556531 | 0.219465 | 20 |
| 21 | 59.717530 | 273.104791 | 0.003662 | 0.016746 | 4.573277 | 0.218662 | 21 |
| 22 | 72.556799 | 332.822321 | 0.003005 | 0.013782 | 4.587059 | 0.218005 | 22 |
| 23 | 88.156511 | 405.379120 | 0.002467 | 0.011343 | 4.598403 | 0.217467 | 23 |
| 24 | 107.110161 | 493.535631 | 0.002026 | 0.009336 | 4.607739 | 0.217026 | 24 |
| 25 | 130.138845 | 600.645791 | 0.001665 | 0.007684 | 4.615423 | 0.216665 | 25 |
| 26 | 158.118697 | 730.784636 | 0.001368 | 0.006324 | 4.621747 | 0.216368 | 26 |
| 27 | 192.114217 | 888.903333 | 0.001125 | 0.005205 | 4.626952 | 0.216125 | 27 |
| 28 | 233.418773 | 1081.017550 | 0.000925 | 0.004284 | 4.631237 | 0.215925 | 28 |
| 29 | 283.603809 | 1314.436323 | 0.000761 | 0.003526 | 4.634763 | 0.215761 | 29 |
| 30 | 344.578628 | 1598.040132 | 0.000626 | 0.002902 | 4.637665 | 0.215626 | 30 |
| 31 | 418.663034 | 1942.618761 | 0.000515 | 0.002389 | 4.640053 | 0.215515 | 31 |
| 32 | 508.675586 | 2361.281794 | 0.000423 | 0.001966 | 4.642019 | 0.215423 | 32 |
| 33 | 618.040837 | 2869.957380 | 0.000348 | 0.001618 | 4.643637 | 0.215348 | 33 |
| 34 | 750.919617 | 3487.998217 | 0.000287 | 0.001332 | 4.644969 | 0.215287 | 34 |
| 35 | 912.367334 | 4238.917834 | 0.000236 | 0.001096 | 4.646065 | 0.215236 | 35 |
| 36 | 1108.526311 | 5151.285168 | 0.000194 | 0.000902 | 4.646967 | 0.215194 | 36 |
| 37 | 1346.859468 | 6259.811479 | 0.000160 | 0.000742 | 4.647709 | 0.215160 | 37 |
| 38 | 1636.434254 | 7606.670947 | 0.000131 | 0.000611 | 4.648321 | 0.215131 | 38 |
| 39 | 1988.267618 | 9243.105200 | 0.000108 | 0.000503 | 4.648823 | 0.215108 | 39 |
| 40 | 2415.745156 | 11231.372819 | 0.000089 | 0.000414 | 4.649237 | 0.215089 | 40 |
| 41 | 2935.130365 | 13647.117975 | 0.000073 | 0.000341 | 4.649578 | 0.215073 | 41 |
| 42 | 3566.183393 | 16582.248339 | 0.000060 | 0.000280 | 4.649859 | 0.215060 | 42 |
| 43 | 4332.912822 | 20148.431732 | 0.000050 | 0.000231 | 4.650089 | 0.215050 | 43 |
| 44 | 5264.489079 | 24481.344554 | 0.000041 | 0.000190 | 4.650279 | 0.215041 | 44 |
| 45 | 6396.354231 | 29745.833634 | 0.000034 | 0.000156 | 4.650436 | 0.215034 | 45 |
| 46 | 7771.570391 | 36142.187865 | 0.000028 | 0.000129 | 4.650564 | 0.215028 | 46 |
| 47 | 9442.458025 | 43913.758256 | 0.000023 | 0.000106 | 4.650670 | 0.215023 | 47 |
| 48 | 11472.586500 | 53356.216281 | 0.000019 | 0.000087 | 4.650757 | 0.215019 | 48 |
| 49 | 13939.192598 | 64828.802781 | 0.000015 | 0.000072 | 4.650829 | 0.215015 | 49 |
| 50 | 16936.119006 | 78767.995379 | 0.000013 | 0.000059 | 4.650888 | 0.215013 | 50 |

22.00% ANNUAL INTEREST RATE

| | 1<br>Future Value<br>of $1 | 2<br>Future Value<br>Annuity of<br>$1 per Year | 3<br>Sinking<br>Fund<br>Factor | 4<br>Present Value<br>of $1<br>(Reversion) | 5<br>Present Value<br>Annuity of<br>$1 per Year | 6<br>Installment<br>to<br>Amortize $1 | |
|---|---|---|---|---|---|---|---|
| Years | | | | | | | Years |
| 1 | 1.220000 | 1.000000 | 1.000000 | 0.819672 | 0.819672 | 1.220000 | 1 |
| 2 | 1.488400 | 2.220000 | 0.450450 | 0.671862 | 1.491535 | 0.670450 | 2 |
| 3 | 1.815848 | 3.708400 | 0.269658 | 0.550707 | 2.042241 | 0.489658 | 3 |
| 4 | 2.215335 | 5.524248 | 0.181020 | 0.451399 | 2.493641 | 0.401020 | 4 |
| 5 | 2.702708 | 7.739583 | 0.129206 | 0.369999 | 2.863640 | 0.349206 | 5 |
| 6 | 3.297304 | 10.442291 | 0.095764 | 0.303278 | 3.166918 | 0.315764 | 6 |
| 7 | 4.022711 | 13.739595 | 0.072782 | 0.248589 | 3.415506 | 0.292782 | 7 |
| 8 | 4.907707 | 17.762306 | 0.056299 | 0.203761 | 3.619268 | 0.276299 | 8 |
| 9 | 5.987403 | 22.670013 | 0.044111 | 0.167017 | 3.786285 | 0.264111 | 9 |
| 10 | 7.304631 | 28.657416 | 0.034895 | 0.136899 | 3.923184 | 0.254895 | 10 |
| 11 | 8.911650 | 35.962047 | 0.027807 | 0.112213 | 4.035397 | 0.247807 | 11 |
| 12 | 10.872213 | 44.873697 | 0.022285 | 0.091978 | 4.127375 | 0.242285 | 12 |
| 13 | 13.264100 | 55.745911 | 0.017939 | 0.075391 | 4.202766 | 0.237939 | 13 |
| 14 | 16.182202 | 69.010011 | 0.014491 | 0.061796 | 4.264562 | 0.234491 | 14 |
| 15 | 19.742287 | 85.192213 | 0.011738 | 0.050653 | 4.315215 | 0.231738 | 15 |
| 16 | 24.085590 | 104.934500 | 0.009530 | 0.041519 | 4.356734 | 0.229530 | 16 |
| 17 | 29.384420 | 129.020090 | 0.007751 | 0.034032 | 4.390765 | 0.227751 | 17 |
| 18 | 35.848992 | 158.404510 | 0.006313 | 0.027895 | 4.418660 | 0.226313 | 18 |
| 19 | 43.735771 | 194.253503 | 0.005148 | 0.022865 | 4.441525 | 0.225148 | 19 |
| 20 | 53.357640 | 237.989273 | 0.004202 | 0.018741 | 4.460266 | 0.224202 | 20 |
| 21 | 65.096321 | 291.346913 | 0.003432 | 0.015362 | 4.475628 | 0.223432 | 21 |
| 22 | 79.417512 | 356.443234 | 0.002805 | 0.012592 | 4.488220 | 0.222805 | 22 |
| 23 | 96.889364 | 435.860746 | 0.002294 | 0.010321 | 4.498541 | 0.222294 | 23 |
| 24 | 118.205024 | 532.750110 | 0.001877 | 0.008460 | 4.507001 | 0.221877 | 24 |
| 25 | 144.210130 | 650.955134 | 0.001536 | 0.006934 | 4.513935 | 0.221536 | 25 |
| 26 | 175.936358 | 795.165264 | 0.001258 | 0.005684 | 4.519619 | 0.221258 | 26 |
| 27 | 214.642357 | 971.101622 | 0.001030 | 0.004659 | 4.524278 | 0.221030 | 27 |
| 28 | 261.863675 | 1185.743978 | 0.000843 | 0.003819 | 4.528096 | 0.220843 | 28 |
| 29 | 319.473684 | 1447.607654 | 0.000691 | 0.003130 | 4.531227 | 0.220691 | 29 |
| 30 | 389.757894 | 1767.081337 | 0.000566 | 0.002566 | 4.533792 | 0.220566 | 30 |
| 31 | 475.504631 | 2156.839232 | 0.000464 | 0.002103 | 4.535895 | 0.220464 | 31 |
| 32 | 580.115650 | 2632.343863 | 0.000380 | 0.001724 | 4.537619 | 0.220380 | 32 |
| 33 | 707.741093 | 3212.459512 | 0.000311 | 0.001413 | 4.539032 | 0.220311 | 33 |
| 34 | 863.444133 | 3920.200605 | 0.000255 | 0.001158 | 4.540190 | 0.220255 | 34 |
| 35 | 1053.401842 | 4783.644738 | 0.000209 | 0.000949 | 4.541140 | 0.220209 | 35 |
| 36 | 1285.150248 | 5837.046581 | 0.000171 | 0.000778 | 4.541918 | 0.220171 | 36 |
| 37 | 1567.883302 | 7122.196829 | 0.000140 | 0.000638 | 4.542555 | 0.220140 | 37 |
| 38 | 1912.817629 | 8690.080131 | 0.000115 | 0.000523 | 4.543078 | 0.220115 | 38 |
| 39 | 2333.637507 | 10602.897760 | 0.000094 | 0.000429 | 4.543507 | 0.220094 | 39 |
| 40 | 2847.037759 | 12936.535267 | 0.000077 | 0.000351 | 4.543858 | 0.220077 | 40 |
| 41 | 3473.386066 | 15783.573025 | 0.000063 | 0.000288 | 4.544146 | 0.220063 | 41 |
| 42 | 4237.531000 | 19256.959091 | 0.000052 | 0.000236 | 4.544382 | 0.220052 | 42 |
| 43 | 5169.787820 | 23494.490091 | 0.000043 | 0.000193 | 4.544575 | 0.220043 | 43 |
| 44 | 6307.141140 | 28664.277911 | 0.000035 | 0.000159 | 4.544734 | 0.220035 | 44 |
| 45 | 7694.712191 | 34971.419051 | 0.000029 | 0.000130 | 4.544864 | 0.220029 | 45 |
| 46 | 9387.548873 | 42666.131243 | 0.000023 | 0.000107 | 4.544970 | 0.220023 | 46 |
| 47 | 11452.809626 | 52053.680116 | 0.000019 | 0.000087 | 4.545058 | 0.220019 | 47 |
| 48 | 13972.427743 | 63506.489742 | 0.000016 | 0.000072 | 4.545129 | 0.220016 | 48 |
| 49 | 17046.361847 | 77478.917485 | 0.000013 | 0.000059 | 4.545188 | 0.220013 | 49 |
| 50 | 20796.561453 | 94525.279331 | 0.000011 | 0.000048 | 4.545236 | 0.220011 | 50 |

22.50% ANNUAL INTEREST RATE

| | 1<br>Future Value<br>of $1 | 2<br>Future Value<br>Annuity of<br>$1 per Year | 3<br>Sinking<br>Fund<br>Factor | 4<br>Present Value<br>of $1<br>(Reversion) | 5<br>Present Value<br>Annuity of<br>$1 per Year | 6<br>Installment<br>to<br>Amortize $1 | |
|---|---|---|---|---|---|---|---|
| Years | | | | | | | Years |
| 1 | 1.225000 | 1.000000 | 1.000000 | 0.816327 | 0.816327 | 1.225000 | 1 |
| 2 | 1.500625 | 2.225000 | 0.449438 | 0.666389 | 1.482716 | 0.674438 | 2 |
| 3 | 1.838266 | 3.725625 | 0.268411 | 0.543991 | 2.026707 | 0.493411 | 3 |
| 4 | 2.251875 | 5.563891 | 0.179730 | 0.444074 | 2.470781 | 0.404730 | 4 |
| 5 | 2.758547 | 7.815766 | 0.127947 | 0.362510 | 2.833291 | 0.352947 | 5 |
| 6 | 3.379221 | 10.574313 | 0.094569 | 0.295926 | 3.129217 | 0.319569 | 6 |
| 7 | 4.139545 | 13.953534 | 0.071666 | 0.241572 | 3.370789 | 0.296666 | 7 |
| 8 | 5.070943 | 18.093079 | 0.055270 | 0.197202 | 3.567991 | 0.280270 | 8 |
| 9 | 6.211905 | 23.164022 | 0.043170 | 0.160981 | 3.728972 | 0.268170 | 9 |
| 10 | 7.609584 | 29.375927 | 0.034041 | 0.131413 | 3.860386 | 0.259041 | 10 |
| 11 | 9.321740 | 36.985510 | 0.027038 | 0.107276 | 3.967662 | 0.252038 | 11 |
| 12 | 11.419131 | 46.307250 | 0.021595 | 0.087572 | 4.055234 | 0.246595 | 12 |
| 13 | 13.988436 | 57.726381 | 0.017323 | 0.071488 | 4.126722 | 0.242323 | 13 |
| 14 | 17.135834 | 71.714817 | 0.013944 | 0.058357 | 4.185079 | 0.238944 | 14 |
| 15 | 20.991396 | 88.850651 | 0.011255 | 0.047639 | 4.232717 | 0.236255 | 15 |
| 16 | 25.714461 | 109.842047 | 0.009104 | 0.038889 | 4.271606 | 0.234104 | 16 |
| 17 | 31.500214 | 135.556508 | 0.007377 | 0.031746 | 4.303352 | 0.232377 | 17 |
| 18 | 38.587762 | 167.056722 | 0.005986 | 0.025915 | 4.329267 | 0.230986 | 18 |
| 19 | 47.270009 | 205.644485 | 0.004863 | 0.021155 | 4.350422 | 0.229863 | 19 |
| 20 | 57.905761 | 252.914494 | 0.003954 | 0.017269 | 4.367691 | 0.228954 | 20 |
| 21 | 70.934557 | 310.820255 | 0.003217 | 0.014098 | 4.381789 | 0.228217 | 21 |
| 22 | 86.894833 | 381.754812 | 0.002619 | 0.011508 | 4.393297 | 0.227619 | 22 |
| 23 | 106.446170 | 468.649645 | 0.002134 | 0.009394 | 4.402691 | 0.227134 | 23 |
| 24 | 130.396558 | 575.095815 | 0.001739 | 0.007669 | 4.410360 | 0.226739 | 24 |
| 25 | 159.735784 | 705.492373 | 0.001417 | 0.006260 | 4.416621 | 0.226417 | 25 |
| 26 | 195.676335 | 865.228157 | 0.001156 | 0.005110 | 4.421731 | 0.226156 | 26 |
| 27 | 239.703511 | 1060.904492 | 0.000943 | 0.004172 | 4.425903 | 0.225943 | 27 |
| 28 | 293.636801 | 1300.608003 | 0.000769 | 0.003406 | 4.429309 | 0.225769 | 28 |
| 29 | 359.705081 | 1594.244804 | 0.000627 | 0.002780 | 4.432089 | 0.225627 | 29 |
| 30 | 440.638724 | 1953.949885 | 0.000512 | 0.002269 | 4.434358 | 0.225512 | 30 |
| 31 | 539.782437 | 2394.588609 | 0.000418 | 0.001853 | 4.436211 | 0.225418 | 31 |
| 32 | 661.233485 | 2934.371046 | 0.000341 | 0.001512 | 4.437723 | 0.225341 | 32 |
| 33 | 810.011019 | 3595.604531 | 0.000278 | 0.001235 | 4.438958 | 0.225278 | 33 |
| 34 | 992.263499 | 4405.615551 | 0.000227 | 0.001008 | 4.439965 | 0.225227 | 34 |
| 35 | 1215.522786 | 5397.879049 | 0.000185 | 0.000823 | 4.440788 | 0.225185 | 35 |
| 36 | 1489.015413 | 6613.401836 | 0.000151 | 0.000672 | 4.441460 | 0.225151 | 36 |
| 37 | 1824.043881 | 8102.417249 | 0.000123 | 0.000548 | 4.442008 | 0.225123 | 37 |
| 38 | 2234.453754 | 9926.461130 | 0.000101 | 0.000448 | 4.442455 | 0.225101 | 38 |
| 39 | 2737.205849 | 12160.914884 | 0.000082 | 0.000365 | 4.442821 | 0.225082 | 39 |
| 40 | 3353.077165 | 14898.120733 | 0.000067 | 0.000298 | 4.443119 | 0.225067 | 40 |
| 41 | 4107.519527 | 18251.197897 | 0.000055 | 0.000243 | 4.443362 | 0.225055 | 41 |
| 42 | 5031.711420 | 22358.717424 | 0.000045 | 0.000199 | 4.443561 | 0.225045 | 42 |
| 43 | 6163.846490 | 27390.428845 | 0.000037 | 0.000162 | 4.443723 | 0.225037 | 43 |
| 44 | 7550.711950 | 33554.275335 | 0.000030 | 0.000132 | 4.443856 | 0.225030 | 44 |
| 45 | 9249.622139 | 41104.987285 | 0.000024 | 0.000108 | 4.443964 | 0.225024 | 45 |
| 46 | 11330.787120 | 50354.609424 | 0.000020 | 0.000088 | 4.444052 | 0.225020 | 46 |
| 47 | 13880.214223 | 61685.396545 | 0.000016 | 0.000072 | 4.444124 | 0.225016 | 47 |
| 48 | 17003.262423 | 75565.610767 | 0.000013 | 0.000059 | 4.444183 | 0.225013 | 48 |
| 49 | 20828.996468 | 92568.873190 | 0.000011 | 0.000048 | 4.444231 | 0.225011 | 49 |
| 50 | 25515.520673 | 113397.869658 | 0.000009 | 0.000039 | 4.444270 | 0.225009 | 50 |

23.00% ANNUAL INTEREST RATE

| | 1<br>Future Value<br>of $1 | 2<br>Future Value<br>Annuity of<br>$1 per Year | 3<br>Sinking<br>Fund<br>Factor | 4<br>Present Value<br>of $1<br>(Reversion) | 5<br>Present Value<br>Annuity of<br>$1 per Year | 6<br>Installment<br>to<br>Amortize $1 | |
|---|---|---|---|---|---|---|---|
| Years | | | | | | | Years |
| 1 | 1.230000 | 1.000000 | 1.000000 | 0.813008 | 0.813008 | 1.230000 | 1 |
| 2 | 1.512900 | 2.230000 | 0.448430 | 0.660982 | 1.473990 | 0.678430 | 2 |
| 3 | 1.860867 | 3.742900 | 0.267173 | 0.537384 | 2.011374 | 0.497173 | 3 |
| 4 | 2.288866 | 5.603767 | 0.178451 | 0.436897 | 2.448272 | 0.408451 | 4 |
| 5 | 2.815306 | 7.892633 | 0.126700 | 0.355201 | 2.803473 | 0.356700 | 5 |
| 6 | 3.464826 | 10.707939 | 0.093389 | 0.288781 | 3.092254 | 0.323389 | 6 |
| 7 | 4.259276 | 14.170765 | 0.070568 | 0.234782 | 3.327036 | 0.300568 | 7 |
| 8 | 5.238909 | 18.430041 | 0.054259 | 0.190879 | 3.517916 | 0.284259 | 8 |
| 9 | 6.443859 | 23.668950 | 0.042249 | 0.155187 | 3.673102 | 0.272249 | 9 |
| 10 | 7.925946 | 30.112809 | 0.033208 | 0.126168 | 3.799270 | 0.263208 | 10 |
| 11 | 9.748914 | 38.038755 | 0.026289 | 0.102576 | 3.901846 | 0.256289 | 11 |
| 12 | 11.991164 | 47.787669 | 0.020926 | 0.083395 | 3.985240 | 0.250926 | 12 |
| 13 | 14.749132 | 59.778833 | 0.016728 | 0.067801 | 4.053041 | 0.246728 | 13 |
| 14 | 18.141432 | 74.527964 | 0.013418 | 0.055122 | 4.108163 | 0.243418 | 14 |
| 15 | 22.313961 | 92.669396 | 0.010791 | 0.044815 | 4.152978 | 0.240791 | 15 |
| 16 | 27.446172 | 114.983357 | 0.008697 | 0.036435 | 4.189413 | 0.238697 | 16 |
| 17 | 33.758792 | 142.429529 | 0.007021 | 0.029622 | 4.219035 | 0.237021 | 17 |
| 18 | 41.523314 | 176.188321 | 0.005676 | 0.024083 | 4.243118 | 0.235676 | 18 |
| 19 | 51.073676 | 217.711635 | 0.004593 | 0.019580 | 4.262698 | 0.234593 | 19 |
| 20 | 62.820622 | 268.785311 | 0.003720 | 0.015918 | 4.278616 | 0.233720 | 20 |
| 21 | 77.269364 | 331.605932 | 0.003016 | 0.012942 | 4.291558 | 0.233016 | 21 |
| 22 | 95.041318 | 408.875297 | 0.002446 | 0.010522 | 4.302079 | 0.232446 | 22 |
| 23 | 116.900822 | 503.916615 | 0.001984 | 0.008554 | 4.310634 | 0.231984 | 23 |
| 24 | 143.788010 | 620.817437 | 0.001611 | 0.006955 | 4.317588 | 0.231611 | 24 |
| 25 | 176.859253 | 764.605447 | 0.001308 | 0.005654 | 4.323243 | 0.231308 | 25 |
| 26 | 217.536881 | 941.464700 | 0.001062 | 0.004597 | 4.327839 | 0.231062 | 26 |
| 27 | 267.570364 | 1159.001581 | 0.000863 | 0.003737 | 4.331577 | 0.230863 | 27 |
| 28 | 329.111547 | 1426.571945 | 0.000701 | 0.003038 | 4.334615 | 0.230701 | 28 |
| 29 | 404.807203 | 1755.683492 | 0.000570 | 0.002470 | 4.337086 | 0.230570 | 29 |
| 30 | 497.912860 | 2160.490695 | 0.000463 | 0.002008 | 4.339094 | 0.230463 | 30 |
| 31 | 612.432818 | 2658.403555 | 0.000376 | 0.001633 | 4.340727 | 0.230376 | 31 |
| 32 | 753.292366 | 3270.836373 | 0.000306 | 0.001328 | 4.342054 | 0.230306 | 32 |
| 33 | 926.549610 | 4024.128738 | 0.000249 | 0.001079 | 4.343134 | 0.230249 | 33 |
| 34 | 1139.656020 | 4950.678348 | 0.000202 | 0.000877 | 4.344011 | 0.230202 | 34 |
| 35 | 1401.776905 | 6090.334368 | 0.000164 | 0.000713 | 4.344724 | 0.230164 | 35 |
| 36 | 1724.185593 | 7492.111273 | 0.000133 | 0.000580 | 4.345304 | 0.230133 | 36 |
| 37 | 2120.748279 | 9216.296866 | 0.000109 | 0.000472 | 4.345776 | 0.230109 | 37 |
| 38 | 2608.520383 | 11337.045145 | 0.000088 | 0.000383 | 4.346159 | 0.230088 | 38 |
| 39 | 3208.480071 | 13945.565528 | 0.000072 | 0.000312 | 4.346471 | 0.230072 | 39 |
| 40 | 3946.430488 | 17154.045599 | 0.000058 | 0.000253 | 4.346724 | 0.230058 | 40 |
| 41 | 4854.109500 | 21100.476087 | 0.000047 | 0.000206 | 4.346930 | 0.230047 | 41 |
| 42 | 5970.554685 | 25954.585587 | 0.000039 | 0.000167 | 4.347098 | 0.230039 | 42 |
| 43 | 7343.782263 | 31925.140272 | 0.000031 | 0.000136 | 4.347234 | 0.230031 | 43 |
| 44 | 9032.852183 | 39268.922535 | 0.000025 | 0.000111 | 4.347345 | 0.230025 | 44 |
| 45 | 11110.408185 | 48301.774718 | 0.000021 | 0.000090 | 4.347435 | 0.230021 | 45 |
| 46 | 13665.802068 | 59412.182903 | 0.000017 | 0.000073 | 4.347508 | 0.230017 | 46 |
| 47 | 16808.936543 | 73077.984971 | 0.000014 | 0.000059 | 4.347567 | 0.230014 | 47 |
| 48 | 20674.991948 | 89886.921514 | 0.000011 | 0.000048 | 4.347616 | 0.230011 | 48 |
| 49 | 25430.240096 | 110561.913462 | 0.000009 | 0.000039 | 4.347655 | 0.230009 | 49 |
| 50 | 31279.195318 | 135992.153559 | 0.000007 | 0.000032 | 4.347687 | 0.230007 | 50 |

23.50% ANNUAL INTEREST RATE

| | 1<br>Future Value<br>of $1 | 2<br>Future Value<br>Annuity of<br>$1 per Year | 3<br>Sinking<br>Fund<br>Factor | 4<br>Present Value<br>of $1<br>(Reversion) | 5<br>Present Value<br>Annuity of<br>$1 per Year | 6<br>Installment<br>to<br>Amortize $1 | |
|---|---|---|---|---|---|---|---|
| Years | | | | | | | Years |
| 1 | 1.235000 | 1.000000 | 1.000000 | 0.809717 | 0.809717 | 1.235000 | 1 |
| 2 | 1.525225 | 2.235000 | 0.447427 | 0.655641 | 1.465358 | 0.682427 | 2 |
| 3 | 1.883653 | 3.760225 | 0.265942 | 0.530883 | 1.996241 | 0.500942 | 3 |
| 4 | 2.326311 | 5.643878 | 0.177183 | 0.429865 | 2.426106 | 0.412183 | 4 |
| 5 | 2.872994 | 7.970189 | 0.125468 | 0.348069 | 2.774175 | 0.360468 | 5 |
| 6 | 3.548148 | 10.843184 | 0.092224 | 0.281837 | 3.056012 | 0.327224 | 6 |
| 7 | 4.381963 | 14.391332 | 0.069486 | 0.228208 | 3.284220 | 0.304486 | 7 |
| 8 | 5.411724 | 18.773295 | 0.053267 | 0.184784 | 3.469004 | 0.288267 | 8 |
| 9 | 6.683479 | 24.185019 | 0.041348 | 0.149623 | 3.618627 | 0.276348 | 9 |
| 10 | 8.254097 | 30.868498 | 0.032395 | 0.121152 | 3.739779 | 0.267395 | 10 |
| 11 | 10.193810 | 39.122596 | 0.025561 | 0.098099 | 3.837878 | 0.260561 | 11 |
| 12 | 12.589355 | 49.316406 | 0.020277 | 0.079432 | 3.917310 | 0.255277 | 12 |
| 13 | 15.547854 | 61.905761 | 0.016154 | 0.064318 | 3.981627 | 0.251154 | 13 |
| 14 | 19.201599 | 77.453615 | 0.012911 | 0.052079 | 4.033706 | 0.247911 | 14 |
| 15 | 23.713975 | 96.655214 | 0.010346 | 0.042169 | 4.075876 | 0.245346 | 15 |
| 16 | 29.286760 | 120.369190 | 0.008308 | 0.034145 | 4.110021 | 0.243308 | 16 |
| 17 | 36.169148 | 149.655949 | 0.006682 | 0.027648 | 4.137669 | 0.241682 | 17 |
| 18 | 44.668898 | 185.825097 | 0.005381 | 0.022387 | 4.160056 | 0.240381 | 18 |
| 19 | 55.166089 | 230.493995 | 0.004339 | 0.018127 | 4.178183 | 0.239339 | 19 |
| 20 | 68.130120 | 285.660084 | 0.003501 | 0.014678 | 4.192860 | 0.238501 | 20 |
| 21 | 84.140698 | 353.790203 | 0.002827 | 0.011885 | 4.204745 | 0.237827 | 21 |
| 22 | 103.913762 | 437.930901 | 0.002283 | 0.009623 | 4.214369 | 0.237283 | 22 |
| 23 | 128.333496 | 541.844663 | 0.001846 | 0.007792 | 4.222161 | 0.236846 | 23 |
| 24 | 158.491867 | 670.178159 | 0.001492 | 0.006309 | 4.228470 | 0.236492 | 24 |
| 25 | 195.737456 | 828.670026 | 0.001207 | 0.005109 | 4.233579 | 0.236207 | 25 |
| 26 | 241.735758 | 1024.407482 | 0.000976 | 0.004137 | 4.237716 | 0.235976 | 26 |
| 27 | 298.543662 | 1266.143241 | 0.000790 | 0.003350 | 4.241066 | 0.235790 | 27 |
| 28 | 368.701422 | 1564.686902 | 0.000639 | 0.002712 | 4.243778 | 0.235639 | 28 |
| 29 | 455.346256 | 1933.388325 | 0.000517 | 0.002196 | 4.245974 | 0.235517 | 29 |
| 30 | 562.352626 | 2388.734581 | 0.000419 | 0.001778 | 4.247752 | 0.235419 | 30 |
| 31 | 694.505494 | 2951.087207 | 0.000339 | 0.001440 | 4.249192 | 0.235339 | 31 |
| 32 | 857.714285 | 3645.592701 | 0.000274 | 0.001166 | 4.250358 | 0.235274 | 32 |
| 33 | 1059.277142 | 4503.306986 | 0.000222 | 0.000944 | 4.251302 | 0.235222 | 33 |
| 34 | 1308.207270 | 5562.584127 | 0.000180 | 0.000764 | 4.252066 | 0.235180 | 34 |
| 35 | 1615.635978 | 6870.791397 | 0.000146 | 0.000619 | 4.252685 | 0.235146 | 35 |
| 36 | 1995.310433 | 8486.427376 | 0.000118 | 0.000501 | 4.253186 | 0.235118 | 36 |
| 37 | 2464.208385 | 10481.737809 | 0.000095 | 0.000406 | 4.253592 | 0.235095 | 37 |
| 38 | 3043.297356 | 12945.946194 | 0.000077 | 0.000329 | 4.253921 | 0.235077 | 38 |
| 39 | 3758.472234 | 15989.243550 | 0.000063 | 0.000266 | 4.254187 | 0.235063 | 39 |
| 40 | 4641.713209 | 19747.715784 | 0.000051 | 0.000215 | 4.254402 | 0.235051 | 40 |
| 41 | 5732.515813 | 24389.428993 | 0.000041 | 0.000174 | 4.254577 | 0.235041 | 41 |
| 42 | 7079.657030 | 30121.944807 | 0.000033 | 0.000141 | 4.254718 | 0.235033 | 42 |
| 43 | 8743.376431 | 37201.601836 | 0.000027 | 0.000114 | 4.254832 | 0.235027 | 43 |
| 44 | 10798.069893 | 45944.978268 | 0.000022 | 0.000093 | 4.254925 | 0.235022 | 44 |
| 45 | 13335.616318 | 56743.048160 | 0.000018 | 0.000075 | 4.255000 | 0.235018 | 45 |
| 46 | 16469.486152 | 70078.664478 | 0.000014 | 0.000061 | 4.255061 | 0.235014 | 46 |
| 47 | 20339.815398 | 86548.150630 | 0.000012 | 0.000049 | 4.255110 | 0.235012 | 47 |
| 48 | 25119.672017 | 106887.966029 | 0.000009 | 0.000040 | 4.255150 | 0.235009 | 48 |
| 49 | 31022.794941 | 132007.638045 | 0.000008 | 0.000032 | 4.255182 | 0.235008 | 49 |
| 50 | 38313.151752 | 163030.432986 | 0.000006 | 0.000026 | 4.255208 | 0.235006 | 50 |

24.00% ANNUAL INTEREST RATE

| | 1<br>Future Value<br>of $1 | 2<br>Future Value<br>Annuity of<br>$1 per Year | 3<br>Sinking<br>Fund<br>Factor | 4<br>Present Value<br>of $1<br>(Reversion) | 5<br>Present Value<br>Annuity of<br>$1 per Year | 6<br>Installment<br>to<br>Amortize $1 | |
|---|---|---|---|---|---|---|---|
| Years | | | | | | | Years |
| 1 | 1.240000 | 1.000000 | 1.000000 | 0.806452 | 0.806452 | 1.240000 | 1 |
| 2 | 1.537600 | 2.240000 | 0.446429 | 0.650364 | 1.456816 | 0.686429 | 2 |
| 3 | 1.906624 | 3.777600 | 0.264718 | 0.524487 | 1.981303 | 0.504718 | 3 |
| 4 | 2.364214 | 5.684224 | 0.175926 | 0.422974 | 2.404277 | 0.415926 | 4 |
| 5 | 2.931625 | 8.048438 | 0.124248 | 0.341108 | 2.745384 | 0.364248 | 5 |
| 6 | 3.635215 | 10.980063 | 0.091074 | 0.275087 | 3.020471 | 0.331074 | 6 |
| 7 | 4.507667 | 14.615278 | 0.068422 | 0.221844 | 3.242316 | 0.308422 | 7 |
| 8 | 5.589507 | 19.122945 | 0.052293 | 0.178907 | 3.421222 | 0.292293 | 8 |
| 9 | 6.930988 | 24.712451 | 0.040465 | 0.144280 | 3.565502 | 0.280465 | 9 |
| 10 | 8.594426 | 31.643440 | 0.031602 | 0.116354 | 3.681856 | 0.271602 | 10 |
| 11 | 10.657088 | 40.237865 | 0.024852 | 0.093834 | 3.775691 | 0.264852 | 11 |
| 12 | 13.214789 | 50.894953 | 0.019648 | 0.075673 | 3.851363 | 0.259648 | 12 |
| 13 | 16.386338 | 64.109741 | 0.015598 | 0.061026 | 3.912390 | 0.255598 | 13 |
| 14 | 20.319059 | 80.496079 | 0.012423 | 0.049215 | 3.961605 | 0.252423 | 14 |
| 15 | 25.195633 | 100.815138 | 0.009919 | 0.039689 | 4.001294 | 0.249919 | 15 |
| 16 | 31.242585 | 126.010772 | 0.007936 | 0.032008 | 4.033302 | 0.247936 | 16 |
| 17 | 38.740806 | 157.253357 | 0.006359 | 0.025813 | 4.059114 | 0.246359 | 17 |
| 18 | 48.038599 | 195.994162 | 0.005102 | 0.020817 | 4.079931 | 0.245102 | 18 |
| 19 | 59.567863 | 244.032761 | 0.004098 | 0.016788 | 4.096718 | 0.244098 | 19 |
| 20 | 73.864150 | 303.600624 | 0.003294 | 0.013538 | 4.110257 | 0.243294 | 20 |
| 21 | 91.591546 | 377.464774 | 0.002649 | 0.010918 | 4.121175 | 0.242649 | 21 |
| 22 | 113.573517 | 469.056320 | 0.002132 | 0.008805 | 4.129980 | 0.242132 | 22 |
| 23 | 140.831161 | 582.629836 | 0.001716 | 0.007101 | 4.137080 | 0.241716 | 23 |
| 24 | 174.630639 | 723.460997 | 0.001382 | 0.005726 | 4.142807 | 0.241382 | 24 |
| 25 | 216.541993 | 898.091636 | 0.001113 | 0.004618 | 4.147425 | 0.241113 | 25 |
| 26 | 268.512071 | 1114.633629 | 0.000897 | 0.003724 | 4.151149 | 0.240897 | 26 |
| 27 | 332.954968 | 1383.145700 | 0.000723 | 0.003003 | 4.154152 | 0.240723 | 27 |
| 28 | 412.864160 | 1716.100668 | 0.000583 | 0.002422 | 4.156575 | 0.240583 | 28 |
| 29 | 511.951559 | 2128.964828 | 0.000470 | 0.001953 | 4.158528 | 0.240470 | 29 |
| 30 | 634.819933 | 2640.916387 | 0.000379 | 0.001575 | 4.160103 | 0.240379 | 30 |
| 31 | 787.176717 | 3275.736320 | 0.000305 | 0.001270 | 4.161373 | 0.240305 | 31 |
| 32 | 976.099129 | 4062.913037 | 0.000246 | 0.001024 | 4.162398 | 0.240246 | 32 |
| 33 | 1210.362920 | 5039.012166 | 0.000198 | 0.000826 | 4.163224 | 0.240198 | 33 |
| 34 | 1500.850021 | 6249.375086 | 0.000160 | 0.000666 | 4.163890 | 0.240160 | 34 |
| 35 | 1861.054026 | 7750.225106 | 0.000129 | 0.000537 | 4.164428 | 0.240129 | 35 |
| 36 | 2307.706992 | 9611.279132 | 0.000104 | 0.000433 | 4.164861 | 0.240104 | 36 |
| 37 | 2861.556670 | 11918.986124 | 0.000084 | 0.000349 | 4.165211 | 0.240084 | 37 |
| 38 | 3548.330270 | 14780.542793 | 0.000068 | 0.000282 | 4.165492 | 0.240068 | 38 |
| 39 | 4399.929535 | 18328.873064 | 0.000055 | 0.000227 | 4.165720 | 0.240055 | 39 |
| 40 | 5455.912624 | 22728.802599 | 0.000044 | 0.000183 | 4.165903 | 0.240044 | 40 |
| 41 | 6765.331653 | 28184.715222 | 0.000035 | 0.000148 | 4.166051 | 0.240035 | 41 |
| 42 | 8389.011250 | 34950.046876 | 0.000029 | 0.000119 | 4.166170 | 0.240029 | 42 |
| 43 | 10402.373950 | 43339.058126 | 0.000023 | 0.000096 | 4.166266 | 0.240023 | 43 |
| 44 | 12898.943698 | 53741.432076 | 0.000019 | 0.000078 | 4.166344 | 0.240019 | 44 |
| 45 | 15994.690186 | 66640.375775 | 0.000015 | 0.000063 | 4.166406 | 0.240015 | 45 |
| 46 | 19833.415831 | 82635.065961 | 0.000012 | 0.000050 | 4.166457 | 0.240012 | 46 |
| 47 | 24593.435630 | 102468.481791 | 0.000010 | 0.000041 | 4.166497 | 0.240010 | 47 |
| 48 | 30495.860181 | 127061.917421 | 0.000008 | 0.000033 | 4.166530 | 0.240008 | 48 |
| 49 | 37814.866624 | 157557.777602 | 0.000006 | 0.000026 | 4.166556 | 0.240006 | 49 |
| 50 | 46890.434614 | 195372.644226 | 0.000005 | 0.000021 | 4.166578 | 0.240005 | 50 |

24.50% ANNUAL INTEREST RATE

| | 1<br>Future Value<br>of $1 | 2<br>Future Value<br>Annuity of<br>$1 per Year | 3<br>Sinking<br>Fund<br>Factor | 4<br>Present Value<br>of $1<br>(Reversion) | 5<br>Present Value<br>Annuity of<br>$1 per Year | 6<br>Installment<br>to<br>Amortize $1 | |
|---|---|---|---|---|---|---|---|
| Years | | | | | | | Years |
| 1 | 1.245000 | 1.000000 | 1.000000 | 0.803213 | 0.803213 | 1.245000 | 1 |
| 2 | 1.550025 | 2.245000 | 0.445434 | 0.645151 | 1.448364 | 0.690434 | 2 |
| 3 | 1.929781 | 3.795025 | 0.263503 | 0.518193 | 1.966557 | 0.508503 | 3 |
| 4 | 2.402578 | 5.724806 | 0.174678 | 0.416220 | 2.382777 | 0.419678 | 4 |
| 5 | 2.991209 | 8.127384 | 0.123041 | 0.334313 | 2.717090 | 0.368041 | 5 |
| 6 | 3.724055 | 11.118593 | 0.089939 | 0.268524 | 2.985614 | 0.334939 | 6 |
| 7 | 4.636449 | 14.842648 | 0.067373 | 0.215682 | 3.201297 | 0.312373 | 7 |
| 8 | 5.772379 | 19.479097 | 0.051337 | 0.173239 | 3.374535 | 0.296337 | 8 |
| 9 | 7.186611 | 25.251475 | 0.039602 | 0.139148 | 3.513683 | 0.284602 | 9 |
| 10 | 8.947331 | 32.438087 | 0.030828 | 0.111765 | 3.625448 | 0.275828 | 10 |
| 11 | 11.139427 | 41.385418 | 0.024163 | 0.089771 | 3.715220 | 0.269163 | 11 |
| 12 | 13.868587 | 52.524845 | 0.019039 | 0.072105 | 3.787325 | 0.264039 | 12 |
| 13 | 17.266391 | 66.393432 | 0.015062 | 0.057916 | 3.845241 | 0.260062 | 13 |
| 14 | 21.496657 | 83.659823 | 0.011953 | 0.046519 | 3.891760 | 0.256953 | 14 |
| 15 | 26.763338 | 105.156480 | 0.009510 | 0.037365 | 3.929124 | 0.254510 | 15 |
| 16 | 33.320355 | 131.919817 | 0.007580 | 0.030012 | 3.959136 | 0.252580 | 16 |
| 17 | 41.483842 | 165.240173 | 0.006052 | 0.024106 | 3.983242 | 0.251052 | 17 |
| 18 | 51.647384 | 206.724015 | 0.004837 | 0.019362 | 4.002604 | 0.249837 | 18 |
| 19 | 64.300993 | 258.371398 | 0.003870 | 0.015552 | 4.018156 | 0.248870 | 19 |
| 20 | 80.054736 | 322.672391 | 0.003099 | 0.012491 | 4.030647 | 0.248099 | 20 |
| 21 | 99.668146 | 402.727127 | 0.002483 | 0.010033 | 4.040680 | 0.247483 | 21 |
| 22 | 124.086842 | 502.395273 | 0.001990 | 0.008059 | 4.048739 | 0.246990 | 22 |
| 23 | 154.488118 | 626.482115 | 0.001596 | 0.006473 | 4.055212 | 0.246596 | 23 |
| 24 | 192.337707 | 780.970233 | 0.001280 | 0.005199 | 4.060411 | 0.246280 | 24 |
| 25 | 239.460445 | 973.307940 | 0.001027 | 0.004176 | 4.064588 | 0.246027 | 25 |
| 26 | 298.128254 | 1212.768385 | 0.000825 | 0.003354 | 4.067942 | 0.245825 | 26 |
| 27 | 371.169677 | 1510.896640 | 0.000662 | 0.002694 | 4.070636 | 0.245662 | 27 |
| 28 | 462.106248 | 1882.066316 | 0.000531 | 0.002164 | 4.072800 | 0.245531 | 28 |
| 29 | 575.322278 | 2344.172564 | 0.000427 | 0.001738 | 4.074538 | 0.245427 | 29 |
| 30 | 716.276236 | 2919.494842 | 0.000343 | 0.001396 | 4.075934 | 0.245343 | 30 |
| 31 | 891.763914 | 3635.771079 | 0.000275 | 0.001121 | 4.077056 | 0.245275 | 31 |
| 32 | 1110.246073 | 4527.534993 | 0.000221 | 0.000901 | 4.077956 | 0.245221 | 32 |
| 33 | 1382.256361 | 5637.781066 | 0.000177 | 0.000723 | 4.078680 | 0.245177 | 33 |
| 34 | 1720.909170 | 7020.037427 | 0.000142 | 0.000581 | 4.079261 | 0.245142 | 34 |
| 35 | 2142.531916 | 8740.946597 | 0.0C0114 | 0.000467 | 4.079728 | 0.245114 | 35 |
| 36 | 2667.452236 | 10883.478513 | 0.000092 | 0.000375 | 4.080102 | 0.245092 | 36 |
| 37 | 3320.978033 | 13550.930749 | 0.000074 | 0.000301 | 4.080404 | 0.245074 | 37 |
| 38 | 4134.617652 | 16871.908782 | 0.000059 | 0.000242 | 4.080645 | 0.245059 | 38 |
| 39 | 5147.598976 | 21006.526434 | 0.000048 | 0.000194 | 4.080840 | 0.245048 | 39 |
| 40 | 6408.760725 | 26154.125410 | 0.000038 | 0.000156 | 4.080996 | 0.245038 | 40 |
| 41 | 7978.907103 | 32562.886136 | 0.000031 | 0.000125 | 4.081121 | 0.245031 | 41 |
| 42 | 9933.739344 | 40541.793239 | 0.000025 | 0.000101 | 4.081222 | 0.245025 | 42 |
| 43 | 12367.505483 | 50475.532582 | 0.000020 | 0.000081 | 4.081303 | 0.245020 | 43 |
| 44 | 15397.544326 | 62843.038065 | 0.000016 | 0.000065 | 4.081368 | 0.245016 | 44 |
| 45 | 19169.942686 | 78240.582391 | 0.000013 | 0.000052 | 4.081420 | 0.245013 | 45 |
| 46 | 23866.578644 | 97410.525077 | 0.000010 | 0.000042 | 4.081462 | 0.245010 | 46 |
| 47 | 29713.890412 | 121277.103721 | 0.000008 | 0.000034 | 4.081495 | 0.245008 | 47 |
| 48 | 36993.793562 | 150990.994132 | 0.000007 | 0.000027 | 4.081522 | 0.245007 | 48 |
| 49 | 46057.272985 | 187984.787395 | 0.000005 | 0.000022 | 4.081544 | 0.245005 | 49 |
| 50 | 57341.304867 | 234042.060680 | 0.000004 | 0.000017 | 4.081561 | 0.245004 | 50 |

25.00% ANNUAL INTEREST RATE

| | 1<br>Future Value<br>of $1 | 2<br>Future Value<br>Annuity of<br>$1 per Year | 3<br>Sinking<br>Fund<br>Factor | 4<br>Present Value<br>of $1<br>(Reversion) | 5<br>Present Value<br>Annuity of<br>$1 per Year | 6<br>Installment<br>to<br>Amortize $1 | |
|---|---|---|---|---|---|---|---|
| Years | | | | | | | Years |
| 1 | 1.250000 | 1.000000 | 1.000000 | 0.800000 | 0.800000 | 1.250000 | 1 |
| 2 | 1.562500 | 2.250000 | 0.444444 | 0.640000 | 1.440000 | 0.694444 | 2 |
| 3 | 1.953125 | 3.812500 | 0.262295 | 0.512000 | 1.952000 | 0.512295 | 3 |
| 4 | 2.441406 | 5.765625 | 0.173442 | 0.409600 | 2.361600 | 0.423442 | 4 |
| 5 | 3.051758 | 8.207031 | 0.121847 | 0.327680 | 2.689280 | 0.371847 | 5 |
| 6 | 3.814697 | 11.258789 | 0.088819 | 0.262144 | 2.951424 | 0.338819 | 6 |
| 7 | 4.768372 | 15.073486 | 0.066342 | 0.209715 | 3.161139 | 0.316342 | 7 |
| 8 | 5.960464 | 19.841858 | 0.050399 | 0.167772 | 3.328911 | 0.300399 | 8 |
| 9 | 7.450581 | 25.802322 | 0.038756 | 0.134218 | 3.463129 | 0.288756 | 9 |
| 10 | 9.313226 | 33.252903 | 0.030073 | 0.107374 | 3.570503 | 0.280073 | 10 |
| 11 | 11.641532 | 42.566129 | 0.023493 | 0.085899 | 3.656403 | 0.273493 | 11 |
| 12 | 14.551915 | 54.207661 | 0.018448 | 0.068719 | 3.725122 | 0.268448 | 12 |
| 13 | 18.189894 | 68.759576 | 0.014543 | 0.054976 | 3.780098 | 0.264543 | 13 |
| 14 | 22.737368 | 86.949470 | 0.011501 | 0.043980 | 3.824078 | 0.261501 | 14 |
| 15 | 28.421709 | 109.686838 | 0.009117 | 0.035184 | 3.859263 | 0.259117 | 15 |
| 16 | 35.527137 | 138.108547 | 0.007241 | 0.028147 | 3.887410 | 0.257241 | 16 |
| 17 | 44.408921 | 173.635684 | 0.005759 | 0.022518 | 3.909928 | 0.255759 | 17 |
| 18 | 55.511151 | 218.044605 | 0.004586 | 0.018014 | 3.927942 | 0.254586 | 18 |
| 19 | 69.388939 | 273.555756 | 0.003656 | 0.014412 | 3.942354 | 0.253656 | 19 |
| 20 | 86.736174 | 342.944695 | 0.002916 | 0.011529 | 3.953883 | 0.252916 | 20 |
| 21 | 108.420217 | 429.680869 | 0.002327 | 0.009223 | 3.963107 | 0.252327 | 21 |
| 22 | 135.525272 | 538.101086 | 0.001858 | 0.007379 | 3.970485 | 0.251858 | 22 |
| 23 | 169.406589 | 673.626358 | 0.001485 | 0.005903 | 3.976388 | 0.251485 | 23 |
| 24 | 211.758237 | 843.032947 | 0.001186 | 0.004722 | 3.981111 | 0.251186 | 24 |
| 25 | 264.697796 | 1054.791184 | 0.000948 | 0.003778 | 3.984888 | 0.250948 | 25 |
| 26 | 330.872245 | 1319.488980 | 0.000758 | 0.003022 | 3.987911 | 0.250758 | 26 |
| 27 | 413.590306 | 1650.361225 | 0.000606 | 0.002418 | 3.990329 | 0.250606 | 27 |
| 28 | 516.987883 | 2063.951531 | 0.000485 | 0.001934 | 3.992263 | 0.250485 | 28 |
| 29 | 646.234854 | 2580.939414 | 0.000387 | 0.001547 | 3.993810 | 0.250387 | 29 |
| 30 | 807.793567 | 3227.174268 | 0.000310 | 0.001238 | 3.995048 | 0.250310 | 30 |
| 31 | 1009.741959 | 4034.967835 | 0.000248 | 0.000990 | 3.996039 | 0.250248 | 31 |
| 32 | 1262.177448 | 5044.709793 | 0.000198 | 0.000792 | 3.996831 | 0.250198 | 32 |
| 33 | 1577.721810 | 6306.887242 | 0.000159 | 0.000634 | 3.997465 | 0.250159 | 33 |
| 34 | 1972.152263 | 7884.609052 | 0.000127 | 0.000507 | 3.997972 | 0.250127 | 34 |
| 35 | 2465.190329 | 9856.761315 | 0.000101 | 0.000406 | 3.998377 | 0.250101 | 35 |
| 36 | 3081.487911 | 12321.951644 | 0.000081 | 0.000325 | 3.998702 | 0.250081 | 36 |
| 37 | 3851.859889 | 15403.439555 | 0.000065 | 0.000260 | 3.998962 | 0.250065 | 37 |
| 38 | 4814.824861 | 19255.299444 | 0.000052 | 0.000208 | 3.999169 | 0.250052 | 38 |
| 39 | 6018.531076 | 24070.124305 | 0.000042 | 0.000166 | 3.999335 | 0.250042 | 39 |
| 40 | 7523.163845 | 30088.655381 | 0.000033 | 0.000133 | 3.999468 | 0.250033 | 40 |
| 41 | 9403.954807 | 37611.819226 | 0.000027 | 0.000106 | 3.999575 | 0.250027 | 41 |
| 42 | 11754.943508 | 47015.774033 | 0.000021 | 0.000085 | 3.999660 | 0.250021 | 42 |
| 43 | 14693.679385 | 58770.717541 | 0.000017 | 0.000068 | 3.999728 | 0.250017 | 43 |
| 44 | 18367.099232 | 73464.396926 | 0.000014 | 0.000054 | 3.999782 | 0.250014 | 44 |
| 45 | 22958.874039 | 91831.496158 | 0.000011 | 0.000044 | 3.999826 | 0.250011 | 45 |
| 46 | 28698.592549 | 114790.370197 | 0.000009 | 0.000035 | 3.999861 | 0.250009 | 46 |
| 47 | 35873.240687 | 143488.962747 | 0.000007 | 0.000028 | 3.999888 | 0.250007 | 47 |
| 48 | 44841.550858 | 179362.203434 | 0.000006 | 0.000022 | 3.999911 | 0.250006 | 48 |
| 49 | 56051.938573 | 224203.754292 | 0.000004 | 0.000018 | 3.999929 | 0.250004 | 49 |
| 50 | 70064.923216 | 280255.692865 | 0.000004 | 0.000014 | 3.999943 | 0.250004 | 50 |